American Poetry to 1914

Titles in the CRITICAL COSMOS series include

AMERICAN FICTION

American Fiction through 1914
American Fiction, 1914–1945
American Fiction, 1946–1965
American Fiction, 1966 to the Present
American Jewish Literature
American Women Novelists and Short
  Story Writers
Black American Fiction

AMERICAN POETRY, DRAMA,
  AND PROSE

American Drama to 1945
American Drama 1945 to the Present
American Poetry through 1914
American Poetry, 1915–1945
American Poetry, 1946–1965
American Poetry, 1966 to the Present
American Prose and Criticism to 1945
American Prose and Criticism, 1945 to
  the Present
American Women Poets
Black American Poetry

BRITISH LITERATURE THROUGH 1880

British Drama: 18th and 19th Centuries
Eighteenth-Century Fiction and Prose
Eighteenth-Century Poetry
Elizabethan and Jacobean Drama
Elizabethan Poetry
Elizabethan Prose and Fiction
English Romantic Fiction and Prose
English Romantic Poetry
Medieval Literature
Seventeenth-Century Poetry
Seventeenth-Century Prose
Victorian Fiction
Victorian Poetry
Victorian Prose

FRENCH LITERATURE

French Drama through 1915
French Fiction through 1915
French Poetry through 1915
French Prose and Criticism through 1789
French Prose and Criticism, 1790 to the
  Present
Modern French Drama
Modern French Fiction
Modern French Poetry
Modern French Prose and Criticism

GERMAN LITERATURE

German Drama through 1915
German Fiction through 1915
German Poetry through 1915
German Prose and Criticism through 1915
Modern German Drama
Modern German Fiction
Modern German Poetry
Modern German Prose and Criticism

MODERN BRITISH AND
  COMMONWEALTH LITERATURE

Anglo-Irish Literature
British Prose, 1880–1914
British World War I Literature
Canadian Fiction
Canadian Poetry and Prose
Commonwealth Poetry and Fiction
Contemporary British Drama, 1946 to the
  Present
Contemporary British Fiction, 1946 to the
  Present
Contemporary British Poetry
Contemporary British Prose
Edwardian and Georgian Fiction,
  1880–1914
Edwardian and Georgian Poetry,
  1880–1914
Modern British Drama, 1900–1945
Modernist Fiction, 1920–1945
Modern Poetry and Prose, 1920–1945

OTHER EUROPEAN AND LATIN
  AMERICAN LITERATURE

African Anglophonic Literature
Dadaism and Surrealism
Italian Drama
Italian Fiction
Italian Poetry
Jewish Literature: The Bible through 1945
Modern Jewish Literature
Modern Latin American Fiction
Modern Scandinavian Literature
Modern Spanish Fiction
Modern Spanish and Latin American
  Poetry
Russian Drama
Russian Fiction
Russian Poetry
Scandinavian Literature through 1915
Spanish Fiction through 1927
Spanish Poetry through 1927

American Poetry to 1914

Edited and with an introduction
by *HAROLD BLOOM*
Sterling Professor of the Humanities
Yale University

CHELSEA HOUSE PUBLISHERS
New York ◇ *Philadelphia*

Printed and bound in the United States of America

10   9   8   7   6   5   4   3

∞The paper used in this publication meets the minimum
requirements of the American National Standard for
Permanence of Paper for Printed Library Materials,
Z39.48-1984.

Library of Congress Cataloging-in-Publication Data
American poetry to 1914.
    (The Critical cosmos)
    Bibliography: p.
    Includes index.
    Summary: A collection of critical essays on American
poetry from its earliest examples to the era of the First
World War.
    1. American poetry—History and criticism.
[1. American poetry—History and criticism]   I. Bloom,
Harold.   II. Series.
PS305.A54   1986   811′.009   86–17113
ISBN 0–87754–951–6

Contents

Editor's Note

This volume gathers together what I judge to be the best criticism available upon American poetry from its inception, with Anne Bradstreet and Edward Taylor, through the era that ended with our entry into the First World War. Though the early poetry of Edwin Arlington Robinson can be regarded as the natural culmination of this first phase of our national poetry, Robinson's later work falls in the period after 1914, and so he has been reserved for the next volume in this Critical Cosmos series.

Three essays each are given to Walt Whitman and Emily Dickinson, who are still our major poets, despite the achievements of such strong figures as Frost, Stevens, Eliot, Pound, W. C. Williams, Marianne Moore, Hart Crane, Robert Penn Warren, Elizabeth Bishop, John Ashbery, and James Merrill, among others in our century. Two essays each are given to Bryant, Melville, and Lanier, because of the high quality of the criticism available, even though I scarcely would argue for the poetic superiority of Bryant, Melville, and Lanier, in comparison to Emerson, Jones Very, Tuckerman, and Trumbull Stickney. Considerations of space have confined me to one essay only for each of the other poets in this volume and have caused me to exclude poets as interesting as Holmes, Chivers, Sill, and Santayana.

I am grateful to Susan Lasher for her aid in researching and editing this volume. My introduction centers upon the poetry of Emerson, Whitman, and Dickinson, and seeks to define their relationship both to the American and the British poetic traditions.

Anne Bradstreet, the forerunner of all our subsequent poets, is studied by Robert Daly as an exquisite balance between the things of this world and the pilgrimage to heaven, a balance he finds representative of the Puritan middle way. Louis L. Martz, our foremost scholar of the meditative poem as a genre, analyzes the Puritan Edward Taylor in terms of his apprehension of the spiritual life in sensory and colloquial language.

Philip Freneau, our leading Jeffersonian poet, is read by the feminist critic Annette Kolodny as an interesting but failed quester for "an appropriate and enduring pastoral landscape in the New World." Our first black poet, Phillis Wheatley, leaves to her critic Terrence Collins a legacy that is a dark image, a testimony "to the insidious, self-destroying nature of even the most subtle, most gentle of racially oppressive conditions."

Whatever the limitations of Bradstreet, Taylor, Freneau, and Wheatley, there is no question of the poetic achievement of William Cullen Bryant, even if he is more the American Cowper than the American Wordsworth. Donald Davie's exegesis of the splendid "To a Waterfowl" rather undervalues the lyric, in my opinion, but it is a very responsible and useful close reading, while Rebecca Rio-Jelliffe considers the rugged and moving "Thanatopsis" in its full context both of Bryant's vision of nature and of the American poetry for which Bryant helped to clear a new vision of landscape.

Emerson's poetry, which is studied in my introduction as a precursor to so many of Emerson's heirs, receives a masterly overview by David Porter, who is sympathetic to Emerson's own sense of failure as a poet but nevertheless rigorously explores the actual limitations of the work. It may be that Porter, like Emerson himself, is too severe, but the severity is soundly based upon the high expectations for poetry of the Sage of Concord himself. Emerson, though a good poet, largely matters as a poet because he is still our essential American theorist—of literature, of the spirit, of life.

Henry Wadsworth Longfellow, as absurdly undervalued now as once he was overpraised, is described by the poet Howard Nemerov as being imaginatively "just," a lyrical perceiver whose best poems remain forever valid. An even stronger defense is made for the Quaker poet Whittier by Robert Penn Warren, our most eminent living poet (indeed now our Poet Laureate). Warren gives us a Whittier whose deep intuition of what it meant to be an American associates him with Hawthorne and Melville, even if he lacks their power and their dialectical irony.

Poe, our largest poetic disaster, receives his classical defense from the accomplished poet Richard Wilbur, who is compelled to rest his case however not on the verse but on the "prose allegories of psychic conflict." Jones Very, a much better poet than Poe, is described by Lawrence Buell in the context of Whitman's more overwhelming transcendental egoism, an inevitable mode for both poets since they stemmed alike from the prophetic Emerson. Another Emersonian disciple, Thoreau, is evaluated as a poet by Henry W. Wells, who perhaps sets Thoreau too high, yet who writes in something of Thoreau's own spirit.

The greatness of our poetry begins with Walt Whitman, who is seen here first by Roy Harvey Pearce in an essay on the great third edition of *Leaves of Grass*, where "Out of the Cradle Endlessly Rocking" and "As I Ebb'd with the Ocean of Life" and the "Calamus" poems joined the Whitman canon. R. W. B. Lewis presents a comprehensive overview of Whitman's work, emphasizing both his poetic origins and the recurrent waves of his returns to those origins. My own essay on our national poet centers on the great "Lilacs" elegy for Lincoln, and on the trope of the "tally" which seems to me Whitman's unique and deliberate image for his own poetic voice.

Melville, as powerful a writer as Whitman but not in verse, is defended as a poet by Robert Penn Warren, whose generous overpraise continues to be influential. The long poem *Clarel*, at once Melville's major yet most problematic work in verse, is accorded the best analysis it has so far received in an essay by Bryan C. Short.

James Russell Lowell, a poet who is unlikely ever to be revived, is sensibly extolled by George Arms as an excellent writer of the familiar verse essay. The rather more interesting and original Frederick Goddard Tuckerman, who has survived the astonishing overpraise of Yvor Winters, is temperately viewed by Denis Donoghue as an author of exemplary American poems, and of "The Cricket" in particular. Another accurate and moderate estimate, of the Confederate poet Henry Timrod, is made by Roy Harvey Pearce, who sees Allen Tate's favorite southern poet (before our century) as a representative of southern culture so central that a minor but persuasive "people's poetry" could come into being through him.

Emily Dickinson, still the only rival to Walt Whitman in our poetry, is analyzed by Charles R. Anderson, her best close reader to date, as an unmatched lyrist of despair. Two rather different feminist exegeses follow, with Margaret Homans centering upon Dickinson's struggle for poetic identity, against her male precursors and their tradition, and with Joanne Feit Diehl persuasively particularizing Dickinson's intimate agon with Emerson, American theorist of the Abyss of the self.

Sidney Lanier, in my own judgment a suggestive but failed poet, is scarcely praised by Robert Penn Warren, who nevertheless sees him as a case worth some meditation. John Hollander, our foremost student of images of music in poetry, ponders Lanier's last poems and makes a surprising defense of them. The rather more impressive if less euphonious Stephen Crane is presented by Daniel G. Hoffman as a religious ironist of considerable power. In this book's final essay, John Hollander returns with a marvelous reading of Trumbull Stickney's beautiful "Mnemosyne," one of the best American elegiac lyrics. Hollander's intricate analysis is both a model of poetic criticism and a fit tribute to Stickney. As such, it brings this volume concerning our earlier national poetry to a gracious and distinguished conclusion.

Introduction

That far-reaching idea of time, which seems to expand our thoughts with limitless existence, gives to our mental struggles a greatness they could not have before had. We each of us feel within our own bosoms a great, an immortal foe, which if we have subdued, we may meet with calmness every other, knowing that earth contains no greater; but which if we have not, it will continually appear in those petty contests with others by which we do but show our own cowardice.

—JONES VERY (1838)

Emerson. *Much more enlightened, more roving, more manifold, subtler than Carlyle; above all, happier. One who instinctively nourishes himself only on ambrosia, leaving behind what is indigestible in things . . . he simply does not know how old he is already and how young he is still going to be.*

—NIETZSCHE

I

On Christmas Day, 1846, Emerson's *Poems* appeared. The poet was forty-three and had published much of his most characteristic prose; *Nature* in 1836, and the two series of *Essays* in 1841 and 1844. Like so many American poets, Emerson was a late starter; few of his important poems precede his thirtieth year, and most were written after he turned forty. The few early exceptions would include "The River" (1827) and some extraordinary chants of self-recognition in the 1831 *Journals*, which resemble certain sermons of Meister Eckhart in their dangerously intense realization that the soul's substance is uncreated, and their conclusion that the soul alone is the Law. By 1832, the *Journals* show a dialectical recoil: "It is awful to look into the mind of man and see how free we are. . . . inside, the terrible freedom!" Throughout Emerson's great period (1832–41, with a sudden but brief resurgence in 1846) there is a dialectic or interplay between the assertion of imagination's autonomy, and a shrewd skepticism of any phenomenon reaching too far into the unconditioned. This rhythm appears again in the Emersonian Whitman in his great years (1855–60), in Dickinson throughout her life, and in every Emersonian poet we have enjoyed since (Cummings, Hart Crane, Roethke) except for poets who stem from the later, resigned Emerson (*The Conduct of Life*, particularly the essay "Fate"), including Robinson and Frost. The relation of Stevens to Emerson, perhaps partly an unconscious one, early and late, is too complex for summary, being hidden, and will receive some consideration further on in this essay.

1

The notable poems in Emerson's first volume are "The Sphinx" (probably 1840), "Uriel" (1845), "Hamatreya" (1845–46), "The Humble-Bee" (1837), "Woodnotes" (1840–41), "Monadnoc" (1845), "Ode: Inscribed to William H. Channing" (1846), "The Forerunners" (date unknown), "Merlin" (1846), "Bacchus" (1846), "Saadi" (1842), and "Threnody" (1842–43). From late in 1845 and almost all through 1846, Emerson seems to have revived in himself something of his earlier Transcendental fury. Stephen Whicher dated 1841 as the end of Emerson's "Period of challenge" and the start of his long "Period of acquiescence," a useful enough categorizing if we grant the year 1846 as an exception. The year's prelude is in "Uriel," a late response to the furor following the Divinity School Address, and Frost's candidate for the best American poem. The poem turns on Uriel's "sentiment divine":

> "Line in nature is not found;
> Unit and universe are round;
> In vain produced, all rays return;
> Evil will bless, and ice will burn."

The poem is deliberately and successfully comic in a unique mode, indeed, the positive magic of poetic influence (as exalted by Borges) appears to be at work, and at moments Frost is writing the poem, even as Yeats writes certain passages in "The Witch of Atlas" or Stevens in "The Recluse," or Dickinson in Emerson's "The Humble-Bee." But "Uriel" (again like some Frost) is very dark in its comedy, and records the inner cost of angelic defiance:

> A sad self-knowledge, withering, fell
> On the beauty of Uriel;
> In heaven once eminent, the god
> Withdrew, that hour, into his cloud;
> Whether doomed to long gyration
> In the sea of generation,
> Or by knowledge grown too bright
> To hit the nerve of feebler sight.

Line in human nature is not to be found either, least of all in Emerson's spiral of a spirit. The Eternal Return is perpetual in the single soul, and Emerson anticipates the doctrines of Yeats as well as Nietzsche. Self-knowledge withers because it teaches the terrible truths of the grand essay, "Circles"; Uriel too is only a proud ephemeral whose revelation must be superseded. Emerson's wisdom, by limiting the self's discourse, gives the poem firm outline; Uriel sings out when possessed but then gyres into a cloudy silence.

"Monadnoc," a powerful ramble of a poem, now absurdly undervalued, shows the same discretion, allowing much everyday lumber to ballast the ascents to vision. Its direct modern descendant, Stevens's

"Chocorua to Its Neighbor," suffers from refusing similar ballast; it is a purer but not a better poem. Monadnoc expects to disappear in the mightier chant of the Major Man it awaits, a god no longer in ruins. Chocorua celebrates only the shadow of the Major Man, but already begins to disappear in that celebration:

> Upon my top he breathed the pointed dark.
> He was not man yet he was nothing else.
> If in the mind, he vanished, taking there
> The mind's own limits, like a tragic thing
> Without existence, existing everywhere.

This is painfully said, but since the mind is the mountain's, Chocorua himself is being skeptically raised to sublimity, where limits vanish. Monadnoc is a sturdier Titan, and sees a form, not a shadow of centrality. In Emerson's poem, we find the shadow, in the mountain:

> Thou seest, O watchman tall,
> Our towns and races grow and fall,
> And imagest the stable good
> For which we all our lifetime grope,
> In shifting form the formless mind,
> And though the substance us elude,
> We in thee the shadow find.

Probably Emerson was not aware he echoed the "Intimations" Ode here, as in so many other places:

> thou Eye among the blind,
> That, deaf and silent, read'st the eternal deep,
> Haunted for ever by the eternal mind,—
> Mighty Prophet! Seer blest!
> On whom those truths do rest,
> Which we are toiling all our lives to find,
> In darkness lost, the darkness of the grave;

Wordsworth addresses the Child, Emerson addresses Monadnoc, but the Other is the same; Monadnoc is a "Mute orator," sending "conviction without phrase," to "succor and remede/The shortness of our days," promising "long morrow" to those of "mortal youth." The Child, though silent, prophesies the same good news. The movement from "Intimations" to "Monadnoc" to "Chocorua" is not one of successive *clinamens*, of swerves away from a downward course, but of what students pursuing Poetic Influence might term the *tessera* or link, a different and subtler kind of revisionary ratio. In the *tessera*, the later poet provides what his imagination tells him would complete the otherwise "truncated" precursor poem and poet, a "completion" that is as much misprision as a revisionary swerve is. I take the term *tessera* from the psychoanalyst Jacques Lacan, whose own revisionary relationship to Freud might be given as an instance of *tessera*. In his *Discours de Rome* (1953), Lacan cites a remark of Mallarmé's, which "compares the common use of Language to the exchange of a coin whose obverse and reverse no longer bear any but worn effigies, and which people pass from hand to hand 'in silence.' " Applying this to the discourse, however reduced, of the analytic subject, Lacan says: "This metaphor is sufficient to remind us that the Word, even when almost completely worn out, retains its value as a *tessera*." Lacan's translator, Anthony Wilden, comments that this "allusion is to the function of the *tessera* as a token of recognition, or 'password.' The *tessera* was employed in the early mystery religions where fitting together again the two halves of a broken piece of pottery was used as a means of recognition by the initiates." In this sense of a completing link, the *tessera* represents any later poet's attempt to persuade himself (and us) that the precursor's Word would be worn out if not redeemed as a newly fulfilled and enlarged Word of the ephebe.

By concluding "Monadnoc" with a *tessera* related to Wordsworth's Great Ode, Emerson overcomes not only the dominant (if hidden) major influence upon his mature poetry, but frees his greater poems of the following year from the excessive authority of the single poem that haunts all of the Transcendentalists. Here is part of a memorable disaster of influence, Christopher Pearse Cranch's "The Ocean," where the Intimations Ode and "Asia's Song" from "Prometheus Unbound" oddly combine:

> Now we've wandered from the shore,
> Dwellers by the sea no more;
> Yet at times there comes a tone
> Telling of the visions flown,
> Sounding from the distant sea
> Where we left our purity:
> Distant glimpses of the surge
> Lure us down to ocean's verge;
> There we stand with vague distress,
> Yearning for the measureless,
> By half-wakened instincts driven,
> Half loving earth, half loving heaven,
> Fearing to put off and swim,
> Yet impelled to turn to Him,
> In whose life we live and move,
> And whose very name is Love.

Thoreau, a stronger poet, handles the Great Ode (in pieces like "Music" and "Manhood") by swerving from it, a *clinamen* already remarked by his editor Carl Bode when he speaks of the "striking bias" the Wordsworthian theme takes on in such poems. But Emerson was as close as Cranch to the "Ode"; it was not to him a point of departure, but a finality, and he handles it accordingly. Thoreau, throughout his use of the "Ode" in his *Journal*, emphasizes a music within, remembering that "There was a time when the beauty and the music were all within. . . . When you were an organ of which the world was but one poor broken pipe." Wordsworth turns to a music in the later time, but emphasizes the lost glory as a light, something seen. What for Wordsworth is a movement from the despotic eye to the liberating ear becomes in Thoreau a double loss, involving both senses. Emerson, from 1831 on a more consistent Wordsworthian than the more drastic (and even more American) Thoreau, wavers more cunningly from the "Ode." Monadnoc takes the Child's place, for the stone Titan is free of the tragic rhythm by which the Child is father of the Man. In this *tessera*, Wordsworthian Nature is perhaps overhumanized, and Monadnoc becomes a Transcendentalist rather too benign, less a flaw in the poem than it might be, since the whole work demands so generous a suspension of our skepticism.

Skepticism, the powerful undersong in Emerson's dialectic, returns in "Hamatreya," as awesome a rebuff to a naturalistic humanism as Yeats's great sonnet "Meru" in the *Supernatural Songs*, and proceeding from much the same sources as "Meru." "Hamatreya" is the necessary prelude to what is most difficult yet inviting in Emerson's two supreme poems, "Merlin" and "Bacchus." Because of the dominance of certain pseudocritical shibboleths for several decades, there is a certain fashion still to deprecate all of Emerson's poetry, with the single exception of "Days." Mathiessen pioneered in grudgingly accepting "Days" as the one Emerson poem that seemed readable by Eliotic standards. I suspect the poem passed because Emerson condemns himself in it, though only for not being Emersonian enough. "Days," in Emerson's canon, is a miniature of his later retreat into the acceptance of Necessity. Necessity speaks as the Earth-Song in "Hamatreya," is defied by the Dionysiac spirit of the poet in "Bacchus," but then subsumes that spirit in "Merlin." The three poems together evidence Emerson's major venture into his own cosmos in the *Poems* of 1846, and are the furthest reach of his imagination beyond his Wordsworthian heritage, since the *May-Day* volume and later work largely return to the Wordsworthianism of "Monadnoc" and "Woodnotes."

The passage copied from the *Vishnu Purana* into his 1845 *Journal* by Emerson has one crucial sentence: "Earth laughs, as if smiling with autumnal flowers to behold her kings unable to effect the subjugation of themselves." In Emerson's poem, this laughter is darkened, for this is a Mortality Ode:

> Earth laughs in flowers, to see her boastful boys
> Earth-proud, proud of the earth which is not theirs;
> Who steer the plough, but cannot steer their feet
> Clear of the grave.

The Earth-Song ends in the spirit of Stevens's "Madame La Fleurie," provoking an extraordinary quatrain that presents Emerson's savage *tessera* to the conclusion of Wordsworth's "Ode":

> When I heard the Earth-song
> I was no longer brave;
> My avarice cooled
> Like lust in the chill of the grave.

The forsaken courage here is Wordsworth's Stoic comfort at the close of the "Ode." "Thoughts that do often lie too deep for tears," prompted by a flower that *blows*, that still lives, become only "avarice," unsuited to our deep poverty, when we hear the earth's true song in its laughing flowers. Since Emerson is to American Romanticism what Wordsworth is to the British or parent version, a defining and separating element in later American poetry begins to show itself here. Emerson had more cause, always, to fear an imminent mortality than Wordsworth did (though in fact both poets lived to be quite old), but he shared with Wordsworth a healthy realism toward natural dangers. I cannot think of another major American writer who is so little credulous in regard to preternatural phenomena as Emerson, who had no patience for superstition, even when manifested as folklore. As an admirer of Sir Thomas Browne, Emerson might have been expected to be at least a touch Yeatsian in this region, but every journal reference to the occult is strongly disparaging. Wordsworth too is reluctant, even when he approaches the form of romance. The largest aspect of the supernatural, the life-after-death, so pervasive in romance traditions as well as folk superstitions, makes no thematic appeal to Emerson or Wordsworth, neither of whom could imagine a life apart from the natural. Wordsworth's "immortality," as many critics have noted, is less Platonic or Christian than it is primordial, personal, almost literal, resembling most closely the child's undivided consciousness, not yet sundered to the self-realization of mortality. But Emerson, though he longed for this, and loved the "Ode" as much as any poem, could not as a poet accept this "immortality" either. Robert C. Pollock, in his fine study of Emerson's "Single Vision," shows how much that vision emphasizes man's "continual self-recovery." Wordsworth's vision declined to offer so much, for his temperament was harsher and his experience less exuberant. But Pollock is writing of the earlier Emerson, whose last major expression is in "Bacchus," not the Emerson who is partly inaugurated by "Merlin," the essay "Experience," and the essay on Montaigne in "Representative Men." "Hamatreya" is another prelude to this Emerson, who speaks his whole mind in the great essay "Fate":

> But Fate against Fate is only parrying and defence: there are also the noble creative forces. The revelation of Thought takes man out of servitude into freedom. We rightly say of ourselves, we were born and afterward we were born again, and many times. We

have successive experiences so important that the new forgets the old, and hence the mythology of the seven or the nine heavens. The day of days, the great day of the feast of life, is that in which the inward eye opens to the Unity in things, to the omnipresence of law:—see that what is must be and ought to be, or is the best. This beatitude dips from on high down on us and we see. It is not in us so much as we are in it. If the air come to our lungs, we breathe and live; if not, we die. If the light come to our eyes, we see; else not. And if truth come to our mind we suddenly expand to its dimensions, as if we grew to worlds. We are as lawgivers; we speak for Nature; we prophesy and divine.

This insight throws us on the party and interest of the Universe, against all and sundry; against ourselves as much as others. A man speaking from insight affirms of himself what is true of the mind: seeing its immortality, he says, I am immortal; seeing its invincibility, he says, I am strong. It is not in us, but we are in it. It is of the maker, not of what is made. All things are touched and changed by it. This uses and is not used. It distances those who share it from those who share it not.

Wordsworth, with his extraordinary precision in measuring the spirit's weather, said of his "spots of time" that they gave knowledge of to what extent and how the mind held mastery over outward sense. In the passage above, the spirit's weather is perpetual cyclone, and the mind's mastery is beyond extent or means. This is more than very American; for glory and loss, it is as central a passage as American literature gives, more so even than the splendid and much-maligned "transparent eyeball" passage in *Nature,* which is to the earlier Emerson what being thrown "on the party and interest of the Universe . . . against ourselves" is to the later. Though the Stevens of *Ideas of Order* mocks the first Emerson (see "Sailing after Lunch": "To expunge all people and be a pupil/Of the gorgeous wheel and so to give/That slight transcendence to the dirty sail,/By light . . . ") the greater Stevens of *The Auroras of Autumn* reaches the resolution of "Fate," precisely attaining the late Emersonian balance (or rather oscillation) between Fate and Freedom. The anxiety of influence abided in Stevens, who continued to satirize his American ancestor (as in the Mr. Homburg of "Looking across the Fields and Watching the Birds Fly," whose enterprise is "To think away the grass, the trees, the clouds,/Not to transform them into other things"). Burrowing away somewhere in Stevens's imagination were memories of reading *The Conduct of Life* (where the essay "Illusions" contains "The Rock" in embryo) and *Letters and Social Aims* (where the long, meandering "Poetry and Imagination" holds more of Stevens's poetics than Valéry or Santayana do). I instance Stevens in relation to "Fate," but the essay touches, directly or dialectically, a company of American poets that includes also Whitman, Dickinson, Melville, Tuckerman, Robinson, Frost,

Jeffers, Aiken, Crane, Roethke, and Ammons, none of whom would have completed the self's circle without it, or at least without modifying into a somewhat different self. That this influence was neither as benevolent as a confirmed Emersonian would have it (see H. H. Waggoner's *American Poets*) nor as destructive as Yvor Winters insisted (*In Defense of Reason*) need not surprise anyone who has reflected upon the long course of Wordsworth's influence upon British poets (or Milton's, before that).

The central passage of "Fate" exhilarates and dismays, as it should; Emerson's "Fate" is Indian enough to be at last unassimilable by him or by us. A *Journal* entry contrasts the Greek "Fate" as "private theatricals" in contrast to India, where "it is the dread reality, it is the cropping-out in our planted gardens of the core of the world: it is the abysmal Force, untameable and immense." This Force inspires a shaman rather than a humanizing poet, an augurer not a prophet, the poet of "Merlin" but not of the misnamed and sublime "Bacchus." Force is irrational, but the inspiration of Bacchus, though more than rational, is the "later reason" of Stevens's *Notes*, or more historically the Idealist Reason that Coleridge and Wordsworth took (though only in part) from assorted Germans. With the contrast between "Bacchus" and "Merlin," we can attempt to clarify two allied strains in Emerson (they cannot be regarded only as early and late, *Nature* and "Self-Reliance" against *The Conduct of Life,* because traces of each can be found from youth through age). Clarification must begin with the 1846 *Journal,* where something of the complexity of Emerson's last great year can be recovered.

In his disgust with the politics of Polk and Webster, in the year of our aggression against Mexico, Emerson consciously turned to the Muse, but with a skeptical reserve: "The life which we seek is expansion; the actual life even of the genius or the saint is obstructive." But, in some mysterious passages, as in the one on the Central Man, . . . the reserve vanishes. Here is another passage, premonitory of Nietzsche's Overman, of Whitman's Self, and (much diminished) of Stevens's Major Man (particularly in the second and third paragraphs, with which compare *Notes toward a Supreme Fiction,* part 1, sections 9–10):

> He lurks, *he* hides,—he who is success, reality, joy, power, that which constitutes Heaven, which reconciles impossibilities, atones for shortcomings, expiates sins, or makes them virtues, buries in oblivion the crowded historical Past, sinks religions, philosophies, nations, persons to legends; reverses the scale of opinion, of fame; reduces sciences to opinion, and makes the thought of the moment the key to the universe and the egg of history to come. . . .
>
> This is he that shall come, or if he come not, nothing comes; he that disappears on the instant that we go to celebrate him. If we go to burn those that blame our celebration, he appears in them.
>
> Hoe and spade; sword and pen; cities, pictures, gardens, laws,

bibles, are prized only because they were means he sometimes used: so with astronomy, arithmetic, caste, feudalism. We kiss with devotion these hems of his garment. They crumble to ashes on our lips.

This is not Christ, but rather an Orphic god-poet, such a divinity as Emerson assumed Hafiz to have celebrated. This is also not the Force or Necessity apotheosized by shamans and bards. Is Emerson constant in distinguishing the three: Christ, Central Man, *Ananke?* As a poet, yes; in prose, not always, for there (despite the fallacious assumptions of Winters) he refuses to "label and ticket, one thing, or two," as he rightly charges the mystic with doing. The 1846 *Journal* frequently approximates Blake, not least when it attacks the mystic, like Swedenborg, as being a Devil turned Angel: "The mystic, who beholds the flux, yet becomes pragmatist on some one particular of faith, and, what is the mischief, seeks to accredit this new jail because it was builded by him who has demolished so many jails." Fearing even an antinomian or visionary dogmatism, the mature Emerson refuses distinctions where we, as his ephebes, badly want and need them. Uriel, like Nature, hates lines, knowing that all new generation comes when matter rolls itself into balls. In the midst of the 1846 *Journal,* there is a great antithetical prayer: "O Bacchus, make them drunk, drive them mad, this multitude of vagabonds, hungry for eloquence, hungry for poetry." The great poem "Bacchus," to me Emerson's finest, comes in answer to this prayer. As I have commented on it elsewhere, I wish here only to look again at its marvelous close:

> Let wine repair what this undid;
> And where the infection slid,
> A dazzling memory revive;
> Refresh the faded tints,
> Recut the aged prints,
> And write my old adventures with the pen
> Which on the first day drew,
> Upon the tablets blue,
> The dancing Pleiads and eternal men.

Stevens's "Large Red Man Reading" aloud "the great blue tabulae" gives to earth-returning ghosts "the outlines of being and its expressings, the syllables of its law," a characteristic reduction of the greater Emersonian dream. Emerson's poem goes as far as apocalyptic poetry can go, but the impulse for refreshing and recutting was stronger even than "Bacchus," and gave Emerson "Merlin," scarcely a lesser poem, but a dangerous and divided work. "Bacchus" asks for more than Wordsworth did, for a renovation as absolute as Blake's vision sought. The poetic faculty is to free man from his own ruins, and restore him as the being Blake called Tharmas, instinctual innocence triumphantly at home in his own place. Stevens, at his most hopeful, asserted that the poem refreshes life so that we share, but only for a moment, the First Idea, which belonged to Tharmas. Like Wordsworth, Stevens yields to a version of the Reality Principle. Blake and Emerson do not, but Emerson departs from Blakean affinities when, in his extraordinary impatience, most fatedly American of qualities, he seeks terms with his Reality Principle only by subsuming it, as he does in "Merlin." Not "Bacchus" but "Merlin" seems to me the archetypal American poem that our best poets keep writing, once they have passed through their crises of individuation, have found their true limit, and then fail to accept any limit as their own. The American Muse is a *daimon* of disorder, whose whispered counsel in the dark is "Evade and multiply." Young and old at once, bewilderingly from their start, the great among our poets seek to become each a process rather than a person, Nemesis rather than accident, as though it could be open to any imagination to be enthroned where only a handful have ever come.

If a single American has incarnated our *daimon*, it is Emerson, not our greatest writer but merely our only inescapable one, to be found always where Whitman asked to be sought, under our boot-soles, effused and drifted all through our lives and our literature, just as he is to be found on every page, almost in every line, of Whitman. Denied or scorned, he turns up again in every opponent, however orthodox, classical, conservative or even just southern. Why he stands so much at the center may always be a mystery, but who else can stand in his place? Nineteenth-century American culture is the Age of Emerson, and what we undergo now seems more than ever his. A good part of what has been urged against him, even by very negative critics like James Truslow Adams and Winters, is true, but this appears to mean mostly that Emerson did subsume something inevitable in the national process, that he joined himself forever to the American version of what Stevens called "fatal Ananke . . . the final god."

"Merlin," a text in which to read both the American Sublime and the American poetic disaster, was finished in the summer of 1846, but had its origins in the *Journal* of 1845, in a strong doggerel:

> I go discontented thro' the world
> Because I cannot strike
> The harp to please my tyrannous ear:
> Gentle touches are not wanted,
> These the yielding gods had granted.
> It shall not tinkle a guitar,
> But strokes of fate
> Chiming with the ample winds,
> With the pulse of human blood,
> With the voice of mighty men,
> With the din of city arts,
> With the cannonade of war,
> With the footsteps of the brave

And the sayings of the wise,
Chiming with the forest's tone
When they buffet boughs in the windy wood,
Chiming with the gasp and moan
Of the ice-imprisoned flood.
I will not read a pretty tale
To pretty people in a nice saloon
Borrowed from their expectation,
But I will sing aloud and free
From the heart of the world.

It is almost the universal motto of the American poet, from Whitman down to the recent transformation of W. S. Merwin into the nearly impersonal bard of *The Lice* and *The Carrier of Ladders*. From the "gentle touches" of *Green with Beasts* ("the gaiety of three winds is a game of green / Shining, of grey-and-gold play in the holly-bush") Merwin has gone to Emersonian "strokes of fate" ("We are the echo of the future / On the door it says what to do to survive / But we were not born to survive / Only to live") and Merwin is probably the representative poet of my own generation. Learned accomplishment will not suffice where the Muse herself masks as Necessity; if Emerson was aware that this was a masking, he failed to show it, an imaginative failure, fine as the finished "Merlin" is:

Thy trivial harp will never please
Or fill my craving ear;
Its chords should ring as blows the breeze,
Free, peremptory, clear. . . .
The kingly bard
Must smite the chords rudely and hard,
As with hammer or with mace;
That they may render back
Artful thunder, which conveys
Secrets of the solar track,
Sparks of the supersolar blaze.
Merlin's blows are strokes of fate.

"Artful thunder" is cousin to "fearful symmetry," reversing the parodistic awe of an argument from apparent design but still mockingly urging us to yield to an other-than-human splendor and terror. Power is "Merlin" 's subject, "strokes of fate" as the essay "Fate" defines them: "why should we fear to be crushed by savage elements, we who are made up of the same elements?" We are ourselves strokes of fate, on this view, and most ourselves in Merlin the Bard, whose "mighty line / Extremes of nature reconciled." The dangers, social and solipsistic, of so amazingly unconditioned a bardic vision crowd upon us in the poem's second part, with great eloquence:

> Perfect-paired as eagle's wings,
> Justice is the rhyme of things;
> Trade and counting use
> The self-same tuneful muse;
> And Nemesis,
> Who with even matches odd,
> Who athwart space redresses
> The partial wrong,
> Fills the just period,
> And finishes the song.

No reader of Emerson ought to brood on these lines without juxtaposing them to the magnificent and famous *Journal* entry of April 1842, in which Emerson gave his fullest dialectic of Nemesis, which "Merlin" seems to slight:

> In short, there ought to be no such thing as Fate. As long as we use this word, it is a sign of our impotence and that we are not yet ourselves. There is now a sublime revelation in each of us which makes us so strangely aware and certain of our riches that although I have never since I was born for so much as one moment expressed the truth, and although I have never heard the expression of it from any other, I know that the whole is here,—the wealth of the Universe is for me, everything is explicable and practicable for me. And yet whilst I adore this ineffable life which is at my heart, it will not condescend to gossip with me, it will not announce to me any particulars of science, it will not enter into the details of my biography, and say to me why I have a son and daughters born to me, or why my sons dies in his sixth year of joy. Herein, then, I have this latent omniscience coexistent with omni-ignorance. Moreover, whilst this Deity glows at the heart, and by his unlimited presentiments gives me all Power, I know that tomorrow will be as this day, I am a dwarf, and I remain a dwarf. That is to say, I believe in Fate. As long as I am weak, I shall talk of Fate; whenever the God fills me with his fulness, I shall see the disappearance of Fate.
>
> I am *Defeated* all the time; yet to Victory I am born.

But Merlin, who can no more be defeated than Nemesis can be thwarted, becomes one with the spirit that "finishes the song." There is nothing like this unity with the serpent Ananke before Emerson in American poetry (or in English) but all too much after. Before Emerson, we can take Bryant and Poe as representative of the possibilities for Romantic poetry in America, and see in both of them a capable reservation that Emerson abolished in himself. Bryant's "The Poet" is very late (1863) but presents a stance firmly established by more than fifty years of composing good poetry. "Make thyself a part/Of the great tumult," Bryant tells the poet, but the same poem severely contrasts the organized violence within the mind and the unorganized violence of nature:

> A blast that whirls the dust
>   Along the howling street and dies away;
> But feelings of calm power and mighty sweep,
> Like currents journeying through the windless deep.

Poe, despite his celebrated and angelic ambitions for the poet, follows Shelley and Byron in emphasizing the pragmatic sorrows of Prometheanism, even as Bryant follows Cowper and Wordsworth in a Stoic awareness of the mind's separation from its desired natural context. "Israfel" remains a poem of real excellence because in it the mind is overwhelmed by auguries of division, between the angelic bard and his wistfully defiant imitator below, who is reduced to doubting his divine precursor's powers where they are to be brought down into nature: "He might not sing so wildly well/A mortal melody." Bryant and Poe are both of them closer to English Romantic consciousness than the Emerson of "Merlin" and "Fate," who thus again prophesied what Wright Morris calls "the territory ahead," the drastic American Romanticism of heroic imaginative failure, or perhaps a kind of success we have not yet learned to apprehend. For the doctrine of "Merlin" is dangerous in that it tempts our poets to a shamanism they neither altogether want nor properly can sustain.

The best Emersonian poets are, by rationally universal agreement, Whitman and Dickinson, who found their own versions of a dialectic between Bacchus and Merlin. . . . But the oscillation between poetic incarnation (Bacchus) and the merging with Necessity (Merlin) is most evident and crucial in each new poet's emergence and individuation. Emerson our father, more than Whitman the American Moses, has become the presiding genius of the American version of poetic influence, the anxiety of originality that he hoped to dispel, but ironically fostered in a more virulent form than it has taken elsewhere.

II

As poet and as person, Walt Whitman remains large and evasive. We cannot know, even now, much that he desired us not to know, despite the best efforts of many devoted and scholarly biographers. The relation between his life and his poetry is far more uncertain than most of his readers believe it to be. Yet Whitman is so important to us, so crucial to an American mythology, so absolutely central to our literary culture, that we need to go on trying to bring his life and his work together. Our need might have delighted Whitman, and might have troubled him also. Like his master, Emerson, Whitman prophesied an American religion that is post-Christian, but while Emerson dared to suggest that the Crucifixion was a defeat and that Americans demand victory, Whitman dared further, and suggested that he himself had satisfied the demand. Here is Emerson:

> The history of Christ is the best document of the power of character which we have. A youth who owed nothing to fortune and who was "hanged at Tyburn"—by the pure quality of his nature has shed this epic splendor around the facts of his death which has transfigured every particular into a grand universal symbol for the eyes of all mankind ever since.
>
> He did well. This great Defeat is hitherto the highest fact we have. But he that shall come shall do better. The mind requires a far higher exhibition of character, one which shall make itself good to the senses as well as to the soul; a success to the senses as well as to the soul. This was a great Defeat; we demand Victory.

This grand journal entry concludes with the magnificent "I am *Defeated* all the time; yet to Victory I am born." And here is Whitman, "he that shall come," doing better:

> That I could forget the mockers and insults!
> That I could forget the trickling tears and the blows of the
>   bludgeons and hammers!
> That I could look with a separate look on my own crucifixion
>   and bloody crowning.
>
> I remember now,
> I resume the overstaid fraction,
> The grave of rock multiplies what has been confided to it, or
>   to any graves,
> Corpses rise, gashes heal, fastenings roll from me.
>
> I troop forth replenish'd with supreme power.

This is Walt Whitman "singing and chanting the things that are part of him,/The worlds that were and will be, death and day," in the words of his involuntary heir, Wallace Stevens. But which Walt Whitman is it? His central poem is what he finally entitled "Song of Myself," rather than, say, "Song of My Soul." But which self? There are two in the poem, besides his soul, and the true difficulties of reading Whitman begin (or ought to begin) with his unnervingly original psychic cartography which resists assimilation to the Freudian maps of the mind. Freud's later system divides us into the "I" or ego, the "above-I" or superego, and the "it" or id. Whitman divided himself (or recognized himself as divided) into "my self," "my soul," and the "real Me" or "Me myself," where the self is a kind of ego, the soul not quite a superego, and the "real Me" not at all an id. Or to use a vocabulary known to Whitman, and still known to us, the self is personality, the soul is character, and again the "real Me" is a mystery. Lest these difficulties seem merely my own, and not truly Whitman's, I turn to the text of "Song of Myself." Here is Walt Whitman, "My self," the *persona* or mask, the personality of the poet:

> Walt Whitman, a kosmos, of Manhattan the son,
> Turbulent, fleshy, sensual, eating, drinking and breeding,
> No sentimentalist, no stander above men and women or
>   apart from them,
> No more modest than immodest.

That is Walt Whitman, one of the roughs, an American, but hardly Walter Whitman, Jr., whose true personality, "real Me" or "Me myself," is presented in the passage I love best in the poem:

> These come to me days and nights and go from me again,
> But they are not the Me myself.
>
> Apart from the pulling and hauling stands what I am,
> Stands amused, complacent, compassionating, idle, unitary,
> Looks down, is erect, or bends an arm on an impalpable
>   certain rest,
> Looking with side-curved head curious what will come next,
> Both in and out of the game and watching and wondering
>   at it.

This "Me myself" is not exactly "hankering, gross, mystical, nude," nor quite "turbulent, fleshy, sensual, eating, drinking and breeding." Graceful and apart, cunningly balanced, charming beyond measure, this curious "real Me" is boylike and girllike, very American yet not one of the roughs, provocative, at one with itself. Whatever the Whitmanian soul may be, this "Me myself" evidently can have no equal relationship with it. When the Whitmanian "I" addresses the soul, we hear a warning:

> I believe in you my soul, the other I am must not abase itself
>   to you,
> And you must not be abased to the other.

The "I" here is the "Myself" of "Song of Myself," poetic personality, robust and rough. "The other I am" is the "Me myself," in and out of the game, and clearly not suited for embraces with the soul. Whitman's wariness, his fear of abasement, whether of his soul or of his true, inner personality, one to the other, remains the enigma of his poetry, as of his life, and accounts for his intricate evasions both as poet and as person.

Whitman's critics thus commence with a formidable disadvantage as they attempt to receive and comprehend his work. The largest puzzle about the continuing reception of Whitman's poetry is the still prevalent notion that we ought to take him at his word, whether about his self (or selves) or about his art. No other poet insists so vehemently and so continuously that he will tell us all, and tell us all without artifice, and yet tells us so little, and so cunningly. Except for Dickinson (the only American poet comparable to him in magnitude), there is no other nineteenth-century poet as difficult and hermetic as Whitman; not Blake, not Browning, not Mallarmé. Only an elite can read Whitman, despite the poet's insistence that he wrote for the people, for "powerful uneducated persons," as his "By Blue Ontario's Shore" proclaims. His more accurate "Poets to Come" is closer to his readers' experience of him:

> I am a man who, sauntering along without fully stopping,
>   turns a casual look upon you and then averts his face.

Whitman was surely too sly to deceive himself, or at least both of his selves, on this matter of his actual poetic evasiveness and esotericism. Humanly, he had much to evade, in order to keep going, in order to start writing and then to keep writing. His biographers cannot give us a clear image of his childhood, which was certainly rather miserable. His numerous siblings had mostly melancholy life histories. Madness, retardation, marriage to a prostitute, depressiveness, and hypochondria figure among their fates. The extraordinary obsession with health and cleanliness that oddly marks Whitman's poetry had a poignant origin in his early circumstances. Of his uneasy relationship with his father we know a little, though not much. But we know nothing really of his mother, and how he felt towards her. Perhaps the most crucial fact about Whitman's psyche we know well enough; he needed, quite early, to become the true father of all his siblings, and perhaps of his mother also. Certainly he fathered and mothered as many of his siblings as he could, even as he so beautifully became a surrogate father and mother for thousands of wounded and sick soldiers, Union and Confederate, white and black, in the hospitals of Washington, D.C., throughout the Civil War.

The extraordinary and truthful image of Whitman that haunts our country; the vision of the compassionate, unpaid, volunteer wound-dresser comforting young men in pain and soothing the dying, is the climax of Paul Zweig's book on how the man Walter Whitman, Jr., became the poet Walt Whitman. This vision informs the finest pages of Zweig's uneven but moving study; I cannot recall any previous Whitman biographer or critic so vividly and humanely portraying Whitman's hospital service. Searching for the authentic Whitman, as Zweig shows, is a hopeless quest; our greatest poet will always be our most evasive, and perhaps our most self-contradictory. Whitman, at his greatest, has overwhelming pathos as a poet; equal I think to anything in the language. The *Drum-Taps* poem called "The Wound-Dresser" is far from Whitman at his astonishing best, and yet its concluding lines carry the persuasive force of his poetic and human images for once unified:

> Returning, resuming, I thread my way through the
>   hospitals,

The hurt and wounded I pacify with soothing hand,
I sit by the restless all the dark night, some are so young,
Some suffer so much, I recall the experience sweet and sad,
(Many a soldier's loving arms about this neck have cross'd
       and rested,
Many a soldier's kiss dwells on these bearded lips.)

Zweig is admirably sensitive in exploring the ambiguities in Whitman's hospital intensities, and more admirable still in his restraint at not voicing how much all of us are touched by Whitman's pragmatic saintliness during those years of service. I cannot think of a western writer of anything like Whitman's achievement who ever gave himself or herself up so directly to meeting the agonized needs of the most desperate. There are a handful of American poets comparable to Whitman in stature: Emily Dickinson certainly, Wallace Stevens and Robert Frost perhaps, and maybe one or two others. Our image of them, or of our greatest novelists, or even of Whitman's master, Emerson, can move us sometimes, but not as the image of the wound-dresser Whitman must move us. Like the Lincoln whom he celebrated and lamented, Whitman is American legend, a figure who has a kind of religious aura even for secular intellectuals. If Emerson founded the American literary religion, Whitman alone permanently holds the place most emblematic of the life of the spirit in America.

These religious terms are not Zweig's, yet his book's enterprise usefully traces the winding paths that led Whitman on to his apotheosis as healer and comforter. Whitman's psychosexuality, labyrinthine in its perplexities, may have been the central drive that bewildered the poet into those ways, but it was not the solitary, overwhelming determinant that many readers judge it to have been. Zweig refreshingly is not one of these overdetermined readers. He surmises that Whitman might have experienced little actual homosexual intercourse. I suspect none, though Whitman evidently was intensely in love with some unnamed man in 1859, and rather differently in love again with Peter Doyle about five years later. Zweig accurately observes that: "Few poets have written as erotically as Whitman, while having so little to say about sex. For the most part, his erotic poetry is intransitive, self-delighting." Indeed, it is precisely autoerotic rather more than it is homoerotic; Whitman overtly celebrates masturbation, and his most authentic sexual passion is always for himself. One would hardly know this from reading many of Whitman's critics, but one certainly knows it by closely reading Whitman's major poems. Here is part of a crucial crisis-passage from "Song of Myself," resolved through successful masturbation:

I merely stir, press, feel with my fingers, and am happy,
To touch my person to some one else's is about as much as I
       can stand.
Is this then a touch? quivering me to a new identity,
Flames and ether making a rush for my veins,

Treacherous tip of me reaching and crowding to help them,
My flesh and blood playing out lightning to strike what is
    hardly different from myself,

. . . .

I went myself first to the headland, my own hands carried
    me there.
You villain touch! what are you doing? my breath is tight
    in its throat,
Unclench your floodgates, you are too much for me.
Blind loving wrestling touch, sheath'd hooded sharp-
    tooth'd touch!
Did it make you ache so, leaving me?
Parting track'd by arriving, perpetual payment of perpetual
    loan,
Rich showering rain, and recompense richer afterward.
Sprouts take and accumulate, stand by the curb prolific and
    vital,
Landscapes projected masculine, full-sized and golden.

I take it that this celebratory mode of masturbation, whether read metaphorically or literally, remains the genuine scandal of Whitman's poetry. This may indeed be one of the kernel passages in Whitman, expanded and elaborated as it is from an early notebook passage that invented the remarkable trope of "I went myself first to the headland," the headland being the psychic place of *extravagance*, of wandering beyond limits, from which you cannot scramble back to the shore, place of the father, and from which you may topple over into the sea, identical with night, death, and the fierce old mother. "My own hands carried me there," as they fail to carry Whitman in "When Lilacs Last in the Dooryard Bloom'd":

O great star disappear'd—O the black murk that hides the
    star!
O cruel hands that hold me powerless—O helpless soul
    of me!

These are Whitman's own hands, pragmatically cruel because they cannot hold him potently, disabled as he is by a return of repressed guilt. Lincoln's death has set going memories of filial guilt, the guilt that the mortal sickness of Walter Whitman, Sr., should have liberated his son into the full blood of creativity that ensued in the 1855 first edition of *Leaves of Grass* (the father died a week after the book's publication). What Whitman's poetry does not express are any reservations about autoeroticism, which more than sadomasochism remains the last western taboo. It is a peculiar paradox that Whitman, who proclaims his love for all men, women, and children, should have been profoundly solipsistic, narcissistic, and self-delighting, but that paradox returns us to the Whitmanian self or rather selves, the cosmological *persona* as opposed to the daemonic "real Me."

The most vivid manifestation of the "real Me" in Whitman comes in the shattering *Sea-Drift* poem, "As I Ebb'd with the Ocean of Life":

O baffled, balk'd, bent to the very earth,
Oppress'd with myself that I have dared to open my mouth,
Aware now that amid all that blab whose echoes recoil upon
    me I have not once had the least idea who or what I
    am,
But that before all my arrogant poems the real Me stands yet
    untouch'd, untold, altogether unreach'd,
Withdrawn far, mocking me with mock-congratulatory signs
    and bows,
With peals of distant ironical laughter at every word I have
    written,
Pointing in silence to these songs, and then to the sand
    beneath.
I perceive I have not really understood any thing, not a
    single object, and that no man ever can,
Nature here in sight of the sea taking advantage of me to
    dart upon me and sting me,
Because I have dared to open my mouth to sing at all.

It is Walt Whitman, Kosmos, American, rough, who is mocked here by his real self, a self that knows itself to be a mystery, because it is neither mother, nor father, nor child; neither quite female nor quite male; neither voice nor voicelessness. Whitman's "real Me" is what is best and oldest in him, and like the faculty Emerson called "Spontaneity," it is no part of the creation, meaning both nature's creation and Whitman's verbal cosmos. It is like a surviving fragment of the original Abyss preceding nature, not Adamic but pre-Adamic. This "real Me" is thus also presexual, and so plays no role either in the homoerotic "Calamus" poems or in the dubiously heterosexual "Children of Adam" group. Yet it seems to me pervasive in the six long or longer poems that indisputably are Whitman's masterpieces: "The Sleepers," "Song of Myself," "Crossing Brooklyn Ferry," "As I Ebb'd with the Ocean of Life," "Out of the Cradle Endlessly Rocking," and "When Lilacs Last in the Dooryard Bloom'd." Though only the last of these is overtly an elegy, all six are in covert ways elegies for the "real Me," for that "Me myself" that Whitman could not hope to celebrate as a poet and could not hope to fulfill as a sexual being. This "real Me" is not a spirit that denies, but rather one that always remains out of reach, an autistic spirit. In English Romantic poetry and in later nineteenth-century prose romance there is the parallel being that Shelley called "the Spirit of Solitude," the daemon or shadow of the self-destructive young Poet who is the hero of Shelley's *Alastor*. But Whitman's very American "real Me" is quite unlike a Shelleyan or Blakean Spectre. It does not quest or desire, and it does not want to be wanted.

Though Zweig hints that Whitman has been a bad influence on other writers, I suspect that a larger view of influence would reverse this implicit judgment. Whitman has been an inescapable influence not only for most significant American poets after him (Frost, indebted directly to Emerson, is the largest exception) but also for the most gifted writers of narrative fiction. This influence transcends matters of form, and has everything to do with the Whitmanian split between the *persona* of the rough Walt and the ontological truth of the "real Me." Poets as diverse as Wallace Stevens and T. S. Eliot have in common perhaps only their hidden, partly unconscious reliance upon Whitman as prime precursor. Hemingway's acknowledged debt to *Huckleberry Finn* is real enough, but the deeper legacy came from Whitman. The Hemingway protagonist, split between an empirical self of stoic courage and a "real Me" endlessly evasive of others while finding its freedom only in an inner perfection of loneliness, is directly descended from the dual Whitman of "Song of Myself." American elegiac writing since Whitman (and how surprisingly much of it *is* covertly elegiac) generally revises Whitman's elegies for the self. *The Waste Land* is "When Lilacs Last in the Dooryard Bloom'd" rewritten, and Stevens's "The Rock" is not less Whitmanian than Hart Crane's *The Bridge*.

Zweig's book joins itself to the biographical criticism of Whitman by such scholars as Bliss Perry, Gay Wilson Allen, Joseph Jay Rubin, Justin Kaplan, and others whose works are part of a useful tradition that illuminates the Americanism of Whitman and yet cannot do enough with Whitman's many paradoxes. Of these, I judge the most crucial to be expressed by this question: how did someone of Whitman's extraordinarily idiosyncratic nature become so absolutely central to nearly all subsequent American literary high culture? This centrality evidently cannot ebb among us, as can be seen in the most recent poems of John Ashbery in his book *The Wave* or in the stories of Harold Brodkey, excerpted from his vast and wholly Whitmanian work-in-progress. Whitman's powerful yet unstable identities were his own inheritance from the Orphic Emerson, who proclaimed the central man or poet-to-come as necessarily metamorphic, Bacchic and yet original, and above all American and not British or European in his cultural vistas. This prescription was and is dangerous, because it asks for pragmatism and yet affirms impossible hopes. The rough Whitman is democratic, the "real Me" an elitist, but both selves are equally Emersonian.

Politically, Whitman was a Free Soil Democrat who rebelled against the betrayal by the New York Democratic Party of its Jacksonian tradition, but Zweig rightly emphasizes the survival of Emersonian "Prudence" in Whitman which caused him to oppose labor unions. I suspect that Whitman's politics paralleled his sexual morality: the rough Walt homoerotic and radical, the "real Me" autoerotic and individualistically elitist. The true importance of this split emerges neither in Whitman's sexuality nor in his politics, but in the delicacy and beauty of his strongest poems. Under the cover of an apparent rebellion against traditional literary form, they extend the poetic tradition without violating it. Whitman's elegies for the self have much in common with Tennyson's, but are even subtler, more difficult triumphs of High Romanticism. Here I dissent wholly from Zweig, who ends his book with a judgment I find both wrong and puzzling:

> *Leaves of Grass* was launched on a collision course with its age. Whitman's work assaulted the institution of literature and language itself and, in so doing, laid the groundwork for the anticultural ambition of modernist writing. He is the ancestor not only of Henry Miller and Allen Ginsberg but of Kafka, Beckett, Andre Breton, Borges—of all who have made of their writing an attack on the act of writing and on culture itself.

To associate the subtle artistry, delicate and evasive, of Whitman's greatest poems with Miller and Ginsberg rather than with Hemingway, Stevens, and Eliot is already an error. To say that Kafka, Beckett, and Borges attack, by their writing, the act of writing and culture, is to mistake their assault upon certain interpretive conventions for a war against literary culture. But the gravest misdirection here is to inform readers that Whitman truly attacked the institutions of language and literature. Whitman's "real Me" has more to do with the composition of the great poems than the rough Walt ever did. "Lilacs," which Zweig does not discuss, is as profoundly traditional an elegy as *In Memoriam* or *Adonais*. Indeed, "Lilacs" echoes Tennyson, while "As I Ebb'd" echoes Shelley and "Crossing Brooklyn Ferry" invokes *King Lear*. Zweig is taken in by the prose Whitman who insists he will not employ allusiveness, but the poet Whitman knew better, and is brilliantly allusive, as every strong poet is compelled to be, echoing his precursors and rivals but so stationing the echoes as to triumph with and in some sense over them.

Zweig's study is an honorable and useful account of Whitman's poetic emergence, but it shares in some of the severe limitations of nearly all Whitman criticism so far published. Whitman's subtle greatness as a poet seems to me not fully confronted, in Zweig's work or elsewhere. The poetry of the "real Me," intricate and forlorn, is addressed to the "real Me" of the American reader. That it reached what was oldest and best in Eliot and Stevens is testified to by their finest poetry, in contradistinction to their prose remarks upon Whitman. Paradoxically, Whitman's best critic remains, not an American, but D. H. Lawrence, who lamented that, "The Americans are not worthy of their Whitman." Lawrence believed that Whitman had gone further, in actual living expression, than any other poet. The belief was extravagant, certainly, but again the Whitmanian poems of Lawrence's superb final phase show us what Lawrence meant. I give the last word here though, not to Lawrence, but to Emerson, who wrote the first words about Whitman in his celebrated 1855 letter to the poet, words that remain true nearly 130 years further on in our literary culture:

I am not blind to the worth of the wonderful gift of *Leaves of Grass*. I find it the most extraordinary piece of wit and wisdom that America has yet contributed.

III

It is not a rare quality for great poets to possess such cognitive strength that we are confronted by authentic intellectual difficulties when we read them. "Poems are made by fools like me," yes, and by Dante, Milton, Blake, and Shelley, but only God can make a tree, to reappropriate a rejoinder I remember making to W. H. Auden many years ago, when he deprecated the possibilities of poetry as compared with the awful truths of Christian theology. But there are certainly very grand poets who are scarcely thinkers in the discursive modes. Tennyson and Whitman are instances of overwhelming elegiac artists who make us fitful when they argue, and the subtle rhetorical evasions of Wallace Stevens do not redeem his unfortunate essay, "A Collect of Philosophy."

Of all poets writing in English in the nineteenth and twentieth centuries, I judge Emily Dickinson to present us with the most authentic cognitive difficulties. Vast and subtle intellect cannot in itself make a poet; the essential qualities are inventiveness, mastery of trope and craft, and that weird flair for intuiting significance through rhythm to which we can give no proper name. Dickinson has all these, as well as a mind so original and powerful that we scarcely have begun, even now, to catch up with her.

Originality at its strongest—in the Yahwist, Plato, Shakespeare, and Freud—usurps immense spaces of consciousness and language, and imposes contingencies upon all who come after. These contingencies work so as to conceal authentic difficulty through a misleading familiarity. Dickinson's strangeness, partly masked, still causes us to wonder at her, as we ought to wonder at Shakespeare or Freud. Like them, she has no single, overwhelming precursor whose existence can lessen her wildness for us. Her agon was waged with the whole of tradition, but particularly with the Bible and with Romanticism. As an agonist, she takes care to differ from any male model, and places us upon warning:

> I cannot dance upon my Toes—
> No Man instructed me—
> But oftentimes, among my mind,
> A Glee possesseth me,
>
> Nor any know I know the Art
> I mention—easy—Here—
> Nor any Placard boast me—
> It's full as Opera—

The mode is hardly Whitmanian in this lyric of 1862, but the vaunting is, and both gleeful arts respond to the Emersonian prophecy of American Self-Reliance. Each responds with a difference, but it is a perpetual trial to be a heretic whose only orthodoxy is Emersonianism, or the exaltation of whim:

> If nature will not tell the tale
> Jehovah told to her
> Can human nature not survive
> Without a listener?
>
>   (1748)

Emerson should have called his little first book *Nature* by its true title of *Man*, but Dickinson in any case would have altered that title also. Alas, that Emerson was not given the chance to read the other Titan that he fostered. We would cherish his charmed reaction to:

> A Bomb upon the Ceiling
> Is an improving thing—
> It keeps the nerves progressive
> Conjecture flourishing—
>
>   (1128)

Dickinson, after all, could have sent her poems to Emerson rather than to the nobly obtuse Higginson. We cannot envision Whitman addressing a copy of the first *Leaves of Grass* to a Higginson. There is little reason to suppose that mere diffidence prevented Miss Dickinson of Amherst from presenting her work to Mr. Emerson of Concord. In 1862, Emerson was still Emerson; his long decline dates from after the conclusion of the War. A private unfolding remained necessary for Dickinson, according to laws of the spirit and of poetic reason that we perpetually quest to surmise. Whereas Whitman masked his delicate, subtle, and hermetic art by developing the outward self of the rough Walt, Dickinson set herself free to invest her imaginative exuberance elsewhere. The heraldic drama of her reclusiveness became the cost of her confirmation as a poet more original even than Whitman, indeed more original than any poet of her century after (and except) Wordsworth. Like Wordsworth, she began anew upon a *tabula rasa* of poetry, to appropriate Hazlitt's remark about Wordsworth. Whitman rethought the relation of the poet's self to his own vision, whereas Dickinson rethought the entire content of poetic vision. Wordsworth had done both, and done both more implicitly than these Americans could manage, but then Wordsworth had Coleridge as stimulus, while Whitman and Dickinson had the yet more startling and far wilder Emerson, who was and is the American difference personified. I cannot believe that even Dickinson would have written with so absolutely astonishing an audacity had Emerson not insisted that poets were as liberating gods:

Because that you are going
And never coming back
And I, however absolute,
May overlook your Track—

Because that Death is final,
However first it be,
This instant be suspended
Above Mortality—

Significance that each has lived
The other to detect
Discovery not God himself
Could now annihilate

Eternity, Presumption
The instant I perceive
That you, who were Existence
Yourself forgot to live—

These are the opening quatrains of poem 1260, dated by Thomas Johnson as about 1873, but it must be later, if indeed the reference is to the dying either of Samuel Bowles (1878) or of Judge Otis Lord (1884), the two men Richard Sewall, Dickinson's principal biographer, considers to have been her authentic loves, if not in any conventional way her lovers. The poem closes with a conditional vision of God refunding to us finally our "confiscated Gods." Reversing the traditional pattern, Dickinson required and achieved male Muses, and her "confiscated Gods" plays darkly against Emerson's "liberating gods." Of Emerson, whose crucial work (*Essays, The Conduct of Life, Society and Solitude,* the *Poems*) she had mastered, Dickinson spoke with the ambiguity we might expect. When Emerson lectured in Amherst in December 1857, and stayed next door with Dickinson's brother and sister-in-law, he was characterized by the poet: "as if he had come from where dreams are born." Presumably the Transcendental Emerson might have merited this, but it is curious when applied to the exalter of "Fate" and "Power" in *The Conduct of Life,* or to the dialectical pragmatist of "Experience" and "Circles," two essays that I think Dickinson had internalized. Later, writing to Higginson, she observed: "With the Kingdom of Heaven on his knee, could Mr. Emerson hesitate?" The question, whether open or rhetorical, is dangerous and wonderful, and provokes considerable rumination.

Yet her subtle ways with other male precursors are scarcely less provocative. Since Shelley had addressed *Epipsychidion* to Emilia Viviani, under the name of "Emily," Dickinson felt authorized to answer a poet who, like herself, favored the image of volcanoes. Only ten days or so before Judge Lord died, she composed a remarkable quatrain in his honor (and her own):

> Circumference thou Bride of Awe
> Possessing thou shalt be
> Possessed by every hallowed Knight
> That dares to covet thee
>
> (1620)

Sewall notes the interplay with some lines in *Epipsychidion:*

> Possessing and possessed by all that is
> Within that calm circumference of bliss,
> And by each other, till to love and live
> Be one:—
>
> (ll. 549–52)

Shelley's passage goes on to a kind of lovers' apocalypse:

> One hope within two wills, one will beneath
> Two overshadowing minds, one life, one death,
> One heaven, one Hell, one immortality,
> And one annihilation.
>
> (ll. 584–87)

In his essay "Circles," Emerson had insisted "there is no outside, no inclosing wall, no circumference to us." The same essay declares "the only sin is limitation." If that is so, then there remains the cost of confirmation, worked out by Dickinson in an extraordinary short poem that may be her critique of Emerson's denial of an outside:

> I saw no Way—The Heavens were stitched—
> I felt the Columns close—
> The Earth reversed her Hemispheres—
> I touched the Universe—
>
> And back it slid—and I alone
> A Speck upon a Ball—
> Went out upon Circumference—
> Beyond the Dip of Bell—
>
> (378)

"My Business is Circumference—" she famously wrote to Higginson, to whom, not less famously, she described herself as "the only Kangaroo among the Beauty." When she wrote, to another correspondent, that "The Bible dealt with the Centre, not with the Circumference—," she would have been aware that the terms were Emerson's, and that Emerson also dealt only with the Central, in the hope of the Central Man who would come. Clearly, "Circumference" is her trope for the Sublime, as consciousness and as achievement or performance. For Shelley, Circumference was a Spenserian cynosure, a Gardens of Adonis vision, while for Emerson it was no part of us, or only another challenge to be overcome by the Central, by the Self-Reliant Man.

If the Bible's concern is Centre, not Circumference, it cannot be because the Bible does not quest for the Sublime. If Circumference or Dickinson is the bride of Awe or of the authority of Judge Lord, then Awe too somehow had to be detached from the Centre:

> No man saw awe, nor to his house
> Admitted he a man
> Though by his awful residence
> Has human nature been.
>
> Not deeming of his dread abode
> Till laboring to flee
> A grasp on comprehension laid
> Detained vitality.
>
> Returning is a different route
> The Spirit could not show
> For breathing is the only work
> To be enacted now.
>
> "Am not consumed," old Moses wrote,
> "Yet saw him face to face"—
> That very physiognomy
> I am convinced was this.
>
> (1733)

This might be called an assimilation of Awe to Circumference, where "laboring to flee" and returning via "a different route" cease to be antithetical to one another. "Vitality" here is another trope for Circumference or the Dickinsonian Sublime. If, as I surmise, this undated poem is a kind of proleptic elegy for Judge Lord, then Dickinson identifies herself with "old Moses," and not for the first time in her work. Moses, denied entrance into Canaan, "wasn't fairly used—," she wrote, as though the exclusion were her fate also. In some sense, she chose this fate, and not just by extending her circumference to Bowles and to Lord, unlikely pragmatic choices. The spiritual choice was not to be post-Christian, as with Whitman or Emerson, but to become a sect of one, like Milton or Blake. Perhaps her crucial choice was to refuse the auction of her mind through publication. Character being fate, the Canaan she would not cross to was poetic recognition while she lived.

Of Dickinson's 1,775 poems and fragments, several hundred are authentic, strong works, with scores achieving an absolute aesthetic dignity. To choose one above all the others must reveal more about the critic than he or she could hope to know. But I do not hesitate in my choice, poem 627, written probably in her very productive year, 1862. What precedents are there for such a poem, a work of unnaming, a profound and shockingly original cognitive act of negation?

> The Tint I cannot take—is best—
> The Color too remote
> That I could show it in Bazaar—
> A Guinea at a sight—
>
> The fine—impalpable Array—
> That swaggers on the eye
> Like Cleopatra's Company—
> Repeated—in the sky—
>
> The Moments of Dominion
> That happen on the Soul
> And leave it with a Discontent
> Too exquisite—to tell—
>
> The eager look— on Landscapes—
> As if they just repressed
> Some Secret—that was pushing
> Like Chariots—in the West—
>
> The Pleading of the Summer—
> That other Prank— of Snow—
> That Cushions Mystery with Tulle,
> For fear the Squirrels—know.
>
> Their Graspless manners—mock us—
> Until the Cheated Eye
> Shuts arrogantly—in the Grave—
> Another way—to see—

It is, rugged and complete, a poetics, and a manifesto of Self-Reliance. "The poet did not stop at the color or the form, but read their meaning; neither may he rest in this meaning, but he makes the same objects exponents of his new thought." This Orphic metamorphosis is Emerson's, but is not accomplished in his own poetry, nor is his radical program of unnaming. Dickinson begins by throwing away the lights and the definitions, and by asserting that her jocular procreations are too subtle for the Bazaar of publication. The repetition of colors (an old word, after all, for tropes) remains impalpable and provokes her into her own Sublime, that state of Circumference at once a divine discontent and a series of absolute moments that take dominion everywhere. Better perhaps than any other poet, she knows and indicates that what is worth representing is beyond depiction, what is worth saying cannot be said. What she reads, on landscapes and in seasons, is propulsive force, the recurrence of perspectives that themselves are powers and instrumentalities of the only knowledge ever available.

The final stanza does not attempt to break out of this siege of perspectives, but it hints again that her eye and will are receptive, not plundering, so that her power to unname is not Emersonian finally, but something different, another way to see. To see feelingly, yes, but beyond the arrogance of the self in its war against process and its stand against other selves. Her interplay of perspectives touches apotheosis not in a Nietzschean or Emersonian exaltation of the will to power, however receptive and reactive, but in suggestions of an alternative mode, less an interpretation than a questioning, or an othering of natural process. The poem, like so much of Dickinson at her strongest, compels us to begin again in rethinking our relation to poems, and to the equally troubling and dynamic relation of poems to our world of appearances.

Anne Bradstreet and the Practice of Weaned Affections

Robert Daly

I have not studied in this you read to show my skill, but to declare the truth, not to set forth myself, but the glory of God.

The spring is a lively emblem of the resurrection.

Were earthly comforts permanent, who would look for heavenly?

—ANNE BRADSTREET

Though her fellow Puritans both in England and America thought Anne Bradstreet an excellent and orthodox poet, commentators in the nineteenth century so thoroughly established the generalization that Puritan theology vitiated poetry that some twentieth-century critics have often praised her poetry by impugning her orthodoxy or praised those poems that apparently have least to do with religion. In his prefatory commendation to the Boston edition of her poems, her fellow Puritan John Rogers praised the power of her art:

> Thus weltring in delight, my virgin mind
> Admits a rape; truth still lyes undiscri'd,
> Its singular, that plural seem'd, I find,
> 'Twas Fancies glass alone that multipli'd;
> Nature with Art so closely did combine,
> I thought I saw the Muses trebble trine,
> Which prov'd your lonely Muse, superior to the nine.

Less enthusiastically, but still with no hint that her poetry contradicted her orthodoxy, Cotton Mather wrote in 1702 that "her poems . . . have afforded . . . a monument for her memory beyond the stateliest marbles." By the nineteenth century, however, it was widely believed that Puritans could not have written lasting poetry. Evert and George Duyckinck turned to the one extant poem by Anne's father, Thomas Dudley, for a verse to "exhibit the severity of his creed and practice." His daughter's poems they considered more domestic than religious. At best and "with a little more taste" she "might have been a happy describer of nature for she had a warm

---

From *God's Altar: The World and the Flesh in Puritan Poetry.* © 1978 by The Regents of the University of California. The University of California Press, 1978.

29

heart and a hearty view of things." As it was, however, she "writes as if under bonds to tell the whole truth, which she does without any regard to the niceties or scruples of the imagination." Bradstreet was a minor domestic poet whose Puritanism was apparently quite beside the point.

That her Puritanism ruined her poetry was the central judgment of Moses Coit Tyler in 1878. The "narrow and ferocious creed" which destroyed the poetry of such as Michael Wigglesworth severely limited that of Anne Bradstreet: "Literature, for her, was not a republic of letters, hospitable to all forms of human thought, but a strict Puritan commonwealth, founded on a scheme of narrow ascetic intolerance, and excluding from its citizenship some of the sublimest, daintiest, and most tremendous types of literary expression." That her poetry broke free from the restraints of her Puritanism and recorded her rebellion has been the conclusion of some subsequent critics. Stanley Williams wrote of her poetry to her husband: "The warm, human lines seem to snap the chains of current poetic theory; for the moment seventeenth-century American verse ceases to be the prisoner of religion." And Ann Stanford asserted that her heart "rebelled" at something in Puritan dogma, that "it is this clash of feeling and dogma that keeps her poetry alive," and that "no better description could be found for the poetry of Anne Bradstreet" than the Lawrencian concept of duplicity, "a tight mental allegiance to a morality which all their passion goes to destroy."

Others have either based their readings upon the quiet recognition of her orthodoxy or vigorously defended it. Samuel Eliot Morison, writing before the picture of Anne Bradstreet-as-poetic-rebel had been drawn, could quietly state that "her art was not an escape from life, but an expression of life. It was shot through and through with her religious faith." The endurance of her poetry "was proof, if it were needed, that creative art may be furthered by religion." But Robert Richardson had to argue insistently, and persuasively, that Bradstreet wrote "from what might be called the Puritan sensibility" and that in her "Contemplations" Bradstreet "has reached that ideal but rare state of Puritan consciousness, a carefully reasoned and emotionally convincing resolution of the problem of how to live in the world without being of it." For Richardson, Bradstreet's poetry records not the poet's resistance to Puritan dogma but her struggle toward and attainment of the moral imperatives of that dogma. And William J. Irvin has argued, in reading the "Contemplations," that "one should see . . . the entire emotional structure of the poem, as well as the epistemological one, as part of the Puritan psychology." But we need not examine further the fairly simple question of whether Bradstreet happened to believe in the general framework of theological attitudes that—pluralist arguments about specific matters of church polity notwithstanding—we still label "orthodox." She did. We need to examine the more subtle question of what she, as practicing poet, made of her theology. We need to examine where experientially her religion took her and where poetically she took her religion.

Though the question of Bradstreet's orthodoxy, then, has been argued in some detail, and though her poetry has attracted more critical attention than that of any other Puritan poet save Taylor, no one has yet examined the ways in which her Puritanism illuminates not only the substance of her poems but also their imagery, structure, and dynamics. In Bradstreet's work, theology became poetics as well as poetry, [she makes] poetic uses of the natural world as [well as] purely religious uses of it.

Her attitude toward the things of this world was certainly orthodox enough. Like Augustine, the Puritans considered the creatures of the sensible world the creations of a good and provident God. Since the sensible world depended for its existence and continuance upon the *concursus Dei*, the sensible world was essentially good, and man was to love it. As Perry Miller has recognized, the real danger besetting the Puritans in their relation to the world was not Gnosticism but pantheism: "always they verge so close to pantheism that it takes all their ingenuity to restrain themselves from identifying God with the creation." That ingenuity remains manifest in Puritan statements that, though the world itself is temporally good and is ordered by God for the good of man, it is not ultimately good: compared with its Creator it is empty and cannot satisfy man's restless soul. Though man is permitted, indeed required, to love the world, then, he must "wean" his affections from the unmixed love of it if he is to pass from this world to the next. The man who cannot do so gives to the creature a complete love rightfully belonging to the Creator and therefore commits idolatry.

Puritan preachers distinguished clearly between proper and idolatrous love of the creature: "He doth not forbid mercy or love to Beasts or Creatures, but he would not have your love terminated in them, bounded in them, he would not have you rejoice or delight in the Creature, before you have part in the Creator, for if you affect these things for themselves, the love of God is not in you." Commanded to love the world with weaned affections, the Puritan struggled, not to work up a little love for himself and his farm, pets, children and wife, but to accept in the love of God the fact that all these things were transitory, to wean his affections from them so that he could without rancor bid goodby at death to things he loved all too well. In *The Soules Justification* (London, 1638), Thomas Hooker explained that one should love the creatures as well as God: "Will you love your friends that are dear unto you, or your Parents that do provide for you, or your wife that is loving and merciful to you? you will love these, as there is good cause you should." Love of God should differ from love of the creatures only in degree, and Hooker concludes merely that one should "love Christ more than all these." The Puritan's struggle was to wean his affections from the unmixed love of such creatures, to convince himself that finally the world he loved was subordinate to its Creator. Though the beauties of the world were the creations of God, the command was clear: "Get thy heart more and more weaned from the Creature, the Creature is empty, it's not able to satisfy thee fully, nor make thee happy."

That the command to love the world with weaned affections did not prevent the Puritans' loving the world is evident in much Puritan literature and can be exemplified, for our purposes, in two otherwise dissimilar sources, Cotton's sermon on calling and Sewall's *Phaenomena quaedam Apocalyptica*, a pamphlet explicating in tireless detail the prophecies in Revelation. Cotton urged his hearers, not to forsake their "natural" and "civil" lives in order to perfect their spiritual lives, but to live both fully. In an illuminating allusion to Paul and Augustine, Cotton described the "natural life" as "that, by which we do live this bodily life, I mean, by which we live a life of sense, by which we go through all conditions, from our birth to our grave, by which we live, and move, and have our being. And now both these a justified [elect] person lives by faith." Leaving aside the difficult questions of intention and audience, we may be sure that Cotton alluded to the description of God as One in Whom "we live, move, and have our being" (Acts 17:28), which Augustine repeated in his *Confessions:* "in Thee we live and move and have our being." His allusion linked living the natural life in the world to living in God. For Cotton, then, the natural life, the life of sense, was also a part of God, a way of serving Him, an expression of faith. Sewall's love of the sensible world and his belief in the intrinsic harmony of this world and the next are rendered more imagistically than Cotton's. In a pamphlet "devoted," as Miller wrote, "to rendering mystical visions into dull prose," Sewall took sudden leave of his dullness to sing a hymn to the sensuous beauties of Plum Island and to its fitness as a place for the work of redemption:

> As long as *Plum Island* shall faithfully keep the commanded post; Notwithstanding all the hectoring Words and hard Blows of the proud and boisterous Ocean. . . . As long as Sea-Fowl shall know the Time of their coming, and not neglect seasonably to visit the Places of their Acquaintance: As long as any Cattle shall be fed with the Grass growing in the Meadows, which do humbly bow down themselves before *Turkey-Hill;* As long as any Sheep shall walk upon *Old Town Hills,* and shall from thence pleasantly look down upon the River *Parker,* and the fruitful Marshes lying beneath; As long as any free and harmless Doves shall find a White Oak, or other Tree within the Township, to perch, or feed, or build a careless Nest upon; and shall voluntarily present themselves to perform the office of Gleaners after Barley-Harvest; As long as Nature shall not grow Old and dote; but shall constantly remember to give the rows of Indian Corn their education, by Pairs: So long shall Christians be born there; and being first made meet, shall from thence be Translated, to be made partakers of the Inheritance of the Saints in Light.

Loving Plum Island with weaned affections would not keep one from his inheritance.

Bradstreet's prose statements place her within the tradition of orthodox

Puritans who loved the sensible world but knew that it could not compare with its Maker. In her "Meditations Divine and Moral" she used the conventional figure of weaning to describe the process through which the Christian, who loves the things of this world, learns ultimately to give them up for the joys of the next:

> Some children are hardly weaned; although the teat be rubbed with wormwood or mustard, they will either wipe it off, or else suck down sweet and bitter together. So is it with some Christians: let God embitter all the sweets of this life, that so they might feed upon more substantial food, yet they are so childishly sottish that they are still hugging and sucking these empty breasts that God is forced to hedge up their way with thorns or lay affliction on their loins that so they might shake hands with the world, before it bid them farewell.

For Bradstreet, then, the things of the world were good and wholesome in their place and for a time. They become a hindrance to growth in God only when loved foolishly, when clung to as if there were nothing beyond them. Her attitude toward the things of this world was clearly orthodox.

What we need to realize now is that her far more complex attitude toward the religious and poetic uses of the sensible world was also orthodox, that Puritan orthodoxy was conducive to the production of poetry, and that Bradstreet's poetry is illuminated by an understanding of the theology which structured the experiences her poetry expressed. . . . Puritan preaching and precedent sanctioned certain uses of the sensible world. Bradstreet, as a Puritan poet, could celebrate the world, could use images drawn from it to figure spiritual states and truths, even in poems on its ultimate vanity, and could ascend from love of the creatures to love of the Creator through her contemplations of the former.

Though delight in the beauty of the world pervades much of her poetry, Bradstreet (unlike the Romantics and several of her fellow Puritans) wrote no poems intended simply to celebrate the sensible world. But neither is her poetry a collection of religious or philosophical abstractions: never her ultimate goal, the sensible world was always her point of departure; it was where she began. In such beginnings we find her celebrations of the natural world, her sense of herself as a fellow creature:

> Some time now past in the autumnal tide
> When Phoebus wanted but one hour to bed,
> The trees all richly clad, yet void of pride,
> Where gilded o'er by his rich golden head.
> Their leaves and fruits seemed painted, but was true,
> Of green, of red, of yellow, mixed hue;
> Rapt were my senses at this delectable view.

Now neither the senses nor the objects that delighted them were at all evil, and Bradstreet would later in the same poem salute the sun as a fellow creature: "Hail creature, full of sweetness, beauty, and delight." But Bradstreet was no Walt Whitman, no H. D.; such was her Puritan habit of mind that she could never rest content with the image itself. For her the image shadowed forth its Maker; its goodness and beauty constituted an *a fortiori* argument for the goodness and beauty (predicated univocally) of God, and in the stanza just after her celebration of "this delectable view" she immediately thought of its *glossa*, or spiritual interpretation:

> I wist not what to wish, yet sure thought I,
> If so much excellence abide below,
> How excellent is He that dwells on high,
> Whose power and beauty by his works we know?
> Sure he is goodness, wisdom, glory, light,
> That hath this under world so richly dight;
> More heaven than earth was here, no winter and no night.

Imbued with divine meaning, the world was to be not only appreciated but understood. Man was to make sense of his earthly experience in the service of his religion.

As Bradstreet made explicit in her "Meditations Divine and Moral," the world was to be used: "There is no object that we see, no action that we do, no good that we enjoy, no evil that we feel or fear, but we may make some spiritual advantage of all." One valid use of the sensible world was figuration. Images could figure, as they had in Scripture, purely human experiences: "We read in Scriptures of three sorts of arrows: the arrow of an enemy, the arrow of pestilence, and the arrow of a slanderous tongue. The first two kill the body, the last the good name; the two former leave a man when once he is dead, but the last mangles him in his grave." They could figure the spiritual states of man: "We often see stones hang with drops not from any innate moisture, but from a thick air about them; so may we sometime see marble-hearted sinners seem full of contrition, but it is not from any dew of grace within but from some black clouds that impends them, which produces these sweating effects"; and "As man is called a little world, so his heart may be called a little commonwealth." They could figure man's quest for salvation: "The hireling that labours all the day comforts himself that when night comes he shall both take his rest and receive his reward; the painful Christian that hath wrought hard in God's vineyard and hath born the heat and drought of the day, when he perceives his sun apace to decline and the shadows of his evening to be stretched out, lifts up his head with joy, knowing his refreshing is at hand"; and "We see in orchards some trees so fruitful that the weights of their burden is the breaking of their limbs, some again are meanly loaden, and some have nothing to show but leaves only, and some among them are dry stock; so it is in the church, which is God's orchard," and Bradstreet's different types of trees become different types of Christians.

Images in the perceived world figured even the "irradiations," the communicable glories of God, Who is portrayed in Bradstreet more as a wise and loving parent than as the celestial lunatic so often foisted off on the Puritans by their modern detractors: "A prudent mother will not cloth her little child with a long and cumbersome garment. . . . Much more will the allwise God proportion His dispensations according to the stature and strength of the person He bestows them on"; and "A wise father will not lay a burden on a child of seven years old which he knows is enough for one twice his strength; much less will our heavenly Father (who knows our mold) lay such afflictions upon his weak children as would crush them to the dust, but according to the strength he will proportion the load." Indeed, Bradstreet insisted that man's relation to God was familial, even physical: "Lord why should I doubt any more when Thou hast given me such assured pledges of Thy love? First, Thou art my Creator, I Thy creature, Thou my master, I Thy servant. But hence arises not my comfort, Thou art my Father, I Thy child; 'Ye shall be My sons and daughters,' saith the Lord Almighty. Christ is my brother, I ascend unto my Father, and your Father, unto my God and your God; but lest this should not be enough, thy Maker is thy husband. Nay more, I am a member of His body, He my head." Lower world and higher were linked by figuration; God's investing the lower world with such divine meaning was an act of love.

One last example illustrates the habit of mind that informed Bradstreet's perception and her poetry. Even the wheeling of the seasons manifested to her the facts of her religion, had been intended by God to manifest them: "The spring is a lively emblem of the resurrection: after a long winter we see the leafless trees and dry stocks (at the approach of the sun) to resume their former vigor and beauty in a more ample manner than what they lost in autumn; so shall it be at that great day after a long vacation, when the Sun of righteousness shall appear; those dry bones shall arise in far more glory than that which they lost at their creation, and in this transcends the spring that their leaf shall never fail nor their sap decline." Bradstreet was aware that such figuration did not imply complete metaphysical identity and was able, as this example shows, to turn dissimilarity to figurative advantage: the resurrection of the body into heaven was after all, a more perfect spring than spring itself. But throughout her prose and poetry she was concerned with figuration, not as a verbal trick the limitations of which gave her opportunity to display her ingenuity, but as a basic principle operative in her perceived universe. She lived in a world in which several orders of reality now often separate—the worldly or earthly or natural or sensible, the biblical, and the eschatological—were the harmonious creation of a single God and were held together by Him in a web of intrinsic correspondence. The worldly season, spring, was intended by God to figure forth both Christ's resurrection in the Bible and the resurrection of the saint after death. Perceptive Christian that she was, Bradstreet could hardly have thought of one without immediately thinking of the other two, not because of a tidy list such as those offered in typological dictionaries, but because of a pervasive habit of mind that lay behind both Puritan poetry and the typological dictionaries. In Puritan poems, symbolic correspondences occur, not at the level of trope, but at the level of perception.

The relevance of this habit of mind to our understanding of Puritan poetry becomes clear if we consider the well-known critical dictum of Allen Tate that good poetry possesses a characteristic that he named "tension," a word formed by "lopping the prefixes off the logical terms *ex*tension and *in*tension." "Tension," wrote Tate, was the coherence of all denotative meanings no matter how far one chose to extend them, the coherence of all connotative intensional meanings, and the coherence of the one set of meanings with the other. In our attempt fully to understand a poem, we must explore both the intensional and extensional meanings of its imagery. In order to understand Bradstreet's poetry, we need to be aware of the implicit symbolism that pervades it.

Three poems afford us a clear example of the way her symbols link the different orders of reality, the way earthly experiences resonate with biblical and eschatological significances. In her "Contemplations" Bradstreet described the sun in the figure of the Bridegroom, a figure taken from the nineteenth psalm of David. But Bradstreet developed the figure far more than the psalmist had, and her description of the sun and earth in spring centered on marriage and impregnation:

> Thou as a bridegroom from thy chamber rushes,
> And as a strong man joys to run a race;
> The morn doth usher thee with smiles and blushes;
> The Earth reflects her glances in thy face.
> Birds, insects, animals with vegative,
> Thy heat from death and dullness doth revive,
> And in the darksome womb of fruitful nature dive.

That both sun and bridegroom were equally real to Bradstreet is evident in "A Letter to Her Husband, Absent upon Public Employment," in which she likened her own bridegroom to the warm and fecund spring sun, now absent in winter:

> I, like the Earth this season, mourn in black,
> My Sun is gone so far in's zodiac,
> Whom whilst I 'joyed, nor storms, nor frost I felt,
> His warmth such frigid colds did cause to melt.
> My chilled limbs now numbed lie forlorn;
> Return, return, sweet Sol, from Capricorn;
> In this dead time, alas, what can I more
> Than view those fruits which through thy heat I bore?

If the warming sun is like a bridegroom, her own husband partakes of the warmth and fertility of the sun, and both can be seen and figured in terms of sensual love and the production of children. For the Puritans, moreover, the sun was frequently used as an admittedly imperfect figure for God, and Christ was of course the bridegroom, come to marry His church and her saints. Death was a spiritual marriage. It is appropriate, then, that in "As Weary Pilgrim," written only three years before her death, she figured her approach to death as the approach of a bride to her wedding. Her grave is "the bed Christ did perfume," which shall receive her withered and "corrupt" body only to yield forth "a glorious body" on the day when "soul and body shall unite / And of their Maker have the sight." Because of this promise, a song of age and death could become a song of love and approaching union: "Lord make me ready for that day, / Then come, dear Bridegroom, come away."

In "As Spring the Winter Doth Succeed," the revivification of nature, the return of her husband and Christ's love, her recovery from physical illness and from doubt about her election, and the biblical pilgrimage through the valley of Baca (Ps. 84:5–6) all resonate through a single set of coherent images:

> My sun's returned with healing wings,
> My soul and body doth rejoice,
> My heart exults and praises sings
> To Him that heard my wailing voice.
>
> O hath Thou made my pilgrimage
> Thus pleasant, fair, and good,
> Blessed me in youth and elder age,
> My Baca made a springing flood.

Sun God bridegroom husband and Christ, and spring health reunion and confidence of election—these image clusters were linked in the poet's perception of the created universe. Once we understand that such linkings take place in the human imagination rather than in some adventitious and rigid typological dictionary, once we see that we too call a charitable person a Good Samaritan, a sanctimonious hypocrite a Pharisee, a traitor Judas, because that is how we see them, because that in our perceived world is what they are, we are ready to read the poetry of Anne Bradstreet, to appreciate both the rendered experiences and the verbal correlatives she found to express them, and to participate, however partially, in the consciousness that created that poetry.

Vanity was one of the most common themes of Bradstreet's poetic career. The vanity of all earthly things, the imperative that man wean his affections from the things of this world may seem less than ideal as a theme for poetry. Allen Tate has shown us the dangers of what he called "the angelic imagination" of Poe, who allegedly "circumvented the natural world" and refused "to see nature," who immersed himself in "a subjectivism which denies the sensible world," which operates "at a high level of abstraction, in which 'clear and distinct ideas' only are workable." Quite apart from the debatable proposition that Poe exemplified the "angelic" rather than the "symbolic" imagination is the more certain proposition that the author who rejects the reality of the sensible world and the figurative validity of images drawn from it must either agree with Rimbaud, Mallarmé, and Stevens that language itself can be or create reality (a secular version of the Christian doctrine of *logos*) or must content himself with a literature of "real" abstractions, a literature in which the sensible world functions only to destroy itself so that Eiros and Charmion or Monos and Una can get together and talk about it, functions only as a conversation piece for retrospective spooks.

As an orthodox Puritan, Bradstreet could not adumbrate the French symbolists by arguing that her words created meaning; the meaning of the sensible world was in the things of the sensible world themselves. It had been put there by God before all time; it was seen and uttered by the poet. To follow the latter course she would have to ignore the tradition that the world was a message sent to man from God; she would have to ignore Paul's admonition in Rom. 1:20 to seek the invisible things of God through the visible things that He made; she would have to ignore Calvin, Richardson, and the preachers of her own time. . . . It was, of course, possible though unlikely for a Puritan poet to take this latter course: I know of only one who did so (Michael Wigglesworth). And he wrote terrible poetry. In writing on the vanity of earthly things from the point of view of one intent on weaning her affections from them, Mistress Bradstreet was courting poetic disaster.

The poetics that enabled her to avoid such disaster is revealed quite clearly in one of her most carefully wrought poems, "The Vanity of All Worldly Things." As reference to the tenth satire of Juvenal and to Samuel Johnson's imitation of it indicates, the theme is hardly original, but Bradstreet's treatment of it is quite original and distinctly Puritan. Having demonstrated with some ferocity that all human wishes are vain, Juvenal suggested a presumably valid wish, a wish that was not vain: "Ask for a stout heart that has no fear of death, and deems length of days the least of Nature's gifts; that can endure any kind of toil; that knows neither wrath nor desire, and thinks that the wars and hard labours of Hercules are better than the loves and banquets of Sardanapalus." He recommended the stoic solution of banishing vain wishes for pleasure, riches, love, and honor, of ceasing to wish for them. Though Johnson's stoicism was Christian, it was stoicism nonetheless. Finding his desire for pleasure thwarted again and again, the reader was advised by Johnson to stop desiring pleasure.

Bradstreet's poem begins within this tradition. After an initial statement that no one can find "on brittle earth a consolation sound," the speaker dismisses the consolations offered by honor, wealth, pleasures, and beauty.

> What is't in honour to be set on high?
> No, they like beasts and sons of men shall die,
> And whilst they live, how oft doth turn their fate;
> He's now a captive that was king of late.
> What is't in wealth great treasures to obtain?
> No, that's but labour, anxious care, and pain.
> He heaps up riches, and he heaps up sorrow,
> It's his today, but who's his heir tomorrow?
> What then? Content in pleasures canst thou find?
> More vain than all, that's but to grasp the wind.
> The sensual senses for a time they please
> Meanwhile the conscience rage, who shall appease?
> What is't in beauty? No that's but a snare,
> They're foul enough today, that once were fair.

So far the poem represents a rejection of earthly vanities, but the grounds for that rejection are somewhat unusual. Worldly pleasures are rejected, not because they are evil, or demean man, or bring about damnation, not because they are illusory, but because they are transient, because they do not last. A person set on high in honor will find his privileged position and the joys of it cut short by death. Political reversals may cut short the joys of kingship. The wealthy person may lose his money or die without heirs. Pleasures, like the wind, cannot be made to stay. Sensual pleasures please, but only for a time. (Here Bradstreet loaded the case somewhat, since the conscience would presumably rate only at fornication or adultery, not at love between husband and wife.) And beauty withers with age and disease. Earthly joys are vain, then, because they do not endure, and Bradstreet's statement of vanity, though it contains allusions to Ecclesiastes, differs from that of Solomon who had tasted the joys of life and found them wanting, not merely transient. The statement that youth, for example, is vain because it does not last is less an indictment of youth than of old age. In this poem, earthly joys are vain because they are deficient as pleasures.

For one whose statement of vanity is based on such a criterion, the stoic solution of ceasing to desire satisfaction is ludicrous because such a cessation is against the nature of man and therefore impossible:

> What is it then? to do as stoics tell,
> Nor laugh, nor weep, let things go ill or well?
> Such stoics are but stocks, such teaching vain,
> While man is man he shall have ease or pain.

Since man was built to seek joy, the stoic center of indifference is impossible. Like Richard Steere, then, Bradstreet rejected the stoic solution as fit perhaps for "stocks" but not for human beings. Man will seek lasting satisfaction, but will not find it in this world. This rejection of stoicism is the turning point of the poem. The speaker continues to see "that *summum bonum* which may stay my mind" and finds it in heavenly joys which are figured as lasting versions of those earthly joys rejected in the first section of the poem:

> It brings to *honour* which shall ne'er decay,
> It stores with *wealth* which time can't wear away.
> It yieldeth *pleasures* far beyond conceit,
> And truly *beautifies* without deceit,
> Nor strength, nor wisdom, nor fresh youth shall fade,
> Nor death shall see, but are immortal made.
> This pearl of price, this tree of life, this spring,
> Who is possessed of shall reign a king.
> Nor change of state nor cares shall ever see,
> But wear his crown unto eternity.
> This satiates the soul, this stays the mind,
> And all the rest, but vanity we find.
>
> (italics added)

In this poem, one is led to heaven by his desire for earthly joys, a desire unsatisfied on earth, not because the things of earth are bitter, delusory, or sinful, but because, though sweet, they do not endure. Heaven in this poem consists of earthly joys uninterrupted by pain, change, and death.

Once we understand this we are in a position to read other poems that hinge on the same distinction between the ultimate value of earthly things (they are worthless compared to the joys of heaven) and their immediate value (they are made by God to delight men and to whet men's hunger for heaven). In one of her prose meditations, Bradstreet made this distinction explicit: "All the comforts of this life may be compared to the gourd of Jonah, that notwithstanding we take great delight for a season in them and find their shadow very comfortable, yet there is some worm or other, of discontent, of fear, or grief that lies at the root, which in great part withers the pleasure else we should take in them, and well it is that we perceive a decay in their greenness, for were earthly comforts permanent, who would look for heavenly?" The figure of the gourd of Jonah is well chosen. When Jonah, outraged at the Lord's having dragged him to Nineveh to prophesy the destruction of the city and then having made a fool of him by deciding not to destroy it, prayed for death, the Lord made life more pleasant for him by causing a large-leaved plant to grow up and give him shade. Jonah was exceeding glad of the plant and enjoyed it for a full day before the Lord, to help him wean his affections from immoderate love of the creature, sent a worm to wither the plant. The point of this story for us is that the plant was the good gift of a good God to a man whom God intended to enjoy it. It functioned to lead Jonah back to the love of God by way of love of the creature, and its function required that it not last. Because the delights of earth are used by God to remind man of the delights of heaven, the Puritan poet could use images of the very objects she rejected to figure the joys she sought.

Nearly all of her poems on vanity hinge on just such a progression. They take love of the creature for granted, and become the poetic exercise through which the poet argues herself from that penultimate love to the ultimate love of the Creator. "My straying soul," wrote Bradstreet, "is too much in love with the world." That soul must wean its affections from the transient delights of this world in order to partake of the lasting delights of the next. For that reason, the Spirit in "The Flesh and the Spirit" rejects the "pearls, and gold" of this world in order to fix her attention upon heaven with its "gates of pearl" and streets of "transparent gold." In "Upon the Burning of our House," the temporal house taken away by God is mourned in quiet understatement. "My pleasant things in ashes lie," observes the speaker; then she addresses the burned house:

> Under thy roof no guest shall sit,
> Nor at thy table eat a bit.
> No pleasant tale shall e'er be told,
> Nor things recounted done of old.
> No candle e'er shall shine in thee,
> Nor bridegroom's voice e'er heard shall be.
> In silence ever shall thou lie.

But such reflections are "vanity," and the speaker, faced with the grim fact of the destruction, begins "my heart to chide" with harsh questions and commands:

> Didst fix thy hope on mold'ring dust?
> The arm of flesh didst make thy trust?
> Raise up thy thoughts above the sky
> That dunghill mists away may fly.

She compares her love for her house and her pain at its passing to Christ's love for man and His suffering on the cross; this comparison is a terribly powerful argument for the ultimate triviality of the house. It enables the speaker to achieve the perspective she seeks. Raising her thoughts, then, from such "dunghill mists" as the memory of a well-loved house, she finds "above the sky" the promise of heaven, figured appropriately as a house:

> Thou hast a house on high erect,
> Framed by that mighty Architect
> With glory richly furnished,
> Stands permanent though this be fled.

Again the heaven the poet seeks is figured by images drawn from the earth she must ultimately leave and differs from it chiefly by being a better, that is a "permanent," version of it. The balanced imagery and the clear progression indicate that in Bradstreet's poetry a Puritan habit of mind became a subtle and powerful poetic strategy.

Before discussing the ways in which Bradstreet's recognition of the poetic and religious uses of the creatures illuminates several of her other poems—notably those to her husband and her elegies on the deaths of her grandchildren—it is worth noting how often her poetry expresses a harmonious interplay between the worldly concerns of the poet as creature and the spiritual concerns of the poet as Christian, an interplay likely to be ignored in a discussion which emphasizes, as mine does, the poems on vanity. Where the poems on vanity center on the next world and contributions of the creatures to the Puritan's understanding of and progress toward it, these poems center on the next world and contributions of providence toward the temporal satisfaction of earthly desires. In "Upon Some Distemper of Body," the God praised is One "Who sendeth help to those in misery." Since the misery derives both from physical illness and from concomitant doubts about her election, the provident God has seen to both and is thanked for both:

> He eased my soul of woe, my flesh of pain,
> And brought me to the short from troubled main.

In a poem of gratitude "For Deliverance from a Fever," Bradstreet told of her fear, when ill, that she was not elect:

> Beclouded was my soul with fear
> Of Thy displeasure sore,
> Nor could I read my evidence
> Which oft I read before.

In terror the poet cried out, as she should have, for God to spare her soul "thought flesh consume to naught," but again God linked physical with spiritual deliverance, "spared my body frail," showed "to me Thy tender love, / My heart no more might quail." Again and again God is thanked for His earthly gifts and petitioned for others:

> My wasted flesh Thou didst restore,
> My feeble loins didst gird with strength.

> My feeble spirit Thou didst revive,
>   My doubting Thou didst chide,
> And though as dead mad'st me alive,
>   I here a while might 'bide.

Instead of praising some neoplatonic God for revealing to her the vanity of earthly things, Bradstreet sang hymns of praise and gratitude to an anthropomorphic God Who often answered petitions for such worldly gifts as health and long life. She gave thanks "For the Restoration of My Dear

Husband from a Burning Ague," for "My Daughter Hannah Wiggin Her Recovery from a Dangerous Fever," for "My Son's Return out of England":

> In sickness when he lay full sore,
> His help and his physician wert.
> When royal ones that time did die
> Thou healed'st his flesh and cheered his heart.

She petitioned Him for the safe return of her husband from England, and gave thanks for letters from him and finally for his safe return. As these examples indicate, God often abetted Bradstreet in her love of the creature even as He had brought Jonah back from his angry prayers for death by sending him a creature to love.

Such a love and use of the creatures lies behind and illuminates Bradstreet's poems to her husband and her elegies on her grandchildren. In both sets of poems, love of the creature is taken for granted as a God-wrought part of human nature and is considered a part of love of God. We have already seen that Bradstreet saw and expressed the intrinsic correspondences between loving a creature such as the Sun, which in Ps. 19:5 is likened to a bridegroom, loving Simon, her earthly bridegroom, and loving God, who is both the sun of Righteousness (Mal. 4:2) and the bridegroom of His faithful (Matt. 2:5, Mark 2, Luke 3, Rev. 18:23). Her love for her husband should, according to Puritan creed, be less intense and lasting than her love for God and would end with her death, with her marriage to God. But during her life that love was, doctrinally as well as symbolically, part of the evidence of her election. Puritan ministers, as Edmund Morgan has noted, preached that conjugal love "was a duty imposed by God on all married couples: . . . If a husband and wife failed to love each other they disobeyed God." As Benjamin Wadsworth warned his congregation, a person who had too thoroughly weaned his affections from his spouse, was not holy but wicked. The wife, for example, "who neglects to manifest real love and kindness" is "a shame to her profession of Christianity; . . . she . . . not only affronts her Husband, but also God . . . by this her wicked behaviour." In Puritan sermons, moreover, "the relation between husband and wife furnished the usual metaphor by which the relationship between Christ and the believer was designated." In symbol and in doctrine, then, Bradstreet's loving her husband was linked to her loving God.

In "To My Dear and Loving Husband," Bradstreet wrote of a real human love carefully subordinated to but completely in harmony with love of God:

> If ever two were one, then surely we.
> If ever man were loved by wife, then thee;
> If ever wife was happy in a man,
> Compare with me, ye women, if you can.

> Thy love is such I can no way repay,
> The heavens reward thee manifold I pray.
> Then while we live, in love let's so persevere
> That when we live no more, we may live ever.

Commenting on the closing couplet, Ann Stanford has written: "There are two possible interpretations of these lines: first, she may mean that they may have children, who will produce descendants, so that they may live on in their line. This is similar to the idea of some of Shakespeare's sonnets, for example. Second, it may mean that they will become famous as lovers, and live in fame. This would hardly seem to be a good Puritan idea, but the Cavalier idea of immortality through fame is not one Mistress Bradstreet would scorn." No one knows what Anne Bradstreet might have thought of this "Cavalier idea," since she never discussed it. She mentioned Sidney's fame in her epitaph on him but dealt more with the moral example of his life and, repeatedly, with the tragedy of his death than with the conventional consolation that his name would be remembered. Nowhere did she make Shakespeare's claim that her verse would live "so long as men can breathe and eyes can see," and nowhere did she ask that any but her immediate family remember her. Her closing lines, then, might have had the meanings Stanford imputed to them if they had been appended to Donne's "The Canonization," but Bradstreet's poem does not prepare us for such an interpretation.

Instead, the lines immediately preceding the closing couplet express the hope that her husband will receive from "the heavens" a meet reward for his love. The last two lines, then, clearly express the hope that, by persevering in their love in a characteristically Puritan way, by loving each other as God has commanded them but not letting an immoderate love of the creature idolatrously supercede their love of God, they will live forever in heaven. They will love just "so"; they will "so persevere" that their love will serve God as He intended that it should. Wife and husband will, when they die, be taken up to heaven where they will "live ever," neither through the biological immortality conferred by their descendants nor through the fame conferred by future lovers who have canonized them for their love, but through the immortality conferred by God on His elect. Whatever its effect on modern readers, Bradstreet's closing couplet surely meant this to her fellow Puritans, especially to her husband for whom the poem was written. Simon Bradstreet—the son of a nonconformist minister and himself an A.B. and A.M. from Emmanuel College, Cambridge, the training ground for most of the first-generation New England ministers—was no doubt alert to the religious allusions of Anne's verse. Writing for such an audience, she could afford to use understatement in matters of religion.

In "A Letter to Her Husband, Absent upon Public Employment," for example, earthly love is figured through the images and language of divine love. We have already seen the associations called up in Puritan religion and in Bradstreet's poetry by the sun, its fertilization of the earth in spring, and the bridegroom. If we add to these the associations engendered by Christ's parable (Matt. 22:2–14) identifying those whom God's love bids enter heaven with the wedding guests of a king, we can appreciate the richness of Bradstreet's language:

> My head, my heart, mine eyes, my life, nay, more,
> My joy, my magazine of earthly store,
> If two be one, as surely thou and I,
> How stayest thou there, whilst I at Ipswich lie?
> So many steps, head from the heart to sever,
> If but a neck, soon should we be together.
> I, like the Earth this season, mourn in black,
> My Sun is gone so far in's zodiac,
> Whom whilst I 'joyed, nor storms, nor frost I felt,
> His warmth such frigid colds did cause to melt.
> My chilled limbs now numbed lie forlorn;
> Return, return, sweet Sol, from Capricorn;
> In this dead time, alas, what can I more
> Than view those fruits which through thy heat I bore?
> Which sweet contentment yield me for a space,
> True living pictures of their father's face.
> O strange effect! now thou art southward gone,
> I weary grow the tedious day so long;
> But when thou northward to me shalt return
> I wish my Sun may never set, but burn
> Within the Cancer of my glowing breast,
> The welcome house of him my dearest guest.
> Where ever, ever stay, and go not thence,
> Till nature's sad decree shall call thee hence;
> Flesh of thy flesh, bone of thy bone,
> I here, thou there, yet both but one.

Though the biblical referents are too numerous to catalog, the progression of attitude in this poem, and the use of the language of religious love to express a love that remains primarily earthly deserve some comment. It is clear from the beginning that Simon is not God, not even her God. He is her "magazine of *earthly* store." Yet their love becomes, in the powerful central section of the poem, a similitude of the love between God and man. Simon's going southward to Boston, like the sun's going southward to Capricorn, or God's withdrawing His love, brings on a winter. When that love was present, winter melted to spring; the Sun, like a bridegroom, rushed from his chamber to make the earth fertile; so Simon sired Children, made them in his own image and likeness, "true living pictures of their father's face." Like the sun's, the bridegroom's, God's, their love brings about creation. Her heart becomes "Cancer," or the place of the summer zenith of the Sun, the guest chamber Christ sought at Passover, the banquet hall to which the king of parable called his guests, the heaven to which God calls His elect, a place of eternal welcome and love where one may "ever, ever stay." All these images connote perfection, eternity. Then, having modulated from the opening, in which their love is her "earthly store," to a central section filled with images of God, salvation, and eternal joy, the poem modulates again, this time back to the recognition that both are subject to "natures's sad decree." But in that central section, the joys of human love were figured in a complex of perfectly coherent images linking the love of the earth and the sun (figured elsewhere in Puritan poetry as the love of Tellus and Apollo), wife and husband, man and God.

Such coherent resonances of symbolism exemplify both the verbal realization of Puritan love (which was human as well as spiritual, for one's spouse as well as one's God) and the verbal realization of such criteria as Tate's theory of "tension," the coherence of all denotations and connotations of one's imagery. Since literature records significant human experience and since criticism records the attempt to understand literature, it is not surprising that a fine poem lives in all three worlds. What is surprising is that Bradstreet has said so much in so quiet a voice, has spoken through such quiet understatement. If one does not listen carefully, one may translate a moving expression of the essential univocity of love—love of God is univocally human love—into a Cavalier convention about the immortality conferred by fame. I do not mean to imply that understatement is a dominant standard of value or that Bradstreet's love and poetry are somehow better than the overstated love and poetry of, say, Walt Whitman, who bared his omnivorous breast and embraced the universe with pantoscopic ardor. Both are fine poets. I mean only to state that Bradstreet's characteristic mode is understatement, and that to understand her, we must listen carefully.

This is especially true of her poems on the deaths of her grandchildren. Perhaps such understatement led Hyatt Waggoner to conclude that "Puritan poetry in general tends to find this world so radically imperfect as not to be worth saving or grieving for." Of Bradstreet's poem on the burning of her house, he wrote that "the conflict of values was almost completely suppressed, but the same theology may be seen at work, denying the significance of a conflict actually felt. . . . Except for one line, we have to *guess* that the poet felt grief at the loss of her worldly goods." Roy Harvey Pearce took the same tack in his reading of Bradstreet's poems on the deaths of her grandchildren: "She would give the impression that her acquiescence in God's dealing with her has been achieved without much effort. She rests assured in the inevitability of her all too human fate." Both men criticized Bradstreet's poems of acceptance and would have preferred verbal correlatives for anguish. Before examining the poems themselves, we need to recognize that this type of argument has been made and answered before, most decisively in Brooks and Warren's *Understanding Poetry*.

In their discussion of Ben Jonson's elegy "On My First Son," Brooks and Warren answered Elizabeth Drew's criticism that "somehow the emotion is weakened by the obvious artfulness of it. The poet can think too cleverly about the situation to carry conviction." Suggesting as a parallel Milton's intricate Petrarchan sonnet "On His Blindness," a carefully wrought poem in which the emotional shock Milton felt is understated, Brooks and Warren answered that Jonson's poem is a "mature effort to make sense of an emotional shock" and that, had he chosen to dwell only on his grief, he might have produced a poem as unarguably wretched as James Russell Lowell's "After the Burial." An intellectual descendant of the Puritans, Lowell, too, was faced with the death of a child and was offered, as was Bradstreet, the consolations of faith. Unlike Bradstreet, he wrote the poem of struggle, of fully stated grief. "In the breaking gulfs of sorrow," he expressed in thirteen pounding quatrains the "sweet despair" of the flesh as the father gazes at "the thin-worn locket / With its anguish of deathless hair," remembers the "touch of her hand on my cheek" for which he "would give all my incomes from dreamland," gazes at "that little shoe in the corner, / So worn and wrinkled and brown" and tells the part of his mind which has tried to comfort him that "that little shoe . . . with its emptiness confutes you, / And argues your wisdom down." No one has to guess at the speaker's grief: it drenches us. Yet his is clearly an inferior poem. Its hackneyed imagery, pile-driver rhythms, and self-indulgent repetitiveness take us nowhere, tell us nothing. Without depth or control, the poem is an amplified verbal correlative of uncontrolled screaming, and as Brooks and Warren quite rightly argue: "The purest and most instinctive expression of emotion is a scream, and a scream is not poetry."

Now poetry does not operate at the level of critical generalization, and the mere facts that the mode of statement urged on Bradstreet by Pearce and Waggoner usually results in bad poetry and that the mode of understatement and control practiced by Bradstreet has in the past characterized some fine poetry by such as Jonson and Milton are not offered as evidence for the excellence of her verse. They are offered merely to counter the assumption that we may dismiss Bradstreet's poems because she does not scream. That assumption is also a critical generalization and, as we have seen, not a very good one.

To understand Bradstreet's elegies, then, we must look closely both at the text itself and at its historical context. One of her characteristic elegies is "In Memory of My Dear Grandchild Elizabeth Bradstreet, Who Deceased August, 1665, Being a Year and Half Old":

> Farewell dear babe, my heart's too much content,
> Farewell sweet babe, the pleasure of mine eye,
> Farewell fair flowers that for a space was lent,
> Then ta'en away unto eternity.

Blest babe, why should I once bewail thy fate,
Or sigh thy days so soon were terminate,
Sith thou are settled in an everlasting state.

By nature trees do rot when they are grown,
And plums and apples thoroughly ripe do fall,
And corn and grass are in their season mown,
And time brings down what is both strong and tall.
But plants new set to be eradicate,
And buds new blown to have so short a date,
Is by His hand alone that guides nature and fate.

The tone of this poem is carefully controlled. Rosemary Laughlin has noted that the stanzaic form itself is difficult and intricate: "the rhyme scheme is *ababccc,* with the last line an alexandrine." The six pentameter lines center on earthly, temporal matters, "while the alexandrines effect a contrast of the eternal with the transient." It is clear from the pentameter lines of the first stanza that Bradstreet loved the child and joyed in her presence. Her question—"why should I once bewail thy fate, / Or sign thy days were so soon terminate"—indicates that to do so was her natural reaction to the child's death. Rosemary Laughlin has observed that even the prosody suggests grief: "The slow alexandrines might also suggest that resignation to God's will was a heavy thing for the poet to bear, especially since the slight irregularity of the meter produces a somewhat tortured hesitation." Her grief, then, is present in the poem and requires some controlling if the poem is not to lapse into sentimentality.

But it is controlled; that resignation is achieved. Through the intricate rhyme scheme, through the closing alexandrines, through the internal rhyme on "blown" and "alone" that doubly knits together the last two lines of the closing triplet, Bradstreet achieved the sense of distance and order that enabled her to make some sense of the emotional shock, to avoid merely wallowing in grief as Lowell would two centuries later. Her argument for resignation is sane and convincing, granted her premises. If one happens to believe in God and heaven, and feels certain that one's grandchild has been taken by God to heaven, wailing and sighing because one misses the child and begrudges God the joys of her presence are not only inappropriate but selfish, self-indulgent. Why should one wail? Having stated in stanza 1 the argument that the child's death is providential and therefore not to be mourned, the poet supported the argument in stanza 2 by giving evidence that God had in fact taken the child, that her death was not merely in the order of nature. In the order of nature, trees, plums, apples, corn, and grass die in old age, after maturity. For a creature to die young, then, God must providentially intervene in the order of nature, must suspend it, not merely allow it to function through the *concursus Dei.* All the evidence indicates that God, who controls both "nature and fate," has done so in taking the child so early. The closing lines, then, are not a sudden abdication to the will of God by a rebellious poet: they are rather the best argument that can be made, the best consolation for the survivors— that the child's untimely death is a clear act of providence, not merely a regrettable part of the order of nature. Those who truly love the child will of course miss her, but they should be consoled that she was singled out by God for an early entrance into heaven.

If we consider the contexts of this elegy, we shall find more evidence that its tone is one of willed resignation and we shall be better able to understand the *donnée* from which Bradstreet's elegies proceeded. One context can only be called that of human expectation. The assumption that an elegist should work toward expressing grief, rather than begin with it and try to resolve it, seems to me wrongheaded. Whether or not there *are* human givens, we tend to live as if there were and to assume that grief at the death of one we love is one of them. Indeed, part of the grisly humor in Arthur Kopit's *Oh Dad, Poor Dad, Mamma's Hung You in the Closet and I'm Feelin' So Sad* is that Jonathan feels compelled to explain to us that his mother's having killed his father, had Dad stuffed, and hung Dad in the closet makes him sad. Another context is that of the Puritan attitude toward love of the creatures. We have already noted Perry Miller's observation that the Puritan theology bordered on pantheism, on the identity of the sensible creation with God; the numerous exhortations of Puritan ministers to wean one's affections from the immoderate love of one's family, for example, presupposed the very love they sought to moderate. We have already seen that Bradstreet's meditations and poetry were full of concern for creatures, of petitions for the health, safety, and continued earthly life of herself and her family, and of hymns of thanksgiving for the continued life of her husband for his love of her, a love commanded by God. Love of one's family and resistance to and grief at their deaths were to be expected among Puritans. But a willed resignation to those deaths was also expected.

Contained in a private autobiography written for his son, Thomas Shepard's description of his wife's death makes painfully clear both his grief and his determination to accept his wife's death: "He took away my most dear precious meek and loving wife. . . . In it the Lord seemed to withdraw his tender care for me and mine, which he graciously manifested by my dear wife; also refused to hear prayer, when I did think he would have hearkened and let me see his beauty in the land of the living, in restoring her to health again." Like Bradstreet, Shepard had petitioned God for earthly favors, for the return of a spouse to health. But God had ignored him, "taking her away in the prime time of her life when she might have lived to have glorified the Lord long." Shepard made explicit the sense of loss that Bradstreet had understated: for him "this loss was very great; she was a woman of incomparable meekness of spirit, toward myself especially and very loving." She had read over Shepard's notes for his sermons, had shared his life, and had told him when she first became ill "that we should love exceedingly together because we should not live long together." But in her final delirium she had not recognized her husband, but had prayed to Christ. Whatever the effect of this information on a modern sensibility, it is clear that Shepard did not turn to Promethean defiance. He argued himself toward acceptance: "I am the Lord's, and he may do with me what he will. . . . Thus god hath visited and scourged me for my sins and sought to wean me from this world, but I have ever found it a difficult thing to profit ever but a little by the sorest and sharpest afflictions." In 1663, his wife had been quite ill, and though Shepard found "the affliction . . . very bitter," he was able to say at last: "I had need of it for I began to grow secretly proud and full of sensuality delighting my soul in my dear wife more than in my god whom I had promised better unto." So now, after his wife's death, he had finally won his way to a willed resignation: "This made me resolve to delight no more in the creature but in the Lord." Shepard had meditated his way from a real grief to an equally real acceptance. As a meditative Puritan poet, Bradstreet might well be expected to follow this movement from grief to resolution in the elegy we have just examined.

Bradstreet's other elegies follow the same movement. Her elegy on her granddaughter Anne Bradstreet begins, not with the easy acceptance imputed to her by Pearce, but with grief:

> With troubled heart and trembling hand I write,
> The heavens have changed to sorrow my delight.

That grief is mitigated somewhat by the realization that on this earth joy simply does not last: "Was ever stable joy yet found below?" The child, though beautiful, was fragile "as a withering flower . . . as a bubble, or the brittle, / Or like a shadow turning as it was." The failure to accept the frangibility and transience of earthly joy is not heroic but foolish:

> More fool then I to look on that was lent
> As if mine own, when thus impermanent.

And persistence in grief or defiance of providence is selfish, for though her grandmother is bereaved, the child is happy:

> Farewell dear child, thou ne'er shall come to me,
> But yet a while, and I shall go to thee;
> Mean time my throbbing heart's cheered up with this:
> Thou with thy Saviour art in endless bliss.

From an earth where joy is never stable, the child has been taken to a heaven where "bliss" differs from earthly joy only in that it is "endless," uninterrupted by imperfection or time, by pain or death. Faced with the absence of a child so taken, the adult survivors are faced with the choice described in her elegy "On My Dear Grandchild Simon Bradstreet." They can either be "mute" toward a providential act the purpose of which passes their understanding, or they can "dispute." The first choice requires trust, that temporary suspension of curiosity that we can manage only toward those we love and believe in. One whose love of and belief in God are not sufficient to enable him to trust in God, to suspend his curiosity about God's motives and methods, can refuse to face the facts of God's will which for the Puritan were the facts of life, death among them. He can, like Ahab, Manfred, and the unnamed quester in Frost's "The Most of It," demand that the universe give some account of itself. Such demands however, are unlikely to be answered in any satisfactory detail, and the Puritans, who were not Romantics, never glorified them, always tried to argue themselves into the acceptance of what pagans called fate, what they called God's will, what we might call the facts of life. Bradstreet wrote:

> With dreadful awe before Him let's be mute
> Such was His will, but why, let's not dispute.

Resigned to death and parting as necessary parts of her life in the world of time, Bradstreet could bid farewell to the child, taking comfort in the belief that he was translated to a world where joys were endless:

> Go pretty babe, go rest with sisters twain;
> Among the blest in endless joys remain.

In heaven God provided, not the revelation that earthly joys were not worth desiring, but joys more satisfactory as joys, because they were perfect and because they lasted.

In her "Meditations Divine and Moral," Bradstreet made explicit the attitude implicit in her poetry: she stressed to her son the necessity of trusting in God, even when no human sense can be made of His providential dispensations, of believing without seeing: "There is nothing admits of more admiration than God's various dispensation of His gifts among the sons of men." By human standards, some are treated well, some horribly. "And no other reason can be given of all this but so it pleased Him whose will is the perfect role of righteousness." At times God's will remains inscrutable and His actions against all reason. Though Bradstreet wrote to her children that she was tempted "many times by atheism," she resisted such an answer and argued that when God has temporarily veiled His face and "we cannot behold the light of His countenance, . . . when He seems to set and to be quite gone out of sight, then must we needs walk in darkness and see no lights; yet then must we trust in the Lord and stay upon our God, and when the morning (which is the appointed time) is come, the Sun of righteousness will arise with healing in His wings." For Bradstreet, then, resignation to the will of God required a difficult and conscious act of her own will; to believe what one had not yet seen was something to be struggled for and achieved. All her elegies begin with her intense grief at the death of her grandchildren, then discipline that grief by moving through a series of controlled arguments expressed in tightly ordered verse forms to a final willed and genuine resignation. Each poem is a part of the difficult process it records, a method for achieving the resignation it expresses.

It is appropriate that a poet who was able to figure the eternal things of God by the temporal things of earth, who considered earthly joys vain because they were transient and divine joys preferable because permanent—she wrote "were earthly comforts permanent, who would look for heavenly?"—and who steeled herself to accept the deaths of those she loved by reflecting that death was just part of this temporal world and that the children had gone to a world free of the pain of time, would write her greatest poem on the theme of time. Bradstreet's "Contemplations" is a single, unified poem about the temporal and the eternal, about their intersection in man who must, like Browne's "amphibium," live in both worlds at once.

The poem begins completely within the world of time:

> Sometime now past in the autumnal tide,
> When Phoebus wanted but one hour to bed.
> (ll. 1–2)

Though it is nearly winter and nearly night, the sensible world is beautiful in purely human terms: "Rapt were my senses at this delectable view" (l. 7). The beauty of the sensible world, as we have seen before, is an *a fortiori* argument for the beauty, predicated univocally, of God:

> If so much excellence abide below,
> How excellent is He that dwells on high,
> Whose power and beauty by his works we know?
> Sure he is goodness, wisdom, glory, light,
> That hath this under world so richly dight;
> More heaven than earth was here, no winter and no night.
> (ll. 10–15)

We know from the first stanza that both winter and night are near, but so fully is the world charged with the grandeur of God that the speaker has forgotten that temporarily, and finds herself in a natural world so thoroughly satisfying as to seem eternal. In the next two stanzas (stanzas 3 and 4) the speaker begins her hymn to the beauty of nature, a beauty conferred on nature by God to figure forth His own beauty and to lead men to Him. Nature's beauty seems eternal: the "stately oak" seems limitlessly old:

> Hath hundred winters past since thou wast born?
> Or thousand since thou brakest thy shell of horn?

But in the alexandrine the speaker recognizes that the oak, though created by God to figure forth His own eternity is not God, is not itself eternal: "If so, all these as nought, eternity doth scorn" (l. 22). So with the sun, which seems a God and is a God-wrought symbol for Himself, but which is not itself divine:

> Then higher on the glistering Sun I gazed,
> Whose beams was shaded by the leavie tree;

> The more I looked, the more I grew amazed,
> And softly said, "What glory's like to thee?"
> Soul of this world, this universe's eye,
> No wonder some made thee a deity;
> Had I not better known, alas, the same had I.
>
> (ll. 23–29)

Again, the alexandrine serves to qualify the claims of divinity made for the creature in the pentameters. In the world of time, the sun seems but is not the Creator. In stanza 5, the sun is likened, as in the nineteenth psalm of David, to the bridegroom who warms and makes fertile, an act of earthly creation. In stanza 6 the sun is presented as a source of comfort and light for human kind and as the power that divides day from night and orders the circle of the seasons, but again the alexandrine functions to remind us (and perhaps the speaker) that the sun is, after all, only a "creature," though "full of sweetness, beauty, and delight" (l. 41). In stanza 7, the speaker returns to the argument of stanza 2—that the beauty and glory of the sensible world have been created by God as an act of love toward His creatures, to show forth to them a metaphor for Himself that they can understand:

> How full of glory then must thy Creator be,
> Who gave this bright light, luster unto thee?
> Admired, adored for ever, be that Majesty.
>
> (ll. 48–50)

This first section of the poem, then, is a hymn to the communicable glory of the eternal God as that glory is reflected in the temporal universe. Neither a hymn to nature nor a hymn (based on analogy) to God Himself, it begins with the sensible universe and praises it as a suitable vehicle for the divine metaphor. Nowhere does it presuppose the analogical method of Aquinas and therefore claim to praise God Himself through the analog of the created universe; at all times the speaker is aware of the difference between the eternal God and the temporal vehicle He has chosen for His metaphor. Neither a Thomist nor a pantheist, the speaker is a careful Puritan who at all times has her theology well in hand.

In stanzas 8 and 9, however, the tone changes. Her first impulse is to sing a song meet or appropriate to the poem of God's creation:

> Silent alone, where none or saw, or heard,
> In pathless paths I lead my wand'ring feet,
> My humble eyes to lofty skies I reared
> To sing some song, my mazed Muse thought meet.
> My great Creator I would magnify,
> That nature had thus decked liberally;
> But Ah, and Ah, again, my imbecility!
>
> (ll. 51–57)

Though she can see the glory of God in the sensible world, she cannot adequately praise the Creator Himself. She sees that other creature can:

> I head the merry grasshopper then sing.
> The black-clad cricket bear a second part;
> They kept one tune and played on the same string,
> Seeming to glory in their little art.
> Shall creatures abject thus their voices raise
> And in their kind resound their Maker's praise,
> Whilst I, as mute, can warble forth no higher lays?
> (ll. 58–64)

Why can nature, and even the lowest of creatures in it, sing praise of the Creator when man cannot?

The answer is clearly the central event that separated man from the rest of creation, the Fall. The answer is that these other creatures, having never fallen into disobedience, retain the pristine glory they had at their creation, while man has fallen below nature. The Fall, then, neither diminished nature nor man's perception of it: the Fall significantly altered man's relation to nature. Before the Fall, man had been lord of nature and it had served him: after the Fall, man was inferior in the natural order, unable to obey and praise God unconsciously, as all of nature still did. Since the poem records contemplations rather than structured argument, the speaker, without explicit transition, begins to trace man's fall into the consciousness of time.

Stanzas 10 through 17 are a retrospective view of man's history, a history characterized as a continuing descent from the primal perfection in which God created him. We see the Fall, the effect of which was to transform "glorious Adam," who was in Eden "made Lord of all" into the fallen man,

> Who like a miscreant's driven from that place,
> To get his bread with pain, and sweat of face,
> A penalty imposed on his backsliding race.
> (ll. 76–78)

This event placed man in a new relation to nature and God, a relation different from that of the grasshopper and cricket. Where before, man had been the lord of all natural creatures, he now became inferior to them, at least in the order of nature.

Man's history after the Fall is one of long declension. Man's consciousness, his perception of the temporal world, causes him to become obsessed with time and affords him a specious glimpse of eternity:

> When present times look back to ages past,
> And men in being fancy those are dead,
> It makes things gone perpetually to last,
> And calls back months and years that long since fled.

It makes a man more aged in conceit
Than was Methuselah, or's grandsire great,
While of their persons and their acts his mind doth treat.

(ll. 65–71)

But that mind merely enables man to view the long decline of his race. When Adam looked ahead upon "their long descent," he "sighed to see his progeny" (ll. 108, 111). When the speaker looks back upon the Fall and subsequent decline, the history itself answers her question; it explains her inability to sing like the grasshopper and cricket.

Her question answered, the speaker turns in stanza 18 from her historical reflections back to her observations of man and nature. Again, on its own terms, nature seems immortal and man an inferior and short-lived creature:

When I behold the heavens as in their prime,
And then the earth (though old) still clad in green,
The stones and trees, insensible of time,
Nor age nor wrinkle on their front are seen;
If winter come and greenness then do fade,
A spring returns, and they more youthful made;
But man grows old, lies down, remains where once he's laid.

(ll. 121–27)

As the speaker realizes in the appropriately halting alexandrine, fallen man is lower than nature, judged only in terms of the temporal world. Her reaction is not to envy that natural world, which is timeless and seems eternal on its own terms, but to judge man and nature by a more cosmic set of terms, those of her religion:

Shall I then praise the heavens, the trees, the earth
Because their beauty and their strength last longer?

(ll. 135–36)

Nay, they shall darken, perish, fade and die,
And when unmade, so ever shall they lie,
But man was made for endless immortality.

(ll. 139–41)

Man lives in two worlds. In the natural world, the world of time, he is a frail and short-lived creature, fallen, no longer "lord of all" (l. 73). In the timeless world of eternity, however, he can share with God joys that never fade; from this point of view the speaker can see that nature's apparent timelessness is only its lack of consciousness, that nature will die, never to rise again. As a part of the natural order, man is inferior; he has, after Adam, fallen below the other creatures and has steadily declined. As part of the supernatural order, however, he is superior to nature; he is immortal, and if elect, destined for endless joys of which nature can know nothing.

If the poem were merely a rejection of the world, an expression of the unmitigated desire to flee the natural order for the supernatural, it could end here.

But the speaker is still on earth, is still a part of both orders. In stanzas 21 through 33 the speaker expresses this double life, predicts the Romantic solution which would affirm the order of quasi-eternal nature and man's part in it, rejects that secular solution as an affirmation of man's death, and comes at last to her own Puritan resolution. At first, the natural order affords her real, though transient, satisfactions:

> Under the cooling shadow of a stately elm
> Close sat I by a goodly river's side,
> Where gliding streams the rocks did overwhelm,
> A lonely place, with pleasures dignified.
> I once that loved the shady woods so well,
> Now thought the rivers did the trees excel,
> And if the sun would ever shine, there would I dwell.
>
> (ll. 142–48)

If these "pleasures dignified" would last forever, earth would be heaven, and man's double nature would be reconciled for him: the temporal world and the eternal would be one. In the alexandrine, the speaker makes her acceptance of this world ("there would I dwell") conditional upon an impossibility. The sun will not shine forever; man's place in the order of nature commits him to death.

Still, the natural world is a message sent by God to lead man to Him, and the speaker is right in supposing the river (in stanzas 22 and 23) a symbol of man's route to heaven. But the fish within that river are, unlike man, unconscious. Symbolic characters figuring forth the eternal joys God has stored up for man, the fish themselves can neither partake of the joys they symbolize nor understand the message: "nature taught . . . you know not why, / You wat'ry folk that know not your felicity" (ll. 168–69). The relation of the temporal world to the timeless is, in the mind of the speaker, not dichotomy but hierarchy, even as it was in the poems on vanity and death. Though her recognition of nature's transience is understated, it is always there, even in her most apparently Romantic celebrations of the natural order. Like Keats, the speaker has heard the voice of the nightingale and longed to join in its song:

> The sweet-tongued Philomel perched o'er my head
> And chanted forth a most melodious strain
> Which rapt me so with wonder and delight,
> I judged my hearing better than my sight,
> And wished me wings with her a while to take my flight.
>
> (ll. 179–83)

Though several critics have referred to the "Contemplations" as a Romantic poem, and have made much of the similarities between Bradstreet's bird and Keats's (both are nightingales, for example), their differences are more telling. Keats clearly considered the nightingale a messenger from an immortal world: "Thou wast not born for death, immortal Bird!" ("Ode to a Nightingale," l. 61). He considered flying away with it a death to the world of time and an entrance into the timeless world of eternity. Bradstreet's nightingale, like her trees and fish, is clearly terrestrial, and the speaker considers joining it in flight only for "a while." For the Romantic, moreover, affirming the order of nature and himself as a part of it took the place of affirming God and the supernatural order: nature offered man the same rewards that God used to. In his "Prospectus," Wordsworth wrote that man, "When wedded to this goodly universe" (*The Recluse*, l. 806), would find himself in "Paradise, and groves / Elysian, Fortunate Fields" (ll. 800–801), regions of the eternally blessed, worlds without time. In his "Dejection: An Ode," Coleridge wrote that "wedding Nature to us gives in dower / A new Earth and new Heaven" (ll. 68–69).

For the Puritans, God, not man and nature, authored the eternal "new heaven and a new earth" of Revelation (21:1). As the speaker has already said, nature is mortal and shall "darken, perish, fade, and die. . . . But man was made for endless immortality" (ll. 138, 140). Her relation to the natural world is real, but temporary and as such subordinate to her relation to the eternal order of God. The point of man's apparent inferiority to nature is not that he should strive to wed himself to nature. To do so would be to affirm his own death since the things of nature die forever: "when unmade so ever shall they lie" (l. 140). The point of that apparent inferiority is that from it he learn to look elsewhere for his superiority. He must learn to look to his election. Time is

> the fatal wrack of mortal things . . .
> But he whose name is graved in the white stone
> Shall last and shine when all of these are gone.
> (ll. 226, 232–33)

The "white stone" from Rev. 2:17 was identified with election in a marginal gloss in the Geneva Bible: "Such a stone signifieth here a token of God's favor and grace; also it was a sign that one was cleared in judgment." As Elizabeth Wade White has noted, these closing lines of the poem "firmly state the Puritan way of thought."

That way of thought valued the sensible world as the earnest of a loving God, to be read for what it revealed of Him, to be used and loved while one abode in it. But the Puritan was not to become trapped in his love for this frangible and transient world: he was to wean his affections, to subordinate his love for this world to his love for its Maker and to prepare himself to leave these temporal joys for the eternal ones of heaven. In stanzas 1 through 6 the speaker celebrates the beauty of God's metaphorical world. In stanzas 8 and 9 she asks why man cannot praise God as nature does, and in stanzas 10 through 17 answers that the Fall separated man from nature. In stanzas 18 through 33 she returns from her historical reverie to her contemplations of man and nature and works out her resolution. Bradstreet's speaker moves from her contemplations on the happiness of the creatures, a happiness based on their ignorance of the time that traps them, to contemplations of the happiness of the elect, an eternal happiness based on wisdom, on the wise use of this temporal world. She neither affirms nor rejects the order of nature. Only the dead can be done with the things of this world. She lives in it, loves it, and prepares herself to transcend it when she fulfills her human identity as one of the elect.

This preparation, as we have seen, is the great theme of Bradstreet's poetry. The struggle to wean one's affections from the real and good things of this world, without ceasing to love them, be grateful for them, and understand them as transient earnests of eternal joys to come provided much of the theme and technique of her poems on vanity, on her love for her husband, on the deaths of her grandchildren, and on time itself. Like her fellow Puritans, Bradstreet had to steer a middle course between two sinful extremes: loving the creatures too little was an affront to God, Who had created them and commanded man to love them; loving them too much, without subordinating that love to the love of their Maker, was idolatry. Her poems were records of that middle course; they were prayers, religious acts, her version of the altar commanded in Exodus. God's altar was intended to lead man to heaven, but it was made of earth or stone. So Bradstreet's poetry was essentially about and part of her pilgrimage to heaven. The pilgrimage and the poetry necessarily took place on earth, among the things of this world.

Edward Taylor:
Preparatory Meditations

Louis L. Martz

Edward Taylor's major work, *Preparatory Meditations*, is made up of 217 poems, written from 1682 to 1725, while Taylor was serving as minister to the frontier settlement of Westfield, Massachusetts. Since 128 of these Meditations were published for the first time in Donald Stanford's edition of 1960, until then the full range and power of this work had not been manifested; and, as a result, students of Taylor had tended to give at least equal attention to his long doctrinal allegory, *Gods Determinations*, which has been available in its entirety in Thomas Johnson's selection from Taylor's poetry. *Gods Determinations* is a significant work, unique in English poetry; it reveals the workings of the Puritan doctrine of Grace through a framework derived from the old devices of medieval allegory; and it develops, by the blunt insistence of its verse, a certain crude and battering strength. Yet when all is said, *Gods Determinations* remains, I think, a labor of versified doctrine; only a few of its lyrics can approach the best of the *Meditations* in poetical quality. In the end, Taylor's standing as a poet must be measured by a full and careful reading of the *Meditations*.

Such a reading leaves no doubt that Taylor is a true poet, and yet it is a strange experience, hard to evaluate and explain. For Taylor leads us, inevitably, to compare his achievement with the consummate artistry of George Herbert, whose poetry Taylor echoes throughout the *Meditations*, as well as in his other poems. The example of Herbert appears with special force in the "Prologue," where Taylor five times repeats Herbert's phrase "crumb of dust":

> Lord, Can a Crumb of Dust the Earth outweigh,
>   Outmatch all mountains, nay the Chrystall Sky?

From *The Poem of the Mind*. © 1966 by Louis L. Martz. Oxford University Press, 1966.

It seems a clear echo of Herbert's "The Temper" (I), which also deals with the speaker's sense of inadequacy in attempting the praise of his Lord:

> Wilt thou meet arms with man, that thou dost stretch
> A crumme of dust from heav'n to hell?

And the whole conception of Taylor's poem is perhaps influenced also by a stanza from Herbert's "Longing":

> Behold, thy dust doth stirre,
> It moves, it creeps, it aims at thee:
> Wilt thou deferre
> To succour me,
> Thy pile of dust, wherein each crumme
> Sayes, Come?

The "Prologue" thus prepares us for the strongly Herbertian mode of the first Meditation, with its theme of Love and its familiar exclamations in the presence of the Lord: "Oh! that thy Love might overflow my Heart!" Then, shortly after, we have the three poems that Taylor entitled "The Experience," "The Return," and "The Reflexion"—the only poems in the sequence thus entitled—with their clear reminiscence of the many titles of this kind among Herbert's poetry: "The Answer," "The Reprisall," "The Glance." But these and the other particular echoes of Herbert pointed out in Mr. Stanford's annotations are only the most evident aspects of a pervasive influence. Like Henry Vaughan, Edward Taylor appears to have had a mind saturated with Herbert's poetry, and the result is that a thousand tantalizing echoes of Herbert remain for the most part untraceable because the meditative voice of Herbert has been merged with Taylor's own peculiar voice.

"How sweet a Lord is mine?" "I'le be thy Love, thou my sweet Lord shalt bee." "Then let thy Spirit keepe my Strings in tune." "Blushes of Beauty bright, Pure White, and Red." "My Dear, Deare, Lord I do thee Saviour Call." "What Glory's this, my Lord?" "Oh! Bright! Bright thing! I fain would something say." "Lord speake it home to me, say these are mine." "Oh! that I ever felt what I profess." "What rocky heart is mine?" "Was ever Heart like mine?" "Fain I would sing thy Praise, but feare I feign." "Strang, strang indeed." "I fain would prize and praise thee." "What love, my Lord, dost thou lay out on thine."

> Dull, Dull indeed! What shall it e're be thus?
>   And why? Are not thy Promises, my Lord,
> Rich, Quick'ning things? How should my full Cheeks blush
>   To finde mee thus? And those a lifeless Word?
>   My Heart is heedless: unconcernd hereat:
>   I finde my Spirits Spiritless, and flat.
>
>   (2.12)

All the quotations above are by Taylor; they would not disrupt the harmony of Herbert's *Temple*, and they could be multiplied a hundred times. Yet the full effect of any single poem by Taylor is never quite Herbertian.

Taylor has, first of all, very little of Herbert's metrical skill. In *Gods Determinations* and in the series of short poems on various "occurrants" Taylor attempts to deal with a great variety of stanza forms in Herbert's way, but with only moderate success. In his *Meditations* no such variety is tried: every poem is written in the popular six-line stanza used in Herbert's "Church-porch." Taylor's handling of this stanza seldom rises above competence, and all too often he gives a lame effect of counting syllables and forcing rimes:

> I needed have this hand, that broke off hath
> This Bud of Civill, and of Sacred Faith.

> untill my Virginall
> Chime out in Changes sweet thy Praises shall.

> To view those glories in thy Crown that vapor,
> Would make bright Angells eyes to run a-water.

This sort of clumsiness, in some degree, is found in most of the poems.

Another problem arises when we compare the language of Herbert and Taylor, especially their use of terms from daily speech. As the examples above indicate, Taylor frequently attains the neat and flexible delicacy of Herbert's conversations with God, where the poet speaks in the presence of a familiar friend, as in Herbert's "Easter":

> I got me flowers to straw thy way;
> I got me boughs off many a tree:
> But thou wast up by break of day,
> And brought'st thy sweets along with thee.

This is colloquial, but chastened and restrained: Herbert's language never strays far from the middle way of educated conversation. Herbert was bred in courtly circles, and though he knows that "Kneeling ne'er spoil'd silk stocking," he does not allow slang, dialect, or "low" terms to spoil his neatness. If he allows a line like "The worky-daies are the back-part," this is exceptional: it is at once absorbed into a more discreet context. But consider these lines by Taylor:

> Thus my leane Muses garden thwarts the spring
>   Instead of Anthems, breatheth her ahone.
>   But duty raps upon her doore for Verse.
>   That makes her bleed a poem through her searce.
>   (2.30)

Terms like "ahone" and "searce" bring us up abruptly; they lie outside the mainstream of the language, along with dozens of other terms scattered profusely throughout the poetry: *I'st, bedotcht, brudled, crickling, flur, frim, gastard, glout, keck, paintice, riggalld, skeg, slatch, snick-snarls, tantarrow'd, weddenwise, an hurden haump*. Words like these, whether coinages, phonetic spellings, or Leicestershire dialect, require a sizable glossary, such as that provided at the end of Mr. Stanford's volume. And the problem is compounded by the fact that Taylor's range runs at the same time to the far end of the learned spectrum: *epinicioum, dulcifi'de, enkentrism, enucleate, officine, fistulate, obsignation, aromatize, theanthropie, bituminated*. Even John Donne, who likes to mingle learned and colloquial terms, does not display in his poetry so wide a range as this; and for Herbert, of course, extremes in either direction are to be avoided: he follows Ben Jonson's dictum: "Pure and neat language I love, yet plain and customary."

The problems presented by Taylor's strangely assorted diction are inseparable from a third difficulty: his use of the homeliest images to convey the most sacred and reverend themes. Here again Herbert leads the way, with his "Elixir":

> All may of thee partake:
> Nothing can be so mean,
> Which with his tincture (for thy sake)
> Will not grow bright and clean.
>
> A servant with this clause
> Makes drugerie divine:
> Who sweeps a room, as for thy laws,
> Makes that and th' action fine.

But with Herbert these homely images are handled with a bland understatement, a deft restraint:

> You must sit down, sayes Love, and taste my meat:
>   So I did sit and eat.
> And in this love, more then in bed, I rest.
>
>   This day my Saviour rose,
> And did inclose this light for his:
> That, as each beast his manger knows,
> Man might not of his fodder misse.
> Christ hath took in this piece of ground,
> And made a garden there for those
>   Who want herbs for their wound.
>
>   ("Sunday")

Herbert thus succeeds by the total poise of his poem: where every syllable is taut, we cannot doubt the speaker's word. But what shall we say of Taylor's treatment of Jonah as the "type" of Christ?

The Grave him swallow'd down as a rich Pill
    Of Working Physick full of Virtue which
Doth purge Death's Constitution of its ill.
      And womble-Crops her stomach where it sticks.
      It heaves her stomach till her hasps off fly.
      And out hee comes Cast up, rais'd up thereby.

                                             (2.30)

Or this treatment of the sinner's state?

Mine Heart's a Park or Chase of sins: Mine Head
    'S a Bowling Alley. Sins play Ninehole here.
Phansy's a Green: sin Barly breaks in't led.
      Judgment's a pingle. Blindeman's Buff's plaid there.
      Sin playes at Coursey Parke within my Minde.
      My Wills a Walke in which it aires what's blinde.

                                             (2.18)

Or this account of the operations of Grace?

Shall things run thus? Then Lord, my tumberill
    Unload of all its Dung, and make it cleane.
And load it with thy wealthi'st Grace untill
      Its Wheeles do crack, or Axletree complain.
      I fain would have it cart thy harvest in,
      Before its loosed from its Axlepin.

                                             (1.46)

    A brief acquaintance with Taylor's poetry might easily lead us to dismiss him as a burlap version of Herbert, a quaint primitive who somehow, despite the Indians, managed to stammer out his rude verses well enough to win the title of "our best Colonial poet." Such a judgment would be utterly wrong. Taylor is not a primitive: he is a subtle, learned man who kept his Theocritus and Origen, his Augustine and Horace, with him in the wilderness. We have the inventory of his library: it would have done credit to a London clergyman, and for one on the Westfield frontier it is all but incredible—until we realize that the Puritan minister of New England did not come to make terms with the wilderness: he came to preserve the Truth in all its purity and wonder. Taylor's Meditations represent a lifelong effort of the inner man to apprehend that Truth.

II

As we read more deeply and more widely in Taylor's poetry, we gradually become aware of the tenacious intelligence that underlies these surface crudities: a bold, probing, adventurous intellect that deliberately tries to bend the toughest matter toward his quest for truth. Consider closely, as a representative example, Meditation 32 of the first series, on the text: "1 Cor. 3:22. Whether Paul or Apollos, or Cephas." We need the whole context of those names: *For all things are yours; whether Paul, or Apollos, or Cephas, or the world, or life, or death, or things present, or things to come; all are yours; and ye are Christ's; and Christ is God's.*

> Thy Grace, Deare Lord's my golden Wrack, I finde
>   Screwing my Phancy into ragged Rhimes,
> Tuning thy Praises in my feeble minde
>   Untill I come to strike them on my Chimes.
>   Were I an Angell bright, and borrow could
>   King Davids Harp, I would them play on gold.
>
> But plung'd I am, my minde is puzzled,
>   When I would spin my Phancy thus unspun,
> In finest Twine of Praise I'm muzzled.
>   My tazzled Thoughts twirld into Snick-Snarls run.
>   Thy Grace, my Lord, is such a glorious thing,
>   It doth Confound me when I would it sing.

There is an effect of deliberate roughness here, of struggling for adequate expression, climaxed in the vigorous line: "My tazzled Thoughts twirld into Snick-Snarls run." And now, to work his way out of this ragged state, the speaker in the next two stanzas turns to analyze the meaning of God's Love and Grace in lines that gradually become clear, more harmonious, more fluent:

> Eternall Love an Object mean did smite
>   Which by the Prince of Darkness was beguilde,
> That from this Love it ran and sweld with spite
>   And in the way with filth was all defilde
>   Yet must be reconcild, cleansd, and begrac'te
>   Or from the fruits of Gods first Love displac'te.
>
> Then Grace, my Lord, wrought in thy Heart a vent,
>   Thy Soft Soft hand to this hard worke did goe,
> And to the Milke White Throne of Justice went
>   And entred bond that Grace might overflow.
>   Hence did thy Person to my Nature ty
>   And bleed through humane Veans to satisfy.

There, in the middle stanza of the poem, the central act of Grace is brought home, with perfect clarity and cadence, to the speaker's mind. As a result, his "Snick-Snarls" disappear, and he bursts forth into spontaneous praise:

> Oh! Grace, Grace, Grace! this Wealthy Grace doth lay
>   Her Golden Channells from thy Fathers throne,
> Into our Earthen Pitchers to Convay
>   Heavens Aqua Vitae to us for our own.
>   O! let thy Golden Gutters run into
>   My Cup this Liquour till it overflow.

He pauses, then, to analyze the meaning of these images which have burst out so unexpectedly:

> Thine Ordinances, Graces Wine-fats where
> > Thy Spirits Walkes, and Graces runs doe ly
> And Angells waiting stand with holy Cheere
> > From Graces Conduite Head, with all Supply.
> > These Vessells full of Grace are, and the Bowls
> > In which their Taps do run, are pretious Souls.

The term "Ordinances" refers specifically to the sacraments of Communion and Baptism, held by Taylor to be the "Seales of the Covenant of Grace." More generally, the term includes the Decrees and Determinations signified by those sacraments. These are the vats of wine from which Grace runs to save the human soul. Realizing now the immensity and the richness of the gift, the speaker has achieved his wish to "play on gold": Grace conveyed through those "Golden Channells" and "Golden Gutters" has brought to the speaker's soul a "Golden Word":

> Thou to the Cups dost say (that Catch this Wine,)
> > This Liquour, Golden Pipes, and Wine-fats plain,
> Whether Paul, Apollos, Cephas, all are thine.
> > Oh Golden Word! Lord speake it ore again.
> > Lord speake it home to me, say these are mine.
> > My Bells shall then thy Praises bravely chime.

The poem, I believe, creates a total effect of rough integrity, moving from a ragged opening to the smooth Herbertian phrasing of the close. The rough phrasing, the colloquialism, the vividly concrete imagery, the Herbertian echoes all play their part in a total pattern. I will not argue that such a control is always present in Taylor's *Meditations:* there is, as I have implied, a frequent clumsiness that has no function; and one cannot defend his excesses in developed imagery, as when he shows the prisoners of sin thus released by "the Blood of thy Covenant":

> And now the Prisoners sent out, do come
> > Padling in their Canooes apace with joyes
> Along this blood red Sea, Where joyes do throng
> > > > > (2.78)

But frequently, even in poems with grave flaws, the underlying control is greater than we might at first think, and sometimes the flaws recede into insignificance as the whole poem comes into focus.

At the same time, we must reckon with the fact that the *Meditations* are written in sequences, sometimes with tight links between the poems. The poem we have just considered, for example, is part of a sequence of seven Meditations (1.31–7) written on consecutive aspects of the above-quoted passage from 1 Cor. 3:21–3. What I have called the tenacity of Taylor's intelligence is enforced when we realize that these seven Meditations, like the others, were composed at intervals of about two months, and sometimes longer, for Communion Sundays; in this case the poems are dated as follows: 17 February 1688/9; 28 April 1689; 7 July 1689; 25 November 1689; 19 January 1689/90; 16 March 1689/90; and 4 May 1690. These Meditations, then, are the outgrowth of a planned series on sequential texts, running over a period of fifteen months. Longer and more striking sequences appear: the thirty meditations on "Types" that begin Taylor's second series; the subsequent series on the nature, love, and power of Christ (2.31–56), which includes the sequence (2.42–56) associated with a group of fourteen sermons preserved by Taylor under the title *Christographia;* the series (2.102–11) in which Taylor deals with the doctrine of the Lord's Supper; and lastly, the long series on sequential texts from Canticles (2.115–53), running from September 1713 to February 1719.

It is worth noting, too, that Taylor started renumbering his *Meditations* when he began the series of poems on typology—that is to say, on events and personages of the Old Testament that were interpreted as prefigurations of the New Testament. This would seem to be a clear indication that the 49 opening meditations constitute a unit of some kind. The number 49 is probably significant after the manner of the times; it is the perfect multiple of seven, a number whose significance Taylor celebrates in Meditation 21 of the second series:

> What Secret Sweet Mysterie under the Wing
> Of this so much Elected number lies?

In seventeenth-century thought the number 7 and its multiples signified perfection, and it may be that a meditative quest toward the perfect apprehension of God's Love is the key to this opening series. Certainly Love is its theme, as the opening Meditation declares, foreshadowing the struggle of the whole series toward a joyous realization of this Love:

> Oh! that thy Love might overflow my Heart!
> To fire the same with Love: for Love I would.
> But oh! my streight'ned Breast! my Lifeless Sparke!
> My Fireless Flame! What Chilly Love, and Cold?
> In measure small! In Manner Chilly! See.
> Lord blow the Coal: Thy Love Enflame in mee.

Toward the close of the series, after many expressions of desire and longing, the efforts of the lover come to focus more and more upon the promised glories in Heaven, beginning with Meditation 41, on the text "I go to prepare a Place for you":

> Reason, lie prison'd in this golden Chain,
> Chain up thy tongue, and silent stand a while.
> Let this rich Love thy Love and heart obtain
> To tend thy Lord in all admiring Style.

Then the sequence moves through meditations on the "Throne," the "Crown of Life," the "Crown of Righteousness," the "Crown of Glory," and the "White Raiment," to conclude with a sequence of three poems on the text "Enter thou into the joy of thy Lord." Meditation 48 achieves the assurance of an affectionate realization:

> When I, Lord, eye thy Joy, and my Love, small,
>   My heart gives in: what now? Strange! Sure I love thee!
> And finding brambles 'bout my heart to crawl
>   My heart misgives mee. Prize I ought above thee?
>   Such great Love hugging them, such small Love, thee!
>   Whether thou hast my Love, I scarce can see.
>
> Yet when the beamings, Lord, of thy rich Joys,
>   Do guild my Soule, meethinks I'm sure I Love thee.
> They Calcine all these brambly trumperys
>   And now I'm sure that I prize naught above thee.

And Meditation 49 gives the effect of a formal conclusion, since it offers a sustained prayer for the continued operations of Grace upon his sinful soul:

> A Lock of Steel upon my Soule, whose key
>   The serpent keeps, I fear, doth lock my doore.
> O pick't: and through the key-hole make thy way
>   And enter in: and let thy joyes run o're.

Thus, as the full effect of an individual Meditation often enfolds and sustains a number of flaws in detail, so a weak poem may be enfolded and sustained by the part it plays in a developing sequence. The flaws are there, and we do not overlook them; yet the poems, in the large, succeed in creating a highly original world, designed upon a special plan. It is a world where the Puritan doctrine of Grace operates to consecrate, within the soul of one of the Elect, every object, every word, every thought that passes through his anguished, grateful, loving mind. To understand the workings of that world, we need to explore the meaning of that key word which Taylor repeated in his titles more than two hundred times: "meditation."

III

For a Puritan minister of New England in the year 1682, the word "meditation" would have retained, certainly, some of the grimmer implications that it held among the older generation of Puritan ministers, for whom the word signified, primarily, a rigorous self-examination designed to uncover the sins of fallen man. The eminent Connecticut divine Thomas Hooker, for example, devotes seventy-five pages of his treatise *The Application of Redemption* (London, 1657) to a vigorous exhortation toward the "Meditation of sins" as "a special means to break the heart of a sinner." Meditation, he declares, "is as it were the register and remembrancer, that looks over the records of our daily corruptions, and keeps them upon file." Moreover, "Meditation is that which encreaseth the weight of the evil of sin, presseth it down upon the Conscience, and burdens the heart with it until it break under it. It gleans up, and rakes together al the particulars, adds dayly to the load, and laies on until the Axletree split asunder, and the heart fails and dies away under the apprehension of the dreadfulness of the evil." Thus "daily meditation flings in one terror after another," "holds the heart upon the rack under restless and unsupportable pressures," with the result that "the sinner is forced to walk and talk with [sin], to wake and sleep with it, to eat and drink his sins." In this way, "by serious meditation we sew them all up together, we look back to the linage and pedigree of our lusts, and track the abominations of our lives, step by step, until we come to the very nest where they are hatched and bred, even of our original corruption."

But in Edward Taylor's day other aspects of the word "meditation" were operating in Puritan circles, aspects that served to modify and ameliorate the rigor of the older generation. The clearest indication of these newer tendencies, I think, may be found by turning to the most important Puritan treatise on meditation written during the seventeenth century, the fourth part of Richard Baxter's famous work *The Saints Everlasting Rest* (London, 1650). Baxter's works were well known in New England; Taylor's own library contained two of Baxter's treatises, although the *Everlasting Rest* is not one of them. We should recall, too, that Taylor did not leave England until 1668, when he was about the age of 25; he was already highly educated and apparently designed for the ministry; he is said to have attended Cambridge University, and he was at once admitted to Harvard with advanced standing. Taylor, then, came to maturity in England at just the time when the temporary victory of the Puritan Commonwealth had released into new areas the powerful energies of English Puritanism, long constricted by the fierce struggle for survival.

Baxter's treatise on meditation is one of many signs that English Puritanism, in its midcentury moment of dominance, was reaching out into areas hitherto neglected: the place of the mystical Platonist Peter Sterry as Cromwell's chaplain and the presence of John Milton and Andrew Marvell in the inner circles of Cromwell's government will testify to the rich expansion of outlook that occurred in this brief interval. Richard Baxter's treatise, with ten editions appearing in the years 1650–70, played its part in this development by urging Puritans to undertake what his title page calls "the Diligent Practice of that Excellent unknown Duty of *heavenly Meditation*"—formal meditation on the joys of Heaven. A brief account of Baxter's mode of meditation will help to show how closely Taylor's poetry accords with the expanding outlook of contemporary Puritanism.

Puritanism, of course, was never the solid phalanx of rigorous doctrine that our studies sometimes make it appear: there were always flexible spirits, always exceptions, always examples in earlier Puritans of the kind of advice that Baxter formulated and brought forward into a central influence. Baxter himself cites some of his predecessors to justify his arguments for a different kind of meditation. But when Baxter says that this way of meditation is "unknown" among his people, we may believe that in general he is right: it is impossible to find a shrewder or a better-informed witness.

Meditation in his sense of the term, Baxter declares, is "unknown" among his people largely because they have spent so much time in running "from Sermon to Sermon," or in examining their souls for "signs of their sincerity," or in passively awaiting the gift of "Enthusiastick Consolations" (pt. 4, pp. 5, 147; I quote from the London edition of 1653). Baxter is clearly attempting to add another dimension to the state of mind that Perry Miller has acutely described in the second chapter of *The New England Mind: The Seventeenth Century*, where he deals with that "unceasing self-examination" by which the Puritan attempted to assure himself that he was indeed regenerated, sanctified, elected. To be sure, the word "meditation" is well known and often used among these people, but, Baxter says, they do not understand its true meaning: "They have thought that Mediation is nothing but the bare thinking on Truths, and the rolling of them in the understanding and memory" (4, 151). And no one, he notes, in a passage that may bear a special import for the study of Taylor's poetry, no one is more prone to this error than "those that are much in publick duty, especially Preachers of the Gospel."

> O how easily may they be deceived here, while they do nothing more then reade of Heaven, and study of Heaven, and preach of Heaven, and pray, and talk of Heaven? what, is not this the Heavenly Life? O that God would reveal to our hearts the danger of this snare! Alas, all this is but meer preparation: This is not the life we speak of, but it's indeed a necessary help thereto. I entreat every one of my Brethren in the Ministry, that they search, and watch against this Temptation: Alas, this is but gathering the materials, and not the erecting of the building it self; this is but gathering our Manna for others, and not eating and digesting our selves.
>
> (4, 122)

And therefore Baxter says to all his people: "this is the great task in hand, and this is the work that I would set thee on; to get these truths from thy head to thy heart, and that all the Sermons which thou hast heard of Heaven, and all the notions that thou hast conceived of this Rest, may be turned into the bloud and spirits of Affection, and thou maist feel them revive thee, and warm thee at the heart" (4, 151).

Taylor's *Meditations* seem to bear exactly this relation to his sermons, as his full title makes clear: "Preparatory Meditations before my Approach to the Lords Supper. Chiefly upon the Doctrin preached upon the Day of administration." Norman Grabo, in his edition ɔf Taylor's *Christographia*, shows how sermon and Meditation correspond, bearing the same dates and, with one exception, the same biblical texts. The sermon prepares the ground, the doctrine, for the Meditation; while the act of meditation in turn prepares the preacher to receive and administer the sacrament, and to deliver his sermon on that day with "the bloud and spirits of Affection." These poems, then, are properly called *Preparatory Meditations* (not *Sacramental Meditations*, as they used to be called, after a title added by another hand above Taylor's own title): they preserve, in the finest verbal form that Taylor could give, his efforts "to get these truths" from his head to his heart.

Baxter, in a long exposition, makes clear every aspect of the art of meditation as he wished his people to practice it. The method is essentially the same as that which had been advocated, over the preceding century, by Catholic handbooks of devotion. It consists of three essential acts, corresponding to the old division of the faculties or "powers" of the soul into memory, understanding, and will. Thus the work of meditation, for Baxter, proceeds by "the set and solemn acting of all the powers of the soul" (4, 146). This meditation, he explains, is "set and solemn" because it is performed "when a Christian observing it as a standing duty, doth resolvedly practise it in a constant course" (4, 153). First, he directs, "you must by *cogitation* go to the Memory (which is the Magazine or Treasury of the Understanding); thence you must take forth those *heavenly doctrines*, which you intend to make the subject of your *Meditation*." Then, after "you have fetcht from your memory the *matter* of your *Meditation*, your next work is to present it to your *Judgment:* open there the case as fully as thou canst" (4, 186–87). He has explained earlier that the "great Instrument that this Work is done by, is Ratiocination, Reasoning the case with your selves, Discourse of mind, Cogitation, or Thinking; or, if you will, call it Consideration." This consideration, he declares, "doth, as it were, open the door, between the Head and the Heart" (4, 178–79).

He particularly urges that the work of consideration be carried on by means of "Soliloquy," "which is nothing but a pleading the case with our own Souls," or, he adds, "a Preaching to ones self." "Why thus must thou do in thy *Meditation* to quicken thy own *heart:* Enter into a serious debate with it: Plead with it in the most moving and affecting language: Urge it with the most weighty and powerful *Arguments*" (4, 209–10). And so, through the vigorous use of the understanding, the soul is aroused to feel the affections (emotions or feelings) of the will, which, according to Baxter, should be developed in a certain order: love, desire, hope, courage (resolution), and, lastly, joy.

I believe that anyone who reads carefully through the first 49 Meditations of Edward Taylor will quickly sense how closely the poetry accords with such advice by Baxter. It is not essential, of course, to believe that Taylor learned this mode of meditation from Baxter's treatise. By 1682 Baxter's influence had been widely disseminated throughout English Puritan-ism; and during Taylor's youth in England exhortations to this kind of meditation were available in Catholic or Anglo-Catholic treatises. The chief point is that both Baxter and Taylor, while maintaining all the central Pu-ritan tenets, were participating in one of the central movements of religious devotion in the seventeenth century.

The entire process is accompanied by two other elements which are, in Baxter's view, essential to success in meditation, and are of the utmost importance for Taylor's poetry. The first of these is prayer: requests to God "may be intermixed or added, and that as a very part of the duty it self." Such constant prayer, Baxter says, "keeps the Soul in mind of the *Divine Presence*; it tends also exceedingly to quicken and raise it; so that as God is the highest Object of our *Thoughts*, so our viewing of him, and our speaking to him, and pleading with him, doth more elevate the soul, and actuate the affections, then any other part of *Meditation* can do" (4, 214).

And secondly, we have the advice stressed by Kenneth Murdock in the second chapter of his study *Literature and Theology in Colonial New England*. As one is aided by the upward looks of prayer, so the meditative man may be constantly aided by downward looks: the senses themselves should be used "to make your *thoughts* of *Heaven* to be piercing, affecting, raising *thoughts*." The time has come, Baxter believes, for Puritanism to moderate its mistrust of sensory aids in the service of religion. "Why sure it will be a point of our Spiritual prudence, and a singular help to the furthering of the work of Faith, to call in our Sense to its assistance. . . . Sure it is both possible and lawful, yea, and necessary too, to do something in this kind; for God would not have given us either our senses themselves, or their usual objects, if they might not have been serviceable to his own Praise, and helps to raise us up to the apprehension of higher things" (4, 216–17). Following the lead of Scriptural imagery, we must make every effort to apprehend the joys of heaven with our senses: "get the liveliest Picture of them in thy minde that possibly thou canst; meditate of them, as if thou were all the while beholding them, and as if thou were even hearing the *Hallelujahs*, while thou art thinking of them; till thou canst say, Methinks I see a glimpse of the Glory! Methinks I hear the shouts of Joy and Praise!" (4, 220–21). And he continues for twenty more pages to suggest various ways in which sensory objects and personal experiences may be used constantly "to quicken your affections, by comparing the unseen delights of Heaven, with those smaller which you have seen, and felt in the flesh" (4, 242).

IV

In Baxter's arguments for the use of sensory images in meditation we have, I believe, the grounds of justification for Taylor's bold and often unseemly use of common imagery. For Baxter's support of this way of meditation is

thoroughly and vehemently argued: "He that will speak to mans understanding must speak in mans language, and speak that which he is capable
to conceive." "Go to then," he exclaims, "When thou settest thy self to
meditate on the joyes above, think on them boldly as Scripture hath expressed them. Bring down thy conceivings to the reach of sense, Excellency
without familiarity, doth more amaze then delight us: Both Love and Joy
are promoted by familiar acquaintance" (4, 218–19). Baxter is speaking at
this point particularly of meditation upon the Everlasting Rest in Heaven;
but he points out elsewhere (4, 208) that the same methods may be used
"for the acting of the contrary and more mixed passions"—such as "hatred
and detestation of sin," grief, shame, repentance, and so on.

The whole of the spiritual life, then, is to be apprehended in sensory
and colloquial terms. Everything that exists may be used to promote this
"familiar acquaintance": thus Taylor uses a rolling pin, roast mutton, a
bowling alley, a "Bucking tub," a "Titimouses Quill," milk pails, a "Drippen
pan," a "Dish clout," a "Trough of Washing-Swill." "Nothing that is available in human experience is to be legislated out of poetry," says R. P.
Warren in a classic essay of modern criticism; Edward Taylor clearly agrees.
Are we searching for the nature of Love? Here is the way to bring it home
to the heart:

> O! what a thing is Love? who can define
>   Or liniament it out? Its strange to tell.
> A Sparke of Spirit empearld pill like and fine
>   In't shugard pargings, crusted, and doth dwell
>   Within the heart, where thron'd, without Controle
>   It ruleth all the Inmates of the Soule.
>
> It makes a poother in its Secret Sell
>   Mongst the affections: oh! it swells, its paind,
> Like kirnells soked untill it breaks its Shell
>   Unless its object be obtained and gain'd.
>   Like Caskd wines jumbled breake the Caske, this Sparke
>   Oft swells when crusht: untill it breakes the Heart.
>   (2.66)

Or perhaps we are searching for a way to drive home the horrors of sin:

> My Sin! my Sin, My God, these Cursed Dregs,
>   Green, Yellow, Blew streakt Poyson hellish, ranck,
> Bubs hatcht in natures nest on Serpents Eggs,
>   Yelp, Cherp and Cry; they set my Soule a Cramp.
>   I frown, Chide, strik and fight them, mourn and Cry
>   To Conquour them, but cannot them destroy.
>
> I cannot kill nor Coop them up: my Curb
>   'S less than a Snaffle in their mouth: my Rains

> They as a twine thrid, snap: by hell they're spurd:
>> And load my Soule with swagging loads of pains.
>> Black Imps, young Divells, snap, bite, drag to bring
>> And pick mee headlong hells dread Whirle Poole in.
>>> (1.39)

As these examples indicate, Taylor has a way of shifting impetuously from image to image in this effort to define and bring home the spiritual import; in the above four stanzas the images work without confusion, but elsewhere, as earlier critics of Taylor have noted, he jumps from image to image in a way that tends to shake the poem apart: Meditation 37 in the first series will provide examples of this weakness. But a more serious flaw in Taylor's handling of imagery seems to arise from the opposite tendency: he frequently hangs on to an image until he has strained it by excessive ingenuity: Meditation 38 in the first series seems to me an example of this sort of excess.

Yet when all his flaws in dealing with imagery have been acknowledged, even at his worst he retains an attractive vigor; and at his best he can produce an analyzed image of a subtlety that equals Herbert:

> I have no plea mine Advocate to give:
>> What now? He'l anvill Arguments greate Store
> Out of his Flesh and Blood to make thee live.
>> O Deare bought Arguments: Good pleas therefore.
>> Nails made of heavenly Steel, more Choice than gold
> Drove home, Well Clencht, eternally will hold.
>>> (1.39)

Thus the nails driven through the flesh of Christ on the Cross are made to symbolize the certainty, as well as the means, of Christ's effective advocacy.

At other times the casual introduction of a homely image or expression is enough to give life to a passage that seems doomed to dryness; thus Taylor deals with Joseph as a Type of Christ:

> Is Josephs glorious shine a Type of thee?
>> How bright art thou? He Envi'de was as well.
> And so was thou. He's stript, and pick't, poore hee,
>> Into the pit. And so was thou. They shell
>> Thee of thy Kirnell. He by Judah's sold
>> For twenty Bits, thirty for thee he'd told.
>
> Joseph was tempted by his Mistress vile.
>> Thou by the Divell, but both shame the foe.
> Joseph was cast into the jayle awhile.
>> And so was thou. Sweet apples mellow so.
>>> (2.7)

Sweet apples mellow so. One can endure a good deal of Taylor's clumsiness for one such effect of "familiar acquaintance."

But in the final analysis the success of Taylor's homely images and earthy language must depend on how they function in the whole poem. Here again, I believe, the meditative discipline that lies behind and within the poetry has enabled Taylor to give many of his poetical meditations a firm and operative structure. For the most part, his Meditations are working at the achieved level of the affections. Like the "Divine Meditations" (Holy Sonnets) of John Donne, the sonnets of Gerard Manley Hopkins, or the poems of George Herbert, Taylor's Meditations represent the peaks and pinnacles of the meditative process on which the poet's spiritual life is based:

> And now his shining Love beams out its rayes
> > My Soul, upon thy Heart to thaw the same:
> To animate th'Affections till they blaze;
> > To free from Guilt, and from Sins Slough, and Shame.
> > Open thy Casement wide, let Glory in,
> > To Guild thy Heart to be an Hall for him.
>
> My Breast, be thou the ringing Virginalls:
> > Ye mine Affections, their sweet Golden Strings,
> My Panting Heart, be thou for Stops, and Falls:
> > Lord, let thy quick'ning Beams dance o're the Pins.
> > > > > (1.18)

But at the same time this music of the affections will frequently, and indeed usually, reflect in some measure the stages by which the soul has reached such a level of religious experience. Consequently, in Taylor's meditative poems, as in Donne's or Herbert's or Hopkins's, we can often trace clearly, preserved in miniature, the whole process of a meditation, in Baxter's meaning of the term. One example must serve: Meditation 29 of the first series, on the text: "Joh. 20.17. My Father, and your Father, to my God, and your God." The context is important, for the words are spoken by the risen Jesus in the garden of the sepulcher, after Mary Magdalene has mistaken him for the gardener; the garden of the Gospel has provided Taylor with a setting from which the hand of meditation can draw forth from the memory the following vivid picture:

> My shattred Phancy stole away from mee,
> > (Wits run a Wooling over Edens Parke)
> And in Gods Garden saw a golden Tree,
> > Whose Heart was All Divine, and gold its barke.
> > Whose glorious limbs and fruitfull branches strong
> > With Saints, and Angells bright are richly hung.

With the situation thus firmly established, consideration then projects the speaker's own plight upon the scene, and explains, with careful analysis, the exact relation of Man to God by developing the central image of a "Grafft" upon that Tree.

Thou! thou! my Deare-Deare Lord, art this rich Tree
    The Tree of Life Within Gods Paradise.
I am a Withred Twig, dri'de fit to bee
    A Chat Cast in thy fire, Writh off by Vice.
    Yet if thy Milke white-Gracious Hand will take mee
    And grafft mee in this golden stock, thou'lt make mee.

Thou'lt make me then its Fruite, and Branch to spring.
    And though a nipping Eastwinde blow, and all
Hells Nymps with spite their Dog's sticks thereat ding
    To Dash the Grafft off, and it's fruits to fall,
    Yet I shall stand thy Grafft, and Fruits that are
    Fruits of the Tree of Life thy Grafft shall beare.

I being grafft in thee there up to stand
    In us Relations all that mutuall are.
I am thy Patient, Pupill, Servant, and
    Thy Sister, Mother, Doove, Spouse, Son, and Heire.
    Thou art my Priest, Physician, Prophet, King,
    Lord, Brother, Bridegroom, Father, Ev'ry thing.

I being grafft in thee am graffted here
    Into thy Family, and kindred Claim
To all in Heaven, God, Saints, and Angells there.
    I thy Relations my Relations name.
    Thy Father's mine, thy God my God, and I
    With Saints, and Angells draw Affinity.

Reason has opened the case as fully as it can, and the door between the
head and the heart now stands ajar: the poem concludes with a surge of
the affections toward gratitude and praise:

My Lord, what is it that thou dost bestow?
    The Praise on this account fills up, and throngs
Eternity brimfull, doth overflow
    The Heavens vast with rich Angelick Songs.
    How should I blush? how Tremble at this thing,
    Not having yet my Gam-Ut, learnd to sing.

But, Lord, as burnish't Sun Beams forth out fly
    Let Angell-Shine forth in my Life out flame,
That I may grace thy gracefull Family
    And not to thy Relations be a Shame.
    Make mee thy Grafft, be thou my Golden Stock.
    Thy Glory then I'le make my fruits and Crop.

V

Some readers will no doubt prefer to describe the action of this analyzed
conceit as "metaphysical" or, perhaps, "baroque." I do not mean to quarrel

with these terms, both well established in critical discussion, and each with its own particular use. I must confess, however, that both seem less accurate than the term "meditative," when applied to Taylor's *Preparatory Meditations*. For Baxter's kind of meditation is, like poetry, a verbal action developed through every resource that language can offer.

Near the close of his treatise Baxter sets forth an elementary "Example" of a full meditation "for the help of the unskilful." This is written in concrete, colloquial, highly charged language which in places sounds like Taylor's poetry—or even like Herbert's poetry—turned into prose:

> What thinkest thou, O my Soul, of this most blessed state? What! Dost thou stagger at the *Promise of God* through unbelief? . . . Can *God* lie? or he that is the *Truth* it self, be false? Foolish wretch! What need hath God to flatter thee, or deceive thee? why should he promise thee more then he will perform? Art thou not his *Creature?* a little crumb of dust?
>
> (4, 259)

One might hesitate to attribute that phrase "crumb of dust" to a memory of Herbert, were it not for the fact that later in the meditation (4, 278) we find Baxter quoting a whole stanza from "*Herberts Poems*, The Glance," and three pages after this, Herbert's entire poem "Dotage," and ten pages after this, a stanza (considerably altered) from Herbert's "Mans medley." Then, after a few pages of concluding advice, Baxter places at the very end of his volume "A Poem of Master G. Herbert; In His Temple": one of Herbert's longest poems, covering three pages here—the poem "Home":

> Come dearest Lord; pass not this holy season;
>   My flesh and bones and joynts do pray;
> And even my verse, when by the rhyme and reason
>   The word is, Stay, say's ever, Come.
>   *O shew thy self to me,*
>   *Or take me up to thee.*

Thus Baxter himself indicates how meditation and poetry converge. Baxter, Herbert, the Psalms, the Canticles—these are enough to suggest the literary traditions which made it possible for Edward Taylor to compose his poetical meditations in the wilderness. They will suggest, too, Taylor's place in literary history as the last heir of the great tradition of English meditative poetry that arose in the latter part of the sixteenth century, with Robert Southwell as its first notable example, continued on through the religious poetry of John Donne (and also in those of his secular poems that have meditative elements), reached a fulfillment in the *Temple* of George Herbert, went abroad to include the baroque motifs of Richard Crashaw, found another home in Henry Vaughan's uneven but inspired meditations on the "creatures," strengthened the fiber of Andrew Marvell's slender muse, and, so far as England was concerned, died at the death of Thomas Traherne in 1674, with both his prose meditations and their companionate poems unpublished. But as Crashaw had gone abroad to preserve and extend his Catholic allegiance, so, at the end of the line, in 1668, Edward Taylor sailed for New England, and there, surrounded by the rude and dangerous life of the frontier, composed his Puritan and meditative poems.

What I have said thus far has been concerned with enforcing Taylor's relation to the traditions of English culture. Is there anything in Taylor's poetry that could be called distinctively American? In the whole large range of his *Preparatory Meditations* and *Gods Determinations*, there is almost nothing (except for an occasional canoe or rattlesnake) that one could single out to suggest a specifically American allusion. In some ways Edward Taylor may seem to bear out the charge brought against New England Puritanism by William Carlos Williams in his *In the American Grain:* that the Puritans refused to *touch*—that they set up a "resistance to the wilderness"—"with a ground all blossoming about them." Williams speaks of the "rigid clarity" of their religion, "its *inhuman* clarity, its steel-like thrust from the heart of each isolate man straight into the tabernacle of Jehovah without embellishment or softening." "Its firmness is its beauty. . . . Its virtue is to make each man stand alone, surrounded by a density as of the Lord: a seed in its shell." It is true that, so far as local allusion is concerned, Taylor's *Meditations*, one might think, could as well have been written in England— or in India, or in Egypt.

Yet the fact remains that no such poetry was being written in the England of Taylor's day; and indeed, poetry with Taylor's peculiar quality could not, I think, have been written at all in England, even by Taylor himself. For the writer in England, wherever he may be living, works within a certain conditioning imposed by the context of that intimate island's culture: he knows the ways of other learned, literary men; he senses the current modes of writing; and even though he believes in freedom of language, as Baxter does, the writer is nevertheless tacitly and unconsciously influenced by the accepted conventions of public speech and writing in that culture. George Herbert lived in Bemerton, a country parson, and yet he could walk from there to the high and ancient culture of Salisbury. But in Taylor's frontier settlement these guidelines fall away; cultivated conversation becomes rare; the minister's work is solely occupied with humble folk; his daily life is rude, simple, concerned with the bare, stark facts of survival in a village that is at times little more than a stockade. Even the intellectual life must be limited to theology and the classics; Taylor's library at his death contained only one work of English poetry: the poems of Anne Bradstreet.

Thus the poet's conversations with God are spoken in a language that the meditative poet, living in England, would never use. For the soul, in meditation, is to speak as the man himself has come to speak; any other language would be dishonest and pretentious. So Taylor speaks in this peculiar mixture of the learned and the rude, the abstract and the earthy, the polite and the vulgar; for such distinctions do not exist in the wilderness.

The result is often lame and crude; in some respects the writer needs the support and guidance of an established culture; but since he in himself is almost the sole bearer and creator of whatever culture his village will possess, he must do what he can with whatever materials lie at hand. Out of his very deficiencies he creates a work of rugged and original integrity. The result helps to mark the beginning of an American language, an American literature.

The Visionary Line:
The Poetry of Philip Freneau

Annette Kolodny

Beautiful world of new superber birth that rises to my eyes,
Like a limitless golden cloud filling the western sky,
Emblem of general maternity lifted above all,
Sacred shape of the bearer of daughters and sons,
Out of thy teeming womb thy giant babes in ceaseless
procession issuing.
>   —WALT WHITMAN, "Thou Mother with Thy
>   Equal Brood," *Leaves of Grass*

One of his more enthusiastic biographers [Mary S. Austin] tells us that "from Concord to Yorktown, during the bleak winter at Valley Forge, and round the campfires on Temple Hill, [Freneau's] verses encouraged the desponding soldiers. The newspapers widely published them, and they were written on slips of paper and distributed throughout the army, or posted in some conspicuous place to be memorized." His appeal was to the heroism of protecting an injured woman from invading British; in "America Independent," written in 1778, he told the partisans, "Your injured country groans while yet [the British] stay," and encouraged them to "Attend her groans, and force their hosts away." Only then, the poem concluded, would "the streams of plenty" again flow "through our soil." In 1782, in a rather weak political allegory employing figures from the Greek pantheon (called "The Political Balance"), he again depicted America as a weak woman, raped and assaulted, requiring succour [all poetry references are to *The Poems of Philip Freneau* (2 vols.), ed. Fred Lewis Pattee, Princeton, N.J., 1903]:

> And the demons of murder her honours defaced.
> With the blood of the worthy her mantle was stained,
> And hardly a trace of her beauty remained.
>
> Her genius, a female, reclined in the shade,
> And, sick of oppression, so mournfully played.
>   (*PPF* 2.134)

From *The Lay of the Land: Metaphor as Experience and History in American Life and Letters.*
© 1975 by the University of North Carolina Press.

As late as 1795, in a poem "On the Approaching Dissolution of Transatlantic Jurisdiction in America," he hailed the signing of the Jay Treaty as the final freeing of vulnerable femininity from tyrant toils:

> From Britain's grasp forever freed,
> COLUMBIA glories in the deed:
> From her rich soil, each tyrant flown,
> She finds this fair estate her own.

The personification of the new nation as feminine was hardly original with Freneau and, in fact, followed the contemporary habit of picturing Liberty, Justice, indeed all the republican virtues, as latterday Greek goddesses. What Freneau consistently and insistently infused into that image, however, was its inextricable connection to the larger femininity of soil and landscape, so that, whatever the ostensible object of the poem, the image of the nation as woman became one and the same with the image of the landscape; the stanza quoted above, motivated by an impending treaty with England, which was supposed to protect American shipping rights on the high seas, is a case in point. Freneau the political activist had made effective journalistic and propagandistic use of the pastoral impulse, while Freneau the poet was to confront over and over again, through the years, the problems that would inevitably trouble "the happy people" who hoped to "find secure repose" in the New World garden (*PPF* 1.83. 458–59).

Born in New York, in 1752, Freneau spent a good part of his youth in rather comfortable circumstances on a family estate in New Jersey; at the age of sixteen he entered Princeton and came in contact both with literary and with "radical" political enthusiasts. His first major attempt at poetry, written during his last year at Princeton and recited at the 1771 class commencement by its sometime collaborator, H. H. Brackenridge, does in fact give quiet voice to the "Whiggish" tendencies then echoing on that campus. What "The Rising Glory of America" also reveals, however, is the pastoral substructure that governed both Freneau's patriotism and his aesthetic.

Encumbered as it is by an unnecessary dialogue structure and by anachronistic English pastoral diction, the poem nevertheless displays a conscious attempt to experience on the new continent the "sylvan settlements" that, if they were ever to become a daily reality, had only this one last opportunity, here on the world's last frontier, in "the last, the best / Of countries" (*PPF* 1.61.159; 1.74.322–23). American history, as Eugenio depicts it, begins with a movement away from an ungiving, unprotective and unloving mother, Britain, to a more genial feminine ambience, America. Britain is cast in the role of the mother abandoning her children—

> She will not listen to our humble prayers,
> Though offered with submission:
>
> . . . .
> She casts us off from her protection,
> (*PPF* 1.78.380–81, 384)

—while America, although an "injured country," nevertheless promises to be "A new Jerusalem," a "land, / Whose ample bosom shall receive" her children in peace and plenty, so that, finally, "Paradise anew / Shall flourish" (*PPF* 1.78.379; 1.82.438–44). That paradise, of course, is essentially agricultural, with conventional pastoral virtues imputed to

> the industrious swain,
> Who tills the fertile vale, or mountain's brow,
> Content to lead a safe, a humble life.
>   (*PPF* 1.67–68.236–38)

In utilizing pseudohistorical and mythical materials to precedent his vision, however, Freneau makes no attempt to distinguish between the pastoral as a literary convention and the pastoral as a possible real-world experience:

> Long has the rural life been justly fam'd,
> And bards of old their pleasing pictures drew
> Of flowery meads, and groves, and gliding streams:
> Hence, old Arcadia—wood-nymphs, satyrs, fauns;
> And hence Elysium, fancied heaven below!—
> Fair agriculture.
>   (*PPF* 1.68.243–48)

In short, by citing "old Arcadia" and "Elysium" as models for a future agrarian America, he compounds real and ideal in his "visions of the rustic reign" (*PPF* 1.71.283). Countering this romantic history and its implicit insistence on agrarian economy are alternate attitudes, including Acasto's argument for the importance of commerce (*PPF* 1.71–72.283–94) and Eugenio's praise of "fair Science!" (*PPF* 1.73.307); but the overall impact of the poem is clearly an argument that "these northern realms demand our song" because they were "designed by nature for the rural reign, / For agriculture's toil" (*PPF* 1.50.19–21). What the pastoral vision promises Freneau is escape from aggression, politics, ambition, greed, and all the forms of self-assertion that "prompts mankind to shed their kindred blood" (*PPF* 1.51.24). And whether we read a young man's claim to seek escape "from the noisy Forum" and "from busy camps, and sycophants, and crowns" (*PPF* 1.69.262–63) as no more than an accepted literary pose, as suggested a few lines later by Acasto ("But this alone, . . . / Would scarce employ the varying mind of man" [*PPF* 1.71.284–85]), it is nevertheless true that the poem's most attractive scenes are those " 'Midst woods and fields," where only, Leander claims, may one experience "full enjoyment" (*PPF* 1.70.264–65).

And yet there is an unexplored contradiction in the poem; the picture of pleasurable toil, which constitutes the initial vision of a pastoral America, is finally superseded by Acasto's vision of a future America in which

> The happy people, free from toils and death,
> Shall find secure repose.
>   (*PPF* 1.83.458–59)

It is, admittedly, a scriptural millennial vision he hopes

> America at last shall have
> When ages, yet to come, have run their round,
> And future years of bliss alone remain.
>
> (*PPF* 1.84.470–73)

And it is, furthermore, a millennium supported not only by nature's "fair fruits" and health-giving climate, but by a new and different mankind also:

> The fiercer passions of the human breast
> Shall kindle up to deeds of death no more,
> But all subside in universal peace.
>
> (*PPF* 1.83.466–68)

"The Rising Glory of America" predicted, in short, beyond the "rural reign" of an America compounded of Arcadia and Elysium, still another "Paradise anew," this one compounded of Canaan and Jerusalem, creating another, unfallen Eden, without thorn or briar:

> the lion and the lamb
> In mutual friendship linked, shall browse the shrub,
> And timorous deer with softened tygers stray
> O'er mead, or lofty hill, or grassy plain;
> Another Jordan's stream shall glide along,
> And Siloah's brook in circling eddies flow:
> Groves shall adorn their verdant banks, on which
> The happy people, free from toils and death,
> Shall find secure repose.
>
> (*PPF* 1.83.451–59)

It is not a millennium restricted to American shores, but somehow, the poem suggests, it is only made possible by the purifying influences of a prior "rural reign" in "the last, the best / Of countries" (*PPF* 1.74.322–23). America thereby becomes at once the appropriate religious ground and the proper political context for realizing the rebirth image—the political and religious so inextricably intertwined as to be almost indistinguishable. All of which merely repeats the contemporary attitude that America, as a matter of course, would prove the hope of the human race. But if Freneau intended to take this possibility seriously, then he was in some way bound to present a more coherent picture of that landscape in which "secure repose" might eventually be experienced; and this he attempted in 1772, with "The American Village," a work that, as he wrote to his old college friend, James Madison, was being "damned by all good and judicious judges."

What damned it was Freneau's own inability to choose between the poem's two competing pastoral landscapes—the first, a conventional cultivated landscape, "Made fertile by the labours of the swain," and the second, a primitive island paradise of free-roaming hunters and herdsmen, with only limited agriculture. Ostensibly replying to Goldsmith's lament for "Deserted Auburn and forsaken plains" by laying claim to the American continent as the rightful heir to Europe's own imaginative, and now diminished, pastoral landscape, Freneau finds himself first peopling "this western land" with "woodland nymphs" and "Dryads fair," and then altering its wild landscape completely in order to sustain his claim to an American Auburn (*PPF* 3.381–82).

> The soil which lay for many thousand years
> O'er run by woods, by thickets and by bears;
> Now reft of trees, admits the chearful light,
> And leaves long prospects to the piercing sight;
> Where once the lynx nocturnal sallies made,
> And the tall chestnut cast a dreadful shade:
> No more the panther stalks his bloody rounds,
> Nor bird of night her hateful note resounds;
> Nor howling wolves roar to the rising moon,
> As pale arose she o'er yon eastern down.
> Some prune their trees, a larger load to bear
> Of fruits nectarine blooming once a year:
> See groaning waggons to the village come
> Fill'd with apple, apricot or plumb;
>
> . . . .
>
> Or see the plough torn through the new made field,
> Ordain'd a harvest, yet unknown to yield.
>
> (*PPF* 3.382–83)

Had the poem ended with the third stanza, from which these lines are quoted, "The American Village" would have stood simply as another in a long line of American replies to Goldsmith, and only later generations would have read with unease of the silencing of the "bird of night" and the wide woods "Now reft of trees." It was not until 1823, after all, that Cooper's Natty Bumppo first declared himself "weary of living in clearings, . . . where the hammer is sounding in my ears from sunrise to sundown."

But Freneau seems to have anticipated that later attitude here, as evidenced by his abrupt departure from the scenes of forced cultivation in favor of his imagined "LOVELY island [that] once adorn'd the sea, / Between New-Albion and the Mexic' Bay" (*PPF* 3.383). The very lack of widespread cultivation leaves the island almost virginally attractive: "ev'ry wind, conspir'd to shade a brook," while "Wild plumb trees flourish'd on the shaded soil." Happily contented "In the dark bosom of this sacred wood," are natives who know only "agriculture's first fair service."

> Small fields had then suffic'd, and grateful they,
> The annual labours of his hands to pay;
> And free his right to search the briny flood
> For fish, or slay the creatures of the wood.
>
> (*PPF* 3.384–85)

But this, too, Freneau was determined to fit under the umbrella of conventional pastoral, and so he labels its hero "the homely shepherd swain." Unfortunately for all its idyllic beauty, the island never "such souls sublime contain'd" and never could, for

> envious time conspiring with the sea,
> Wash'd all it's landscapes, and it's groves away.
> (*PPF* 3.385)

Of course, history, with its implications of progress, cultivation and urbanization, would have served equally well; but it was precisely these aspects of contemporary America that he had tried to ignore earlier, turning instead to this imagined primitive landscape. When, finally, he tells the reader—

> THUS, tho' my fav'rite isle to ruin gone,
> Inspires my sorrow and demands my moan;
> Yet this wide land it's place can well supply
> With landscapes, hills and grassy mountains high.
> (*PPF* 3.386)

—he effectively leaves us uncertain as to which "isle" it is he refers: England or that which "once adorn'd the sea, / Between New-Albion and the Mexic' Bay." America is supposed to supply its restoration, but just *which* pastoral he wants to see restored here, the cultivated Auburn or the primitive wild, he never makes clear. Probably, he wanted at least a little of each. If, on the one hand, he was committed to answering Goldsmith, he was also aware that the success of Auburn only slightly preceded that age when "dread commerce stretch'd the nimble sail, / And sent her wealth with ev'ry foreign gale" (*PPF* 3.386). In short, Auburn seemed just a bit too far removed from "the golden season" or primitive pastoral that also had its appeals and that, in some sense, seemed more appropriate to the new, untamed continent. At the same time, he was clearly unable (or perhaps unwilling?) to project what would happen to America when all the forests had been cleared and all the soil cultivated; that is, what would happen when America caught up to Europe. Should this occur, as his own choice of grammar implies it must, then there will be a millennium—but not the lovely Jerusalem predicted in the earlier poem; should America follow in Europe's path, "The American Village" asserts, it will prove not mankind's salvation, but his ultimate destruction:

> When [America] has seen her empires, cities, kings,
> Time must begin to flap his weary wings;
> The earth itself to brighter days aspire,
> And wish to feel the purifying fire.
> (*PPF* 3.387)

And yet, even with this apocalyptic prediction, he could not abandon his emotional commitment to a pastoral America; turning to a 150-line miniepic of love and heroism, he attempted once again to validate its possibility. Briefly, he retells the story of Colma and her husband, Caffraro, who, with their child, are thrown into Arctic seas during a fierce storm. A small boat approaches to rescue them, but has room only for two; the heroic Colma sacrifices herself that her beloved husband and child might live, asking only that Caffraro embrace "no future bride," but always "Remember Colma, and her beauteous face" (*PPF* 3.390). It is not a particularly interesting tale, nor does Freneau's poetry do much to improve it. And only if we realize how Freneau intends it to sustain his confused pastoral vision can we begin to understand how it relates to the rest of the poem. What Freneau has done is to once again go backward in time, into the primitive, linking America (in sentiment, at least) to the noble and "Renowned SACHEMS" who once ruled the continent—before, that is, "rav'nous nations with industrous toil, / Conspir'd to rob them of their native soil" (*PPF* 3.387). The implication, clearly, is that anyone affected by this Indian tale is then empathically linked to the innocence of the primitive "northern shepherd," and, hence, to the harmonious intimacy inherent in the primitive pastoral he represents.

If Freneau learned anything from struggling with this poem it was not, as he had assumed at the outset, a knowledge of how American history would fulfill the dreams of European pastoral; instead, he confronted—perhaps for the first time—the inevitable clash between his own pastoral images and the demands of history. If America in 1772 appeared comparatively wild and untamed, a fact that coincided with Freneau's theories of primitive simplicity and innocence, he nevertheless found himself describing shepherd swains in the process of destroying the "primæval majesty" (*PPF* 3.386). To preserve both competing landscapes and also, perhaps, his political commitment to Jeffersonian theories of agrarian democracy, he imposed the identical pastoral labels on pioneers, farmers, and Indians alike—but the tensions attendant on such arbitrary labelings were never resolved.

At the end of the poem, the best Freneau can do is to invoke the classic pastoral moment, the moment of stasis, committing himself at once to poetry and to fantasy:

> Long, long ago with [Poetry] I could have stray'd,
> To woods, to thickets or the mountain shade;
> Unfit for cities and the noisy throng,
> The drunken revel and the midnight song;
>
> . . . .
> Here then shall center ev'ry wish, and all
> The tempting beauties of this spacious ball:
> No thought ambitious, and no bold design,
> But heaven born contemplation shall be mine.

> In yonder village shall my fancy stray,
> Nor rove beyond the confines of to-day.
> (*PPF* 3.392–93)

In order to achieve this kind of contentment, however, he had both to sacrifice the reality of the untamed American landscape and to ignore the inevitability of historical processes; as a result, the idealized American village becomes insubstantial and unlocated, existing, if at all, in poetic diction and imagination. With the final lines, this too is denied, as the youthful poet, apparently tired of the rather uneventful scene he had created, or perhaps, simply tired of maintaining his impossible dream, seeks other realms and different subjects:

> Now cease, O muse, thy tender tale to chaunt,
> The smiling village, or the rural haunt;
> New scenes invite me, and no more I rove,
> To tell of shepherds, or the vernal grove.
> (*PPF* 3.394)

That same year, 1772, also saw the publication of "Discovery," a poem in which Freneau clearly pitted the wild American landscape against its human destroyers. Here, the projective, expansive activities of a mankind "Fond of exerting power untimely shewn," in order "to conquer what remains unknown" (*PPF* 1.86), results in the rape of a decidedly and alluringly feminine island:

> Some gay *Ta-ia* on the watery waste,
> Though Nature clothes in all her bright array,
> Some proud tormentor steals her charms away:
> Howe'er she smiles beneath those milder skies,
> Though men decay the monarch never dies!
> Howe'er the groves, how'er the gardens bloom,
> A monarch and a priest is still their doom!
> (*PPF* 1.88)

The confrontation reveals, in miniature, both the inescapable threat to pastoral possibilities and the resulting quiet despair that echoes throughout so much of the later poetry. Monarch and priest, for Freneau, are repeatedly symbols of the aggressively destructive masculine orientation of history, before which anything suggestively feminine must fall victim. As a virtually archetypal confrontation, it was, he admitted in "Pictures of Columbus," one in which the lady had been doomed from the first.

The various poems that comprise the "Pictures of Columbus" (written and published just two years after "The American Village" and "Discovery"), show us another dreamer who, like the poet, had pursued "Imaginary worlds through boundless seas." When finally given a promise of their substantial reality in the Inchantress's mirror, Columbus sees, before he ever sets out, "Fine islands,"

Cover'd with trees, and beasts, and yellow men;
Eternal summer through the vallies smiles
And fragrant gales o'er golden meadows play!—
                    (*PPF* 1.96, picture 3, "The Mirror")

Recapitulating a previous century's experience, Freneau's Columbus moves too quickly from the reactivation of universal, but often suppressed, human longings to a guilt-ridden outcry against the violation he had thereby unwittingly made possible. His arrival "In these green groves . . . / Where guardian nature holds her quiet reign" (*PPF* 1.115–16) results in only a momentary sojourn amid "Sweet sylvan scenes of innocence and ease, . . . / Their works unsullied by the hands of men" (*PPF* 1.117, picture 14, "Columbus at Cat Island"). For almost immediately he is confronted by that from which he had so happily thought himself escaped. At his feet lies the body of a native, murdered by one of his own crew, for the gold trinkets adorning his body. Crying out, "Is this the fruit of my discovery!," the anguished captain predicts all the devastations to follow—

If the first scene is murder, what shall follow
But havock, slaughter, chains and devastation
In every dress and form of cruelty!
                    (*PPF* 1.117)

By having his character experience his crewman's crime as a stab at the bounteous landscape itself, Freneau creates a Columbus who, in attempting to flee the sight of "injur'd Nature," prophecies the migrations that were to become the hallmark of American history:

away, away!
And southward, pilots, seek another isle,
Fertile they say, and of immense extent:
There we may fortune find without a crime.
                    (*PPF* 1.118, picture 14)

With fortune from the first confused with pastoral impulses, Freneau seems to be saying here, Columbus's pursuit, like that of later Americans, would never find a resting place.

But, like his protagonist, Freneau himself could never abandon the search nor, once he had found them, the islands that promised pastoral realities. Even during the difficult years of revolution, Freneau described his repeated residences in the West Indies, on Santa Cruz, Jamaica, and Bermuda, as "all too pleasing." Turning from the woman who was then being raped and pillaged by invading British, he sought that tiny landscape in the ocean where "Fair Santa Cruz, arising, laves her waist" (*PPF* 1.251. st. 8). What he finds so appealing about "The Beauties of Santa Cruz," which he praised in 1776, was obviously its invitation to totally passive, but luxurious, repose.

> Sweet orange grove, the fairest of the isle,
> In thy soft shade luxuriously reclin'd,
> Where, round my fragrant bed, the flowrets smile,
> In sweet delusions I deceive my mind.
>
> *(PPF* 1.249)

The nature of those "sweet delusions" is never made explicit, but one can ascertain from the quality of the descriptions that the poet is thoroughly enjoying a kind of passive and infantile orality, available in a landscape so abundantly generous that it appears to demand no human labor whatever. "Pomegranates . . . / Ready to fall," "the papaw or mamee" *(PPF* 1.259. st. 53), offer a maternal Eden of exotic nurture:

> Those shaddocks juicy shall thy taste delight,
> And yon' high fruits, the richest of the wood,
> That cling in clusters to the mother tree,
> The cocoa-nut; rich, milky, healthful food.
>
> *(PPF* 1.259. st. 54)

What the feminine embrace also provided, especially in 1776, was a refuge from the world of "tyrants," and political strife; here "bloody plains, and iron glooms," might be forgotten in a "land of love." The appeal, then, goes beyond the merely physical sating of hunger and corresponds to the universal urge to return, tantalizing us with its dim reminders of a totality of gratifications, experienced only once, in the dim past of infancy. Then, only, were we innocent of "Absence and death, and heart-corroding care, / . . . [which] cloud the sun-shine of the mind" *(PPF* 1.267. st. 98). Sadly, inevitably, of course, that sunshine *is* clouded, and even here, as in childhood, an ugly reality intrudes itself upon the primal harmony: a "slave that slowly bends this way" leaves the poet's "heart distrest" *(PPF* 1.262. st. 72). And, like Columbus, he too seeks another, still innocent paradise:

> Give me some clime, the favorite of the sky,
> Where cruel slavery never sought to reign.
>
> *(PPF* 1.264. st. 79)

But, having written Columbus's story, Freneau knows that no such paradises remain; and so he "shun[s] the theme" (stanza 79), and turns instead to scenes of a hurricane's devastation:

> These isles, lest Nature should have prov'd too kind,
> Or man have sought his happiest heaven below,
> Are torn with mighty winds, fierce hurricanes,
> Nature convuls'd in every shape of woe.
>
> *(PPF* 1.264. st. 80)

The suggestion, clearly, is that Nature herself has conspired to defeat the realization of pastoral impulses. But it is a suggestion the poet neither explores nor continues; instead, he turns to his more usual villain, proud princes—in this case, England—and hopes that even if they "o'er the globe . . . extend [their] reign," they spare "one grotto" in Santa Cruz as a haven for the poet:

> Here—though thy conquest vex—in spite of pain,
> I quaff the enlivening glass, in spite of care.
>
> *(PPF* 1.266. st. 96)

The end of the poem, apparently encouraging the patriots at home while the speaker remains happily embraced by his island paradise, could appear supercilious or even hypocritical—but only if we ignore the powerfully seductive and embracing qualities attributed to the landscape in the earlier stanzas and fail to acknowledge how their imagery suggests the processes by which the mind reasserts infantile configurations and the claim of infantile gratifications even amid adult experience:

> Still there [i.e., in the colonies] remain—thy native air enjoy,
> Repell the tyrant who thy peace invades,
> While, pleas'd, I trace the vales of Santa Cruz,
> And sing with rapture her inspiring shades.
>
> *(PPF* 1.268. st. 108)

Given the fact that Freneau did return to his native shore and engage actively in the politics of founding the new republic, we must see these lines as an expression of his continuing commitment to pastoral pleasures, a fit habitation for which he was hard-pressed to discover on the mainland. His subsequent incarceration on a British prison-ship, of course, fanned the patriotic fires and, without further delay, Freneau once more actively defended the woman assaulted, "her honours defaced" *(PPF* 2.134).

By 1782, however, we can see him struggling to maintain his initial revolutionary zeal. Wearied, or even angry, that the "war still rages and the battle burns," he questions the possibility of ever seeing happiness reign. In "A Picture of the Times, With Occasional Reflections," published that year, he admits that "Discord" is no longer specific to European shores; it now "flies" "round the world triumphant" *(PPF* 2.165). In "every breast" Passion and Reason wage battle. Once, however, he maintains, all men lived harmoniously in an "age of innocence and ease," an innocence made possible by the very primitiveness of its setting. Then, "The hoary sage beneath his sylvan shade" governed, like a good son of Thomas Paine, with the consent of the governed. He "Impos'd no laws but those which reason made; . . . He judg'd his brethren by their own consent; . . . In virtue firm, and obstinately just." But this primitive preagricultural communal pastoral "Of some small tribe" is finally destroyed by Freneau's all-purpose enemy, "Ambition," which, in this poem, takes the particular form of "regal pride" denying "equal right to equal men" *(PPF* 2.166, 167, 165). More anger is directed at those "servile souls" who "basely own'd a brother for a lord," however, than at the monarchs themselves (*PPF* 2.165). Nevertheless, the result of breaking up the original fraternal community, for Freneau, is a heritage of "wrath, and blood, and feuds and wars," "And man turned monster to his fellow man" (*PPF* 2.165). If Freneau's summary history of mankind strikes us as hopelessly naive, it nevertheless points up that communal aspect of golden-age mythology that still held its grip on the American imagination.

At the writing of this poem, however, Freneau saw no such happy possibility around him; instead, after a brief diatribe against George III, "the tyrant," he closes on a note of hopelessness. "Ambition!," both for power and for wealth, everywhere "Tempts the weak mind, and leads the heart astray!" As a result, happiness is relegated to the realm of fond illusion,

> still sought but never found,
> We, in a circle, chase thy shadow round;
> Meant all mankind in different forms to bless,
> Which yet possessing, we no more possess.
> (*PPF* 2.167)

Happiness becomes, in the last lines, a kind of visionary dream, like pastoral itself, the impulse for which, firmly possessed by the mind or imagination, is yet sought vainly in everyday reality:

> Thus far remov'd and painted on the eye
> Smooth verdant fields seem blended with the sky,
> But where they both in fancied contact join
> In vain we trace the visionary line;
> Still as we chase, the empty circle flies,
> Emerge new mountains or new oceans rise.
> (*PPF* 2.167)

What arrests the attention in the final line (if the wording is intentional, that is, and not merely the accident of hurried composition) is the suggestion that the landscape itself presents a physical barrier, separating the poet from "the visionary line." If we see in the blending of "Smooth verdant fields" with sky a visual emblem for the meeting of real and ideal, analogous perhaps to the kinds of happiness the poem had earlier praised, then we see another instance of what pastoral has always been for Freneau—reluctant though he was to admit it; but here the landscape itself hinders access to that union of reality and ideality, much as the Mother must finally reject the erotic claims of a loving son. If such a reading is permitted, then we have one of the few early examples of Freneau's intuition that Nature herself might throw up barriers to men's fondest dreams. It was a proposition he had quickly abandoned in the earlier "Beauties of Santa Cruz," and which, even here, he only vaguely suggests. In later years, of course, he refined it into a philosophical principle. In 1782, however, he contented himself by relegating his visions of happiness and ideal landscapes to the world to come, a stance with its heritage in Christian as well as Stoic writing:

> Then seek no more for bliss below,
>   Where real bliss can ne'er be found,
> Aspire where sweeter blossoms blow
>   And fairer flowers bedeck the ground.
>   (*PPF* 2.107)

What these lines "To an Old Man" predicted was the general trend of Freneau's nature poetry after the war. His intense awareness of the transitory, fleeting quality of the world may be seen in this light, then, not only as an aesthetic comment on "The Vanity of Existence," as one title suggests, but also as a generalized and regretful emotional response to the very real and inescapable destruction of pastoral possibilities that he saw going on all about him.

As though to partially compensate for that loss, Freneau seems to have invented for himself a primitivist *persona*, "The Pilgrim," a lover of wild nature and a biting critic of civilization. In a series of nineteen essays that appeared from November 21, 1781, through August 14, 1782, in the *Freeman's Journal*, Freneau addressed his countrymen through the voice of a man who claimed to live in a forest north of Philadelphia, happily sequestered in a cavern or grotto near a stream, and chary of his solitude; if anyone attempts to find him, he warns, he will leave the country. In the first essay of the series, as Philip Marsh summarizes it, the Pilgrim "describes himself as a lover of all men and animals and an enemy to kings, ambitious men, all war and bloodshed, even the eating of flesh": "I subsist wholly upon roots and vegetables . . . I have not had an hour's sickness these forty years past, am altogether devoid of ambition, and have never experienced the least inclination to shed the blood of any man, or injure him in the slightest degree." He is, in short, a European version of the happy island primitives earlier pictured in "The American Village." But, even as that island was washed away by the sea, so too, this primitive idyll is gradually diluted, until, as Marsh points out, "the pilgrim becomes less a primitivist and more a man-about-town," his subjects turning from the forest to "the manners, morals, and politics of Philadelphia." Clearly, the politics of the new nation now commanded Freneau's attention and, with the 1780s, the promising poet became a fulltime essayist.

The events of the years to follow, including the signing of the Treaty of Paris in 1783, his brief appointment as clerk for foreign languages to Jefferson (then secretary of state) from 1791 to 1793, his various editing activities and repeated involvements in political causes, and the War of 1812—all promoted the oscillations of renewed hopes and enthusiasms, followed by the inevitable disillusionments and renunciations, until finally, in 1815, he attempted a kind of tentative truce with his warring impulses. A few poems will suffice to outline the process. With the new nation finally, if precariously, on its feet, he optimistically hailed "the EMIGRATION TO AMERICA and Peopling the Western Country." Published in 1785, the ten short stanzas of the poem by that title easily accept the need "to tame the soil, and plant the arts" amid the "western woods, and lonely plains" (*PPF* 2.280). Unlike the mood of misgiving that was given expression in the earlier "American Village," here there is only calm acceptance of the alteration of nature for human use and the advent of commerce. "No longer," he declares, "shall [the waters of the Mississippi] useless prove, / Nor idly through the forests rove." Now, at last, they shall be put to use, as "commerce plans new freights for them]." But, recalling his own suspicions of "dread commerce," he immediately qualifies the line by claiming for America the moral protections of "virtue," generosity, and "heaven-born freedom." The new nation, he insists, will be innocent of "the voice of war" and "Europe's all-inspiring pride," a place where "Reason shall new laws devise." How this political and moral paradise is to be maintained he never explains more than to applaud the colonies for having forsaken "kings and regal stage." The only blight on the landscape that he will admit is the African who "still . . . complains, / And mourns his yet unbroken chains." When his contemporary, Crevecoeur, described the caged and dying black in Charlestown, it forced his readers to reassess and finally abandon the paradisal picture that had preceded; for Freneau, however, the slave stands only as an unpleasant fact of present life that, he optimistically assumes, "a future age" will improve. The poem ends, in fact, with his muse predicting for America "happier systems . . . / Than all the eastern sages knew" (*PPF* 2.281–82).

What remnant of pastoral gratification he is able to protect amid the necessities of political upheaval and economic progress is consigned now to the rural, semicultivated landscape of sparse population, "that Nature for her happiest children made" (*PPF* 3.46). First published in 1790, "The Bergen Planter" pictures a humble "rustic," happily watching "the seasons come and go, / His autumn's toils returned in summer's crops" (*PPF* 3.45). Comparing the simplicities of the planter's life to the vanities and indignities of "distant forms and modes," the poem makes an effective political statement for the Jeffersonian agrarian democracy that Freneau had always espoused:

> In humble hopes his little fields were sown,
> A trifle, in your eye—but all his own.
>
> (*PPF* 3.46)

Typical of the type is Freneau's address "To Crispin O'Conner, A Back-Woodsman," written two years later. Having left Ireland, "Where mother-country acts the step-dame's part, . . . / Hatch[ing] sad wars to make her brood the thinner," Crispin had sought happier scenes "Far in the west." There, "a paltry spot of land" becomes, through Crispin's unremitting labor, a prosperous garden, until, finally, the proud owner "Bids harvests rise where briars and bushes grew" (*PPF* 3.74–75). Both the poet's address to Crispin and "Crispin's Answer," also published in 1792, approve the need for Crispin to alter the wilderness in order to make it bountiful. In fact, claims Crispin, he came not only in search of "Equal Rights" but in search of a place "my axe to ply" (*PPF* 3.75).

Taken as a group, then, the poems written approximately between 1785 and 1795 reveal a quiet, if growing, discomfort at the consequences of human mastery and cultivation. If, in 1785, he could still look with equanimity at the progress of "Emigration to America and Peopling the Western Country," seeing "Where Nature's wildest genius reigns" the acceptable necessity "To tame the soil, and plant the arts" (*PPF* 2.280), by 1790, in "LINES, Occasioned by a Law passed by the Corporation of New York, . . . for cutting down the trees in the streets of that City," he bewails the fact that human civilization inevitably destroys the desired union with the land. Written as a "Citizen's Soliloquy," the lines nostalgically regret the abandoned pastoral vision—

> "Thrice happy age, when all was new,
> And trees untouched, unenvied grew,"
> (*PPF* 3.53)

—and see, in the trees' imminent destruction, a negation of many years' intimacy and friendship:

> "The fatal Day, dear trees, draws nigh,
> When you must, like your betters, die,
> Must die!—and every leaf will fade
> That many a season lent its shade,
> To drive from hence the summer heat,
> And made my porch a favorite seat."
> (*PPF* 3.53)

The loss is at once personal and political, suggesting (if not explicitly) the guilt that was to emerge at the beginning of the next century as so much a part of the American fictional self-image.

> "And you, my trees, in all your bloom,
> Who never injured small or great,
> Be murdered at so short a date!"
> (*PPF* 3.55)

In the course of civilizing the landscape, the poem implies, man makes of it his helpless victim and inevitably betrays an earlier or hoped-for intimacy.

Once more, therefore, he tried to grasp the illusive primitive pastoral, projecting himself, in 1795, into the mind and experiences of "TOMO CHEEKI, the CREEK INDIAN in Philadelphia." Beginning with the May 23, 1795, issue of the *Jersey Chronicle*, Freneau published a series of fourteen essays that purported to be "translations" from a manuscript by Tomo Cheeki, a Creek

Indian who had previously visited the city "to settle a treaty of amity," and then departed, leaving in his hotel room "a large bundle of papers," As Philip Marsh points out, the device of the discovered Indian manuscript was not original with Freneau and probably owed its conception to an earlier attempt of Addison's. The use Freneau made of the device, however, is important because it succinctly foreshadows what were to become the major themes of American pastoral fiction. The note of nostalgia for an irrevocably lost pastoral landscape, which was to echo through Cooper, is here in the second number, as the Indian emerges from "many pathless woods" into the city and exclaims, "But what is all this I behold!—how changed is the country of my fathers!" The romantic depictions of a landscape nurturing and protecting human children, with which Cooper was to surround Natty Bumppo and Simms his Revolutionary War partisans, is also here in what Philip Marsh describes as "a fine utopia of Indian natural living": "Wherever we run it is amidst the luxuriant vegetation of Nature, the delectable regale of flowers and blossoms, and beneath trees bending with plump and joyous fruits." Anticipating Natty Bumppo's quarrel with Judge Temple, Tomo Cheeki insists, "in the forests, we acknowledge no distinction of property. The woods are as free as the waters." More interesting still is the anticipation of Faulkner's vision of an earth that abides and takes back its own, despite the human illusion of mastery and possession: in contemplating the many changes of inhabitants the land has already known, the Indian predicts that yet another time will come, after the whites have gone, "when the ancient chaos of woods will in its turn, take [the] place of all this fantastic finery; when the wild genius of the forest will reassume his empire." For Freneau, the Indian *persona* provided a way of expressing what later became the religious and philosophical mediator between the world he had hoped for and the one he knew: "CHANGE," says Tomo Cheeki, "seems to be the system of Nature in this world."

Having imaginatively participated, through the Indian, in the history of the continent itself, then, Freneau was finally able to put aside the conflicting millennial visions of his early poetry and compose, in 1797, still another "millennium," this one giving evidence of a single unifying and pervasive "system" behind all the confusion and "apparent discord" that "still prevails" in both man and nature (*PPF* 3.176). Possibly following the model of the Indian's perceptions, Freneau now espouses a "system" that, in its wake, effectively dooms the pastoral possibility altogether—

> The forest yields to active flame,
> The ocean swells with stormy gales.
> (*PPF* 3.176)

And man himself, as part of that same "system," cannot escape its inherent disharmonies:

> And do you think that human kind
>   Can shun the all-pervading law—
> That passion's slave we ever find—
>   Who discord from their nature draw:—
> Ere discord can from man depart
> He must assume a different heart.
>
> (PPF 3.177)

Nothing that he wrote after this, however, suggests that he saw either a "different heart," or any withdrawal of "passion's" claims upon the human or the natural.

What remained as a real-world fit habitation for his pastoral impulses by the end of the century were, essentially, those same few landscapes—in the South or West Indies—that he had praised twenty years earlier; and to one of these he traveled in 1798, ostensibly to visit relatives, but, perhaps, as his poem commemorating the occasion claimed, also in hopes of finding there "a happier home, / Retirement for the days to come" (*PPF* 3.200). In recalling his joy "On Arriving in South Carolina, 1798," he sounds once again like the young man who could not bear to leave the seductive embrace of Santa Cruz:

> The fairest, loveliest, scenes disclose—
>   All nature charms us here.
>
> (PPF 3.201)

Its fertile fields boast the traditional southern plenty and temperate climate; and echoing the sentiments of the first English explorers to the region, Freneau declares the land "a paradise restored" (*PPF* 3.201). Its pastoral implications are made clear by the invocation of the conventional diction, with "rural love . . . bless[ing] the swains," but what strikes him as more attractive still is not the cultivated "paradise," but the "lofty hills" of "sweet nature's wilderness." There, only, the poem suggests, does he feel really secure "from wars and commerce far away." The suggestively erotic waters of undammed rivers roam "the prospect to the western glade," and fructify "the ancient forest, undecay'd." And it is "these the wildest scenes" he claims, which "awed the sight" (*PPF* 3.201–2). The poem ends with a wish for possession—but precisely which he wished to possess, the cultivated "paradise" or "the wildest scenes . . . / That ever awed the sight," he does not say. Perhaps we are to hear some impossible combination of the two in the acres "where all nature's fancies join":

> But, where all nature's fancies join,
> Were but a single acre mine,
> Blest with the cypress and the pine,
>   I would request no more;
> And leaving all that once could please,
> The northern groves and stormy seas—

> I would not change such scenes as these
> For all that men adore.
>
> (*PPF* 3.202)

If we want, we can say the poem is hypocritical for refusing to explain what precisely has made "the northern groves" less attractive. His own earlier poetry and essays would suggest that commerce had damaged the possibility of pastoral for him in the fast-growing urban centers of the Northeast, while the South, with its continued agrarian economy, could still claim the mythic and poetic associations of "rural haunts" and "fragrant woods" (*PPF* 3.200). That this was made possible by an economy dependent on slave labor this poem ignores. As it also ignores the inevitable consequences of the possession he so ardently desires; clearly, increased possession of the land would lead to more cultivation until, finally, the cultivated acres would edge out "sweet nature's wilderness" (*PPF* 3.202). But Freneau refuses to abandon either landscape or to see beyond his own stubbornly maintained commitment to a pastoral "retirement for the days to come." It was a stubbornness supported perhaps by the vagaries of a life that had led him not to the farm, but to the city. As more than one biographer has noted, Freneau was essentially a wanderer and, unlike Crevecoeur, "he was not even a true farmer, only a resident on a farm."

Still, the kinds of contentment and the life of contemplation that pastoral had always seemed to offer remained, throughout his work, at least an imaginative conception to which he could turn. And, as the poems of his last, active years, collected and published in two tiny volumes in 1815, attest, he had, in fact, turned to the kinds of contemplation he had predicted for himself as early as 1772, in "The American Village." While poems of war, politics, and patriotism dominate the second volume, the first is devoted to questions of belief and faith, with such titles as "On the Uniformity and Perfection of Nature" and "On the Universality and Other Attributes of the God of Nature" indicating the general areas of concern. And here, as Philip M. Marsh has pointed out, was "where the author's real interest lay." What they also reveal, amid the more optimistic Deist sentiments, was a final admission that pastoral impulses could never be realized in the real world, doomed as they were both by the nature of man and by the larger order of things. The War of 1812 had prompted him to complain,

> The world has wrangled half an age,
> And we again in war engage.
>
> (*PPF* 3.376)

In "The Brook of the Valley," from which these lines are quoted, he sought some refuge near a "sweet, sequester'd rill [that] / Murmurs through the valley still" (*PPF* 3.376). But even untamed nature now offers no escape, having become instead an emblem for "the human passions" (*PPF* 3.377). Like the restless and changing activities of human civilization, so, too, he realizes, the brook is at one time "flowing, peaceful," at another, "angry" or "overflow'd" (*PPF* 3.376–77).

> Emblem, thou, of restless man;
> What a sketch of nature's plan!
> Now at peace, and now at war,
> Now you murmur, now you roar;
>
> Muddy now, and limpid next,
> Now with icy shackles vext—
> What a likeness here we find!
> What a picture of mankind!
> (*PPF* 3.377)

If the intimate harmony between man and the landscape still evaded him, at least he could contemplate their analogies; to see this as either a reconciliation between his pastoral impulse and the pressures of history or as a repression of that impulse altogether, however, is inadequate. To the last, Freneau struggled to proclaim the pastoral possibility of America, his verses marked, as one contemporary critic noted, "with a certain rusticity" that had long been out of date. His last known poem, a manuscript fragment dated November 28, 1827, still invoked "Nymphs and Swains on Hudson's quiet shore," and asked, "Blest in your *Village*, who would wish for more?" But the absoluteness of the happiness is subtly qualified by the following suggestion:

> Compare your state with thousands of our kind;
> How happy are you in the lot you find!—

That Crispin O'Conner or the Bergen planter were called upon to compare their state with the starving poor of Europe made good polemical sense during the years of revolution and early federalist struggles. But why did he feel it necessary to bolster his pastoral assertion with comparisons now, when democracy had apparently triumphed and the republic stood on firm foundations? The first lines of the poem provide a kind of answer: it is a poem of winter, the winter of the year, the winter of an old man's life, the dormancy of dreams.

> The sun hangs low!—so much the worse, we say,
> For *those* whose pleasure is a Summer's day;
> Few are the Joys which stormy Nature yields
> From blasting winds and desolated fields;
> *Their* only pleasure in that season found
> When orchards bloom and flowers bedeck the ground.

"For *those* whose pleasure is a Summer's day" and the feminine ambience of fertile orchards, whose ideal retreat had from the first been "Some gay *Ta-ia* on the watery waste, . . . clothe[d] in all her bright array" (*PPF* 1.88), the "blasting winds and desolated fields" of a wintery New York landscape could only have proved a disappointment. And so, to make it all just a little less disappointing, he turned to comparisons, a device he had used with great success at an earlier date, and finally broke off the fragment when the task became hopeless:

> Contrast the Scene with Greenland's wastes of Snow
> Where darkness rules and oceans cease to flow.

Still, for all its limitations, its awkwardnesses, its archaic diction, its proclivities for grandiose, overgeneralized statement, Freneau's poetry exposed that single tension that was to structure so much American literature to follow: the growing disillusionment with the pastoral possibility in conflict with a commitment to maintain that possibility—almost at any cost. And were we to look for a compendium of what constituted the threats to a pastoral America, we would not have to go beyond Freneau; from the first he struggled not only to describe a pastoral landscape appropriate to the New World experience, but, more important still, to delineate what one could or would actually do in the garden. Over and over again, he pitted his own delight in the passivity to be enjoyed within the luxuriously feminine ambiences of tropical islands against the various human urges toward mastery and progress, both political and agricultural, which he saw all around him—conflicts that Simms and Cooper would later convert to the uses of fiction. And finally, if reluctantly, he gave the lie to the myth that mankind had been reborn in the New World paradise; not so, declared Freneau, he had simply brought his European corruptions with him and, slowly but surely, was laying waste the garden.

Freneau, of course, was only the first of many who failed to locate an appropriate and enduring pastoral landscape in the New World; but while later dreamers came up against the brick walls of politics or industrial progress, Freneau, in the eighteenth century, was also forced to joust with language. Like so many of his contemporaries, he wanted to perceive America as the realization of a European pastoral mythology. In trying to visualize an American Auburn, however, he saw that the price of such a pastoral was the destruction of what made "this wide land" so appealing in the first place, "with [its] landscapes, hills and grassy mountains high" (*PPF* 3.386). He therefore tried to use the diction to describe *both* the primitive and untamed continent *and* the contemporary eagerness to clear the forests and cultivate the soil; but it would not work. The imported Arcadia tended to constrict and stylize the kinds of possibilities that an American landscape might really offer, and, too, an archaic literary convention was simply not adequate to the task of exploring the various, and sometimes conflicting, configurations of filial and erotic responses. What was truly the subject matter of his poetry—the tension between the primitive, passive pastoral and the active, cultivated Arcadia—existed in a psychological landscape he could never quite render.

He did, however, make excellent political and propagandistic use of a diction that, as Harold Toliver points out, had always had a tendency to level "all social elements to an Arcadian democracy and [bring] into question the value of honor and fame when the simple pleasures of shepherdom are so readily available." What strikes us as out of place and even absurd, as when Freneau calls the Indian "The Shepherd of the Forest" or the country inn a rural temple, becomes, in this light, an aesthetic appeal to that quality of fraternal and communal democracy that has always been an element of pastoral, both European and American. The Bergen planter or Crispin O'Conner may indeed have been the political heirs of knights masquerading as shepherd swains, but Freneau's adoption of conventional pastoral vocabulary repeatedly proved inadequate to the complexities of American experience. Struggling to depict some kind of real-world landscape in which to experience the pastoral impulse and thus forge a pastoral "vision" for the new nation, he succeeded only in tracing a "visionary line," flying in "the empty circle" of language that had no clear external reference. Obviously, Freneau had neither the talent nor the insight to forge a new, specifically American pastoral diction and a new, appropriately indigenous, "shepherd swain." That remained a task for the nineteenth century.

Phillis Wheatley: The Dark Side of the Poetry

Terrence Collins

In a recent article in *Phylon* [3 (Fall 1972): 222–30], R. Lynn Matson credibly argues that the poems of Phillis Wheatley exhibit the beginning of a poetry of protest, albeit surreptitiously. Though he rightly dismisses much Wheatley criticism as overlooking essential elements discoverable in the poems and letters (more readily available now with Julian D. Mason's fine edition of the poems and letters), on the whole one senses throughout Matson's presentation an element of wishful thinking that finds in Wheatley a racial and political precocity difficult to reconcile with the facts of her slave life and with the evidence of the poems and letters themselves. In interpreting the thrust of Phillis Wheatley's consciousness of race as disguised resentment of the institution of slavery, he has addressed only one aspect of a highly ambivalent attitude. A more educative purpose to which a reexamination of Wheatley's life and work might be put is to see in the poems a gauge of the depths to which what has come to be called the slave mentality—or self-hate by blacks based on introjection of the dominant culture's estimate of their worth—penetrated and to some extent, we are told, still penetrates the collective mind of Black America.

Since her enslavement was hardly typical of even the mildest versions of New England slavery, a short biographical sketch, implied in many of Matson's comments, seems essential for inquiry into the racial attitudes of Wheatley as they emerge in the poems and as they relate to her estimate of her own worth as a black person.

Phillis Wheatley was owned by the Boston tailor John Wheatley. Mr. Wheatley gave the following sketch of her origins in a letter of introduction to the 1773 edition of her poems:

From *Phylon: The Atlanta University Review of Race and Culture* 36, no. 1 (March 1975). © 1975 by Atlanta University.

> Phillis was brought from Africa to America, in the year 1761, be-
> tween seven and eight years of age. Without any assistance from
> school education and by only what she was taught in the family,
> she, in sixteen months time from her arrival attained the English
> language, to which she was an utter stranger before, to such a
> degree, as to read any, the most difficult part of the sacred writ-
> ings, to the great astonishment of all who heard her.
>
> As to her writing, her own curiosity led her to it; and this she
> learned in so short a time, that in the year 1765, she wrote a letter
> to the Rev. Mr. Occum, the Indian minister, while in England.

The tone of this letter as well as the indication that she was admitted to
the inner circle of family education and religion suggest that hers was not
a life typical of American slavery.

Such indeed was the case. When the Wheatley family obtained her,
she was sickly and weak, fitted only for housework, and soon became the
personal attendant for Mrs. Wheatley and a companion for a daughter,
Mary Wheatley. In this capacity she was exempted from the usual lot of
slaves and was encouraged toward refinement and cultivation. Margaretta
Matilda Odell, an abolitionist biographer, relates the following:

> A daughter of the family, not long after the child's first introduc-
> tion to the family, undertook to learn her to read and write; and
> while she astonished her instructress by her rapid progress, she
> won the good will of her kind mistress by her amiable disposition
> and the propriety of her behavior. She was not devoted to menial
> occupations, as was first intended; nor was she allowed to associate
> with other domestics of the family, who were of her own color
> and condition, but was kept constantly about the person of her
> mistress.

Odell further indicates that Wheatley was nurtured on "the best English
writers" with Mary, and that she was "encouraged to converse freely with
the wise and learned" of Boston's polite circles. She further notes that
Phillis, unlike slaves prior to that time, was received as a member of Boston's Old South Church congregation with the Wheatley family. Significantly, all of these tokens of special favor were shown to the slave Phillis
prior to the added notoriety afforded her by the publication of her poems
in the 1773 volume.

During 1773, Phillis was sent to England in the company of Nathaniel
Wheatley, a son in the family, in order that she might recover her health—
a further indication that her position as a slave was indeed out of the
ordinary. While in England she was befriended by Selina Hastings, the
Countess of Huntingdon, who introduced her to London polite society and
who eventually arranged for the publication of her poems. The extent to
which she was encouraged to mix freely in these aristocratic circles is in-

dicated by the gifts she received (the Lord Mayor of London presented her with a folio copy of *Paradise Lost*, for instance) and by her being favored with an audience with George III, which was prevented only by her premature return to America at the news of Mrs. Wheatley's impending death.

Thus Phillis Wheatley's life during the years in which all but a few of her extant poems were written was both comfortable and cultivated. From 1774 until her death, however, her fortune changed for the worse. Still popular enough to be noticed by George Washington in 1776 as the result of a flattering poem in his honor, little is known of her after her manumission and marriage in 1778, except that her husband was an unsuccessful dabbler who brought Phillis to poverty and to a premature death, nearly unnoticed, in a cheap boarding house in 1784.

The few details of Wheatley's life which are available to us suggest that she was in no ordinary sense of the word a slave, nor was she in any way subject to the more tangible hardships characteristic of even New England slavery during the years in which she wrote the poems of the 1773 collection. In fact, if the account of Odell (a relative of the Wheatley's) is accurate, Phillis was entirely cut off from the slaves around her (her correspondence with Arbour Tanner being the one noticeable exception). On the other hand, she was not in any real way a part of the dominant culture: although she mixed with white society, it was always as an exception, as a guest, as a showpiece novelty. As a result, one must guess that she lived in a neutral zone, neither black nor white—and her poems stand as a record of this ambivalence, as an indication that the slave mentality went deeper than the surface of her life.

Not surprisingly, then, Wheatley stands at the head of a long line of black American artists who, more or less unwittingly, give expression in their work to hatred of or at least an ambivalence toward their blackness. J. Saunders Redding generalizes about the literature of black Americans and calls it a "literature of necessity," a literature "motivated by the very practical desire to adjust to the American environment." The literature that springs from the unique motivation is likewise unique. In Redding's analysis, it is marked by a "cultural dualism":

> Of course writing by Negroes is different. The difference stems from the fact of their distinctive group experience in America. The cultural dualism of the American Negro is very real, and nearly all the Negro writers of more than local reputation have expressed it in one form or another.

Redding's assertion that there exists in the work of black authors a strain of racial alienation finds eloquent affirmation in James Baldwin's "Autobiographical Notes." Generalizing from his own experience, Baldwin says of the dilemma faced by the black artist in America:

The most crucial time in my development came when I was forced to recognize that I was a kind of bastard of the West; when I followed the line of my development I did not find myself in Europe but in Africa. And this meant that in some subtle way, in some really profound way, I brought to Shakespeare, Bach, Rembrandt, to the stones of Paris, a special attitude. Those were not really my creations, they did not contain my history, I might search in them in vain for any reflection of myself. . . . At the time I saw that *I* had no other heritage which I could possibly hope to use. . . . I would have to appropriate those white centuries, I would have to make them mine—I would have to accept my special attitude, my special place in this scheme—otherwise I would have no place in any scheme. What was the most difficult was the fact that I was forced to admit something I had always hidden from myself, which the American Negro has always had to hide from himself as the price of his public progress: that I hated and feared white people. This did not mean that I loved black people: on the contrary, I despised them.

Phillis Wheatley, as a black, and especially as a black cut off from her racial fellows in a slave society, wrote verse permeated with this social ambivalence, by what Baldwin and others suggest is a self-hatred motivated by the factor of race.

The poem "To Maecenas," which opens the 1773 edition of her work and which Matson sees as an example of the flight-to-freedom strain in the poem is, for the attentive reader, an initiation into Wheatley's racial ambivalence. A glance at "To Maecenas" will show that the poem is meant to be a dedicatory piece in imitation of the standard Augustan enshrinement of the benefactor's many virtues as a patron of the arts. The reader is not surprised, then, when Phillis assumes the self-demeaning posture so characteristic of the style:

> Great Maro's strain in heavenly numbers flows,
> The Nine inspire, and all the bosom glows.
> O could I rival thine and Virgil's page,
> Or claim the Muses with the Mantuan Sage;
> Soon the same beauties should my mind adorn,
> And the same ardors in my soul should burn:
> Then should my song in bolder notes arise,
> And all my numbers pleasingly surprise;
> But here I sit, and mourn a grov'ling mind,
> That fain would mount and ride upon the wind.

However, she ties this sense of inadequacy to her being black, and in doing so goes beyond the demands of the convention. Her otherwise standard lament over her "grov'ling mind" is impossible to divorce from the specifically racial content of the fifth stanza:

> The happier Terence all the choir inspired,
> His soul replenish'd and his bosom fir'd;
> But say ye Muses, why this partial grace,
> To one alone of Afric's sable race;
> From age to age transmitting thus his name
> With the first glory in the rolls of fame?

She presents Terence, an African by birth, as having exhausted the poetic gifts available to Africans. Thus her "grov'ling mind" is the child of a lack of talent which she attributes to her being of the "sable race." The solution she seeks to this racial quandary is to turn to the master's patronage:

> I'll snatch a laurel from thine honor'd head,
> While you indulgent smile upon the deed.

While flattery of the patron is certainly commonplace within the convention, it is noteworthy here in the context of the racial character of her complaint: she as a black cannot expect to write well, and the best she can do is to hope that the master will be indulgent in her defense.

A different sort of poem, "To the University of Cambridge in New England," contains a dimension of Wheatley's demeaning of her blackness that goes beyond the "smug contentment at her own escape from Africa" that James Weldon Johnson found in her poems. The poem is a moral admonition to the students at Harvard and is, for the most part, predictably Christian in its warning:

> Improve your privileges while they stay,
> Ye pupils, and each hour redeem, that bears
> Or good or bad report of you to heaven.
> Let sin, that baneful evil to the soul,
> By you be shunned, nor once remit your guard;
> Suppress the deadly serpent in its egg.

The significance of the poem in the context of the present discussion, though, lies not in the conventional moral statement but rather in the rationale used to justify such a warning. In the opening stanza she uses her African origins to establish her credibility as one who knows evil and who therefore feels impelled to warn others:

> While an intrinsic ardor prompts to write,
> The muses promise to assist my pen;
> 'Twas not long since I left my native shore
> The land of errors and Egyptian gloom:
> Father of mercy, 'twas thy gracious hand
> Brought me in safety from those dark abodes.

From this opening she makes no transition, but merely begins her admonition. She neither elaborates nor explains why Africa and her being from

Africa have thus enabled her to warn, but implies that her having recently been brought from Africa is justification enough for her to speak on evil and its consequences. She also assumes that her readers will make the same association and equate her origin in the "dark abodes" of Africa with an intimate acquaintance with evil not available to the white American Harvard students that are her peers.

The third stanza makes it clear that the thrust of the opening carries beyond an identification of her African background with paganism to a rejection of Africa as not only the land of pagan error, but also of satanic evil. She indicates that in delivering her from Africa's "Egyptian gloom" the "gracious hand" of God did more than rescue her from the dimly remembered doctrinal deficiencies of pagan cults. The passage of warning quoted above concludes as follows:

> Supress the deadly serpent in its egg.
> Ye blooming plants of human race divine,
> An Ethiop tells you 'tis your greatest foe;
> Its transient sweetness turns to endless pain,
> And immense perdition sinks the soul.

Once more, without elaboration or explanation, she assumes that her being an "Ethiop" is sufficient credential to speak familiarly of the "deadly serpent" and the state of a soul sunk in perdition. And finally, in identifying herself as an African, she implicitly excludes herself from the class "blooming plants of human race divine" who she addresses, underscoring the assumed moral distinction she has made based on color. In doing so, she transforms an otherwise religious warning into an indictment of her color and her African heritage.

"On Being Brought from Africa to America" is similar to the "Cambridge" poem in its gratuitous alignment of blackness and evil. The first half of this short poem is another of Wheatley's predictable religious verses. The tone of her calling Africa a "Pagan land," and of her declaration of happiness at having come to know God and salvation in America, is matter of fact. The second half of the poem, though, is devastating in its assumptions about black people:

> Some view our sable race with scornful eye,
> "Their color is a diabolic die."
> Remember, Christians, Negroes, black as Cain,
> May be refined, and join th' angelic train.

On the surface, this might pass with the first four lines as a vote of confidence in the salvation of black men through the mercy of God's deliverance. It might even seem to be a rather presumptuous reminder to white people by an adolescent slave girl that they ought not judge blacks too harshly. But, significantly, Wheatley's reminder includes an implicit affirmation of the very indictment she seeks to refute. That is, she does not

attempt to discredit the myth that the black man's color reflects a special
moral inheritance from Cain the murderer, marked by God in Genesis as
a sign of his fratricide (though no mention is made in the biblical story of
the skin marking being total pigmentation differentiation). On the contrary,
she apparently accepts the myth, dubious as it is, and in doing so affirms
that in its native state the "diabolic die" of black people reflects an essentially corrupt moral nature specifically related to the mere fact of blackness.
These final four lines indicate that blacks have value not in their origins
and in their humanity, but only in so far as they can be "refined" to fit
into the "angelic train" of the white Christians she addresses—in other
words, only to the degree to which they can reject their African origins
and assume the moral values of the white Christians.

Another of her "address" poems, "To the Right Honorable William,
Earl of Dartmouth, His Majesty's Principle Secretary of State for North
America" proves, upon close inspection, to be unintentionally ironic and
not, as Matson suggests, rebellious. The poem, largely a celebration of
freedom, was written in anticipation of what the colonists hoped would
be a vigorous effort by Dartmouth to work on their behalf. As such, it
serves to illustrate how far removed from the issue of slavery and from her
African origins Phillis had become by 1772.

In a letter accompanying the poem she requests that Dartmouth be
indulgent in perusing the poem, an address by a presumptuous African,
and she goes on in the poem to express her hopes that freedom might
return to New England. There is no suggestion in the poem that the freedom
of which she speaks is related to the issue of slavery. On the contrary, the
remarks in the letter and in the poem indicate that the freedom of which
she speaks is limited to an anticipated resolution of the political and economic conflicts between the colonists and the crown during the years preceding the revolution:

> No more, America, in mournful strain
> Of wrongs, and grievance unredress'd complain,
> No longer shalt thou dread the iron chain,
> Which wanton Tyranny with lawless hand
> Has made, and with it meant t' enslave the land.

Wheatley introduces the slavery question in the third stanza as a means of
justifying her presuming to speak on the topic of freedom and tyranny.
Clearly distinct from the plea for a return of liberties by King George to
the colonists, her claim to authority in discussing tyrants is surprisingly
empty of commentary on the question of freedom as it related to the slaves:

> Should you, my lord, while you peruse my song,
> Wonder from whence my love of Freedom sprung,
> Whence flow these wishes for the common good,
> By feeling hearts alone best understood,

> I, young in life, by seeming cruel fate,
> Was snatch'd from Afric's fancy'd happy seat:
> What pangs excruciating must molest,
> What sorrows labour in my parents' breast?
> Steel'd was that soul and by no misery mov'd
> That from a father seiz'd his babe belov'd:
> Such, such my case. And can I then but pray
> Others may never feel tyrannic sway?

She does not claim her authority to speak of freedom from her experience as a slave, nor does she draw on observations of the less comfortable lot of those slaves around her as one might expect her to. Rather, hers is a secondhand authority derived from her sorrow at imagining what her parents must have suffered at her loss. She implies that her own fate as a slave has not been cruel: Africa is only a "fancy'd happy" place; moreover, her indication that it was a "seeming cruel fate" that snatched her away suggests that it was, indeed, a fortunate day that saw her sold into slavery and removed from her African heritage.

One might object that it was not the prerogative of the slave Phillis to criticize such institutions as slavery. However, in the same poem she does not shrink from criticizing the "wanton Tyranny," of the crown—statements which are, as she reminds us several times, presumptuous for a slave to make. The disregard for the issue of slavery which this inconsistency implies is very aptly described by Saunders Redding:

> If the degree to which she felt herself a Negro poet was slight, the extent to which she was attached spiritually and emotionally to the slaves is even slighter. By 1761 slavery was an important, almost daily topic. The Boston home of the Wheatley's, intelligent and alive as it was, could not have been deaf to the discussions of restricting the slave trade. . . . Not once, however, did she express either in word or action a thought on the enslavement of her race; not once did she utter a straightforward word for the freedom of the Negro. . . . It is this negative, bloodless, spirit-denying-the-flesh attitude that somehow cannot seem altogether real in one whose life should have made her sensitive to the thing she denies.

The Dartmouth poem in particular, then, serves as one measure of how far removed from the reality of her blackness Phillis had become, at least intellectually, during the period in which she wrote. Matson's suggestion, tempting though it is, that Wheatley is protecting herself by her indirectness, seems to have an element of conjecture not really supported by biographical or textual evidence.

Besides the rather direct inferences treated thus far, there are less significant indications of Phillis Wheatley's racial ambivalence scattered throughout her other poems. Some of these will be noted briefly. In "A Hymn to Humanity," a poem similar to "To Maecenas" in its conventional tone of praise of a benefactor, she again asserts the specifically racial cause of her deficiencies as a poet. "Afric's muse" of the sixth stanza is the "languid muse of low degree" which she claims earlier on in the poem as her own. As in "To Maecenas," she is rescued by the white patron whom she lauds. Similar to the Harvard poem discussed earlier is "On the Death of the Rev. Mr. George Whitefield." In closing a catalogue of appeals which she uses to convey a sense of Whitefield's preaching voice, she writes:

> Take [Jesus] my dear Americans, he said,
> Be your complaints on his kind bosom laid:
> Take him, ye Africans, he longs for you,
> Impartial Saviour in his title due:
> Wash'd in the fountain of redeeming blood,
> You shall be sons, and kings, and priests to God.

The assumption is the same as that made in the Harvard poem: Americans—the white colonists—come to Jesus to air complaints, for a reason that is larger than the mere fact of their being Americans or human; the Africans come to Jesus, apparently, because they are Africans—no other reason is given. Wheatley once again infers an immediate relationship between being African and the moral evil which stands so gratuitously in need of washing.

As a sort of footnote to the discussion just concluded, it might be appropriate to comment on the possibility of racial undercurrents in the light/darkness images so pervasive in Phillis Wheatley's poetry. The validity of reading a racial significance in the use of images of light and dark in the poetry of one who was an admirer of Milton and who knew the scriptures is questionable indeed. However, in view of the more tenable indications of racial ambivalence on Wheatley's part already mentioned, it is not unreasonable to at least mention the possibility of a connection. That is, assuming that images derive their power from some referent in the experience of the author or of the reader of a given poem, the proliferation of images which ally light with the good, the intelligent, and the divine and dark with error, damnation, and chaotic evil might very well be significant in a racial context in the writings of one who was cut off from her black fellows, who was estranged from, who perhaps hated the blackness which separated her from the white world into which she was only partially impressed and toward which she apparently looked with admiration and gratitude. Psychoanalyst Joel Kovel and historian Winthrop Jordan have argued persuasively in, respectively, *White Racism: A Psychohistory* and *White over Black* that in the American experience it is impossible to dissociate the respective value placed on black and white persons from the traditional associations of black-bad, dirty, dead and white-good, clean, alive. When such equations are reinforced by religious symbolism and by cultural and economic devaluation of black people in the institution of slavery and its heirs, the racial significance of a poetic vocabulary permeated by such equations might be credibly posited. The possibility of such a significance, at least, will be assumed in the discussion of Wheatley's religion which follows.

In a letter to Arbour Tanner, Wheatley indicates that the religion in which she believed was one area in which her attitude toward her blackness and her being of African origins played a significant role:

> Let us rejoice in and adore the wonders of God's infinite love in bringing us from a land semblent of darkness itself, and where the divine light of revelation (being obscured) is as darkness. Here the knowledge of the true God and eternal life are made manifest; but there, profound ignorance overshadows the land. Your observation is true, namely, that there was nothing in us to recommend us to God. . . . It gives me very great pleasure to hear of so many of my nation seeking with eagerness the way of true felicity.

Her comment that there "was nothing in us to recommend us to God," a sentiment common to the New England protestantism in which she was formed, is especially significant in the racial context in which she was writing in that part of the letter. Her derogatory references to Africa are familiar from the ambivalence expressed in the poems. Here, though, the sense of the prose suggests that it was in their state of African ignorance that there was nothing to recommend them to God. The thrust of the passage, it seems, is one of seeing in religion an escape not from their condition of servitude but from the conditions of their Africanism—an escape they rejoice to see so many blacks accepting. Matson sees the escapist elements in the religious poems, in general, as having connotations of protest: the repeated assertion of escapist motifs being seen, "after a fashion," as protest against the condition of slavery. Again one must, at least in part, disagree: the escape Wheatley envisions is one that will purify her of the evil she sees as intrinsic to her blackness and her African origins.

In discussing the religion of Phillis Wheatley in his classic study of black religion in literature, Benjamin Mays employs the term "compensatory." He describes the function of this compensatory religion in this way:

> Miss Wheatley's religion is one of sweetness and affection. Her ideas of God help one to endure suffering and to bear up under it. They are capable of lending sweetness to life, giving it an elegant tone. . . . She is hardly concerned about transforming society. She is more interested in the individual and his soul's salvation.

The evidence from the poetry substantiates Mays's observations. Two types of religious concern are found in Phillis Wheatley's poetry: the delineation of a cosmology in which the primary fact is God's providential management and the vision of a corrupt world from which Providence eventually will deliver the virtuous believer. Repeatedly, in the many poems written on the deaths of various persons, these two strains join with the matrix of light/dark imagery to create a pattern of imagery in which the conventional themes of man's insignificance and God's providential concern reflect as well Wheatley's ambivalence over and desire to escape from her own blackness. Perhaps most typical is "To a Lady on the Death of Three Relations":

> We trace the pow'r of Death from tomb to tomb,
> And his are all the ages yet to come.
> 'Tis his to call the planets from on high,
> To blacken Phoebus, and dissolve the sky;
> His too, when all in his dark realms are hurl'd,
> From its firm base to shake the solid world;
> His fatal sceptre rules the spacious whole,
> And trembling nature rocks from pole to pole.

From this sombre beginning the poem moves to hope, the mourner admonished to "smile on the tomb, and sooth the raging pain" in a vision of the ethereal world. Significant for our purpose is the typical alignment of imagery along the lines of the equation observed by Kovel and Jordan: death and perdition converge in the image of blackness. For Wheatley, the terms of religious escape and racial denial of the self are, here and elsewhere, the same. Traditional and familiar though the religious sentiments be, the existence of a racial significance in their expression is more than mildly suggested when viewed from the perspective of the demeaned blackness present in the poems discussed earlier.

No doubt Phillis Wheatley was a bright young lady—perhaps, as Matson properly suggests in her evaluation of the poetry, a genius. To master English in sixteen months at the age of eight years was and still is an admirable accomplishment. Moreover, to produce even second-rate poetry in a milieu in which most blacks were oppressed and illiterate was at least a social, if not exactly a literary, triumph. Only occasionally worth reading for its aesthetic value (like indeed most Colonial poetry), her poetry retains a cultural significance beyond its literary merit that will insure its perpetuation as a proper object of study in the cultural history of black people in America. Literary phenomenon though she might have been, Wheatley's true legacy is the testimony her poetry gives to the insidious, self-destroying nature of even the most subtle, most gentle of racially oppressive conditions. It is in this aspect, although entirely remote from her conscious aims as a poet, that her poetry has its rich and alarming educative value today.

William Cullen Bryant:
"To a Waterfowl"

Donald Davie

Whither, 'midst falling dew,
While glow the heavens with the last steps of day,
Far, through their rosy depths, dost thou pursue
    Thy solitary way?

Vainly the fowler's eye
Might mark thy distant flight to do thee wrong,
As, darkly seen against the crimson sky,
    Thy figure floats along.

Seek'st thou the plashy brink
Of weedy lake, or marge of river wide,
Or where the rocking billows rise and sink
    On the chafed ocean side?

There is a Power whose care
Teaches thy way along that pathless coast,—
The desert and illimitable air,—
    Lone wandering, but not lost.

All day thy wings have fanned
At that far height, the cold thin atmosphere,
Yet stoop not, weary, to the welcome land,
    Though the dark night is near.

And soon that toil shall end;
Soon shalt thou find a summer home and rest,
And scream among thy fellows; reeds shall bend,
    Soon, o'er thy sheltered nest.

Thou'rt gone, the abyss of heaven
Hath swallowed up thy form; yet, on my heart
Deeply hath sunk the lesson thou hast given,
    And shall not soon depart.

He who, from zone to zone,
Guides through the boundless sky thy certain flight,
In the long way that I must tread alone,
    Will lead my steps aright.

It is convenient to point to the sixth stanza as the point at which we feel a more than usual honesty in the poet: "And scream among thy fel-

From *Interpretations: Essays on Twelve English Poems*, edited by John Wain. © 1955 by Routledge & Kegan Paul, Ltd.

lows. . . ." Screaming, with its connotations of rage and terror, seems not at all appropriate to Bryant's intention in this place, where "rest" in the line before, and "sheltered" in the following line, carry the idea of earned repose, wings folding, and the fall to rest. But the moment is beautifully controlled; for the implications of earned repose are there, but qualified and sharpened by the word "scream." We are only too ready to lapse with the bird into shelter, into the arms of a comfortable Providence; but Bryant will not allow it, demanding that we remain alert, aware of the bird in itself as a foreign creation, not only as a text for the poet's discourse. How easy, and how dishonest, would have been the word "cry," falling fitly into place with the tired lapse upon the lap of nature. But in that case it would have been a tired child that lapsed upon a mother's lap, the lap of "mother Nature" or a maternal God. And the cry would not have been what it purports to be, the cry of a bird, but a human cry, or a bird's cry treated as if human. Waterfowl *do* scream. Yet it is not true that the word denotes only. It carries connotations, though not the ones expected. It connotes the bird's "beastliness," its otherness, its existence in and for itself, as well as in the eyes of man. There is no question of our entering into this otherness by an effort of sympathy. We are only to remember that a bird is not a man. So we are not invited to identify ourselves with the bird, only, while keeping our distance, to take it for a sign. "Summer home" has the same effect.

This is enough to show Bryant disowning the indulgence of the neo-Georgian poet. It is just as important to notice how he avoids the self-indulgence of another kind of poet, how the surprising word draws no attention to itself, how the temptingly *recherché* epithet is avoided, so that the momentary pungency does not halt the exposition. So I said that it is convenient to regard this point as the one at which our attention is forced to be close. It is convenient so to regard it. But in fact there is no forcing here or anywhere else. The demand for attention does not assert itself. It is easy to read this poem carelessly and pass it off as merely creditable or even dull.

One could for instance equally well take the last line of the fourth stanza, "Lone wandering, but not lost." If we look back on this from the end of the poem, we perceive that "lost" is something not far short of a pun. Here the word has the homely tang of "Lost in a wood"; but after the rest of the poem has been read, it takes on also the other meanings or the other shades of meaning represented by "the lost tribes," or even by "lost" = "damned." For the moment what is pleasing is the approach to popular idiom in a poem up to this point couched in rather literary diction. The word demands once again an alertness in the reader, a keeping of one's wits about one, a refusal to go all the way after the easily cheapened emotional appeal of "lone." And on the other hand the pun or near-pun is submerged, refusing the opposite temptation to stand and preen upon a slick smartness. The poet can have it both ways.

It may be here, then, that the careful reader first becomes aware of having to deal with something more than a didactic set piece. Certainly the first stanzas seem to promise no more, if even so much. "Rosy depths" is weak, and so is "crimson sky," while it is only the vagueness of the second line which prevents the reader from asking whether "steps" is the right word for a progress which leaves a glow. At this point we do not know what we are in for, and later, when we realize that it is no part of the poet's intention to be vivid or "concrete," our objections to "rosy depths," for instance, may disappear. (Of course if we are of those readers for whom all poetry must be "concrete," we shall continue to object; but that is our funeral.) Still, the language of the first two stanzas is no more than tolerable at best. And "Thy figure floats along" is perhaps unacceptable on any terms. "Falling dew" may be called artificial, in the sense that it does not appeal to sense experience (no one sees the dew falling) but to deductions from that experience. "Thy figure floats along" is artificial in another and less excusable sense. It does not appeal beyond experience to a known fact. It does not appeal to experience, for "floating" does not adequately represent the experience of seeing a bird in flight; it is as vague as "figure." Still less, on the other hand, does it appeal to a known fact, belying experience, about the flight of a bird. The appearance is of ease, the fact is effort. But neither ease nor effort is represented by "floats." Moreover there is the disagreeable association of the "Gothick" heroine seen as a floating form down a perspective of dank arches. This precariousness has its own charm; but it is charming not to the reader of poetry but to the antiquarian amateur. And the image causes discomfort.

What I have called "precariousness" may deserve a harsher name. At any rate the third stanza explains and confirms it. For this stanza dates the poem and so establishes its convention. It substantiates the Gothick lady. "Weedy lake" and "rocking billows" are locutions which show the poet still in touch with the characteristic diction of the eighteenth century; yet "plashy" and "marge of river wide," with their Spenserian air, place the poem very late in that tradition, when it was no longer sure of itself. I will play fair here and admit that one of the few things I know about Bryant is that he read and admired Blair and Kirke White, poets in whom the Augustan diction has become corrupted. And of course one of the principal ingredients of that diction, even so early as Dryden, was borrowings from the language of Spenser. Still I think it true that the diction of this third stanza is enough to place the poem at or about the end of the eighteenth-century tradition. It could have been written quite a long time after 1800, but only by a poet who was behind the times or out of touch, a sort of provincial. If we were ignorant of the author, I believe we could go so far as this towards dating the piece on internal evidence. But by "dating" I do not mean so much assigning a period in time. Rather it is a matter of assigning the poem to its appropriate tradition, so that we may know what conventions are being observed, what to look for and what not to expect, what sort of objective the poet is aiming at.

But it is just here that we run into difficulties. For if my analysis holds so far, it appears that this poem appeals clearly to no one tradition, and abides unreservedly by no one system of conventions. It exists in a sort of hiatus between two traditions and in a makeshift convention compounded of elements from both. This is the secret of that precariousness which manifests itself in such uneasy locutions as "Thy figure floats along"; and it is this that makes the right reading of the poem such an exacting test of taste, difficult but also salutary.

"Weedy lake," for instance, goes along with the "falling dew" of the first line. It appeals beyond sense-experience in just the same way. "Rushy" or "reedy" would have been the Romantic word. And bullrushes are weeds. But to call them so shuts out Sabrina and Midas and their whispering, and places them firmly in the vegetable kingdom, where, for this poet as for the botanist, they belong. "Chafed" does just the same. The chafing of land by the sea is not an observed fact, but a deduction from many observed facts. "Chafed" is a dry, merely descriptive word. "Weedy" and "chafed," then, belong to one convention, as the appropriate diction of an age concerned not so much with experience as with the lessons to be drawn from it. "Plashy," on the other hand, and "marge," familiar archaisms, seem to invite just those legendary and literary associations that the other epithets so sternly suppressed. These are not *dry* words at all; they yearn out at the reader, asking him to colour with inarticulate feeling the things to which they refer. They thus appeal to quite another convention. Some readers may feel this betwixt-and-between air unsettling; others may think the poet deserves credit for bringing the two conventions into harmony. I will say only that the harmony, if it is achieved, is precarious, in the sense that while the poet may sustain it throughout his poem (and the reader feels that it is touch and go with him all the way), his success will not help him with the next poem he writes—he is as far as ever from perfecting a style that he can trust, a reliable tool. He is even further from himself contributing to a tradition in the shape of a heritable body of techniques; no later poet will be able to take his procedure as a model.

One sort of poet works his way to God by learning the lessons of experience, drawing conclusions from it, and so coming upon the moral laws behind it. Another sort of poet leaps up to God by dwelling with a fervent intensity upon experience as it is offered to him, not for the lessons it can give, but for what it is in itself. In the first stanzas of this poem, the reader is uncertain which sort of poet he is dealing with, so uncertain that he wonders if the poet himself knows. But the balance of probability was always towards the first alternative, because of the ceremonious tone and stately movement, and the rigidity of the metrical arrangement. For the leap to God would have to be made in the verse, and so it would demand, not Bryant's stanza, but some larger unit which would provide for a gathering impetus and *élan*.

Poet and reader alike begin to move with more assurance in the fourth stanza. Here, for the first time in the poem, we encounter something in the nature of Mr. Empson's ambiguities. For "teaches thy way" appears as an impurity, an awkward construction forced upon the poet by the exigencies of metre and rhyme, until we remember the usage "teaching the way to do." And this, once remembered, gives to the phrase the sense not only of guiding along a navigated track, but of teaching wings how to fly. In the same way, the seacoast is not pathless, but only the coast imagined as duplicated at the altitude of the bird's flight. And once the idea of altitude is introduced, there is the merest hint, no more, of that other "coast" which comes with "coasting," so obviously a better word for the flight of a bird than that "floating" of six lines before.

Only now can the point of the pun on "lost" be properly taken. For in the third line of this stanza the equable flow and the subdued tone are abandoned. "The desert and illimitable air"—a reverberation, a powerful élan; and fine, but at once controlled and valued by the earthy and quaint tang of the colloquial "lost." The Miltonic blast has been worked for, and is paid for; at the same time it asserts magnificently the importance and the glory of what the poet has in hand. And so it is possible to talk in a heightened tone, to move into "that far height, the cold thin atmosphere," and for the wings to grow into sails, into a dragon's vans, "fanning" the air. So the subsidence is effected upon several different levels. First the movement subsides after the beautiful break at "weary." Second, the flight subsides to the nest. Third, the vaulting human thought subsides, to a need for shelter. And finally, with "scream among thy fellows," the bird subsides, from a dragon or an angel, fanning the wheat from the chaff in lofty speculation, to being, precisely, once more a bird, a brute creature.

Thus, when,

> Thou'rt gone, the abyss of heaven
> Hath swallowed up thy form,

not only is the flying bird lost to sight, but the symbol too is lost to the eye of the mind. The abyss is not only the blue depth, but also the profundity of paradox in which the questions of destiny evade answer. Only so, having realized the incomplete and arbitrary nature of the "lessons" given, can Bryant's certainty ("And shall not soon depart") appear heroic and admirable, more than a windy gesture. The certainty of conviction impresses the more, not because of the uncertainty of the revelation, but because of the poet's acknowledgment of what in it would seem uncertain to others.

Or so we might have said, were it not for the last stanza. It is difficult to be fair to this. The moral is thumped home very pat indeed, but I think we deceive ourselves if we suppose that this is what offends us. We should not mind the certainty if the moral itself were more acceptable. Perhaps most readers will agree with me in thinking the migratory instinct in birds is no just analogy for the provisions made by divine solicitude for the guidance of the human pilgrim. And Bryant seems to assert something closer than analogy. In fact he seems now, at the end, to approach that identification of himself with the bird, that earlier he took care to avoid. Yet we cannot but think that the human being has a margin of choice for good and evil, that a bird has not. Hence divine guidance in the human soul must work in a way very different from the automatic and undeviating operation of instinct in migratory birds. To think otherwise is to cheapen alike the idea of Providence and the idea of human dignity—a dignity which depends, by the traditional paradox, upon the possibility of human depravity.

All this, however, is quite extraneous to the poem as poem. In raising these objections, we are in fact asking Bryant, not only to write a different poem from the one he has written, but to believe in a different god from the "Power" that he offers to us. My disappointment with the last stanza is relevant to the poem as poem, only if I can show that the expectations which it disappoints are such as earlier passages have entitled me to entertain. Only then can my objections stand as a valid criticism of the poem.

I think this can be shown. For if the lesson to be drawn is as straightforward as this, if supernatural guidance in human life is no more of a mystery than the migratory instinct in waterfowl (mysterious as that is), then "the abyss of heaven" is surely not deep enough. It is no longer the profundity of paradox, only those "rosy depths" of the first stanza, which have grown, in the interim, no ruddier and hardly any deeper. "Abyss" now comes to seem a pretentious word, too effusive, making promises that cannot be redeemed.

Thus the piece is seriously flawed both first and last. It is not a great poem, it is only just, perhaps, a good one. Just for that reason it demands very careful reading. When a poet's achievement is precarious at best, he requires in especial degree the cooperation of his readers. Not that he should be repeatedly given the benefit of the doubt; that would be not cooperation but indulgence. Rather it is a question of permitting the poem to establish its own convention; and where a poet is himself uncertain about the convention he is writing in (having perhaps to express something for which the established conventions are inadequate, yet lacking the energy to break wholly free of them), the reader has to be patient while the poet feels his way towards the convention he wants. Bryant feels his way through three or four stanzas.

Ultimately every poem establishes its own convention, dictates its own terms. But in a period when certain conventions (of diction, for instance) are shared by almost all the poets of one or more generations, the reader can with ease take his first rough bearings, and the poet can rely upon his doing so. When poets and readers agree, for instance, that certain metres, certain rhetorical figures, a certain vocabulary, go along with elegy, certain others with satire, the poet can expect his reader to understand quite quickly how any one poem he writes is to be "taken." But in periods such as our own, or Bryant's, when the genres are being reshuffled so that they are no longer mutually exclusive, the poet finds it much harder, not just to hold, but to direct the reader's attention, so that he shall know what to look for, what not to expect. Even in these cases, however, the poem establishes a convention for itself by, in effect, challenging comparison with certain poems and not with others. We begin to get somewhere with Bryant's poem only when he brings it home to us (and perhaps to himself) that, although this poem could never have been written in the eighteenth century, yet it belongs, and is to be taken, along with an eighteenth-century poem such as Gray's "On the Spring," not with Shelley's "To a Skylark."

From this point of view, to offer to read a poem "in isolation" is really a piece of trickery. For a great part of any careful reading consists in setting the poem among its fellows, that is, with those poems, in that genre, where it belongs. This has the effect, not of multiplying the meanings to be found, but rather of limiting the meanings to those which are really there, excluding those that come from reading it in the wrong way, expecting things that the poem (not the poet) tells us, by implication, not to expect.

Bryant's "Thanatopsis" and the Development of American Literature

Rebecca Rio-Jelliffe

On reading an anonymous poem brought by Willard Phillips, his coeditor with Edward Channing of the *North American Review*, Richard Henry Dana, Jr., is said to have exclaimed: "Ah! Phillips, you have been imposed upon; no one on this side of the Atlantic is capable of writing such verses" (1.150). [All references to Parke A. Godwin, *The Life and Works of William Cullen Bryant* (New York, 1883), six volumes, are indicated in this manner, with Roman numeral for volume and Arabic numeral for page.] Dana's skeptical remark identifies in the unknown author, soon discovered as the young William Cullen Bryant, the presence of a new voice, the promise of a new direction in American letters. Other critics have since concurred with Dana's estimate. H. M. Jones takes the first publication of "Thanatopsis" in 1817 as "the landmark . . . from which many are inclined to date the beginnings of a truly national American letters." In Bryant's first collection and Cooper's *The Spy*, both published in 1821, F. O. Matthiessen detects "the literature of the new nation, as distinct from colonial literature, [beginning] to find its voice."

"Thanatopsis" is also significant for adumbrating a concept of nature and art which generated over half a century a coherent poetic theory and practice denoting the character of the yet unborn American literature. While the historical significance of "Thanatopsis" is generally acknowledged, its artistic structure and the relation of that structure to the development of American literature remain undefined. This paper examines the artistic structure of "Thanatopsis," a pattern of tension created by contradiction and paradox (I); and notes the relation of that structure to Bryant's theory of poetry and language, and of his theory and poetry to the development

From *William Cullen Bryant and His America: Centennial Conference Proceedings 1878–1978*, edited by Stanley Brodwin and Michael D'Innocenzo. © 1983 by AMS Press, Inc.

of American literature (II). Limited by space to a summary of my evidence, the paper is based on a full-length study of Bryant's concept of nature and its relation to poetic theory and practice.

Literary historians detect in the attempts of early nineteenth-century writers to assimilate and order a confusion of inherited and indigenous literary crosscurrents the beginnings of an American literature. The works of Brown, Irving, Cooper, Bryant, and others record the propaedeutic struggle toward artistic independence. Bryant's precursive discovery of a subjective locus for synthesizing borrowed and native elements, of an aesthetic for giving voice to innate experience of American nature, points the way to artistic identity and integrity. His coherent system of poetics and poetry, probably the first in America, exemplifies the process of assimilation and naturalization indispensable for the advent of the great writers in the "renaissance."

At a time when American "criticism was preoccupied with the social implications of literature" and "questions of art and technique were too often neglected," Bryant discoursed on literary technique, language, and form. Contradictory assessments of Bryant's critical position and tenets require a coherent and thorough consideration of his theory and poetry. For Bryant, like Wordsworth, is a transitional writer who sets traditional material in new orientations and thus recasts them with fresh significance. Both show the influence of associational writers, the English poet primarily of the mechanist Hartley, and the American of the later intuitive-idealist Alison, whose theories anticipate romantic aesthetics. Bryant's critical and poetic works center around and are informed by an innate feeling for American nature and its implications for art. His poetic theory and practice, founded on romantic principles of emotional expression, naturalness, simplicity, spontaneity, irregularity, and freedom, set him squarely in the romantic movement which he anticipates in America by over a decade.

I

After the first publication of the body of the poem in 1817, generally assumed to be a fair copy of the original draft, two other versions preceded the 1821 "Thanatopsis" with its now famous introduction and conclusion. Two manuscripts, dated 1813–15 and 1818–20, contain prototypal versions of the introduction and conclusion. These variants contravene assumptions made by some readers that the 1821 introduction and conclusion were "additions . . . hastily composed" under Wordsworth's influence for the collection Dana had commissioned. The variants give evidence of an evolving view of nature which structures and informs the poem, and lies at the heart of Bryant's poetic theory and practice.

The introduction of the 1821 "Thanatopsis" opens with a general statement on nature's "various language" which breaks down into detailed components of gladness, beauty, sympathy, and consolation:

To him who in the love of Nature holds
Communion with her visible forms, she speaks
A various language; for his gayer hours
She has a voice of gladness, and a smile
And eloquence of beauty, and she glides   5
Into his darker musings, with a mild
And gentle sympathy, that steals away
Their sharpness, ere he is aware. When thoughts
Of the last bitter hour come like a blight
Over thy spirit, and sad images   10
Of the stern agony, and shroud, and pall,
And breathless darkness, and the narrow house,
Make thee to shudder, and grow sick at heart;—
Go forth, under the open sky, and list
To Nature's teachings, while from all around—   15
Earth and her waters, and the depths of air—
Comes a still voice—

The next abstract reference to "thoughts of the last bitter hour" modulate from the vague "sad images" and "stern agony" to the concrete "shroud, and pall" and "narrow house." Embedded in these concrete images, and countering the impersonal generalization, are feelings of terror and grief. Material objects convert universal fact into personal experience. The movement from abstract generalities to sensuous, emotionally connotative particulars is a structural pattern reenforced by contrasting tones of detachment and involvement, and by rhythm congruent with imagery: gentle cadence among cheerful images in the first half, spasmodic rhythm among sorrowful, harsh images in the second half. These contrastive patterns recur consistently throughout the poem in various forms of expansion and development.

The body of the 1821 "Thanatopsis" (17–73) originally published in 1817, likewise opens on an impersonal assertion of universal fact which shades into details connoting loss and grief: "cold ground," "lost each human trace," "brother to th'insensible rock." Kinetic imagery in "The oak / Shall send his roots abroad, and pierce thy mould" (29–30) renders general truth into dread. No emotions are overtly named; they are inherent in particularized or concrete images. Discourse enunciates an objective cognition of ultimate doom, while poetic texture sounds undertones of feeling.

The paradoxical interplay of intellectual and emotional elements is reenforced by the contrast in landscape of eternal cosmos and transient being doomed to dissolution:

Yet a few days, and thee
The all-beholding sun shall see no more
In all his course; nor yet in the cold ground,
Where thy pale form was laid with many tears,   20

Nor in the embrace of ocean shall exist
Thy image. Earth, that nourished thee, shall claim
Thy growth, to be resolv'd to earth again;
And, lost each human trace, surrend'ring up
Thine individual being, shalt thou go   25
To mix forever with the elements,
To be a brother to th'insensible rock
And to the sluggish clod, which the rude swain
Turns with his share, and treads upon. The oak
Shall send his roots abroad, and pierce thy mould.   30

Nature the consoler in the introduction turns in this section of the body into an enemy. Imagery corroborates antithetical design in yet another way. Large natural entities of sun, ocean, earth dwindle to rock, clod, roots. The living body fades into pale form and vanishes in "mould." Contracting immensity and reducing "individual being" to mere shade underscore the sense of subsidence and deprivation.

The same contrastive patterns structure the second section which argue against grief and fear (31–48). The generalization on the magnificent sepulcher of the dead break down into component images of hills, woods, rivers, brooks, and sun, planets, stars. Yet their glory make them no less the "sad abodes of death." In the third section (48–57), the general abstraction on the infinite dead crystallizes in images of time and space whose grandeur, again paradoxically, intensifies the human being's sense of loss. The remote, impersonal background modulates to felt life in sensuous objects. In the concluding section, an abstract common destiny takes substantial form in specific details.

The conclusion of the poem repeats the pattern in preceding sections with an impersonal injunction and vague "pale realms of shade" which resolve into kinetic images celebrating nature's triumph over man's enemy:

So live, that when thy summons comes to join
The innumerable caravan, that moves   75
To the pale realms of shade, where each shall take
His chamber in the silent halls of death,
Thou go not, like the quarry-slave at night,
Scourged to his dungeon; but sustain'd and sooth'd
By an unfaltering trust, approach thy grave,   80
Like one who wraps the drapery of his couch
About him, and lies down to pleasant dreams.

Two obverse images render the theme of the whole poem: negatively in the quarry slave, and positively in actions encapsulating nature's lessons on how to die and how to live.

The tensional interplay of intellectual abstraction and sensuous emotional objects, general and particular, detachment and involvement, eternal and transient, converts the poem from a versified disquisition on death, a commonplace at the time, to a record of dissonances in mind and heart. A structural pattern of contrast and paradox transforms intellectual discourse into a "structure of emotion" where, in Alison's terms, external objects function as "emotion-bearing" vehicles.

Consistent with the structural pattern, the dialectic, which centers on the role of nature, hinges as well on opposition and paradox. Postulated in the introduction as premise of the whole poem, nature is benefactor of human spirit, particularly in the extremity of death. Yet in the first verse paragraph of the body, the benign comforter disappears behind an indifferent cosmos threatening the individual with loss of every "human trace." The "all-beholding Sun" the transient Self "shall see no more." In the premise set by the introduction, the end of consciousness turns into the ultimate deprivation of nature herself, of access to spiritual aid. The role of nature in the first section of the poem contradicts her role premised in the introduction.

The temporary reversal in nature's role reflects the way the human being, overwhelmed with fear, views the natural universe. In contrast, nature's cosmic, timeless perspective subsumes human fear and grief in the common destiny of all things. This universal vision counters the individual's view of nature as an impersonal threat. Natural beauty, magnified in detail after concrete detail, is a metaphor of nature's all-encompassing beneficence. The sun, symbol of individual extinction in the first section now glorifies man's eternal home. Forbidding immensity and solitude on earth and sky, as in "Take the wings of morning . . ." (45–54), are transformed into nature's enthralling world. Changes in descriptive mood reflect the individual's subjective alteration from fear and regret to assurance.

With this development the major paradox of the poem becomes clear. For over these natural scenes of beauty lies the shadow of grief and loss evoked in the first section. Enhancing nature's grandeur heightens the attractiveness of man's final resting place, but contrarily, intensifies rather than mitigates feelings of sorrow and loss which, from the start, imbues natural objects in the body of the poem. Working against nature's rational precepts are countersignals of feeling embedded in imagistic particulars. The rhetorical question in the final section of the body (58–60) reiterates the loneliness and bitter regret of one cut off from the living. Nature's arguments address human reason, but the language of the poem betrays instinctual undertones of dismay and terror past rational argument.

The intellectual reasoning culminates in the concluding image of one who "lies down to pleasant dreams." The understructure of counterfeeling climaxes in the opposite image of a quarry slave "Scourged to his dungeon." Both, not one or the other, encapsulate the paradoxical theme of "Thanatopsis." This conclusion may not be what the poet had consciously intended to leave with the reader. But Bryant's own theory of language, of imagery in particular, and the preeminent role of emotion in the creative process, recognizes the power of words as accessible only to partial control. "Symbols of words," Bryant says, "suggest both the sensible object and the association" (V.5). It is those associations that could undermine sense.

In style, technique, and thought, the 1821 introduction is more successfully integrated with the body than earlier variants. In the variants, a "better genius" mediates for nature whose ministry on spirit is contingent on the poet's voluntary return to the "repose of nature," a condition that holds in the later work. For the surrogate, a being with complex attributes appears in the 1821 poem, attesting to the poet's increased faith in nature as generative source of his art. This inner history is recorded in the early poems and confirmed in the centrality of nature in Bryant's critical theory.

An incremental dialectic from the introduction through the body rises to a point in the conclusion. Considered by many readers as a didactic excrescence, the conclusion brings nature's injunctions to its logical issue: in life alone man may learn how to die. To complete the lesson on death, nature must instruct man to "so live" that he dies in peace. The lesson on dying, the conclusion establishes, is primarily a lesson on living. In the context of the whole poem, from nature's ministry on spirit in the introduction to the influence of her "still voice" in the body, the conclusion clearly affirms "an unfaltering trust" in nature alone. From beginning to end, man's ultimate recourse in life or death is nature's benign government.

The introduction, body, and conclusion are integrally joined to one another with consistent structural patterns and antithetical stresses in technique and dialectic. Balanced contrast is reflected as well in diction which deviates markedly from Bryant's immediate legacies of English poetic tradition and its transplants in America. The language of "Thanatopsis" demonstrates the American poet's functional naturalization of poetic diction and more recent realistic modes from favorites like Cooper, Burns, and Wordsworth. In the descriptive passages, the realistic "Rock-ribb'd" operates with formulas, "ancient as the sun" and "venerable woods" (38–40). Inert epithets like "th'insensible rock" obtain conceptual and affective life in the vivid actions of the "rude swain" who "turns with his share and treads upon" the "sluggish clod." In contrast to flaccid images of "cold ground" and "pale form," kinetic energy in the image of oak roots spreading out and piercing the human mould sharpens the sense of horror (19–30). Interacting with sensuous immediacy in natural or human actions, poetic diction acquires fresh viability.

Bryant prunes poetic convention to its functional essence, using formulaic simplicity to reinforce imagistic impression and consonant thought. Prosopopoeia, the preeminent figure of late eighteenth-century ornamental poetry, is transformed in Bryant's handling of personified nature into a functional device to set the premise of the poem and inform the whole structure.

Strategic placement of conventional phrases also contributes to unfolding dialectic and mood, as the infinite hosts of heaven (45–48) convey as well immensity of space and eternal time; and "the continuous woods/ Where rolls the Oregon" (52–53) picture infinity and solitude of the dead. The two modes of language function conjointly to intensify paradoxical dissonance of universal fate and individual resistance to it in design and thought.

What might appear to modern readers as an unusual handling of nineteenth-century poetic language and form sets Bryant apart from the prevailing practice of this time. "Thanatopsis" diverges markedly from antecedent traditions in England. The most direct lines are the graveyard school, and the didactic strains of popular nature poetry with their sentimental, hyperbolic rhetoric, excessive analogizing of nature and human life; deliberate elevation of language with cumulative similes; periphrases, abstract personifications, extended descriptions; and loose, discursive form.

At a time when poetic diction was of universal currency, and preromantic and romantic writers like Cowper, Burns, Wordsworth, and Coleridge were generally unknown or unwelcome to American readers, Bryant fashions a multivalent language closer to the bone of American experience. Tempered language, restrained, dignified tone, and controlled structure distinguishes "Thanatopsis" from the prevailing poetic practice of the period. In this literary phenomenon, Bryant forges material and form, both inherited and original, in the shape of an American artist's vision of life and death.

The artistic qualities of "Thanatopsis" confirm the unique position accorded to it in the history of American literature. The poem is important in other ways not generally recognized. It adumbrates fundamental principles of Bryant's theory and poetic practice, a congruent system based on his concept of nature and its implications for poetic form portending the character of a national literature. The discussion below outlines basic theoretical principles of Bryant's theory of language and related technique.

II

The original draft of "Thanatopsis" (1811) precedes by almost a decade and a half, the 1821 version by four years, Bryant's formulation of his critical theory. The four "Lectures on Poetry" (1825–26) is a comprehensive statement of theory drawing together dispersed ideas, and in the next five decades, consistently applied and reaffirmed in criticism and poetry. The concept of nature which unifies "Thanatopsis" becomes the fundamental principle of theory and practice grounded on the "premise of feeling" in associational and romantic aesthetics. Already germinal in the early poem are principles and tenets which bear on the development of American literature.

Bryant echoes an associational principle in postulating that the "great spring of poetry is emotion" (V.10); but he locates the "living and inexhaustible sources of poetic inspiration" (V.40) in nature. The creative process generated by nature-inspired feelings mirrors the spontaneity of natural processes. Poetry is the product of mind quickened by nature. On these premises lies the touchstone for poetic language, style, and structure: the "natural." Bryant's organic view of mind and art prefigures the principle of organicism central to American critical theory from the renaissance to later periods.

The coadunation of mind and nature in Bryant's theory occasions a concept of poetic form now known as the doctrine of analogies or correspondences. Over a decade before the doctrine becomes central to American criticism, Bryant defines a poetic technique which exhibits "analogies and correspondences . . . between the things of the moral and of the natural worlds," and "connects all the varieties of human feelings with the works of creation" (V.19), "moral associations with inanimate objects." Metaphoric analogy combines at once the main elements of Bryant's poetics: instigating and unifying emotion; nature, source, and norm of art; language and technique congruent to union of feeling and nature. It also achieves the immediate and ultimate ends of poetry, aesthetic experience, and moral elevation.

The poetic structure blueprinted in the doctrine of analogies opens on a natural scene imbued with congruous feelings and thoughts, or posits an idea associated with feelings which permeate natural objects in the poem, as in "Thanatopsis." The fusion conjures up analogous scenes embodying inner responses. Poetic form emerges with the accretion of congruent details reenforcing the original fusion, and by accumulation grows in intensity. The "leitmotif of romantic thought about art," the doctrine is an aesthetic formulation of the romantic vindication of mind over physical world, and outlines romantic structural forms.

In theory the doctrine of analogies combines discrete elements. In Bryant's practice, intense feeling inundates natural objects, and natural images are infused with feeling-thought. A new reality transcends the objective-subjective dualism. Irradiated with mind and feeling, imagery speaks the language of the inner world. The majestic beauty of the prairies becomes an agency of mind for projecting its own life. Under the fusion force of emotion, material and immaterial conjoin, and words function polysemously.

Anticipating in theory the metaphoric and symbolic modes of later poetry, Bryant applies the doctrine of analogies in poetic form distinguishing his nature poems from traditional descriptive-mediative types, where natural scene provides the setting for moral or intellectual reflections, or occasions a literal, often mechanical analogizing of nature. In most Bryant nature poems (except in the rare instance of a work like "Monument Mountain"), emotion unifies natural scene and subjective experience. From early works like "I Cannot Forget the High Spell" (1815) to great middle period works like "A Forest Hymn" (1825) and "The Prairies" (1832), landscape and cogitation mingle and illuminate one another.

All other components of Bryant's theory stem from the principle of emotion as unifier of mind and art. Since emotion and other mental constituents are "embodied in language" so as to affect another mind, the nature of poetic language engages Bryant over several decades. Emotion, he postulates, is the unfailing guide to poetic expression analogous to originating experience.

Bryant defines language as "the symbols of thought." Poetry selects and arranges these "arbitrary symbols" which are "as unlike as possible to the things with which it deals," and by this very limitation may render the immaterial in material "images" and "pictures" (V.5–6). This view of poetic language as symbol advances beyond the associationists toward the romantic theory of Coleridge. It also suggests modern views on the nonrepresentational character of language.

Images or pictures are the heart of poetic language. Emotion opens up "the storehouse where the mind has laid up its images" (V.10); while imagination "shapes materials . . . into pictures of majesty and beauty" (V.26). The poet's "sketches of beauty" are transformed in the reader's imagination to "noblest images" brought forward "from its own stores" (V.6–7). Bryant, however, dissenting from writers of the time, distinguishes a poem "affluent" with "mere imagery" from the "language of passion" framed in "spontaneity or excitement" (V.8–10). Supplanting the vogue of ornamental language and extended pictorial description, Bryant's imagism relies on a "few touches to delineate both external reality and subjective response, and thus to activate simultaneously sense, imagination, feeling, and moral sensibility. Imagery whose materiality calls up "the idea of certain emotions" (V.7) exemplifies Bryant's principle of synchronous operation in creative mind and poem.

The image, furthermore, concretizes general "lessons of wisdom" or "moral truth" in objects or particulars (V.11). Like Wordsworth, Bryant regards universal and permanent features of human and natural life as proper subjects of poetry, but requires that they be manifested in the particular or specific.

In depicting both particular and universal, outer and inner worlds, transient and permanent, imagery achieves the suggestive and effective ends of poetry. Both "picturesque and impassioned," a well-wrought image "touches the heart and kindles the imagination" (V.52). The polyphonic function of imagery adumbrated in "Thanatopsis" appears in varying degrees of concentration in nature poems of the following decades. Bryant's view of image prefigures a line of thought from the renaissance to the present, as in Pound's definition of image as "an intellectual and emotional complex in an instant of time."

In accord with the informing principle of his thought and art, Bryant locates the source of functional imagery in nature, the "original fountain" and "standard of perfection" for poetry. He urges the poet to "go directly to nature" for original imagery true to experience, instead of the current dependence on "the common stock of the guild of poets" (V.158).

Related to these tenets is Bryant's contention that only brief poems or those of moderate length may touch mind and heart. Despite the popular taste for epics of the revolutionary poets, or tales such as those he himself composed, Bryant asserts, "There is no such thing as a long poem" (I.186). Presaging Poe's famous dictum by a decade, Bryant sets down a primary tenet of early nineteenth-century poetics on the lyric.

While Bryant advocates "simplicity and clearness" in language (V.19), he would admit "obscurity . . . in the phrase" and "recondite or remote allusions" (V.157) to heighten poetic effect. He allows poetry to "transgress arbitrary rules" so long as it "speaks a language which reaches the heart" (V.10). The end of poetry, to make the "fullest effect upon the mind," is thus attained "no matter by what system of rules" (V.45). His radical prescriptions for prosody abrogate current rules and open the way for freer forms.

Even more revolutionary for his age where "artificial elevation of style" with "meretricious decorations" prevailed in poetic practice (V.51–52) is Bryant's vehement advocacy of "simple and severe" style (V.51), or "simple and natural . . . style" (V.155). He repeatedly inveighs against "strained, violent contrivances," "florid and stately" imagery and epithet popular with American poets. "Too far removed from the common idiom of our tongue" (V.157–58), the "false sublime" subverts "pathos and feeling" (V.52–53), and is therefore—a heinous sin in the Bryant creed—"out of nature" or "unnatural" (V.49). Like Wordsworth, Bryant believes "the language of poetry is naturally figurative," but figures must be used only "to heighten the intensity of expression. . . ." Unless forged in the heat of feeling they turn into "cold conceits" or "extravagance" (V.10).

Bryant's obsessive demand for "simple and natural" language rests on a principle of marked historical significance: the organic correlation of verbal expression to originating emotion. From early to late critical works, he censures the "artificial and mechanical" in poetic language, and recommends "a natural and becoming dress for the conceptions of the writer" (V.54), an "honest expresion of meaning." Only "natural" language gains the end Bryant extols, as did Coleridge before and Poe after him, "unity of effect." As no American writer of the time held so inflexibly, Bryant requires the language of poetry to be an organic expression of and commensurate to the originating subjective state.

Bryant locates the sources of "natural" language "in the organic expression of the people," in "the vernacular language of the poet" (V.36–37). Consistent with his organicism, Bryant resolves the fundamental issue in the search for national literature. For all the causes adduced to account for its absence, and all the solutions to bring it about, the problem hinges primarily on locating an indigenous language to give intrinsic expression to American experience. An advanced pioneer on this question, Bryant renounces the prevailing dependence on English heritage, and locates an American language in "the copious and flexible dialect we speak" (V.36). "It has grown up . . . among a simple and unlettered people," and has "accommodated itself, in the first place to things of nature, and, as civilization advanced, to the things of art. . . ." It has thus "become a language full of picturesque forms of expression . . ." (V.34). While the language of "Thanatopsis" is hardly the vernacular, still its chaste diction and controlled form deviates markedly from ornate expression and loose structure in similar works. Nature poems after "Thanatopsis" move closer to common speech in diction and rhythm. Departing from contemporary theory and poetic practice, Bryant's views on language presage the language of the emergent American literature.

Bryant addresses another question in the search for national literature when he directs American writers to draw "their subjects from modern manners and the simple occurrences of common life" (V.33). He anticipates the shift at about the fourth decade from elegant or sublime subjects to "real life" (V.55), to "familiar and domestic life." Portending the practice of many American novelists, he claims romance puts "familiar things in a new and striking yet natural light," for its subject is not the "supernatural and the marvelous" but the "manners of our countrymen" (V.55). The romancer is an "anatomist of the human heart," a title befitting such writers as Hawthorne, Melville, James, and Faulkner. Bryant grounds both language and subject matter in the life of "human beings, placed among the things of this earth" (V.29).

As the demand for American literature rose in the early decades, the idea of an indigenous literature became increasingly identified with romantic spirit and modes. A complex of ideas and trends—elevation of feeling and imagination over reason; power of mind to link man and nature; with democratic socio-political ideals, the rise of the common man, and the divinity of common things; resurgence of American nature as source of poetic inspiration and expression; location of literary language rooted in American soil; subsidence of neoclassicism in literary art and taste; shifts in critical norms from absolute universal standards to historic relativism and subjective or impressionistic appeal; the moral ends of literature balanced with aesthetic pleasure; the turn from nationalism to universalism; the concept of organicism in government and art—these constituents of Bryant's thought and art identify the search for national literature with romantic confluences.

Enunciating romantic tenets in the twenties, Bryant may have promoted the shift from the rational-mechanistic to an organic view of mind and art. His poetics, grounded on emotion as the unitary creative principle, and poetry as analogue of mind quickened by nature, prefigure other major statements of organicism in America, and precede the belated reception of

Alison and romantic theorists like Wordsworth and Coleridge. From the forties on, when romanticism had become "the positive movement of the time," organic unity and its allied doctrine of analogies echo in the works of Emerson, Melville, Lowell, Whitman, and others. Holding to the life principle as spirit, and to objects as symbols of inner or higher reality, Bryant prefigures transcendental organicism.

His organicism, however, falls short of the radical totality of All in Each espoused by Emerson and some contemporaries. Still relying on the human imagination to unite nature and mind, and to effect the same unity in the poem, Bryant adumbrates only in part the metaphysics to come. Similarly, his poetry in general merely foreshadows the symbolic mode after him. Still dwelling on natural beauty for its own sake as well as for its spiritual significance, the poems are essentially metaphoric in function. The nature poems nonetheless inaugurate "the organic union of art, nature, and mind of man," the salient mark of organicism in American literature.

Bryant's theory and art typifies one of two contemporaneous streams of American romanticism: an "organic emotional romanticism . . . of a slow but indigenous growth," and the imitative romanticism of Freneau, Halleck, Willis, Drake, Percival, and somewhat later, Poe, who exploited medievalism, the gothic, and other exotic trends in Europe. Two main branches of American poetry stem from Bryant and Poe, the first important poets of early nineteenth century. Poe initiates art for art's sake, the use of technique to achieve supernal beauty transcending mundane reality. Bryant inaugurates a poetic tradition founded on a total view of reality encompassing natural world and human mind. Where Poe in his poetic practice bypasses nature, Bryant takes nature for the main constituent of his art.

Bryant keeps faith in the literary potential of America when writers, misled by early associational thought, despair over a landscape empty of hoary legend and history. Virtually alone among the poets of the first three decades, he makes American landscape viable for poetry, not by drumming up external attributes of historic or mythic values, but by recreating natural scene in the crucible of impassioned imagination. For Bryant, the quest for nationality is the quest for personal artistic integrity. He discovers an inner locus for assimilating American nature and life, and for rendering it in art forms accordant to its spirit. His philosophy, aesthetics, and poetry offer a way to release American writers "from the sterile obligation to express what their own experience had not nurtured." Within the limited scope of his vision and achievement lay the seeds of the future.

Readers of his day find Bryant's poetry "complex and difficult," a testimony to the unique character of his work. For modern readers, Bryant's poems are loosely knit, lacking the tension of paradox, the oblique curve of irony, the concentration of symbol, the power of Adamic self-parturitions in Emerson, Whitman, Melville, and Dickinson. Yet for all their faults, the poems manifest a viable synthesis of tradition and innovation which prepares the ambience necessary for the great writers to come. His poetry describes and states, like poetry of the past; it also embodies, like much of the poetry to come. His "organic style," issuing from his search for language commensurate with his experience of American landscape and life, opens the way to an American literature sought after in his age, and claimed with pride in our own.

The Muse Has a Deeper Secret:
Emerson's Poetry

David Porter

The death of young Waldo was only the most tragic of all the experiences that were absorbed by Emerson's aesthetic concentration. The poems assimilated experience to the introspective life of his poetic imagination. No matter what the ostensible subject—a walk in the countryside, a snowstorm, a camping trip, a commemorative verse, even the death of a son—the deep determining subject remained constant. But the great writers, as Proust's narrator explains somewhere, have never written more than a single work, expressing rather through diverse transformations the unique ardor by which they are animated. This observation in no way denies the useful groupings of the poems which Emerson scholars have made according to such categories as the domestic poems (say "Threnody"), political ("Ode to W. H. Channing"), descriptive ("May-Day"), or philosophical ("Brahma"). Firkins argued that "the number of *species* in Emerson's verse is large in proportion to the number of poems. He is always doing something not quite like other people and not quite like himself."Others have enumerated the poetic genres at some length. But within the poems exists a structural sameness that organizes the apparent distinctions at the surface.

Detecting Emerson's brooding search for ways to allow the unimpeded outlet of the poetic imagination is quite different from concluding, as readers have, that Emerson's poems are mostly distilled philosophy. They are, in fact, transformings of a persistent inner imperative that lodged below the level of Emerson's conscious aim. Jonathan Bishop's observation on Emerson's preoccupation with the process of the Soul is on the mark exactly: "The metamorphosis of circumstances into consciousness is the consum-

From *Emerson and Literary Change.* © 1978 by the President and Fellows of Harvard College. Harvard University Press, 1978.

mation of the Soul's great act. The trajectory of that act is sketched in a hundred remarks." The fixation was stronger than that: it was single, intense, distracting. This is why, as Arnold implied when he said the reader of "The Titmouse" never quite arrives at learning what the bird in the poem actually did for the man, many poems are so curiously indecisive. Labeling the poems "philosophical" seems to have been a way of getting at this indeterminate quality that is marked in poems like "The Sphinx" and "The Problem." They are surely not philosophical in the way Wordsworth's poems are, turning identifiable issues in explicit development; they are as inconclusive in statement as they are earnest in tone.

Emerson's poems took their mode from his world of stratified values and of stratified mind. The structure of the mind became the structure of the poems. The basic binarism was mapped out in the poem "Merlin": nature comes in ascending pairs, a kind of moral double helix through which the mind rises, and in this doubled world, "like the dancers' ordered band, thoughts come also hand in hand." Emerson's twoness comprised for him a symmetry that produced balance, replication, and joy, and thus "The animals are sick with love / Lovesick with rhyme." Furthermore, because the doubles reproduce themselves, they are immortal, they repeat truth, keep it "undecayed," triumph over time, and establish the Universal harmony. Like the Platonists, in whose system justice resides in the stable order beneath Truth and Love, Emerson plots that same abstract virtue in the symmetrical structure of nature. "Justice is the rhyme of things," he says in "Merlin."

It was a dynamic order in which the things that rhymed were not nearly so important as the rhyming itself. Emerson's younger contemporary, Matthew Arnold, sought to fix a multitudinous world, to establish for things, as Richard Ohmann has put it, "the fixity of being properly named" and not "to let concepts, actions, properties, or groups of people drift in a limbo of namelessness." Emerson's aim was to keep dissolving those constraining definitions, to break down barriers and life-denying rituals, to rediscover one's manifold being in the universal circuit, and to yield oneself to the perfect whole. It is a powerful vision whose central light was Emerson's conception of the poetic imagination in the act of conversion. This was the enormously beneficent process of savage nature itself. In art, he believed, a comparable, radical transforming primitivism was needed. In "The American Scholar," which, together with "Poetry and Imagination," forms the central document in the radical poetics of Emerson, we read this: "Not out of those on whom systems of education have exhausted their culture, comes the helpful giant to destroy the old or to build the new, but out of unhandselled savage nature; out of terrible Druids and Berserkers come at last Alfred and Shakespeare" [vol. 1, pp. 99–100 of *The Complete Works of Ralph Waldo Emerson*, ed. Edward Waldo Emerson, 12 vols., Boston and New York, 1903–4; hereafter abbreviated as *W*].

That helpful giant is Emerson's wonderfully muscular embodiment of the imagination, filled with power to convert, to liberate, to build the new out of the old, to reject all systems of established religions, able indeed to convert the world. He is the heroic figure of the artist's imagination, and he secretly inhabits almost every poem. Some poems relinquish their own power because they serve the giant and not their particular selves. Others, like "Merlin" and "The Snow-Storm," take on a powerful aesthetic significance.

This covert allegory explains in part why the world has so little reality in Emerson's poems. It is a bright rhyming world a long way from Charles Olson's "In cold hell, in thicket." What the poems lose in worldliness, however, they gain as an artist's concern with the working of creative energy. The discussion that follows is a new look at Emerson's poems as they distractedly circle again and again the three basic aspects of the poet's imagination: how it is structured, how it operates, and what its goal is.

In "Threnody" two levels of mind frame the dialogue of the poem and provide the poles between which the abrupt confrontation takes place. One way to identify these poles is by their Platonic designations of Being and Becoming. The father-mourner is the consciousness directly involved in the experience, actively mourning the death of the son. He confronts the loss and suffers the torments. Yet he fails to see the tragedy in its larger reconciling aspect, which is the function of the "deep Heart." This second consciousness perceives the significance of the death and offers the reconciliation for the mourner. The dramatic basis of the poem and the stage on which the performance takes place come directly from Emerson's idea of the low and high steps of the poetic imagination. . . . The genetic action of "Threnody" is not the death itself but the negotiation of these levels of the imagination that lead to elevation, understanding, and resolution.

Emerson identified these layers in many ways, always maintaining the distinction that the experiencing stage of the imagination was the lower, the resolving level the higher. In "Poetry and Imagination" he saw them reflected in the separation of science and art. "The solid men," he says, "complain that the idealist leaves out the fundamental facts; the poet complains that the solid men leave out the sky. To every plant there are two powers; one shoots down as rootlet, and one upward as tree. You must have eyes of science to see in the seed its nodes; you must have the vivacity of the poet to perceive in the thought its futurities" (*W* 8.71). In attempting to analyze precisely how contemporary events are transformed to thought, Emerson had earlier employed a similar vertical division, resorting finally to the orchard metaphor:

> The actions and events of our childhood and youth are now matters of calmest observation. They lie like fair pictures in the air. Not so with our recent actions,—with the business which we now have in hand. On this we are quite unable to speculate. Our affections as yet circulate through it. We no more feel or know it than we feel the feet, or the hand, or the brain of our body. The new deed is yet a part of life,—remains for a time immersed in

our unconscious life. In some contemplative hour it detaches itself from the life like a ripe fruit, to become a thought of the mind. Instantly it is raised, transfigured; the corruptible has put on incorruption. Henceforth it is an object of beauty, however base its origin and neighborhood.

(*W* 1.96)

This process of transformation, both moral and aesthetic as the quotation indicates, habitually informs Emerson's poetry. The separation of functions between the lower experiencing consciousness and the higher perceiving consciousness marks the distinction Emerson defined variously as that between talent and genius, fancy and the imagination, Understanding and Reason. It is the very armature and substance of the poem "The Problem." The speaker's cherished deep truth and creative act rise not from "a vain or shallow thought" but rather issue from fundamental and terrifying sources:

> Out from the heart of nature rolled
> The burdens of the Bible old;
> The litanies of nations came,
> Like the volcano's tongue of flame,
> Up from the burning core below.

Part of the "problem" is that the churchman's cowl signifies a deep consort with primal laws that no one would casually presume to possess. That sort of genius is not acquired simply by choice of the clerical profession. Emerson abhorred that presumption, and the argument of the poem, very much like that in "Threnody" (note the similar humbling rhetorical questions: "Know'st thou what wove yon woodbird's nest / . . . Or how the fish outbuilt her shell [?]"), divides between the lesser powers of mere preaching and the powers of genius, whose love and terror create wonders equal to Nature's.

Ambivalent as the poem is, despite its decisive opening and closing lines, it argues finally the speaker's desire to be an original *maker* and not simply a *transmitter*. It is an artist's poem, for inside its somewhat indeterminate exterior, the poem celebrates beauty and not religion.

"Give All to Love" contains a similar divided structure, based on the same model of the imagination. The poem also proceeds from the lower power to the higher. In the beginning, it cheerfully promotes the human proclivity to give all to love and to the things of the day, ascending in experience with them:

> Obey thy heart;
> Friends, kindred, days,
> Estate, good-fame,
> Plans, credit and the Muse,—
> Nothing refuse.

By its end, abruptly, in that slackening of intention we have seen, the poem urges freedom from those lower claims:

> Keep thee to-day,
> To-morrow, forever,
> Free as an Arab
> Of they beloved.

The two-staged experience comes directly to the surface in the final lines where the choice between an earthly love and the ideal is made clear:

> Though thou loved her as thyself,
> As a self of purer clay,
> Though her parting dims the day,
> Stealing grace from all alive;
> Heartily know,
> When half-gods go,
> The gods arrive.

Once again Emerson draws the distinction between a half-perception and the full ideal one. The half-gods, corrupted and partial by definition, are kin to those Plato describes in the *Apology* as the demi-gods who are the illegitimate sons of the gods sired on nymphs or mortals. Here they are embodiments of that familiar Emersonian choice between the half-sight focused on means and the full perception open to truth. Of George Herbert's idea of man as microcosm ("Man is one world, and hath / Another to attend him"), Emerson says in *Nature*: "The perception of this class of truths makes the attraction which draws men to science, but the end is lost sight of in attention to the means. In view of this half-sight of science, we accept the sentence of Plato, that 'poetry comes nearer to vital truth than history' " (W 1.69). In Emerson's aesthetic equation, that half-sight of science equals poetic talent as opposed to genius, literary convention as opposed to prophetic content. The hierarchy thus had its personifications not only in the father-mourner as opposed to the deep Heart, but also the work-a-day preacher as opposed to the genius in possession of the word, the sensuous mortal pursuing the half-god of profane love as opposed to the idealist in quest of the gods themselves. The intention of each poem is thus linear, often abruptly so, proceeding from a first state of confusion, ignorance, or paralysis (sometimes all three) to a state of clarity, revelation, and liberation.

This basic structural model provides the armature in almost all of Emerson's poetry. In "Each and All," it is the speaker of simple talent or fancy who "aggregates" experiences, collecting a sparrow and seashells without discerning the plan of "the perfect whole" from which they are organically inseparable. Here again, the speaker starts out misled into thinking he can possess things as he pleases; he soon discovers that removed from their place in the great circuit, they become, like the shells, "poor, unsightly, noisome things." Through a slow, deliberate version of the eyeball experience, the speaker's consciousness finally rises so that he "sees" the larger beauty. Again we confront Emerson's world as it was limited to experiences that could be used to demonstrate the two levels of the imagination. But there was an opening in Emerson's scheme that will be important to us later and is appropriately to be noted here. The philosophical assumption of an organic universe had extremely significant ramifications in Emerson's developing aesthetics of poetic form. He says in a journal entry of May 16, 1834: "I learned that Composition was more important than the beauty of individual forms to effect" [vol. 4, p. 291 of *The Journals and Miscellaneous Notebooks of Ralph Waldo Emerson*, ed. William H. Gilman et al., 16 vols., Cambridge, Mass., 1960–82; hereafter abbreviated as *JMN*]. The poem "Each and All" enacts this credo by an allegory of what was essentially an aesthetic tenet of Emerson's, perhaps the most important and most "modern" one, the need for more aggregate and fully receptive forms.

"Brahma" is a late example of his structural obsession. Despite its Möbius loop view of the universe where all things turn on their opposites— it is the insight of genius that Brahma possesses—the poem rests on that familiar ladder of the ascending consciousness. At its conclusion, the half-perception is associated with "heaven" and a partial way of seeing. Brahma in effect says at the end, "Turn your back on single systems of thought exemplified by the idea of heaven and be liberated into the realm of total perceptions with me." The sweep toward revelation and thus at least a theoretical liberation from confinement is both a formal and philosophical paradigm here, as in other Emerson poems. Brahma urges a full and knowing receptiveness to this world below. It is the lower order of mind that thinks it can slay or be slain; the higher order sits where all the contraries converge. We hear in the poem another not so simple version of the deep Heart in "Threnody"; we stand at the burning core in "The Problem"; we face the gods in "Give All to Love."

The overheard Poet in that most inconclusive of all of Emerson's published poems, "The Sphinx," gives us a gloss on the higher sight of Brahma:

> "To vision profounder,
>   Man's spirit must dive;
> His aye-rolling orb
>   At no goal will arrive;
> The heavens that now draw him
>   With sweetness untold,
> Once found,—for new heavens
>   He spurneth the old."

By that marvelous etherializing process of conversion that Emerson never ceased portraying, the drowsy Sphinx finally "melts," "silvers," "spires," "flowers," "flows" into nature's forms. From a stony mystery she becomes the airy spiritual truth of nature, a not unfamiliar progression in the poetry of Emerson. Again he has moved along the trajectory from ignorance to revelation. "The Sphinx" is a paradigm itself of Emerson's conception of the poetic function. For this reason if for no other, Emerson was justified in placing it at the beginning of his first volume of poems in 1846.

But Emerson's contemporaries found the poem impenetrable, as most readers have since. Ambiguous, apparently contradictory in viewpoint, it did not provide a welcome entry to his other poems, and later editors moved it back from the head position. Edward Emerson said it "cut off, in the very portal, readers who would have found good and joyful words for themselves, had not her riddle been beyond their powers" (*W* 9.403). The poem's vexing ambiguity comes largely because it is unclear whether or not the Poet solves the Sphinx's riddle. The Poet seems to defeat the Sphinx ("Dull Sphinx, Jove keep thy five wits") and to be defeated (the Sphinx replies: "Thou art the unanswered question. . . . And each answer is a lie."). Yet encompassing the two-level structures of the supernatural riddler and the human riddle-solver, joyful nature and melancholy man, is a primary consciousness. This all-seeing maker of the poem contains the dull Sphinx's opacity as well as its protean dynamism, the picture of oafish man as well as the cheerful poet's confident reply. That primary speaker, part Emerson and part an idealization, knows both the Poet's craving for universal principles and the Sphinx's knowledge of infinite forms and transformations. It is this speaker, then, who sees the truth that nature is incessant change and has no single identifiable center such as Love, as the overheard Poet says. And it is this super Emersonian speaker presumably who was intended to preside over the poems in the book. "The Sphinx" was the essential statement and act of all the other poems that accompanied it. In it, Emerson's speaker is the Central Poet outside his two-tiered system for once, living fully in the world, serene in its flux, beyond grasping after absolutes.

The drama between the grasping but ignorant low mind and the enduring, all-perceiving imagination or high mind is played out later in "Hamatreya" by the farmers on the one hand and the earth on the other. Emerson, we recall, said near the conclusion of "Poetry and Imagination" that "Men are facts as well as persons, and the involuntary part of their life is so much as to fill the mind and leave them no countenance to say aught of what is so trivial as their selfish thinking and doing" (*W* 8.75). In the poem this "trivial doing" is the vain regard of the farmers soon to die. The facticity of their lives is established at the beginning with drumming directness (and no little humor) as their names form a list exactly parallel to the "things" of their toil:

> Bulkeley, Hunt, Willard, Hosmer, Meriam, Flint,
> Possessed the land which rendered to their toil
> Hay, corn, roots, hemp, flax, apples, wool, and wood.

In Emerson's equation men are the facts while the Earth (yet another disembodied voice out of the deep) stands for the larger and finally absorbing truth. In a further parallel, the aggregating lower mind is mirrored in the farmers' vain and possessive beliefs, while the Imagination has knowledge like the enduring Earth's:

> "They called me theirs,
> Who so controlled me;
> Yet every one
> Wished to stay, and is gone,
> How am I theirs,
> If they cannot hold me,
> But I hold them?"

To the extent that Emerson conceived of men as convertible elements in an eternal scheme, they were indeed facts. Both Alcott and Parker remarked that he thought of men as ideas, but Emerson's conception was always a part of a higher humanism. When he saw individual men, like the farmers in "Hamatreya," blinded by their vanity, Emerson's moral wrath could explode. Sampson Reed, his early guide, when he displayed his own kind of vanity in dogmatic narrowness, Emerson condemned in outrage in the poem "S. R.," calling him "Sleek deacon of the New Jerusalem" and "A blind man's blind man." In aesthetic terms, all these men are failed poets, captives of their fancies, unable to liberate themselves from petty vanities and ascend to the higher imagination.

The rural man in nature displayed for Emerson the clear sight of the imagination, while the grasping city man among the money-mad crowd collected wealth but not sane contentedness. The city dweller in "Woodnotes II" does not see beyond his acquisitions. The forester has acquired qualities of the supernatural Sphinx:

> Whoso walks in solitude
> And inhabiteth the wood,
> Choosing light, wave, rock and bird,
> Before the money-loving herd,
> Into that forester shall pass,
> From these companions, power and grace.
> Clean shall he be, without, within,
> From the old adhering sin,
> All ill dissolving in the light
> Of his triumphant piercing sight:
> Not vain, sour, nor frivolous;
> Not mad, athirst, nor garrulous.

The seemingly blessed possessor in "Guy" is another version of factual man mistaking his material abundance for the higher power he lacks. Prosperous but not quite an example of "the balanced soul in harmony with nature," as Edward Emerson describes him in a note on the poem, Guy is rather another vain fact in an allegory of the lower mind. Emerson is careful in the poem to have us distinguish between fancy and genius. Guy's enormous vanity is established at the outset:

> Mortal mixed of middle clay,
> Attempered to the night and day,
> Interchangeable with things,
> Needs no amulets nor rings.
> Guy possessed the talisman
> That all things from him began.

He prospers in all he does, and it appears he has "caught Nature in his snares." In his vanity he supposes, like the farmers of "Hamatreya," that "fortune was his guard and lover." Indeed, he thinks himself (lovely parody of the eyeball) concentric with the universe:

> In strange junctures, felt, with awe,
> His own symmetry with law.

He believes he shares God's genius:

> It seemed his Genius discreet
> Worked on the Maker's own receipt.

But his end, one infers from the repeated overstatements, will be that of Polycrates, who suffered a cruel death despite his unbroken good fortune. Mere possessiveness and smug satisfaction with the lower virtues are not to be confused with the higher humbling power to see the larger plan. The swelled pride is wonderfully punctured by the Byronic rhyme at the end where Guy's values converge on the single word: "Belonged to wind and world the toil / And venture, and to Guy the oil."

The model of mind was the stage for Emerson's actors, and he directs them in the poems with varying degrees of obviousness. The allegory determined the characters he chose and comprised the shadowy significance of the subjects he presented. The philosophy behind this divided model of the imagination as it perceived a convertible world had more significance for the artist, however, than simply the matters of vain possession and spiritual insight. The two levels of mind were the basis for an aesthetics that was part of the allegory.

Characteristically, the aesthetic suppositions take protean forms, and if we follow his principal ones we will end up seeing in Emerson's cherished snowstorm, of all places, the acting out of a forceful poetics. The way to this disclosure begins with Emerson's idea of the function of a college and his image of a fire. Colleges, he said in "The American Scholar," "only highly serve us when they aim not to drill, but to create; when they gather from far every ray of various genius to their hospitable halls, and by the concentrated fires, set the hearts of their youth on flame" (W 1.93). He describes the ideal college not as a simple aggregating fancy but, like genius, as a distiller and transformer of those aggregated elements to inspiring flame. Only a little leap from this analogy is necessary to see the aesthetic meaning of the famous humble-bee. Emerson calls the bee "rover of the underwoods" and describes him as gatherer of all nature's sweetnesses, who by leaving the chaff and taking the wheat (in the poet's strained metaphor) transforms the gatherings to honey. The bee is his own self-reliant generator of heat ("Thou animated torrid-zone!"), the center of his society ("Joy of thy dominion!"), and perceiver of the ideal ("Yellow-breeched philosopher!"). There is a classical origin of course for these metaphorical associations of the bee, but in Emerson the figure embodies his constant vision of the transforming power of the imagination as it operates on the aggregations of the fancy.

In the aesthetic application of this model, we understand that genius transforms the gathered experiences into art. By way of the bee, we see also the naturalness of this transforming process; its wider analogy is the workings of nature, and these are visible most dramatically in Emerson's snowstorm. That equating of artistic creation with some form of great power appears repeatedly in the prose. In "The American Scholar" Emerson identified "the helpful giant" with the primitive force of the unschooled and natural. Only a transfer of metaphor is needed to make the snowstorm. Or it can be reached by the architecture metaphor with which the snowstorm poem ends. Emerson, in "The Poet," says of the poet that he "does not wait for the hero or the sage, but, as they act and think primarily, so he writes primarily what will and must be spoken, reckoning the others, though primaries also, yet, in respect to him, secondaries and servants; as sitters or models in the studio of a painter, or as assistants who bring building-materials to an architect" (*W* 3.7–8). Overlapping, merging, the analogues crowd forth—college, bumblebee, giant, painter-artist, and architect. They are the gatherers and transformers, the honeymakers and the builders, all those who make a new construction out of their gathered materials. The fury of this creation and its identification with nature come in a passage of prose on the great poets. All the emblems converge. "Every good poem that I know," says Emerson in "Poetry and Imagination," "I recall by its rhythm also [as well as its rhyme]. Rhyme is a pretty good measure of the latitude and opulence of a writer. If unskillful, he is at once detected by the poverty of his chimes. . . . Now try Spenser, Marlowe, Chapman, and see how wide they fly for weapons, and how rich and lavish their profusion. In their rhythm is no manufacture, but a vortex or musical tornado, which, falling on words and the experience of a learned mind, whirls these materials into the same grand order as planets and moons obey, and seasons, and monsoons" (*W* 8.49–50). Here is that habitual movement from flux and chaos to the orderly, from the changeable to the systematic or monumental. That conversion of the mind and the correlative binary view of nature's own processes are ultimately founded in the basic elements that structured Emerson's thought: movement and stasis, chaos and order, the passing and the permanent. The writer, says Emerson in "Poetry and Imagination," "needs a frolic health . . . he must be at the top of his condition. In that prosperity he is sometimes caught up into a perception of . . . funds of power hitherto utterly unknown to him, whereby he can transfer his visions to mortal canvas, or reduce them into iambic or trochaic, into lyric or heroic rhyme. These successes are not less admirable and astonishing to the poet than they are to his audience" (W 8.40). We have now in aggregate all of the primary analogies that structure the snow-storm poem, and, whereas earlier we were concerned with discovering the Emersonian linear arrangement and deliverance scheme of the poem, here it stands forth also as a concentrated poetics. While students may search the meteorological records of Concord for the early 1830s in search of an actual snowstorm source, we can satisfy ourselves that the much more demanding subject was Emerson the Artist's, and that was the idealized storm of poetic creation to which he yearned to submit. The poem is about a snowstorm and it is a program for poetry. It is worth quoting in its entirety:

> Announced by all the trumpets of the sky,
> Arrives the snow, and, driving o'er the fields,
> Seems nowhere to alight: the whited air
> Hides hills and woods, the river, and the heaven,
> And veils the farm-house at the garden's end.
> The sled and traveller stopped, the courier's feet
> Delayed, all friends shut out, the housemates sit
> Around the radiant fireplace, enclosed
> In a tumultuous privacy of storm.
>
>   Come see the north wind's masonry.
> Out of an unseen quarry evermore
> Furnished with tile, the fierce artificer
> Curves his white bastions with projected roof
> Round every windward stake, or tree, or door.
> Speeding, the myriad-handed, his wild work
> So fanciful, so savage, nought cares he
> For number or proportion. Mockingly,
> On coop or kennel he hangs Parian wreaths;
> A swan-like form invests the hidden thorn;
> Fills up the farmer's lane from wall to wall,
> Maugre the farmer's sighs; and at the gate
> A tapering turret overtops the work.
> And when his hours are numbered, and the world
> Is all his own, retiring, as he were not,
> Leaves, when the sun appears, astonished Art
> To mimic in slow structures, stone by stone,
> Built in an age, the mad wind's night-work,
> The frolic architecture of the snow.

Emerson's superb oxymorons—"tumultuous privacy," "fierce artificer," "so fanciful, so savage," "astonished Art," "slow structures," and "frolic architecture"—combine in a severely compacted way his idealized contraries of free imagination and ordered art. What seems chaotic, the storm, in the final perception is ordered, still, graceful, a part of nature itself in the way the Pyramids, St. Peter's, and the Parthenon are in the poem "The Problem." There is more: those freely formed contours of the snow sculpture rest upon but at the same time *obliterate* the rigid supporting forms beneath:

> So fanciful, so savage, nought cares he
> For number or proportion. Mockingly,
> On coop or kennel he hangs Parian wreaths;
> A swan-like form invests the hidden thorn;
> Fills up the farmer's lane from wall to wall.

The aesthetic principle behind the metaphor of the storm is central to Emerson's move toward more open compositional forms. He admonished writers not so much to await inspiration (this is a superficial view of Emerson's hardheaded methods) as to allow language strings, like snow, to fall into mimetic shapes: "Shun manufacture or the introducing an artificial arrangement in your thoughts, it will surely crack and come to nothing, but let alone tinkering and wait for the natural arrangement of your treasures." In the light of the poetics within the poem, we see as much an *aesthetic* sense in the famous thorn passage as a moral one. Emerson's moral stance was one with his aesthetics: poetry rightly shows the beautiful and ideal, and they in turn are moral because the humdrum and base are raised to the spiritual level. The moral and the aesthetic were to Emerson inseparable, as were the forces both of nature and human genius. As in "The Problem," it was an artist's philosophical system that had at its center not a moral point but the sensuous ideal of Beauty.

One final association and I shall be done with this line of exposition. When Emerson says in the essay "The Poet" that he sees nowhere among his contemporaries the poet of America, that is, the *genius* of the country, we understand now that he is calling for that great converting consciousness figured in the poetic snowstorm and in the great creative act of the helpful giant. The poet is to transform, like the bee, like the architect, like the storm itself, the vast and varied materials of the country into an aesthetic and visionary whole. That deep impulse to transform America to its noblest essence—at the same time to see it as an aesthetic whole—is Emerson's meaning when he says "America is a poem in our eyes." "We have yet had," he said, "no genius in America, with tyrannous eye, which knew the value of our incomparable materials" (W 3.37). What Emerson missed in the poets of past ages, as he contemplated the kind of ideal imagination needed to convert the diverse nation to *its* ideal, were the basic qualities that emerge in "The Snow-Storm": the epic-sized transforming imagination with language equal to the task. "If I have not found that excellent combination of gifts in my countrymen which I seek," Emerson said, "neither could I aid myself to fix the idea of the poet by reading now and then in Chalmer's collection of five centuries of English poets. These are wits more than poets, though there have been poets among them. But when we adhere to the ideal of the poet, we have our difficulties even with Milton and Homer. Milton is too literary, and Homer to literal and historical" (*W* 3.38). Emerson glimpsed that ideal poet in himself, animated as he was by a vision of what was possible. He had already freed himself from the literal by his constant process of transforming to the essence; he sought in theory a way to free himself also from the literary past that had no voice for his age. In the poems is the tirelessly worked ground of that theme.

The seer-genius stage of the imagination found expression in Emerson's structural drama through a dissociated voice, in a curious but habitual separation from his poet-speaker. We took account [elsewhere] of the admonitory voice of the deep Heart in "Threnody" which catechizes the mourning father and argues the way to consolation for the death of the son. That strategy of the wise countervoice has deep roots in Emerson's poetry. In his journal for 1845 he saw his own poetic role as that of a reporter of this voice of natural wisdom: "I will sing aloud and free / From the heart of the world" (*JMN* 9.168). Much earlier, in "The American Scholar," he considered this transmitting of the heart's voice to be one of the principal functions of the scholar: "Whatsoever oracles the human heart, in all emergencies, in all solemn hours, has uttered as its commentary on the world of actions,—these he [Man Thinking] shall receive and impart" (*W* 1.102). The schema of the separated poetic consciousness appears almost everywhere in the poetry. The dissociated voice, which is the expression of that schema, sounds conspicuously in "Hamatreya" (fancy speaks in the person of the farmers, the earth is the imagination), "Monadnoc" (the mountain speaks), "Woodnotes II" (the pinetree speaks), "To Ellen at the South" (flowers), "Hermione" (the dying Arab and Nature), "Celestial Love III" (God), "Saadi" (fakirs and the muse), "Dirge" (the bird), "May-Day" (old man), "Freedom" (spirit), "Boston Hymn" (God), "Voluntaries" (Destiny), "Boston" (the mountain, Boston, King George), "Solution" (the muse), "The Titmouse" (bird), "Seashore" (the sea), "Song of Nature" (nature), "Terminus" (the god Terminus), "The Poet" (the mighty). Even so selective a list indicates the fixity of Emerson's preoccupation.

Confronting a voice out of the heart of things was not uncommon in the work of Emerson's contemporaries, but it was less programmatic. The enchanting paradigm of the encounter occurs in the "Spring" section of *Walden,* where Thoreau finds himself present at Creation. The railroad bank thaws, flows into primal forms, and thereby speaks to Thoreau the language of the earth's original plan. "No wonder that the earth expresses itself outwardly in leaves, it so labors with the idea inwardly." Inwardly the earth speaks liquid words; outwardly they are leaves and wing feathers. Wet *love* becomes dry *leaf*. Thoreau's literal-mindedness was, characteristically, total. There are comparable meetings in Emily Dickinson, the essential text being "Further in Summer than the Birds," where the voice is the cricket nation's in a canticle of death. A similar encounter takes place in Frederick Tuckerman's great poem "The Cricket." In a rapt moment, the poet feels himself on the verge of conversing in the secret language of nature, drawn toward its mystery, and tempted finally to die into it (the dissolution that Yvor Winters called moral failure). In a later day, it is this direct encounter . . . that Robert Frost's solitary characters seek in the woods, even cry out for as in "The Most of It" but, with the exception of the mower in "The Tuft of Flowers," never accomplish. Because revelation, the eyeball experience, does not really come, Frost's is a poetry of aborted communion. A contemporary version of the instinctual heart-actor—predatory, brooding, bereft of light, yet stubborn, unkillable, wily, surviving—is Ted Hughes's crow.

Merlin is the lately-at-court figure in whom Emerson's own emblematic deep Heart, the technique of the separated voice, and his idea of the poet come together. The identification is most fully apparent if the poem "Merlin" is held alongside Emerson's extended remarks in "Poetry and Imagination." Emerson quotes in the essay as a high and memorable experience the section in *Morte d'Arthur* when Merlin speaks for the last time to Gawain from his enchanted prison in the forest. "Whilst I served King Arthur, I was well known by you and by other barons, but because I have left the court, I am known no longer, and put in forgetfulness, which I ought not to be if faith reigned in the world." The similarity to Emerson's leaving the ministry and his later ostracism because of the lecture to the divinity students is striking. Merlin continues: "you will never see me more, and that grieves me, but I cannot remedy it, and when you shall have departed from this place, I shall nevermore speak to you nor to any other person, save only my mistress; for never other person will be able to discover this place for anything which may befall; neither shall I ever go out from hence, for in the world there is no such strong tower as this wherein I am confined; and it is neither of wood, nor of iron, nor of stone, but of air" (W 8.61). This voice literally imprisoned in the heart of nature is Emerson's exemplary voice. He described that particular passage from *Morte d'Arthur* as the "height which attracts more than other parts, and is best remembered" (W 8.60). It is concerned with the voice Emerson believed poets should strive to hear and to transmit. Aspects of it rise again and again from other poems, most fervently in "Threnody," very pointedly in "The Problem," where the seer inside nature is the very figure the speaker cannot presume to be, even though he might wear the cowl that signifies it. The humbling voice issues from the center of all the circles: "Out from the heart of nature rolled / The burdens of the Bible old." But it also sounds in the forest, like Merlin's, to the lover's ear:

> The word by seers or sibyls told,
> In groves of oak, or fanes of gold,
> Still floats upon the morning wind,
> Still whispers to the willing mind.

Emerson sought that willing mind in the poem and in himself and elaborately projected it as Man Thinking. The poet of willing mind will earn his freedom and learn his craft from that voice of knowing nature. Merlin, then, is the exemplary poet, and in the Merlin poem Emerson stresses liberation from constraints of form, calls for artful thunder, and specifies the goal: "Great is the art, / Great be the manners, of the bard." Merlin is the authentic voice, Guy's is delusive, for despite all his pride of nature's cooperation, Guy gets only the oil. Merlin's

> blows are strokes of fate,
> Chiming with the forest tone,
> When boughs buffet boughs in the wood;
> Chiming with the gasp and moan
> Of the ice-imprisoned flood.

No simple meddling wit can stand with the angels, but rather only the propitious mind.

> There are open hours
> When the God's will sallies free,
> And the dull idiot might see
> The flowing fortunes of a thousand years.

Emerson also knew the blind moments. He experienced the failure of nature's language and the blockage of the poetic imagination when communication is shut down. The ambivalence cuts into the lines of "Merlin" which follow immediately and end the positive first section:

> Sudden, at unawares,
> Self-moved, fly-to the doors,
> Nor sword of angels could reveal
> What they conceal.

Edward Emerson accurately described Merlin as typifying for Emerson "the haughty, free and liberating poet, working the magic of thought through the charm of Art" (W 9.440). Merlin says the primal word because he is unencumbered by the courtly restraints of artifice. In Emerson's early journal version of the poem, the poet is admonished to reject the devices of the merely talented poets—"gentle touches," the tinklings of a guitar, telling "a pretty tale" only to "pretty people in a nice saloon," all false creations "borrowed from their expectation" (JMN 9.167–68). There are, instead, qualities of the self-reliant, manly figure in Emerson's poet. He described that unfettered myth-phallic figure in the powerful essay "Experience":

"The great and crescive self, rooted in absolute nature, supplants all relative existence and ruins the kingdom of mortal friendship and love" (*W* 3.77).

Among Emerson's constructs of the poetic imagination, the central one is Merlin. All those dissociated voices speaking out of his poems are versions of that central poet.

The figures crowd Emerson's verse. In "Threnody" alone . . . there are three: young Waldo as the budding poet dead before his time, the desperate father as the failed poet-seer, and the deep Heart as the thunder-poet out of the volcano.

The variety of forms this allegory takes attests to the obsessiveness of the poet's role in Emerson's thought. He could be quite literal-minded in pointing out likenesses. Some of the psychological faddists of his time—people he believed capable of controlling other individuals because they possessed an absolute "natural" power—share, perhaps debased a bit, the ways of the poet. Among examples of "the action of man upon nature with his entire force,—with reason as well as understanding" Emerson includes "Animal Magnetism" and "the miracles of enthusiasm" as reported by Swedenborg, Hohenloke, and the Shakers. These, say Emerson, are examples of "Reason's momentary grasp of the sceptre; the exertions of a power which exists not in time or space, but an instantaneous in-streaming causing power" (*W* 1.73).

Emerson's literal-mindedness in this respect is unique. It was his attempt to make his insights available to the common man, *to make the poet's revelation a democratic enterprise*. This distinguishes him in a fundamental way from the willfully alienated poet-seers of the Romantic temper. The convention of isolation was a concomitant of the higher vision with its sight of revelation. Frank Kermode defines the direct correlation between "these two beliefs—in the Image as a radiant truth out of space and time, and in the necessary isolation or estrangement of men who can perceive it." Not so with Emerson. He refused to promote the fanciful isolation of the seer-poet but rather, as he says in "Merlin," strove to open the doors, making the vision available to all who would attempt it. In so doing, he staked out the fundamental American variant to the central Romantic myth.

Carl Strauch calls Emerson's poet figures masks: "Uriel, Merlin, Saadi, these are poetic masks for the attributes and functions of the poet as Emerson saw them. Uriel is an archetypal emblem of the rebellious intellect, Merlin typifies power, and Saadi represents the cheerful acceptance of isolation until the propitious moment has arrived for the poet to deliver his message." Beyond these, however, and enclosing them all is the basic figure of the perceiving imagination. The variety of versions indicates how obsessive this theoretical subject was for Emerson. Uriel, for example, who possessed a "look that solved the sphere" and who is able to declare "Line in nature is not found" and "Evil will bless, and ice will burn," acts as much the role of a conscious eyeball as a resigned minister or the rebellious deliverer of the Divinity School address. Each role contributes to his conception of the liberated and liberating poet, which is to say that while the free and imaginative man took many forms in Emerson, he was never distinct from the poet, whether Man Thinking or angel rebelling.

One inevitably sees "Brahma" as a version of the poet. Here again is Emerson on the eye: "The eye is the best of artists. By the mutual action of its structure and of the laws of light, perspective is produced, which integrates every mass of objects, of what character soever, into a well colored and shaded globe, so that where the particular objects are mean and unaffecting, the landscape which they compose is round and symmetrical" (W 1.15). Condensed here is every basic element of Emerson's structural poetics: the converting imagination as the eyeball, its structure integral with nature, its highly selective and transforming power over reality, the consequent reduction of reality to a symmetrical moral equation. The prose contains the aesthetic and the moral geometry of the poem "Brahma," with the Oriental consciousness as the transforming center of the poem. It is Emerson's basic model of the world as seen through a shaping eyeball that merges the moral and aesthetic imagination and inevitably abstracts reality to a scheme inseparable from that vision. Brahma is one of Emerson's ultimate poets and, not surprisingly, the poem for all its economy and control presents the moral and aesthetic problem of his poetry. The final line, in that habitual Emersonian movement, dismisses the half-god of a human belief ("turn thy back on heaven") for the whole but abstract purity of the ideal vision.

There are yet other poet figures. The poet in "The Sphinx," overheard by the yet more complete mind of the poet's maker, literally converts the beast from ugliness to beauty, from mystery to intelligibility, liberating mankind as befits the poet Emerson described as a liberating god. The Sphinx is ponderous fact; the poet transforms it into bright Truth. In a similar plot, though less dramatic, the protagonists in "The Rhodora" and "Each and All" who are failed poets as the poems begin, come, through the auspices of nature, to their own revelation of the natural symmetry of the world's beauty and the imagination ("Rhodora": "The self-same Power that brought me there brought you"), and a fresh recognition that the higher unity includes man ("Each and All": "Beauty through my senses stole; / I yielded myself to the perfect whole").

Nonhuman actors embody types of the artist, as we saw in "The Snow-Storm." Another actor is the humble-bee. As he transforms the materials of his foraging, he plays the part of the imagination. The same qualities of intellectual nomadism, in characteristic Emerson fashion, circulate in all his actors. The "forest seer" in "Woodnotes I," while justifiably identified as Thoreau in literal readings of the poem (see Edward Emerson's note, W 9.420), is very much the poet as a personified bee! The terms are identical:

> It seemed that Nature could not raise
> A plant in any secret place . . .
> But he would come in the very hour
> It opened in its virgin bower . . .
> It seemed as if the breezes brought him,
> It seemed as if the sparrows taught him;
> As if by secret sight he knew
> Where, in far fields, the orchis grew . . .
> What others did at distance hear,
> And guessed within the thicket's gloom,
> Was shown to this philosopher,
> And at his bidding seemed to come.

"In poetry," Emerson says, "we say we require the miracle. The bee flies among the flowers, and gets mint and marjoram, and generates a new product, which is not mint and marjoram, but honey . . . and the poet listens to conversation and beholds all objects in Nature, to give back, not them, but a new and transcendent whole" (W 8.16–17). There is a further loop in this skein of concern with the poet and the imagination. Emerson says in the essay "The Poet" that the Ancients remind us that poets speak "not with intellect alone but with the intellect inebriated by nectar" (W 3.27). In the Emersonian aesthetic, the nectar is visionary. Having come round by way of snowstorm, Brahma, and bee, we recognize how deep-drawing is the concern in the poem "Bacchus" with the poetic enterprise. A colossal ballast of aesthetic rumination feeds the urgent imperatives of the poet-speaker:

> Give me of the true . . .
> Wine of wine,
> Blood of the world,
> Form of forms, and mould of statures,
> That I intoxicated,
> And by the draught assimilated,
> May float at pleasure through all natures;
> The bird-language rightly spell,
> And that which roses say so well.

A circuit closes between this poem and the Sphinx poem that Emerson had placed at the head of the 1846 edition:

> I thank the joyful juice
> For all I know,—
> Winds of remembering
> Of the ancient being blow,
> And seeming-solid walls of use
> Open and flow.

"Imagination intoxicates the poet," Emerson tells us (W 3.30), and the poet in turn, by his clarifying symbols, intoxicates and therefore liberates men. The poetic act centers in the plenitude of the single imagination, self-intoxicating. This is the aesthetic equivalent in his poetics of what Emerson called in social and moral contexts the self-reliant man.

We are not done with versions of the poet. The pinetree in "Woodnotes II" admonishes the poet-listener in a long discourse marked by some of Emerson's most egregious rhymes and meters:

> "Come learn with the fatal song
> Which knits the world in music strong,—
> Come lift thine eyes to lofty rhymes . . .
> I, that to-day am a pine,
> Yesterday was a bundle of grass.
> He [God, the eternal Pan] is free and libertine,
> Pouring of his power the wine
> To every age, to every race;
> Unto every race and age
> He emptieth the beverage;
> Unto each, and unto all,
> Maker and original."

God, Bacchus, humble-bee, forest seer, Uriel, Brahma, pinetree: all are versions of the poet and types of the imagination just as Bulkeley, Hunt, and Willard, Guy, the mourning father, the hiker in the snowy woods (and many more both early and late) are figures of the merely acquisitive or perceiving sense. Ideas of the aesthetic transaction were so crucial to Emerson's imagination that even the rifles that fire the shot in "Concord Hymn," as we shall discover, inescapably figure as yet another version of the imagination. We shall reach that disclosure by leaving off now the examples of structures of the imagination in the poems to see how Emerson's conception of the *process* of the poetic alembic lies equally deep and formative in the poetry.

Wordsworth said that objects should be reported not as they are but as they seem, and it is the seeming that is literally reported. In Emerson's poetry, the process of conversion is reported, the apparent subjects being thus quite interchangeable. The poems, no matter what objects occupy their vision, enact the process of the beholding and coenergizing mind as it transforms reality on the way from the nerve ends to the mind in that now familiar train of conversion from sensation to experience to thought.

This transfer of energy inevitably rests on the pairs that stand behind the spirals that Emerson's figurative thought favored. These different structural metaphors are related. His circles and spirals are the connecting motions of the mind as it plays over the fundamental dialectic, which takes the form of horizontal and vertical dualities. The horizontal doubleness embraces the reassuring paired structure of nature that everywhere manifests the universal symmetry. Emerson located himself pleasurably in that cosmic rhyme. As he put it in a marvelous lexical playback: "The animals are sick with love, / Lovesick with rhyme." The vertical duality consists in the Platonic division of experience into lower shadows of Becoming and the higher light of Being. Across this grid of two dimensions Emerson conceived the imagination playing its constant act of conversion. In the poems, the conversion arcs again and again.

The more complicated motions of conversion I traced in several poems: facts transformed to principle in "The Snow-Storm," "Humble-bee," "Each and All," "Rhodora." Its outline rationalizes the otherwise awkward and even fractured progress of "Threnody," a major display of the powerful structural set of Emerson's aesthetic beliefs. A revealing occasion occurs in "Each and All," where the conversion seems made with little conviction, almost as a gratuitous assertion. It is in fact the structure of Emerson's poetics right on the surface, with no shadowing allegory. Instead, in a kind of eyeball instance, there is an abrupt transfer of fact into thought at the end of the poem. The revelation arrives out of the blue with no explanation of how the "facts" fly together in the viewer's mind to make the instructive principle.

> I said, "I covet truth;
> Beauty is unripe childhood's cheat;
> I leave it behind with the games of youth:"—
> As I spoke, beneath my feet
> The ground-pine curled its pretty wreath,
> Running over the club-moss burrs;
> I inhaled the violet's breath;
> Around me stood the oaks and firs;
> Pine-cones and acorns lay on the ground;
> Over me soared the eternal sky,
> Full of light and of deity;
> Again I saw, again I heard,
> The rolling river, the morning bird;—
> Beauty through my senses stole;
> I yielded myself to the perfect whole.

We can see in this apparently random list of natural things the familiar Platonic structure of the high and low: the ground-pine beneath the towering trees; the fallen acorns beneath the soaring and eternal sky. In what seems a casual but is surely a deliberate symmetry are what Emerson called the visual rhymes of nature. Out of the details of this picture, the cosmic coherence is more or less taken on trust. The viewer in the poem, at the outset a poet lacking imagination and possessing a fragmenting scientific mind, wins through despite himself to a final ideal vision. Because the process is so mechanically delivered here, "Each and All" discloses the assumptions in the deeper part of Emerson's consciousness. There is almost no surface enactment of the process of conversion. In a revealing prose passage, Emerson came no closer to explaining that buried transfer: "It is easier to read Sanscrit, to decipher the arrow-head character, than to interpret . . . familiar sights. It is even much to name them. Thus Thomson's 'Seasons' and the best parts of many old and many new poets are simply enumerations by a person who felt the beauty of the common sights and sounds, without any attempt to draw a moral or affix a meaning" (W 8.22–23).

The most fully drawn conversion unfolds in "The Snow-Storm." It is a process that reaches back to the mythopoeic confrontation in "The Sphinx," the individual deciphering the code of his existence. Poem after poem, as it enacts the conversion, points to the centrality of this movement in Emerson's mind. In "Berrying" the occasion is virtually identical to that in "Each and All," revealing now as well its links to other poems, like "The Titmouse":

> "May be true what I had heard,—
> Earth's a howling wilderness,
> Truculent with fraud and force,"
> Said I, strolling through the pastures,
> And along the river-side.
> Caught among the blackberry vines,
> Feeding on the Ethiops sweet,
> Pleasant fancies overtook me.
> I said, "What influence me preferred,
> Elect, to dreams thus beautiful?"
> The vines replied, "And didst thou deem
> No wisdom from our berries went?"

The poem "Étienne de la Boéce," based on a friendship of Montaigne's, is a rare and stunning example where the process obsessive to Emerson the artist dominated even the treatment of this historical relationship. Once again the goal of the poem is to disclose the essential value of the experience, which for the Montaigne-Emerson figure is the divine spark that makes a "resistant" manhood, not simply a shadow of Boéce but his equal in inspiration. We recognize how much like Brahma is that miraculously transforming sour Emerson ascribes to Montaigne:

> if I could,
> In severe or cordial mood,
> Lead you rightly to my altar,
> Where the wisest Muses falter,
> And worship that world-warming spark
> Which dazzles me in midnight dark,
> Equalizing small and large,
> While the soul it doth surcharge,
> Till the poor is wealthy grown,
> And the hermit never alone,—
> The traveller and the road seem one

> With the errand to be done,—
> That were a man's and lover's part,
> That were Freedom's whitest chart.

The same converting process exists as a plaintive fixation of the artist who speaks in "Blight." The poem begins with what is now familiar to us as the act of drawing the visionary out of the factual. Again, the syntax is demanding because completion is deliberately suspended:

> Give me truths;
> For I am weary of the surfaces,
> And die of inanition. If I knew
> Only the herbs and simples of the wood,
> Rue, cinquefoil, gill, vervain and agrimony,
> Blue-vecht and trillium, hawkweed, sassafras,
> Milkweeds and murky brakes, quaint pipes and sundew,
> And rare and virtuous roots, which in these woods
> Draw untold juices from the common earth,
> Untold, unknown, and I could surely spell
> Their fragrance, and their chemistry apply
> By sweet affinities to human flesh,
> Driving the foe and stablishing the friend,—
> O, that were much, and I could be a part
> Of the round day, related to the sun
> And planted world, and full executor
> Of their imperfect functions.

Here is the characteristic recognition once more of the deep forces that generate the green outer world's language. It was the way Emerson sought the significance of the life around him, and it was the way of his poems.

The conversion act is imminent in "Days." He described the scholar as "watching days and months sometimes for a few facts" (*W* 1.101). His speaker in "May-Day" saw hidden in the spring days the gods themselves:

> I saw them mask their awful glance
> Sidewise meek in gossamer lids . . .
> It was as if the eternal gods,
> Tired of their starry periods,
> Hid their majesty in cloth
> Woven of tulips and painted moth.

The man in his pleached garden is one more Emersonian poet waiting for the revelation. The association is suggested by an 1843 journal entry: "Somebody . . . saw in a dream a host of angels descending with salvers of glory in their hands. On asking one of them for whom those were intended, he answered, 'for Shaikh Saadi of Shiraz, who has written a stanza of poetry that has met the approbation of God Almighty' "

(W 9.447–448). The same archetypal visitation constitutes the central metaphor in the early poem "The Day's Ration." As in "Days," the awaiting consciousness, the mind's chalice, cannot take the inflow:

> To-day, when friends approach, and every hour
> Brings book, or starbright scroll of genius,
> The little cup will hold not a bead more,
> And all the costly liquor runs to waste.

A specific emphasis in "Days" is worth noting: the imagination confronts not only visionary moments but actual days. Emerson, as his journals show, was acutely aware of the facts of his own days, from political and economic to intellectual, and he searched them with the poet's transfiguring imagination for their essential truth. He urged the same on every poet. The pleached garden of his poem was already implicit in a passage from the essay "The Poet" seven years earlier: "I look in vain for the poet whom I describe. We do not with sufficient plainness or sufficient profoundness address ourselves to life, nor dare we chaunt our own times and social circumstance. If we filled the day with bravery, we should not shrink from celebrating it. Time and nature yield us many gifts" (W 3.37). I shall have more to say [elsewhere] about Emerson's occasional depiction of the poet as a reluctant converter, for this passivity is one of the crucial aspects of the deeply idealistic structure of the imagination. For the present, we can see that "Days" provides the quintessential converting situation undisguised. The poem has no diversionary subject—a walk, a bereavement, a characterization—but like "The Sphinx" deals directly with a conspicuous allegory of the imagination confronting reality. The conversion fails, and we are surprised by Emerson's explicit depiction of the defeat:

> I, in my pleached garden, watched the pomp,
> Forgot my morning wishes, hastily
> Took a few herbs and apples, and the Day
> Turned and departed silent. I, too late,
> Under her solemn fillet saw the scorn.

"Days" takes account of untranslatable realities rarely brought into Emerson's poetry. Here is an occasion when experience presents itself but is not taken up, as if it were unintelligible to the poet-viewer. This is a lurking nightmare in Emerson that readers often miss. The balletic imagery of "Days" does not penetrate to the depth . . . in "Threnody," but the desperation over a whole reality that goes unperceived and unconverted is as genuine.

Successful conversion takes place almost everywhere else in Emerson's poetry. The opening of second sight into the compensatory plan of nature manages to occur. As each poem makes its drama out of that process, each then is a variation of the transparent-eyeball experience at the visionary heart of *Nature*. The eyeball conversion is the accelerated ideal. The others in the individual poems, though they may be extended out in time for dramatic purposes, are in fact deliberately slackened examples of that one ecstatic act of the poetic imagination.

Seen in its full coherence, the eyeball process defines the aesthetics of Emerson's moral beliefs by establishing the emblematic equation between the physical eye and the poetic imagination. It is the single, homely metaphor in which the Platonic terms Emerson adopted for himself converge in an instant dependence of form upon soul. Once we see the centrality of this crucial image, we recognize how it ramifies into other analogies. The pleached garden of "Days," in which the poet stands passively and enclosed, is itself a sort of enlarged eyeball and the two figures in turn make a metaphor for the receiving consciousness. In the allegory of "Days," that consciousness confronts reality in the form of maidens. Exotic, their appearance distracts the fancy of the waiting man, and the encounter fails of revelation. What did *not* happen is the poem's subject, and we find it described in "Poetry and Imagination": "The test of the poet is the power to take the passing day, with its news, its cares, its fears, as he shares them, and hold it up to a divine reason, till he sees it to have a purpose and beauty, and to be related to astronomy and history and the eternal order of the world"(*W* 8.35).

There are inescapable consequences, both for Emerson's view of reality and for his perception of contemporary culture, in this idea of the poetic imagination and its relation to reality. He called the eye the best of artists, integrating groups of things so that where particular objects are mean and unaffecting, the landscape they compose is round and symmetrical. That vision of balanced wholeness composes the "each" and the "all"; the individual reality, of whatever form or moral state, is part of the whole, being swept up in a final aesthetic incorporation. Particulars are sacrificed to the demands of the symmetrical, dramatic, and moral whole. The perceiving eye registers a world whose moral and cultural disparities, whose tragic possibilities, and whose grey ambiguities and indefiniteness disappear in the aesthetic compass and balance. The overviewing eye has no vision capable of rendering the finer lines of reality. If the world we live in is the words we use, then the world Emerson's poetry saw is the poetry that Emerson wrote. The vision sacrificed the possible subjective life of individual poems to the underlying structure of a harmonizing aesthetic theory.

Emerson returned again and again in the poems to the image of monumentality. It seems a repudiation of the dynamism in the essay "Circles," for instance, and in the circular poems "Brahma" and "Uriel," where perceptual motion pushes out from concentrated centers of self-knowledge to the edges of dispersal. That yielding to the perfect whole is the plot of many familiar outward-flowing passages from the poems, but the little-noticed monument image . . . came out of the poetics and determined the focus of some of the poems. The monument stands against the flux, providing stasis amid the onwardness and outwardness of Emerson's contrary images. It is an integral part of the mind's converting process even though it seems a compromise of Emerson's concept of natural organicism. It most certainly is a departure from the biological figure upon which Coleridge depended in discussing art. There is a strong sense of deliberate craftsmanship in Emerson's view of the artist. A monument stands at the end of "Threnody," an objective parallel to the consolation of the deep Heart as it unfolds the larger purpose in which the boy's death is made intelligible as well as blessed.

The snowstorm poem follows the metaphor of architecture, the graceful forms taking shape by the savage and chaotic labors of the storm. The oxymoron "frolic architecture" captures that instantaneous creation of stasis from movement, order from chaos, and beauty from savagery. The contradictory joining of "fierce" and "artificer" holds the paradox of wild genius issuing in graceful form. In "The Problem" the most noble expression of genius takes the form of buildings: the Parthenon, the Pyramids, St. Peter's, and England's abbeys. "Out of Thought's interior sphere / These wonders rose to upper air." Buildings, then, are emblems of inspired genius. In Emerson's ordering system, as in Pythagoras's, the fixed is associated with the preferred (bright, straight, male) and with eternal values (the good, the one). The realm of shifting values and Becoming (many, female, moving) is associated with flux. But Emerson, like Swedenborg, could sit without terror in the midst of flux, among the "hated waves." The poem "Illusions" speaks of "the endless imbroglio" of this universe where "no anchorage is." But the vision leads Emerson not to existential terror, but rather to the durable confidence that Arnold admired.

> first shalt thou know,
> That in the wild turmoil,
> Horsed on the Proteus,
> Thou ridest to power,
> And to endurance.

Monumentality has two principal associations for Emerson, and they merge in the figure of the poet. The first association is philosophical, that monumentality is a way of standing in the world. The second association is aesthetic, that monumentality is a way of conceiving art in its relationship to that world. Philosophically, the monumental is principled firmness. In "Ode: Inscribed to W. H. Channing," for example, whoever does not stand fast to principle is on the side of ignorance, slavery, and chaos. In Emerson's bitter closing parable, the Muse is the solid mooring point when the victors divide and "Half for freedom strike and stand." The positive philosophical association is emphatic in "Monadnoc" where the poet-speaker proclaims the virtues of the mountain:

> Man in these crags a fastness find
> To fight pollution of the mind;

> In the wide thaw and ooze of wrong,
> Adhere like this fountain strong,
> The insanity of towns to stem
> With simpleness for strategem.

This is a virtuous monumentality to set beside Robert Frost's definition of poetry as a momentary stay against confusion. It is Platonic Being set against Becoming. The man who sees the immutable and can make the permanent symbol of it is the poet. Emerson says in the essay "The Poet": "He is the poet and shall draw us with love and terror, who sees through the flowing vest the firm nature, and can declare it" (W 3.37). Swedenborg . . . was one of Emerson's early heroes who fulfilled that role: "Swedenborg, of all men in the recent ages, stands eminently for the translator of nature into thought. . . . Before him the metamorphosis continually plays" (W 3.35).

To Emerson, the thought that is taken from the flowing metamorphosis was the artifact itself, and that is the aesthetics of his monumentality. Thought put into language—poem, essay, lecture—was a fixed entity, a verbal monument. There was no doubt the biblical association: "The word unto the prophet spoken / Was writ on tables yet unbroken." In "Uriel," with spirited humor, Emerson parodied the lesser documents of order, the "Laws of form, and metre first," even the calendar of months and days, which the vain young gods discuss. It is Uriel who "solves the sphere" with his higher knowledge ("Line in nature is not found"), and immediately Fate's balance beam gives way and heaven slides to confusion.

In the poem "To Ellen," the lives of the two lovers are intelligible only as they are recorded on a page:

> And Ellen, when the graybeard years
>   Have brought us to life's evening hour
> And all the crowded Past appears
>   A tiny scene of sun and shower,
> Then, if I read the page aright
>   Where Hope, the soothsayer, reads our lot,
> Thyself shalt own the page was bright
>   Well that we loved, woe had we not.

Emerson's neoclassical predilection for attaching general values to monuments, seeing life over the shoulder as exemplum, straitjacketed his poetry. The fixity at the end of "The Snow-Storm," despite the summoning of savage genius and colossal artistic energy, makes the closing exclusionary, cold, and inanimate. Whitman managed a more difficult unity by inclusion. His reality was not abstracted into monuments but, by a new linguistic drift and sweep, caught up not only the contradictions but the wayward drama of experience taking form.

Emerson's impulse toward liberation in his philosophy, in his life, and in his art equaled his need for monuments. Structure and constraint, the "virtue of self-trust," appear in the middle essays "Montaigne" and "Experience" as necessary modes for life, just as the young Emerson acknowledged the utility of custom, as here in the early poem "Grace":

> How much, preventing God, how much I owe
> To the defences thou has round me set;
> Example, custom, fear, occasion slow.

But Emerson's compulsion toward liberation in the name of imaginative exploration and deep-diving moral and aesthetic discovery, the discovery of self, was the dynamo of his existence. It sounded in his poems at times with exultant tones. More often it was a plaintive undertheme in which the artist considered the ideal ability to feel fully and to give fully in his art.

Liberation paired in Emerson's mind with power, as if the imagination, once freed from material vanities, could possess the resources of nature itself. The circulation of nature's forces concentrated and replenished the sources of imaginative energy. The poet, Emerson wrote, "is capable of a new energy . . . by abandonment to the nature of things" (W 3.26). In "The American Scholar," he saw no dissipation of this energy once tapped: "There is never a beginning, there is never an end, to the inexplicable continuity of this web of God, but always circular power returning into itself" (W 1.85). Once gathered by the poetic imagination, ideally transformed into poetry, this concentrated power liberates mankind. Readers of poetry, he said, are like persons who come out of a cave or cellar into the open air. It was a new way of seeing that comes when men are freed, as Gertrude Stein was to say about Picasso's revolution, from the habit of knowing what they are looking at. Emerson's dilemma, then, was not in the theory of goals, but in the creation of a language that could grasp the energies of liberation.

In the geology of his poems this liberation from closed forms recurs as the principal but sometimes buried meaning. In "Brahma," as I pointed out earlier, the admonition "turn thy back on heaven" is less a rejection of Christian doctrine than a summons to the higher imagination to turn away from single forms of seeing. "Form is imprisonment and heaven itself a decoy," he wrote in his journal a decade earlier (*JMN* 9.322). And before that, in the essay "The Poet," he said: "Every thought is also a prison; every heaven is also a prison (W 3.33). The admonition in "Brahma" is echoed earlier still in "The Sphinx" as the Poet describes man's instinctual restlessness:

> The heavens that now draw him
>   With sweetness untold
> Once found,—for new heavens
>   He spurneth the old.

"The Sphinx" was a bold credo of the poet's liberating crusade. By a parable, because to be explicit about the poet as the converter of the world was absurdly heady, the poem set out the goal of the poet, the goal of Emerson's book of poems, the goal of Emerson the artist. Other poets, extending out to the limits of Emerson's poetic canon, by one plot or another follow the same impulse. In "Bacchus" it takes the form of intoxication; in "Give All to Love" it is transacted in the exchange of half-gods for the gods. Each was a reenactment of the archetypal release from the cave into the sun. As in "Threnody" and all the others, that linear arrangement of dramatic action led in the same direction. With such assumptions so dominant in Emerson's vision, it is not surprising that in poems like "Rhodora" and "Each and All" the revelation arrives presumptuously. The archetype is more integral in the structure of "Uriel" and "The Snow-Storm." Rarely, however, was that mental chain that leads to revelation broken or distorted.

Emerson, to our great relief, took account of the contrary workings of fate and the preposterous optimism of his poet's credo. In "Nemesis," following the rhetorical question "Will a woman's fan the oceans smooth?" we find the counterclaim:

> In spite of Virtue and the Muse,
> Nemesis will have her dues,
> And all our struggles and our toils
> Tighter wind the giant coils.

This dire aspect Harold Bloom emphasizes in plotting the dark-bright dialectic in Emerson's world. But though Emerson came to grips with the negation of his idealist philosophy, the set of his deepest beliefs assumed a powerful converting imagination whose function in turn necessarily assumed the free state into which art was to liberate all men.

Emerson's poetic theory was so powerful a generator of his poems that it molded to its own shape even the goegraphical and historical facts of the Concord battle that opened the Revolutionary War. The landscape, the action, and the actors he selected for the ceremonial poem "Concord Hymn" were an artist's choice. It was an unlikely vehicle for a theory of poetry, but there was no material that could withstand alteration in the deep set of Emerson's mind.

Most famous of all American works of the artistic mind, "Concord Hymn" took its shape and hidden concerns from the poetics. Emerson wrote the poem in 1837 when he was thirty-four for the dedication of the Revolutionary battle monument raised at Concord on July Fourth of that year. The citizens of Concord sang the poem's sixteen lines to the tune of the familiar hymn "Old Hundred." There were prayers and an address by a congressman. The local paper said the hymn spoke for itself, exciting "ideas of originality" and "poetic genius." Emerson himself was absent from the ceremony, visiting his in-laws in Plymouth and trying to get over a cold.

This year was the watershed of Emerson's life. On April 21, 1837, he wrote in his journal his own declaration of independence from guilt over his choice of writing as a profession. Like the Massachusetts industrialists, Emerson surmised, the writer did not depend on the weather. He could stop his own "morbid sympathy" for the farmers every time New England temperatures fell. "Climate touches not my own work," he concluded. "Where they have the sun, let them plant; we who have it not, will drive our pens." He declared with elation, "I am gay as a canary bird with this new knowledge." And then he announced: "I will write and so teach my countrymen their office" (*JMN* 5.301).

While Emerson prepared his hymn, his great address "The American Scholar" was also taking form in his journal. He had been invited on June 22, at short notice, to be a substitute speaker and deliver the Phi Beta Kappa address at Harvard College on August 31. That speech, as Holmes said, was America's intellectual Declaration of Independence. The audacity of it still shocks us if we look at the proposition Emerson makes. The work of the native scholar was to be nothing less than "the conversion of the world." Emerson's purpose, he announced at the beginning, was to awaken "the sluggard intellect of this continent," and to free it from subservience to the Old World. "We will walk on our own feet; we will work with our own hands," he declared. "It is for you," he charged the young men at Cambridge, "to dare all."

At this high-running time of his life, Emerson's journal is filled with the urgent language from which he eventually extracted passages for more than three dozen essays and lectures. His personal life was equally crowded. Among his many activities, he finished delivering a series of lectures in Boston on the philosophy of history, planted thirty-one fruit trees near his house, corresponded with Thomas Carlyle in London, took lessons in German pronunciation from the formidable Margaret Fuller, and resisted his brother's entreaties to put some of the inheritance from his deceased first wife into a real-estate venture on Staten Island.

He records his alarm at the condition of the country. The times are bleak with fear of economic collapse. Men are breaking, and there is a run on banks in Boston and New York. The Exchange in New Orleans is burned. Emerson grieves for "the desponding hearts of the people in these black times." Yet "Concord Hymn" with its soaring affirmation never swerved from Emerson's first concern, freedom from stifling conventions. Here is the complete poem:

> By the rude bridge that arched the flood,
>   Their flag to April's breeze unfurled,
> Here once the embattled farmers stood
>   And fired the shot heard round the world.
>
> The foe long since in silence slept;
>   Alike the conqueror silent sleeps;
> And Time the ruined bridge has swept
>   Down the dark stream which seaward creeps.

> On this green bank, by this soft stream,
>   We set to-day a votive stone;
> That memory may their deed redeem,
>   When, like our sires, our sons are gone.
>
> Spirit, that made those heroes dare
>   To die, and leave their children free,
> Bid Time and Nature gently spare
>   The shaft we raise to them and thee.

"Concord Hymn" is an Emersonian conversion poem. The several binary pairings mirror the same pattern in his other poems. "Justice is the rhyme of things" he said in "Merlin," which keeps "truth undecayed." Those paired elements—in setting, actors, action, and time—are visible in "Concord Hymn": the river and the land, the soft stream and the stone shaft, the conqueror and the foe, the deed and the memory, sires and their sons, the battlefield and the wide round world, the stream and the sea, the heroes and their children, Time and Nature (the *rude* bridge becomes in line seven a *ruined* bridge), then and now. The close interior rhyme of bridge *swept* and votive stone *set* focuses, perhaps without Emerson's conscious design, his basic opposition of what is in motion and what holds fast. Symbolically, every pair divides in Pythagorean fashion along Emerson's line between the transient and the permanent.

The conversion process goes on everywhere. The flux of battle becomes the stasis of the monument, the fact becomes the ideal of freedom, matter becomes spirit, the stream finds its way to the world-coiling sea, and Concord's battle becomes the world's battle cry. The arching conversion is the death and transubstantiation of the original actors who, like Bulkeley, Hunt, and Willard of "Hamatreya," pass into dust and are held by the abiding earth. Foe and conqueror alike have become one. The high truth has been revealed in the Concord fight. Every element participates in the elaborate process.

Because it is under the dictate of that deep structure, the shot heard round the world sets up a veritable hum of resonances from other poems. The shot is an audible variant of "that world-warming spark / Which dazzles me in midnight dark, / Equalizing small and large" from the poem "Étienne de la Boéce." Twenty years to the day after the monument ceremony, Emerson picked up the analogy in the recently laid Atlantic cable, commemorated in his "Ode: Sung in the Town Hall, Concord, July 4, 1857." Cannons boom from town to town in that poem, but the cable is to carry the earth-circling song:

> henceforth there shall be no chain,
>   Save underneath the sea
> The wires shall murmur through the main
>   Sweet songs of liberty.

Emerson himself got word of the cable hookup to America while he was on the camping trip to the Adirondacks in 1858. He reports in his poetic account that two campers return with news of

> the wire-cable laid beneath the sea,
> And landed on our coast, and pulsating
> With ductile fire.

"We have few moments in the longest life," he then declares, "Of such delight and wonder as there grew." Electricity was now schooled to spell "with guided tongue man's messages / Shot through the weltering pit of the salt sea." These echoing lines transmit a single idea and share visual forms and symbolic associations, for the trajectory of the bullet and the path of the cable make actual arcs that become conceptual circles that travel around the world.

Uriel, a poet figure, sees a world whose apparently straight lines bend into the closing arcs that structure the universe. His voice has the effect of a shot, and the result parallels the Emersonian revelatory "shudder of joy":

> As Uriel spoke with piercing eye,
> A shudder ran around the sky.

Stephen Whicher suggested the relationship of this shooting figure to Emerson's poetics. Referring to the essay "Circles" and to "Uriel" he wrote: "Both speak for Emerson's pride in the explosive properties of his thought, and his ill-concealed delight at the thought of the havoc he could weak— if people were once to listen to him."

Emerson's prose repeatedly links poets and soldiers. He conceived his self-reliant man as an embattled defender at the parapets. He says in the lecture series he began in Boston in 1836, entitled "The Philosophy of History," "Society must come again under the yoke of the base and selfish, but the individual heart faithful to itself is fenced with a sacred palisado not to be traversed or approached unto, and is free forevermore." To his mind the thundering affectiveness of the poet was a manly virtue to be preferred to the character of Bryant's poems, Greenough's sculpture, and Dr. Channing's preaching. Of these he said: "They are all *feminine* or receptive and not masculine or creative" (*JMN* 5.195). He idealized the devastating power possible in public address, whose form he described in his journal as "a panharmonicon,—every note on the longest gamut, from the explosion of cannon to the tinkle of a guitar. Let us try it Folly, Custom, Convention and Phlegm cannot hear our sharp artillery" (*JMN* 7.265). The orator feels the discharge the same as the soldier: "The least effect of the oration is on the orator. Yet it is something; a faint recoil; a kicking of the gun" (*JMN* 5.362). To reestablish Adam in the garden, to recover our power and mission as divine beings, he says elsewhere, we "must fire . . . the artillery of sympathy and emotion" against "the mechanical powers and the mechanical philosophy of this time" (*JMN* 7.271)

The poets are liberating gods. The Concord minutemen are liberating poets. At the heart of the identification is the chief element in Emerson's concept of the poetic imagination: power and the ability to convert the present act into the ideal vision it contains. Emerson's passage in "Poetry and Imagination" now rings with added resonance: the poet "reads in the word or action of the man its yet untold results. His inspiration is power to carry out and complete the metamorphosis" (*W* 8.39). The crucial passage describing conversion in "The American Scholar" reveals how he identified Man Thinking, poet in action, and soldier with his musket: the world "came into him life; it went out from him truth. It came to him short-lived actions; it went out from him immortal thoughts. It came to him business; it went from him poetry. It was dead fact; now, it is quick thought" (*W* 1.87). The shot at Concord is like a poem of freedom, the riflemen are figures of the imagination. What came to them as lead musketballs went from them as the force that would convert the world. It was a marvelous allegory of the brave belief in "Poetry and the Imagination," that poetry could trigger the conversion of the world: "Is not poetry the little chamber in the brain where is generated the explosive force which, by gentle shocks, sets in action the intellectual world?" (*W* 8.64).

New power is the good which the soul seeks, Emerson announced. It was the gigantic duty of his poet. As Emerson inevitably associated the farmer-rifleman with the American poets, he called upon them to overthrow the foes of literary freedom. In the Concord battle poem not only are Minutemen firing on British redcoats, but, I unabashedly propose, rebel American poets are shooting down the stiff, ornamented troops of poetic tradition.

That breakthrough into freedom is the principal quality by which we know the open-form poetry we call modern. William Carlos Williams carried the rebellion forward. In the mid-twentieth century he is the great hater of blockages. *Paterson* (1956–1958), his splendid, sprawling poem of release, sings of

> —a dark flame,
> a wind, a flood—counter to all staleness.

Two marvelously subversive lines in *Paterson* sum up the American aesthetic that began with the revolutionary ferment in Emerson's stirring hymn:

> beauty is
> a defiance of authority.

Oliver Wendell Holmes said that the poem's "one conspicuous line— 'And fired the shot heard round the world'—must not take to itself all the praise deserved by this perfect little poem." The syntax of that most famous American line, however, holds emblematically the trajectory of the poetics. So powerful is the conversion structure of Emerson's poetic forms that inevitably his syntax duplicates that structure. In "Threnody," the paradox at the end of the poem sets out a compact linguistic model of the conversion toward which the poem works. "Lost in God, in Godhead found" holds syntactically the movement from material dissolution to spiritual fulfillment and from the mistaken idea of "loss" to the spiritual revelation of discovery. In "Concord Hymn," the famous line compacts the Emersonian conversion process, its syntax acting out the basic movement of the conversion. The "plot" of this crucial line proceeds precisely from the fact to the truth. The actual line, with the one preceding it, has undergone fairly complicated transformations to achieve this. The deep content structure would look something like this: (Someone) embattle(d) the farmers. The farmers (stood) here once. The farmers fire(d) the shot. (Someone)(heard) round the world the shot. But because Emerson conceived the process of conversion always as from fact to truth, from the act to its significance, he wrote what he did. Its order is exact as the flowing of the stream to the sea, another linear and transmutive image in the poem. As the shot becomes the idea of freedom, the syntax manifests the movement from act to idea, from the farmers to the world, from the smaller to the larger, from the small musket ball to the great globe itself.

The poem's larger transaction (from adversity to triumph, from the embattled to the redemptive) parallels in an extraordinarily close way the structure of "The Snow-Storm." Both poems move from frantic activity to stasis and from confusion and paralysis to liberation. The monument of "Concord Hymn" is a model for that aspect of Emerson's poetics in which the poet extracts the lasting from the transient, making art the votive stone of experience. The poet "sees through the flowing vest the firm nature, and can declare it" (W 3.37). The shaft fills the now familiar objective of Emerson's poetics by its upward idealizing sign toward the Platonic realm. The activity in "Concord Hymn" is quintessentially Emersonian, as the generalized citizen-speaker gathers his crucial elements from the horizontal landscape for the purpose of building the vertical shaft of significance. It is the literal setting-up of the moral coordinates from a journal entry of the same year: "Pride, and Thrift, and Expediency, who jeered and chirped and were so well pleased with themselves, and made merry with the dream, as they termed it, of Philosophy and Love,—behold they are all flat, and here is the Soul erect and unconquered still" (*JMN* 5.332). Sherman Paul discerned the basic structural alignments in Emerson's moral space: "The paradoxes and polarity of his thought reflect [the] struggle to inform the life of the horizontal with the quality of the vertical, and by means of the horizontal to raise himself into the erect position." Whereas Whitman's poems pushed out to preserve the full process of experience, Emerson's monument poems carved closely to preserve the meaning. In the hymn, the shaft is the artifact, literally the truth of the matter.

The poem, with all its associations, is an intricate model of the poetics. The two Emersonian forces, one outward toward fluid dissipation and the other inward toward concentration and fixity, work simultaneously. The obsessive design of the poem, its surface faultlessly crafted as a communal tribute for a public ceremony, is fundamentally that of a poet commemorating the poetic enterprise. Ralph Rusk said of "Concord Hymn" that "Though it was to become a part of the American tradition and deserved immortality," the poem "offered Emerson no pattern for his future verse." Quite to the contrary, the poem reflects in every element—its structure, players, images, syntax, its *idea*—the poetics that presided over Emerson's craft. The poem's deepest springs, as we have seen, fed his other aesthetic pronouncements. It would be remarkable, in fact, if this were not so, for the poem was composed at a highly charged time when Emerson's theoretical energies and sense of mission were beaming out in every direction. Within a year and a few days he was to deliver both "The American Scholar" address, his credo on the artist's imagination, and the Divinity School address, his explosive call to liberation from the old forms. When those Concord worthies sang the hymn for their dead heroes, they were also singing of Emerson's hopes for a new poetry. A remarkable occasion indeed. But knowing that Emerson's poetics was the dynamo that energized all he did, we also know it could not have been otherwise.

On Longfellow

Howard Nemerov

Great reputation is perhaps the most curious as well as the most volatile product of civilized society; lives of great men very often remind us, Longfellow's celebrated "Psalm" to the contrary, what a vast deal of illusion their energy sustains around them while they live, and how perishable a commodity it proves to be after they die. William Blake put the matter with characteristic clarity:

> When Sir Joshua Reynolds died
> All Nature was degraded:
> The King drop'd a tear into the Queen's ear,
> And all his pictures faded.

But the fame of a great poet in the nineteenth century seems to us, a hundred years after, peculiarly productive of the grotesque and absurd, and of a nature extremely ready to be degraded. Here, for example, is Queen Victoria's comment on Longfellow's visit to Windsor Castle (this happened, with more or less tact, on the Fourth of July in 1868): "I noticed an unusual interest among the attendants and servants. I could scarcely credit that they so generally understood who he was. When he took leave, they concealed themselves in places from which they could get a good look at him as he passed. I have since inquired among them, and am surprised and pleased to find that many of his poems are familiar to them. No other distinguished person has come here that has excited so peculiar an interest. Such poets wear a crown that is imperishable."

Alas.

And here is a description even more revealing, in my opinion, of the

From *Poetry and Fiction: Essays.* © 1963 by Rutgers, The State University. Rutgers University Press, 1963.

strangeness of this kind of fame. I am quoting an early biographer and critic, George Lowell Austin, writing in the year after the poet's death:

"It is about seven inches in height, and is broad, stout, and capacious. It holds, when filled to the brim, about five pints; has an honest handle; and is, of course, of the usual color of Wedgwood ware. . . . The jug exhibits two panels, one presenting a most admirable portrait of Mr. Longfellow, and the other the following familiar verse from the poem 'Kéramos':

> Turn, turn, my wheel! Turn round and round
> Without a pause, without a sound:
>   So spins the flying world away!
> This clay, well mixed with marl and sand,
> Follows the motion of my hand;
> For some must follow, and some command,
>   Though all are made of clay!

"One is tempted to say of the portrait, that it is one of the best, if not the best, that has been made of the poet. The remaining decorations of the jug comprise scrolls intertwined with flowers, on which are imprinted the titles of some of Mr. Longfellow's most popular poems: 'The Golden Legend,' 'Hiawatha,' 'Evangeline,' 'Psalm of Life,' etc. As a specimen of art production, the jug is certainly one of the most beautiful and desirable, and will immensely please all lovers of Mr. Longfellow's poetry."

Alas for the jug, the specimen of art production!

Even the beard, the universal and encyclopedic beard behind which, in our childhood, half the poets of the world seemed to be hiding, is only falsely and as it were "historically" characteristic of Longfellow, who grew it only when in his fifties, as a consequence of burns suffered in the fire which killed his wife; these burns made it impossible for him to shave. As simple as that!

And so it is possible, barely possible, that behind the jug, the world-renown, the official beard, there exists another poet, smaller but truer than the impressive representations of his time would allow.

It would not be quite true to say that no one nowadays reads Longfellow. A while ago, between the halves of a football game, some fifty thousand persons—I was one of them—heard great swatches of "Hiawatha" droned out over the public address system while several hundred drum majorettes twirled their batons; this was, to be sure, in Minnesota, which is Hiawatha country.

But it is probably true, as this example suggests, that Longfellow is not fashionable among literary people, is in fact regarded by them slightly, scornfully, or not at all; and in this situation I find a problem or two, which I shall try to describe in these pages.

I am certain that the last thing Longfellow wanted was to be a problem. He was a man of very settled dispositions, and what he wanted from very early days was to be a poet—as he put it in a letter to his father, written while he was still an undergraduate at Bowdoin College, "I most eagerly aspire after future eminence in literature." In the course of a long, honorable career at teaching and writing he then achieved this eminence step by step, in a steady upward progression, until, nearing the end of his life, he was clearly one of the great poets of the world, not to America only but to England and all Europe—admired, as we have seen, by Queen Victoria and by her servants; by Saintsbury and by King Leopold of Belgium; by Baudelaire and the Princess Royal of Russia. Greater even than these, the heroine of a novel by Charles Kingsley, on her way to the Crimea to be a nurse with Florence Nightingale, took with her two books, *The Bible* and *Evangeline*. Longfellow's "eminence in literature," then, was in every way comparable with that attained to by his contemporaries (and acquaintances), Browning, Tennyson, and Dickens. Nothing problematic in that!

And yet—and yet. Fifty years after his death in 1882, the writer of a popular history of American literature disposes of Longfellow in a few pages of severities, breaking off in the midst to ask himself, "Am I slaying the thrice slain? Who, except wretched schoolchildren, now reads Longfellow?" And he supplies this justification for going on: "The thing to establish in America is not that Longfellow was a very small poet, but that he did not partake of the poetic character at all." (Ludwig Lewisohn, *The Story of American Literature*, first published 1932, Modern Library Edition, 1939.)

That is more or less how the matter stands at present. The world went a long way, from the schoolgirl of the seventies who unhesitatingly chose Mr. Longfellow's *Poems* as "the book that all good people loved to read" to the wretched schoolchildren of 1932, and long ways, where the world is concerned, have a trick of curving back; but it is doubtful that Longfellow will ever again achieve his past eminence. It is all very well to think of the fluctuations of the literary market as the whirligig of time brings in his revenges, but in this instance we must content ourselves with a more limited revision of judgment. Possibly, indeed, the appropriate lesson to be drawn from this history has less to do with rehabilitating Longfellow than with imposing a certain missing modesty and reasonableness upon contemporary pretensions in the same line of work.

There are at least two problems here, though they are closely related ones. First, there is the question of a violent change in literary fashion between the Victorian period and the period, if it is one, which with a prolonged optimism keeps calling itself "the modern." Second, and symptomatic of this change in literary fashion, there is an increased distance, perhaps a near-absolute separation, between what I shall have to call, having failed to find any noninvidious terms to convey my meaning, popular poetry and good poetry. Longfellow's renown, spread, like that of Browning and Tennyson, through all classes of society, suggests that for the Victorian era the two terms were very nearly synonymous, or could become synonymous, at least, in the case of these poets who were thought of, surely, as "broad" as well as "lofty" and "deep." This kind of reputation, compared with that accorded, say, Ezra Pound or William Carlos Williams on the one hand, and Edgar Guest, Ella Wheeler Wilcox, or Robert W. Service on the other, suggests the magnitude of the change, the definite nature of the separation between what have become two quite different arts, whose audiences exclude one another.

The kind of difference involved, and the tension produced, are well expressed by Cleanth Brooks and Robert Penn Warren in their influential handbook *Understanding Poetry*, where they begin a detailed and destructive analysis of Joyce Kilmer's "Trees" by writing: "This poem has been very greatly admired by a large number of people. The fact that it has been popular does not necessarily condemn it as a bad poem. But it is a bad poem." The essay which follows, brilliant as it is, cannot of course get around the difficulty that the more "objective" determinants you bring up to show that "Trees" is a bad poem, the more you must convince your readers, so far as you convince them of anything at all, that the popularity of this bad poem rests on a sentimental popular misconception of what poetry is and does; and a similar demonstration might be made, with the same justice and the same implications about popular taste, upon certain of Longfellow's "best-loved" poems.

My object in this discussion of Longfellow's work is to exhibit a poet somewhat different from the one who wrote, e.g., "A Psalm of Life," "Hiawatha," "The Wreck of the Hesperus." Without trying to present him, in the result, as anything like a great poet (there are fewer of these than formerly thought), I shall claim for some of his productions an interest other than historical, scholarly, or biographical—an interest truly poetical, and undiminished by time.

Longfellow was a good minor poet, at times a very good one indeed, who succumbed to the characteristic disease of minor poets especially of the nineteenth century (it would be invidious to speak of the twentieth in this connection), the fevered wish to be a major poet, accompanied quite often by the hallucination that he was. Why this kind of thing happens and goes on happening will perhaps never be altogether clear: we may remark that the ambition in itself is not blameworthy, and that knowledge, in this of all endeavors, is precisely what comes too late to be of any use; but in attempting to say why it happened to Longfellow I find that three sorts of cause become visible. These do not exist in isolation but are much interwoven, yet they may be broadly named as the encouragement of history, the encouragement of popularity, and the encouragement of literature.

1. The Encouragement of History. "Surely," writes Longfellow to his father, from Bowdoin College, "surely there was never a better opportunity offered for exertion of literary talent in our own country than is now offered. To be sure, most of our literary men thus far have not been profoundly so, until they have studied and entered the practice of theology, law, or medicine. I do believe that we ought to pay more attention to the opinion of philosophers, that 'nothing but nature can qualify a man for knowledge.' " In other words, America in the 1820s is thought to have so far entered civilization as to be able to support poetry; and not only so, but to support a poetry which is not merely the by-product or graceful accompaniment of the practical life of the professions, but a something in itself—a true art, and "profoundly so."

Still quite early in his career, in 1849, through the mouth of a character in his novel *Kavanagh*, Longfellow invests his wish with the questionable authority of the *Zeitgeist*: "We want a national literature commensurate with our mountains and rivers . . . a national epic that shall correspond to the size of the country . . . a national drama in which scope shall be given to our gigantic ideas and to the unparalleled activity of our people. . . . In a word, we want a national literature altogether shaggy and unshorn, that shall shake the earth, like a herd of buffaloes thundering over the prairies."

This has a pathos in the midst of its generous absurdity, "shaggy and unshorn" being perhaps the qualities we are least likely to think of in connection with Longfellow's poetry, for which, as Howard Mumford Jones has said, the canonical adjective is "gentle." Such a program for literature will sound to some like Walt Whitman, whom it anticipates, and to others like a pronouncement of the Supreme Soviet; it had been, in fact, an extremely popular idea since the formation of the Republic (on this point, see R. W. B. Lewis, *The American Adam*), and it continues to be heard among us year by year, despite our extreme modernity. Though Longfellow is capable of viewing the matter with some detachment—"a man will not necessarily be a great poet because he lives near a great mountain," says another character in the same novel—the subjects he chose for the larger works of his middle period seem to show the American theme as equivocally appealing and summoning, a desire and a duty at once ("Evangeline," "Hiawatha," "The Courtship of Miles Standish," "The New England Tragedies"), while his treatment of these—the hexameters, the measure of the *Kalevala*, the imitation Elizabethanism, a generally pervasive atmosphere of almost scholarly caution—suggests the strain attendant on becoming a great national poet and harmonizing Europe and the past with America and the future.

His solution, or one of his solutions, to this problem is quite simply to become universal and do everything, and so he writes, over a long period of time, *Christus: A Mystery*, of which the three parts, "The Divine Tragedy," "The Golden Legend," and "The New England Tragedies," are designed to represent the theological virtues of Faith, Hope, and Charity as respectively characteristic of antiquity, the Middle Ages, and modern times. But the connection of the parts seems, unhappily, more accidental and arbitrary than the grand design of this program would indicate, nor do the parts themselves come off so much better if considered as separate pieces. "The Golden Legend" is the most attractive, as it is the most fully imagined of the three; even so, the influence of Goethe's *Faust*, especially upon Longfellow's conception of Lucifer, is quite plain to be seen. "The Divine Tragedy" seems a mere mechanical repetition of the sources shuffled into verse, while "The New England Tragedies" sufficiently illustrate that Longfellow shared with many poets of the nineteenth century the inability as well as the desire to write dramatically.

2. The Encouragement of Popularity. Given the ambition of making a national literature, and given the response of all sorts of readers not only to the idea but to the productions, such as "Hiawatha" and "Evangeline," which embodied the idea, we can scarcely blame Longfellow for accepting success as it came. His earnest sincerity, and somewhat simplistic spirit, are not in question; he was neither writing down to his audience nor posing as a prophet among the people. But he was stretching a relatively small gift over a very large frame.

This was indeed noticed, not at all uncertainly, by Edgar Allan Poe and Margaret Fuller among others. Poe, varying between a carefully limited admiration of Longfellow and a bitter resentment extending as far as a reckless and unproven charge of plagiarism, yet noted something essential: "didacticism is the prevalent tone of his song." Margaret Fuller, in an essay which Longfellow privately described as "a bilious attack," wrote an appraisal very judicious in some points, and the more damaging for the impression it gives of deep hostility straining to be fair: "Longfellow is artificial and imitative. He borrows incessantly, and mixes what he borrows, so that it does not appear at the best advantage. He is very faulty in using broken or mixed metaphors. The ethical part of his writing has a hollow, second-hand sound. He has, however, elegance, a love of the beautiful, and a fancy for what is large and manly, if not a full sympathy with it. His verse breathes at times much sweetness; and if not allowed to supersede what is better, may promote a taste for good poetry. Though imitative, he is not mechanical."

But the detractors died; Longfellow and the admirers lived on, and presently the poet's fame was beyond effective question in his day: "surely," he heard from a friend, "no poet was ever so fully recognized in his lifetime as you."

An immense, a world-wide reputation must be a difficult thing to bear gracefully; it is my impression that Longfellow took it all with a beautiful modesty so far as the personal life was concerned. If he was (and he was) a trifle vain in trifles, he had never been swollen with pride, never been self-idolatrous, and was not so in the time of his greatest fame. But professionally, in the image of the poet at his work, he may have succumbed and received the enormous reverberations of his worth for the thing itself; at all events, his very success involved him in a relation with the public, a commitment to the public, to its idea of what a poet is and does, which to later judgment appears as a misfortune. The same overencouraged ambition of an obvious fame, where largeness is taken for greatness, profundity for accuracy, importance for truth, also affected his great contemporaries Tennyson and Browning, and seems to be responsible for those large, facile gestures which we now find so oppressive in the works of those poets. The situation of Victorian poetry ought perhaps to be construed as in large part the result of a false idea (one still very common) of the poet's relation with his audience: the idea that, instead of seeking patiently the truth of the matter at hand, the poet is a repository of "values," which he affirms "in beautiful language" *pour encourager les autres.*

This is not to say that the poet, on this view of him, is insincere. But there exists a curious and even tragic tension between poetry and value. In the work of very great poets we seem to find ideas of order, harmonious articulations of our experience, inextricably involved with the poetry; these poets are admirable not because they present values (though they do) but because they *become* values. I mean by this simply that after a certain point in our reading we cease to judge them in the light of our experience and begin instead to judge our experience in the light of their poems.

Lesser poets, in attempting to attain this distinction, are deceived into philosophizing, or poetizing philosophically, and when time has worked a little on their poems it comes to seem as though their finest poetry escaped them by accident, when they had forgotten for some reason to conclude the poem by orienting it with explicit reference to their beliefs, their values, or when the poem had somehow evaded the censorship of "ideas." This may be one meaning of a phrase from the *Kena Upanishad* which Yeats renders so beautifully: "The living man who finds spirit, finds truth. But if he fail, he falls among fouler shapes."

This may or may not be essential among Longfellow's difficulties; I think, myself, that it is. But it is not the business of criticism to practice preventive medicine by saying Thou Shalt Not to anyone's future; so that the poet's attempt to exceed his limitations is always necessary, and knowledge, after all the returns are in, always too late.

3. The Encouragement of Literature. Longfellow was from the beginning of his career as a teacher a learned and a studious man, who became accustomed to viewing the world of experience with an immediate, almost automatic reference to a wide range of books, a range much extended by his study of languages, his travels in Europe, his love of history, and his work as a translator. A few samples, drawn from among many, will show not only his scrupulousness about giving sources, but also his positive delight in doing so; the following are the opening lines of the poems in which they occur:

> Have you read in the Talmud of old . . . ?

> In Mather's Magnalia Christi,
>   Of the old colonial time,
> May be found in prose the legend
>   That is here set down in rhyme.

> Saint Augustine! well hast thou said.

Another poem, "The Discoverer of the North Cape," is prefaced with the subtitle "A Leaf from King Alfred's Orosius"; and in his diary he notes about "My Lost Youth" his particular pleasure at "the bringing in of the two lines of the old Lapland song." It is also observable in this connection, about the *Tales of a Wayside Inn*, that the interludes between tales not infrequently resemble seminars in criticism and comparative literature—for example:

> "A pleasant and a winsome tale,"
> The Student said, "though somewhat pale
> And quiet in its coloring,
> As if it caught its tone and air
> From the gray suits that Quakers wear;
> Yet worthy of some German bard,
> Hebel or Voss or Eberhard,
> Who love of humble themes to sing,
> In humble verse; but no more true
> Than was the tale I told to you."

The Theologian (who had told the pleasant and winsome tale) replies "with some warmth":

> "That I deny;
> 'Tis no invention of my own,
> But something well and widely known
> To readers of a riper age,
> Writ by the skilful hand that wrote
> The Indian tale of Hobomok,
> And Philothea's classic page."

That is, by "the folk."

Now there is nothing wrong with this in itself. Poets have always taken their stories from past literature and history and tradition. Dante and Shakespeare no less than Longfellow relied on what they read; people who believe otherwise, and think that poets write out of some simple, untutored relation with nature, are making a mistake. But the point scarcely needs to be insisted on, I hope, that when Dante read Ovid or Statius, when Shakespeare read Cinthio or Plutarch, something quite new happened; while with Longfellow, all too often, no transformation takes place in the passage from source to poem, and the result is a mere mechanical "putting into verse," a patient but routine setting down of the external facts of the matter, with nothing problematic about it, no inwardness, as though the transaction between the poet and his subject were primarily a measuring-out of feet and rhymes to be applied to something already in all essentials existing.

This doesn't by any means happen all the time, and the reference to literature is responsible for some of Longfellow's finest things as well as some of his worst; but the point here is that his love for literature, his knowledge of it, his piety toward it, may have suggested to him that the achievement of poetry was after all a simpler matter than it is generally thought to be, and may have encouraged him in a facility which by nature he already amply had.

Our attempt to find a workable relation with poets of the past is always likely to produce embarrassment at the start—and we might in charity admit that if it were possible the embarrassment would be on both sides. Words change, and the habit of speech changes. Dr. Johnson, for example, can no longer commend Dr. Levet to us by calling him "officious," because officious has ceased to mean "kind; doing good offices," which is what it meant to Dr. Johnson. In the same way, when Longfellow calls this life "a suburb of the life elysian" our dismay probably has less to do with our view of immortality than with our view of suburbs. When he continues, however, writing of his dead daughter:

> She is not dead—the child of our affection,—
>   But gone unto that school
> Where she no longer needs our poor protection,
>   And Christ himself doth rule,

we may have to see our difficulty, if we dislike the lines, as a difficulty of attitude, and that it is somewhat snobbish in us to refuse from Longfellow what we should gladly accept from Dante, who also speaks of heaven as a school: *nel quale é Cristo abate del collegio,* "where Christ is abbot of the college" (*Purgatorio* 26.129).

It will be helpful to be as clear as possible about such distinctions, lest on the one hand we reject our poet altogether and uncritically because we do not share his beliefs, or are embarrassed by the form in which he expresses them, lest on the other hand we admire him uncritically for things he cannot truly give us. So, for example, I have seen Longfellow praised as a pioneer imagist for the following lines:

> In broad daylight, and at noon,
> Yesterday I saw the moon
> Sailing high, but faint and white,
> As a school-boy's paper kite.
>   ("Daylight and Moonlight")

Whether these lines do in fact anticipate the practice of Amy Lowell, or whether anyone ought to be praised for the anticipation, I am uncertain; but I am quite certain that this sort of imagery is uncharacteristic in Longfellow's work. Nor is he a poet of brilliant or subtle or elaborated metaphor, though there are occasional miracles of fused vision like this one:

> A memory in his heart as dim and sweet
> As moonlight in a solitary street,
> Where the same rays, that lift the sea, are thrown
> Lovely but powerless upon walls of stone.
>   ("Torquemada," from *Tales of a Wayside Inn*)

His more usual practice is to limit his metaphors immediately by an application, by drawing out their meaning, by moralizing upon them; and this is of course what most offends against the taste of the present age, and makes us look with especial disfavor upon the conclusions of many of his poems as being comically reductive in their insistence on pointing the moral:

> By the mirage uplifted, the land floats vague in the ether,
> Ships and the shadows of ships hang in the motionless air;
> So by the art of the poet our common life is uplifted,
> So, transfigured, the world floats in a luminous haze.
>
> ("Elegiac Verse vi")

I suppose that the attitude of many modern readers toward what is represented here would be in favor of the first two lines and against the last two; substantially the attitude of Longfellow himself in the fourth and fourteenth of these same "Elegiac Verses":

> Let us be grateful to writers for what is left in the inkstand;
> When to leave off is an art only attained by the few.

And

> Great is the art of beginning, but greater the art is of ending;
> Many a poem is marred by a superfluous verse.

Now it is certainly true that some of Longfellow's poems are spoiled for us by their endings which are so explicit and sententious; and this is especially sad in poems which otherwise attain to a considerable and convincing eloquence, such as "The Lighthouse" and "The Golden Milestone." As to the former in particular, after an achievement of the following order,

> Even at this distance I can see the tides,
>   Upheaving, break unheard along its base,
> A speechless wrath, that rises and subsides
>   In the white lip and tremor of the face,

it is very disappointing to be brought down to the conclusion in which the lighthouse "hails the mariner with words of love" which turn out to be platitudes.

Yet, when I consider the general question involved, of morality and statement in poetry, I am not altogether convinced of the absolute rightness of the modern attitude, or that it ought to be applied, without many reservations, to such a poet as Longfellow. He is perhaps most immediately impressive, or at any rate most accessible to us, in those relatively few poems, such as "The Harvest Moon" and "Chaucer" and "Aftermath," which remain steadfastly with their minute particulars. "Aftermath" especially seems to me to have a very moving sort of melancholy, a music in which more is suggested than said. The aftermath is the second mowing of the fields, in late fall; beyond this, perhaps, the poet's work in old age; and the second of the two stanzas deals with it this way:

> Not the sweet, new grass with flowers
> Is this harvesting of ours;
>   Not the upland clover bloom;
> But the rowen mixed with weeds,
> Tangled tufts from marsh and meads,
> Where the poppy drops its seeds
>   In the silence and the gloom.

I shall risk saying that that is first-rate writing. It is not typical of Longfellow's style or way of concluding; yet there are more examples of the kind than people nowadays incline to acknowledge.

And in the other kind, the explicit and moralizing kind of verse, the standard idea of his being "gentle" ought not to blind us to a sometimes considerable strength. For example, in "The Challenge," the "ancient Spanish legend" he begins with is a mere excuse, an occasion only, and the poem exists as a sermon on riches and poverty, as he sees

> The living, in their houses,
>   And in their graves, the dead!
> And the waters of their rivers,
>   And their wine, and oil, and bread!

The challenge is from the poor, who "impeach us all as traitors, / Both living and the dead," leading to this decisive and not especially gentle conclusion:

> And there in the camp of famine,
>   In wind and cold and rain,
> Christ, the great Lord of the army,
>   Lies dead upon the plain!

Generally, then, though Longfellow is not a poet of great dramatic powers, he does have in good measure the essential lyrical equivalent of those powers, the ability to make his moral reflections arise out of experience, emerge from the substance of the stories he tells, the images he presents. Though he is sometimes sentimental, and though it is true that "didacticism is the prevalent tone of his song," yet the substance of his teaching is often poetically just, that is, relevant to the material. Though he is more explicit about drawing the moral than is now the fashion, it may be a false romanticism in the present taste, a desire to indulge the spirit in pseudomysteries, which is embarrassed by plain statements and wants everything "left implicit."

This justice, indeed, is the virtue of Longfellow's poetry that I most wish to call attention to. It seems to me the constant element common to good poetry everywhere and always, and I would define this justice as the poet's acceptance of the consequences of his poem, his will to submit his will to the matter at hand, and follow where the thought will lead him. This quality will demand, no doubt, the sacrifice of incidental beauties, spectacular surprises, especially toward the end of a poem, where the consequences are most powerfully to be felt; and a poet subjected to this discipline will incline to finish his poems rather formally, definitely, explicitly, even with "a message" if that seems an appropriate result of the pressure of what has gone before. When this is properly accomplished, the reader should feel the force of the formal close as rather conventional and distant, bring the measure and the meaning to a resolution together; as in the conventional endings decreed for eighteenth-century music.

Consider in this connection "The Fire of Drift-Wood." The friends sitting before the fire rehearse their memories, and this naturally leads them on to think of themselves as changing in their relations with one another, and to feel "The first slight swerving of the heart, / That words are powerless to express." Then, looking into the fire, they think of the driftwood feeding it, thus of "wrecks upon the main, / Of ships dismasted, that were hailed / And sent no answer back again."

Outward and inward images come together now, in "The long-lost ventures of the heart, / That send no answers back again." And the close of the poem is a very simple placing of the one against the other:

> O flames that glowed! O hearts that yearned!
>   They were indeed too much akin,
> The drift-wood fire without that burned,
>   The thoughts that burned and glowed within.

It is quiet, but it does its work, it exactly resolves the elements of the poem, and does so without any gorgeous or spectacular fussing.

The same is true of a much better poem, "The Ropewalk," where the spinners are seen in a figure subtly involving time and fate:

> In that building, long and low,
> With its windows all a-row,
>   Like the port-holes of a hulk,
> Human spiders spin and spin,
> Backward down their threads so thin
>   Dropping, each a hempen bulk.

It is not going to be a "metaphysical" or conceited poem; its development will be more diffuse than that; but the quality of the world is here nevertheless a quality of thought; the wheel going round suggests that "All its spokes are in my brain."

> As the spinners to the end
> Downward go and reascend,
>   Gleam the long threads in the sun;

> While within this brain of mine
> Cobwebs brighter and more fine
> By the busy wheel are spun.

In the development, which is perhaps overextended and too cataloguelike, the rope being spun is related metaphorically to experience, as to gallows-rope and dragging anchor-cable; again the conclusion is deliberate, conventional, quiet:

> All these scenes do I behold,
> These, and many left untold,
>   In that building long and low;
> While the wheel goes round and round,
> With a drowsy, dreamy sound,
>   And the spinners backward go.

Here the reminder of the spinners going backward throws retrospectively a mysterious air, almost of paradox, over the details of the poem, life having been seen simultaneously as remembered, as lived, as spun, or fated, in the spinning of the rope.

Nor does even "The Ropewalk," good as it is, define the limit of Longfellow's achievement. On the one hand, I have not touched on his humor, which is often much livelier than his present reputation allows us to believe, and shows especially well in some of the *Tales of a Wayside Inn*, e.g., "The Monk of Casal-Maggiore," "The Cobbler of Hagenau," and the Landlord's final Tale of Sir Christopher Gardiner, Knight of the Holy Sepulchre,

> The first who furnished this barren land
> With apples of Sodom and ropes of sand.

On the other hand, this "gentle" and melancholy Christian poet now and then, though rarely, touches simultaneously on tragedy and greatness. "The Chamber over the Gate," simple, reserved, yet, at its end, passionate quite beyond sentimentality, is a lyric poem of the first rank. And in the vast meditation "Michael Angelo," which Longfellow left unfinished at his death, the relation of art and mortality produces, in addition to a sardonic and critical humor not felt in his poetry before, moments which have a claim to be considered the equal of the best in nineteenth-century poetry:

> All things must have an end; the world itself
> Must have an end, as in a dream I saw it.
> There came a great hand out of heaven, and touched
> The earth, and stopped it in its course. The seas
> Leaped, a vast cataract, into the abyss;
> The forests and the fields slid off, and floated
> Like wooded islands in the air. The dead
> Were hurled forth from their sepulchres; the living

Were mingled with them, and themselves were dead,—
All being dead; and the fair, shining cities
Dropped out like jewels from a broken crown.
Naught but the core of the great globe remained,
A skeleton of stone. And over it
The wrack of matter drifted like a cloud,
And then recoiled upon itself, and fell
Back on the empty world, that with the weight
Reeled, staggered, righted, and then headlong plunged
Into the darkness, as a ship, when struck
By a great sea, throws off the waves at first
On either side, then settles and goes down
Into the dark abyss, with her dead crew.

This entire scene, indeed, the meditation on the Coliseum in the fourth section of part 3, is a study of art and life of a profound beauty rare not only for this poet but for any.

Unfashionable Longfellow is a poet of allegory rather than of symbol, of personification rather than of metaphor, of anecdote rather than myth. His ways are plain so far as he can make them so. I have tried to suggest in these prefatory observations what the differences and difficulties are which will make the modern reader impatient very often with this poet, but also what the rewards may be for those who, sick of the fashion, are willing to take a fresh view of the matter, and who may find, as I have found, that Longfellow, gentle as he is, maintains beneath his gentleness a fair share of that unyielding perception of reality which belongs to good poetry wherever and whenever written.

John Greenleaf Whittier

Robert Penn Warren

When Whittier, at the age of twenty-six, came to knock "Pegasus on the head," the creature he laid low was, indeed, not much better than the tanner's superannuated donkey. In giving up his poetry he gave up very little. Looking back on the work he had done up to that time, we can see little achievement and less promise of growth. He had the knack, as he put it in "The Nervous Man," for making rhymes "as mechanically as a mason piles one brick above another," but nothing that he wrote had the inwardness, the organic quality, of poetry. The stuff, in brief, lacked content, and it lacked style. Even when he was able to strike out poetic phrases, images, or effects, he was not able to organize a poem; his poems usually began anywhere and ended when the author got tired. If occasionally we see a poem begin with a real sense of poetry, the poetry gets quickly lost in some abstract idea. Even a poem as late as "The Last Walk in Autumn" (1857) suffers in this way. It opens with a fine stanza like this:

> O'er the bare woods, whose outstretched hands
>   Plead with the leaden heavens in vain,
>   I see beyond the valley lands,
>   The sea's long level dim with rain,
>   Around me, all things, stark and dumb,
>   Seem praying for the snows to come,
> And for the summer bloom and greenness, gone,
> With winter's sunset lights and dazzling morn atone.

But after five stanzas, the poem dies and the abstractions take over for some score of stanzas.

From *The Sewanee Review* 79 (January–March 1971). © 1971 by Robert Penn Warren.

For a poet of natural sensibility, subtlety, and depth to dedicate his work to propaganda would probably result in a coarsening of style and a blunting of effects, for the essence of propaganda is to refuse qualifications and complexity. But Whittier had, by 1833, shown little sensibility, subtlety, or depth, and his style was coarse to a degree. He had nothing to lose, and stood to gain certain things. To be effective, propaganda, if it is to be more than random vituperation, has to make a point, and the point has to be held in view from the start; the piece has to show some sense of organization and control, the very thing Whittier's poems had lacked. But his prose had not lacked this quality, nor, in fact, a sense of the biting phrase; now his verse could absorb the virtues of his prose. It could learn, in addition to a sense of point, something of the poetic pungency of phrase and image, and the precision that sometimes marked the prose. He had referred to his poems as "fancies," and that is what they were, no more. Now he began to relate poetry, though blunderingly enough, to reality. The process was slow. It was ten years—1843—before Whittier was able to write a piece as good as "Massachusetts to Virginia." This was effective propaganda; it had content and was organized to make a point.

Whittier had to wait seven more years before, at the age of forty-three, he could write his first really fine poem. This piece, the famous "Ichabod," came more directly, and personally, out of his political commitment than any previous work. On March 7, 1850, Daniel Webster, senator from Massachusetts, spoke on behalf of the more stringent Fugitive Slave Bill that had just been introduced by Whittier's ex-idol Henry Clay; and the poem, which appeared in March in the *Washington National Era*, a paper of the "political" wing of the abolition movement, deals with the loss of the more recent and significant idol. "This poem," Whittier wrote years later, "was the outcome of the surprise and grief and forecast of evil consequences which I felt on reading the Seventh of March Speech by Daniel Webster. . . ." But here the poet remembers his poem, which does dramatically exploit surprise and grief, better than he remembers the facts of its origin; he could scarcely have felt surprise at Webster's speech, for as early as 1847, in a letter to Sumner, Whittier had called Webster a "colossal coward" because of his attitude toward the annexation of Texas and the Mexican War.

Here is the poem:

> So fallen! so lost! the light withdrawn
>   Which once he wore!
> The glory from his gray hairs gone
>   Forevermore!
>
> Revile him not, the Tempter hath
>   A snare for all;
> And pitying tears, not scorn and wrath,
>   Befit his fall!

Oh, dumb be passion's stormy rage,
    When he who might
Have lighted up and led his age,
    Falls back in night.

Scorn! would the angels laugh, to mark
    A bright soul driven,
Fiend-goaded, down the endless dark,
    From hope and heaven!

Let not the land once proud of him
    Insult him now,
Nor brand with deeper shame his dim,
    Dishonored brow.

But let its humbled sons, instead,
    From sea to lake,
A long lament, as for the dead,
    In sadness make.

Of all we loved and honored, naught
    Save power remains;
A fallen angel's pride of thought,
    Still strong in chains.

All else is gone; from those great eyes
    The soul has fled;
When faith is lost, when honor dies,
    The man is dead!

Then, pay the reverence of old days
    To his dead fame;
Walk backward, with averted gaze,
    And hide the shame!

The effectiveness of "Ichabod," certainly one of the most telling poems of personal attack in English, is largely due to the dramatization of the situation. At the center of the dramatization lies a division of feeling on the part of the poet: the poem is not a simple piece of vituperation, but represents a tension between old trust and new disappointment, old admiration and new rejection, the past and the present. The biblical allusion in the title sets this up: "And she named the child Ichabod, saying, the glory is departed from Israel (1 Sam. 4:21). The glory has departed, but grief rather than rage, respect for the man who was once the vessel of glory rather than contempt, pity for his frailty rather than condemnation—these are the emotions recommended as appropriate. We may note that they are appropriate not only as a generosity of attitude; they are also the emotions that are basically condescending, that put the holder of the emotions above the object of them, and that make the most destructive assault on the ego of the object. If Webster had been motivated by ambition, then pity is the one attitude unforgivable by his pride.

The biblical allusion at the end offers a brilliant and concrete summary of the complexity of feeling in the poem. As Notley Sinclair Maddox has pointed out (*Explicator*, April 1960), the last stanza is based on Gen. 9:20–25. Noah, in his old age, plants a vineyard, drinks the wine, and is found drunk and naked in his tent by his youngest son, Ham, who merely reports the fact to his brothers Shem and Japheth. Out of filial piety, they go to cover Noah's shame, but "their faces were backward, and they saw not their father's nakedness." Ham, for having looked upon Noah's nakedness, is cursed as a "servant to servants" to his "brethren."

The allusion works as a complex and precise metaphor: The great Webster of the past, who, in the time of the debate with Robert Young Hayne (1830), had opposed the slave power and thus established his reputation, has now become obsessed with ambition (drunk with wine) and has exposed the nakedness of human pride and frailty. The conduct of Shem and Japheth sums up, of course, the attitude recommended by the poet. We may remember as an ironical adjunct that the biblical episode was used from many a pulpit as a theological defense of slavery; Ham, accursed as a "servant to servants," being, presumably, the forefather of the black race.

We may look back at the first stanza to see another complex and effective metaphor, suggested rather than presented. The light is withdrawn, and the light is identified, by the appositive construction, with the "glory" of Webster's gray hair—the glory being the achievement of age and the respect due to honorable age, but also the image of a literal light, an aureole about the head coming like a glow from the literal gray hair. This image fuses with that of the "fallen angel" of line 27 and the dimness of the "dim,/ Dishonored brow" in lines 19 and 20. In other words, by suggestion, one of the things that hold the poem together (as contrasted with the logical sequence of the statement) is the image of the angel Lucifer, the light-bearer, fallen by excess of pride. Then in lines 29 and 30, the light image, introduced in the first stanza with the aureole about the gray hair, appears as an inward light shed outward, the "soul" that had once shone from Webster's eyes (he had remarkably large and lustrous dark eyes). But the soul is now dead, the light "withdrawn," and we have by suggestion a death's-head with the eyes hollow and blank. How subtly the abstract ideas of "faith" and "honor" are drawn into this image, and how subtly the image itself is related to the continuing play of variations of the idea of light and dark.

From the point of view of technique this poem is, next to "Telling the Bees," Whittier's most perfectly controlled and subtle composition. This is true not only of the dramatic ordering and interplay of imagery, but also of the handling of rhythm as related to meter and stanza, and to the verbal texture. For Whittier, in those rare moments when he could shut out the inane gabble of the sweet singers like Lydia Sigourney, and of his own incorrigible meter-machine, could hear the true voice of feeling. But how rarely he heard—or trusted—the voice of feeling. He was, we may hazard, afraid of feeling. Unless, of course, a feeling had been properly disinfected.

In the "war with wrong," Whittier wrote a number of poems that were, in their moment, effectively composed, but only two (aside from "Ichabod") that survive to us as poetry. To one, "Song of Slaves in the Desert," we shall return; but the other, "Letter from a Missionary of the Methodist Episcopal Church South, in Kansas, to a Distinguished Politician," not only marks a high point in Whittier's poetic education but may enlighten us as to the relation of that education to his activity as a journalist and propagandist.

The "Letter," as the full title indicates, grew out of the struggle between the pro-slavery and the free-state forces for the control of "Bleeding Kansas." Though the poem appeared in 1854, four years after "Ichabod," it shows us more clearly than the earlier piece how the realism, wit, and irony of Whittier's prose could be absorbed into a composition that is both polemic and poetry. The polemical element is converted into poetry by the force of its dramatization—as in the case of "Ichabod": but here specifically by an ironic ventriloquism, the device of having the "Letter" come from the pen of the godly missionary:

> Last week—the Lord be praised for all His
>   mercies
> To His unworthy servant!—I arrived
> Safe at the Mission, *via* Westport; where
> I tarried over night, to aid in forming
> A Vigilance Committee, to send back,
> In shirts of tar, and feather-doublets quilted
> With forty stripes save one, all Yankee comers,
> Uncircumcised and Gentile, aliens from
> The Commonwealth of Israel, who despise
> The prize of the high calling of the saints,
> Who plant amidst this heathen wilderness
> Pure gospel institutions, sanctified
> By patriarchal use. The meeting opened
> With prayer, as was most fitting. Half an hour,
> Or thereaway, I groaned, and strove, and wrestled,
> As Jacob did at Penuel, till the power
> Fell on the people, and they cried "Amen!"
> "Glory to God!" and stamped and clapped their hands;
> And the rough river boatmen wiped their eyes;
> "Go it, old hoss!" they cried, and cursed the niggers—
> Fulfilling thus the word of prophecy,
> "Cursed be Canaan."

By the ventriloquism the poem achieves a control of style, a fluctuating tension between the requirements of verse and those of "speech," a basis for the variations of tone that set up the sudden poetic, and ironic, effect at the end:

> P.S. All's lost. Even while I write these
> lines,
> The Yankee abolitionists are coming
> Upon us like a flood—grim, stalwart men,
> Each face set like a flint of Plymouth Rock
> Against our institutions—staking out
> Their farm lots on the wooded Wakarusa,
> Or squatting by the mellow-bottomed Kansas;
> The pioneers of mightier multitudes,
> The small rain-patter, ere the thunder shower
> Drowns the dry prairies. Hope from man is not.
> Oh, for a quiet berth at Washington,
> Snug naval chaplaincy, or clerkship, where
> These rumors of free labor and free soil
> Might never meet me more. Better to be
> Door-keeper in the White House, than to dwell
> Amidst these Yankee tents, that, whitening, show
> On the green prairie like a fleet becalmed.
> Methinks I hear a voice come up the river
> From those far bayous, where the alligators
> Mount guard around the camping filibusters:
> "Shake off the dust of Kansas. Turn to Cuba—
> (That golden orange just about to fall,
> O'er-ripe, into the Democratic lap;)
> Keep pace with Providence, or, as we say,
> Manifest destiny. Go forth and follow
> The message of our gospel, thither borne
> Upon the point of Quitman's bowie-knife,
> And the persuasive lips of Colt's revolvers.
> There may'st thou, underneath thy vine and fig-tree,
> Watch thy increase of sugar cane and negroes,
> Calm as a patriarch in his eastern tent!"
> Amen: So mote it be. So prays your friend.

Here quite obviously the ventriloquism is what gives the poem a "voice," and the fact instructs us as to how Whittier, less obviously, develops through dramatization a voice in "Ichabod." The voice of a poem is effective—is resonant—insofar as it bespeaks a life behind that voice, implies a dramatic issue by which that life is defined. We have spoken of the complexity of feeling behind the voice of "Ichabod," and in the present case we find such a complexity in the character of the missionary himself.

At first glance, we have the simple irony of the evil man cloaking himself in the language of the good. But another irony, and deeper, is implicit in the poem: the missionary may not be evil, after all; he may even be, in a sense, "good"—that is, be speaking in perfect sincerity, a man good but misguided; and thus we have the fundamental irony of the relation of evil and good in human character, action, and history. Whittier was a polemicist, and a very astute one, as the "Letter" in its primary irony exemplifies. But he was also a devout Quaker, and by fits and starts a poet, and his creed, like his art, would necessarily give a grounding for the secondary, and deeper, irony, and irony that implies humility and forgiveness.

What we have been saying is that by repudiating poetry Whittier became a poet. His image of knocking Pegasus on the head tells a deeper truth than he knew; by getting rid of the "poetical" notion of poetry, he was able, eventually, to ground his poetry on experience. In the years of his crusade and of the Civil War, he was, bit by bit, learning this, and the process was, as we have said, slow. It was a process that seems to have been by fits and starts, trial and error, by floundering, rather than by rational understanding. Whittier was without much natural taste and almost totally devoid of critical judgment, and he seems to have had only a flickering awareness of what he was doing—though he did have a deep awareness, it would seem, of his personal situation. As a poet he was trapped in the automatism and compulsiveness that, in "Amy Wentworth," he defined as the "automatic play of pen and pencil, solace in our pain"— the process that writing seems usually to have been for him. Even after a triumph, he could fall back for another fifty poems into this dreary repetitiveness.

The mere mass of his published work in verse between 1843 and the Civil War indicates something of this. In 1843 appeared *Lays of My Home*, in 1848 what amounted to a collected edition, in 1850 *Songs of Labor*, in 1853 *The Chapel of the Hermits, and Other Poems*, in 1856 *The Panorama, and Other Poems*, in 1857 the *Political Works*, in two volumes, and in 1860, *Home Ballads, Poems and Lyrics*.

But in this massive and blundering production there had been a growth. In 1843 even poems like "To My Old Schoolmaster," "The Barefoot Boy," "Maud Muller," "Lines Suggested by Reading a State Paper," and "Kossuth" would have been impossible, not to mention "Skipper Ireson's Ride," which exhibits something of the élan of traditional balladry and something of the freedom of living language of "Ichabod" and the "Letter." But nothing short of miracle, and a sudden miraculous understanding of Wordsworth and the traditional ballad, accounts for a little masterpiece like "Telling the Bees." There had been the technical development, but something else was happening too, something more difficult to define; Whittier was stumbling, now and then, on the subjects that might release the inner energy necessary for real poetry.

There was, almost certainly, a deep streak of grievance and undischarged anger in Whittier, for which the abolitionist poems (and editorials) could allow a hallowed—and disinfected—expression; simple indignation at fate could become "righteous indignation," and the biting sarcasm was redeemed by the very savagery of the bite. But there was another subject which released, and more deeply, the inner energy—the memory of the past, more specifically the childhood past, nostalgia, shall we say, for the happy, protected time before he knew the dark inward struggle, the outer struggle with "strong-willed men" (as he was to put it in "To My Sister") to which he had to steel himself, the collapses, and the grinding headaches. Almost everyone has an Eden time to look back on, even if it never existed and he has to create it for his own delusion; but for Whittier the need to dwell on this lost Eden was more marked than is ordinary. If the simple indignation against a fate that had deprived him of the security of childhood could be transmuted into righteous indignation, both could be redeemed in a dream of Edenic innocence. This was the subject that could summon up Whittier's deepest feeling and release his fullest poetic power.

Furthermore, if we review the poems after 1850, we find a subsidiary and associated theme, sometimes in the same poem. In poems like "Maud Muller," "Kathleen," "Mary Garvin," "The Witch's Daughter," "The Truce of Piscataqua," "My Playmate," "The Countess," and "Telling the Bees," there is the theme of the lost girl, a child or a beloved, who may or may not be, in the course of a poem, recovered. Some of these poems, notably "Maud Muller" and "Kathleen," raise the question of differences of social rank, as do "The Truce of Piscataqua" if we read "blood" for *social difference*, and "Marguerite" and "Mary Garvin" if we read the bar of religion in the same way. This last theme, in fact, often appears; we have it in "Amy Wentworth," "The Countess," and "Among the Hills," all of which belong to the mature period of Whittier's work, when he was looking nostalgically backward. But this theme of the lost girl, especially when the loss is caused by difference in social rank or the religious bar, even though it clearly repeats a theme enacted in Whittier's personal life, never really touched the spring of poetry in him except in "Telling the Bees," where it is crossed with the theme of childhood to reduce the pang of the sexual overtones. The theme of the lost girl, taken alone, belonged too literally, perhaps, to the world of frustration. In life Whittier had worked out the problem and had survived, by finding the right kind of action for himself, a "sanctified" action, and this action could, as we have seen, contribute to some of his best poetry; but, more characteristically, his poetic powers were released by the refuge in assuagement, the flight into Eden, and this was at once his great limitation and the source of his success.

For the poems specifically of nostalgia for childhood, we have "Too My Old Schoolmaster," "The Barefoot Boy," "The Playmate," "The Prelude" (to "Among the Hills"), "To My Sister, with a Copy of 'The Supernaturalism of New England,' " "School-Days," "Telling the Bees," and, preeminently, *Snow-Bound*. It is not so much the number of poems involved that is significant, but the coherent quality of feeling and, by and large, the poetic quality in contrast to the other work. As Whittier puts it in "The Prelude," he was more and more impelled to

> idly turn
> The leaves of memory's sketch-book, dreaming o'er
> Old summer pictures of the quiet hills,
> And human life, as quiet, at their feet.

He was, as he shrewdly saw himself in "Questions of Life," an "over-wearied child," seeking in "cool and shade his peace to find," in flight

> From vain philosophies, that try
> The sevenfold gates of mystery,
> And, baffled ever, babble still,
> Word-prodigal of fate and will;
> From Nature, and her mockery, Art
> And book and speech of men apart,
> To the still witness in my heart.

As a young man hot with passion and ambition, and later as a journalist, agitator, and propagandist, he had struggled with the world, but there had always been the yearning for the total peace which could be imaged in the Quaker meetinghouse, but more deeply in childhood, as he summarized it in "To My Sister":

> And, knowing how my life hath been
> A weary work of tongue and pen,
> A long, harsh strife with strong-willed men,
>   Thou wilt not chide my turning
> To con, at times, an idle rhyme,
> To pluck a flower from childhood's clime,
> Or listen, at Life's noonday clime,
>   For the sweet bells of Morning!

The thing which he fled from but did not mention was, of course, inner struggle, more protracted and more bitter than the outer struggle with "strong-willed men."

"To My Old Schoolmaster," which appeared in 1851, just after Whittier's great poetic breakthrough with "Ichabod," is the germ of *Snow-Bound*, the summarizing poem of Whittier's basic impulse. It can be taken as such a germ not merely because it turns back to the early years, but because Joshua Coffin, the schoolmaster, was a person associated with certain of Whittier's rites of passage, as it were. It was Coffin who, when Whittier was a boy of fourteen, sat by the family fire and read aloud from Burns. It was Coffin who was with Whittier at the founding of the American Anti-Slavery Society in Philadelphia, in 1833. Furthermore, Coffin early encouraged Whittier's historical and antiquarian interests (a fact that explains certain passages in the poem), and shared in his religious sense of the world; and in this last connection it is logical to assume that when, late in life, Coffin, a sweet-natured and devout man, fell prey to the conviction that he was not among the "elect" and would be damned, the fact would stir the aging Whittier's deepest feelings about the meaning of his own experience. Be that as it may, when Coffin died, in June 1864, just before the death of Whittier's sister Elizabeth, which provoked *Snow-Bound*, Whittier felt, as he said in a letter, that he had lost "one of the old landmarks of the past." This bereavement would be absorbed into the more catastrophic one about to occur, just as the figure of Coffin would be absorbed into that of the schoolmaster in the poem that is ordinarily taken to refer, as we shall see, to a certain George Haskell.

We have remarked that "To My Old Schoolmaster," composed shortly after "Ichabod," may in one sense be taken also as contributing to *Snow-Bound*. But an even earlier poem, "Song of the Slaves in the Desert" (1847), indicates more clearly the relation of the poems inspired by Whittier's "war on wrong" to the poems of personal inspiration. The "Song" is, as a matter of fact, the best poem done by Whittier up to that time; and here the homesickness of the slaves gives a clear early example of the theme of nostalgia. Furthermore, since the slaves are, specifically, female, here is the first example of the theme of the lost girl:

> Where are we going? where are we going,
>   Where are we going, Rubee?
>
> Lord of peoples, lord of lands,
> Look across these shining sands,
> Through the furnace of the noon,
> Through the white light of the moon.
> Strong the Ghiblee wind is blowing,
> Strange and large the world is growing!
> Speak and tell us where we are going,
>   Where are we going, Rubee?
>
> Bornou land was rich and good,
> Wells of water, fields of food,
> Dourra fields, and bloom of bean,
> And the palm-tree cool and green:
> Bornou land we see no longer,
> Here we thirst and here we hunger,
> Here the Moor-man smites in anger:
>   Where are we going, Rubee?
>
> When we went from Bornou land,
> We were like the leaves and sand,
> We were many, we are few;
> Life has one, and death has two:

Whitened bones our path are showing,
Thou All-seeing, thou All-knowing!
Hear us, tell us, where are we going,
    Where are we going, Rubee?

Moons of marches from our eyes
Bornou land behind us lies;
Stranger round us day by day
Bends the desert circle gray;
Wild the waves of sand are flowing,
Hot the winds above them blowing,—
Lord of all things! where are we going?
    Where are we going, Rubee?

We are weak, but Thou art strong;
Short our lives, but Thine is long;
We are blind, but Thou hast eyes;
We are fools, but Thou art wise!
Thou, our morrow's pathway knowing
Through the strange world round us growing,
Hear us, tell us where are we going,
    Where are we going, Rubee?

The relation of "Ichabod" to the theme of nostalgia is somewhat more indirect and complex, but we may remember that, as the title declares, the theme is a lament for departed glory. Literally the glory is that of Webster, who has betrayed his trust, but also involved is the "glory" of those who trusted, who had trailed their own clouds of glory, not of strength and dedication, but of innocence, simplicity, and faith. The followers are betrayed by their natural protector, for, as the biblical reference indicates, they are the sons of the drunken Noah. In the massiveness of the image, however, the father betrays the sons not only by wine but by death, for it is a death's-head with empty eye-sockets that is the most striking fact of the poem. Here the evitable moral betrayal is equated, imagistically, with the inevitable, and morally irrelevant, fact of death. But by the same token, as a conversion of the proposition, the fact of death in the morally irrelevant course of nature is, too, a moral betrayal. The child, in other words, cannot forgive the course of nature—the fate—that leaves him defenseless.

In connection with this purely latent content of the imagery, we may remark that Whittier, in looking back on the composition of the poem, claimed that he had recognized in Webster's act the "forecast of evil consequences" and knew the "horror of such a vision." For him this was the moment of confronting the grim actuality of life. It was, as it were, a political rite of passage. Here the protector has become the betrayer—has "died." So, in this recognition of the isolation of maturity, we have the beginning of the massive cluster of poems of the nostalgia of childhood.

Let us glance at a later poem, "The Pipes of Lucknow: An Incident of the Sepoy Mutiny," that seems, at first glance, even more unrelated to the theme of childhood than does "Ichabod." But as "Ichabod" is associated with "To My Old Schoolmaster," a more explicit poem of childhood, so "Lucknow" is associated with "Telling the Bees." If we translate "Lucknow," we have something like this: The Scots have left home (*i.e.*, grown up) and are now beleaguered.

> Day by day the Indian tiger
> Louder yelled, and nearer crept;
> Round and round the jungle-serpent
> Nearer and nearer circles swept.

The "Indian tiger" and the "jungle-serpent" are melodramatic versions of the "strong-willed men" and other manifestations of the adult world that Whittier had steeled himself to cope with, and had turned from, as the Scots turn now, on hearing the pipes, to seek assuagement in the vision of home. As another factor in this equation, we may recall that Whittier had early identified his father's rocky acres with the Scotland of Burns, and so the mystic "pipes o' Havelock" are the pipes of Haverhill.

With one difference: the pipes of Havelock announce not merely a vision of assuagement but also a vengeful carnage to be wrought on all those evil forces and persons that had robbed the child of "home," on the "strong-willed men" and the "Indian tiger" and the "jungle-serpent." Furthermore, since in the inner darkness, where its dramas are enacted, desire knows no logic or justice beyond its own incorrigible nature, we may see distorted in the dark face of the "Indian tiger" and the "jungle-serpent" the dark faces of those poor slaves in Dixie—for it was all their fault; they were the enemy—if it had not been for them Whittier would never have been drawn forth from the daydreams and neurotic indulgences of his youth into the broad daylight of mature and objective action.

Whittier recognized in himself an appetite for violence. "I have still strong suspicions," he would write in the essay "The Training," "that somewhat of the old Norman blood, something of the grim Berserker spirit, has been bequeathed to me." So, paradoxically, but in the deepest logic of his being, this strain of violence is provoked against these forces that would threaten the "peace" of childhood, and it is to the "air of Auld Lang Syne," rising above the "cruel roll of war-drums," that the vengeful slaughter is released and the gentle Quaker poet breaks out in warlike glee in such lines as:

> And the tartan clove the tartan
> As the Goomtee cleaves the plain.

"Lucknow," in fact, seems nearer to Kipling than to the saint of Amesbury, the abolitionist, and the libertarian poet who, in this very period, was writing poems deeply concerned with the freedom of Italians ("From Perugia," 1858, and "Italy," 1860), if not with that of Sepoys. But it is no mystery that in 1858, the year of "Lucknow," Whittier should have written the gentle little masterpiece of nostalgia "Telling the Bees," for both would seem to have been conditioned by the same traumatic event: the death of Whittier's mother, which occurred in December 1857.

On February 16, 1858, Whittier sent "Telling the Bees" to James Russell Lowell, at the *Atlantic Monthly*, saying, "What I call simplicity may be only silliness." It was not silliness. It was a pure and beautiful little poem informed by the flood of feeling that broke forth at the death of his mother.

> Here is the place; right over the hill
>   Runs the path I took;
> You can see the gap in the old wall still,
>   And the stepping-stones in the shallow brook.
>
> There is the house, with the gate red-barred,
>   And the poplars tall;
> And the barn's brown length, and the cattle-yard,
>   And the white horns tossing above the wall.
>
> There are the beehives ranged in the sun;
>   And down by the brink
> Of the brook are her poor flowers, weed-o'errun,
>   Pansy and daffodil, rose and pink.
>
> A year has gone, as the tortoise goes,
>   Heavy and slow;
> And the same rose blows, and the same sun glows,
>   And the same brook sings of a year ago.
>
> There's the same sweet clover-smell in the breeze;
>   And the June sun warm
> Tangles his wings of fire in the trees,
>   Setting, as then, over Fernside farm.
>
> I mind me how with a lover's care
>   From my Sunday coat
> I brushed off the burrs, and smoothed my hair,
>   And cooled at the brookside my brow and throat.
>
> Since we parted, a month had passed,—
>   To love, a year;
> Down through the beeches I looked at last
>   On the little red gate and the well-sweep near.
>
> I can see it all now,—the slantwise rain
>   Of light through the leaves,
> The sundown's blaze on her window-pane,
>   The bloom of her roses under the eaves.

Just the same as a month before,—
    The house and the trees,
The barn's brown gable, the vine by the door,—
    Nothing changed but the hives of bees.

Before them, under the garden wall,
    Forward and back,
Went drearily singing the chore-girl small,
    Draping each hive with a shred of black.

Trembling, I listened: the summer sun
    Had the chill of snow;
For I knew she was telling the bees of one
    Gone on the journey we all must go!

Then I said to myself, "My Mary weeps
    For the dead to-day:
Haply her blind old grandsire sleeps
    The fret and the pain of his age away."

But her dog whined low; on the doorway sill,
    With his cane to his chin,
The old man sat; and the chore-girl still
    Sung to the bees stealing out and in.

And the song she was singing ever since
    In my ear sounds on:—
"Stay at home, pretty bees, fly not hence!
    Mistress Mary is dead and gone!"

The setting of the poem is a scrupulous re-creation of the farmstead where Whittier spent his youth. The poem was composed almost thirty years after Whittier had gone out into the world, and some twenty-two years after he had sold the home place and moved the family to Amesbury. Not only is the same nostalgia that informs *Snow-Bound* part of the motivation of this poem, but also the same literalism. But more than mere literalism seems to be involved in the strange fact that Whittier keeps his sister Mary—or at least her name—in the poem, and keeps her there to kill her off; and there is, of course, the strange fact that he cast a shadowy self—the "I" of the poem—in the role of the lover of Mary, again playing here with the theme of lost love, of the lost girl, but bringing the story within the family circle, curiously coalescing the youthful yearning for sexual love and the childhood yearning for love and security within the family circle. And all this at a time when Mary was very much alive.

Just as the shock of his mother's death turned Whittier's imagination back to the boyhood home and released the energy for "Telling the Bees," so the death of his sister Elizabeth lies behind *Snow-Bound*. The relation of

Whittier to this sister, who shared his literary and other tastes, who herself wrote verses (often indistinguishable in their lack of distinction from the mass of her brother's work), who was a spirited and humorous person, and who, as a spinster, was a companion to his bachelorhood, was of a more complex and intimate kind than even that of Whittier to his mother. She was "dear Lizzie, his sole home-flower, the meek lily-blossom that cheers and beautifies his life"—as was observed in the diary of Lucy Larcom, a poetess of some small fame and one of the ladies who, along the way, was in love, to no avail, with the poet himself. When Elizabeth died, on September 3, 1864, Whittier said, "The great motive of my life seems lost."

Shortly before Elizabeth's death there had been another crisis in Whittier's life, the end of his second and final romance with Elizabeth Lloyd, whom we have already mentioned. The relation with that lady was something more than merely one among his numerous frustrated romances. He had known her for some twenty-five years, from the time when he was thirty. She was good-looking, wrote verses, painted pictures, believed ardently in abolition, and was a Quaker to boot. What could have been more appropriate? She even fell in love with him, if we can judge from the appeals in her letters toward the end of the first connection with her: "Spirit, silent, dumb and cold! What hath possessed thee?" Or: "Do come, Greenleaf! I am almost forgetting how thee looks and seems." But Greenleaf was beating one of his strategic retreats; so she cut her losses, got to work and made a literary reputation of sorts, married a non-Quaker, and got "read out of meeting."

After her husband's death, however, Elizabeth Lloyd, now Howell, reappeared in Whittier's life. They became constant companions. Both suffered from severe headaches, but they found that if they caressed each other's hair and massaged each other's brows, the headaches would go away. Or at least Whittier's headache would, and he proposed to her. She refused him, but not definitively, and the dalliance went on. Even a quarrel about Quakerism did not end it. But it did end; or perhaps it merely petered out. In any case, in later years the lady nursed a grievance, and spoke bitterly of the old sweetheart.

So in spite of Elizabeth Howell's healing hands, Whittier again took up his solitude, and if he still clung to the explanation that his bachelorhood had been due to "the care of an aged mother, and the duty owed a sister in delicate health," the last vestige of plausibility was, ironically enough, now to be removed by the sister's sudden death. He was now truly alone, with no landmarks left from the Edenic past except those of memory.

Before the end of the month in which Elizabeth died, Whittier sent to the *Atlantic* a poem which he said had "beguiled some weary hours." It was "The Vanishers," based on a legend he had read in Schoolcraft's famous *History, Condition, and Prospects of the American Indians* about the beautiful spirits who fleetingly appear to beckon the living on to what Whittier calls "The Sunset of the Blest." To the Vanishers, Whittier likens the beloved dead:

> Gentle eyes we closed below,
>   Tender voices heard once more,
> Smile and call us, as they go
>   On and onward, still before.

The poem is, in its basic impulse, a first draft of *Snow-Bound*.

In a very special way *Snow-Bound* summarizes Whittier's life and work. The poem gives the definitive expression to the obsessive theme of childhood nostalgia. As early as 1830, in "The Frost Spirit," we find the key situation of the family gathered about a fire while the "evil power" of the winter storm (and of the world) goes shrieking by. Already, too, Whittier had long been fumbling toward his great question of how to find in the contemplation of the past a meaning for the future. In "My Soul and I" (1847), the soul that turns in fear from the unknown future to seek comfort in the "Known and Gone" must learn that

> The past and the time to be are one,
>   And both are now.

The same issue reappears in "The Garrison of Cape Ann":

> The great eventful present hides the past; but through the
>   din
> Of its loud life hints and echoes from the life behind steal
>   in;
> And the lore of home and fireside, and the legendary rhyme,
> Make the task of duty lighter which the true man owes his
>   time.

And it appears again in "The Prophecy of Samuel Sewall" (1859).

As for the relation to the poet's personal life, *Snow-Bound* came after another manifestation of the old inhibition that forbade his seeking solace from Elizabeth Lloyd's healing hands (and this as he neared the age of sixty, when the repudiation of the solace must have seemed more nearly and catastrophically final). It came after the death of the sister had deprived him of the motive of his life. And it came, too, toward the end of the Civil War, when he could foresee the victory of the cause to which he had given his energies for more than thirty years and which had, in a sense, served as his justification for life, and as a substitute for other aspects of life. Now the joy of victory would, necessarily, carry with it a sense of emptiness. Furthermore, the victory itself was in terms sadly different, as Whittier recognized, from those that he had dreamed.

Snow-Bound is, then, a summarizing poem for Whittier; but it came, also, at a summarizing moment for the country. It came when the country—at least all the country that counted, the North—was poised on the threshold of a new life, the world of technology, big industry, big business, finance capitalism, and urban values. At that moment, caught up in the promises of the future, the new breed of American could afford to look back on his innocent beginnings; and the new breed could afford to pay for the indulgence of nostalgia—in fact, in the new affluence, paid quite well for it. Whittier's book appeared on February 17, 1866, and the success was immediate. For instance, in April, J. T. Fields, the publisher, wrote to Whittier: "We can't keep the plaguey thing quiet. It goes and goes, and now, today, we are bankrupt again, not a one being in crib." The first edition earned Whittier ten thousand dollars—a sum to be multiplied many times over if translated into present values. The poor man was, overnight, modestly rich.

The scene of the poem, the "Flemish picture," as Whittier calls it, the modest genre piece, is rendered with precise and loving care, and this scene had its simple nostalgic appeal for the generation who had come to town and made it, and a somewhat different appeal, compensatory and comforting no doubt, for the generation that had stayed in the country and had not made it. But the poem is not simple, and it is likely that the appeals would have been far less strong and permanent if Whittier had not set the "idyl" in certain "perspectives" or deeper interpretations. In other words, it can be said of this poem, as of most poetry, that the effect does not depend so much on the thing looked at as on the way of the looking. True, if there is nothing to look at, there can be no looking, but the way of the looking determines the kind of feeling that fuses with the object looked at.

Before we speak of the particular "perspectives" in which the poem is set, we may say that there is a preliminary and general one. This general perspective, specified in Whittier's dedicatory note to his "Winter Idyl," denies that the poem is a mere "poem." The poem, that is, is offered as autobiography with all the validation of fact. In other words, the impulse that had appeared in "The Vanishers" as fanciful is here given a grounding in the real world, and in presenting that world the poem explores a complex idea—how different from the vague emotion of "The Vanishers"—concerning the human relation to Time.

The literalness of that world is most obviously certified by the lovingly and precisely observed details: the faces sharpened by cold, the "clashing horn on horn" of the restless cattle in the barn, the "grizzled squirrel" dropping his shell, the "broad nails snapping in the frost" at night. The general base of the style is low, depending on precision of rendering rather than on the shock and brilliance of language or image; but from this base certain positive poetic effects emerge as accents and point of focus. For instance:

A chill no coat, however stout,
Of homespun stuff could quite shut out,
A hard, dull bitterness of cold,
That checked, mid-vein, the circling race
Of life-blood in the sharpened face,
The coming of the snow-storm told.
The wind blew east; we heard the roar
Of Ocean on his wintry shore,
And felt the strong pulse throbbing there
Beat with low rhythm our inland air.

Associated with this background realism of the style of the poem we find a firm realism in the drawing of character. Three of the portraits are sharp and memorable, accented against the other members of the group and at the same time bearing thematic relations to them: the spinster aunt, the schoolmaster, and Harriet Livermore.

The aunt, who had had a tragic love affair but who, as the poem states, has found reconciliation with life, bears a thematic relation to both Elizabeth Whittier and Whittier himself. The schoolmaster, whose name Whittier could not remember until near the end of his life, was a George Haskell, who later became a doctor, practiced in New Jersey and Illinois, and died in 1876 without even knowing, presumably, of his role in the poem; but as we have pointed out, there are echoes here, too, of Joshua Coffin. As for Harriet Livermore, Whittier's note identifies her. The fact that the "warm, dark languish of her eyes" might change to rage is amply documented by the fact that at one time, before the scene of *Snow-Bound*, she had been converted to Quakerism, but during an argument with another Quaker on a point of doctrine she asserted her theological view by laying out with a length of stove wood the man who was her antagonist. This action, of course, got her out of the sect. In her restless search for a satisfying religion, she represents one strain of thought in nineteenth-century America, and has specific resemblances to the characters Nathan and Nehemiah in Melville's *Clarel*. As a "woman tropical, intense," and at the same time concerned with ideas and beliefs, she is of the type of Margaret Fuller, the model for Zenobia in the *Blithedale Romance* of Hawthorne.

To return to the structure of the poem, there are three particular "perspectives"—ways in which the material is to be viewed—that can be localized in the body of the work. These perspectives operate as inserts that indicate the stages of the dialectic of this poem. The first appears in lines 175 to 211, the second in lines 400 to 437, and the third in lines 715 to the end.

The first section of the poem (up to the first perspective) presents a generalized setting: the coming of the storm, the first night, the first day, and the second night. Here the outside world is given full value in contrast to the interior, especially in the following passage, which is set between two close-ups of the hearthside, that Edenic spot surrounded by the dark world:

The moon above the eastern wood
Shone at its full; the hill-range stood
Transfigured in the silver flood,
Its blown snows flashing cold and keen,
Dead white, save where some sharp ravine
Took shadow, or the sombre green
Of hemlocks turned to pitchy black
Against the whiteness at their back.
For such a world and such a night
Most fitting that unwarming light,
Which only seemed where'er it fell
To make the coldness visible.

The setting, as we have said, is generalized; the individual characters have not yet emerged, the father having appeared in only one line of description and as a voice ordering the boys (John and his only brother, Matthew) to dig a path, with the group at the fireside only an undifferentiated "we." This section ends with the very sharp focus on the mug of cider simmering between the feet of the andirons and the apples sputtering—the literal fire, the literal comfort against the threat of literal darkness and cold outside.

Now the first perspective is introduced:

What matter how the night behaved?
What matter how the north-wind raved?
Blow high, blow low, not all its snow
Could quench our hearth-fire's ruddy glow.

But immediately, even as he affirms the inviolability of the fireside world, the poet cries out:

O Time and Change!—with hair as gray
As was my sire's that winter day,
How strange it seems, with so much gone
Of life and love, to still live on!

From this remembered scene by the fireside only two of the participants survive, the poet and his brother, who are now as gray as the father at that snowfall of long ago; for all are caught in Time, in this less beneficent snowfall that whitens every head, as the implied image seems to say. Given this process of the repetition of the pattern of Time and Change, what, the poet asks, can survive? The answer is that "love can never lose its own."

After the first perspective has thus grafted a new meaning on the scene of simple nostalgia by the fire, the poem becomes a gallery of individual portraits, the father, the mother, the uncle, the aunt, the elder sister (Mary), and the younger (Elizabeth), the schoolmaster, and Harriet Livermore. That is, each individual brings into the poem a specific dramatization of the problem of Time. In the simplest dimension, they offer continuity and repetition: they, the old, were once young, and now, sitting by the fire with the young, tell of youth remembered against the background of age. More specifically, each of the old has had to try to come to terms with Time, and their portraits concern this past.

When the family portraits have been completed, the second perspective is introduced; this is concerned primarily with the recent bereavement, with the absent Elizabeth, and with the poet's personal future as he walks toward the night and sees (as an echo from "The Vanishers") Elizabeth's beckoning hand. Thus out from the theme of Time and Change emerges the theme of the Future, which is to be developed in the portraits of Haskell and Harriet Livermore.

The first will make his peace in Time, by identifying himself with progressive social good (which, as a matter of fact, George Haskell had done by 1866). Harriet Livermore, though seeking, by her theological questing, a peace out of Time, has found no peace in Time, presumably because she cannot seek in the right spirit; with the "love within her mute," she cannot identify herself with the real needs of the world about her (as Aunt Mercy can and George Haskell will); she is caught in the "tangled skein of will and fate," and can only hope for a peace in divine forgiveness, out of Time. After the portrait of Harriet Livermore, we find the contrast in the mother's attitude at the goodnight scene: unlike Harriet she finds peace in the here-and-now, "food and shelter, warmth and health" and love, with no "vain prayers" but with a willingness to act practically in the world— an idea that echoes the theme of "My Soul and I," which we have already mentioned. And this is followed with the peace of night and the "reconciled" dream of summer in the middle of the winter.

With dawn, the present—not the past, not the future—appears, with its obligations, joys, and promises. Here there is a lag in the structure of the poem. When the snowbound ones awake to the sound of "merry voices high and clear," the poem should, logically, move toward its fulfilment. But instead, after the gay and active intrusion of the world and the present, we have the section beginning "So days went on," and then the dead "filler" for some twenty lines. Whittier's literalism, his fidelity to irrelevant fact rather than to relevant meaning and appropriate structure of the whole, here almost destroys both the emotional and the thematic thrust, and it is due only to the power of the last movement that the poem is not irretrievably damaged.

The third "perspective" (lines 715–59), which ends the poem, is introduced by the eloquence of these lines:

> Clasp, Angel of the backward look
> And folded wings of ashen gray
> And voice of echoes far away,
> The brazen covers of thy book.

Then follow certain new considerations. What is the relation between the dream of the past and the obligations and actions of the future? The answer is, of course, in the sense of continuity of human experience, found when one stretches the "hands of memory" to the "wood-fire's blaze" of the past; it is thus that one may discover the meaningfulness of obligation and action in Time, even as he discovers in the specific memories of the past an image for the values out of Time. The "idyl" is more than a "Flemish picture"; it is an image, and a dialectic, of one of life's most fundamental questions that is summed up in the haunting simplicity of the end:

> Sit with me by the homestead hearth,
> And stretch the hands of memory forth
>   To warm them at the wood-fire's blaze!
> And thanks untraced to lips unknown
> Shall greet me like the odors blown
> From unseen meadows newly mown,
> Or lilies floating in some pond,
> Wood-fringed, the wayside gaze beyond;
> The traveller owns the grateful sense
> Of sweetness near, he knows not whence,
> And, pausing, takes with forehead bare
> The benediction of the air.

As a corollary to the third "perspective" generally considered, Whittier has, however, ventured a specific application. He refers not merely to the action in the future, in general, in relation to the past, but also, quite clearly, to the Civil War and the new order with its "larger hopes and graver fears"—the new order of "throngful city ways" as contrasted with the old agrarian way of life and thought. He invites the "worldling"—the man who, irreligiously, would see no meaning in the shared experience of human history, which to Whittier would have been a form of revelation—to seek in the past not only a sense of personal renewal and continuity, but also a sense of the continuity of the new order with the American past. This idea is clearly related to Whittier's conviction, which we have already mentioned, that the course of development for America should be the fulfilling of the "implied intent" of the Constitution in particular, of the American revelation in general, and of God's will. And we may add that Whittier, by this, also gives another "perspective" in which his poem is to be read.

If we leave *Snow-Bound*, the poem, and go back again to its springs in Whittier's personal story, we may find that is recapitulates in a new form an old issue. The story of his youth is one of entrapments—and of his failure to break out into the world of mature action. In love, politics, and poetry, he was constantly being involved in a deep, inner struggle, with the self-pity, the outrage, the headaches, the breakdowns. He was, to no avail, trying to break out of the "past" of childhood into the "future" of manhood—to achieve, in other words, a self.

The mad ambition that drove him to try to break out of the entrapments, became in itself, paradoxically, another entrapment—another dead hand of the past laid on him. He cried out, "Now, now!"—not even knowing what he cried out for, from what need, for what reality. But nothing worked out, not love, nor politics, nor even poetry, that common substitute for success of a more immediate order. In poetry, in fact, he could only pile up words as a mason piles up bricks; he could only repeat, compulsively, the dreary clichés; his meter-making machine ground on, and nothing that came out was, he knew, real: his poems were only "fancies," as he called them, only an echo of the past, not his own present. And if he set out with the declared intention of being the poet of New England, his sense of its history was mere antiquarianism, mere quaintness—no sense of an abiding human reality. Again he was trapped in the past. All his passions strove, as he put it, "in chains." He found release from what he called "the pain of disappointment and the temptation to envy" only in repudiating the self, and all the self stood for, in order to save the self. He could find a cause that, because it had absorbed (shall we hazard?) all the inner forces of the "past" that thwarted his desires, could free him into some "future" of action.

So much for the story of the young Whittier.

But what of the old?

He had, in the end, fallen into another entrapment of the past. All action—and the possibility of action and continuing life—had been withdrawn: the solacing hands of Elizabeth Lloyd, the "great motive of . . . life" that the other Elizabeth represented, old friends such as Joshua Coffin, even the "cause" to which he had given his life and which had given his life meaning. Only memory—the past—was left. To live—to have a future—he had to refight the old battle of his youth on a new and more difficult terrain. He had to find a new way to make the past nourish the future.

It could not be the old way. The old way had been, in a sense, merely a surrender. By it, Whittier had indeed found a future, a life of action. But the victory had been incomplete, and the cost great; for we must remember that the grinding headaches continued and that the solacing hands of Elizabeth Lloyd had been, in the end, impossible for him.

The new way was more radical. That is, Whittier undertook to see the problem of the past and future as generalized rather than personal, as an issue confronting America, not only himself: furthermore, to see it *sub specie aeternitatis*, as an aspect of man's fate. And he came to see—how late!—that man's fate is that he must learn to accept and use his past completely, knowingly, rather than to permit himself to be used, ignorantly, by it.

Having struggled for years with the deep difficulties of his own life, Whittier at last found a way fruitfully to regard them, and *Snow-Bound* is the monument of this personal victory. No, it may be the dynamic image of the very process by which the victory itself was achieved. But there is another way in which we may regard it. It sees Whittier into relation to an obsessive and continuing theme in our literature, a theme that most powerfully appears in Cooper, Hawthorne, Melville, and Faulkner: what does the past mean to an American?

The underlying question is, of course, why a sense of the past should be necessary at all. Why in a country that was new—was all "future"—should the question have arisen at all? Cooper dealt with it in various dramatizations, most obviously in the figures of Hurry Harry and the old pirate in *Deerslayer* and of the squatter in *The Prairie*, who are looters, exploiters, and spoilers of man and nature: none of these men has a sense of the pride and humility that history may inculcate. How close are these figures to those of Faulkner's world who have no past, or who would repudiate the past, who are outside history—for example, the Snopeses (descendants of bushwhackers who had no "side" in the Civil War), Popeye of *Sanctuary*, Jason and the girl Quentin of *The Sound and the Fury* (who repudiate the family and the past), and of course poor Joe Christmas of *Light in August*, whose story is the pathetic struggle of a man who, literally, has no past, who does not know who he is or his own reality. Whittier, too, understood the fate of the man who has no past—or who repudiates his past. This is his "worldling" of *Snow-Bound* (whom we may also take as an image of what the past might have been had the vainglorious dreams of his youth been realized), whom he calls to spread his hands before the warmth of the past in order to understand his own humanity, to catch the sweetness coming "he knows not where," and the "benediction of the air."

But, on the other side of this question, Whittier understood all too well the danger of misinterpreting the past—in his own case the danger of using the past as a refuge from reality. Faulkner, too, fully understood this particular danger and dramatized it early in *Sartoris* and later in "The Odor of Verbena." But the theme appears more strikingly and deeply philosophized in characters like Quentin Compson in *The Sound and the Fury*, and Hightower in *Light in August*. But Faulkner understood other kinds of dangers of misinterpretation. Sutpen, with his "design" and no comprehension of the inwardness of the past, suggests, in spite of all differences, a parallel with Cooper's squatter in *The Prairie*, whose only link with the past is some tattered pages from the Old Testament that serve, in the end, to justify his killing of the brother-in-law (the pages having no word of the peace and brotherhood of the New Testament). But Faulkner's most complex instance of the misinterpretation of the past occurs with Ike McCaslin, who, horrified by the family crime of slavery and incest, thinks he can buy out simply by refusing his patrimony: he does not realize that a true understanding of the past involves both an acceptance and a transcendence of the acceptance.

If we turn to Melville, we find in *Pierre, or The Ambiguities* the story of a man trapped, as Whittier was, in the past and desperately trying to free himself for adult action, just as we find in *Battle-Pieces,* in more general terms, the overarching ironical idea of the vanity of human action set against man's need to validate his life in action. And, for a variation, in *Clarel* we find the hero (who has no "past"—who is fatherless and has lost his God, and who does not know mother or sister) seeking in history a meaning of life, this quest occurring in the Holy Land, the birthplace of the spiritual history of the Western world; and it is significant that Clarel finds his only answer in the realization that men are "cross-bearers all"—that is, by identifying himself with the human community, in its fate of expiatory suffering—an answer very similar to, though in a different tonality from, that of *Snow-Bound.*

With Hawthorne the same basic question is somewhat differently framed. We do not find figures with roles like those of Hurry Harry, the squatter, Joe Christmas, Hightower, or Clarel, but we find, rather, a general approach to the meaning of the past embodied in Hawthorne's treatment of the history of New England. Nothing could be further than his impulse from the antiquarian and sentimental attitude of Whittier in his historical pieces or from that of Longfellow. What Hawthorne found in the past was not the quaint charm of distance but the living issues of moral and psychological definition. What the fact of the past meant to him was a perspective on the present which gives an archetypal clarity and a mythic force. The sentimental flight into an assuagement possible in the past was the last thing he sought. He could praise the ancestors, but at the same time thank God for every year that had come to give distance from them. In his great novel and the tales the underlying theme concerns "legend" as contrasted with "action," the "past" as contrasted with the "future," as in the works of Cooper, Melville, and Faulkner; and sometimes, most obviously in "My Kinsman, Major Molyneux," with this theme is intertwined the psychological struggle to achieve maturity, with the struggle seen as a "fate."

Whittier, though without the scale and power of Cooper, Hawthorne, Melville, and Faulkner, and though he was singularly lacking in their sense of historical and philosophic irony, yet shared their deep intuition of what it meant to be an American. Further, he shared their intuitive capacity to see personal fate as an image for a general cultural and philosophic situation. His star belongs in their constellation. If it is less commanding than any of their, it yet shines with a clear and authentic light.

The House of Poe

Richard Wilbur

A few weeks ago, in the *New York Times Book Review*, Mr. Saul Bellow expressed impatience with the current critical habit of finding symbols in everything. No self-respecting modern professor, Mr. Bellow observed, would dare to explain Achilles's dragging of Hector around the walls of Troy by the mere assertion that Achilles was in a bad temper. That would be too drearily obvious. No, the professor must say that the circular path of Achilles and Hector relates to the theme of circularity which pervades *The Iliad*.

In the following week's *Book Review*, a pedantic correspondent corrected Mr. Bellow, pointing out that Achilles did not, in Homer's *Iliad*, drag Hector's body around the walls of Troy; this perhaps invalidates the Homeric example, but Mr. Bellow's complaint remains, nevertheless, a very sensible one. We are all getting a bit tired, I think, of that laboriously clever criticism which discovers mandalas in Mark Twain, rebirth archetypes in Edwin Arlington Robinson, and fertility myths in everybody.

Still, we must not be carried away by our impatience, to the point of demanding that no more symbols be reported. The business of the critic, after all, is to divine the intention of the work, and to interpret the work in the light of that intention; and since some writers are intentionally symbolic, there is nothing for it but to talk about their symbols. If we speak of Melville, we must speak of symbols. If we speak of Hawthorne, we must speak of symbols. And as for Edgar Allan Poe, whose sesquicentennial year we are met to observe, I think we can make no sense about him until we consider his work—and in particular his prose fiction—as deliberate and often brilliant allegory.

Not everyone will agree with me that Poe's work has an accessible

From *Anniversary Lectures 1959*. © 1966 by Richard Wilbur. The Library of Congress, 1959.

allegorical meaning. Some critics, in fact, have refused to see any substance, allegorical or otherwise, in Poe's fiction, and have regarded his tales as nothing more than complicated machines for saying "boo." Others have intuited undiscoverable meanings in Poe, generally of an unpleasant kind: I recall one Freudian critic declaring that if we find Poe unintelligible we should congratulate ourselves, since if we *could* understand him it would be proof of our abnormality.

It is not really surprising that some critics should think Poe meaningless, or that others should suppose his meaning intelligible only to monsters. Poe was not a wide-open and perspicuous writer; indeed, he was a secretive writer both by temperament and by conviction. He sprinkled his stories with sly references to himself and to his personal history. He gave his own birthday of January 19 to his character William Wilson; he bestowed his own height and color of eye on the captain of the phantom ship in "Ms. Found in a Bottle"; and the name of one of his heroes, Arthur Gordon Pym, is patently a version of his own. He was a maker and solver of puzzles, fascinated by codes, ciphers, anagrams, acrostics, hieroglyphics, and the Kabbala. He invented the detective story. He was fond of aliases; he delighted in accounts of swindles; he perpetrated the famous Balloon Hoax of 1844; and one of his most characteristic stories is entitled "Mystification." A man so devoted to concealment and deception and unraveling and detection might be expected to have in his work what Poe himself called "undercurrents of meaning."

And that is where Poe, as a critic, said that meaning belongs: not on the surface of the poem or tale, but below the surface as a dark undercurrent. If the meaning of a work is made overly clear—as Poe said in his "Philosophy of Composition"—if the meaning is brought to the surface and made the upper current of the poem or tale, then the work becomes bald and prosaic and ceases to be art. Poe conceived of art, you see, not as a means of giving imaginative order to earthly experience, but as a stimulus to unearthly visions. The work of literary art does not, in Poe's view, present the reader with a provisional arrangement of reality; instead, it seeks to disengage the reader's mind from reality and propel it toward the ideal. Now, since Poe thought the function of art was to set the mind soaring upward in what he called "a wild effort to reach the Beauty above," it was important to him that the poem or tale should not have such definiteness and completeness of meaning as might contain the reader's mind within the work. Therefore Poe's criticism places a positive value on the obscuration of meaning, on a dark suggestiveness, on a deliberate vagueness by means of which the reader's mind may be set adrift toward the beyond.

Poe's criticism, then, assures us that his work does have meaning. And Poe also assures us that this meaning is not on the surface but in the depths. If we accept Poe's invitation to play detective, and commence to read him with an eye for submerged meaning, it is not long before we sense that there *are* meanings to be found, and that in fact many of Poe's stories, though superficially dissimilar, tell the same tale. We begin to have this sense as we notice Poe's repeated use of certain narrative patterns; his repetition of certain words and phrases; his use, in story after story, of certain scenes and properties. We notice, for instance, the recurrence of the *spiral* or *vortex.* In "Ms. Found in a Bottle," the story ends with a plunge into a whirlpool; the "Descent into the Maelström" also concludes in a watery vortex; the house of Usher, just before it plunges into the tarn, is swaddled in a whirlwind; the hero of "Metzengerstein," Poe's first published story, perishes in "a whirlwind of chaotic fire"; and at the close of "King Pest," Hugh Tarpaulin is cast into a puncheon of ale and disappears "amid a whirlpool of foam." That Poe offers us so many spirals or vortices in his fiction, and that they should always appear at the same terminal point in their respective narratives, is a strong indication that the spiral had some symbolic value for Poe. And it did: What the spiral invariably represents in any tale of Poe's is the loss of consciousness, and the descent of the mind into sleep.

I hope you will grant, before I am through, that to find spirals in Poe is not so silly as finding circles in Homer. The professor who finds circles in Homer does so to the neglect of more important and more provable meanings. But the spiral or vortex is a part of that symbolic language in which Poe said his say, and unless we understand it we cannot understand Poe.

But now I have gotten ahead of myself, and before I proceed with my project of exploring one area of Poe's symbolism, I think I had better say something about Poe's conception of poetry and the poet.

Poe conceived of God as a poet. The universe, therefore, was an artistic creation, a poem composed by God. Now, if the universe is a poem, it follows that the one proper response to it is aesthetic, and that God's creatures are attuned to Him in proportion as their imaginations are ravished by the beauty and harmony of his creation. Not to worship beauty, not to regard poetic knowledge as divine, would be to turn one's back on God and fall from grace.

The planet Earth, according to Poe's myth of the cosmos, has done just this. It has fallen away from God by exalting the scientific reason above poetic intuition, and by putting its trust in material fact rather than in visionary knowledge. The Earth's inhabitants are thus corrupted by rationalism and materialism; their souls are diseased; and Poe sees this disease of the human spirit as having contaminated physical nature. The woods and fields and waters of earth have thereby lost their first beauty, and no longer clearly express God's imagination; the landscape has lost its original perfection of composition, in proportion as men have lost their power to perceive the beautiful.

Since Earth is a fallen planet, life upon Earth is necessarily a torment for the poet: neither in the human sphere nor in the realm of nature can he find fit objects for contemplation, and indeed his soul is oppressed by everything around him. The rationalist mocks at him; the dull, prosaic spirit of the age damps his imaginative spark; the gross materiality of the world crowds in upon him. His only recourse is to abandon all concern for Earthly things, and to devote himself as purely as possible to unearthly visions, in hopes of glimpsing that heavenly beauty which is the thought of God.

Poe, then, sees the poetic soul as at war with the mundane physical world; and that warfare is Poe's fundamental subject. But the war between soul and world is not the only war. There is also warfare within the poet's very nature. To be sure, the poet's nature was not always in conflict with itself. Prior to his earthly incarnation, and during his dreamy childhood, Poe's poet enjoyed a serene unity of being; his consciousness was purely imaginative, and he knew the universe for the divine poem that it is. But with his entrance into adult life, the poet became involved with a fallen world in which the physical, the factual, the rational, the prosaic are not escapable. Thus, compromised, he lost his perfect spirituality, and is now cursed with a divided nature. Though his imagination still yearns toward ideal beauty, his mortal body chains him to the physical and temporal and local; the hungers and passions of his body draw him toward external objects, and the conflict of conscience and desire degrades and distracts his soul; his mortal senses try to convince him of the reality of a material world which his soul struggles to escape; his reason urges him to acknowledge everyday fact, and to confine his thought within the prison of logic. For all these reasons it is not easy for the poet to detach his soul from earthly things, and regain his lost imaginative power—his power to commune with that supernal beauty which is symbolized, in Poe, by the shadowy and angelic figures of Ligeia, and Helen, and Lenore.

These, then, are Poe's great subjects: first, the war between the poetic soul and the external world; second, the war between the poetic soul and the earthly self to which it is bound. All of Poe's major stories are allegorical presentations of these conflicts, and everything he wrote bore somehow upon them.

How does one wage war against the external world? And how does one release one's visionary soul from the body, and from the constraint of the reason? These may sound like difficult tasks; and yet we all accomplish them every night. In a subjective sense—and Poe's thought is wholly subjective—we destroy the world every time we close our eyes. If *esse est percipi*, as Bishop Berkeley said—if to be is to be perceived—then when we withdraw our attention from the world in somnolence or sleep, the world ceases to be. As our minds move toward sleep, by way of drowsiness and reverie and the hypnagogic state, we escape from consciousness of the world, we escape from awareness of our bodies, and we enter a realm in which reason no longer hampers the play of the imagination: we enter the realm of dream.

Like many romantic poets, Poe identified imagination with dream. Where Poe differed from other romantic poets was in the literalness and absoluteness of the identification, and in the clinical precision with which he observed the phenomena of dream, carefully distinguishing the various states through which the mind passes on its way to sleep. A large number of Poe's stories derive their very structure from this sequence of mental states: "Ms. Found in a Bottle," to give but one example, is an allegory of the mind's voyage from the waking world in to the world of dreams, with each main step of the narrative symbolizing the passage of the mind from one state to another—from wakefulness to reverie, from reverie to the hypnagogic state, from the hypnagogic state to the deep dream. The departure of the narrator's ship from Batavia represents the mind's withdrawal from the waking world; the drowning of the captain and all but one of the crew represents the growing solitude of reverie; when the narrator is transferred by collision from a real ship to a phantom ship, we are to understand that he has passed from reverie, a state in which reality and dream exist in a kind of equilibrium, into the free fantasy of the hypnagogic state. And when the phantom ship makes its final plunge into the whirlpool, we are to understand that the narrator's mind has gone over the brink of sleep and descended into dreams.

What I am saying by means of this example is that the scenes and situations of Poe's tales are always concrete representations of states of mind. If we bear in mind Poe's fundamental plot—the effort of the poetic soul to escape all consciousness of the world in dream—we soon recognize the significance of certain scenic or situational motifs which turn up in story after story. The most important of these recurrent motifs is that of *enclosure* or *circumscription;* perhaps the latter term is preferable, because it is Poe's own word, and because Poe's enclosures are so often more or less circular in form. The heroes of Poe's tales and poems are violently circumscribed by whirlpools, or peacefully circumscribed by cloud-capped paradisal valleys; they float upon circular pools ringed in by steep flowering hillsides; they dwell on islands, or voyage to them; we find Poe's heroes also in coffins, in the cabs of balloons, or hidden away in the holds of ships; and above all we find them sitting alone in the claustral and richly furnished rooms of remote and mouldering mansions.

Almost never, if you think about it, is one of Poe's heroes to be seen standing in the light of common day; almost never does the Poe hero breathe the air that others breathe; he requires some kind of envelope in order to be what he is; he is always either enclosed or on his way to an enclosure. The narrative of William Wilson conducts the hero from Stoke Newington to Eton, from Eton to Oxford, and then to Rome by way of Paris, Vienna, Berlin, Moscow, Naples, and Egypt: and yet, for all his travels, Wilson seems never to set foot out-of-doors. The story takes place in a series of rooms, the last one locked from the inside.

Sometimes Poe emphasizes the circumscription of his heroes by multiple enclosures. Roderick Usher dwells in a great and crumbling mansion from which, as Poe tells us, he has not ventured forth in many years. This mansion stands islanded in a stagnant lake, which serves it as a defensive moat. And beyond the moat lies the Usher estate, a vast barren tract having its own peculiar and forbidding weather and atmosphere. You might say that Roderick Usher is defended in depth; and yet at the close of the story Poe compounds Roderick's inaccessibility by having the mansion and its occupant swallowed up by the waters of the tarn.

What does it mean that Poe's heroes are invariably enclosed or circumscribed? The answer is simple: circumscription, in Poe's tales, means the exclusion from consciousness of the so-called real world, the world of time and reason and physical fact; it means the isolation of the poetic soul in visionary reverie or trance. When we find one of Poe's characters in a remote valley, or a claustral room, we know that he is in the process of dreaming his way out of the world.

Now, I want to devote the time remaining to the consideration of one kind of enclosure in Poe's tales: the mouldering mansion and its richly furnished rooms. I want to concentrate on Poe's architecture and décor for two reasons: first, because Poe's use of architecture is so frankly and provably allegorical that I *should* be able to be convincing about it; second, because by concentrating on one area of Poe's symbolism we shall be able to see that his stories are allegorical not only in their broad patterns, but also in their smallest details.

Let us begin with a familiar poem, "The Haunted Palace." The opening stanzas of this poem, as a number of critics have noted, make a point-by-point comparison between a building and the head of a man. The exterior of the palace represents the man's physical features; the interior represents the man's mind engaged in harmonious imaginative thought.

> In the greenest of our valleys
>   By good angels tenanted,
> Once a fair and stately palace—
>   Radiant palace—reared its head.
> In the monarch Thought's dominion—
>   It stood there!
> Never seraph spread a pinion
>   Over fabric half so fair!
>
> Banners yellow, glorious, golden,
>   On its roof did float and flow,
> (This—all this—was in the olden
>   Time long ago,)
> And every gentle air that dallied,
>   In that sweet day,
> Along the ramparts plumed and pallid,
>   A wingéd odor went away.
>
> Wanderers in that happy valley,
>   Through two luminous windows, saw

> Spirits moving musically,
>   To a lute's well-tunéd law,
> Round about a throne where, sitting,
>   Porphyrogene,
> In state his glory well befitting,
>   The ruler of the realm was seen.
>
> And all in pearl and ruby glowing
>   Was the fair palace door,
> Through which came flowing, flowing, flowing,
>   And sparkling evermore,
> A troop of Echoes, whose sweet duty
>   Was but to sing,
> In voices of surpassing beauty,
>   The wit and wisdom of their king.

I expect you observed that the two luminous windows of the palace are the eyes of a man, and that the yellow banners on the roof are his luxuriant blond hair. The "pearl and ruby" door is the man's mouth—ruby representing red lips, and pearl representing pearly white teeth. The beautiful Echoes which issue from the pearl and ruby door are the poetic utterances of the man's harmonious imagination, here symbolized as an orderly dance. The angel-guarded valley in which the palace stands, and which Poe describes as "the monarch Thought's dominion," is a symbol of the man's exclusive awareness of exalted and spiritual things. The valley is what Poe elsewhere called "that evergreen and radiant paradise which the true poet knows . . . as the limited realm of his authority, as the circumscribed Eden of his dreams."

As you all remember, the last two stanzas of the poem describe the physical and spiritual corruption of the palace and its domain, and it was to this part of the poem that Poe was referring when he told a correspondent, "By the 'Haunted Palace' I mean to imply a mind haunted by phantoms—a disordered brain." Let me read you the closing lines:

> But evil things, in robes of sorrow,
>   Assailed the monarch's high estate.
> (Ah, let us mourn!—for never morrow
>   Shall dawn upon him desolate!)
>
> And round about his home the glory
>   That blushed and bloomed,
> Is but a dim-remembered story
>   Of the old time entombed
>
> And travellers, now, within that valley,
>   Through the red-litten windows see

Vast forms, that move fantastically
To a discordant melody,
While, like a ghastly rapid river,
Through the pale door
A hideous throng rush out forever
And laugh—but smile no more.

The domain of the monarch Thought, in these final stanzas, is disrupted by civil war, and in consequence everything alters for the worse. The valley becomes barren, like the domain of Roderick Usher; the eye-like windows of the palace are no longer "luminous," but have become "red-litten"—they are like the bloodshot eyes of a madman or a drunkard. As for the mouth of our allegorized man, it is now "pale" rather than "pearl and ruby," and through it come no sweet Echoes, as before, but the wild laughter of a jangling and discordant mind.

The two states of the palace—before and after—are, as we can see, two states of mind. Poe does not make it altogether clear *why* one state of mind has given way to the other, but by recourse to similar tales and poems we can readily find the answer. The palace in its original condition expresses the imaginative harmony which the poet's soul enjoys in early childhood, when all things are viewed with a tyrannical and unchallenged subjectivity. But as the soul passes from childhood into adult life, its consciousness is more and more invaded by the corrupt and corrupting external world: it succumbs to passion, it develops a conscience, it makes concessions to reason and to objective fact. Consequently, there is civil war in the palace of the mind. The imagination must now struggle against the intellect and the moral sense; finding itself no longer able to possess the world through a serene solipsism, it strives to annihilate the outer world by turning in upon itself; it flees into irrationality and dream; and all its dreams are efforts both to recall and to simulate its primal, unfallen state. "The Haunted Palace" presents us with a possible key to the general meaning of Poe's architecture; and this key proves, if one tries it, to open every building in Poe's fiction. Roderick Usher, as you will remember, declaims "The Haunted Palace" to the visitor who tells his story, accompanying the poem with wild improvisations on the guitar. We are encouraged, therefore, to compare the palace of the poem with the house of the story; and it is no surprise to find that the Usher mansion has "vacant eye-like windows," and that there are mysterious physical sympathies between Roderick Usher and the house in which he dwells. The House of Usher *is*, in allegorical fact, the physical body of Roderick Usher, and its dim interior *is*, in fact, Roderick Usher's visionary mind.

The House of Usher, like many edifices in Poe, is in a state of extreme decay. The stonework of its facade has so crumbled and decomposed that it reminds the narrator, as he puts it, "of the specious totality of old woodwork which has rotted for long years in some neglected vault." The Usher mansion is so eaten away, so fragile, that it seems a breeze would push it over; it remains standing only because the atmosphere of Usher's domain is perfectly motionless and dead. Such is the case also with the "time-eaten towers that tremble not" in Poe's poem "The City in the Sea"; and likewise the magnificent architecture of "The Domain of Arnheim" is said to "sustain itself by a miracle in mid-air." Even the detective Dupin lives in a perilously decayed structure: the narrator of "The Murders in the Rue Morgue" tells how he and Dupin dwelt in a "time-eaten and grotesque mansion, long deserted through superstitions into which we did not enquire, and tottering to its fall in a retired and desolate portion of the Faubourg St. Germain." (Notice how, even when Poe's buildings are situated in cities, he manages to circumscribe them with a protective desolation.)

We must now ask what Poe means by the extreme and tottering decay of so many of his structures. The answer is best given by reference to "The Fall of the House of Usher," and in giving the answer we shall arrive, I think, at an understanding of the pattern of that story.

"The Fall of the House of Usher" is a journey into the depths of the self. I have said that all journeys in Poe are allegories of the process of dreaming, and we must understand "The Fall of the House of Usher" as a dream of the narrator's, in which he leaves behind him the waking, physical world and journeys inward toward his *moi intérieur*, toward his inner and spiritual self. That inner and spiritual self is Roderick Usher.

Roderick Usher, then, is part of the narrator's self, which the narrator reaches by way of reverie. We may think of Usher, if we like, as the narrator's imagination, or as his visionary soul. Or we may think of him as a *state of mind* which the narrator enters at a certain stage of his progress into dreams. Considered as a state of mind, Roderick Usher is an allegorical figure representing the hypnagogic state.

The hypnagogic state, about which there is strangely little said in the literature of psychology, is a condition of semiconsciousness in which the closed eye beholds a continuous procession of vivid and constantly changing forms. These forms sometimes have color, and are often abstract in character. Poe regarded the hypnagogic state as the visionary condition *par excellence*, and he considered its rapidly shifting abstract images to be—as he put it—"glimpses of the spirit's outer world." These visionary glimpses, Poe says in one of his *Marginalia*, "arise in the soul . . . only . . . at those mere points of time where the confines of the waking world blend with those of the world of dreams." And Poe goes on to say: "I am aware of these 'fancies' only when I am upon the very brink of sleep, with the consciousness that I am so."

Roderick Usher enacts the hypnagogic state in a number of ways. For one thing, the narrator describes Roderick's behavior as inconsistent, and characterized by constant alternation: he is alternately vivacious and sullen; he is alternately communicative and rapt; he speaks at one moment with "tremulous indecision," and at the next with the "energetic concision" of an excited opium-eater. His conduct resembles, in other words, that wavering between consciousness and subconsciousness which characterizes the hypnagogic state. The trembling of Roderick's body, and the floating of his silken hair, also bring to mind the instability and underwater quality of hypnagogic images. His improvisations on the guitar suggest hypnagogic experience in their rapidity, changeableness, and wild novelty. And as for Usher's paintings, which the narrator describes as "pure abstractions," they quite simply *are* hypnagogic images. The narrator says of Roderick, "From the paintings over which his elaborate fancy brooded, and which grew, touch by touch, into vaguenesses at which I shuddered the more thrillingly because I shuddered without knowing why—from these paintings (vivid as their images now are before me) I would in vain endeavor to educe more than a small portion which should lie within the compass of merely written words." That the narrator finds Roderick's paintings indescribable is interesting, because in that one of the *Marginalia* from which I have quoted, Poe asserts that the only things in human experience which lie "beyond the compass of words" are the visions of the hypnagogic state.

Roderick Usher stands for the hypnagogic state, which as Poe said is a teetering condition of mind occurring "upon the very brink of sleep." Since Roderick is the embodiment of a state of mind in which *falling*—falling asleep—is imminent, it is appropriate that the building which symbolizes his mind should promise at every moment to fall. The House of Usher stares down broodingly at its reflection in the tarn below, as in the hypnagogic state the conscious mind may stare into the subconscious; the house threatens continually to collapse because it is extremely easy for the mind to slip from the hypnagogic state into the depths of sleep; and when the House of Usher *does* fall, the story ends, as it must, because the mind, at the end of its inward journey, has plunged into the darkness of sleep.

We have found one allegorical meaning in the tottering decay of Poe's buildings; there is another meaning, equally important, which may be stated very briefly. I have said that Poe saw the poet as at war with the material world, and with the material or physical aspects of himself; and I have said that Poe identified poetic imagination with the power to escape from the material and the materialistic, to exclude them from consciousness and so subjectively destroy them. Now, if we recall these things, and recall also that the exteriors of Poe's houses or palaces, with their eye-like windows and mouth-like doors, represent the physical features of Poe's dreaming heroes, then the characteristic dilapidation of Poe's architecture takes on sudden significance. The extreme decay of the House of Usher—a decay so extreme as to approach the atmospheric—is quite simply a sign that the narrator, in reaching that state of mind which he calls Roderick Usher, has very nearly dreamt himself free of his physical body, and of the material world with which that body connects him.

This is what decay or decomposition mean everywhere in Poe; and we find them almost everywhere. Poe's preoccupation with decay is not, as some critics have thought, an indication of necrophilia; decay in Poe is a symbol of visionary remoteness from the physical, a sign that the state of mind represented is one of almost pure spirituality. When the House of Usher disintegrates or dematerializes at the close of the story, it does so because Roderick Usher has become all soul. "The Fall of the House of Usher," then, is not really a horror story; it is a triumphant report by the narrator that it *is* possible for the poetic soul to shake off this temporal, rational, physical world and escape, if only for a moment, to a realm of unfettered vision.

We have now arrived at three notions about Poe's typical building. It is set apart in a valley or a sea or a waste place, and this remoteness is intended to express the retreat of the Poet's mind from worldly consciousness into dream. It is a tottery structure, and this indicates that the dreamer within is in that unstable threshold condition called the hypnagogic state. Finally, Poe's typical building is crumbling or decomposing, and this means that the dreamer's mind is moving toward a perfect freedom from his material self and the material world. Let us now open the door—or mouth—of Poe's building and visit the mind inside.

As we enter the palace of the visionary hero of "The Assignation," or the house of Roderick Usher, we find ourselves approaching the master's private chamber by way of dim and winding passages, or a winding staircase. There is no end to dim windings in Poe's fiction: there are dim and winding woods paths, dim and winding streets, dim and winding watercourses—and, whenever the symbolism is architectural, there are likely to be dim and winding passages or staircases. It is not at all hard to guess what Poe means by this symbol. If we think of waking life as dominated by reason, and if we think of the reason as a daylight faculty which operates in straight lines, then it is proper that reverie should be represented as an obscure and wandering movement of the mind. There are other, and equally obvious meanings in Poe's symbol of dim and winding passages: to grope through such passages is to become confused as to place and direction, just as in reverie we begin to lose any sense of locality, and to have an infinite freedom in regard to space. In his description of the huge old mansion in which William Wilson went to school, Poe makes this meaning of winding passages very plain:

> But the house!—how quaint an old building was this!—to me how veritable a palace of enchantment! There was no end to its windings—to its incomprehensible subdivisions. It was difficult, at any given time, to say with certainty upon which of its two stories one happened to be. From each room to every other there were sure to be found three or four steps either in ascent or descent. Then the lateral branches were innumerable—inconceivable—and so returning in upon themselves, that our most exact ideas in regard to the whole mansion were not very far different from those with which we pondered on infinity.

Dim windings indicate the state of reverie; they point toward that infinite freedom in and from space which the mind achieves in dreams; also, in their curvature and in their occasional doubling-back, they anticipate the mind's final spiralling plunge into unconsciousness. But the immediate goal of reverie's winding passages is that magnificent chamber in which we find the visionary hero slumped in a chair or lolling on an ottoman, occupied in purging his consciousness of everything that is earthly.

Since I have been speaking of geometry—of straight lines and curves and spirals—perhaps the first thing to notice about Poe's dream rooms is their shape. It has already been said that the enclosures of Poe's tales incline to a curving or circular form. And Poe himself, in certain of his essays and dialogues, explains this inclination by denouncing what he calls "the harsh mathematical reason of the schools," and complaining that practical science has covered the face of the earth with "rectangular obscenities." Poe quite explicitly identifies regular angular forms with everyday reason, and the circle, oval, or fluid arabesque with the otherworldly imagination. Therefore, if we discover that the dream chambers of Poe's fiction are free of angular regularity, we may be sure that we are noticing a pointed and purposeful consistency in his architecture and décor.

The ballroom of the story "Hop-Frog" is circular. The Devil's apartment in "The Duc de l'Omelette" has its corners "rounded into niches," and we find rounded corners also in Poe's essay "The Philosophy of Furniture." In "Ligeia," the bridal chamber is a pentagonal turret room; however, the angles are concealed by sarcophagi, so that the effect is circular. The corners of Roderick Usher's chamber are likewise concealed, being lost in deep shadow. Other dream rooms are either irregular or indeterminate in form. For example, there are the seven rooms of Prince Prospero's imperial suite in "The Masque of the Red Death." As Poe observes, "in many palaces . . . such suites form a long and straight vista"; but in Prince Prospero's palace, as he describes it, "the apartments were so irregularly disposed that the vision embraced but little more than one at a time. There was a sharp turn at every twenty or thirty yards, and at each turn a novel effect." The turret room of "The Oval Portrait" is not defined as to shape; we are told, however, that it is architecturally "bizarre," and complicated by a quantity of unexpected nooks and niches. Similarly, the visionary's apartment in "The Assignation" is described only as dazzling, astounding and original in its architecture; we are not told in what way its dimensions are peculiar, but it seems safe to assume that it would be a difficult room to measure for wall-to-wall carpeting. The room of "The Assignation," by the way—like that of "Ligeia"—has its walls enshrouded in rich figured draperies which are continually agitated by some mysterious agency. The fluid shifting of the figures suggests, of course, the behavior of hypnagogic images; but the agitation of the draperies would also produce a perpetual ambiguity of architectural form, and the effect would resemble that which Pevsner ascribes to the interior of San Vitale in Ravenna: "a sensation of uncertainty [and] of a dreamlike floating."

Poe, as you see, is at great pains to avoid depicting the usual squarish sort of room in which we spend much of our waking lives. His chambers of dream either approximate the circle—an infinite form which is, as Poe somewhere observes, "the emblem of Eternity"—or they so lack any apprehensible regularity of shape as to suggest the changeableness and spatial freedom of the dreaming mind. The exceptions to this rule are few and entirely explainable. I will grant, for instance, that the iron-walled torture chamber of "The Pit and the Pendulum" portrays the very reverse of spatial freedom, and that it is painfully angular in character, the angles growing more acute as the torture intensifies. But there is a very good allegorical reason for these things. The rooms of "Ligeia" or "The Assignation" symbolize a triumphantly imaginative state of mind in which the dreamer is all but free of the so-called "real" world. In "The Pit and the Pendulum," the dream is of quite another kind; it is a nightmare state, in which the dreamer is imaginatively impotent, and can find no refuge from reality, even in dream. Though he lies on the brink of the pit, on the very verge of the plunge into unconsciousness, he is still unable to disengage himself from the physical and temporal world. The physical oppresses him in the shape of lurid graveyard visions; the temporal oppresses him in the form of an enormous and deadly pendulum. It is altogether appropriate, then, that this particular chamber should be constricting and cruelly angular.

But let us return to Poe's typical room, and look now at its furnishings. They are generally weird, magnificent, and suggestive of great wealth. The narrator of "The Assignation," entering the hero's apartment, feels "blind and dizzy with luxuriousness," and looking about him he confesses, "I could not bring myself to believe that the wealth of any subject in Europe could have supplied the princely magnificence which burned and blazed around." Poe's visionaries are, as a general thing, extremely rich; the hero of "Ligeia" confides that, as for wealth, he possesses "far more, very far more, than ordinarily falls to the lot of mortals"; and Ellison, in "The Domain of Arnheim," is the fortunate inheritor of 450 million dollars. Legrand, in "The Gold Bug," with his treasure of 450 *thousand,* is only a poor relation of Mr. Ellison; still, by ordinary standards, he seems sublimely solvent.

Now, we must be careful to take all these riches in an allegorical sense. As we contemplate the splendor of any of Poe's rooms, we must remember that the room is a state of mind, and that everything in it is therefore a thought, a mental image. The allegorical meaning of the costliness of Poe's décor is simply this: that his heroes are richly imaginative. And since imagination is a gift rather than an acquisition, it is appropriate that riches in Poe should be inherited or found, but never earned.

Another thing we notice about Poe's furnishings is that they are eclectic in the extreme. Their richness is not the richness of Tiffany's and Sloan's, but of all periods and all cultures. Here is a partial inventory of the fantastic bridal chamber in "Ligeia": Egyptian carvings and sarcophagi; Venetian glass; fretwork of a semi-Gothic, semi-Druidical character; a Saracenic chandelier; Oriental ottomans and candelabra; an Indian couch; and figured draperies with Norman motifs. The same defiance of what interior decorators once called "keeping" is found in the apartment of the visionary hero of "The Assignation," and one of that hero's speeches hints at the allegorical meaning of his jumbled décor:

> To dream [says the hero of "The Assignation"]—to dream has been the business of my life. I have therefore framed for myself, as you see, a bower of dreams. In the heart of Venice could I have erected a better? You behold around you, it is true, a medley of architectural embellishments. The chastity of Ionia is offended by antediluvian devices, and the sphynxes of Egypt are outstretched upon carpets of gold. Yet the effect is incongruous to the timid alone. Proprieties of place, and especially of time, are the bugbears which terrify mankind from the contemplation of the magnificent.

That last sentence, with its scornful reference to "proprieties of place, and . . . time," should put us in mind of the first stanza of Poe's poem "Dream-Land":

> By a route obscure and lonely,
> Haunted by ill angels only,
> Where an Eidolon, named NIGHT,
> On a black throne reigns upright,
> I have reached these lands but newly
> From an ultimate dim Thule—
> From a wild weird clime that lieth, sublime,
> Out of SPACE—out of TIME.

In dreamland, we are "out of SPACE—out of TIME," and the same is true of such apartments or "bowers of dreams" as the hero of "The Assignation" inhabits. His eclectic furnishings, with their wild juxtapositions of Venetian and Indian, Egyptian and Norman, are symbolic of the visionary soul's transcendence of spatial and temporal limitations. When one of Poe's dream rooms is *not* furnished in the fashion I have been describing, the idea of spatial and temporal freedom is often conveyed in some other manner: Roderick Usher's library, for instance, with its rare and precious volumes belonging to all times and tongues, is another concrete symbol of the timelessness and placelessness of the dreaming mind.

We have spoken of the winding approaches to Poe's dream chambers, of their curvilinear or indeterminate shape, and of the rich eclecticism of their furnishings. Let us now glance over such matters as lighting, soundproofing, and ventilation. As regards lighting, the rooms of Poe's tales are never exposed to the naked rays of the sun, because the sun belongs to the waking world and waking consciousness. The narrator of "The Murders in the Rue Morgue" tells how he and his friend Dupin conducted their lives in such a way as to avoid all exposure to sunlight. "At the first dawn of the morning," he writes, "we closed all the massy shutters of our old building; lighting a couple of tapers which, strongly perfumed, threw out only the ghastliest and feeblest of rays. By the aid of these we then busied our souls in dreams . . . "

In some of Poe's rooms, there simply are no windows. In other cases, the windows are blocked up or shuttered. When the windows are not blocked or shuttered, their panes are tinted with a crimson or leaden hue, so as to transform the light of day into a lurid or ghastly glow. This kind of lighting, in which the sun's rays are admitted but transformed, belongs to the portrayal of those half-states of mind in which dream and reality are blended. Filtered through tinted panes, the sunlight enters certain of Poe's rooms as it might enter the half-closed eyes of a daydreamer, or the dream-dimmed eyes of someone awakening from sleep. But when Poe wishes to represent that deeper phase of dreaming in which visionary consciousness has all but annihilated any sense of the external world, the lighting is always artificial and the time is always night.

Flickering candles, wavering torches, and censers full of writhing vari-colored flames furnish much of the illumination of Poe's rooms, and one can see the appropriateness of such lighting to the vague and shifting perceptions of the hypnagogic state. But undoubtedly the most important lighting-fixture in Poe's rooms—and one which appears in a good half of them—is the chandelier. It hangs from the lofty ceiling by a long chain, generally of gold, and it consists sometimes of a censer, sometimes of a lamp, sometimes of candles, sometimes of a glowing jewel (a ruby or a diamond), and once, in the macabre tale "King Pest," of a skull containing ignited charcoal. What we must understand about this chandelier, as Poe explains in his poem "Al Aaraaf," is that its chain does not stop at the ceiling: it goes right on through the ceiling, through the roof, and up to heaven. What comes down the chain from heaven is the divine power of imagination, and it is imagination's purifying fire which flashes or flickers from the chandelier. That is why the immaterial and angelic Ligeia makes her reappearance directly beneath the chandelier; and that is why Hop-Frog makes his departure for dreamland by climbing the chandelier chain and vanishing through the skylight.

The dreaming soul, then, has its own light—a light more spiritual, more divine, than that of the sun. And Poe's chamber of dream is auton-omous in every other respect. No breath of air enters it from the outside world: either its atmosphere is dead, or its draperies are stirred by magical and intramural air currents. No earthly sound invades the chamber: either it is deadly still, or it echoes with a sourceless and unearthly music. Nor does any odor off lower or field intrude: instead, as Poe tells in "The Assignation," the sense of smell is "oppressed by mingled and conflicting perfumes, reeking up from strange convolute censers."

The point of all this is that the dreaming psyche separates itself wholly from the bodily senses—the "rudimental senses," as Poe called them. The bodily senses are dependent on objective stimuli—on the lights and sounds and odors of the physical world. But the sensuous life of dream is self-sufficient and immaterial, and consists in the imagination's Godlike enjoyment of its own creations.

I am reminded, at this point, of a paragraph of Santayana's, in which he describes the human soul as it was conceived by the philosopher Leibniz. Leibniz, says Santayana, assigned

> a mental seat to all sensible objects. The soul, he said, had no windows and, he might have added, no doors; no light could come to it from without; and it could not exert any transitive force or make any difference beyond its own insulated chamber. It was a *camera obscura*, with a universe painted on its impenetrable walls. The changes which went on in it were like those in a dream, due to the discharge of pent-up energies and fecundities within it.

Leibniz's chamber of the soul is identical with Poe's chamber of dream: but the solipsism which Leibniz saw as the normal human condition was for Poe an ideal state, a blessed state, which we may enjoy as children or as preexistent souls, but can reclaim in adult life only by a flight from everyday consciousness into hypnagogic trance.

The one thing which remains to be said about Poe's buildings is that cellars or catacombs, whenever they appear, stand for the irrational part of the mind; and that is so conventional an equation in symbolic literature that I think I need not be persuasive or illustrative about it. I had hoped, at this point, to discuss in a leisurely way some of the stories in which Poe makes use of his architectural properties, treating those stories as narrative wholes. But I have spoken too long about other things; and so, if you will allow me a few minutes more, I shall close by commenting briskly on two or three stories only.

The typical Poe story occurs *within* the mind of a poet; and its characters are not independent personalities, but allegorical figures representing the warring principles of the poet's divided nature. The lady Ligeia, for example, stands for that heavenly beauty which the poet's soul desires; while Rowena stands for that earthly, physical beauty which tempts the poet's passions. The action of the story is the dreaming soul's gradual emancipation from earthly attachments—which is allegorically expressed in the slow dissolution of Rowena. The result of this process is the soul's final, momentary vision of the heavenly Ligeia. Poe's typical story presents some such struggle between the visionary and the mundane; and the duration of Poe's typical story is the duration of a dream.

There are two tales in which Poe makes an especially clear and simple use of his architectural symbolism. The first is an unfamiliar tale called "The System of Dr. Tarr and Prof. Fether," and the edifice of that tale is a remote and dilapidated madhouse in southern France. What happens, in brief, is that the inmates of the madhouse escape from their cells in the basement of the building, overpower their keepers, and lock them up in their own cells. Having done this, the lunatics take possession of the upper reaches of the house. They shutter all the windows, put on odd costumes, and proceed to hold an uproarious and discordant feast, during which there is much eating and drinking of a disgusting kind, and a degraded version of Ligeia or Helen does a strip tease. At the height of these festivities, the keepers escape from their cells, break in through the barred and shuttered windows of the dining room, and restore order.

Well: the madhouse, like all of Poe's houses, is a mind. The keepers are the rational part of that mind, and the inmates are its irrational part. As you noticed, the irrational is suitably assigned to the cellar. The uprising of the inmates, and the suppression of the keepers, symbolizes the beginning of a dream, and the mad banquet which follows is perhaps Poe's least spiritual portrayal of the dream state: *this* dream, far from being an escape from the physical, consists exclusively of the release of animal appetites— as dreams sometimes do. When the keepers break in the windows, and subdue the revellers, they bring with them reason and the light of day, and the wild dream is over.

"The Masque of the Red Death" is a better-known and even more obvious example of architectural allegory. You will recall how Prince Prospero, when his dominions are being ravaged by the plague, withdraws with a thousand of his knights and ladies into a secluded, impregnable and windowless abbey, where after a time he entertains his friends with a costume ball. The weird décor of the seven ballrooms expresses the Prince's own taste, and in strange costumes of the Prince's own design the company dances far into the night, looking, as Poe says, like "a multitude of dreams." The festivities are interrupted only by the hourly striking of a gigantic ebony clock which stands in the westernmost room; and the striking of this clock has invariably a sobering effect on the revellers. Upon the last stroke of twelve, as you will remember, there appears amid the throng a figure attired in the blood-dabbled graveclothes of a plague-victim. The dancers shrink from him in terror. But the Prince, infuriated at what he takes to be an insolent practical joke, draws his dagger and pursues the figure through all of the seven rooms. In the last and westernmost room, the figure suddenly turns and confronts Prince Prospero, who gives a cry of despair and falls upon his own dagger. The Prince's friends rush forward to seize the intruder, who stands now within the shadow of the ebony clock; but they find nothing there. And then, one after the other, the thousand revellers fall dead of the Red Death, and the lights flicker out, and Prince Prospero's ball is at an end.

In spite of its cast of one thousand and two, "The Masque of the Red Death" has only one character. Prince Prospero is one-half of that character, the visionary half; the nameless figure in graveclothes is the other, as we shall see in a moment.

More than once, in his dialogues or critical writings, Poe describes the earth-bound, time-bound rationalism of his age as a *disease*. And that is what the Red Death signifies. Prince Prospero's flight from the Red Death is the poetic imagination's flight from temporal and worldly consciousness into dream. The thousand dancers of Prince Prospero's costume ball are just what Poe says they are—"dreams" or "phantasms," veiled and vivid creatures of Prince Prospero's rapt imagination. Whenever there is a feast, or carnival, or costume ball in Poe, we may be sure that a dream is in progress.

But what is the gigantic ebony clock? For the answer to that, one need only consult a dictionary of slang: we call the human heart a *ticker*, meaning that it is the clock of the body; and that is what Poe means here. In sleep, our minds may roam beyond the temporal world, but our hearts tick on, binding us to time and mortality. Whenever the ebony clock strikes, the dancers of Prince Prospero's dream grow momentarily pale and still, in half-awareness that they and their revel must have an end; it is as if a sleeper should half-awaken, and know that he has been dreaming, and then sink back into dreams again.

The figure in blood-dabbled graveclothes, who stalks through the terrified company and vanishes in the shadow of the clock, is waking temporal consciousness, and his coming means the death of dreams. He breaks up Prince Prospero's ball as the keepers in "Dr. Tarr and Prof. Fether" break up the revels of the lunatics. The final confrontation between Prince Prospero and the shrouded figure is like the terrible final meeting between William Wilson and his double. Recognizing his adversary as his own worldly and mortal self, Prince Prospero gives a cry of despair which is also Poe's cry of despair: despair at the realization that only by self-destruction could the poet fully free his soul from the trammels of this world.

Poe's aesthetic, Poe's theory of the nature of art, seems to me insane. To say that art should repudiate everything human and earthly, and find its subject matter at the flickering end of dreams, is hopelessly to narrow the scope and function of art. Poe's aesthetic points toward such impoverishments as *poésie pure* and the abstract expressionist movement in painting. And yet, despite his aesthetic, Poe is a great artist, and I would rest my case for him on his prose allegories of psychic conflict. In them, Poe broke wholly new ground, and they remain the best things of their kind in our literature. Poe's mind may have been a strange one; yet all minds are alike in their general structure; therefore we can understand him, and I think that he will have something to say to us as long as there is civil war in the palaces of men's minds.

Transcendental Egoism
in Very and Whitman

Lawrence Buell

Jones Very and Walt Whitman would certainly have disliked sharing an [essay] with each other, even though one of the Very family's cats, "an enormous grey woolly" animal, was named after Walt. Very's austere pietism and Whitman's metropolitan expansiveness do not mix. But they resemble each other in the lengths to which they go in experimenting poetically with the idea of the self. Emerson invented the equation which all such experiments assume, i = I (or self = Self, soul = Soul), but modestly refrained from exploiting it in his own person, except in a limited way. Thoreau presented a version of himself as a representative man, but did not press his claims to prophetic status beyond a point. Whitman and Very, however, both regarded themselves as charismatic figures called to be spokesmen, through their poetry, of the divine word. Not that this was the only view they had of themselves: in Very's case, it lasted with full intensity only for a brief period; in Whitman's, it alternated with more modest images of himself as lyrist and language experimenter. Partly because of these complicating factors, one of the salient features of the poetry of both is a fascinating interplay of voices. Now the poet speaks from one side of his mind, now from another; now he speaks in his own person, now he is prophet or God.

In their development of the possiblities of the poetic speaker's role, Very and Whitman suggest Tennyson and Browning's contemporaneous achievements in the dramatic monologue. The four poets share in common the impulse to project themselves imaginatively into as many forms of experience as possible. The main difference is that the Victorians maintain a certain ironic distance from their poetic masks, while Very and Whitman

From *Literary Transcendentalism.* © 1973 by Cornell University. Cornell University Press, 1973.

express lyric empathy with theirs. This latter characteristic can be traced back to the idea of cosmic unity-in-diversity discussed in part 3 [elsewhere]. According to this principle, the individual may stand before all the monuments of the past, as Emerson puts it, and tell himself, " 'Under this mask did my Proteus nature hide itself.' " There is no identity in nature or history which the inspired soul may not assume. Hence one finds Emerson in his poetry speaking in the person of Alphonso of Castile, Mithridates, Montaigne, Merlin, Saadi, Brahma, Nature, a nun, and other identities.

But as Jonathan Bishop points out, often Emerson's "projected identities are playful, even capricious." Emerson writes in an increasing awareness of the insufficiency of the individual perception and therefore the inevitability of role-playing when one assumes a given stance or identity. In his later writing, accordingly, the figure of Proteus stands no longer for unity-in-variety but for the elusiveness of truth and the illusoriness of appearances. But while Emerson himself thus becomes something of a Victorian, detaching himself from the identities he momentarily assumes, his successors take their "I" more seriously and attempt to orient their creative worlds around it. Thus the poetic stance of Very and Whitman is truer to the original Transcendentalist idea of self, and it is in their writings rather than in Emerson's or Thoreau's that one sees the literary possibilities of this idea exploited to the fullest.

Jones Very was temperamentally much less urbane and more intense than Emerson, and far less inclined to view man's relation to God and nature in impersonal terms. For Emerson, God was a "sublime It"; Very, as a self-professed Channing Unitarian, experienced God as a father and was therefore much more likely to write about spiritual experience in familiar terms. As for Very's attitude toward nature, he seems to have held that nature is a stumbling block for man in his fallen or unenlightened condition (a notion which Emerson would have rejected as a Calvinistic anachronism), but that regenerated man is restored to Adam's position of mastery over the things of nature:

> For he who with his maker walks aright
> Shall be their Lord as Adam was before.

This sentiment seems identical with Emerson's position in *Nature*, but in fact there is an implicit difference. For Very is deeply committed to the idea of man's relationship to nature as a kind of personal mastery (though he would reject this way of putting it), while Emerson sticks rather closely to an impersonal view of this relationship as spirit answering to spirit. Superficially, this claim will seem paradoxical, since Emerson frequently expresses an admiration of the great man who dominates his environment, whereas Very's extreme pietism keeps him from such hero worship. But that same pietism made Very more aware of spiritual grandeur as a personal feeling.

A comparison of the essays each man wrote about Shakespeare will give a better sense of this difference between them. To a large extent they are interested in Shakespeare for the same reasons: his creative range or negative capability, the way in which he seems to illustrate the idea of the creative process as inspired and spontaneous, and the alarming discrepancy between his genius and his "immorality." The difference is that Emerson is content to know nothing of the "real" Shakespeare. He sees it rather as a virtue that "Shakespeare is the only biographer of Shakespeare." Very, on the other hand, is intensely concerned with reconstructing and typing Shakespeare's mind. Even his negative capability Very insists on seeing as a mark of personality: "In this activity of mind, then, in this childlike superiority to the objects by which it was attracted, we find Shakespeare," although Very goes on to concede that "this condition of mind might perhaps be designated as an impersonal one, so strongly is it always possessed by that which is before it, as to seem for the time to have no other individuality.

The standard by which Very finally judges Shakespeare is also instructive. He sees Shakespeare as a spiritual child, as representing "that primaeval state of innocence from which we have fallen," but by the same token having the moral limitations of a child. In the sense that a child's mind spontaneously and amorally reflects everything in its environment, Shakespeare represented both the pure and the impure. "In Wordsworth and Milton, on the contrary, we see the struggle of the child to become the perfect man in Christ Jesus," which is a higher aspiration. This intermediate stage of development is something of a declension also, in that the poet loses his power of total empathy and becomes trapped in self-consciousness, "but when the war of self which these and other bards have so nobly maintained shall have ceased, and the will of the Father shall be done on earth as it is in heaven . . . then shall the poet again find himself speaking with many tongues: . . . Each soul shall show in its varied action the beauty and grandeur of Nature; and shall live forever a teacher of the words it hears from the Father." This formulation contains an interesting and characteristic mixture of the ideas of self-abasement and self-glorification. Very had more of both than Emerson, insisting on the necessity both of absolute submission to the will of God and the infallible authority of him who had done so, as Very believed himself to have done.

Very's peculiar brand of intoxication with the self comes out most strikingly in the last of three unpublished letters "To the Unborn," evidently designed as a preface to the 1839 *Essays and Poems* but rejected by Emerson. These letters (on "Birth," "Prayer," and "Miracles"), called "Epistles" after St. Paul but written in the style of St. John, are in effect three minisermons on redemption. Each of his three subjects Very interprets metaphorically in the transcendental or post-Unitarian manner. Real birth is the new birth; true prayer is the total action of the reborn man; the true miracle is the unity of the self with God which awaits the reborn. To dramatize this last idea, Very abruptly drops his role as preacher and speaks with the tone of

God himself. Just as Jesus told his hearers "I am the Resurrection and the Life," Very says:

> So say *I* to you to whom as the unborn I stand in a similar position. *I* am your Resurrection and life, believe in *Me* that speaks and you though unborn, shall be born. . . . "He that receives you," said he to his disciples, receives *Me* and he that receives *Me* receives Him that sent *Me*. These *Me*'s and *I*'s are the *I*'s and *Me*'s of the persons in the different worlds or states of which I have spoken and which because they are used are confounded by you and you are led to think that the person who speaks is like yourself.

For the moment his unborn audience will fail to recognize the speaker's divine authority, but they surely will perceive it when they themselves are reborn to his estate: Now you *make* me what I am to you; then you shall see me as I *am*; for you yourself will be made like unto me." What Very has done is to push the Unitarian view of Jesus as representative man, as extended by the Transcendentalist idea of God's potential immanence, to its uttermost limits, and dare to assert that he too has His authority. This Very had been doing in the flesh for some time, to the confusion of his friends and neighbors; "The Epistle on Miracles" simply represents his nearest attempt to explain himself deliberately in writing.

Like Emerson, Very was a poet before he was a mystic, and his vision necessarily expressed itself more compellingly (at least to an unbeliever) in poetry than in prose, because it was profoundly metaphorical. When he looked at nature he saw emblems; when he looked at the self he saw God; when he looked at society he saw parables of spiritual death, or the potential for regeneration. It is no wonder that when his talent dwindled he became an occasional poet, because it seems always to have been instinctive with him to convert the external stimuli of the moment into tropes: biblical phrases, natural images, popular sayings, and the like. But his most distinctive hallmark as a poet is the reinterpretation of scripture and the creation from the perspective of one who has merged with God.

On one level, the speaker travels at will through a circuit of identities. He assumes the role of any or all the prophets: John the Baptist, Isaiah, Noah, Moses. Adamlike he dreams:

> I saw the spot where our first parents dwelt,
> And yet it wore to me no face of change.

The speaker here is not the old Adam but the new man in Christ, himself a kind of deity. Elsewhere he becomes God the Father:

> I am the First and Last declare my Word

> There is no voice but it is born of Me
> I am there is no other God beside
> Before Me all that live shall bow the knee

Wouldst thou behold my features cleanse thy heart

or Christ the son:

> This is the rock where I my church will build
>
> Come then partake the feast for you prepared
> I have come down to bid you welcome there
>
> Why come you out to me with clubs and staves,
> That you on every side have fenced me so

or the Holy Ghost:

> I come the rushing wind that shook the place
> Where those once sat who spake with tongues of fire
> Oer thee to shed the freely given grace.

It is surely no accident that all but one of the seven sonnets just excerpted remained unpublished during the nineteenth century, as they are among the most daring Very ever wrote. Most of the fifty or so in which the speaker impersonates the deity do not live up to their extraordinary beginnings and become vitiated by filler lines and overuse of biblical phraseology, but in conception they are a remarkable group of poems. (Incidentally, Emerson was wrong in insisting that the Spirit be grammatical. These poems read best without punctuation, just as Bartlett printed them from the manuscript.)

Very's prophetic speaker does not always ventriloquize through the mask of deity or biblical figure, by any means. He has an identity of his own, albeit of a somewhat generalized sort. One often finds him having millennial visions of "The White Horse," "The New Jerusalem," the resurrection of the dead, and the like; decrying "The Unfaithful Servants," "The Glutton," and other avatars of sin, even to the point of presenting himself as the scourge of God; comforting the people with words of encouragement; petitioning God to use him as an instrument or aid mankind Himself. The most interesting poems of this group, because they come closest to breaking the Old Testament stereotype Very usually sets for himself, are those in which the prophet attempts to establish some sort of human relationship with his audience in addition to his official capacity.

> My brother, I am hungry,—give me food
> Such as my Father gives me at his board;
> He has for many years been to thee good,
> Thou canst a morsel then to me afford;
>
> . . . .
> I ask the love the Father has for thee,
> That thou should'st give it back to me again;
> This shall my soul from pangs of hunger free,
> And on my parched spirit fall like rain;
> Then thou wilt prove a brother to my need,
> For in the cross of Christ thou too canst bleed.

A poem like this makes it clear that the speaker has a personal investment in his mission. He is not merely reenacting the role of Jesus for the benefit of the unborn (although the poem is based on the gospel maxim that what is done for the least of mankind is done for the Lord); he himself, the poem suggests, has a genuine need for reciprocal communication with the neighbor he has come to admonish, as indeed Very seems to have had in life.

Frequently, indeed, the speaker does not appear at all in the role of deity or prophet, but as a single person, in a variety of mental states. The most common of these is a prayerful attitude, either of praise or petition to God. In "The Prisoner," he is "a slave to mine own choice," who looks forward only distantly to his transfiguration; in "The Presence" he is the solitary worshiper suffused with a sense of the protecting spirit. In another group of poems he presents himself as a soul seeking to emulate Christ, anticipating a similar crucifixion, either for his own salvation ("That I through Christ the victory may win") or, less often, to serve as a model for the rest of mankind. Another series of poems portrays the speaker in contemplation of or in an active relationship with nature; in still another, smaller group, but more interesting as far as self-dramatization is concerned, the speaker pictures himself in an unstable relationship with others. Significantly, the speaker does not attain intimacy with those to whom he speaks to the extent that he does with God and nature. Usually he sees himself as rejected or rejecting; at most, he issues us invitations to come with him on a "ramble" through the fields or to join him in his spiritual quest.

The alternation between divine, prophetic, and human voices from poem to poem to have a provocatively disorienting effect on the reader, who sometimes becomes unsure just who is speaking. For example, the poems in which God apparently speaks have been interpreted as dialogues between God and the poet, rather than as monologues in which the poet assumes the role of God. On the other hand, a poem which seems to begin on the human level may turn out to be a divine communication.

> I knock, but knock in vain; there is no call
> Comes from within to bid Me enter there.

Not until one comes to "Me" is it clear that this is the complaint of Christ, not of the frustrated soul. Again, the opening of "To-Day"—"I live but in the present; where art thou?"—might seem to express the confusion of a superficial mind, but it turns out to be the call of the omnipresent God to the distant sinner, who is "far away and canst not hear." In a few poems, it is finally impossible to resolve the speaker into a single voice. "Terror," for example, seems to begin with a prophet or onlooker witnessing the apocalypse:

> There is no safety! fear has seized the proud;
> The swift run to and fro but cannot fly;
> Within the streets I hear no voices loud,
> They pass along with low, continuous cry.

Yet at the end of the poem God himself emerges as the speaker:

> Repent! why do ye still uncertain stand,
> The kingdom of My Son is nigh at hand.

But to take God as the speaker throughout would be to deny the note of awe in the tone at the outset.

Very's use of the speaker is altogether sufficiently versatile and subtle as to suggest conscious manipulation of the persona for literary effect, despite his professed disinterest in revision and his friends' claims that he "composed without a thought of literary form." For example, his two haunting sonnets on the I-Thou relationship, "Yourself" and "Thy Neighbor," read like exercises in wit. Here is the latter:

> I am thy other self; what thou wilt be
> When thou art I, the one thou seest now;
> In finding thy true self thou wilt find me,
> The springing blade where now thou dost but plow;
> I am thy neighbor, a new house I've built
> Which thou as yet hast never entered in;
> I come to call thee; come in when thou wilt,
> The feast is always waiting to begin;
> Thou shouldst love me, as thou dost thyself;
> For I am but another self beside;
> To show thee him thou lov'st in better health,
> What thou wouldst be when thou to him hast died;
> Then visit me, I make thee many a call;
> Nor live I near to thee alone but all.

Who speaks here? Is it the local prophet, or Christ speaking through him, or does one first of all imagine one's own neighbor speaking, and then see Christ standing behind him? The three types of persona intermingle here; the invitation is essentially to the heavenly banquet, but it has overtones of a New England dinner. In a faint way, Very anticipates Whitman in saying that you will find "myself" everywhere: in the speaker-countryman who has come to call on the farmer-reader; in yourself; even under your bootsoles, in "the springing blade." These multiple suggestions show Very's considerable gift for swerving away from outright didacticism in the direction of wit and emotional complexity. Not that the content of the poem is hard to grasp; it all opens up quite easily as soon as one perceives the biblical associations of self-neighbor-Jesus. The complexity consists in the dislocating effect of having a poet, or rather a poem, express this idea in its own person; and in the laconic way in which it is expressed, so that the poem seems halfway in between an exhortation and a riddle.

In view of what we know about Very's moral seriousness, it is quite unlikely that he intended to exploit the element of ambiguity in his personae for its own sake, or that he published his poetry under the pseudonym of

"I" for literary effect. When Sophia Peabody and her brother expressed "our enjoyment of his sonnets," for example, Very replied that "unless we thought them beautiful because we also heard the Voice in reading them, they would be of no avail." The strong probability is that Very was simply intoxicated by the mystical relationships between self and Self, oneself and oneSelf, so that in certain situations it was instinctive for him to elaborate these relationships poetically in what seems to us a very modern way. In any case, Very almost never fails to create an arresting effect when he writes of the disparity between the temporal and spiritual aspects of the I and the I-Thou relation, particularly in those peoms which begin with an ostensibly mundane speaker making what would be an outrageous statement if interpreted in less prophetic terms:

> 'Tis to yourself I speak; you cannot know
> Him whom I call in speaking such an one,
> For thou beneath the earth liest buried low,
> Which he alone as living walks upon
>
> I have no Brother,—they who meet me now
> Offer a hand with their own wills defiled
>
> I weigh out my love with nicest care
>
> I do not need thy food, but thou dost mine

As these lines suggest, Very's specialty as a poet, just as in life, was self-righteousness, justified (in his mind, anyhow) by the spiritual authority with which he felt himself to be invested. The incongruity of a Harvard tutor speaking as the Messiah was a practical stumbling block to his mission among the Reverends Charles Wentworth Upham and John Brazer and other Salem worthies, but a poetic asset in the long run.

In his excellent study of Very, Edwin Gittleman suggests that Very intended in the late 1830s to publish his poems in an arrangement whereby the spiritual cycle outlined in the "Letters to the Unborn" "would be unfolded in systematic fashion," but that Emerson refused. However well thought out Very's scheme actually was, Gittleman is quite right in pointing out that his holy sonnets, "if arranged without regard for the exact order of composition . . . comprise the only form of epic Very thought still possible in the modern world," a drama of unfolding spiritual consciousness. Very's friend W. P. Andrews, in his edition of Very's poetry, tried to give a sense of what this order might be by organizing the selections into a sequence of categories: "The Call," "The New Birth," "The Message," "Nature," "Song and Praise," and "The Beginning and the End." In Gittleman's somewhat more apocalyptic interpretation, the hypothetical sequence would have been "organized in terms of the promise of the Second Coming," depicting "the prelude and consequences of this manifestation of deity on earth." These conjectures attest to the impression of organic relationship among the poems of this period which anyone who reads them all through is bound to feel. They do invite rearrangement into a sequence, and the sequential approach seems also to be validated by Very's prophecies of imminent millennium during his period of illumination. Actually to reorder Very's work in this manner, however, is to impute to him a degree of calculation which clashes somewhat with one's impression of him as a visionary, and to make his work seem more contrived and less spontaneous. Very may well have had such a poetic plan in mind, judging from his attempts to evangelize his friends. But had he carried it out, his poetry would seem a great deal less transcendental than it now is. The rich interplay of voices and moods which the very confusion of Clarke's edition (bad as it is) preserves would have been regularized and toned down, and the prophetic voice would begin to sound like that of the pitchman.

Carried to its logical conclusion, the idea of the self as God means that the "I" is capable of the same infinite variety as nature and that every thought and act is (at least potentially) significant and holy. The Transcendentalists realized this, but the thought disturbed them. The Transcendentalist ministers from the conservative Clarke to the radical Parker shrank back from cosmic egoism; Emerson and Thoreau and even Very entertained it only under strict conditions. They made a sharp distinction between higher and lower natures and reserved their praise for the first; even Emerson's tributes to instinct and Thoreau's to wildness are based on the assumption that the primitive impulse is essentially chaste. Secondly, though the Transcendentalists delighted in the multiplicity of nature, in seeing Spirit manifest itself in a variety of forms, they preferred to think of the self as essentially unitary, not liable to change, except in the direction of greater purification. Thus Emerson comes very close in "Experience" to the modern idea of a disintegrated self when he describes personality as a succession of moods, but he regards this successiveness as a tragic thing and falls back with relief upon the vision of a Spirit which underlies all such change. The personae of Thoreau and Very have even less tolerance for the chaos of experience. One sees them constantly trying to order their perceptions and maintain their integrity against a hostile and philistine audience. "They were all in some particulars much alike," Whitman said of Emerson, Alcott, and Thoreau. "They all had the same manner—a sort of aloofness: as though they meant me to see they were willing to come only so far: that coming an inch beyond that would mean disaster to us all."

Whitman ventured further. His earlier poetry in particular exploits the literary potential of the Transcendental "I" to its fullest. He was prepared to celebrate a much greater range of human experience, the body as well as the soul; his gift for empathy was unsurpassable; and he was enough of an exhibitionist to make "myself" a much more dominant figure than the New Englanders would have thought to do. One may draw dim analogues between Whitman, Thoreau, Very and the idea of a romantic epic of the self; but only in *Leaves of Grass* (and particularly "Song of Myself") is anything like the feeling of epic scope really attained. In this respect, Whitman's book stands as both the culmination and the epitaph of literary Transcendentalism. A short review of both these aspects here may also serve as a postscript to this survey of the Transcendentalist persona.

Whether or not Emerson was really Whitman's "master," as he averred in 1856, is an unanswerable question. In any event, Whitman can be seen as extending all the creative possibilities of the self which have been discussed so far: its socially representative or democratic aspects; its double or multiple nature; and the mysteriousness of that multiplicity. "Myself" in Whitman's poetry becomes, by turns, a demiurge or Oversoul; an epitome of America; a proteus of vicarious shapes and moods; the book or poem itself; and lastly, you, the reader. As a result, Whitman's speaker comes much closer than the Transcendentalists' to encompassing the whole range of human consciousness. He is not ashamed of his body; he is not so insistent on identifying himself with his best moments; he is willing, indeed eager, to show himself loafing, dreaming, doubting, hungering, masturbating, dying. When it comes to presenting the self in its universal aspects, moreover, Whitman does not merely assert this claim in theory, but has the persona act it out, by imaginatively projecting into a series of identities or situations. In this way, the principle of spiritual metamorphosis which the Transcendentalists celebrated in the activity of nature is at last fully dramatized on the human level. Thus Whitman's speaker seems more pretentious than the Transcendentalists', but the element of moral elitism is largely absent. Unlike the speakers of Very and Thoreau, who think of themselves in the company of heroes and prophets, Whitman's persona embraces even the "cotton-field drudge" and the "cleaner of privies" (1. 1003). One feels too that the speaker genuinely wants this experience of human contact, despite his weakness for factitious rhetoric.

Whitman's powers of empathy also give him a greater awareness of the ineffability and unpredictableness of the self: "I hear and behold God in every object, yet understand God not in the least" (1. 1281). And why should he bother to figure it all out? "To elaborate is no avail, learn'd and unlearn'd feel that it is so" (1. 47). The grass may be any number of things, and all is well; the speaker may be in New York one moment and Montana the next, without knowing how he got there, and it is well; he is "amused, complacent, compassionating, idle, unitary" (1. 76) or "hankering, gross, mystical nude" (1. 389) and it is no real contradiction, but rather a sign of health.

However, the willingness to incorporate the whole of experience into one's self-conception involves certain risks, to which Whitman repeatedly succumbs. Indiscriminateness, for example. When Whitman's empathy becomes fatuous or mechanical, one cries out with D. H. Lawrence, "Oh Walter, Walter, what have you done with it? What have you done with yourself? With your own individual self? For it sounds as if it had all leaked out of you, leaked into the universe." The problem is not merely one of self-parody. Whitman was also aware of the potentially self-destructive consequences of empathy. It can lead to sickness and shame and even death. In "Song of Myself" the speaker is betrayed by his sense of touch into temporary insanity; in "Calamus" he is the victim of his adhesiveness; in "The Wound-Dresser" he presents himself as haunted, years later, by the young men he attended. Partly, perhaps, because of the spiritual exhaustion of being torn apart so many times, Whitman's gift for empathy dwindled as he aged, as was also true of the Transcendentalists. Beginning even before 1860, a sense of weariness begins to creep in. The poet assumes less often the role of multiform cosmic force, more often the role of observer. If he dons a mask in a given poem, it tends to be a single and limited one: Columbus, a dying redwood tree, a November bough, a sailor embarking on the ultimate voyage. Death is of course the linking motif in these examples, just as the thought of death pervades all of Whitman's good poetry and much of the rest after "Out of the Cradle." In different ways, he turns the fact of death to his advantage: by welcoming it, like a mother or protector, by celebrating the persistence of spirit, by looking forward to the continuance of his fame, by seeing himself as a martyr to the Civil War. All the same, *Leaves of Grass* is ultimately a tragic poem compared to the work of Emerson, Thoreau, and Very, in the sense that one sees the godlike hero decline and die. Whitman winds up like the "lonely old grubber" of Allen Ginsberg's poem,

> Soon to be lost for aye in the darkness—loth, O so loth to
>   depart!
> Garrulous to the very last.
>   ("After the Supper and Talk," 11–12)

In such passages as this, *Leaves of Grass* undercuts the Transcendental conception of self and epitomizes in its unfolding the demise of American romanticism. Youthful bravado inevitably sinks into humility as the godlike element in the self shrinks into the more respectable "spark of the divine" and the Oversoul acquires a gray beard and a throne.

To the extent that Whitman and the Transcendentalists took seriously the cosmic dimension of their self-dramatizations they ring less true to a modern reader than, say, Ellery Channing's poetic expressions of self-doubt, or the lyrics of Emily Dickinson. Channing was saved from Transcendental naiveté, as we have seen, by the awareness that he was personally unsuited for the self-reliant life. Dickinson, a parallel product of the heritage of self-examination, also shows what seems to us an authenticity—at the cost of her happiness—in being unable either to accept or break away from an inherited religious framework (orthodox, in her case, not liberal). Like Whitman, she is an experimenter in the first-person, moving through a series of masks: the little girl, the queen, the rebel, the sufferer, the corpse. But one senses in her, as in Channing, a greater awareness of the pose as pose. She admits defeat too often; her moods do not complement each other in the same way as Whitman's—partly because her poems are not run together into sustained visions, as Whitman's often are. She is, in short, more appealingly baffled and lost, in the modern way.

Nevertheless, the Transcendentalist conception of self, however delusory, did lead to some important poetic discoveries, which through Whitman's example have had a permanent impact on literary history. First, it provided a way of talking about the unity-in-diversity of American society. Second and more far-reaching, it made possible the introduction of stream-of-consciousness techniques into western poetry. The psychological basis of this technique is precisely the Transcendentalist idea of self, stripped of its metaphysical basis: the idea that identity consists of one's perceptions of the universe moment by moment. As Emerson saw, if one denies the assumption of unifying, essential soul, personality disintegrates into chaos. Because they rested on this assumption, the Transcendentalists put their trust in the "method" of moment-by-moment inspiration as the most "natural" path for the intellect. Whitman's contribution, in turn, was to use this method more uncompromisingly than the Transcendentalists did except in their journals, and to apply it more directly to the self, and thereby to indulge and express the chaos of experience that Emerson came to fear. The somewhat ironic result was that Transcendentalism's last and greatest celebration of the heroic possibilities of the self also foreshadowed those twentieth-century classics in which the self is shown as finally baffled and lost in its labyrinths of perception. Today the self remains in the same divided condition that Emerson describes at the beginning of "The American Scholar."

An Evaluation of Thoreau's Poetry

Henry W. Wells

Eighty-one years after the death of Henry Thoreau has appeared under the careful editorship of Carl Bode the first edition of Thoreau's verse to provide an adequate view of his poetical attainments. The story is, to say the least, unusual. One recalls that eighty years is more than twice the time required to give due appreciation to the lyric art of Emily Dickinson. At last we are able to arrive at a critical estimate of Thoreau's place in American poetry and to speculate upon how much influence his poems, now that they are fairly available, may exercise.

The long period of tepid praise or total silence has been occasioned not only by inadequate publicity but by inadequate criticism and understanding. He himself gradually yielded to the pressure of circumstances and, as years advanced, largely deserted verse for prose. His poems were commonly accused of rawness and lack of poetical refinement. Whatever their faults, they were not vulgar. The middle-class emotionalism and false optimism, monotonous rhythms and facile sentiments, found no place in his personally sincere, highly imaginative, and deeply expressive lines. His poetic prose the public accepted, but found his verse prosaic. It possessed sterner qualities discoverable only in the most vigorous schools of poetry and foreign not only to the effeminate phase of nineteenth-century taste but to the true comprehension of other leaders of American thought, such as Emerson and Lowell.

When a poet views his own lyrics casually, however carefully he may have produced them, sends few of them to his friends and to but one or two periodicals, and publishes them for the most part as appendages to his prose, his readers can scarcely be expected to weigh their intrinsic value

From *American Literature* 16, no. 2 (May 1944). © 1944, renewed 1971 by Duke University Press.

as literature. Moreover, when such poems do at last see print in a becoming form, they will at first almost inevitably be regarded a bit cavalierly. Even the editor in his introduction scarcely ventures to check a natural impression that they were casual jottings left half finished or in a shape unsatisfying to their author and blithely discarded by him when he reached full maturity of authorship. This view is unhappily furthered by the wholly legitimate inclusion in the collected edition of some fifty or more items of a few lines each which are in truth trifles, abruptly broken off, lacking in their opening lines, or left palpably unrevised. To the enthusiast they may appear precious fragments but to the larger public they may well be the rotten apples which tend to spoil the entire barrel. They tempt us to miss the main point, which is that three-quarters of the poems and some nine-tenths of the total number of lines are of finished workmanship, so far, at least, as the author's taste and judgment admitted. No part of Thoreau's voluminous manuscripts shows such painstaking revision as his verse.

Almost all Thoreau's poetry may be regarded as the achievement of a conspicuously independent young man who resolutely declined to ape the popular fashions of his age. While Emily Dickinson quietly discarded much of the specious writing of her times and country, Thoreau displayed a more vigorous opposition. To a remarkable degree he turned away from the main streams of contemporary taste in poetry as directed by Wordsworth, Byron, and the younger British writers of his own day. To be sure, he loved Wordsworth, and his poetry betrays this love; but in its rugged, terse, and abrupt expression it shows an art fundamentally unlike Wordsworth's. Scarcely a single poem from his hand can be associated with American fashions soon to be securely established by Longfellow, Whittier, and Lowell. In short, he is unregenerately unorthodox so far as midnineteenth-century America is concerned. It is well known that his reading was very little in his contemporary fellow countrymen and widely disseminated among the English classics and the literatures of the world. His unusual grasp of Greek and Latin poetry and his exercises in the translation of classical verse, notably Pindar, at least indicate his scope. It is true that whatever he writes springs from his heart—the clearest evidence of his genuine poetic faculty. Yet one of the outstanding features of his work is this evidence of the fruits of his reading and prophetic insight. Of his major poems not a single specimen adheres narrowly to the norm of romantic verse at the time of its composition, although, as we shall see, some extraordinary variations on romantic themes are to be found. The American environment itself is clearly indicated by his art in only half a dozen pieces, which at least resemble though they do not entirely agree with Emerson's rugged, didactic manner. At least an equal number strongly suggest Horace and the pure classical vein itself. A few stand in a surprising relation to medieval thought, feeling, or verse patterns. Slightly more are in much the same style as the manly verse of the founder of British neoclassicism, Ben Jonson. The more mannered and pseudoheroic eloquence of the English

Augustans, as in James Thomson, is occasionally turned by Thoreau to his own purpose. A larger group of lyrics share the spiritual inwardness, lively imagination, and chaste exterior of the English seventeenth-century metaphysical poets, whom Thoreau read and grasped uncommonly well. The nervous vigor and high excitement of some of the spiritual or didactic poetry of the Revolutionary period, notably William Blake's, has striking analogues in the New England radical. Where his nature poetry and his expressions of exaggerated idealism, optimism, and enthusiasm most approximate the high romantic style, he still shows his characteristic independence in thought and feeling. Finally, the largest group of his most memorable poems, nearly a third of them, belongs when historically considered not so much with the past as with the future. Thoreau, like Emily Dickinson or Baudelaire, anticipates the bold symbolism, airy impressionism, stringent realism, and restless inconsistencies of twentieth-century poetry. In the art of poetry no less than in his metaphysics, the recluse of Walden made the world and its epochs his province.

> If with fancy unfurled
>   You leave your abode,
> You may go round the world
>   By the Old Marlborough Road.

Moreover, he is a spiritual cosmopolitan by virtue of his intuitive grasp of the poetic imagination of other periods than his own and not by any mere wealth of allusions which he plunders from abroad. None of Poe's exotic bric-a-brac glitters from his pages. He makes no display of his internationalism, for it is the most natural and instinctive thing about him. His allusions and images are drawn from common nature and from life as seen in the neighborhood of Concord. It is with the eye of the soul and not of the body that his art looks toward past, future, and the ultramontane world.

His classical studies left him, while still in his teens, with a sense of form sufficiently rare in the comparatively formless nineteenth century. His insight is suggested by a few quatrains with a shapeliness resembling the Greek Anthology. In speaking of Thoreau's epigrams Emerson not unnaturally referred to Simonides. A less derivative and more creative poet than Landor, Thoreau transports the classical form to the New England scene; the form is revitalized, the scene reinterpreted:

> Not unconcerned Wachusett rears his head
>   Above the field, so late from nature won,
> With patient brow reserved, as one who read
>   New annals in the history of man.

The long and impressive ode entitled "Let such pure hate still underprop" is clearly fashioned with the strict Horatian sense of proportion. One of his more romantic nature poems ends with an obvious recollection of Horace; the bare New England trees are pictured thus:

> Poor knights they are which bravely wait
>   The charge of Winter's cavalry,
> Keeping a simple Roman state,
>   Disencumbered of their Persian luxury.

It is worth notice that he refers to several of his poems as odes. Moreover, his lyrics are often classical in content as well as in form. He appropriately expresses Platonic doctrine in a poem of strict classical outline, "Rumors from an Aeolian Harp." Much of the classical morality of life appealed to him, especially in his later years when the extremes of his naturalistic romanticism wore thin. In "Manhood" he sees man and not nature as master of human fate. Man guides nature to do his will, as he might guide a horse. Experience teaches him a doctrine of ripe humanism:

> And it doth more assert man's eminence
> Above the happy level of the brute
> And more doth advertise me of the heights
> To which no natural path doth ever lead,
> No natural light can ever light our steps,
> But the far-piercing ray that shines
> From the recesses of a brave man's eye.

Traces of thought and art more or less deliberately derived from medieval sources may at first seem incongruous in a lover of the Mine woods, but they are present in no negligible degree. Thus a surprising poem entitled "The Virgin" reveals her place in the Catholic system midway between Heaven and Earth, the Old Law and the New. This paradoxical account of Mary resembles her praise as put into the mouth of Saint Bernard by Dante, yet Thoreau follows the spirit rather than the letter of medieval sources:

> With her calm, aspiring eyes
> She doth tempt the earth to rise,
> With humility over all,
> She doth tempt the sky to fall.
>
> In her place she still doth stand
> A pattern unto the firm land
> While revolving spheres come round
> To embrace her stable ground.

If this poem does not consciously refer to the Virgin Mary, it affords at least a remarkable coincidence. Much more usual in his poetry than theological reminiscences are inheritances, conscious or unconscious, from medieval verse patterns, possibly with aid from the German lyric tradition. Thoreau is a keen metrical experimenter, seeking exotic devices, both in rhyme and a free blank verse, to express his highly various moods. He revives Skeltonic measures, dimeter in general, and a dipodic verse typical of medieval poetry no less than of nursery rhymes. Metrically, and to some degree verbally, such a stanza as the following carries us back to the inspired doggerel of medieval mystery plays:

> The axe resounds,
> And bay of hounds
> And tinkling sounds
> Of wintry fame;
> The hunter's horn
> Awakes the dawn
> On field forlorn,
> And frights the game.

But to Thoreau the poetry and culture of the Middle Ages must indeed have seemed an interlude. To his ear as an English-speaking poet the classical manner which he loved was to be heard most forcibly rendered in English by Ben Jonson, father of English neoclassicism, and by Jonson's most intimate followers. Their simple and disciplined style leaves an unmistakable mark upon the wholly unaffected elegy, "Brother Where Dost Thou Dwell." The balanced and severely controlled style is crystalized in "Inspiration":

> I hearing get who had but ears,
>   And sight, who had but eyes before,
> I moments live who lived but years,
>   And truth discern who knew but learning's lore.

Also from the English seventeenth century Thoreau drew a poetic heritage still more congenial to him. Such lucidity and formality as are illustrated in the foregoing quotation, drawn ultimately from ancient models, were transformed by the "metaphysical" poets following Donne into a more sensitive and indigenous English verse, thus bestowing upon our poetry in general and upon Thoreau in particular the most charming of octosyllabic verse and a similarly fluid and controlled stanzaic structure. Marvell or some other poet of his times may be regarded as godfather to such a passage as the conclusion of "The River Swelleth More and More":

> Here Nature taught from year to year,
> When only red men came to hear;
> Methinks 'twas in this school of art
> Venice and Naples learned their part;
> But still their mistress, to my mind,
> Her young disciples leaves behind.

Marvell's school, with its metaphysical and subjective insight, also contributed an important part to the transcendental vision and lusty imagination of the New Englander. His inwardness appears notably in such a poem as "The Inward Morning." A highly fanciful symbolism ingeniously employed to express the mysteries of consciousness appears very much after the pattern of the "metaphysicals" in "Farewell," "Poverty," and "On Ponkawtasset, Since, We Took Our Way." The New Englander, with a realism exceeding Vaughan's, uses in "Upon This Bank at Early Dawn" the same bold and spiritualized image of the cock which Vaughan employs in his memorable "Cock-Crowing." The rigid architecture of the typical metaphysical poem also leaves an imprint on Thoreau's art, as may be seen in "I knew a Man by Sight," with its stanzas in the most logical sequence possible. In one of the most nearly imitative of all his truly successful pieces, "I Am a Parcel of Vain Strivings Tied," he comes strikingly close to the verse forms of Herbert:

> I am a parcel of vain strivings tied
> By a chance bond together,
> Dangling this way and that, their links
> Were made so loose and wide,
> Methinks,
> For milder weather.

He became sensible to the charms of the baroque neoclassical rhetoric of the age and school of James Thomson and William Cowper. The poet who in one lyric employs the simplest and most colloquial manner, in another assumes for gravity's sake the full panoply of Augustan artifice and eloquence. He uses a heroic or an epic diction in treating subjects where such a diction seems far from inevitable. Yet here his warmth of feeling proves his salvation. There is something genuinely poetic and instinctively noble in his style, so that his poetry is seldom frozen into the rhetorical frigidities which occasionally deface not only Lowell but Emerson. "The Sluggish Smoke Curls up from Some Deep Dell" is a piece by Thoreau in this pseudoepic manner. Augustan robes, though worn lightly, are still perceptible. This is his description of smoke at dawn rising from a farmer's chimney:

> It has gone down the glen with the light wind,
> And o'er the plain unfurled its venturous wreath,
> Draped the tree tops, loitered upon the hill,
> And warmed the pinions of the early bird;
> And now, perchance, high in the crispy air,
> Has caught sight of the day o'er the earth's edge,
> And greets its master's eye at his low door,
> As some refulgent cloud in the upper sky.

Thoreau was kindled from the spiritual fires struck by the violence of the French Revolution upon the sterner and more masculine of English minds, such as Blake's. The revolutionary temper, so strong in Thoreau, found in the language of these earlier revolutionaries an inspiration for his own poetic speech. There are revolutionary explosives in the defiant poem which begins:

The Good how can we trust?
Only the Wise are just.

Several of his more reflective quatrains strike with an energy very similar
to that of Blake. Again, in their faith and enthusiasm some of his most
vigorous transcendental verses, as the superb lyric "All Things Are Current
Found," bear the accent of spiritual assertion belonging to the more spiritual
discoveries of the pioneers of the romantic movement.

Although Thoreau is never a strictly representative figure of either the
earlier or later phases of romanticism, he naturally participates to a considerable degree in some of its major trends. An imagery finely descriptive
of nature, a power in this imagery to beget a mood rich in emotion and
vague in intellectual definition, as well as an audacious idealism show him
a cousin, though not quite a brother, to the leading popular romantic poets
in America and Europe. Thus while his remarkable poems on smoke and
clouds bear the strongest marks of his own genius, they obviously stem
from the main body of romantic nature verse. Notable in the same connection is his romantic fondness for autumn, almost as marked as in Corot.
He wrote a cheerful nature lyric, "May Morning," Wordsworthian in its
general intention though hardly in its execution, while the lines, "My Books
I'd Fain Cast Off," praising nature above books, are also Wordsworthian
in content though not in style. In "Walden" he dreams of nature before
and after the Age of Man. The ethical phase of romanticism also affects
him. One of his most notable flights of romantic idealism may be seen in
the strongly imaginative lyric with the rather unfortunate first line, "Away!
Away! Away! Away!"

Thoreau also participated in the rugged but somewhat strident didacticism which entered American poetry with Emerson and his immediate
associates; and once more he reflected a movement without in any way
losing his own individuality. Since he most nearly resembles Emerson yet
differs from him notably, it becomes a nice test of Thoreau's art to place
beside his own pieces Emerson's poems on like themes. Each poet, for
example, wrote a fairly long ode on Mount Monadnock, alike not only in
much of their imagery but in their ideas, language, and, to a rather less
degree, in rhythm. Yet the differences afford an excellent measurement of
the general distinction between the two poets. Emerson's poem is clearer
in meaning and nearer to the usual practices of the times in metre, symbol,
texture, and total effect. A Yankee practicality in his verse withholds it from
the more catholic and liberated imagination conspicuous in all Thoreau's
best lyrics. To his contemporaries Thoreau's poem must certainly have
appeared rough and raw. To us it seems less regular in its beauty, subtler,
more meditative, and, in the very delicacy and elusiveness of its symbolism,
so much the more poetic. Thoreau's picture of mountains as ships pioneer-
ing on strange seas possesses a poetic scope and a richness of imagination
of which Emerson proved incapable.

Thoreau as a poet flourished more in spiritual contact with past and future than with his own present. Hence the largest single group into which his chief poems fall, when considered historically, is that showing him in various ways anticipating the mind of the twentieth century. He touches the poetry of our own times closely largely in terms of its acute tensions. His verse, for example, often directly expresses the abrupt and vivid experience of the moment. Monuments to such sharp and intense experience appear in such pieces as "Music," "The Cliffs and Springs," and that unique poem on the imaginative import of unmusical sounds:

> They who prepare my evening meal below
> Carelessly hit the kettle as they go
> With tongs or shovel,
> And ringing round and round,
> Out of this hovel
> It makes an eastern temple by the sound.

A typical abruptness of phrase and boldness in sound connotative imagery may be seen in the first line of one of his lyrics, "Dong, sounds the brass in the East." The close and astringent conjunction of the concrete and the elusive, so much sought after in the poetry of the present age, may be seen in a poem comprised of six short lines:

> The waves slowly beat,
> Just to keep the noon sweet,
> And no sound is floated o'er,
> Save the mallet on shore,
> Which echoing on high
> Seems a-calking the sky.

As in much twentieth-century verse, nature imagery is first used to produce a mood and then suddenly surprises us by unveiling an imaginative idea, as when, in the lyric "Where Gleaming Fields of Haze," the "ancient" sound of the name "Souhegan" abruptly leads to thoughts of the Xanthus and Meander. The nervous heightening in subjectivity so keenly felt in much poetry of the twentieth century appears foreshadowed in the startling couplet at the end of "I Am the Autumnal Sun":

> And the rustling of the withered leaf
> Is the constant music of my grief.

Some less drastic features of modern verse making it appear more rugged than its nineteenth-century predecessor also give nerve and vigor to Thoreau's lines. These may be seen in bits of light but effective verse where humor comes to the support of idealism, or a homely realism to the aid of a lofty transcendentalism. "My Boots" and "Tall Ambrosia" offer instances. Finally, Thoreau's drastic and startling realistic satire in such highly acid poems as "For Though the Caves Were Rabitted" and "I Am the Little Irish

Boy" resembles in a broad way the forthright manner of the brilliant satires of Yeats.

These powerful projections into the poetic mood of a restless age still almost a century in advance should free the scholar poet from any suspicion that he is merely imitative, overderivative, or immature. It is obviously true that as young man he revolted from most contemporary fashions in letters as well as in life and gave himself to a devoted study of our heritage from Greece and Rome and from all the periods of the English literary record. But his scholarly habits were vitalizing habits, which happily added strength to his strongly creative mind and in no way fettered his creative faculties in chains of pedantic imitation. His scholarship is merely the outward sign of his universality as poet. His occasional lapses owing to bad taste may generally be ascribed to the limitations of his age, from which even so pronounced an individualist as he could not entirely escape. The refinements of his art, on the contrary, may best be discerned in his highly varied and modulated rhythms, his uncommonly flexible vocabulary, and his many unclassifiable nuances. His strength is most intimately associated with his breadth. Thoreau found all schools of poetry his teachers, none his master. The publication at the present time is no accident. Thoreau's breadth of vision is precisely what our own age, tragically seeking a new consolidation of mankind, most of all requires.

Whitman: The Poet in 1860

Roy Harvey Pearce

Was der Mensch sei, sagt ihm nur seine Geschichte.
　　　　—WILHELM DILTHEY, "Der Traum"

As early as February 1857, Walt Whitman was planning a new edition of *Leaves of Grass*. He wanted to give the collection a scope, a range, a quality of completeness which it so far had lacked. By June or July 1857 he had some seventy new poems ready. We presume he could not make arrangements to publish them. Then, from March 1857 to June 1859, he was caught up in the day-to-day business of editing the Brooklyn *Daily Times*, meanwhile relaxing as best he could in the pleasures of being a celebrated, or notorious, young Bohemian. He wrote few poems during this period. Once freed from his editorial duties, he began again to write poems. And sometime between April and December 1859, he had a series of poems set up and printed—with the intention of making revision on the proof sheets, much as writers in our time use fair-copy typescript. Once more he was ready to publish a new, enlarged *Leaves of Grass*. He intended merely to fill out and give substance to the 1856 *Leaves of Grass*, not to reorder and reconstruct the volume—so, as it turned out, to initiate the series of transformations which mark its subsequent history.

That he did actually transform the volume is owing to an unexpected opportunity offered him in a letter, February 10, 1860, he received from a new publishing firm in Boston:

> DR. SIR. We want to be the publishers of Walt. Whitman's Poems—Leaves of Grass.—When the book was first issued we were clerks in the establishment we now own. We read the book with profit and pleasure. It is a true poem and writ by a *true* man.
>
> When a man dares to speak his thought in this day of refinement—so called—it is difficult to find his mates to act amen to it.

Now *we* want to be known as the publishers of Walt. Whitman's books, and put our name as such under his, on title-pages.—If you will allow it we can and will put your books into good form, and style attractive to the eye; we can and will sell a large number of copies; we have great facilities by and through numberless Agents in selling. We can dispose of more books than most publishing houses (we do not "puff" here but speak *truth*).

We are young men. We "celebrate" ourselves by acts. Try us. You can do us good. We can do you good—pecuniarily.

Now Sir, if you wish to make acquaintance with us, and accept us as your publishers, we will offer to either buy the stereo type plates of Leaves of Grass, or pay you for the use of them, in addition to regular copy right.

Are you writing other poems? Are they ready for the press? Will you let us read them? Will you write us? Please give us your residence

> Yours Fraternally
> THAYER & ELDRIDGE.

A month later Whitman was in Boston with his manuscript. (He visited Emerson, who, so he recalled in his old age, tried to dissuade him from putting the "Enfans d'Adam"—later "Children of Adam"—sequence into the new *Leaves of Grass*.) By late April the volume was announced as about to be published; and it was issued in mid-May—the work of Whitman in what I should call his "humanist" phase, a true poem writ by a man who knew that he had, at whatever cost, to be true to his sense of himself as man.

II

This is a Whitman whom we know but little. By now we know well that Whitman of the 1855 *Leaves of Grass*, who is too much shaken by his triumphant discovery of his sense of himself to need to know what he has discovered. And of course we know even better the Whitman of the 1892 *Leaves of Grass* (the last edition), who has moved beyond discovery and knowledge to that stage of prophetic insight and expression wherein the hard truths of merely human existence are so often catalogued and filed away in cosmic consciousness. These introductory notes are intended to suggest how we may come to know the Whitman of the 1860 *Leaves of Grass*. He too can be read "with profit and pleasure," perhaps with higher profit and greater pleasure than our abiding images of Whitman have so far allowed. For this is a Whitman who confronts us on a ground neither of his nor our choosing, the ground of our lives lived through day to day. He is a Whitman who, however briefly, rests satisfied—because there is no alternative to being satisfied—with the fact that the poet, like the rest of us, is always in the middle of his journey.

He looks forward, of course. But at this stage of his career he is over-whelmingly, poignantly, even tragically, aware of the difference between past, present, and future. He freely predicts what is to come, while yet declining to guarantee its coming. Thus in the fourteenth of the "Chants Democratic" (a version of the poem we best know as "Poets to Come"):

> Poets to come!
> Not to-day is to justify me, and Democracy, and what we
>   are for,
> But you, a new brood, native, athletic, continental, greater
>   than before known,
> You must justify me.
>
> Indeed, if it were not for you, what would I be?
> What is the little I have done, except to arouse you?

Whitman is, he concludes, "the bard" of a "future" for which he writes only "one or two indicative words."

The vision is utopian, of course, and became increasingly so in the 1870s and 1880s, when he was not only calling for but guaranteeing a state of things whereby poems would work so as eventually to make for the withering away of poetry. In a preface of 1872 he could claim:

> The people, especially the young men and women of America, must begin to learn that Religion, (like Poetry,) is something far, far different from what they supposed. It is, indeed, too important to the power and perpetuity of the New World to be consigned any longer to the churches, old or new, Catholic or Protestant— Saint this, or Saint that. . . . It must be consigned henceforth to Democracy *en masse*, and to Literature. It must enter into the Poems of the Nation. It must make the Nation.

And by 1888 (in "A Backward Glance O'er Travel'd Roads") he could claim that, contrary to European critical opinion, verse was not a dying technique:

> Only a firmer, vastly broader, new area begins to exist—nay, is already form'd—to which the poetic genius must emigrate. What-ever may have been the case in years gone by, the true use for the imaginative faculty of modern times is to give ultimate vivi-fication to facts, to science, and to common lives, endowing them with glows and glories and final illustriousness which belong to every real thing, and to real things only. Without that ultimate vivification—which the poet or other artists alone can give—reality would seem to be incomplete, and science, democracy, and life itself, finally in vain.

These two statements (and they are quite typical) sum up Whitman's grow-ing sense of the power of poetry, and thus of the poet: religion, operating as poetry—and only as poetry—can make the nation, vivify it, or, in the language of a late poem like "Passage to India," "eclaircise" it.

"In the prophetic literature of these states," he had written in 1871 (in "Democratic Vistas"), ". . . Nature, true Nature, and the true idea of Nature, long absent, must, above all, become fully restored, enlarged, and must furnish the pervading atmosphere to poems." And later in the same essay: "The poems of life are great, but there must be the poems of the purports of life, not only in itself, but beyond itself." Life beyond life, poetry beyond poetry: This idea came to count for more and more in Whitman's conception of his vocation and, accordingly, of that of the poets who were to come. The last edition of *Leaves of Grass* is surely the testament of the sort of "divine literatus" whom he had earlier prophesied. Indeed, he had not only prophesied himself but made the prophecy come true. But, as he acknowledged, this was not the only form of his testament. For, when he wrote of the last edition, "I am determined to have the world know what *I* was pleased to do," he yet recognized: "In the long run the world will do as it pleases with the book." The question remains: how may we use the book so as to know what we please to do with it? And more: what does the book, in its structure and function, in its growth, teach us about the vocation of poet in the modern world? And more: how may it help the poets who are yet to come discover, and so define, their vocation?

The hard fact—my sense of which, I must admit, derives from my admiration for the 1860 *Leaves of Grass*—is that Whitman fails as prophetic poet precisely because he is such a powerfully humane poet. The adjective makes us flinch, perhaps, but only because, like Whitman, we have found the beliefs it implies so difficult to hold to that we have come, if not to seek for the prophetic utterances which will offer us something in their stead, then to discount them as disruptive of the high sense of our private selves on which we ground our hopes for the lives we must live. Still, it might be that a close reading of Whitman, the poet of 1860—for it is he whose advocate I am being—will teach us what it might be like once more to hold to them.

Be that as it may, the record of Whitman's life would suggest that his own power, his own humanity, was in the long run too much for him. When, hoping to look beyond the end of his journey, he tried to write prophetic poetry, he came eventually to sacrifice man—that finite creature, locked in time and history, at once agonized and exalted by his humanity—for what he has encouraged some of his advocates again to call cosmic man, the cosmic man of, say, these final lines from "Passage to India":

> Passage, immediate passage! the blood burns in my veins!
> Away O soul! hoist instantly the anchor!
> Cut the hawsers—haul out—shake every sail!
> Have we not stood here like trees in the ground long
>   enough?

Have we not grovel'd here long enough, eating and drinking
    like mere brutes?
Have we not darken'd and dazed ourselves with books long
    enough?

Sail forth—steer for the deep waters only,
Reckless O soul, exploring, I with thee, and thou with me,
For we are bound where mariner has not yet dared to go,
And we will risk the ship, ourselves and all.

O my brave soul!
O farther farther sail!
O daring joy, but safe! are they not all the seas of God?
O farther, farther, farther sail!

It is the idea of that "daring joy, but safe"—everywhere in the poem—
which prevents one from assenting to this passage and all that comes before
it. The passage of the soul, whether it is everyman's or a saint's, is not
"safe," however "joyful." Whitman cannot focus the poem on the sort of
human experience to which one might assent because one could acknowledge its essential humanity. The figures in the passage proliferate farther
and farther out from whatever center in which they have originated, until
one wonders if there ever was a center. Probably not, because the experience of the protagonist in this poem is that of cosmic man, who, because
he is everywhere, is nowhere; who, because he can be everything, is nothing. This Whitman, I believe, mistakes vivification for creation, the ecstasy
of cadence for the ecstasy of belief, efficient cause for final cause, poet for
prophet. Which is not, I emphasize, the same as conceiving of the poet as
prophet.

Whitman's genius was such as to render him incapable of the kind of
discipline of the imagination which would make for the genuine sort of
prophetic poetry we find in, say, Blake and Yeats: of whom we can say
that they were poets as prophets, for whom we can observe that poetry is
the vehicle for prophecy, not its tenor. Whitman is at best, at his best,
visionary and sees beyond his world to what it might be. Blake and Yeats
are at best, at their best, prophetic and see through their world to what it
really is. Visionary poetry projects a world which the poet would teach us
to learn to acknowledge as our own; it comes to have the uncanniness of
the terribly familiar. Prophetic poetry projects a world which the poet would
teach us is alien to our own yet central to our seeing it as it really is, a
world built upon truths we have hoped in vain to forget. As the characteristic manner of visionary poems makes us feel, we say of the visionary
world that we could have made it, at least in dream-work. We say of the
prophetic world that we could not possibly have made it; for, as the characteristic manner of prophetic poems drives us to assent, it was there already. The ground of visionary poetry is indeed dream-work and magical

thought; the ground of prophetic poetry, revelation, and mythical thought. Thus the special language of prophetic poetry—one of its most marked formal characteristics—must, by the definition of its purpose, be foreign to us (for it reveals a world, and the strange things in it, hidden from us); yet, by the paradox of prophecy, it is a language native to us (for the things it reveals, being universal, out of the realm of day-to-day time, space, and conception, put all of us, all of our "actual" world, under their aegis). That language we can "understand" because its grammar and syntax are analogous to our own; understanding it, we assent to—and perhaps believe in—the metaphysical system which its structure and vocabulary entail; trying to account for its origin, we must grant the justness of the poet's reporting to us that he has been, in some quite literal sense, "inspired." Rob the visionary of his poetry, and only he remains. Rob the prophet of his poetry, and the stuff of his prophecy remains, perhaps as the stuff of philosophy.

When the mood came over him, as it did increasingly, Whitman did claim to have been "inspired" in this literal sense. But even so, his later work fails as prophetic poetry (for that is what it is meant to be) precisely because, like the earlier work, it projects not a world to which the poet stands as witness, but one to which he stands as maker. Without him, without his voice and his vision, it could not exist. But he asks of the world projected in the later work that, in accordance with the requirements of prophetic poetry, it have the effect of revelation given by a source beyond himself, that its language be at once of and not of our workaday world, that it imply what in "Democratic Vistas" he called a "New World metaphysics." Yet the editions of *Leaves of Grass* from 1867 on fail of the centrality and integrity of properly prophetic poetry—fail, I think, because the poet mistakenly assumes that poetry, when it is made to deal with the universe at large, becomes prophecy. For all of his revisions and manipulations of his text, for all his enlargement of his themes, the later Whitman is but a visionary poet. And, since he asks more of it than it can properly yield, the vision, and consequently the poetry, even the conception of the poet, get increasingly tenuous. A certain strength is there, of course, but it is the strength of an earlier Whitman, who perhaps prophesied, but could not bring about, his own metamorphosis from poet to prophet. His genius was too great to let him forget that, after all, it was poets who were to come.

True enough, he wrote toward the end of "A Backward Glance O'er Travel'd Roads":

> But it is not on "Leaves of Grass" distinctively as *literature*, or a specimen thereof, that I feel to dwell, or advance claims. No one will get at my verses who insist upon viewing them as a literary performance, or attempt at such performance, or as aiming mainly toward art or aestheticism.

One says: how right, how sad, how wasteful! For, ironically enough, Whitman's words characterize the failure of the 1892 *Leaves of Grass*. And one turns to the earlier Whitman, I daresay the authentic Whitman, whose verses did aim mainly toward art and aestheticism, toward a definition of the vocation of the poet in that part of the modern world which was the United States.

III

The 1855, 1856, and 1860 editions of *Leaves of Grass* make a complete sequence—in which the poet invents modern poetry, explores its possibility as an instrument for studying his role in the world at large, and comes finally to define, expound, and exemplify his vocation. The sequence, in brief, is from language to argument; and it is controlled at all points by a powerful sense of the ego which is struggling to make the move—thereby to realize the limits of its own humanity, which are the limits of argument. If, as we well know, the vocation of poet envisaged in the 1855 and 1856 editions is to be explicated by Emerson's "The Poet" (1844), that envisaged in the 1860 *Leaves of Grass* is to be explicated by Emerson's account of Goethe in *Representative Men* (1850): not Shakespeare, not Plato, not Swedenborg— so Emerson was sure—would do for the modern world, which yet "wants its poet-priest, a reconciler." Goethe was one such: "the writer or secretary, who is to report the doings of the miraculous spirit of life that everywhere throbs and works. His office is a reception of the facts into the mind, and then a selection of the eminent and characteristic experiences." Note: just a "writer"—what John Holloway in an important book of a few years ago called the Victorian Sage, a philosopher of a kind, but one who constructs his argument according to a grammar of assent. Emerson had concluded:

> The world is young: the former great men call to us affectionately. We too must write Bibles, to unite again the heavens and the earthly world. The secret of genius is to suffer no fiction to exist for us; to realize all that we know; in the high refinement of modern life, in arts, in sciences, in books, in men, to exact good faith, reality and a purpose; and first, last, midst and without end, to honor every truth by use.

The 1860 *Leaves of Grass*, as one of Whitman's notebook entries indicates, was to be a Bible too: "The Great Construction of the New Bible. . . . It ought to be ready in 1859." It was to offer a "third religion," Whitman wrote. And in a way it does; but, for well and for ill, that religion is a religion of man—man as he is, locked in his humanity and needing a religion, yet not claiming to have it by virtue of needing it, not hypnotizing himself into declaring that he has it. (For Whitman a little cadence was a dangerous, if exciting, thing, much cadence, disastrous.) The Whitman of the 1860 *Leaves of Grass* is, par excellence, Emerson's "secretary," reporting "the doings of the miraculous spirit of life that everywhere throbs and works." To accept a miracle, to live in its presence, even to try to comprehend it, this is not the same as trying to work a miracle, even claiming to have worked one. And, as the poets who have come after him have variously testified in the puzzled, ambiguous relation to him, Whitman's way with the language of poetry, going against the grain of mass communications and "positivism," may well teach us how to recognize and acknowledge miracles. It cannot teach us how to work them, or even how to earn them. One can well imagine how hard it must be for a poet to go so far with language, only to discover that he can go no farther. Such a discovery constitutes the principal element of greatness in the 1860 *Leaves of Grass.* I suggest that it is at least worth entertaining the notion that such a discovery constitutes the principal element of greatness in Whitman's poetry as a whole.

I have said that in 1855 Whitman "invented" modern poetry. By this I mean only that, along with other major poets of the middle of the century, he participated, but in a strangely isolated way, in the development of romanticist poetics toward and beyond its symbolist phase. ("To invent" may mean, among other things, "to stumble upon.") I do not mean to claim too much for the word "symbolist" here; I use it only generally to indicate that Whitman too came to realize that a poet's vocation was fatefully tied to the state of the language which constituted his medium. He discovered with Baudelaire—although without Baudelaire's (and incidentally Emerson's) overwhelming sense of the problem of "correspondences"— that as regards language "tout vit, tout agit, tout se correspond." The medium thus had a "life" of its own, and so might generate "life," the "life" of poetry. Poetry on this view thus became *sui generis,* a unique mode of discourse; and the role of the poet became more and more explicitly to be that of the creator, one who might "free" language to "mean," a creator in a medium, pure and simple. We have in Whitman's early work a version of that conception of poet and poetry with which we are now so familiar: to whom was the poet responsible? Not to whom, the reply ran, but to what? And the answer: to language. Language as such was seen to be the sole, overriding means to establish, or reestablish, community. The perhaps inevitable drift—not only in Whitman's work but in that of his contemporaries and of the poets who have come—was toward an idea of poetry as a means of communion, perhaps modern man's sole means of communion, his religion. Professor Meyer Abrams (In *The Mirror and the Lamp*) concludes his account of these developments thus:

> It was only in the early Victorian period, when all discourse was explicitly or tacitly thrown into the two exhaustive modes of imaginative and rational, expressive and assertive, that religion fell together with poetry in opposition to science, and that religion, as a consequence, was converted into poetry, and poetry into a kind of religion.

Professor Abrams is speaking about developments in England. In the United States conditions were somewhat simpler and, withal, more extreme. From the beginning, that is to say, Whitman was sure that the imaginative and rational might well be subsumed under a "higher" category, which was poetry. So that—as I have indicated in my remarks on Whitman and prophetic poetry—for him there was eventually entailed the idea that the New Bible might be just that, a total and inclusive account of cosmic man, of man as one of an infinitude of gods bound up in Nature. It is a nice question whether or not the "symbolist" dedication to the idea of language-as-communion must inevitably lead to a search for a metalinguistic structure of analogies and correspondences and then to an idea of poetry as religion and religion as poetry. And it is a nicer question whether or not "symbolist" poetics—with its emphasis on medium as against matrix, language per se as against language-in-culture—is characterized by a certain weakness in linguistic theory. Whitman's work raises these questions; and a full critique of his work would entail a critique of his theory of poetry, thus of his theory of language, thus of his theory of culture. We will not have that until we begin to read seriously the 1860 *Leaves of Grass*.

In any case, we must grant Whitman his special kind of "unmediated vision." (I am inclined to avoid the phrase "mystical experience" here, for it serves only to raise questions so as to make them unanswerable. Moreover, it is a too-easy means to legitimizing, particularly in terms of the earlier poems, Whitman's later claims to being a prophet.) We are made aware above all that the poet is "in" the world, that if he leaves it he will perforce have to take it with him. His power over language has taught him—and us too, if we can bear the knowledge—that, in a quite naturalistic sense, the world is "in" him. The shock of discovery is terrific: so many presences, so much experience, in a little room! According to the common sense of his culture, it should not have been possible. And the poet, properly grown mistrustful of orthodox principles of selecting and ordering all that he has come to know, will try to contain it all; for he knows that in containing it all he is containing himself, as he is part of it. The means to the containing is the visionary power. At its most telling, Whitman's earlier poetry manifests what has been called (by Erich Kahler) an "existential consciousness," but of a mid-nineteenth-century American sort—its key term, its center of strength and weakness, being not anguish but joy. Or rather, the key term is "triumph"—as suffering, the poet endures, and rejoices, seeing that it is his vocation as poet to teach men that they can endure. The freedom which ensues is wonderful, not dreadful.

Thus I take the 1855 and 1856 editions of *Leaves of Grass*, which most freshly project this mode of consciousness, as stages on the way to the 1860 edition. In 1855 and 1856 Whitman shows that he has learned to report truthfully, and to contain, what he has seen; in 1860, that he has learned to measure its significance for the poet taken as "secretary"—the archetypal "writer." The form of the 1855 and 1856 editions is that of a diary; the form of the 1860 edition, that of an autobiography. Whitman strove to go beyond autobiography, but in vain. The movement from the 1855 to the 1856 editions is the movement from the first "Song of Myself" and the first "The Sleepers" (both originally untitled) to the first "Crossing Brooklyn Ferry" (called in 1856 "Sun-Down Poem"). The poet first learns, as we would put it now, to discipline himself into regressing deeply into his own preconscious; then, with his new-found sense of himself as at once subject and object in his world, he learns to conceive in a new way of the world at large; he is, as though for the first time, "in" the world, even as he discovers that it is "in" him. The crucial factor is a restoration of the poet's vital relationship to language. A good, powerfully naïve account of this discovery is that in Whitman's prose *American Primer*, written in the 1850s but not published until after his death:

> What do you think words are? Do you think words are positive and original things in themselves?—No: words are not original and arbitrary in themselves—Words are a result—they are the progeny of what has been or is in vogue.—If iron architecture comes in vogue, as it seems to be coming, words are wanted to stand for all about iron architecture, for the work it causes, for the different branches of work and of the workman. . . .
>
> A perfect user of words uses things—they exude in power and beauty from him—miracles in his hands—miracles from his mouth: . . .
>
> A perfect writer would make words sing, dance, kiss, do the male and female act, bear children, weep, bleed, rage, stab, steal, fire cannon, steer ships, sack cities, charge with cavalry or infantry, or do any thing, that man or woman or the natural powers can do: . . . [Note the insistence on "natural," not "supernatural," powers.]
>
> Likely there are other words wanted.—Of words wanted, the matter is summed up in this: When the time comes for them to represent any thing or any state of things, the words will surely follow. The lack of any words, I say again, is as historical as the existence of words. As for me, I feel a hundred realities, clearly determined in me, that words are not yet formed to represent.

These sentiments generally, and some of these phrases particularly, got into Whitman's prose meditations. More important, from the beginning they inform the poems. They derive much from Emerson's "The Poet," of course; but they are not tied to even Emerson's modestly transcendental balloon. The power which Whitman discovers is the power of language, fueled by the imagination, to break through the categories of time, space, and matter and to "vivify" (a word, as I have said, he used late in his life—

so close to Pound's "Make it new") the persons, places, and things of his world, and so make them available to his readers. In the process, since the readers would, as it were, be using words for the first time, he would make them available to themselves, as poets in spite of themselves.

It is as regards this last claim, that the reader is a poet in spite of himself, that the 1860 *Leaves of Grass* is all-important. For there Whitman most clearly saw that the poet's power to break through the limiting categories of day-to-day existence is just that: a poet's power, obtaining only insofar as the poem obtains and limited as the poem is limited. In 1860, that is to say, Whitman saw that his Bible was to be a poet's Bible, and had to be built around a conception of the poet's life: his origins, experience, and end; his relation with the persons, places, and things of his world. The 1855 and 1856 volumes are but collections of poems—their organization as rushed and chaotic as is the sensibility of the writer of the *American Primer*. Within individual poems there is form, a form which centers on the moment in the poet's life which they project. But the 1860 *Leaves of Grass* is an articulated whole, with an argument. The argument is that of the poet's life as it furnishes a beginning, middle, and end to an account of his vocation. As I have said, the 1860 volume is, for all its imperfections, one of the great works in that romantic mode, the autobiography. Or, let us give the genre to which it belongs a more specific name: archetypal autobiography. The 1860 volume is autobiographical as, say, *Moby-Dick* and *Walden* are autobiographical; for its hero is a man in the process of writing a book, of writing himself, of making himself, of discovering that the powers of the self are the stronger for being limited. The hero who can say "No!" in thunder discovers that he can say "Yes!" in thunder too, but that the thunderation is his own and no one else's.

To say that the 1860 *Leaves of Grass* is quintessentially autobiographical is to say what has been said before, most notably by Frederik Schyberg, Roger Asselineau, and Gay Wilson Allen. But I mean to say it somewhat differently than they do. For they see in the volume a sign of a crisis in Whitman's personal life; and this is most likely so. Yet I think it is wrong to read the volume as, in this literal sense, personal, that is, "private." (The Bowers edition of the surviving manuscript of the 1860 edition clearly shows that Whitman—naturally enough, most often in the "Calamus" poems—wanted to keep the book clear of too insistently and privately personal allusions. He was, I think, not trying to "conceal," much less "mask," his private personality, but to transmute it into an archetypal personality. It is a mistake to look so hard, as some critics do, for the "private" I.) Thus I should read the volume as not personal but archetypal autobiography, as yet another version of that compulsively brought-forth nineteenth-century poem which dealt with the growth of the poet's mind. (Well instructed by our forebears, we now have a variety of names for the form, all demonstrating how deeply, and from what a variety of nonliterary perspectives, we have had to deal with the issues which it raises for us: *rite de passage*, quest for identity, search for community, and the like.) Whitman's problem, the poet's problem, was to show that integral to the poet's vocation was his life cycle; that, having discovered his gifts, the poet might now use them to discover the relevance of his life, his lived life, his *Erlebnis*, his career, to the lives of his fellows. It is the fact that his newly discovered use of poetry is grounded in his sense of a life lived-through: it is this fact that evidences Whitman's ability here, more than in any other version of *Leaves of Grass*, to contain his gift and use it, rather than be used by it. Of this volume Whitman said:

> I am satisfied with *Leaves of Grass*, (by far the most of it) as expressing what was intended, namely, to express by sharp-cut self assertion, One's Self and also, or may be still more, to map out, to throw together for American use, a gigantic embryo or skeleton of Personaltiy,—fit for the West, for native models.

Later, of course, he wanted more. But, so it seems to me, he never had the means beyond those in the 1860 edition to get what he wanted. And that has made all the difference. Since a reader who comes fresh to the 1860 edition must take that difference into account, I shall venture an outline of the argument and at the end shall give special emphasis to "A Word Out of the Sea"—an early version of "Out of the Cradle Endlessly Rocking"—which marks its turning point.

IV

The 1860 *Leaves of Grass* opens with "Proto-Leaf" (later, much revised, "Starting from Paumanok"). Here Whitman announces his themes and, as he had done before, calls for his new religion; but he gives no indication that it is to be a religion of anything else but the poet's universalized vocation. (My misuse of the word "religion" is his. The nature of the 1860 *leaves of Grass* is such that one is to be neither victimized nor saved by following him here.) It might yet, on this accont, be a precursor to a religion, in the more usual (and I think proper) sense, as well as a substitute for it. "Whoever you are! to you endless announcements," he says. There follows "Walt Whitman," a somewhat modified version of the 1855 poem which became "Song of Myself." It is still close to the fluid version of 1855; strangely enough, it is so overarticulated (with some 372 sections) that it does not have the rather massive, and therefore relatively dogmatic, articulation of the final version. In all, it gives us an account of the poet's overwhelming discovery of his native powers. Then in the numbered (but not separately titled) series of poems called "Chants Democratic," the poet, after an apostrophic salutation to his fellows (it ends "O poets to come, I depend upon you!"), celebrates himself again, but now as he conceives of himself in the act of celebrating his world. The chief among these poems—as usual, much modified later—became "By Blue Ontario's Shore," "Song of the Broad-Axe," A Song for Occupations," "Me Imperturbe," "I Was Looking a Long While," and "I Hear America Singing." Following upon "Walt Whitman," the "Chants Democratic" sequence successfully establishes the dialectical tension between the poet and his world, the tension being sustained as one is made to realize again and again that out of the discovery of his power for making words "do the male and female act" in "Walt Whitman" has come his power to "vivify" his world in the "Chants Democratic."

The transition to the next sequence "Leaves of Grass"—again the poems are numbered but not separately titled—is natural and necessary. For the poet now asks what it is to make poems in the language which has been precipitated out of the communal experience of his age. The mood throughout is one of a mixture of hope and doubt, and at the end it reaches a certitude strengthened by a sense of the very limitations which initially gave rise to the doubt. The first poem opens with two lines expressing doubt; later, when the prophetic Whitman willed himself not to doubt, the lines were dropped, and the poem became the "positive" "As I Ebb'd with the Ocean of Life." The second poem is a version of an 1855 poem, "Great Are the Myths"; and it was finally rejected by Whitman as being, one guesses, too certain in its dismissal of the "mythic" mode toward which he later found himself aspiring. The third poem, which, combined with the sixth, later became "Song of the Answerer," opens up the issue of communication as such. The fourth, a version of an 1856 poem which eventually became "This Compost," conceives of poetry as a kind of naturalistic resurrection. It moves from "Something startles me where I thought I was safest"—"safest," that is, in his relation to the materials of poetry—to a simple acknowledgment at the end that the earth "gives such divine materials to men, and accepts such leavings from them at last." The fifth (later "Song of Prudence") considers the insight central to the poet's vocation. To the categories of "time, space, reality," the poet would add that of "prudence"—which teaches that the "consummations" of poetry must finally entail the necessary relationship of all other "consummations": the imagination's law of the conservation of energy. The sixth (which, as I have said, later became part of "Song of the Answerer") develops an aspect of the theme of the fourth and fifth; but now that theme is interpreted as it is bound up exclusively in the problem of language: "The words of poems give you more than poems, / They give you to form for yourself poems, religions, politics, war, peace, behavior, histories, essays, romances, and everything else." At this depth of discovery there is no possibility of any kind of logically continuous catalogue of what words "give you to form for yourself." Poetry is a means of exhausting man's powers to know the world, and himself in it, as it is. Beyond this, poems

> prepare for death—yet are they not the finish, but rather
> the outset,
> They bring none to his or her terminus, or to be content and
> full;
> Whom they take, they take into space, to behold the birth of
> stars, to learn one of the meanings,
> To launch off with absolute faith—to sweep through the
> ceaseless rings, and never be quiet again.

In the seventh poem (later "Faith Poem") the poet discovers that he needs "no assurances"; for he is (as he says in the eighth poem, later "Miracles") a realist and for him the real (by which he here means phenomena) constitute "miracles." The poet is led in the ninth poem (later "There Was a Child Went Forth") to a recollection of his first discovery of the miraculousness of the real, a discovery he only now understands; this poem, taken in relation to the rest of the sequence, properly anticipates "A Word Out of the Sea," in which Whitman makes so much of the word "now." The tenth poem opens with a passage dropped from the later version, "Myself and Mine," but one which is essential as a transition in the sequence:

> It is ended—I dally no more,
> After to-day I inure myself to run, leap, swim, wrestle, fight.

Simply enough, the poet, having accepted his vocation and its constraints, is now free, free through it, and he must now teach this freedom to others:

> I charge that there be no theory or school founded out
> of me.
> I charge you to leave all free, as I have left all free.

The rest of the sequence, fourteen more poems, celebrate aspects of the poet's new freedom as it might be the freedom of all men. It is the freedom to rejoice in the miraculousness of the real, and has its own costs. The greatest is a terrible passivity, as though in order to achieve his freedom man has to offer himself up as the victim of his own newly vivified sensibility. Being as he is, the poet sees (in twelve) "A vast similitude [which] interlocks all"; yet he must admit (in fifteen) "that life cannot exhibit all to me" and "that I am to wait for what will be exhibited by death." He is (in seventeen) the man who must "sit and look out upon all the sorrows of the world, and upon all oppression and shame"; and he must "See, hear, and [be] silent," only then to speak. He declares (in twenty): "whether I continue beyond this book, to maturity, / . . . / Depends . . . upon you, / . . . / . . . you, contemporary America." Poem 24, wherein the poet completes his archetypal act and so is compelled to give himself over to his readers, tells us:

Lift me close to your face till I whisper,
What you are holding is in reality no book, nor part of a book,
It is a man, flushed and full-blooded—it is I—*So long!*
We must separate—Here! take from my lips this kiss,
Whoever you are, I give it especially to you;
So long—and I hope we shall meet again.

I quote this last poem entire, because I want to make it clear that the lapses into desperate sentimentality—and this poem is a prime example—are intrinsically a part of Whitman's autobiographical mode in the 1860 *Leaves of Grass*, as they are of the mode, or genre, which they represent. It will not do to explain them away by putting them in a larger context, or considering them somehow as masked verses, evidences of Whitman the shape-shifter. (Speaking through a persona, Whitman too often hides behind it.) Caught up in the agonies and ambiguities of his conception of the poet, Whitman too often fell into bathos or sentimentalism. Yet bathos and sentimentalism, I would suggest, are but unsuccessful means—to be set against evidence of successful means—of solving the archetypal autobiographer's central problem, of at once being and seeing himself, or bearing witness to his own deeds. If what he is, as he sees it, is too much to bear, if he is incapable of bearing it, if his genius is such as not to have prepared him to bear it— then his miraculism will fail him precisely because he cannot stand too much reality.

Bathos and sentimentalism—and also anxious, premonitory yearnings for something beyond mere poetry—inevitably mar the rest of the 1860 *Leaves of Grass*, but not fatally, since they are the by-products of its total argument. At some point most foxes want to be hedgehogs. Whitman, in this *Leaves of Grass* as in the others, is a poet who must be read at large. But I suggest that he can be best read at large in the 1860 *Leaves of Grass*. When he can be read in smaller compass, as in "A Word Out of the Sea," it is because in a single poem he realizes that he has come to a turning point in what he is developing at large. Presently I shall consider in detail this poem, which became "Out of the Cradle Endlessly Rocking," and I shall want to suggest that the earlier version, set in its earlier context, is even greater than the later. At this point, I note only that it comes as one of a loosely related series of poems, following the "Leaves of Grass" sequence, in which the poet meditates the sheer givenness of the world his poems have discovered, as though for the first time. In these poems he is even capable of seeing himself as one of the givens. But then he must specify in detail the nature of his kind of givenness, which includes the power to give, to bring the given to a new life.

After "Salut au Monde!" "Poem of Joys," "A Word Out of the Sea," "A Leaf of Faces," and "Europe," there is first the "Enfans d'Adam" sequence; and then, after an interlude of generally celebrative poems, the "Calamus" sequence. These two sequences are passionate in a curiously objective fashion. I have suggested that the proper word for their mood and tone is neither personal nor impersonal, but archetypal. They furnish contrasting analogues—directly libidinal analogues, as it were—for the poet's role, seen now not (as in the earlier sequences) from the point of view of a man telling us how he had discovered his gift, put it to use, and measured the cost of using it properly, but seen rather from the point of view of the reader. The explicit sexuality of the poems surely is Whitman's; and we cannot but be troubled by its frank ambivalence. But there are enough times when, ambivalent or not, it is rendered so as to make it virtually anonymous, so that the reader can acknowledge it at least as potentially his. Libidinal *analogues,* not *metaphors,* I have said; for the only way in which Whitman can teach his readers what it means to participate in "making" something is, through a directly applicable analogue, to evoke in them a response which articulates and thus generalizes all that is involved in moving from sexuality to love. At times in these two sequences Whitman seems driven to conceive of sexuality and love in terms of the making of poems—as though, for whatever reason, he were confused, even frustrated, by his own "procreant urge" (as he calls it in "Walt Whitman" / "Song of Myself"). It is, on the one hand, a matter of so trivial a thing as "poetic diction"; and, on the other, of so all-consuming a thing as the simple acknowledgment of "the pent up rivers of myself" and "the hungry gnaw that eats me night and day." Too often the effect is of protesting too much; but then, it is always so in writing which is directly, not metaphorically, libidinal. As Whitman knew too well for our comfort, the final discrimination has to be ours. The important point is that not only the place of the "Enfans d'Adam" and "Calamus" sequence in the 1860 *Leaves of Grass* but also the generalizing directives that Whitman puts in many of the poems—that place and directives at the very least bid us entertain the possibility of their analogizing function.

Since the problem is great, we might well be justified in looking for outside help in solving it. Such help is at hand in the manuscript versions of many of the 1860 "Enfans d'Adam" and "Calamus" poems, which Professor Bowers has edited. The beginning of the twelfth of the "Calamus" poems reads:

> Are you the new person drawn toward me, and asking
>   something significant from me?
> To begin with, take warning—I am probably far different
>   from what you suppose;
> Do you suppose you will find in me your ideal?
> Do you think it so easy to have me become your lover?

The manuscript version begins, however:

> Be careful—I am perhaps different from what you suppose;
> Do you suppose you will find in me your ideal?
> Do you suppose you can easily be my lover, and I yours?

And the thirty-sixth poem of the sequence begins:

> Earth! my likeness!
> Though you look so impassive, ample and spheric there,
> I now suspect that is not all.

The manuscript version of this poem begins:

> Earth! Though you look so impassive, ample and spheric
>   there—I suspect that is not all.

The crucial revisions are: in the twelfth poem, the addition of the first two lines, centering on "asking something significant . . ."; and in the thirty-sixth, that of "my likeness" in the first line. The tendency here, and throughout the poems of which we have manuscript versions, is to call our attention to the poet's relation to the "other" which he addresses—thus to the reader as he is asked to imagine himself as caught up in the experience of making poems and inquiring what the making might mean.

The "I" of these poems is meant to include the reader, as at once potential poet and reader of poems. The "Efans d'Adam" sequence tells us how it is, what it means, what it costs, to be a maker of poems; and the "Calamus" sequence, how it is to be a reader of poems. In the first instance the analogue is procreation; in the second it is community. If Whitman's homosexuality led him to write more powerfully in the second vein than in the first, we can well afford to be grateful for the fact that we can learn from these poems as from few others, to understand everyman's potential for "alienation" as Whitman has the power to evoke and define it for us. That understanding is carried through to the end, as we are told in the next to last of the "Calamus" sequence that we are to be ready for the poet's most "baffling" words, and then as we are given those words in the last poem of the sequence:

> When you read these, I, that was visible, am become
>   invisible;
> Now it is you, compact, visible, realizing my poems, seeking
>   me,
> Fancying how happy you were, if I could be with you, and
>   become your lover;
> Be it as if I were with you. Be not too certain but I am with
>   you now.

Later Whitman changed "lover" to "comrade"—mistakenly, I think; for, as their function in the 1860 volume shows, the "Calamus" poems were to carry through to completion the poet's conception of his painfully loving relation with his readers.

Having, in the "Enfans d'Adam" and "Calamus" sequences, defined the poetic process itself, as he had earlier defined the poet's discovery of that process, Whitman proceeds variously to celebrate himself and his readers at once under the aegis of the "Enfans d'Adam" and the "Calamus" analogues. Much of the power of the poems, new and old, derives from their place in the sequence. In "Crossing Brooklyn Ferry" and the series of "Messenger Leaves" there are addresses to all and sundry who inhabit Whitman's world, assurances to them that now he can love them for what they are, becaue now he knows them for what they are. There is then an address to Mannahatta, which returns to the problem of naming, but now with an assurance that the problem has disappeared in the solving: "I was asking for something specific and perfect for my city, and behold! here is the aboriginal name!" Then, a little farther on, there is in "Kosmos" an address to the simple, separate persons, to each of his readers who is "constructing the house of himself or herself." Then, after a series of apo-thegm-poems, there is "Sleep-Chasings" (a version of the 1855 "The Sleep-ers"), now a sublime poem, in which the poet can freely acknowledge that the source of his strength is in the relation of his nighttime to his daytime life, the unconscious and conscious. The last stanza reads:

> I will stop only a time with the night, and rise betimes,
> I will duly pass the day, O my mother, and duly return to
>   you.

"Sleep-Chasings" is the more telling for being followed by "Burial" (origi-nally an 1855 poem which eventually became "To Think of Time"). For in his incessant moving between night and day, the poet manages to make poems and so proves immortal. He makes men immortal in his poems, as he teaches them to make themselves immortal in their acts:

> To think that you and I did not see, feel, think, nor bear our
>   part!
> To think that we are now here, and bear our part!

This poem comes virtually at the end of the 1860 volume. Only an address to his soul—immortal, but in a strictly "poetic" sense—and "So long!" follow. In the latter we are reminded once again:

> This is no book,
> Who touches this, touches a man,
> (Is it night? Are we here alone?)
> It is I you hold, and who holds you,
> I spring from the pages into your arms—decease calls me
>   forth.

We are reminded thus, to paraphrase a recent Whitmanian, that in the flesh of art we are immortal—which is a commonplace. We are reminded also that in our age, the role of art, of poetry, is to keep us alive enough to be capable of this kind of immortality—which is not quite a commonplace.

V

The central terms in the argument of the 1860 *Leaves of Grass* run something like this: first, in the poems which lead up to "A Word Out of the Sea," self-discovery, self-love, rebirth, diffusion-of-self, art; and second, in the poems which follow "A Word Out of the Sea," love of others, death, rebirth, reintegration of self, art, immortality. The sequence is that of an ordinary life, extraordinarily lived through; the claims are strictly humanistic. The child manges somehow to achieve adulthood; the movement is from a poetry of diffusion to a poetry of integration. Immortality is the result of art, not its origin, nor its cause. The humanism is painful, because one of its crucial elements (centering on"death" as a "clew" in "A Word Out of the Sea") is an acknowledgment of all-too-human limitations and constraints. So long as Whitman lived with that acknowledgment, lived in that acknowledgment—even when living with it drove him (as it too often did) toward bathos and sentimentalism—he managed to be a poet, a "secretary," a "sage," a seer, a visionary. His religion was the religion of humanity, the only religion that a work of art can directly express, whatever other religion it may confront and acknowledge. Indirectly, it can confront religion in the more usual, and more proper, sense; for it can treat of man in his aspiration for something beyond manhood, even if it cannot claim— since its materials are ineluctably those of manhood—to treat directly of that something-beyond. The burden—someone has called it the burden of incertitude; Keats called it "negative capability"—is a hard one to bear. Whitman, I am suggesting, bore it most successfully, bore it most successfully for us, in the 1860 *Leaves of Grass*.

This brings me to the most important of the poems first collected in this volume, "A Word Out of the Sea." (It was originally published separately in 1859, as "A Child's Reminiscence.") Thus far I have tried to suggest the proper context in which the poem should be read, as part of the volume for which it was originally written, as a turning point in the argument of that book. Note that "A Word Out of the Sea" comes about midway in the book, after "Walt Whitman," the "Chants Democratic," "Leaves of Grass," "Salut au Monde!" and "Poem of Joys"—that is, after those poems which tell us of the poet's discovery of his powers as poet and of his ability to use them to "vivify" his world and himself in it, after his discovery that it is man's special delight and his special agony to be at once the subject and object of his meditations, after his discovery that consciousness inevitably entails self-consciousness and a sense of the strengths and weaknesses of self-consciousness. Moreover, "A Word Out of the Sea" comes shortly before the "Enfans d'Adam" and "Calamus" sequences—that is, shortly before those poems which work out the dialectic of the subject–object relationship under the analogue of the sexuality of man as creator of his world and of persons, places, and things as its creatures. I cannot but think that Whitman knew what he was doing when he placed "A Word Out of the Sea" thus. For he was obliged, in all his autobiographical honesty, to treat directly of man's fallibilities as well as his powers, to try to discover the binding relationship between fallibilities and powers—to estimate the capacity of man to be himself and the cost he would have to pay. The poems which come before "A Word Out of the Sea" have little to do with fallibilities. They develop the central terms of the whole argument only this far: self-discovery, self-love, rebirth, art. Theirs is the polymorph perverse world of the child. In them, death only threatens, does not promise; power is what counts. The turning point in the poet's life can come only with the "adult" sense of love and death, the beginning and the end of things—out of which issues art, now a mode of immortality. In "A Word Out of the Sea" the 1860 volume has its vital center. Beyond this poem, we must remember, are the "Enfans d'Adam" and "Calamus" sequences, and also "Crossing Brooklyn Ferry" and the "Messenger Leaves" sequence.

The 1860 poem begins harshly: "Out of the rocked cradle." The past participle unlike the present participle in the later versions, implies no continuing agent for the rocking. The sea here is too inclusive to be a symbol; it is just a fact of life—life's factuality. Then comes the melange of elements associated with the sea. They are among the realities whose miraculousness the poet is on his way to understanding. Note the third line (omitted in later versions) which clearly establishes the autobiographical tone and makes the boy at once the product of nature at large and a particular nature: "Out of the boy's mother's womb, and from the nipples of her breasts." All this leads to a clear split in point of view, so that we know that the poet-as-adult is making a poem which will be his means to understanding a childhood experience. Initially we are told of the range of experiences out of which this poem comes. The sea as rocked cradle seems at once literally (to the boy) and metaphorically (to the poet) to "contain" the song of the bird, the boy's mother, the place, the time, the memory of the brother, and the as yet unnamed "word stronger and more delicious than any" which marks a limit to the meaning of the whole. This is quite explicitly an introduction. For what follows is given a separate title, "Reminiscence," as though the poet wanted to make quite plain the division between his sense of himself as child and as adult. Then we are presented with the story of the birds, the loss of the beloved, and the song sung (as only *now* the poet knows it) to objectify this loss, thus make it bearable, thus assure that it can, in this life, be transcended. Always we are aware that the poet-as-adult, the creative center of the poem, seeks that "word stronger and more delicious" which will be his means finally to understand his reminiscences and—in the context of *this* volume—serve to define his vocation as poet, at once powerful and fallible. The points of view of bird, child and adult are kept separate until the passage which reads:

> Bird! (then said the boy's Soul,)
> Is it indeed toward your mate you sing? or is it mostly to
>   me?
> For I that was a child, my tongue's use sleeping,
> Now that I have heard you,
> Now in a moment I know what I am for—I awake,
> And already a thousand singers—a thousand songs, clearer,
>   louder, more sorrowful than yours,
> A thousand warbling echoes have started to life within me,
> Never to die.

The boy, even as a man recalling his boyhood, does not, as in later versions, at first address the bird as "Demon." He is at this stage incapable of that "or"—in the later reading "Demon or bird." Even though his soul speaks, he is to discover some lines later his special "poetic" relation to the bird. Moreover, as "boy" he holds toward death an attitude halfway between that of the bird, who is merely "instinctive," and that of the man, who is "reflective," capable of "reminiscence." Yet the points of view begin to be hypnotically merged—after the fact. In the boy's "soul" the poet discovers a child's potentiality for adult knowledge; but he keeps it as a potentiality, and he never assigns it to the bird, who (or which) is an occasion merely. Yet having seen that potentiality as such, he can "now," in the adult present, work toward its realization. He can ask for "the clew," "The word final, superior to all," the word which "now" he can "conquer." I cannot emphasize too much that it is a "word" which he seeks—that the poet is translating the sea (and all it embodies) as prelinguistic fact into a word, knowledge of which will signify his coming to maturity. "Out of," in the original title, is meant quite literally to indicate a linguistic transformation. In the record of the growth of his mind, he sees *now* that the word will once and for all precipitate the meaning he has willed himself to create, and in the creating to discover. And it comes as he recalls that time when the sea, manifesting the rhythm of life and death itself,

> Delaying not, hurrying not,
> Whispered me through the night, and very plainly before
>   daybreak,
> Lisped to me constantly the low and delicious word DEATH,
> And again Death—ever Death, Death, Death.

(Not "Death," merely repeated four times as in later versions—but "ever," beyond counting. The prophetic Whitman was bound to drop that "ever," since for him nothing was beyond counting.)

The merging of the points of view occurs as not only past and present, child and adult, but subject and object (i.e., "The sea . . . whispered me," not "to me") are fused. The poet know knows the word, because he has contrived a situation in which he can control its use; he has discovered (to recall the language of the *American Primer* notes) another reality, one that words until *now* had not been formed to represent. He has, as only a poet can, *made* a word out of the sea, for the duration of the poem understood "sea" as it may be translated into "death," "ever death." His achievement is to have enabled us to put those quotation marks around the word—guided by him, to have "bracketed" with language this portion of our experience. We discover that as language binds us in the poet's time, so it is bound in human time.

If the end of the poem is to understand cosmic process as a continual loss of the beloved through death and a consequent gain of death-in-life and life-in-death, nonetheless it is an end gained through a creative act, an assertion of life in the face of death, and a discovery and acknowledgment of the limits of such an assertion. This act is that of the very person, the poet, whom death would deprive of all that is beloved in life. Moreover, the deprivation is quite literally that, and shows the poet moving, in high honesty, from the "Enfans d'Adam" sequence to "Calamus." In the 1860 volume, "A Word Out of the Sea" entails the "Calamus" sequence.

In any case, at this stage of his career Whitman would not yield to his longing for such comfort as would scant the facts of life and death. There is, I repeat, that opening "rocked," not "rocking," cradle; there is the quite naturalistic acknowledgment of the "boy's mother's womb." And there is stanza 31 (the stanzas in the 1860 poem are numbered, as the stanzas of the final version are not):

> O give me some clew!
> O if I am to have so much, let me have more!
> O a word! O what is my destination?
> O I fear it is henceforth chaos!
> O how joys, dreads, convolutions, human shapes, and all
>   shapes, spring as from graves around me!
> O phantoms! you cover all the land, and all the sea!
> O I cannot see in the dimness whether you smile or frown
>   upon me;
> O vapor, a look, a word! O well-beloved!
> O you dear women's and men's phantoms!

In the final version, the equivalent stanza reads only:

> O give me the clew (it lurks in the night here somewhere,)
> O if I am to have so much, let me have more!

The difference between "some clew" and "the clew" marks the difference between a poet for whom questions are real and one for whom questions are rhetorical, as does the confrontation of "chaos." The later Whitman was convinced that the lurking clew would find him, and to that degree, whatever else he was, was not a poet. The earlier Whitman, in all humility, feared that what might issue out of this experience was "phantoms"—a good enough word for aborted poems. And often, but not too often, he was right.

Finally, there is not in "A Word Out of the Sea" the falsely (and, in the context of the poem, undeservedly) comforting note of "Or like some old crone rocking the cradle, swathed in sweet garments, bending aside." The sentimentality and bathos of this too-much-celebrated line, as I think, is given away by the fact that it is the only simile, the only "like" clause, in the poem. And, in relation to the total effect of the poem, the strategic withdrawal of the "Or" which introduces the line and of the parentheses which enclose it is at least unfortunate, at most disastrous.

VI

I make so much of the kind of disaster, as I think it is, because it became increasingly characteristic of Whitman's way with poetry after the 1860 *Leaves of Grass*. The facts, as I interpret them, show that Whitman, for whatever reason, after 1860 moved away from the mode of archetypal autobiography toward that of prophecy. He worked hard to make, as he said, a cathedral out of *Leaves of Grass*. He broke up the beautifully wrought sequence of the 1860 volume, so that, even when he let poems stand unrevised, they appear in contexts which too often take from them their life-giving mixture of tentativeness and assurance, of aspiration, and render them dogmatic, tendentious, and overweening.

In D. H. Lawrence's word, Whitman "mentalized" his poems. In order, by contrast, to fix the mode of the 1860 *Leaves of Grass* in the mind of a reader coming to it for the first time, I give a few examples of "mentalizing" revisions of 1860 poems. The opening of the third "Enfans d'Adam" poem reads in the 1860 text:

> O my children! O mates!
> O the bodies of you, and of all men and women, engirth
>   me, and I engirth them.

In the 1867 version the lines read:

> I sing the body electric,
> The armies of those I love engirth me and I engirth them.

Another example: the opening line of the fourteenth poem of the same sequence reads in the 1860 version, "I am he that aches with love," and becomes in 1867, "I am he that aches with amorous love." (This is the "amorous" which so infuriated Lawrence.) And another example: the opening lines of the fifteenth poem in the sequence read in the 1860 version, "Early in the morning, / Walking . . . ," and became in 1867, "As Adam early in the morning, / Walking . . . ." Small examples surely. But note the unsupported and unsupportable claims of "body electric," "armies," "amorous," and the Old Testament "Adam."

A larger, but still characteristic, example is Whitman's revision of the first of the 1860 "Leaves of Grass" sequence, which became "As I Ebb'd with the Ocean of Life." The 1860 poem opens thus:

> have just been impressing me.
>
> Elemental drifts!
> O I wish I could impress others as you and the waves
>
> As I ebbed with an ebb of the ocean of life,
> As I wended the shores I know.

In the poem as it appears in the 1892 edition of *Leaves of Grass*, the first two lines (expressing doubt, as I have pointed out) are missing; the third has been simplified to "As I ebb'd with the ocean of life." In effect the poet is no longer conceived as part of an "ebb." The fourth line stands as we have it now. Later, in the seventh line of the 1892 version, the poet says that he is "Held by this electric self out of the pride of which I utter poems." In the 1860 version he says that he is "Alone, held by the eternal self of me that threatens to get the better of me, and stifle me." And so it goes— with all passion beyond spending (unless vivified by a kind of cosmic electroshock), all poetry beyond the mere writing, all life beyond the mere living. The poet's tactic, however unconscious, is to claim to have transcended that which must have been hard to live with, his extraordinarily ordinary self and the ordinarily extraordinary death that awaits him. Granting the mood and movement of the later editions of *Leaves of Grass*, it is only proper that Whitman would have rejected the eighth poem in the 1860 "Calamus" sequence, which begins "Long I thought that knowledge alone would suffice me—O if I could but obtain knowledge!" and ends, as the poet is brought to confront the readers to whom he would offer his poems, "I am indifferent to my own songs—I will go with him I love. . . ."

One more example, this one not of a revision but of an addition to a sequence originating in the 1860 volume. In the 1871 *Leaves of Grass*, Whitman, now wholly committed to making of his poem a series of prophetic books, placed in the "Calamus" sequence the woolly "Base of All Metaphysics," the last stanza of which reads:

> Having studied the new and antique, the Greek and
>   Germanic systems,
> Kant having studied and stated, Fichte and Schelling and
>   Hegel,
> Stated the lore of Plato, and Socrates greater than Plato,
> And greater than Socrates sought and stated, Christ divine
>   having studied long,
> I see reminiscent to-day those Greek and Germanic systems,

See the philosophies all, Christian churches and tenets see,
Yet underneath Socrates clearly see, and underneath Christ
    the divine I see,
The dear love of man for his comrade, the attraction of
    friend to friend.
Of the well-married husband and wife, of children and
    parents,
Of city for city and land for land.

Whitman stuck by this poem until the end, and it went unchanged into the 1892 edition, contributing its bit to the "mentalizing" of the whole. And it is only too typical of additions to the book made from 1867 on.

My comparative observations here derive, of course, from a strong conviction, or prejudice, in favor of the 1860 *Leaves of Grass*. I offer them with a certain diffidence. But, without diffidence, I suggest that the 1860 *Leaves of Grass*, in and of itself, is a great *book*—so I am persuaded, Whitman's greatest.

In any case, the prophetic Whitman begins to take over *Leaves of Grass* in the 1867 edition and is fully in command by the time of the 1871 edition. (We shall know more of the takeover when we are given an edition of Whitman's own copy of the 1860 edition—marked heavily for revision. I have seen a microfilm copy of it and have noted that it manifests a Whitman by 1865, a date given in some of the marginalia, quite conscious of his need to make his poems confirm the redefinition of his role which seems to have been a consequence of his Civil War experiences.) It is, unhappily, still the later Whitman whom we know best. It is he with whom our poets have had to make their pacts and truces—so that during the uneasy peace they may come to know another (and in fact an earlier) Whitman, whose way with poetry they seem to sense but can never quite get to. The way to that Whitman, who emerged in 1855 and came to maturity in 1860, is not impossible, although working with the Inclusive Edition (upon whose variant readings I have depended) is tedious. But there is a yet more direct way— reading not only the 1855 edition (which we should by now know well enough) but the 1860 edition, "a true poem," as his publishers knew it would be, "writ by a *true* man."

Walt Whitman:
Always Going Out and Coming In

R. W. B. Lewis

Walt Whitman is the most blurred, even contradictory figure in the classical or midnineteenth-century period of American literature. Recent scholarship and criticism have been clearing things up a good deal; but both the poet and his work remain something of a jumble. For a number of decades, Whitman was the most misrepresented of our major poets; and the misrepresentation began with Whitman himself, in the last twenty-five years of his life. It was during those years, from 1867 onward, that Whitman— initially a very self-exposed and self-absorbed poet—became willfully self-concealing, while at the same time he asserted in various ways an entity, a being, a persona radically other than the being that lay at the heart of his best poetry.

The chief mode of such concealment and assertion was not creative; it was editorial. Whitman wrote little poetry of lasting value after "Passage to India" (1871); what he did do in those later years was constantly to reshuffle the contents of his expanding book: to disperse the poems out of their original and effective order, to arrange them in new and fundamentally misleading groups, to suppress some of the more telling and suggestive of the items, and to revise or delete a series of key passages. The result of this process was a serious shift of emphasis whereby the authentic Whitman was gradually dismembered and replaced by a synthetic entity that was more posture than poet, more mere representative than sovereign person. It, or he, was the representative—in nearly the conventional political sense—of a rather shallowly and narrowly conceived democratic culture: a hearty voice at the center of a bustling and progressive republic, a voice that saluted the pioneers, echoed the sound of America singing, itself sang songs of joy that foretold the future union of the nation and the world and

From *Trials of the Word*. © 1965 by R. W. B. Lewis. Yale University Press, 1965.

the cosmos, chanted the square deific, and wept over the country's captain lying cold and dead on the deck of the ship of state. Other and truer aspects of Whitman continued to exert an appeal, especially in certain lively corners of Europe. But in the English-speaking world, it was primarily the bombastic, or, as his disciples sometimes said, the "cosmic" Whitman that was better know; and it was this Whitman that was either revered or—in most literary circles after the advent of T. S. Eliot—dismissed or simply disregarded.

So much needs to be said: for our first task is to disentangle Whitman, to separate the real from the unpersuasive, to separate the poet from the posture. To do that, we have, first of all, to put Whitman's poems back into their original and chronological order. It might be argued that we have no right to tamper with the poet's own editorial judgment; that *Leaves of Grass* is, after all, Whitman's book and that we are bound to take it in the order and the form he eventually decided on. The answer to this proposition is that there is no satisfactory way around the critical necessity of discriminating among Whitman's successive revisions of his own work, of appealing from the Whitman of 1867 and 1871 and later to the earlier Whitman of 1855 and 1856 and 1860. The dates just named are all dates of various editions of *Leaves of Grass;* and the latter three, the ones we appeal to, are those of the editions in which most (not all) of the real Whitman is to be found. This Whitman is a great and unique figure who is also the recognizable ancestor of many significant poetic developments since his creative prime—from *symboliste* poetry to imagism to more recent neoromantic and, less interestingly, "beat" writing; a chief, though by no means the only, American begetter of Wallace Stevens and Hart Crane, to some extent of Ezra Pound (as he once reluctantly confessed), and to an obscure but genuine degree of T. S. Eliot.

The importance of chronology, in Whitman's case, cannot be exaggerated. Without it, we can have no clear sense of Whitman's development as a consciousness and as a craftsman: an affair of far graver concern with Whitman than with many other poets of his stature. For, as I shall propose, the development of his consciousness and his craft, from moment to moment and year to year, is the very root of his poetic subject matter. It is what his best poems are mainly about, or what they reenact: the thrust and withdrawal, the heightening and declining, the flowing and ebbing of his psychic and creative energy. Whitman's poetry has to do with the drama of the psyche or "self" in its mobile and complex relation *to* itself, to the world of nature and human objects, and to the creative act. What is attempted here, consequently, is a sort of chart of Whitman's development— in the belief that such a chart is not simply a required preliminary for getting at Whitman, but, rather, that it is the proper way to identify the poetic achievement, and to evaluate it. And in a case like Whitman's, the chart of the development is not finally separable from the graph of the life, or biography; the biographical material, therefore, has likewise been distributed among the successive commentaries on the editions of Whitman's single lifelong book.

I. 1855

When *Leaves of Grass* was published on July 4, 1855, Walt Whitman, now thirty-six years old, was living in Brooklyn, with his parents and brothers, earning an occasional dollar by carpentering. Both his family and his carpentry served as sources of allusion and metaphor in the poetry; but neither—that is, neither his heredity nor his temporary employment—help much to explain how a relatively indolent odd-jobber and sometime journalist named Walter Whitman developed into Walt Whitman the poet. His mother, whom he salutes in "There Was a Child Went Forth" for having "conceiv'd him in her womb and birth'd him" (the birthday being the last day in May 1819; the place, rural Long Island), was of Dutch and Quaker descent, not especially cultivated, and remembered by her son, in the same poem of 1855, as quiet and mild and clean. His father was a farmer of deteriorating fortunes, temper, and health: "manly, mean, anger'd, unjust" in his son's account; and it is a psychological curiosity that the father died within a week of the son's first public appearance, or birth, as a poet. Other members of the family were sources of that compassionate intimacy with the wretched and the depraved reflected, for example, in "Song of Myself ":

> The lunatic is carried at last to the asylum a confirm'd
>   case . . .
> The prostitute draggles her shawl, her bonnet bobs on her
>   tipsy and pimpled neck . . .
> Voices of the diseas'd and despairing and of thieves and
>   dwarfs.

Two of Whitman's brothers were diseased, one of them dying eventually in an insane asylum and the other (who was also a drunkard) married to a woman who became a prostitute. Yet another brother was a congenital idiot; and one of Whitman's sisters suffered from severe nervous melancholy. From these surroundings emerged the figure who, in the carpentering imagery of "Song of Myself," felt "sure as the most certain sure, plumb in the uprights, well entretied, braced in the beams"; a figure who not only felt like that but could write like that.

So remarkable and indeed so sudden has the appearance of Whitman the poet seemed, and out of so unlikely and artistically inhospitable a background, that literary historians have been driven to making spectacular guesses about the miraculous cause of it: an intense love affair, for instance, with a Creole lady of high degree; an intense love affair with an unidentified young man; a mystical seizure; the explosive impact of Emerson or of Carlyle or of George Sand. The literary influences can be documented, though they can scarcely be measured; with the other guesses, evidence is inadequate either to support or altogether to discount them. But perhaps the problem itself has not been quite properly shaped. Whitman's poetic emergence was remarkable enough; but it was not in fact particularly sudden. Nor was the career, seen retrospectively, as haphazard and aimless as one might suppose. Looked at from a sufficient distance, Whitman's life shows the same pattern of thrust and withdrawal, advance and retreat, that pulsates so regularly in the very metrics as well as the emotional attitudes of his verses; and to much the same effect. Up to about 1850, when he was thirty-one, Whitman—like the child in the autobiographical poem already quoted—was always going forth, always brushing up against the numberless persons and things of his world, and always *becoming* the elements he touched, as they became part of him. After 1850, he withdrew for a while into the privacies not only of his family but, more importantly, of his own imagination, in touch now with what he called the "Me myself"—his genius, or muse. It was this latter union between man and muse that, by 1855, produced the most extraordinary first volume of poems this country has so far seen.

One of the things Whitman did not become was a scholar, or even a college graduate. His school days, all spent in the Brooklyn to which his family moved in 1823, ended when he was eleven. Thereafter he was apprenticed as a typesetter for a Long Island newspaper; and characteristically, the boy not only worked at the job, he *became* a typesetter, and typesetting became a part of his imagination. The look of a printed page and the rhetoric of punctuation were integral elements in his poetry—the printing of which he actually set with his own hands or carefully supervised. Between 1831 and 1836, Whitman occasionally wrote articles as well as set type for the paper; and he continued to compose fugitive little pieces from time to time during the five years following, from 1836 to 1841, while he was teaching in a variety of schools in a variety of Long Island villages. Writing, too, became part of him; and Whitman became a writer—at least by intention, announcing very firmly in a newspaper article of 1840, that he "would compose a wonderful and ponderous book . . . [treating] the nature and peculiarities of men, the diversities of their characters. . . . Yes: I *would* write a book! And who shall say that it might not be a very pretty book?"

In 1841, Whitman moved into New York City, where he was absorbed especially by what he called "the fascinating chaos" of lower Broadway, and by the life of saloons and theaters, of operas and art museums. Operatic techniques and museum lore went into his later verses; but what Whitman became at this stage was that elegant stroller, or *boulevardier*, known as a dandy. This role persisted during the five years passed as reporter for a number of New York newspapers; and even after he returned to Brooklyn in 1846 and became editor of the *Eagle*, he came back by ferry to stroll Manhattan on most afternoons. But he was a dandy much caught up in public and political affairs. Among the personae he took on was that of the political activist, an ardent Freesoiler in fact, arguing the exclusion of Negro slavery from the territories with such editorial vehemence that the newspaper's owner fired him in February 1848. Within a matter of days, however, Whitman left for what turned out to be a three-month stay in New Orleans, where he served as assistant editor to that city's *Crescent*. It was there that rumor once assigned him the affair with the Creole lady, that soul-turning initiation into love that is said to have made a poet of him. The legend is almost certainly baseless; but something did happen to Whitman nonetheless. During the long weeks of travel, passing over the vast stretches of land and along the great rivers and the lakes (all that "geography and natural life" he catalogues so lavishly in the 1855 Preface), Whitman had his first encounter with the national landscape, and became (it may be hazarded) another of the personalities announced in *Leaves of Grass:* an American.

Back in Brooklyn, Whitman accepted the post of editor-in-chief on the liberal *Freeman* and stayed with it till he resigned in political outrage the following year. He had clearly "become" a journalist, an uncommonly able and effective one; his best poetry sprang in good part from a journalistic imagination—"I witness the corpse with its dabbled hair, I note where the pistol has fallen." At the same time, the forthgoing impulse was nearly— for the moment—exhausted. After expressing his sense of both national and personal betrayal by the Fugitive Slave Law in 1850, Whitman withdrew from the political arena; withdrew from active or regular journalism, and from the life of the city. He moved back to his family and commenced a leisurely existence in which, according to his brother George, "he would lie abed late, and after getting up would write a few hours, if he took the notion"—or work at "house-building" for a bit, with his father and brothers, if he took that notion. Now he became a workman; and it was in the role of working-class artisan that he presented himself both in the verses of the 1855 *Leaves of Grass* and in the portrait which appeared as substitute for the author's name in the front of the volume.

For Whitman, I am suggesting, the act of becoming a poet was not a sudden or an unpredictable one. He had always been in process of becoming a poet, and the figures he successively became, from his school days onward, were not false starts or diversions, but moments in the major process. Typesetter, reporter, dandy, stroller in the city, political activist, surveyor of the national scenery, skilled editor, representative American workman: none of these was ever fully replaced by any other, nor were all at last replaced by the poet. They were absorbed into the poet; and if they do not explain the appearance of genius (nothing can explain that), they explain to some real degree the kind of writing—observant, ambulatory, varied, politically aware, job-conscious—in which *this* particular genius expressed itself.

Signs and symptoms of the poet proper, however, can also be isolated over a good many years. The determination to write a "wonderful" book, in 1840, has already been mentioned; but that was presumably to be a philosophical disquisition in prose. In the early 1840s, the writer-in-general became a writer of fiction, and Whitman contributed a number of moralistic short stories to different New York periodicals, all signed by "Walter Whitman" and none worth remembering. Not much later than that, certainly not later than 1847, Whitman's aspiration turned toward poetry. He began to carry a pocket-size notebook about with him; in this he would jot down topics for poems as they occurred, experimental lines, and trial workings of new metrical techniques. The process was stepped up from 1850 onward. In June 1850, the New York *Tribune* published two free-verse poems by Whitman, the second—later called "Europe: The 72d and 73d Year of These States," on the uprisings of 1848—to be included as the eighth item in the 1855 *Leaves of Grass*. It was probably in 1852 that he composed, though he did not publish, a fairly long poem called "Pictures," which had everything characteristic of his genuine poetry except its maritime movement. And in 1854, the repeal of the Missouri Compromise, and the arrest in Boston of a runaway slave named Anthony Burns, drew from Whitman a forty-line satiric exclamation that would comprise the ninth poem in the first edition— later called "A Boston Ballad."

These creative forays were increasingly stimulated by Whitman's reading, which was not only wide but, as evidence shows, surprisingly careful. He had reviewed works by Carlyle, George Sand, Emerson, Goethe, and others for the Brooklyn *Eagle*. He had known Greek and Roman literature, in translation, for years. "I have wonder'd since," he remarked in *A Backward Glance* (1888), "why I was not overwhelm'd by these mighty masters. Likely because I read them . . . in the full presence of Nature, under the sun . . . [with] the sea rolling in." (The comment suggests much of the quality of Whitman's poetry, wherein a natural atmosphere and sea rhythms help provide fresh versions of ancient and traditional arhetypes.) It should be stressed that Whitman's literary education at this time, though it was by no means skimpy, was fairly conventional. It included the major English poets, Shakespeare and Milton especially, but it did not include Oriental writing or the literature of the mystical tradition or that of German idealism—except as those sources reached him faintly through his occasional readings in the essays of Emerson. This is probably to be reckoned fortunate: Whitman's mystical instinct, during his best creative years, was held effectively in check by a passion for the concrete, a commitment to the actual; and discussion of his "mysticism" is well advised to follow his example. Whitman became acquainted, too, with such American writers as Longfellow and Bryant, both of whom he came later to know personally. In addition, he took to making extensive notes and summaries of a long list of periodical essays, mostly dealing with art and artists.

"Art and Artists," in fact, was the title of an essay which Whitman himself read to the Brooklyn Art Union in 1851. And it was here that he first developed his large notion of the artist as hero—of the artist, indeed, as savior or redeemer of the community to which he offers his whole being as champion (sacrificial, if necessary) of freedom and humanity and spiritual health. "Read well the death of Socrates," he said portentously, "and of greater than Socrates." The image of the modern poet as godlike—even Christlike ("greater than Socrates")—was to run through and beneath Whitman's poetry from "Song of Myself" to "Passage to India"; and often, as here, it drew added intensity from Whitman's disillusion with other possible sources for that miraculous national transformation scene he seems to have waited for during most of his life. It was an extravagant notion; but it was one that anticipated several not much less extravagant images, in the twentieth century, of the artist as hero. It was this image, anyhow, that Whitman sought to bring into play in the whole body of the 1855 *Leaves of Grass* and particularly in "Song of Myself."

The first edition contained a long preface introducing the poet-hero, who is then imaginatively created in the poems that follow. There were twelve of the latter, unnumbered and untitled and of varying length, with unconventional but effective typography—for example:

> The atmosphere is not a perfume. . . . it has no taste of the
>   distillation. . . . it is odorless,
> It is for my mouth forever. . . . I am in love with it.

The first and by far the longest entry was, of course, the poem that in 1881 was labeled "Song of Myself." It is in part genuine though highly original autobiography; in part, it is a form of wish projection. We may think of it, among many other things, as a free-flowing recapitulation of the two processes I have been describing—the process by which a man of many roles becomes a poet, and the process by which the poet becomes a sort of god. There are as many significant aspects to "Song of Myself" as there are critical discussions and analyses of it; if the comment here is mainly limited to the enlargement of its central figure—that is, to the question of its structure—it is because the structure tends to confirm one's sense of Whitman's characteristic movement both in life and in poetry. For if, again, this strange, sometimes baffling, stream-of-consciousness poem does have a discernible structure, an "action" with a beginning, middle, and end, it is almost certainly one that involves the two events or processes just named.

More than one astute reader, while acknowledging a typical pulse or rhythm in the poem, a tidal ebb and flow, has nonetheless denied to it any sustained and completed design. But it may be ventured, perhaps, that "Song of Myself" has not so much a single structure as a number of provisional structures—partly because Whitman, like Melville, believed in a deliberate absence of finish in a work of art; more importantly because of what we may call Whitman's democratic aesthetic. Just as the political activist was absorbed into the poet at some time after 1850, so, and at the same moment, a practical concern with the workings of a democratic society was carried over into the aesthetic realm and applied to the workings of poetry, to the writing and the reading of it. The shape of "Song of Myself" depended, in Whitman's view, on the creative participation of each reader— "I round and finish little," he remarked in *A Backward Glance*, "the reader will always have his or her part to do, just as much as I have had mine." In a real sense, the poem was intended to have as many structures as there were readers; and the reason was that Whitman aimed not simply to create a poet and then a god, but to assist at the creation of the poetic and godlike in every reader.

Like Emerson, Whitman was here giving a democratic twist to the European Romantic notion of the poet as mankind's loftiest figure. For both Emerson and Whitman the poet's superiority lay exactly in his representativeness. "The poet is representative," Emerson had said, in his essay "The Poet." "He stands among partial men for the complete man, and apprises us not of his wealth, but of the common wealth." This is what Whitman meant when he spoke of "the great poet" as "the equable man"; and it is what he asserted in the opening lines of "Song of Myself":

> I celebrate myself and sing myself
> And what I assume you shall assume.

As one or two commentators—notably Roy Harvey Pearce—have rightly suggested, "Song of Myself" is the first recognizable American epic; but, if so, it is an epic of this peculiar and modern sort. It does not celebrate a hero and an action of ancient days; it creates (and its action *is* creative) a hero of future days—trusting thereby to summon the heroism implicit in each individual.

Considered in these terms, as the epic consequence of a democratic aesthetic, "Song of Myself" shows a variable number of structural parts. This reader discovers but does not insist upon the following. The invocation leads, in sections 1 and 2, into a transition from the artificial to the natural— from perfume in houses to the atmosphere of the woods; uncontaminated nature is the first scene of the drama. Next comes the recollection of the union—mystical in kind, sexual in idiom—between the two dimensions of the poet's being: the limited, conditioned Whitman and the "Me, myself," his creative genius, what Emerson might have called the Over-Soul. This was the union that was consummated somehow and sometime in the early 1850s, and out of which there issued the poem in which the union was itself reenacted.

There follows a long portion, continuing at least through section 17, where—as a result of union—the *man* becomes a *poet*, and by the very act of creation. What is created is a world, an abundant world of persons and places and things—all sprung into existence by the action of seeing and naming:

> The little one sleeps in its cradle,
> I lift the gauze and look a long time . . .
> The suicide sprawls on the bloody floor of the bedroom,
> I witness the corpse with its dabbled hair . . .
> Where are you off to, lady? for I see you.

The democratic aesthetic is most palpably at work here. What we take at first to be sheer disorder, what some early reviewers regarded as simple slovenliness and lack of form, is in fact something rather different. It is the representation of moral and spiritual and aesthetic equality; of a world carefully devoid of rank or hierarchy. In "Song of Myself," this principle of moral equivalence is not so much stated as "suggested" (one of Whitman's favorite words), and suggested by "indirection" (another favorite word)—by the artfully casual juxtaposition of normally unrelated and unrelatable elements, a controlled flow of associations. Thus:

> The prostitute draggles her shawl, her bonnet bobs on her
>   tipsy and pimpled neck . . .
> The President holding a cabinet council is surrounded by the
>   great Secretaries,
> On the piazza walk three matrons stately and friendly with
>   twined arms,
> The crew of the fish-smack pack repeated layers of halibut in
>   the hold,
> The Missourian crosses the plains toting his wares and his
>   cattle

and so on. In the 1855 preface, Whitman was willing to make the case explicit: "Each precise object or condition or combination or process exhibits a beauty." And he there illustrated the idea in a succession of still more surprising incongruities: "the multiplication table. . . . old age. . . . the carpenter's trade. . . . the grand-opera."

When, therefore, toward the end of this phase of the poem, the speaker begins to claim for himself the gradually achieved role of poet, it is as the poet of every mode of equality that he particularly wishes to be acknowledged. The announcement runs through section 25:

> I play not marches for accepted victors only, I play marches
>   for conquer'd and slain persons . . .
> I am the poet of the Body, and I am the poet of the
>   Soul. . . .
> I am the poet of the woman the same as the man . . .
> I am not the poet of goodness only, I do not decline to be
>   the poet of wickedness also.

The *poet* now makes ready for the second great adventure, the long journey, as we may say, toward *godhood*. By way of preparation, he undergoes a second ecstatic experience in sections 26 and following: an experience of an almost overpoweringly sensuous kind, with the sense of touch so keen as to endanger his health or his sanity: "You villain touch! . . . you are too much for me." The poet survives, and in section 33 he is "afoot with [his] vision." In the visionary flight across the universe that is then recounted, the poet enlarges into a divine being by *becoming* each and every element within the totality that he experiences; while the universe in turn is drawn together into a single and harmonious whole since each element in it is invested in common with a portion of the poet's emergent divinity. It is no longer the prostitute who draggles her shawl, the President who holds a cabinet council, the Missourian who crosses the plain: it is "I" who does all that:

> I anchor my ship for a little while only . . .
> I go hunting polar furs and the seal . . .
> I am the man, I suffer'd, I was there . . .
> I am the hounded slave, I wince at the bite of dogs.

And the "I" is itself no longer the individual man-poet; it is the very force or *élan vital* of all humanity.

The journey lasts through section 33; and in its later moments, as will be noticed, the traveler associates especially with the defeated, the wretched, the wicked, the slaughtered. Whitman's poetic pores were oddly open, as were Melville's, to the grand or archetypal patterns common to the human imagination—so psychologists such as Carl Jung tell us—in all times and places; and the journey of "Song of Myself" requires, at this point, the familiar descent into darkness and hell—until (section 33) "corpses rise, gashes heal, fastenings roll from me," and an enormous resurrection is accomplished. But what gets reborn, what "troop[s] forth" from the grave is not the poet simply; it is the poet "replenish'd with supreme power," the poet become a divine figure. Just as, by the poetic act of creating a world, the man had previously grown into a poet; so now, by experiencing and, so to speak, melting into the world's totality to its furthest width and darkest depth, poet expands into a divinity. He has approximated at last that "greater than Socrates" invoked by Whitman in 1851; he has become that saving force which Whitman had proposed was to be the true role of the American poet. It is the divinity who speaks through sections 39 to 51, proclaiming his divine inheritance ("Taking to myself the exact dimensions of Jehovah," etc.), performing as healer and comforter ("Let the physician and the priest go home"), exhorting every man to his supreme and unique effort. For it is a divinity who insists at every turn that he speaks but for the divine potential of all men. And, having done so, in section 52 he departs.

Wallace Stevens, the most sophisticated among Whitman's direct poetic descendants, once specified his ancestor's recurrent and dual subject matter in the course of a resonant salute to him in "Like Decorations in a Nigger Cemetery":

> Walt Whitman walking along a ruddy shore
> . . . singing and chanting the things that are part of him
> The worlds that were and will be, death and day.

"Death and day," with its corollary "life and night," is as apt a phrase as one can think of for the extremes between which Whitman's poetry habitually alternates. "Song of Myself " is Whitman's masterpiece, and perhaps America's, in the poetry of "day"—"the song of me rising from bed and meeting the sun"—while "To Think of Time" or "Burial Poem," as Whitman once called it, belongs initially to the poetry of "death," and "the Sleepers" to the poetry of "night." But although both the latter, in their very different ways, explore in depth the dark undergrounds of experience, both return—as "Song of Myself " does—with the conviction of a sort of absolute life. "I swear I think there is nothing but immortality": so ends the meditation in "To Think of Time." And such is the determining sense everywhere in the 1855 edition; we shall shortly have occasion to contrast it with the sense of things in the edition of 1860. It may be helpful, meanwhile, to glance at the 1855 poem "There Was a Child Went Forth," to see how Whitman's characteristic psychological movement was reflected in his poetic technique—how the shifting play of his consciousness was reflected in the shifting play of his craft.

"There Was a Child Went Forth" is Whitman's most unequivocal account of the thrust toward being. It is a poem about growth, about burgeoning and sprouting; and it grows itself, quite literally, in size and thickness. The difference in the sheer physical or typographical look of the first and last stanzas is an immediate clue to the poem's thematic development. Yet what the poet enacts, on the technical side, is not an altogether uninterrupted increase in substance and vitality. The process is rather one of alternation, of enlarging and retracting, of stretching and shrinking—in which, however, the impulse toward growth is *always* dominant. The quantitatively shrunken fourth stanza, for example, is flanked by the longer eight-line stanza that precedes it and the longest or eighteen-line stanza that follows it and completes the poem's swelling motion: giving us a process in fact of stretching-shrinking-stretching. The same process is present more artfully still within the first stanza, with its rhythmic shift from short line to longer line to still longer and back to shorter once again; but where the line that contains the quantitative shrink is nonetheless a line accentuated by the word "stretching"—"Or for many years or stretching cycles of years." The psychic stretching is thus quietly affirmed at the instant of technical shrinking; and it is the stretching impulse that triumphs and defines the poem.

The same effect is accomplished metrically. "There Was a Child Went Forth" is what is now called free verse; and no doubt the word "free" in this context would have had, had Whitman known the whole term, a political aura, and become a part of his democratic aesthetic. Whitman was the first American poet to break free from the convention of iambic pentameter as the principal and most decorous meter for poetry in English; in so doing he added to the declaration of literary independence—from England, chiefly—that had been triumphantly proclaimed for his generation in Emerson's "The American Scholar" and was the predictable artistic consequence of the political fact. Whitman's was a major gesture of technical liberation, for which every American poet after him has reason to be grateful; every such poet, as William Carlos Williams (a manifest heir of Whitman) has said, must show cause why iambic pentameter is proper for him. But it was not an act of purely negative liberation; it was emancipation with a purpose. It freed Whitman to attempt a closer approximation of metrics and the kind of experience he naturally aimed to express; and it made possible an eventual and occasional return to older and more orderly metrics—to possess them, to use them freshly, to turn them to the poet's established poetic intentions. The long uneven alternations I have been describing could hardly have been conveyed by recurring five- and four-stress lines. Whitman instinctively depended, not on the regular alternating current of the iambic, but on an irregular alternation of *rising* and of *falling* rhythms—which corresponded happily to the rise and fall of the felt life, to the flowing and ebbing—and the rising rhythm, once again, is always in command:

There was a child went forth.

And in the poem's conclusion—when a world and a child have been brought fully to interdependent life—the rhythm settles back in a line that neither rises nor falls; a line that rests in a sort of permanent stillness; a subdued iambic of almost perfectly even stress—a convention repossessed in the last long slow series of monosyllables broken only and rightly by the key words "became," "always," and "every":

> These became part of that child who went forth every day,
> and who now goes, and will always go forth every
> day.

It is not possible to invoke the imagery of stretching and shrinking without being reminded of sexual analogies, and thereby of the sexual element so prevalent in Whitman's poetry. That element was notably, even blatantly more central to the 1856 edition—it was about several poems in this edition that Thoreau, otherwise much taken with Whitman, said that "It is as if the beasts spoke"—and it operated most tellingly in 1860. Still, it was evident enough in 1855 to startle sensibilities. "Song of Myself" exhibits a degree of sexual bravado mixed with a trace of sexual nostalgia. But the sexual aspect is more apparent in the poem that inhabits the world where Freud and Jung would look for signs of the sexual impulse—the world of dreams. "The Sleepers"—or "Sleep-Chasings," according to its 1860 title—is not only a poem of night and death—"I wander all night in my visions . . . the white features of corpses"—it is a poem of profound psychic disturbance, as the speaker makes clear at once in a superb line that gained force from the 1855 typography: "Wandering and confused . . . . lost to myself . . . . ill-assorted . . . . contradictory." A portion of sexual shame contributes to the uncertainty and deepens the sense of terror—the terror, as Richard Chase has usefully hazarded, of the ego, or conscious self, confronting the id, or the unconscious, and being threatened by extinction. But, in the manner typical of the first *Leaves of Grass*, the poem moves to the discovery of solace amid fear, of pattern amid the random. Descending through the planes of night, "The Sleepers" encounters in its own heart of darkness sources of maternal comfort and spiritual revelation. Guilt is transcended and harmony restored. The adjectives of the opening stanza—"wandering and confused, lost to myself, ill-assorted, contradictory"—are matched and overcome by the adjectives of the poem's close: "sane," "relieved," "resumed," "free," "supple," "awake." There has occurred what Jung would call the "reintegration of the personality"; the ill-assorted psyche has become whole again after passing through what Jung would also call the "night journey." In "The Sleepers," Whitman displayed once more his remarkable talent for arriving by intuition at the great archetypes. And the night journey concludes in that confident recovery of day, that perfect reconciliation with night, that is the distinctive mark of the edition of 1855.

II. 1856

The second edition of *Leaves of Grass* appeared in June 1856, less than a year after the first. There had been several more printings of the latter; and, indeed, during the intervening months Whitman was mainly occupied with the new printings and with reading—and writing—reviews of his work. He still lived with his family in Brooklyn, but he had virtually given up any practical employment. He had "no business," as his mother told Bronson Alcott, "but going out and coming in to eat, drink, write and sleep." The same visitor from Concord quoted Whitman himself as saying that he only "lived to make pomes." Over the months he had made twenty new ones, and included them all in the considerably expanded second edition.

Conventional norms of printing crept back a little into this edition. All the poems, old and new, were now numbered and given titles, the new poems always including the word "poem"—a word that obviously had a magical power for Whitman at the time. Among the poems added were: "Poem of Wonder at the Resurrection of Wheat"—to be known more tamely as "This Compost"; "Bunch poem"—later "Spontaneous Me"; and "Sundown Poem"—later "Crossing Brooklyn Ferry." The physical appearance of the poems had also become a trifle more conventional, as the eccentric but effective use of multiple dots was abandoned in favor of semicolons and commas. The poetry lost thereby its vivid impression of sistole and diastole, of speech and silence, of utterance and pause, always so close to Whitman's psychic and artistic intention: for example, "I am the man . . . . I suffered . . . . I was there" gets crowded together by punctuation and contraction into "I am the man, I suffer'd, I was there." But the earlier mode of punctuation might well have become exceedingly tiresome; and Whitman, in any event, had arrived at that necessary combination of originality and convention by which the most vigorous of talents always perpetuates itself.

For the rest, the new poems dilate upon the determining theme and emotion of the first edition. There is still the awareness of evil, both general and personal: "I am he who knew what it was to be evil / . . . Had guile, anger, lust, hot wishes I dared not speak / . . . the wolf, the snake, the hog, not wanting in me" (an unmistakable and highly suggestive borrowing from *King Lear* 3.4. 87 ff.—Whitman drew more on literary sources than he or his critics have normally admitted). There is even a fleeting doubt of his own abilities— "The best I had done seem'd to me blank and suspicious"— a note that would become primary in the 1860 edition. But by and large the compelling emotion is one of unimpeded creative fertility, of irresistible forward-thrusting energy. It registers the enormous excitement of the discovered vocation and of its miracle-making nature: Whitman's response to the experience of having published his first volume and to the headiest of the reviews of the book. Contrary to some reports, including Whitman's forgetful old-age account, the first edition had a reasonably good sale; and among the many reviews in America and England, some were admiring, some were acutely perceptive, and one or two were downright reverential and spoke of Whitman as almost that "greater than Socrates" he had been hoping to become. Much the most stirring for Whitman, of course, was the famous letter from Emerson, which found *Leaves of Grass* "the most extraordinary piece of wit and wisdom that America has yet contributed," with "incomparable things said incomparably well in it." One sentence from this letter—and without Emerson's permission—adorned the back cover of the 1856 edition: "I greet you at the beginning of a great career."

The tone of the new poems, consequently, was one of achieved and boundless fertility. This is the poetry of day and the poetry of unending flow. The feeling, indeed, is so large and intense as to produce a sense of profound awe: a sense, almost, of terror. That sense arises from Whitman's convinced and total association of his own fecundity ("Spontaneous Me") with that of nature at large ("This Compost"), an association itself enough to intoxicate one. It arises, too, from Whitman's startling view that the creative accomplishment—of the man-poet and of nature—issues from something superficially ugly or shameful or diseased or dead. "Spontaneous Me" mingles two kinds of poems: those that result from the artistic act and those that are involved with the physical act. The act of love, the expression of sexual energy, whether metaphorical or physical, whether heterosexual or homosexual, carries with it a sweeping sensation of shame ("the young man all color'd, red, ashamed, angry"). But the experience fulfills itself in triumph and pride, just as Whitman had deliberately expanded the erotic dimension of the new volume in triumph and pride; it leads to a great "oath of procreation," procreation in every sort; it ends in a full consciousness of wholesome abundance. In much the same way, nature, in "This Compost," reproduces life each spring out of the rotting earth: "Every spear of grass rises out of what was once a catching disease." The conduct of nature—creating life out of death, health out of sickness, beauty out of foulness, "sweet things out of such corruption"—provided Whitman with an example, an analogy to his own creative experience, so immense as to terrify him.

The terror, needless to say, did not disempower but electrified him. The most far-ranging and beautiful of the new poems, "Crossing Brooklyn Ferry," shows Whitman writing under the full force of his assurance—of his assured identification with the *élan vital* of all things. The interplay of the self and the large world it thrusts forward into is on a scale not unlike that of "Song of Myself"; the flow of the consciousness merges with the flow of reality. Every item encountered is a "dumb beautiful minister" to Whitman's responsive spirit; all the items in the universe are "glories strung like beads on my smallest sights and hearings." The complex of natural and human and created objects now forms a sort of glowing totality that is always in movement, always frolicking on. "Crossing Brooklyn Ferry" presents a vision of an entirety moving forward: a vision that is mystical in its sense of oneness but that is rendered in the most palpable and concrete language—the actual picture of the harbor is astonishingly alive and visible. And the poem goes beyond its jubilant cry of the soul—"Flow on river!"— to reach a peace that really does surpass any normal understanding. Whitman was to write poetry no less consummate; but he was never again to attain so final a peak of creative and visionary intoxication.

III. 1860

Whitman, as we have heard his mother saying, was always "going out and coming in." She meant quite literally that her son would go out of the house in the morning, often to travel on the ferry to Manhattan and to absorb the spectacle of life, and would come back in to the household to eat and sleep, perhaps to write. But she unwittingly gave a nice maternal formula to the larger, recurring pattern in Whitman's career—the foray into the world and the retreat back into himself and into a creative communion with his genius. The poetry he came in to write—through the 1856 edition just examined—reflected that pattern in content and rhythm, and in a way to celebrate the commanding power of the outward and forward movement. The early poetry bore witness as well, to be sure, of the darker mode of withdrawal, the descent into the abysses of doubt, self-distrust, and the death-consciousness; but it was invariably overcome in a burst of visionary renewal. The poetry of 1855 and 1856 is the poetry of day, of flood tide.

The 1860 *Leaves of Grass,* however, gives voice to genuine desolation. In it, betimes, the self appears as shrunken, indeed as fragmented; the psyche as dying; the creative vigor as dissipated. The most striking of the new poems belong to the poetry not of day but of death. A suggestive and immediate verbal sign of the new atmosphere may be found in the difference of title between so characteristic a poem of 1855 as "There Was a Child Went Forth" and perhaps the key 1860 poem, "As I Ebb'd with the Ocean of Life." Yet the case must be put delicately and by appeal to paradox. For, in a sense, the new death poetry represents in fact Whitman's most remarkable triumph over his strongest feelings of personal and artistic defeat. There has been a scholarly debate over the precise degree of melancholy in the 1860 edition, one scholar emphasizing the note of dejection and another the occasional note of cheerfulness; but that debate is really beside the point. What we have is poetry that expresses the sense of loss so sharply and vividly that substantive loss is converted into artistic gain.

During the almost four years since June 1856, Whitman had once again gone out and come back in; but this time the withdrawal was compelled by suffering and self-distrust. Whitman's foray into the open world, beginning in the fall of 1856, took the form, first, of a brief new interest in the political scene and, second, of a return to journalism, as editor-in-chief of the Brooklyn *Daily Times* from May 1857 until June 1859. In the morning, he busied himself writing editorials and articles for the newspaper; in the afternoon, he traveled into New York, to saunter along lower Broadway and to sit watchful and silent near or amid the literati who gathered in Pfaff's popular Swiss restaurant in the same neighborhood. In the evening, he continued to write—prolifically: seventy poems, more or less, in the first year after the 1856 edition and probably a few more in the months immediately following. Then there occurred a hiatus: a blank in our knowledge of Whitman's life, and apparently a blank in his creative activity. We cannot say just when the hiatus began—sometime in 1858, one judges. It ended, anyhow, at some time before the publication in the December 1859 issue of the New York *Saturday Press* of a poem called "A Child's Reminiscence," its familiar title being "Out of the Cradle Endlessly Rocking."

On the political side, Whitman's disenchantment was even swifter than usual. The choices offered the American public in the election of 1856—Buchanan, Frémont, and Fillmore—seemed to him false, debased, and meaningless; and he called—in an unpublished pamphlet—for a president who might play the part of "Redeemer." His disappointment with the actual, in short, led as before to an appeal for some "greater than Socrates" to arise in America; and, also as before, Whitman soon turned from the political figure to the *poet,* in fact to himself, to perform the sacred function, asserting in his journal that *Leaves of Grass* was to be "the New Bible." (Not until 1866 would the two aspirations fuse in a poem—"When Lilacs Last in the Dooryard Bloom'd"—that found a new idiom of almost biblical sonority to celebrate death in the person of a Redeemer President, Abraham Lincoln.) Meanwhile, however, Whitman's private and inner life was causing him far more grief and dismay than the public life he had been observing.

A chief cause for Whitman's season of despair, according to most Whitman biographers, was a homosexual love affair during the silent months: an affair that undoubtedly took place, that was the source at once of profound joy and profound guilt, and that, when it ended, left Whitman with a desolating sense of loss. Such poems as "A Hand-Mirror" and "Hours Continuing Long, Sore and Heavy-Hearted" testify with painful clarity both to the guilt and to the subsequent misery of loneliness. At the same time, poems such as "As I Ebb'd with the Ocean of Life" and "So Long!" strike a different and perhaps deeper note of loss: a note, that is, of poetic decline, of the loss not so much of a human loved one but of creative energy—accompanied by a loss of confidence in everything that energy had previously brought into being. There had been a hint of this in "Crossing Brooklyn Ferry" in 1856—"The best I had done seem'd to me blank and suspicious"—but there self-doubt had been washed away in a flood of assurance. Now it had become central and almost resistant to hope. It may be that the fear of artistic sterility was caused by the moral guilt; but it seems no less likely that the artistic apprehension was itself at the root of the despair variously echoed in 1860. If so, the apprehension was probably due to a certain climacteric in Whitman's psychic career—what is called *la crise de quarantaine*, the psychological crisis some men pass through when they reach the age of forty. Whitman was forty in May 1859; and it was in the month after his birthday that he wrote two aggressive and, one cannot but feel, disturbed articles for the Brooklyn *Daily Times*—on prostitution and the right to unmarried sexual love—that resulted in his dismissal from the paper. Characteristically dismissed, Whitman characteristically withdrew. But no doubt the safest guess is that a conjunction of these factors—*la quarantaine*, the temporary but fearful exhaustion of talent after so long a period of fertility, the unhappy love affair—begot the new poems that gave "death and night" their prominence in the 1860 edition.

The edition of 1860 contained 154 poems: which is to say that 122 had been composed since 1856, and of these, as has been said, seventy by the summer of 1857. Most of the other fifty, it can be hazarded, were written late in 1859 and in the first six months of 1860. It can also be hazarded that among those latter fifty poems were nearly all the best of the new ones—those grouped under the title "Calamus," the name Whitman gave to his poetry of masculine love. These include "Scented Herbage," "Hours Continuing," "Whoever You Are," "City of Orgies," "A Glimpse," "I Saw in Louisiana," "Out of the Cradle," "As I Ebb'd" (published in the April 1860 issue of the *Atlantic Monthly* as "Bardic Symbols"), and "So Long!"

"A Hand-Mirror" records a feeling of self-loathing almost unequaled in English or American poetry. And it is representative of the entire volume in its emphatic reversal of an earlier work and an earlier course of feeling. In "This Compost," in 1856, Whitman was seized with a wonder verging on terror at the capacity of nature and of man to produce the beautiful out of the foul or shameful; here, in 1860, he is smitten with the dreadful conviction of having, in his own being, produced the foul and the shameful out of the potentially beautiful. "Hours Continuing Long, Sore and Heavy-Hearted" is a statement of pain so severe, so unmitigated, that Whitman deleted the poem from all subsequent editions of *Leaves of Grass*. These poems of pain are uncommonly painful to read; and yet, in the other major new poems of 1860, we find Whitman executing what might be called the grand Romantic strategy—the strategy of converting private devastation into artistic achievement; of composing poetry of high distinction out of a feeling of personal, spiritual, and almost metaphysical *extinction*. Keats's "Ode on a Grecian Urn" offers an example of the same, at one chronological extreme; as, at another, does Hart Crane's "The Broken Tower."

That strategy is, indeed, what the 1860 edition may be said to be about; for more than the other versions of *Leaves of Grass*, that of 1860 has a sort of plot buried in it. The plot—in a very reduced summary—consists in the discovery that "death" is the source and beginning of "poetry"; with "death" here understood to involve several kinds and sensations of loss, of suffering, of disempowering guilt, of psychic fragmentation; and "poetry" as the awakening of the power to catch and to order reality in language. What had so fundamentally changed since 1855 and 1856 was Whitman's concept of reality. In 1855, as we have seen, the thought of death led to a flat denial of it: "I swear I think there is nothing but immortality." But in "Scented Herbage" of 1860 he arrives at an opposite conclusion: "For now," as he says, "it is convey'd to me that you [death] are . . . the real reality." If Whitman's poetic faculty had formerly been quickened by his sense of the absolute life, it now finds its inspiration in the adventure of death. In "So Long!" Whitman confesses to the death of his talent: "It appears to me that I am dying. . . . My songs cease, I abandon them." Yet in "Scented Herbage" poetry is identified as the very herbage and flower of death, as Baudelaire had a few years earlier identified poetry as the flower of evil; his new poems, for Whitman, are "growing up above me above death." By 1860 Whitman had reached the perception of Wallace Stevens—in "Sunday Morning" (1923)—that "death is the mother of beauty."

Stevens's phrase might serve as motto for the 1860 edition; as it might also serve for another of the several titles for the poem that was first called "A Child's Reminiscence," then "A Word Out of the Sea," and finally (in 1871) "Out of the Cradle Endlessly Rocking." Whatever else occurs in this in every sense brilliant poem, there unmistakably occurs the discovery of poetic power, the magical power of the word, through the experience—here presented as vicarious—of the departure and loss, perhaps the death, of the loved one. It is one of the most handsomely *made* of Whitman's poems; the craft is relaxed, firm, and sure. Only an artist in virtuoso control of his technical resources would attempt a poem with such effortless alternation of narrative (or recitatif) and impassioned aria, such dazzling metrical shifts, such hypnotic exactitude of language, not to mention a narrative "point of view" of almost Jamesian complexity: the man of forty recalling the child of, say, twelve observing the calamitous love affair of two other beings, and the same man of forty projecting, one assumes, his own recent and adult bereavement into the experience of an empathic child. Whitman, by 1860, was very impressively the poet in that word's original meaning of "maker," in addition to being still the poet as inspired singer; and "Out of the Cradle Endlessly Rocking"—for all its supple play of shadows and glancing light—will bear the utmost weight of analysis. But it has perhaps been sufficiently probed elsewhere, and I will instead take a longer look at "As I Ebb'd with the Ocean of Life."

We will not be far wrong, and in any case it will illuminate the pattern of Whitman's career, if we take this poem as an almost systematic inversion of the 1855 poem "There Was a Child Went Forth," as well as an inversion of a key moment—sections 4 and 5—in the 1855 "Song of Myself." As against that younger Whitman of morning and of spring, of the early lilacs and the red morning-glories, here is the Whitman of the decline of the day and of the year—a poet now found "musing late in the autumn day" (the phrase should be read slowly, as though the chief words were, in the older fashion, divided by dots). All the sprouts and blossoms and fruit of "There Was a Child Went Forth" are here replaced, in the poetically stunning second stanza by:

> Chaff, straw, splinters of wood, weeds, and the sea-gluten,
> Scum, scales from shining rocks, leaves of salt-lettuce, left by
>   the tide;

to which are added, later, "A few sands and dead leaves," "a trail of drift and debris," and finally:

> loose windrows, little corpses,
> Froth, snowy white, and bubbles,
> (See, from my dead lips the ooze exuding at last. . . .)

The poem's rhythm, instead of pulsating outward in constantly larger spirals (though it seems to try to do that occasionally), tends to fall back on itself, to fall away, almost to disintegrate; no poem of Whitman's shows a more cunning fusion of technique and content. It is here, quite properly, the falling rather than the rising rhythm that catches the ear. As against:

> There was a child went forth,

we now hear:

> Where the fierce old mother endlessly cries for her castaways

—a dying fall that conveys the shrinking away, the psychological slide toward death, the slope into oblivion that the poem is otherwise concerned with.

The major turn in the action appears in the grammatical shift from the past tense of section 1 ("As I ebb'd," etc.) to the present tense of section 2 ("As I wend," etc.). It is a shift from the known to the unknown, a shift indeed not so much from one moment of time to another as from the temporal to the timeless, and a shift not so much accomplished as desired. For what produces in the poet his feeling of near-death is just his conviction that neither he nor his poetry has ever known or ever touched upon the true and timeless realm of reality. The essential reality from which he now feels he has forever been cut off is rendered as "the real Me." To get the full force of the despondent confession of failure, one should place the lines about "the real Me" next to those in sections 4 and 5 in "Song of Myself" where Whitman had exultantly recalled the exact opposite. There he had celebrated a perfect union between the actual Me and the real Me: between the here-and-now Whitman and that timeless being, that Over-Soul or genius that he addressed as the Me myself. *That,* I suggest, was Whitman's real love affair; that was the union that was consummated in 1855 and that ended—so Whitman temporarily felt—in disunion three or four years later; "the real Me" was the loved one that departed. And now, divorced and disjoined from the real Me, the actual Me threatens to come apart, to collapse into a trail of drift and debris, with ooze exuding from dead lips. (So, by analogy, a Puritan might have felt when cut off, through sin, from the God that created him.)

Still, as Richard Chase has insisted, this poem is saved from any suggestion of whimpering self-pity by the astonishing and courageous tone of self-mockery—in the image of the real Me ridiculing the collapsing Me:

> before all my arrogant poems the real Me stands
>   yet untouch'd, untold, altogether unreach'd,
> Withdrawn far, mocking me with mock-congratulatory signs
>   and bows,
> With peals of distant ironical laughter at every word I have
>   written,
> Pointing in silence to these songs, and then to the sand
>   beneath.

It is an image of immeasurable effect. And it is, so to speak, a triumph over its own content. Anyone who could construct an image of the higher power—the one he aspires toward—standing far off and mocking him with litle satiric bows and gestures, comparing and consigning his verses to the sandy debris under his feet: such a person has already conquered his sense of sterility, mastered his fear of spiritual and artistic death, rediscovered his genius, and returned to the fullest poetic authority. Within the poem, Whitman identifies the land as his father and the fierce old sea as his mother;

he sees himself as alienated no less from them than from the real Me, and he prays to both symbolic parents for a rejuvenation of his poetic force, a resumption of "the secret of the murmuring I envy." But the prayer is already answered in the very language in which it is uttered; Whitman never murmured more beautifully; and this is why, at the depth of his ebbing, Whitman can say, parenthetically, that the flow will return.

IV. 1867

If Whitman, by the spring of 1860, had not been "rescued" by his own internal capacity for resurgence, he would, more than likely, have been rescued anyhow by the enormous public event that began the following April with the outbreak of a national civil war. During the war years, Whitman "went forth" more strenuously than in any other period of his life, and he immersed himself more thoroughly in the activities and sufferings of his fellows. The immediate poetic fruit of the experience was a small, separately published volume of fifty-three new poems, in 1865, called *Drum-Taps*, with a *Sequel to Drum-Taps*—containing "When Lilacs Last in the Dooryard Bloom'd"—tacked on to the original in 1866. Both titles were added as an Appendix to the fourth edition of *Leaves of Grass* in 1867, which otherwise contained only a handful of new poems. Several of Whitman's war poems have a certain lyric strength, either of compassion or of sheer imagistic precision; and the meditation occasioned by the death of Lincoln is among his finest artistic achievements. Nonetheless—and however remarkable and admirable his human performance was during the war—it was in this same period that Whitman the poet began to yield to Whitman the prophet, and what had been most compelling in his poetry to give way to the misrepresentation and concealment that disfigured *Leaves of Grass* over the decades to follow.

Until the last days of 1862, Whitman remained in Brooklyn, formally unemployed, making what he could out of earnings from *Leaves of Grass,* and—once the fighting had started—following the course of the war with the liveliest concern. He was initially very much on the side of the North, which he regarded as the side of freedom, justice, and human dignity. But as time went on, he came to be increasingly on the side of the nation as a whole, more anxious to heal wounds than to inflict them—and this, of course, is what he literally turned to doing in 1863. In December of the previous year, he learned that his younger brother Jeff had been wounded. Whitman journeyed south at once, found his brother recuperating satisfactorily near Falmouth, Virginia, and stayed for eight memorable days among the forward troops in the battle area. It was only eight days, but the spectacle of horror and gallantry of which he was the closest eyewitness had an enduring, almost a conversionary effect upon him. He came back north only as far as Washington; and from that moment until 1867, he spent every free moment in the military hospitals, ministering to the needs of the wounded. He became, in fact, a "wound-dresser," though a dresser primarily of spiritual wounds, bearing gifts, writing letters, comforting, sustaining, exhorting; he became, indeed, the physician-priest with whom, in "Song of Myself," he had associated the figure of the poet.

He made a living in Washington through a series of governmental jobs: as assistant to the deputy paymaster for a while; as clerk in the Indian Bureau—a position from which he was summarily dismissed when the bureau chief read *Leaves of Grass* and pronounced it unpardonably obscene; finally in the office of the Department of Interior. Here he stayed, relatively prosperous and content, until he suffered a partly paralyzing stroke in 1873. It was in the same year that, traveling north, ill and exhausted, he settled almost by accident in Camden, New Jersey, where he lived until his death in 1892.

In short, when Whitman went forth this time, or was drawn forth, into the American world of war, he was drawn not merely into New York City but into the center of the country's national life; to the actual battle-fields, to the seat of the nation's political power, to the offices of government, to the hospitals, and into the presence of the men who carried on their bodies the burden of the nation's tragedy. It is not surprising that the outer and public life of the country absorbed most of his energy; it is only regrettable that, as a result, and in the course of time, the solitary singer disappeared into the public bard, into the singer of democracy, of companionship, the singer not of "this compost" but of "these States." This was the figure celebrated by William Douglas O'Connor in a book written as an angry and rhapsodic defense of Whitman at the time of his dismissal from the Indian Bureau; a book which, in its title, provided the phrase which all but smothered the genuine Whitman for almost a century: *The Good Gray Poet* (1866).

There had been a faint but ominous foreshadowing of the good gray poet in the 1860 edition: in the frontispiece, where Whitman appeared for the first time as the brooding, far-gazing prophetic figure; in the first tinkerings with and slight revisions of the earlier poems; and in the group of poems called "Chants Democratic," the volume's major blemish. The 1867 edition had no frontispiece at all; but now the process of revising, deleting, and rearranging was fully at work. A number of the "Calamus" poems on manly love, for example, were removed from *Leaves of Grass* once and for all: those which acknowledged or deplored his erotic attraction to another man—including "Hours Continuing." The sexuality of "Song of Myself" and "The Sleepers" was toned down by deleting in particular the orgasmic imagery in both of them. Much of the bizarre and the frantic was taken out of the 1856 and 1860 poetry, in the interest, as Roger Asselineau has put it, of placing "the accent on the poet-prophet rather than on the lover." In a general way, it was the intense and personal *self* of Whitman that got shaded over by the new editing—that self, in its always rhythmic and sometimes wild oscillations, that was the true source and subject of the true poetry. The private self was reshaped into the public person, and the public stage on which this person chanted and intoned became the major subject of the would-be national bard. Whitman became less and less the original artist singing by indirection of his own psychic advances and retreats; he was becoming and wanted to become the Poet of Democracy. No longer the watchful solitary, he was changing into the Poet of Comradeship.

It should not be assumed that, because these were postures, they were necessarily false or worthless; they were simply uncongenial to Whitman's kind of poetry. In the same year, 1867, that *Leaves of Grass* unveiled the prophet of the democratic culture, Whitman also published in the New York *Galaxy* a prose essay called "Democracy," where he set forth much of the evidence that, a few years later, went into the longer essay "Democratic Vistas"—as cogent and searching an account of the conditions of democracy in American, and of their relation to the life of letters, as any American has ever written. But what Whitman could do with this material in prose, he could not do effectively in verse. The democratic element in the early poems was, as has been suggested, an aesthetic element. It was part of the very stress and rhythm of the verse, implicit in the poet's way of looking at persons and things, in the principle of equality in his catalogues and the freedom of his meters, in the dynamic of his relation to his readers. Tackling democracy head on in poetry, Whitman became unpersuasive, even boring.

In the same way, Whitman's poems about the actual war were least striking when they were least personal. There is critical disagreement on this point, but in one reader's opinion, Melville wrote far more authentic war poetry because he had what Whitman did not—a powerful sense of history as allegory. In "The Conflict of Convictions," for example, Melville could suggest the thrust and scale of the struggle in a frame of grand tragedy and in a somberly prophetic mode that the aspiring prophet, Whitman, could never approach. Whitman, the man, had entered the public arena, but his muse did not follow him there; and the enduring poems culled from the war are rather of the intimate and lyrical variety—tender reminiscences or crisp little vignettes like "Cavalry Crossing a Ford," where the image is everything.

There appears among these poems, however, like an unexpected giant out of an earlier age, the work that is widely regarded as Whitman's supreme accomplishment: "When Lilacs Last in the Dooryard Bloom'd." This poem does not, in fact, have quite the artistic finality of "As I Ebb'd" or "Out of the Cradle"; or, rather, its finality is more on the surface, where it is asserted, than in the interior and self-completing pulse of the verses. But, like the other two poems just named, "When Lilacs Last in the Dooryard Bloom'd"—a string of words, D. H. Lawrence once said, that mysteriously makes the ear tingle—has to do with the relation between death and poetry. The death of Lincoln provided the occasion, and the emergent grief of an entire nation served as large but distant background. What is enacted in the foreground, however, is what so often summoned up Whitman's most genuine power: the effort to come to terms with profound sorrow by converting that sorrow into poetry. By finding the language of mourning, Whitman found the answer to the challenge of death. By focusing not on the public event but rather on the vibrations *of* that event— vibrations converted into symbols—within his private self, Whitman produced one of his masterpieces, and perhaps his last unmistakable one.

V.   1871 and Later

The transformation that both Whitman's figure and his work had slowly undergone was acknowledged by Whitman himself in his Preface to the fifth edition of *Leaves of Grass*, which had two identical printings in 1871 and 1872, while Whitman was still in Washington. The earlier editions, he said, had dealt with the *"Democratic Individual"* (the italics are his); in the new edition, he is concerned instead with the "Vast, composite, electric *Democratic Nationality."* It was never clear just what the latter entity amounted to; and in any case, Whitman was not able to make it susceptible to satisfactory poetic expression. It became the subject not of poetry but of oratory and rant—elements that had always been present in Whitman's work but that, for the most part, had hitherto been sweetened by music and, as it were, liquified by verbal sea-drift.

Oratory and rant were unhappily notable even in the most interesting of the new poems added to the 1871 edition, "Passage to India." But the case of "Passage to India" is peculiar. It was stimulated by several public events (including, for one, the opening of the Suez Canal), stimuli usually dangerous for Whitman unless he could instantly personalize them, as here he could not. The poem not only bespeaks the ultimate union of all times and places and peoples but finds in that condition a universal reality; and as Richard Chase has remarked, "Whenever [Whitman] headed for the universal he was headed for trouble." The poem moves swiftly away from the tough entanglements of the concrete that were the vital strength of works as different as "Song of Myself" or "Crossing Brooklyn Ferry" or "As I Ebb'd"; and, arriving at a realm of bodiless vapor, Whitman can only utter such bodiless lines as: "the past—the infinite greatness of the past!"— which is an exclamation without content. Yet "Passage to India" is interesting, because, while providing an example of Whitman's bombast, it is also technically most accomplished. It completes a kind of parabola of Whitman's craftsmanship: from 1855, where consciousness and craft were discovering each other; through 1856 and 1860, where power and technique were very closely fused; to the later sixties, where technique almost superseded content. The technique in question is primarily a manipulation of sound patterns, something too involved to be analyzed here in detail: an extremely skillful distribution of sheer sounds, without any regard for substance. "Passage to India" is interesting too, by way of historical footnote, for the obsessive effect it was to have more than fifty years later on Hart Crane. It virtually supplied the initiating force for *The Bridge*, especially for the "Atlantis" section, the first portion of his symbolist epic that Crane composed.

Whitman spent the last nineteen years of his life in Camden, New Jersey. He made a partial recovery from the stroke of 1873, but then suffered further seizures from time to time until the one that carried him off. In between these bouts, he continued to "go out" as much as he could: to nearby Philadelphia frequently, to Baltimore and Washington, to New York, and once—in 1879—to Kansas, Colorado, and Canada. Otherwise he remained in Camden, writing short and generally trivial poems, a great amount of prose, and countless letters to friends and admirers all over the world. His old age was punctuated by a series of controversies about him in the public press: in 1876, for example,when a clamor from England to raise a subscription for Whitman was countered by a verbal assault upon him in the New York *Tribune* by Bayard Taylor. The charge was almost always obscenity; in the instance mentioned, the charge only aroused the English to greater efforts, and Whitman was so encouraged as to feel, in his own word, "saved" by the contributions—then and later—of Rossetti, Tennyson, Ruskin, Gosse, Saintsbury, and others. Longfellow and Oscar Wilde, old Dr. Holmes and Henry James, Sr., were among the visitors to his Camden home. He became the genius of the city; and his birthday became an annual celebration. It was amid such flurries of support and defamation, idolatry and contempt, that the old man—cheerful and garrulous to the end—succumbed at last to a horde of diseases that would have killed most men many years sooner.

Whitman *was*, as M. Asselineau says of him, a "heroic invalid." But it may be that his physical and psychological heroism as a man was what produced, by overcompensating for the terrible discomforts he felt, the relentless optimism of so much of his writing in the last two decades— optimism not only about himself and his condition, but about America and about history: for which and in which every disaster, every betrayal was seen by Whitman as a moment in the irresistible progress of things toward the better. The "word signs" of his poetry after 1867 became, as Whitman himself remarked in *A Backward Glance O'er Travel'd Roads* (1888), "Good Cheer, Content and Hope," along with "Comradeship for all lands." Those were also the words that fixed and froze the popular understanding of the poet.

Mention of *A Backward Glance*, however, reminds one that Whitman's most valuable work after 1867 tended to be in prose rather than in verse. The sixth edition of *Leaves of Grass*, printed in 1876 and called the "Centennial Edition" (America's centennial—America now being Whitman's subject), added almost no significant new poetry; but it did include the remarkable essay "Democratic Vistas." The latter poises a noble emphasis upon individual integrity against the moral squalor of a society that was already an impossible mixture of chaos and conformity; and in its plea for "national original archetypes in literature" that will truly "put the nation in form," it presents one of the great statements about the relation between art and culture. The next or seventh edition, that of 1881–82, contained the fine little image of the copulative collision of two eagles—an image based on a written description of such an event by Whitman's friend John Burroughs—and a poem that, with two others, gave cause for the suppression of the entire volume, following a complaint by the Society for the Prevention of Vice. But this edition was also characterized by endless revisions and expurgations and, now especially, regroupings of earlier poems: the process whereby the old man steadily buried his youth. In the same year, though, Whitman also published a separate volume of prose: *Specimen Days and Collect*. In it, along with *Specimen Days* and the several indispensable prefaces to *Leaves of Grass*, were "Democratic Vistas," Civil War reminiscences, and Whitman's annual lecture on Lincoln. *A Backward Glance* first appeared in 1888; the following year it served as the preface to, and was the one memorable new piece of writing in, the *Leaves of Grass* of 1889.

Though it is indeed memorable and even beguiling, *A Backward Glance* is also somewhat misleading. The real motivations and the actual achievement of *Leaves of Grass* lie half-forgotten behind the comradeship, good cheer, and democratic enthusiasm of the ailing elderly bard. Like F. Scott Fitzgerald, Whitman could have said, though one cannot imagine him doing so, that he had found his proper form at a certain moment in his career, but that he had then been diverted into other forms, other endeavors less appropriate to his talent. The fact that it was in these other forms that Whitman's reputation got established make the development more lamentable. At his best, Whitman was not really the bard of the democratic society at all; nor was he the prophet of the country's and the world's glorious future. He was, perhaps, the poet of an aesthetic and moral democracy. But he was above all the poet of the self and of the self's swaying motion—outward into a teeming world where objects were "strung like beads of glory" on his sight; backward into private communion with the "real Me." He was the poet of the self's motion downward into the abysses of darkness and guilt and pain and isolation, and upward to the creative act in which darkness was transmuted into beauty. When the self became lost to the world, Whitman was lost for poetry. But before that happened, Whitman had, in his own example, made poetry possible in America.

Whitman's Image of Voice:
To the Tally of My Soul

Harold Bloom

Where does the individual accent of an American poetry begin? How, then and now, do we recognize the distinctive voice that we associate with an American Muse? Bryant, addressing some admonitory lines, in 1830, "To Cole, the Painter, Departing for Europe," has no doubts as to what marks the American difference:

> Fair scenes shall greet thee where thou goest—fair,
>   But different—everywhere the trace of men,
> To where life shrinks from the fierce Alpine air.
>   Gaze on them, till the tears shall dim thy sight,
>   But keep that earlier, wilder image bright.

Only the Sublime, from which life shrinks, constitutes a European escape from the trace of men. Cole will be moved by that Sublime, yet he is to keep vivid the image of priority, an American image of freedom, for which Emerson and Thoreau, like Bryant before them, will prefer the trope of "wildness." The wildness triumphs throughout Bryant, a superb poet, always and still undervalued, and one of Hart Crane's and Wallace Stevens's legitimate ancestors. The voice of an American poetry goes back before Bryant, and can be heard in Bradstreet and Freneau (not so much, I think, in Edward Taylor, who was a good English poet who happened to be living in America). Perhaps, as with all origins, the American poetic voice cannot be traced, and so I move from my first to my second opening question: how to recognize the Muse of America. Here is Bryant, in the strong opening of his poem "The Prairies," in 1833:

From *Agon.* © 1982 by Oxford University Press.

These are the gardens of the Desert, these
The unshorn fields, boundless and beautiful,
For which the speech of England has no name—
The Prairies. I behold them for the first
And my heart swells, while the dilated sight
Takes in the encircling vastness.

Bryant's ecstatic beholding has little to do with what he sees. His speech swells most fully as he intones "The Prairies," following on the prideful reflection that no English poet could name these grasslands. The reflection itself is a touch awkward, since the word after all is French, and not Amerindian, as Bryant knew. No matter; the beholding is still there, and truly the name is little more important than the sight. What *is* vital is the dilation of the sight, an encircling vastness more comprehensive even than the immensity being taken in, for it is only a New England hop, skip and a jump from this dilation to the most American passage that will ever be written, more American even than Huck Finn telling Aunt Polly that he lies just to keep in practice, or Ahab proclaiming that he would strike the sun if it insulted him. Reverently I march back to where I and the rest of us have been before and always must be again, crossing a bare common, in snow puddles, at twilight, under a clouded sky, in the company of our benign father, the Sage of Concord, teacher of that perfect exhilaration in which, with him, we are glad to the brink of fear:

Standing on the bare ground,—my head bathed by the blithe air and uplifted into infinite space,—all mean egotism vanishes. I become a transparent eyeball; I am nothing; I see all; the currents of the Universal Being circulate through me; I am part or parcel of God.

Why is this ecstasy followed directly by the assertion: "The name of the nearest friend sounds then foreign and accidental . . . "? Why does the dilation of vision to the outrageous point of becoming a transparent eyeball provoke a denaturing of even the nearest name? I hasten to enforce the obvious, which nevertheless is crucial: the name is not forgotten, but loses the sound of immediacy; it becomes foreign or out-of-doors, rather than domestic; and accidental, rather than essential. A step beyond this into the American Sublime, and you do not even forget the name; you never hear it at all:

And now at last the highest truth on this subject remains unsaid; probably cannot be said; for all that we say is the far-off remembering of the intuition. That thought by what I can now nearest approach to say it, is this. When good is near you, when you have life in yourself, it is not by any known or accustomed way; you shall not discern the footprints of any other; you shall not see the face of man; you shall not hear any name;—the way, the thought, the good, shall be wholly strange and new.

"This subject" is self-reliance, and the highest truth on it would appear to be voiceless, except that Emerson's voice does speak out to tell us of the influx of the Newness, in which no footprints or faces are to be seen, and no name is to be heard. Unnaming always has been a major mode in poetry, far more than naming; perhaps there cannot be a poetic naming that is not founded upon an unnaming. I want to leap from these prose unnamings in Emerson, so problematic in their possibilities, to the poem in which, more than any other, I would seek to hear Emerson's proper voice for once in verse, a voice present triumphantly in so many hundreds of passages throughout his prose:

> Pour, Bacchus! the remembering wine;
> Retrieve the loss of me and mine!
> Vine for vine be antidote,
> And the grape requite the lote!
> Haste to cure the old despair,—
> Reason in Nature's lotus drenched,
> The memory of ages quenched;
> Give them again to shine;
> Let wine repair what this undid;
> And where the infection slid,
> A dazzling memory revive;
> Refresh the faded tints,
> Recut the aged prints,
> And write my old adventures with the pen
> Which on the first day drew,
> Upon the tablets blue,
> The dancing Pleiads and eternal men.

But why is Bacchus named here, if you shall not hear any name? My question would be wholly hilarious if we were to literalize Emerson's splendid chant. Visualize the Sage of Concord, gaunt and spare, uncorking a bottle in Dionysiac abandon, before emulating the Pleiads by breaking into a Nietzschean dance. No, the Bacchus of Ralph Waldo is rather clearly another unnaming. As for voice, it is palpably absent from this grand passage, its place taken up not even by writing, but by rewriting, by that revisionary pen which has priority, and which drew before the tablets darkened and grew small.

I am going to suggest shortly that rewriting is an invariable trope for voicing, within a poem, and that voicing and reseeing are much the same poetic process, a process reliant upon unnaming, which rhetorically means the undoing of a prior metonymy. But first I am going to leap ahead again, from Emerson to Stevens, which is to pass over the great impasse of Whitman, with whom I have identified always Hart Crane's great trope: "Oval encyclicals in canyons heaping / The impasse high with choir." Soon enough this discourse will center upon Whitman, since quite simply he *is* the American Sublime, he *is* voice in our poetry, he *is* our answer to the Continent now, precisely as he was a century ago. Yet I am sneaking up on him, always the best way for any critic to skulk near the Sublime Walt. His revisionism, of self as of others, is very subtle; his unnamings and his voices come out of the Great Deep. Stevens's are more transparent:

> Throw away the lights, the definitions,
> And say of what you see in the dark
> That it is this or that it is that,
> But do not use the rotted names.
>
> Phoebus is dead, ephebe. But Phoebus was
> A name for something that never could be named.
> There was a project for the sun and is.
>
> There is a project for the sun. The sun
> Must bear no name, gold flourisher, but be
> In the difficulty of what it is to be.
>
> This is nothing until in a single man contained,
> Nothing until this named thing nameless is
> And is destroyed. He opens the door of his house
>
> On flames. The scholar of one candle sees
> An Arctic effulgence flaring on the frame
> Of everything he is. And he feels afraid.

What have these three unnaming passages most in common? Well, what are we doing when we give pet names to those we love, or give no names to anyone at all, as when we go apart in order to go deep into ourselves? Stevens's peculiar horror of the commonplace in names emerges in his litany of bizarre, fabulistic persons and places, but though that inventiveness works to break casual continuities, it has little in common with the true break with continuity in poets like Lewis Carroll and Edward Lear. Stevens, *pace* Hugh Kenner, is hardly the culmination of the poetics of Lear. He may *not* be the culmination of Whitman's poetics either, since that begins to seem the peculiar distinction of John Ashbery. But like Whitman, Stevens does have a link to the Lucretian Sublime, as Pater the Epicurean did, and such a Sublime demands a deeper break with commonplace continuities than is required by the evasions of nonsense and fantasy. The most authentic of literary Sublimes has the Epicurean purpose of rendering us discontented with easier pleasures in order to prepare us for the ordeal of more difficult pleasures. When Stevens unnames he follows, however unknowingly, the trinity of negative wisdom represented by Emerson, Pater and Nietzsche. Stevens himself acknowledged only Nietzsche, but the unfashionable Emerson and Pater were even stronger in him, with Emerson (and Whitman) repressedly the strongest of strains. Why not, after all, use the rotted names? If the things were things that never could be named, is not one name as bad anyway as another? Stevens's masterpiece is not named. "The Somethings of Autumn," and not only because the heroic desperation of the Emersonian scholar of one candle is not enough. Whether you call the auroras flames or an Arctic effulgence or call them by the trope now stuck into dictionaries, auroras, you are giving your momentary consent to one arbitrary substitution or another. Hence Emerson's more drastic and Bacchic ambition; write your *old* adventures, not just your new, with the Gnostic pen of our forefather and foremother, the Abyss. I circle again the problematic American desire to merge voicing and revisionism into a single entity, and turn to Whitman for a central text, which will be the supposed elegy for Lincoln, "When Lilacs Last in the Dooryard Bloom'd." So drastic is the amalgam of voicing, unnaming and revisionism here that I take as prelude first Whitman's little motto poem, "As Adam Early in the Morning," so as to set some of the ways for approaching what is most problematic in the great elegy, its images of voice and of voicing.

What can we mean when we speak of the *voice* of the poet, or the voice of the critic? Is there a pragmatic sense of voice, in discussing poetry and criticism, that does not depend upon the illusions of metaphysics? When poetry and criticism speak of "images of voice," what is being imaged? I think I can answer these questions usefully in the context of my critical enterprise from *The Anxiety of Influence* on, but my answers rely upon a post-philosophical pragmatism which grounds itself upon what has worked to make up an American tradition. Voice in American poetry always necessarily must include Whitman's oratory, and here I quote from it where it is most economical and persuasive, a five-line poem that centers the canon of our American verse:

> As Adam early in the morning,
> Walking forth from the bower refresh'd with sleep,
> Behold me where I pass, hear my voice, approach,
> Touch me, touch the palm of your hand to my body as
>   I pass,
> Be not afraid of my body.

What shall we call this striding stance of the perpetually passing Walt, prophetic of Stevens's singing girl at Key West, and of Stevens's own Whitman walking along a ruddy shore, singing of death and day? Rhetorically the stance is wholly transumptive, introjecting earliness, but this is very unlike the Miltonic transuming of tradition. Walt is indeed Emerson's new Adam, American and Nietzschean, who can live as if it were morning, but though he is *as* the Biblical and Miltonic Adam, that "as" is one of Stevens's "intricate evasions of as." The Old Adam was not a savior, except in certain Gnostic traditions of Primal Man; the new, Whitmanian Adam indeed is Whitman himself, more like Christ than like Adam, and more like the Whitmanian Christ of Lawrence's "The Man Who Died" than like the Jesus of the Gospels.

Reading Whitman's little poem is necessarily an exercise both in a kind of repression and in a kind of introjection. To read the poem strongly, to voice its stance, is to transgress the supposed boundary between reading or criticism, and writing or poetry. "As" governs the three words of origins—"Adam," "early" and "morning"—and also the outgoing movement of Whitman, walking forth refreshed from a bower (that may be also a tomb), emerging from a sleep that may have been a kind of good death. Whitman placed this poem at the close of the "Children of Adam" division of *Leaves of Grass*, thus positioning it between the defeated American pathos of "Facing West from California's Shores" and the poignant "In Paths Untrodden" that begins the homoerotic "Calamus" section. There is a hint, in this contextualization, that the astonished reader needs to cross a threshold also. Behold Whitman as Adam; do not merely regard him when he is striding past. The injunctions build from that "behold" through "hear" and "approach" to "touch," a touch then particularized to the palm, as the resurrected Walt passes, no phantom, but a risen body. "Hear my voice" is the center. As Biblical trope, it invokes Jehovah walking in Eden in the cool of the day, but in Whitman's American context it acquires a local meaning also. Hear my voice, and not just my words; *hear me as voice*. Hear me, as in my elegy for President Lincoln, I hear the hermit thrush.

Though the great elegy finds its overt emblems in the lilac bush and the evening star, its more crucial tropes substitute for those emblems. These figures are the sprig of lilac that Whitman places on the hearse and the song of the thrush that floods the western night. Ultimately these are one trope, one image of voice, which we can follow Whitman by calling the "tally," playing also on a secondary meaning of "tally," as double or agreement. "Tally" may be Whitman's most crucial trope or ultimate image of voice. As a word, it goes back to the Latin *talea* for twig or cutting, which appears in this poem as the sprig of lilac. The word meant originally a cutting or stick upon which notches are made so as to keep count or score, but first in the English and then in the American vernacular it inevitably took on the meaning of a sexual score. The slang words "tallywoman," meaning a lady in an illicit relationship, and "tallywhack" or "tallywags," for the male genitalia, are still in circulation. "Tally" had a peculiar, composite meaning for Whitman in his poetry, which has not been noted by his critics. In the odd, rather luridly impressive death-poem "Chanting the Square Deific," an amazing blend of Emerson and an Americanized Hegel, Whitman identifies himself with Christ, Hermes and Hercules and then writes: "All sorrow, labor, suffering, I, tallying it, absorb it in myself." My comment would be: "Precisely *how* does he tally it?" and the answer to that question, grotesque as initially it must seem, would be: "Why, first by masturbating, and then by writing poems." I am being merely accurate, rather than outrageous, and so I turn to "Song of Myself," section 25, as first proof-text:

> Dazzling and tremendous how quick the sun-rise would kill
>   me,
> If I could not now and always send sun-rise out of me.
> We also ascend dazzling and tremendous as the sun,
> We found our own O my soul in the calm and cool of the
>   daybreak.
>
> My voice goes after what my eyes cannot reach,
> With the twirl of my tongue I encompass worlds and
>   volumes of worlds.
>
> Speech is the twin of my vision, it is unequal to measure
>   itself,
> It provokes me forever, it says sarcastically,
> *Walt you contain enough, why don't you let it out then?*
>
> Come now I will not be tantalized, you conceive too much of
>   articulation,
> Do you not know O speech how the buds beneath you are
>   folded?
> Waiting in gloom, protected by frost,
> The dirt receding before my prophetical screams,
> I underlying causes to balance them at last,
> My knowledge my live parts, it keeping tally with the
>   meaning of all things,
> Happiness, (which whoever hears me let him or her set out
>   in search of this day.)
>
> My final merit I refuse you, I refuse putting from me what I
>   really am,
> Encompass worlds, but never try to encompass me,
> I crowd your sleekest and best by simply looking toward
>   you.
>
> Writing and talk do not prove me,
> I carry the plenum of proof and every thing else in my face,
> With the hush of my lips I wholly confound the skeptic.

At this, almost the midpoint of his greatest poem, Whitman is sliding knowingly near crisis, which will come upon him in the crossing between sections 27 and 28. But here he is too strong, really too strong, and soon will pay the price of that overstrength, according to the Emersonian iron Law of Compensation, that nothing is got for nothing. Against the sun's mocking taunt: "See then whether you shall be master!" Whitman sends forth his own sunrise, which is a better, a more Emersonian answer than what Melville's Ahab threatens when he cries out, with surpassing Promethean eloquence: "I'd strike the sun if it insulted me!" As an alternative dawn, Whitman crucially identifies himself as a voice, a voice overflowing with presence, a presence that is a sexual self-knowledge: "My knowledge my live parts, it keeping tally with the meaning of all things." His knowledge and sexuality are one, and we need to ask: how does that sexual self-knowing keep tally with the meaning of all things? The answer comes in the crisis sequence of sections 26–30, where Whitman starts with listening and then regresses to touch, until he achieves both orgasm and poetic release through a Sublime yet quite literal masturbation. The sequence begins conventionally enough with bird song and human voice, passes to music, and suddenly becomes very extraordinary, in a passage critics have admired greatly but have been unable to expound:

> The orchestra whirls me wider than Uranus flies,
> It wrenches such ardors from me I did not know I possess'd
>   them,
> It sails me, I dab with bare feet, they are lick'd by the
>   indolent waves,
> I am cut by bitter and angry hail, I lose my breath,
> Steep'd amid honey'd morphine, my windpipe throttled in
>   fakes of death,
> At length let up again to feel the puzzle of puzzles,
> And that we call Being.

This Sublime antithetical flight (or repression) not only takes Whitman out of nature, but makes him a new kind of god, ever-dying and ever-living, a god whose touchstone is of course voice. The ardors wrenched from him are operatic, and the cosmos becomes stage machinery, a context in which the whirling bard first loses his breath to the envious hail, then sleeps a drugged illusory death in uncharacteristic silence, and at last is let up again to sustain the enigma of Being. For this hero of voice, we expect now a triumphant ordeal by voice, but surprisingly we get an equivocal ordeal by sexual self-touching. Yet the substitution is only rhetorical, and establishes the model for the tally in the Lincoln elegy, since the sprig of lilac will represent Whitman's live parts, and the voice of the bird will represent those ardors so intense, so wrenched from Whitman, that he did not know he possessed them.

After praising his own sensitivity of touch, Whitman concludes section 27 with the highly equivocal line: "To touch my person to some one else's is about as much as I can stand." The crisis section proper, 28, centers upon demonstrating that to touch his own person is also about as much as Whitman can stand. By the time he cries out: "I went myself first to the headland, my own hands carried me there," we can understand how the whole 1855 "Song of Myself" may have grown out of an early notebook jotting on the image of the headland, a threshold stage between self-excitation and orgasm. Section 28 ends with frankly portrayed release:

> You villain touch! what are you doing? my breath is tight in
> > its throat,
> Unclench your floodgates, you are too much for me.

The return of the image of breath and throat, of voice, is no surprise, nor will the attentive reader be startled when the lines starting section 29 take a rather more affectionate view of touch, now that the quondam villain has performed his labor:

> Blind loving wrestling touch, sheath'd hooded sharp-tooth'd
> > touch!
> Did it make you ache so, leaving me?

Since Whitman's "rich showering rain" fructifies into a golden, masculine landscape, we can call this sequence of "Song of Myself" the most productive masturbation since the ancient Egyptian myth of a god who masturbates the world into being. I suggest now (and no Whitman scholar will welcome it) that a failed masturbation is the concealed reference in section 2 of the "Lilacs" elegy:

> O powerful western fallen star!
> O shades of night—O moody, tearful night!
> O great star disappear'd—O the black murk that hides the
> > star!
> O cruel hands that hold me powerless—O helpless soul
> > of me!
> O harsh surrounding cloud that will not free my soul.

The cruel hands are Whitman's own, as he vainly seeks relief from his repressed guilt, since the death of Father Abraham has rekindled the death, a decade before, of the drunken Quaker carpenter-father, Walter Whitman, Senior. Freud remarks, in "Mourning and Melancholia," that

> there is more in the content of melancholia than in that of normal grief. In melancholia the relation to the object is no simple one; it is complicated by the conflict of ambivalence. This latter is either constitutional, i.e. it is an element of every love-relation formed by this particular ego, or else it proceeds from precisely those experiences that involved a threat of losing the object. . . . Constitutional ambivalence belongs by nature to what is repressed, while traumatic experiences with the object may have stirred to activity something else that has been repressed. Thus everything to do with these conflicts of ambivalence remains excluded from

consciousness, until the outcome characteristic of melancholia sets in. This, as we know, consists in the libidinal cathexis that is being menaced at last abandoning the object, only, however, to resume its occupation of that place in the ego whence it came. So by taking flight into the ego love escapes annihilation.

Both conflicts of ambivalence are Whitman's in the "Lilacs" elegy, and we will see love fleeing into Whitman's image of voice, the bird's tallying chant, which is the last stance of his ego. Freud's ultimate vision of primal ambivalence emphasized its origin as being the dialectical fusion / defusion of the two drives, love and death. Whitman seems to me profounder even than Freud as a student of the interlocking of these antithetical drives that darkly combine into one Eros and its shadow of ruin, to appropriate a phrase from Shelley. Whitman mourns Lincoln, yes, but pragmatically he mourns even more intensely for the tally, the image of voice he cannot as yet rekindle into being, concealed as it is by a "harsh surrounding cloud" of impotence. The miraculous juxtaposition of the two images of the tally, sprig of lilac and song of the hermit thrush, in sections 3 and 4 following, points the possible path out of Whitman's death-in-life:

> 3
> In the dooryard fronting an old farm-house near the white-
>   wash'd palings,
> Stands the lilac-bush tall-growing with heart-shaped leaves
>   of rich green,
> With many a pointed blossom rising delicate, with the
>   perfume strong I love,
> With every leaf a miracle—and from this bush in the
>   dooryard,
> With delicate-color'd blossoms and heart-shaped leaves of
>   rich green,
> A sprig with its flower I break.
>
> 4
> In the swamp in secluded recesses,
> A shy and hidden bird is warbling a song.
>
> Solitary the thrush,
> The hermit withdrawn to himself, avoiding the settlements,
> Sings by himself a song.
>
> Song of the bleeding throat,
> Death's outlet song of life, (for well dear brother I know,
> If thou wast not granted to sing thou would'st surely die.)

Whitman breaks the *talea*, in a context that initially suggests a ritual of castration, but the image offers more than a voluntary surrender of man-

hood. The broken lilac sprig is exactly analogous to the "song of the bleeding throat," and indeed the analogy explains the otherwise baffling
"bleeding." For what has torn the thrush's throat? The solitary song itself,
image of wounded voice, is the other *talea*, and has been broken so that
the soul can take count of itself. Yet why must these images of voice be
broken? Whitman's answer, a little further on in the poem, evades the
"why" much as he evades the child's "What is the grass?" in "Song of
Myself" 6, for the *why* like the *what* is unknowable in the context of the
Epicurean-Lucretian metaphysics that Whitman accepted. Whitman's answer comes in the hyperbolic, daemonic, repressive force of his copious
over-breaking of the tallies:

> Here, coffin that slowly passes,
> I give you my sprig of lilac.
>
> 7
> (Nor for you, for one alone,
> Blossoms and branches green to coffins all I bring,
> For fresh as the morning, thus would I chant a song for you
>   O sane and sacred death.
>
> All over bouquets of roses,
> O death, I cover you over with roses and early lilies,
> But mostly and now the lilac that blooms the first,
> Copious I break, I break the sprigs from the bushes,
> With loaded arms I come, pouring for you,
> For you and the coffins all of you O death.)

Why should we be moved that Whitman intones: "O sane and sacred
death," rather than: "O insane and obscene death," which might seem to
be more humanly accurate? "Death" here is a trope for the sane and sacred
Father Abraham, rather than for the actual father. Whitman's profuse breaking of the tallies attempts to extend this trope, so as to make of death itself
an ultimate image of voice or tally of the soul. It is the tally and not literal
death, our death, that is sane and sacred. But that returns us to the figuration of the tally, which first appears in the poem as a verb, just before
the carol of death:

> And the charm of the carol rapt me,
> As I held as if by their hands my comrades in the night,
> And the voice of my spirit tallied the song of the bird.

"My knowledge my live parts, it keeping tally with the meaning of all
things" now transfers its knowledge from the vital order to the death drive.
I am reminded that I first became aware of Whitman's crucial trope by
pondering its remarkable use by Hart Crane, when he invokes Whitman
directly in the "Cape Hatteras" section of *The Bridge*:

O Walt!—Ascensions of thee hover in me now
As thou at junctions elegiac, there, of speed,
With vast eternity, dost wield the rebound seed!
The competent loam, the probable grass,—travail
Of tides awash the pedestal of Everest, fail
Not less than thou in pure impulse inbred
To answer deepest soundings! O, upward from the dead
Thou bringest tally, and a pact, new bound
Of living brotherhood!

Crane's allusion is certainly to the "Lilacs" elegy, but his interpretation of what it means to bring tally "upward from the dead" may idealize rather too generously. That Walt's characteristic movement is ascension cannot be doubted, but the operative word in this elegy is "passing." The coffin of the martyred leader passes first, but in the sixteenth and final section it is the bard who passes, still tallying both the song of the bird and his own soul. That the tally is crucial, Crane was more than justified in emphasizing, but then Crane was a great reader as well as a great writer of poetry. Flanking the famous carol of death are two lines of the tally: "And the voice of my spirit tallied the song of the bird" preceding, and "To the tally of my soul" following. To tally the hermit thrush's carol of death *is* to tally the soul, for what is measured is the degree of sublimity, the agonistic answer to the triple question: more? less? equal? And the Sublime answer in death's carol is surely "more":

Come lovely and soothing death,
Undulate round the world, serenely arriving, arriving,
In the day, in the night, to all, to each,
Sooner or later delicate death.

Prais'd be the fathomless universe,
For life and joy, and for objects and knowledge curious,
And for love, sweet love—but praise! praise! praise!
For the sure-enwinding arms of cool-enfolding death.

Dark mother always gliding near with soft feet,
Have none chanted for thee a chant of fullest welcome?
Then I chant it for thee, I glorify thee above all,
I bring thee a song that when thou must indeed come,
        come unfalteringly.

Approach strong deliveress,
When it is so, when thou hast taken them I joyously sing
        the dead,
Lost in the loving floating ocean of thee,
Laved in the flood of thy bliss O death.

If this grand carol, as magnificent as the Song of Songs which is Solomon's, constitutes the tally or image of voice of the soul, then we ought now to be able to describe that image. To tally, in Whitman's sense, is at once to measure the soul's actual and potential sublimity, to overcome object-loss and grief, to gratify one's self sexually by one's self, to compose the thousand songs at random of *Leaves of Grass*, but above all, as Crane said, to bring a new covenant of brotherhood, and here that pact is new bound with the voice of the hermit thrush. The bird's carol, which invokes the oceanic mother of Whitman's *Sea-Drift cosmos*, is clearly not its tally but Whitman's own, the transgressive verbal climax of his own family romance. When, in the elegy's final section, Whitman chants himself as "Passing the song of the hermit bird and the tallying song of my soul," he prepares himself and us for his abandonment of the image of the lilac. And, in doing so, he prepares us also for his overwhelming refusal or inability to yield up similarly the darker image of the tally:

> Yet each to keep and all, retrievements out of the night,
> The song, the wondrous chant of the gray-brown bird,
> And the tallying chant, the echo arous'd in my soul.

The tally is an echo, as an image of voice must be, yet truly it does not echo the carol of the hermit thrush. Rather, it echoes the earlier Whitman, of "Out of the Cradle Endlessly Rocking," and his literary father, the Emerson of the great *Essays*. But here I require an *excursus* into poetic theory in order to explain image of voice and its relation to echo and allusion, and rather than rely upon as recondite a theorist as myself, I turn instead to a great explainer, John Hollander, who seems to me our outstanding authority upon all matters of lyrical form. Here is Hollander upon images of voice and their relation to the figurative interplay I have called "transumption," since that is what I take "tally" to be: Whitman's greatest transumption or introjection or Crossing of Identification, his magnificent overcoming both of his own earlier images of poetic origins and of Emerson's story of how poetry comes into being, particularly American poetry. First Hollander, from his book, *The Figure of Echo*:

> we deal with diachronic trope all the time, and yet we have no name for it as a class. . . . the echoing itself makes a figure, and the interpretive or revisionary power which raises the echo even louder than the original voice is that of a trope of diachrony. . . .
>
> I propose that we apply the name of the classical rhetoricians' trope of *transumption* (or *metalepsis* in its Greek form) to these diachronic, allusive figures. . . .
>
> Proper reading of a metaphor demands a simultaneous appreciation of the beauty of a vehicle and the importance of its freight. . . . But the interpretation of a metalepsis entails the recovery of the transumed material. A transumptive style is to be distinguished radically from the kind of conceited one which we

usually associate with baroque poetic, and with English seven-teenth-century verse in particular. It involves an ellipsis, rather than a relentless pursuit, of further figuration.

Hollander then names transumption as the proper figure for interpre-tive allusion, to which I would add only the description that I gave before in *A Map of Misreading:* this is the trope-undoing trope, which seeks to reverse imagistic priorities. Milton crowds all his poetic precursors together into the space that intervenes between *himself and the truth*. Whitman also crowds poetic anteriority—Emerson and the Whitman of 1855–1860—into a little space between the carol of death and the echo aroused in the soul of the elegist of "Lilacs." Emerson had excluded the questions of sex and death from his own images-of-voice, whether in a verse chant like "Bac-chus" or a prose rhapsody like "The Poet." The earlier Whitman had made of the deathly ocean at night his maternal image of voice, and we have heard the hermit thrush in its culmination of that erotic cry. Whitman's tally transumes the ocean's image of voice, by means of what Hollander calls an ellipsis of further figuration. The tally notches a restored narcissism and the return to the mode of erotic self-sufficiency. The cost is high as it always is in transumption. What vanishes here in Whitman is the presence of others and of otherness, as object-libido is converted into ego-libido again. Father Abraham, the ocean as dark mother, the love of comrades, and even the daemonic alter ego of the hermit thrush all fade away together. But what is left is the authentic American image of voice, as the bard brings tally, alone there in the night among the fragrant pines except for his remaining comrades, the knowledge of death and the thought of death.

In 1934 Wallace Stevens, celebrating his emergence from a decade's poetic silence, boldly attempted a very different transumption of the Whit-manian images of voice:

> It was her voice that made
> The sky acutest at its vanishing.
> She measured to the hour its solitude.
> She was the single artificer of the world
> In which she sang.

The tally, in "The Idea of Order at Key West," becomes the "ghostlier demarcations, keener sounds" ending the poem. A year later, Stevens granted himself a vision of Whitman as sunset in our evening-land:

> In the far South the sun of autumn is passing
> Like Walt Whitman walking along a ruddy shore.
> He is singing and chanting the things that are part of him,
> The worlds that were and will be, death and day.
> Nothing is final, he chants. No man shall see the end.
> His beard is of fire and his staff is a leaping flame.

It is certainly the passing bard of the end of "Lilacs," but did he chant that nothing is final? Still, this is Walt as Moses and as Aaron, leading the poetic children of Emerson through the American wilderness, and surely Whitman was always proudly provisional. Yet, the tally of his soul had to present itself as a finality, as an image of voice that had achieved a fresh priority and a perpetually ongoing strength. Was that an American Sublime, or only another American irony? Later in 1935, Stevens wrote a grim little poem called "The American Sublime" that seems to qualify severely his intense images of voice, of the singing girl and of Whitman:

> But how does one feel?
> One grows used to the weather,
> The landscape and that;
> And the sublime comes down
> To the spirit itself,
>
> The spirit and space,
> The empty spirit
> In vacant space.
> What wine does one drink?
> What bread does one eat?

The questions return us full circle to Emerson's "Bacchus," nearly a century before:

> We buy ashes for bread;
> We buy diluted wine.

This is not transumptive allusion, but a repetition of figurations, the American baroque defeat. But that is a secondary strain in Stevens, as it was in Emerson and in Whitman. I leap ahead, past Frost and Pound, Eliot and Williams, past even Hart Crane, to conclude with a contemporary image-of-voice that is another strong tally, however ruefully the strength regards itself. Here is John Ashbery's "The Other Tradition," the second poem in his 1977 volume, *Houseboat Days*:

> They all came, some wore sentiments
> Emblazoned on T-shirts, proclaiming the lateness
> Of the hour, and indeed the sun slanted its rays
> Through branches of Norfolk Island pine as though
> Politely clearing its throat, and all ideas settled
> In a fuzz of dust under trees when it's drizzling:
> The endless games of Scrabble, the boosters,
> The celebrated omelette au Cantal, and through it
> The roar of time plunging unchecked through the sluices
> Of the days, dragging every sexual moment of it
> Past the lenses: the end of something.
> Only then did you glance up from your book,
> Unable to comprehend what had been taking place, or

Say what you had been reading. More chairs
Were brought, and lamps were lit, but it tells
Nothing of how all this proceeded to materialize
Before you and the people waiting outside and in the next
Street, repeating its name over and over, until silence
Moved halfway up the darkened trunks,
And the meeting was called to order.
                                        I still remember
How they found you, after a dream, in your thimble hat,
Studious as a butterfly in a parking lot.
The road home was nicer then. Dispersing, each of the
Troubadours had something to say about how charity
Had run its race and won, leaving you the ex-president
Of the event, and how, though many of these present
Had wished something to come of it, if only a distant
Wisp of smoke, yet none was so deceived as to hanker
After that cool non-being of just a few minutes before,
Now that the idea of a forest had clamped itself
Over the minutiae of the scene. You found this
Charming, but turned your face fully toward night,
Speaking into it like a megaphone, not hearing
Or caring, although these still live and are generous
And all ways contained, allowed to come and go
Indefinitely in and out of the stockade
They have so much trouble remembering, when your
        forgetting
Rescues them at last, as a star absorbs the night.

I am aware that this charming poem urbanely confronts, absorbs and
in some sense seeks to overthrow a critical theory, almost a critical climate,
that has accorded it a canonical status. Stevens's Whitman proclaims that
nothing is final and that no man shall see the end. Ashbery, a Whitman
somehow more studiously casual even than Whitman, regards the prophets
of belatedness and cheerfully insists that his forgetting or repression will
rescue us at last, even as the Whitmanian or Stevensian evening star absorbs
the night. But the price paid for this metaleptic reversal of American belatedness into a fresh earliness is the yielding up of Ashbery's tally or image
of voice to a deliberate grotesquerie. Sexuality is made totally subservient
to time, which is indeed "the end of something," and poetic tradition
becomes an ill-organized social meeting of troubadours, leaving the canonical Ashbery as "ex-president / Of the event." As for the image of voice
proper, the Whitmanian confrontation of the night now declines into: "You
found this / Charming, but turned your face fully toward night, / Speaking
into it like a megaphone, not hearing / Or caring." Such a megaphone is
an apt image for Paul de Man's deconstructionist view of poetic tradition,

which undoes tradition by suggesting that every poem is as much a random and gratuitous event as any human death is.

Ashbery's implicit interpretation of what he wants to call *The Other Tradition* mediates between this vision of poems as being totally cut off from one another and the antithetical darkness in which poems carry over-determined relationships and progress towards a final entropy. Voice in our poetry now tallies what Ashbery in his "Syringa," a major Orphic elegy in *Houseboat Days,* calls "a record of pebbles along the way." Let us grant that the American Sublime is always also an American irony, and then turn back to Emerson and hear the voice that is great within us somehow breaking through again. This is Emerson in his journal for August 1859, on the eve of being burned out, with all his true achievement well behind him; but he gives us the true tally of his soul:

> *Beatitudes of Intellect.*—Am I not, one of these days, to write con-secutively of the beatitude of intellect? It is too great for feeble souls, and they are over-excited. The wineglass shakes, and the wine is spilled. What then? The joy which will not let me sit in my chair, which brings me bolt upright to my feet, and sends me striding around my room, like a tiger in his cage, and I cannot have composure and concentration enough even to set down in English words that thought which thrills me—is not that joy a certificate of the elevation? What if I never write a book or a line? for a moment, the eyes of my eyes were opened, the affirmative experience remains, and consoles through all suffering.

Melville the Poet

Robert Penn Warren

F. O. Matthiessen has undertaken to give in twenty-two pages [of his Selected Poems of Herman Melville] a cross section of the rather large body of the poetry of Herman Melville. If he had intended to give merely a little gathering of his poet's best blossoms, his task would have been relatively easy. But he has also undertaken, as he says in his brief but instructive preface, to "take advantage of all the various interests attaching to any part of Melville's work." So some items appear because they present the basic symbols which are found in the prose or because they "serve to light up facets of Melville's mind as it developed in the years after his great creative period."

In one sense all one can do is to say that Mr. Matthiessen, with the space permitted by the series to which this book belongs (*The Poets of the Year*), has carried out his plan with the taste and discernment which could have been predicted by any reader of his discussion of Melville's poetry in the *American Renaissance*. But I shall take this occasion to offer a few remarks supplementary to the preface [elsewhere] and to point out other poems and passages in Melville's work which I hope Mr. Matthiessen admires or finds interesting but which could have no place in his arbitrarily limited collection.

First, I wish to comment on Melville's style. It is ordinarily said that he did not master the craft of verse. Few of his poems are finished. Fine lines, exciting images, and bursts of eloquence often appear, but they appear side by side with limping lines, inexpressive images, and passages of bombast. In a way, he is a poet of shreds and patches. I do not wish to deny the statement that he did not master his craft, but I do feel that it needs some special interpretation.

From *Selected Essays*. © 1966 by Vintage Books.

If, for example, we examine the poems under the title "Fruit of Travel Long Ago," in the *Timoleon* volume of 1891, we see that the verse here is fluent and competent. In his belated poetic apprenticeship, he was capable of writing verse which is respectable by the conventional standards of the time. But the effects which he could achieve within this verse did not satisfy him. Let us look at the poem called "In a Bye-Canal." The first section gives us verse that is conventionally competent:

> A swoon of noon, a trance of tide,
> The hushed siesta brooding wide
>   Like calms far off Peru;
> No floating wayfarer in sight,
> Dumb noon, and haunted like the night
>   When Jael the wiled one slew.
> A languid impulse from the car
> Plied by my indolent gondolier
> Tinkles against a palace hoar,
>   And hark, response I hear!
> A lattice clicks; and lo, I see
> Between the slats, mute summoning me,
> What loveliest eyes of scintillation,
> What basilisk glance of conjuration!

But the next eight lines are very different. The metrical pattern is sorely tried and wrenched.

> Fronted I have, part taken the span
> Of portent in nature and peril in man.
> I have swum—I have been
> 'Twixt the whale's black fluke and the white shark's fin;
> The enemy's desert have wandered in,
> And there have turned, have turned and scanned,
> Following me how noiselessly,
> Envy and Slander, lepers hand in hand.

Then the poem returns to its normal movement and tone:

> All this. But at the latticed eye—
> "Hey, Gondolier, you sleep, my man;
> Wake up!" And shooting by, we ran;
> The while I mused, This surely now,
> Confutes the Naturalists, allow!
> Sirens, true sirens verily be,
> Sirens, waylayers in the sea.
> Well, wooed by these same deadly misses,
> Is it shame to run?
> No! Flee them did divine Ulysses,
> Brave, wise, and Venus' son.

The poem breaks up. The central section simply does not go with the rest. It is as though we have here a statement of the poet's conviction that the verse which belonged to the world of respectability could not accommodate the rendering of the experience undergone " 'Twixt the whale's black fluke and the white shark's fin." Perhaps the violences, the distortions, the wrenchings in the versification of some of the poems are to be interpreted as the result not of mere ineptitude but of a conscious effort to develop a nervous, dramatic, masculine style. (In this connection, the effort at a familiar style in *John Marr and Other Sailors*, especially in "Jack Roy," is interesting.) That Melville was conscious of the relation of the mechanics of style to fundamental intentions is ably argued by William Ellery Sedgwick in *Herman Melville: The Tragedy of Mind* in connection with the verse of *Clarel*. Mr. Sedgwick argues that the choice of short, four-beat lines, usually rhyming in couplets, a form the very opposite to what would have been expected, was dictated by a desire to confirm himself in his new perspective. "The form of *Clarel* was prop or support to his new state of consciousness, in which his spontaneous ego or self-consciousness no longer played an all-commanding role." I would merely extend the application of the principle beyond *Clarel*, without arguing, as Mr. Sedgwick argues in the case of *Clarel*, that Melville did develop a satisfactory solution for his problem.

If we return to "In a Bye-Canal," we may observe that the poem is broken not only by a shift in rhythm but also by a shift in tone. The temper of the poem is very mixed. For instance, the lines

> Dumb noon, and haunted like the night
> When Jael the wiled one slew

introduce a peculiarly weighted, serious reference into the casual first section which concludes with the playful *scintillation-conjuration* rhyme. Then we have the grand section of the whale and the shark. Then the realistic admonition to the gondolier. Then the conclusion, with its classical allusion, at the level of *vers de société*. Probably no one would argue that the disparate elements in this poem have been assimilated, as they have, for example, in Marvell's "To His Coy Mistress." But I think that one may be well entitled to argue that the confusions of temper in this poem are not merely the result of ineptitude but are the result of an attempt to create a poetry of some vibrancy, range of reference, and richness of tone.

In another form we find the same effort much more successfully realized in "Jack Roy" in the difference between the two following stanzas:

> Sang Larry o' the Cannakin, smuggler o' the wine,
> At mess between guns, lad in jovial recline:
>
> "In Limbo our Jack he would chirrup up a cheer,
> The martinet there find a chaffing mutineer;
> From a thousand fathoms down under hatches o' your
>   Hades

He'd ascend in love-ditty, kissing fingers to your ladies!"
Never relishing the knave, though allowing for the menial,
Nor overmuch the king, Jack, nor prodigally genial.
Ashore on liberty, he flashed in escapade,
Vaulting over life in its levelness of grade,
Like the dolphin off Africa in a rainbow a-sweeping—
Arch iridescent shot from seas languid sleeping.

Or we find the same fusion of disparate elements in "The March into Virginia," one of Melville's best poems:

Did all the lets and bars appear
To every just or larger end,
Whence should come the trust and cheer?
Youth must its ignorant impulse lend—
Age finds place in the rear.
All wars are boyish, and are fought by boys,
The champions and enthusiasts of the state:
. . . .
No berrying party, pleasure-wooed,
No picnic party in the May,
Ever went less loath than they
Into that leafy neighborhood.
In Bacchic glee they file toward Fate,
Moloch's uninitiate;
. . . .
But some who this blithe mood present,
As on in lightsome files they fare,
Shall die experienced ere three days are spent—
Perish, enlightened by the volleyed glare;
Or shame survive, and, like to adamant,
The throe of Second Manassas share.

On a smaller scale, Melville's effort to get range and depth into his poetry is illustrated by the occasional boldness of his comparisons. For example, in "The Portent," the beard of John Brown protruding from the hangman's cap is like the trail of a comet or meteor presaging doom.

Hidden in the cap
Is the anguish none can draw;
So your future veils its face,
Shenandoah!
But the streaming beard is shown
(Weird John Brown),
The meteor of the war.

Or in one of the early poems, "In a Church of Padua," we find the confessional compared to a diving-bell:

> Dread diving-bell! In thee inurned
> What hollows the priest must sound,
> Descending into consciences
> Where more is hid than found.

It must be admitted that Melville did not learn his craft. But the point is that the craft he did not learn was not the same craft which some of his more highly advertised contemporaries did learn with such glibness of tongue and complacency of spirit. Even behind some of Melville's failures we can catch the shadow of the poem which might have been. And if his poetry is, on the whole, a poetry of shreds and patches, many of the patches are of a massy and kingly fabric—no product of the local cotton mills.

But to turn to another line of thought: Both Mr. Matthiessen and Mr. Sedgwick have been aware of the importance of the short poems in relation to Melville's general development. Mr. Sedgwick does give a fairly detailed analysis of the relation of *Battle-Pieces* to *Clarel*. "Even in the *Battle-Pieces*," he says, "we feel the reservations of this (religious) consciousness set against the easy and partial affirmations of patriotism and partisan conflict." And he quotes, as Mr. Matthiessen has quoted in the preface to the present collection and in the *American Renaissance*, an extremely significant sentence from the prose essay which Melville appended to the *Battle-Pieces*: "Let us pray that the terrible historic tragedy of our time may not have been enacted without instructing our whole beloved country through pity and terror." And Mr. Sedgwick refers to one of the paradoxes of "The Conflict of Convictions," that the victory of the Civil War may betray the cause for which the North was fighting:

> Power unanointed may come—
> Dominion (unsought by the free)
> And the Iron Dome
> Stronger for stress and strain,
> Fling her huge shadow athwart the main;
> But the Founders' dream shall flee.

But even in this poem there are other ideas which relate to Melville's concern with the fundamental ironical dualities of existence: will against necessity, action against ideas, youth against age, the changelessness of man's heart against the concept of moral progress, the bad doer against the good deed, the bad result against the good act, ignorance against fate, etc. These ideas appear again and again, as in "The March into Virginia":

> Did all the lets and bars appear
> To every just or larger end,
> Whence should come the trust and cheer?
> Youth must its ignorant impulse lend—
> Age finds place in the rear.
> All wars are boyish, and are fought by boys,
> The champions and enthusiasts of the state.

Or in "On the Slain Collegians":

> Youth is the time when hearts are large,
> And stirring wars
> Appeal to the spirit which appeals in turn
> To the blade it draws.
> If woman incite, and duty show
> (Though made the mask of Cain),
> Or whether it be Truth's sacred cause,
> Who can aloof remain
> That shares youth's ardour, uncooled by the snow
> Of wisdom or sordid gain?

Youth, action, will, ignorance—all appear in heroic and dynamic form as manifestations of what Mr. Sedgwick has called Melville's "radical Protestantism," the spirit which had informed *Moby Dick*. But in these poems the commitment is nicely balanced, and even as we find the praise of the dynamic and heroic we find them cast against the backdrop of age, idea, necessity, wisdom, fate. Duty may be made the "mask of Cain" and "lavish hearts" are but, as the poem on the Collegians puts it, "swept by the winds of their place and time." All bear their "fated" parts. All move toward death or toward the moment of wisdom when they will stand, as "The March into Virginia" puts it, "enlightened by the volleyed glare."

Man may wish to act for Truth and Right, but the problem of definitions is a difficult one and solution may be achieved only in terms of his own exercise of will and his appetite for action. That is, his "truth" and the Truth may be very different things in the end. "On the Slain Collegians" sums the matter up:

> What could they else—North or South?
> Each went forth with blessings given
> By priests and mothers in the name of Heaven;
>   And honour in both was chief.
> Warred one for Right, and one for Wrong?
> So be it; but they both were young—
> Each grape to his cluster clung,
> All their elegies are sung.

Or there is "The College Colonel," the young officer who returns from the war, a crutch by his saddle, to receive the welcome of the crowd and especially, as "Boy," the salute of age. But to him comes "alloy."

> It is not that a leg is lost
> It is not that an arm is maimed.
> It is not that the fever has racked—
> Self he has long disclaimed.
> But all through the Seven Days' Fight,

> And deep in the Wilderness grim,
> And in the field-hospital tent,
> And Petersburg crater, and dim
> Lean brooding in Libby, there came—
> Ah heaven!—what *truth* to him.

The official truth and the official celebration are equally meaningless to him who has been "enlightened by the volleyed glare"—who has known pity and terror.

The event, the act, is never simple. Duty may be made the mask of Cain. In "The Conflict of Convictions," it is asked:

> Dashed aims, at which Christ's martyrs pale,
> Shall Mammon's slaves fulfill?

And in the same poem, in the passage which Mr. Sedgwick quotes, Melville conjectures that the Iron Dome, stronger for stress and strain, may fling its huge, imperial shadow across the main; but at the expense of the "Founders' dream." But other dire effects of the convulsion, even if it involves Right, may be possible. Hate on one side and Phariseeism on the other may breed a greater wrong than the one corrected by the conflict. The "gulfs" may bare "their slimed foundations," as it is phrased in the same poem in an image which is repeated in "America." The allegorical female figure, America, is shown sleeping:

> But in that sleep contortion showed
> The terror of the vision there—
> A silent vision unavowed,
> Revealing earth's foundations bare,
> And Gorgon in her hiding place.
> It was a thing of fear to see
> So foul a dream upon so fair a face,
> And the dreamer lying in that starry shroud.

Even if the victory is attained, there is no cause for innocent rejoicing. As, in "The College Colonel," the hero looks beyond the cheering crowd to his "truth," so in "Commemorative of a Naval Victory," the hero must look beyond his "festal fame":

> But seldom the laurel wreath is seen
> Unmixed with pensive pansies dark;
> There's a light and shadow on every man
> Who at last attains his lifted mark—
> Nursing through night the ethereal spark.
> Elate he never can be;
> He feels that spirits which glad had hailed his worth,
> Sleep in oblivion.—The shark
> Glides white through the phosphorous sea.

There is more involved here than the sadness over the loss of comrades. The shark comes as too violent and extravagant an image for that. The white shark belongs to the world of "slimed foundations" which are exposed by the convulsion.It is between the whale's black fluke and the white shark's fin that wisdom is learned. He is the Maldive shark, which appears in the poem by that name, the "Gorgonian head" (the "Gorgon in her hiding place" appears too in the bared foundations of earth glimpsed in the dream of "America"), the "pale ravener of horrible meat," the Fate symbol.

We may ask what resolution of these dualities and dubieties may be found in Melville's work. For there is an effort at a resolution. The effort manifests itself in three different terms: nature, history, and religion.

In reference to the first term, we find the simple treatment of "Shiloh":

> Foemen at morn, but friends at eve—
> Fame or country least their care:
> (What like a bullet can undeceive!)
> But now they lie low,
> While over them the swallows skim
> And all is hushed at Shiloh.

Mortal passion and mortal definition dissolve in the natural process, as in "Malvern Hill":

> We elms of Malvern Hill
> Remember everything;
> But sap the twig will fill:
> Wag the world how it will,
> Leaves must be green in Spring.

The focal image at the end of "A Requiem for Soldiers Lost in Ocean Transports" repeats the same effect:

> Nor heed they now the lone bird's flight
> Round the lone spar where mid-sea surges pour.

There is, however, a step beyond this elegiac calm of the great natural process which absorbs the human effort and agony. There is also the historical process. It is possible, as Melville puts it in "The Conflict of Convictions," that the "throes of ages" may rear the "final empire and the happier world." The Negro woman in "Formerly a Slave" looks

> Far down the depth of thousand years,
> And marks the revel shrine;
> Her dusky face is lit with sober light,
> Sibylline, yet benign.

In "America," the last poem of *Battle-Pieces*, the contorted expression on the face of the sleeping woman as she dreams the foul dream of earth's bared foundations, is replaced, when she rises, by a "clear calm look."

> It spake of pain,
> But such a purifier from stain—
> Sharp pangs that never come again—
> And triumph repressed by knowledge meet,
> And youth matured for age's seat—
> Law on her brow and empire in her eyes.
> So she, with graver air and lifted flag;
> While the shadow, chased by light,
> Fled along the far-drawn height,
> And left her on the crag.

"Secession, like Slavery, is against Destiny," Melville wrote in the prose supplement to *Battle-Pieces*. For to him, if history was fate (the "foulest crime" was inherited and was fixed by geographical accident upon its perpetrators), it might also prove to be redemption. In *Mardi*, in a passage which Mr. Sedgwick quotes in reference to the slaves of Vivenza, Melville exclaims: "Time—all-healing Time—Time, great philanthropist! Time must befriend these thralls." Melville, like Hardy, whom he resembles in so many respects and with whose war poems his own war poems share so much in tone and attitude, proclaimed that he was neither an optimist nor a pessimist, and in some of his own work we find a kind of guarded meliorism, like Hardy's, which manifests itself in the terms of destiny, fate, time, that is, in the historical process.

The historical process, however, does not appear always as this mechanism of meliorism. Sometimes the resolution it offers is of another sort, a sort similar to the elegiac calm of the natural process: the act is always poised on the verge of history, the passion, even at the moment of greatest intensity, is always about to become legend, the moral issue is always about to disappear into time and leave only the human figures, shadowy now, fixed in attitudes of the struggle. In "Battle of Stone River, Tennessee," we find the stanzas which best express this.

> With Tewksbury and Barnet heath,
> In days to come the field shall blend,
> The story dim and date obscure;
> In legend all shall end.
> Even now, involved in forest shade
> A Druid-dream the strife appears,
> The fray of yesterday assumes
> The haziness of years.
>> In North and South still beats the vein
>> Of Yorkist and Lancastrian.
>
> . . . .

But Rosecrans in the cedarn glade
And, deep in denser cypress gloom,
Dark Breckinridge, shall fade away
Or thinly loom.
The pale throngs who in forest cowed
Before the spell of battle's pause,
Forefelt the stillness that shall dwell
On them and their wars.
   North and South shall join the train
   Of Yorkist and Lancastrian.

In "The March into Virginia" the young men laughing and chatting on the road to Manassas are "Moloch's uninitiate" who "file toward Fate."

All they feel is this: 'tis glory,
A rapture sharp, though transitory
Yet lasting in belaurelled story.

The glory of the act ends in legend, in the perspective of history, which is fate. Human action enters the realm where it is, to take a line from "The Coming Storm,"

Steeped in fable, steeped in fate.

Nature and history proved the chief terms of resolution in *Battle-Pieces*. Only rarely appears the third term, religion, and then in a conventional form. For instance, there is "The Swamp-Angel," which deals with the bombardment of Charleston:

Who weeps for the woeful City
Let him weep for our guilty kind;
Who joys at her wild despairing—
Christ, the Forgiver, convert his mind.

It is actually in the terms of nature and history that the attitude which characterizes *Clarel* first begins to make itself felt. Mr. Sedgwick has defined Melville's attitude as the result of a "religious conversion to life." In it he renounced the quest for the "uncreated good," the individualistic idealism of *Moby Dick*, the "radical Protestantism." Mr. Sedgwick continues: "Behind *Clarel* lies the recognition that for ripeness, there must be receptivity; that from the point of view of the total consciousness it is not more blessed to give than to receive. One receives in order to be received into life and fulfilled by life. . . . Melville's act was toward humanity, not away from it. He renounced all the prerogatives of individuality in order to enter into the destiny which binds all human beings in one great spiritual and emotional organism. He abdicated his independence so as to be incorporated into the mystical body of humanity." There is the affirmation at the end of *Clarel:*

But through such strange illusions have they passed
Who in life's pilgrimage have baffled striven—
Even death may prove unreal at the last,
And stoics be astounded into heaven.

Then keep thy heart, though yet but ill-resigned—
Clarel, thy heart, the issues there but mind;
That like the crocus budding through the snow—
That like a swimmer rising from the deep—
That like a burning secret which doth go
Even from the bosom that would hoard and keep;
Emerge thou mayst from the last whelming sea,
And prove that death but routs life into victory.

Or we find the same attitude expressed by the comforting spirit which appears at the end of "The Lake":

She ceased and nearer slid, and hung
In dewy guise; then softlier sung:
"Since light and shade are equal set,
And all revolves, nor more ye know;
Ah, why should tears the pale cheek fret
For aught that waneth here below.
Let go, let go!"

With that, her warm lips thrilled me through,
She kissed me while her chaplet cold
Its rootlets brushed against my brow
With all their humid clinging mould.
She vanished, leaving fragrant breath
And warmth and chill of wedded life and death.

And when, in the light of these poems we look back upon "The Maldive Shark" we see its deeper significance. As the pilot fish may find a haven in the serrated teeth of the shark, so man, if he learns the last wisdom, may find an "asylum in the jaws of the Fates."

This end product of Melville's experience has, in the passage which I have already quoted from Mr. Sedgwick, been amply defined. What I wish to emphasize is the fact that there is an astonishing continuity between the early poems, especially *Battle-Pieces*, and *Clarel*. Under the terms of nature and history, the religious attitude of *Clarel* and "The Lake" is already being defined.

Form as Vision
in Herman Melville's *Clarel*

Bryan C. Short

In his forward to Vincent Kenny's book on *Clarel* (*Herman Melville's Clarel: A Spiritual Autobiography* [Hamden, 1973]), Gay Wilson Allen recommends three "routes" for approaching the poem. The first relates *Clarel* to Melville's "spiritual quest for the meaning of existence." The second reaches *Clarel* by way of Melville's actual trip to Palestine. The third explores Melville's anticipation of the pessimism so important to later thought. Efforts by such recent critics as Kenny and William H. Shurr, not to mention all whose contributions Kenny summarizes in his fourth chapter, have moved us far enough along these routes that another can be glimpsed. *Clarel* demands a reading in the light of relationships between Melville's poetic technique and modifications which the practice of verse wrought in his view of literature. A reverence for organic unity pervaded Romantic poetics in America; Melville's changing interpretation of this doctrine determines the adapting of versification to narrative purpose which gives *Clarel* its unique shape. Such a study promises a better understanding of how Melville's later verse grew out of the impatient questing of the novels, an explanation of his curious abandonment of tetrameter in the *Clarel* epilogue, and a more flattering image of his state of mind than has been current. The protean nature of Melville's poetry suggests that the promise of artistic rather than philosophical accomplishment motivated the varied forms of his mature works. Although his themes reflect the depression which adorns his family correspondence, his incessant technical experiments bespeak an undying vitality. Our view of Melville should include the literary interests, both practical and theoretical, which kept him active at his desk in spite of obscurity, money problems, family tragedy, poor health, and civil service.

From *American Literature* 50, no. 4 (January 1979). © 1979 by Duke University Press.

Clarel, with its profound dedication to organic poetics, reveals these springs and motives as well as any other work in the cannon.

Battle-Pieces lays the groundwork for organic form in *Clarel* by achieving a well-tested strategy for facing the terrors of experience, a style which both suits and embodies that strategy, and a new confidence, noted by critics, *vis à vis* the spiritual quest whose enticements survived the foundering of Melville's fiction. Without this foundation, *Clarel* is unthinkable, for *Clarel* presents a world as blasted and a plot as depressing as any met previously in Melville's works. A study of organicism in the epic begins with *Battle-Pieces,* upon whose successes rests Melville's decision, in the teeth of his woes, to grapple with old and crushing obsessions in the medium of eighteen thousand tetrameter lines.

The main strategy carried from *Battle-Pieces* into *Clarel* is the abrogation of "deep diving" after "chronometrical" truths in favor of a disciplined objectivity. Melville signals this strategy in a prefatory note:

> The aspects which the strife as a memory assumes are as manifold as are the moods of involuntary meditation. . . . Yielding instinctively, one after another, to feelings not inspired from any one source exclusively, and unmindful, without purposing to be, of consistency, I seem, in most of these verses, to have but placed a harp in a window, and noted the contrasted airs which wayward winds have played upon the strings.

Poetry responds to the winds of war without forcing an artificial consistency on them. *Battle-Pieces* wagers that clearly "noted" historical movements may reveal the meaning of existence more effectively than the single-minded vision of a Taji, and that a valuable organic bond can unite fact and verse. This is not to say that Melville eschews fictionalization but that fictionalization plays a more limited and descriptive role than in his novels.

Objectivity suits Melville's main *persona,* an aging observer remote from the action. However, during the course of *Battle-Pieces,* Melville discovers important correspondences between poetic and battlefield deeds; the Civil War gives birth to modern man, brave, self-controlled, and fatalistic, and Melville adopts this new hero as a model for his own literary goals. Courageous warriors display the same discipline as the poet, and both stand in the mainstream of history. Praising the pilot of a suicide-launch, Melville writes:

> In Cushing's eager deed was shown
> A spirit which brave poets own—
> That scorn of life which earns life's crown.
> ("At the Cannon's Mouth")

Poetry can strive for an organic encompassing of heroic action because it embodies a parallel heroism.

However brave, neither poet nor soldier, art nor experience, can claim knowledge beyond death; in this objective limitation all share equally. The living must be satisfied with mere hints at the meaning of existence without hoping that some heroic act or literary "deep dive" will yield more:

> Obscure as the wood, the entangled rhyme
>> But hints at the maze of war—
> Vivid glimpses or livid through peopled gloom,
>> And fires which creep and char—
> A riddle of death, of which the slain
>>> Sole solvers are.
>>>> ("The Armies of the Wilderness")

The equality of art and action only partly explains Melville's confidence in an objective, unified poetry. Art goes a step further by so revealing the human heart that it anticipates experience. In " 'The Coming Storm' " Melville takes the example of Shakespeare:

> No utter surprises can come to him
>> Who reaches Shakespeare's core;
> That which we seek and shun is there—
>> Man's final lore.

The truths of the heart cannot transcend mortality, but, as illuminated by art, they predict whatever shocks may come—a function which in *Clarel* takes the place of attempts to penetrate the pasteboard mask of reality. If one picks a great experience—the Civil War, a pilgrimage to the Holy Land—a poetry which reflects its varied aspects organically and without preconception can capture whatever lessons the experience teaches. Imposing transcendental hopes on the experience will only destroy both its heroic discipline and its validity.

In seeking to respond objectively to the winds of history, Melville evolves a style in line with Emerson's organicist dictum that "it is not metres but a metre-making argument which makes a poem." He describes the style in "A Utilitarian View of the Monitor's Fight":

> Plain be the phrase, yet apt the verse,
>> More ponderous than nimble;
> For since grimed War here laid aside
> His painted pomp, 'twould ill befit
>> Overmuch to ply
> The rhyme's barbaric cymbal.

The plain, apt verse of *Battle-Pieces* matures in "Lee in the Capitol," the penultimate poem in the volume, into the full-blown *Clarel* form; loose iambic tetrameter, a prominent line throughout the collection, falls into unequal verse paragraphs; flexible rhyme patterns intrude on the predominant couplets. The poem presents a dramatic yet essentially verbal scene much like those of *Clarel* and reflects a similar relationship between narrator and character. "Lee in the Capitol" presents the final hero of *Battle-Pieces* abandoning his avowed silence to speak before a hostile public. Both the circumstances of Lee's act and the repetition of his views in a prose supplement suggest Melville's identification with him. Hero and poet come together to climax the hope for both art and experience, a hope which rests on the bravery, aptness, and objectivity of Lee's words, compellingly turned into verse. Out of the narrowed horizons and clouded dreams of war comes a vision of honest courage and unified art. Lee's act, like Melville's bow to history, reveals an ability to anticipate if not transcend experience, for his plea catches "the light in the future's skies." Discipline and self-control sustain most of the *Clarel* pilgrims. The belief that a verse like that of "Lee in the Capitol" can contain metaphysical anxieties within an objective framework and thereby anticipate their ravages is the heaviest weapon carried by Melville from *Battle-Pieces* into the epic. Melville's willingness to fictionalize Lee's speech demonstrates his willingness to sum up the lesson of the war as he sees it; the abandonment of preconceived transcendental goals does not stop art from reaching conclusions. *Clarel* begins on the hope that new, if circumscribed, insights into the "meaning of existence" are possible.

In line with the principles of organic unity, Melville's substitution of disciplined objectivity for deep diving dramatically modifies the "diagram" of his characteristic quest. In *Clarel*, the search leads away from rather than toward the symbol which promises resolution. Whereas Taji incessantly follows Yillah, Clarel's pilgrimage leads him from Ruth. This change in direction, to some a structural disharmony, reflects Melville's wish to distinguish spiritual knowledge from emotional satisfaction and to keep the transcendent questing of his earlier works from dominating experience. The lesson of Civil War fatalism permits Melville to build into *Clarel* his misgivings about the nobility of both pilgrims and pilgrimage; vivid adventure gives way to desultory wandering and endless talk; systems of belief no longer command attention on the basis of logical force. Robert Penn Warren comments that "Melville is trying to show ideals not as abstractions but as a function of the life process." This impulse, both objective and organic, leads Melville to conclude that grand ideas have little positive impact on human happiness; they do Clarel no more good than they do the wounded veterans of the war.

Just as the search for knowledge in *Clarel* separates from the promise of satisfaction, the views of the characters have little to do with their importance. The sociability of Derwent, whose meliorism subjects him to derision, keeps him at the center of the group. Vine says so little that his influence on Clarel partakes of the irrational. Rolfe's heartiness outweighs his contradictions. Walter Bezanson concludes that Clarel "goes increasingly from asking whose beliefs are right to asking who is the right kind of man." A concomitant question which Melville asks is not what truth is deepest but what kind of art is both unified and honest, a question which finally undercuts all abstractions. Melville's objectivity challenges even Lee's resigned wisdom. Removed from the realm of historical greatness, experience offers less comfort than blind faith; the wise soldiers of *Battle-Pieces* condense into Ungar, whose heroism is irrelevant to his needs. Versification follows suit by seeking effects of plainness and tension rather than ease or dramatic brilliance. The tetrameters borrowed from "Lee in the Capitol" come to embody, and finally to symbolize, the hard realities of a wasted world.

Clarel is not, however, without a hint of redemption, but redemption, operating within the sphere of satisfaction rather than knowledge, finally contradicts both the experience of its characters and the outcome of its plot, creating a disintegration which threatens to ruin the organic unity at the heart of the work. Redemption comes second hand in Melville's curiously buoyant epilogue. It is here that Melville redefines organic form in order to escape the objective decorum of his narrative. Like the palinode of a medieval allegory or the epilogue of an Elizabethan play, the *Clarel* epilogue removes Melville's conclusion from the context of the tale. Clarel is left alone shouldering a greater burden than ever; none of his friends can comfort him; but Melville blithely tells us that things are not so bad. In reevaluating the search for truth, Melville denies the final value of brave and disciplined objectivity, the archetypal virtues of *Battle-Pieces*; art, in the epilogue, is left alone to find its own satisfactions. Melville salvages the principle of organic unity by shifting to a new and fitting form. He abandons the tetrameters which have stood for "apt" art since their emergence and takes on a pentameter line. Once *Clarel* has conveyed its charge of depressing truth it flees into emotional and stylistic exuberance. If, as the epilogue says, "death but routs life into victory," hard facts seem to rout an art of truth into an art of pleasure in which style answers organically not to experience but to the immediate delights of literature. The *Clarel* epilogue trades tension, plainness, discipline, and objective seriousness for wit, exaggeration, delicate stylistic artifice, and casual sophistication.

In the *Clarel* epilogue, Melville moves away from the typically Romantic organicism of Emerson's "metre-making argument" to a perspective in which poetry, by creating its own decorum, becomes an argument-making meter equally unified but liberated from objectivity. How this happens, and what it implies for Melville's poetics, reflect in the ways by which Melville prepares for the epilogue. Given Melville's doubts, it is hardly surprising objectivity and organic unity result in the bleak finale of *Clarel*, but the ability of art to anticipate this bleakness enables Melville to detach and distance his poetic voice from experience and finally to elevate it, like "the spirit about the dust" over the predetermined ruins surrounding it. Melville knows what is coming and has time to prepare an escape. The heroism of poetry, discovered in *Battle-Pieces*, has given the created world, the world of literature, an immediacy and a power previously reserved for bold adventure and half-glimpsed spiritual forces; when the potential emotional attractiveness of art rather than either mysterious meanings or observed facts determines the style and form of a work, that work can achieve an expressiveness and beauty denied to an art of objective observation. It is in the context of Melville's shift in focus from truth to beauty that the symbolic value of his versification comes into focus.

In *Moby-Dick*, Ishmael's consciousness is a territory in which opposing views conflict; in *Clarel*, verse itself plays a similar role. Poetry transforms Melville's narrative voice from that of a first-person participant or an objective observer into a less well-defined authorial presence. The constraints of meter, rhyme, and third-person detachment make it difficult for the narrator to submerge himself in the events of *Clarel* as Ishmael does when the *Pequod* sets sail; his voice, identified with versification, is less malleable. How Melville defines this voice and makes it embody the conflict between experience and freedom, truth and beauty, is best illuminated by Northrop Frye's apt description of musical rhythm in English epic verse:

> When we find sharp barking accents, crabbed and obscure language, mouthfuls of consonants, and long lumbering polysyllables, we are probably dealing with *melos*, or poetry which shows an analogy to music, if not an actual influence from it.
>
> The musical diction . . . is congenial to a gnarled intellectualism of the so-called "metaphysical" type. It is irregular in metre (because of the syncopation against stress), leans heavily on enjambement, and employs a long cumulative rhythm sweeping the lines up into larger rhythmical units such as the paragraph.

Combined with his assertion that English epic verse naturally tends to a four-beat line, Frye's description suits *Clarel* in all but one respect; the longer line of the English epic tradition—from alliterative to blank verse—permits four accentual stresses to appear in a line less frequently than every other syllable, thus providing a hedge against strict metrics. A pentameter line, for example, can easily show four major accents, without either contradicting or abandoning its meters, simply by deemphasizing one metrical stress. If the octosyllabic line of *Clarel* is to escape from tetrameters into accentual rhythm, it must resort to extra syllables, feminine endings, violent substitutions, and continual enjambement. Although these occur with frequency, they lack the sustained force necessary to efface the movement of Melville's tetrameters, whose effect of disciplined plainness gave few problems in the shorter compass of "Lee in the Capitol." Consequently, the rudiments of accentual rhythm, *melos*, continually struggle against metrics, producing a tension which Melville finds valuable enough to his theme to reinforce through rhyme and indentation.

Melville generally indents or breaks a line whenever his focus shifts from one character to another or to the narrator, and whenever the narrative changes mode (conversation, song, thought, commentary, description). However, indentation also varies the texture of the verse, occurring more frequently in passages of agitation such as that in which Clarel learns of Ruth's death. Indentation speeds the flow of verse by introducing new rhyme sounds and patterns. Melville lends stability to calmer passages by utilizing couplets and quatrains, as in "Clarel and Ruth"; elsewhere, as in "Celio," rhymes change and rhyme patterns mutate so rapidly as to prevent the easy division of the poem into units smaller than the paragraph. Taken together, indentations, breaks, rapid rhyme mutations, and metrical irregularities call attention to the jagged and cumulative effects defined by Frye, and the absence of these devices returns the poem to the unchallenged metrics of "Lee in the Capitol." Regular metrics predominate in many places expressing hope for consolation within the world of objective experience; accentual freedom struggles more violently against meter where the discipline of established doctrines threatens to collapse. When the climax of the tale brings utter despair, Melville escapes to a pentameter in which ease and rhythmic freedom prevail, thus tolling the death of his organic combination of objectivity with stylistic plainness and metrical tension. Melville makes sure that collapses in established order result from events within the sphere of human anticipation, and thus that they pinpoint the poverty of vision which now goes hand-in-hand with both heroic discipline and the commitment of poetry to an organic "noting" of factual trends.

The promise of escape which Melville consummates in the epilogue informs the lyrics of *Clarel*. Although sometimes frivolous, as a group they celebrate freedom from discipline, beauty, and related values which receive little reinforcement from the pilgrims—hedonism as opposed to self-denial, satisfaction as opposed to knowledge, faith as opposed to reason, feeling as opposed to thought. Twenty-two of them, nearly half, are sung by four characters—Glaucon, the Cypriote, the Lesbian, and the Lyonese—who question the asceticism of the pilgrimage; thirteen express a more comforting faith than that of Clarel. The lyrics also give certain characters the opportunity to speak more personally than they can elsewhere. Vine's depth receives a major witness in his two songs; Ungar reveals his hidden wishes in verse. From the beginning, the lyrics undercut the constraint which weighs upon the pilgrimage; they presage Melville's leap into the epilogue by exemplifying the qualities which make art satisfying even in the face of blankness and by employing poetic forms less restrained than that of the narrative.

The first lyric peeps out at Clarel from under the peeling whitewash of his hotel room in Jerusalem. In the only sustained pentameters outside the epilogue, it tells of an answer to doubt found by an earlier tenant who sees the decayed remains of the Biblical world as symbols of a personal, emotional faith:

> So much the more in pathos I adore
> The low lamps flickering in Syria's Tomb.

The lyric embodies the ability to make subjective feelings and alluring symbols into the bases for a satisfying faith—an ability which Clarel lacks. Melville's sophisticated use of alliteration in such lines as "Triumph and taunt that shame the winning side," and "My unweaned thoughts in steadfast trade-wind stream" produces an accentual rhythm which does not jar against metrics. Shortly thereafter, Clarel's actual pilgrimage begins and the message of satisfaction and the pleasing style of the lyric are forgotten.

The start of the journey introduces.Glaucon, Melville's first hedonist, who abandons the group after singing four lyrics warning against the deliberate rejection of beauty for a life of trial. Glaucon's final song suggests that the psychological effect of a blasted landscape is dangerous for those who traverse it:

> Tarry never there
> Where the air
> Lends a lone Hadean spell—
> Where the ruin and the wreck
> Vine and ivy never deck
> And wizard wan and sibyl dwell:
> There, oh, beware!

However, the pilgrims continue in their belief that the search for knowledge supercedes all sensations, a view which prevails until the final section of the poem.

Following Glaucon's departure, a Dominican friar sings a song of praise for the Church which is mocked by Margoth in an important negative example of the lyric promise:

> Patcher of the rotten cloth,
> Pickler of the wing o' the moth,
> Toaster of bread stale in date,
> Tinker of the rusty plate,
> Botcher of a crumbling tomb,
> Pounder with the holy hammer,
> Gaffer-gammer, gaffer-gammer-
> Rome!

Margoth criticizes the Church in a poem whose metrical pounding and short, parallel, end-stopped phrases produce a mechanical effect more rigid than any other in the volume. The oppressive meter of Margoth's poem relates to its meaning in three ways; it symbolizes his view of church activities, it exemplifies his own rigidly dogmatic beliefs, and it embodies the danger that repeated formal patterns can degenerate into empty, deadening convention. Melville satirizes both the Church and Margoth for the programmed nature of their responses to life, and his metrics demonstrate the need for freedom in art, personal attitude, and doctrine. For all his scientific sanctimony, Margoth is as unsatisfied as the others; his trochaic tetrameter merely offers an exaggerated mirror image of the iambic tetrameter of the narrative. Margoth's song makes it clear that an organic fitting of form to theme cannot alone produce a verse of comforting emotional power.

The Dead Sea cantos of *Clarel* contain important lyrics by Nehemiah, and Mortmain, both of which reaffirm the significance of a faith like that in the first lyric. Mortmain laments the death of the now "unadored" Southern Cross as a Christian symbol, and Nehemiah's psalm paraphrase finds comfort in a candle shining in the "valley of shade." Both seek a religion supported by simple affective symbols comparable to the "low lamps flickering in Syria's Tomb" rather than intellectual abstractions—a religion of satisfactions rather than truths. Mortmain's song conveys an impression of the attractiveness of the dead symbol:

> How far removed, thou Tree divine,
> Whose tender fruit did reach so low—
> Love apples of New-Paradise!
> About the wide Australian sea.

Ultimately, Nehemiah's narrow fundamentalism and Mortmain's bitterness prevent them from accepting the emotional and imaginative freedom which is Melville's key to escape from eternal pilgrimage; neither can create his own symbols of faith; both sing in the iambic tetrameter of the narrative, and both die on the journey. The presence of such delicate yet tragic songs in iambic tetrameter implies that the lyric and narrative sensibilities can merge, that experience can lay the groundwork for freedom if one can achieve the proper combination of sensitivity and aesthetic distance—gifts which begin to replace discipline and objectivity at the center of Melville's art.

"Mar Saba" introduces the Cypriote and the Lesbian, whose songs of love and pleasure contrast with the asceticism of the monastery. Their sensuality awakens Clarel to the attractions of a return to Ruth, thus contributing to the erotic theme discussed by Nina Baym. The Cypriote's first song is particularly symbolic; after two stanzas describing the lasting delights enjoyed by the gods, he finishes with an imperative:

> Ever blandly adore them;
> But spare to implore them:
> They rest, they discharge them from time;
>> Yet believe, light believe
>> They would succor, reprieve—
>>> Nay, retrieve—
> Might but revelers pause in the prime!

For the Cypriote, earthly and heavenly revelry provoke comparison, and revelry expresses faith; no gaping dichotomy separates flesh and spirit, satisfaction and knowledge, beauty and truth. The proper approach to the gods combines adoration, affirmed in the first lyric and lamented by Mortmain, with respect for the senses. The Cypriote's anapests and widely varied line lengths again suggest an alternative to tetrameters. Hearing his song, the central group of pilgrims are deeply touched.

"Mar Saba" climaxes when Melville brings Vine, Mortmain, and Rolfe face to face with the famous palm tree of the monastery, while Clarel looks on. Each of the three undergoes a moment of inspiration, a hint at the unity of dream and experience available to the liberated mind, and then each reverts to doubt and questioning. In each, the choice of experience and objective reason over sensuality and emotion prevents the acceptance of a vision woven out of momentary ecstasy. In the face of the most eloquent symbol and the deepest feelings in the poem, they relapse. Mortmain, an Ahab stripped of his command by Melville's objectivity, dies in anguish. Moved, Clarel begins to reflect on his love for Ruth; he acknowledges the importance of erotic symbols to Christianity and the beauty which they possess, but his belief in his own impurity keeps him from rejecting a discipline which, unlike the Cypriote, he identifies with religion. He continues to think of Ruth in abstract terms, as if she too were an item of knowledge. As the pilgrimage leaves Mar Saba, the stage is set for Ungar and the Lyonese, who restate the conflict between order and freedom.

Ungar sings the swansong of Melville's identification with Civil War heroism. His two fragments, both metrically rigid, express a philosophy of resignation and a secret hope for revenge. Ungar senses the vanity of his wish and the split between his knowledge of life and his dream of vindication. Rather than finding a way of uniting himself, he controls his disintegrated personality through relentless mental discipline. He presides over the now stale pilgrimage which, with the coming of the Lyonese, begins to give way to the end of Clarel's quest for knowledge and his concomitant acceptance of satisfaction as a goal.

After arguing with a monk on the importance of sexuality, Clarel dreams of the choice before him:

> And Clarel dreamed, and seemed to stand
> Betwixt a Shushan and a sand;
> The Lyonese was lord of one,
> The desert did the Tuscan own,
> The pale pure monk. A zephyr fanned;
> It vanished, and he felt the strain
> Of clasping arms which would detain
> His heart from each ascetic range.

Just as a movement from end-stopped to run-on lines gives the passage a sense of emerging freedom, Clarel awakens to feel an "organic change" working within him; the arms of love which draw him from Mar Saba promise a unity of spirit unknown to him before; he experiences a sudden impatience with his journey. The Lyonese then sings the folly of a discipline which contradicts nature:

> Rules, who rules?
> Fools the wise, makes wise the fools—
>   Every ruling overrules?
> Who the dame that keeps the house,
>   Provides the diet, and oh, so quiet,
> Brings all to pass, the slyest mouse?
>   Tell, tell it me:
> Signora Nature, who but she!

The four songs of the Lyonese accentuate his freedom from dogma. They employ such rapidly shifting feet and strong alliteration that they often attain an accentual rhythm which obliterates metrics, anticipating Melville's experiments in *John Marr and Other Sailors:*

> Over the river
> In gloaming, ah, still do ye plain?
>   Dove—dove in the mangroves,
>   How dear is thy pain!

Clarel hears the Lyonese without heeding the elegiac tone central to his lyrics. Dame nature both brings all to pass and makes all pass away. The Lyonese, wise compared to all other hedonists, has bought his freedom by a deliberate distancing of himself from the religion which draws him to the Holy Land. His poems acknowledge and integrate his sense of loss, creating out of pain a promise of consoling beauty. Clarel also ignores the power of time sung by the Cypriote, Ungar, and the Lyonese; he attaches his hopes not to freedom, imagination, beauty, and emotion but to Ruth herself. Fellowship and love may well be experiences in which Melville takes unambiguous pleasure, but his works tell us that only the very lucky gather their fruit; we are unprepared for life unless we prepare for loneliness. When Ruth dies, Clarel, like Mortmain, relapses into anguish.

Melville's final lyric, a dirge on the death of Ruth, firmly establishes the value of an art of expressive beauty; in it, Melville's narrative voice takes its new direction. The dirge sings in tetrameters, hinting that disciplined objectivity can coexist with imaginative freedom for those who are not blind. In order to avoid confusing this possibility with the vain hope that experience will reward the resolute, Melville ends his story on an objective note, leaving Clarel to the fate which has been anticipated.

Melville's dirge places Ruth in a sensually pleasing realm of "honey" and "mosses sweet" where her lover may hope to rejoin her. It creates a mental image of death as gentle and feeling, an imaginative leap which it justifies through literary symbolism rather than experiential data. The final image sums up its main affirmation:

> And if, ere yet the lover's free,
> Some added dusk thy rule decree—
> That shadow only let it be
> Thrown in the moon-glade by the palm.

The palm recalls that of Mar Saba, which cast a shadow over the pilgrims by confronting them with the ephemeral nature of their dreams. And yet, that shadow, the despair of Mortmain, the resignation of Vine and Rolfe, proves the imaginative force of those dreams. The dirge, a sophisticated intrusion of art on ritual, affirms the emotional appropriateness of such dreams even in a context which also proves them insubstantial. Only in the world of personal emotion and aesthetic sensitivity do they persist, yet life inhabits this world as well as the objective realm of physical experience. The dirge shows poetry capable of creating an alluring vision in response to the most pressing tragedy, of establishing an organic symbol of hope comparable to the adored symbols of Christianity. The true artist, lover, or worshipper is he who sustains his faith creatively by keeping the Southern Cross, the low lamps, Ruth, imaginatively alive or by replacing them with equally compelling phenomena.

After the dirge, Melville dissociates his viewpoint from that of his less imaginative protagonist; he describes Clarel's Easter Week activities with reserve and artistic distance in order to fulfill his tale of experience before retreating into the epilogue. However, during the Passion Week canto, Melville imbues Christian ritual with the same imaginative grace and delicate sensuality seen in the lyrics and the dirge:

> With the blest anthem, censers sway,
> Whose opal vapor, spiral borne,
> Blends with the heavens' own azure Morn
> Of Palms; for 'twas Palm Sunday bright,
> Though thereof he, oblivious quite,
> Knew nothing.

Clarel, in his depression, ignores the procession—another of the sources of inspiration which experience offers to those who are sensitive to beauty and uncommitted to doubt. Remaining blind, Clarel vanishes into the "obscurer town" a final victim of Melville's molding of heroism, discipline, and objectivity into an organic art.

The epilogue reaffirms the satisfactions of the *Clarel* lyrics. Not only does Melville abandon his jagged tetrameters for an easier, freer-flowing rhythm, but he displays a wit rare in both *Clarel* and his earlier verse:

> But through such strange illusions have they passed
> Who in life's pilgrimage have baffled striven—
> Even death may prove unreal at the last,
> And stoics be astounded into heaven.

Melville playfully mocks the blinding egoism of the intellect; the urbanity of the verse prevents our reading it as either a true confession of newfound religious faith or as an ironic joke. He offers, above all, an elegant and clever literary antidote to the gloom of the narrative. The determinism of "Darwin's year" can be read into "Luther's day" if one wishes, but for the poet history is the raw material of poetry, which stands on imagination, sensual pleasure, and beauty. Life is a victory if celebrated rather than merely endured. Like Glaucon, Melville abandons the pilgrimage with a warning for those who deem it "life's pilgrimage," the only path to walk.

The *Clarel* epilogue in all its conscious artificiality fits form to theme as carefully as any of Melville's verses. Frequent couplets and quatrains reinforce the witty comparisons which give it an Augustan quality. Images and symbols are tossed off or piled on one another with a breezy casualness which challenges intellectual rigor. Vast generalizations explode into aphorism without warning, and disappear as rapidly, hinting at their own insignificance. The verse coolly recommends to Clarel, wracked by anguish,

> Then keep thy heart, though yet but ill-resigned—
> Clarel, thy heart, the issues there but mind.

Lightness of tone gives the caution a hollow ring which even an image from *The Scarlet Letter* ("like a burning secret which doth go / Even from the bosom that would hoard and keep") cannot counteract. Without the amusing stylistic artifice and exaggeration which frames it, Melville's conclusion would demand a deep evaluation. What the style of the epilogue warns us is that such a conclusion, always objectively problematical, is absurd in an art whose job should be to create attractive, emotionally accessible, organic manifestations of whatever it affirms, and not to give sententious speeches. The lesson of Melville's changing art in *Clarel* is that truth-seeking, whether transcendental or objective, too easily produces a truth which is useless while ignoring opportunity after opportunity for beauty and satisfaction. The *Clarel* epilogue, in its marvelously complex self-consciousness, gives the best proof of Melville's faith in literature and playful delight in creative freedom since the early pages of *Moby-Dick*.

Battle-Pieces and *Clarel* tell the tale of Melville's interest in a serious, disciplined, realistic, and organically unified verse; as such, *Clarel* can be called America's greatest Victorian poem. Melville found in *Battle-Pieces* a new approach to the doubts and ambiguities hovering over his later fiction. As reservations about this approach arose, he built them organically into the structure, the versification, and the lyrics of *Clarel*, evolving an alternative vision at the fringes of his epic. By the end, the alternative—faith in the satisfactions of beauty, imaginative freedom, and art—moves from the fringe to the center, and the epilogue gives it the last word. Here, Melville prefigures the witty and technically sophisticated verse of his later years. *Clarel* proves Melville's tenacity and clear-sightedness in bringing to completion a staggeringly difficult work, his alertness to sources of new inspiration, and his willingness to risk stylistic audacity when his vision warrants.

James Russell Lowell

George Arms

In contrast with the public's complete acceptance of his contemporaries, Lowell's place as a schoolroom poet was scarcely warranted by the actual use of his poetry. "I am the first poet," he once boldly prophesied, "who has endeavored to express the American Idea, and I shall be popular by and by." But in the older anthologies we must look for the "American Idea" in the adventures of Sir Launfal, who, far from being native, does not even deserve accreditation as a British envoy to the culture of the United States. And though for the main exhibits of his poetry recent anthologies have shifted to *The Biglow Papers* and *A Fable for Critics*, the connection with the "American Idea" in these topical verses concerned with native wars and authors seems slight at best. Besides as poetry they are admittedly sporting gestures—dialect, propaganda, and miscellany—all very well in their genre but seldom resulting in a "shock of recognition" or a permanent cultivation of response.

My guess is that Lowell received his place of schoolroom poet as a gesture to his general accomplishment in letters and to his association with Holmes and Longfellow. The sentimentalities and didacticisms in which he indulged were neither of the kind nor frequency to secure him a firm place in the schoolroom heart. The public may also have felt that here was a man who ought to be a good poet, even a better one than most of his contemporaries could hope to be. The sense of life and of the word revealed in critical papers, letters, and conversation point to poetry potentially great. But it seldom reached greatness and it failed to achieve a real audience in Lowell's time and ours.

Yet more than most, Lowell has suffered from misrepresentation in

From *The Fields Were Green: A New View of Bryant, Whittier, Holmes, Lowell, and Longfellow, with a Selection of Their Poems*. © 1953 by the Board of Trustees of the Leland Stanford Junior University. Stanford University Press, 1953.

343

anthologies. Usually we find a couple of *Biglow Papers*, the parts of *A Fable for Critics* that characterize other authors appearing in the same volume, and a few shorter pieces in a conventional lyric mood. That is the general pattern, but individually several anthologists do better, though in a sporadic rather than consistent way. Thus George Whicher (1950) prints the Commemoration Ode, by Jay B. Hubbell (1936, 1949) some of the late political satires, Harry Hayden Clark (1936) all the later odes and *The Cathedral*, and William Smith Clark (1948, in a book of Lowell selections) *The Cathedral* and "Fitz Adam's Story." Within its fifteen pages—a generous allotment in the plan of the volumes—the fresh selection of Auden's and Pearson's *Poets of the English Language* (1950) includes "An Oriental Apologue." Each of the poems noted stems from the same root that produced *The Biglow Papers* and *A Fable*, and they deserve their place. But none of the anthologists prints all of these pertinent poems, or even enough of them to represent their man justly. Instead (except for Auden and Pearson) they fill the page allotments with such inferior Lowellisms as "Hebe," "Beaver Brook," "Rhœcus," and "The Petition."

These anthologists do not include, I am happy to say, the poem "After the Burial," which readers of the nineteenth century probably liked best after *The Vision of Sir Launfal*. Today more readers, at least in the university schoolroom, may know the poem than any other, for it appears in Brooks's and Warren's *Understanding Poetry*. One is relieved that these critics make no analysis of "After the Burial" and restrict themselves to a few questions only; but to find Lowell appearing with this poem in this book still disheartens, especially since in 1889 Lowell as president of the Modern Language Association had challenged sterile literary scholarship with ideals anticipating those of Brooks and his associates a half-century later. The questions of *Understanding Poetry* are more lenient, however, than they might be, for they cite two stanzas (3 and 11) as better than the rest of the poem and two stanzas (10 and 12) as especially poor. My own belief is that the first five stanzas are a vulgarly extended mocking of a cliché and the remaining ones are heterogeneous, with the whole dramatic situation of a querulousness ill-conceived for the occasion. It is also true, though, that in one of the stanzas that is particularly reproved, I find an aside ("But not all the preaching since Adam Has made Death other than Death") that as an epigram well bears its own weight.

Lowell has written a worse poem on the death of a child, and it is either good luck that Brooks and Warren did not know "The Changeling" or courteous tact if knowing it they refrained from printing it. The poem is an even drossier mirror of low popular taste than "After the Burial." But badly as Lowell did here, he has done better too. "Agassiz," written in 1874 upon the death of the Harvard scientist, deserves Henry James's epithet "magnificent" and calling it "the truest expression of [Lowell's] poetic nature" after the Commemoration Ode.

"Agassiz" has a quality of full-bodied talk, an educated man's mingling of the colloquial and formal, which seldom falls into prosiness and which still rings upon the ear. We need not wonder that James so unreservedly praised the poem, for in it James probably saw a masterly achievement in that same style which we find in his later fictions. Though except for Agassiz himself the poem offers no controlling image or sequence of images such as in James's novels, it has a passionately intelligent unfolding of a central theme.

That theme may be roughly stated as the need for an awareness of the past in the present, a consolation that in spite of the rather too pat idea of immortality appearing in the last section of the poem seems as hard won a solution as any in the great elegies. The poem starts by anticipating this theme. Using the telegraphed dispatch of Agassiz's death in contrast with the traditional announcement of death in pastoral elegy, Lowell suddenly compares the nature of its shock with a mythic past:

> Earth sentient seems again as when of old
>   The horny foot of Pan
> Stamped, and the conscious horror ran
> Beneath men's feet through all her fibres cold.

This intermingling of past and present marks the whole of the first section. Lowell discards the pastoral appeal to "mountains, woods, and streams, to help us mourn him." Instead he calls upon the "strong poets of a more unconscious day"—Jonson and Chapman— to help him organize the "simpler moods" that "befit our modern themes."

The next three sections center in a description of Agassiz, the second describing the scientist in his social character, the third as a member of the Saturday Club, and the fourth in his relation to New England. For a time Lowell seems to have left his central theme, but as we come to the stanzas on the Saturday Club we begin to realize that Lowell, in writing of it and especially of its members who are no longer alive, urges the living presence of the past. This he makes explicit in the fourth section as the memory of Agassiz returning home with Lowell after one of the dinners is invoked:

> Still can I hear his voice's shrilling might . . .
> Call Oken back, or Humboldt, or Lamarck,
> Or Cuvier's taller shade, and many more
> Whom he had seen, or knew from others' sight
> And make them men to me as ne'er before . . .
> "Good night!" and ere the distance grew too wide,
> "Good night!" again; and now with cheated ear
> I half hear his who mine shall never hear.

Speculating further in this fourth section about the impact of the "grim outcrop" of New England's "granite edge" upon Agassiz, Lowell comes to his two final sections. The first of these offers no consolation, but rather in contrast with the spiritual drive of New England witnessed in the preceding lines hymns pagan praise for life and laments at death.

> Truly this life is precious to the root,
> And good the feel of grass beneath the foot;
> To lie in buttercups and clover-bloom,
>   Tenants in common with the bees,
> And watch while white clouds drift through gulfs
>   of trees,
> Is better than long waiting in the tomb.

Over against this materialism the sixth section offers a concept of immortality. Discarding the pagan possibilities of an "endless slumber" or a sleep in which dreamy consciousness accompanies the reabsorption of the body by nature, Lowell shares Agassiz's own hope:

> And he was sure to be
> Somehow, somewhere, imperishable as He,
> Not with His essence mystically combined,
> As some high spirits long, but whole and free,
>   A perfected and conscious Agassiz.

Such an existence, Lowell also suggests, may be realized on the earthly plane as well, as scholars will "trace his features with an eye less dim Than ours whose sense familiar wont makes dumb." Here the poet enforces the central theme of his elegy by an adumbration of heavenly and earthly immortality that is in keeping with it. It is also a belief that, whatever we think of its snobbish implications, attracted Henry James in his admiration of the poem. A quarter of a century later James was to make full and systematic argument for the survival of consciousness beyond death when it had been adequately cultivated in life.

Yet in spite of an occasional achievement of this sort, which we neglect to out impoverishment, Lowell was a poor poet. To speculate upon the personal reasons behind this failure is for the psychologist rather than the literary critic. But neither Lowell nor the critics have abstained. Lowell himself had many excuses at hand: his early impulse toward reform, the deadening hand of academic routine, the fact that when the muse was invited, she did not appear. Critics have disdained these as rationalizations, but the main reason they generally give—indolence—seems to evade verification just as much. For though this indolence may be regarded as a disinclination to think rather than a disinclination to work, one can easily point to better poets who have done less thinking or raise the question with T. S. Eliot whether it is the business of a poet to do much thinking anyway. About all that seems profitable for literary criticism to observe is that Lowell, if he did not know the reason for his failure, recognized the fact itself. "I am perfectly conscious that I have not yet got the best of my poetry out of me," he wrote to his friend Briggs in 1850. Twenty-five years later he spoke of himself as "but third-rate compared with the masters." Earlier he had penned the epitaph which, though unused, he kept among his papers until his death:

> Here lies that part of J. R. L.
> That hampered him from doing well.

Putting aside the personal reasons, we find public ones present throughout the whole body of the verse. Most specifically we feel Lowell's habit of genteel Romanticism (though this diminished with his growth, as Harry Hayden Clark has shown) and Lowell's inability to cultivate a particular kind of poetry with its obverse in a facile imitation of too many poets ("the chameleon of nineteenth-century literature," as Leon Howard has called him). What emerges from this situation is a general weakness that one feels every time one comes to considering a literary characteristic. The language falls into prosiness or archaism, the morality into tidy didacticism, the ironies into pettiness. Lowell can seldom take an image from the concrete to the universal without diluting its earthiness or muddying its ideal, and he regularly commits himself to formlessness.

Especially since they differentiate his work so largely from his ideals, these two final ineptitudes deserve fuller comment. Lowell edited one of the few nineteenth-century editions of Donne's poetry in 1855, which though in itself of no scholarly value led to the annotations that formed the basis of the Lowell-Norton edition of 1895, a work that Grierson overgenerously declares has such merit that if he had known of its existence earlier he probably would not have undertaken his own definitive text. But if the acquaintance with Donne accounted for some of the "violent phrases" for which contemporaries sometimes upbraided Lowell, it does not inform the greater part of his imagery.

As for Lowell's lack of form, we are surprised at the failing in view of what he says in his prose. In his fine essay on the criticism, Norman Foerster makes it clear that Lowell prized unity—"Lowell's creed is almost the unwritten constitution of the republic of letters." But as Odell Shepard has written, echoing the uneasiness of most writers on the poetry, *The Vision of Sir Launfal* is "one of the worst constructed poems in English." By and large Lowell exhibits neither craftsmanship in form nor the more desirable concord of discordants that lets us think of him as a poet who created artistic designs of self-containment and permanence.

So curious is the structure of *The Vision* that it is well to examine it. Out of such examinations comes the essential method of Lowell which, with but few exceptions, is present in all his poems of merit: the form and tone of the familiar verse essay, emphasizing the digressive and disparate, yet constantly working toward an ultimate unity of effect. In *The Vision* he did not achieve this goal, and certainly the sentimental reform of Sir Launfal cancels incidental merits of the poem. Yet in all its weakness the work has interest as a prestudy of later accomplishment.

Everyone feels the distortion. By line count the prelude to the first part is longer than the first part itself (95 lines to 78), and the prelude to the second part is more than half as long as what follows (66 lines to 108). Lowell recognized this odd apportioning, as his reference to the poem in a letter as "a sort of a story" and his apology for the plot in the preface "if I may give that name to anything so slight" suggest. The poem itself also makes clear that he looked upon it as an improvisation, for the opening stanza describes the organist who "first lets his fingers wander as they list" and then "nearer draws his theme first guessed by faint auroral flushes." Touching upon this key and that, the poet plays upon the theme of man's rebirth in the rebirth of nature.

Yet he does so by starts and jumps, and except for the exultant passage on June in the first prelude makes a creaking and even wretched performance. The banality of the revivifying power of June may be somewhat tempered by the use of winter, but if so, it results in only the slightest sense of resistance. To the extent that Lowell understood what his readers were after (he anticipated that the poem was "more likely to be popular than what I write generally") he had his method. He also had method in knowing he was *not* writing a self-sustaining narrative, but as yet he had not fully discovered his flair for the familiar verse essay. The choice of medieval matter treated in a serious fashion could indeed hardly lend itself to such success. Yet *The Vision of Sir Launfal* points the way.

In 1848, the same year that saw publication of *The Vision*, the two poems by which Lowell is at present recognized also appeared. Neither is of high poetical order, and the value we attach to both is for qualities which, though not antipoetical, are nonpoetical. We like *A Fable for Critics* because it makes shrewd judgments of midnineteenth-century American authors that have stood remarkably well in the critical developments of the past hundred years; and we like *The Biglow Papers*, of which the first part was published in 1848, because it contains incisive writing on the Mexican and Civil Wars.

These are incidental values. To only a slight degree can we speak of the works as poetical units, but somewhat more certainly we may regard them as experiments in the direction of familiar verse essays. *A Fable for Critics* is the better illustration, since from the first Lowell conceived it as a complete piece. Like *The Vision* it has rudiments of plot which the author treats with the same irresponsibility.

> I'd apologize here for my many digressions,
> Were it not that I'm certain to trip into fresh ones.

Toward the end of the work he runs a footnote:

> Turn back now to page—goodness only knows what,
> And take a fresh hold on the thread of my plot.

But unlike *The Vision* Lowell here presents his fable in a comic spirit, not asking the reader to receive—or even remember—the story in the same way that he is asked to respond to that of the serious piece.

Without some awareness of this background, a certain loss occurs in reading the individual judgments that make up each part. One should remember that they come from Phoebus Apollo himself and contrast with the pseudocritical judgments of the day. At the same time Apollo is a humanized god, with foibles to qualify his greatness—a god who watches a pastoral procession of shepherds with a newspaper reporter at his elbow. The setting allows for the mixture of gravity and scurrility that appears in Lowell's evaluations of his contemporaries. Their incisiveness lets them stand alone, and they have rightly become the valued small change of criticism as well as larger bills of credit that we can draw against. But though they stand alone, they still form parts of the larger whole in which Lowell is happily working toward a genre that gives free play to his talent.

As a whole *The Biglow Papers* also accords with the tradition of the familiar essay. Here I omit the word "verse," since the framework is contrived out of prose letters which present Hosea Biglow partly in his own person and partly through the auspices of his father and his pastor. But as with *The Vision of Sir Launfal*, if with different particulars, the framework succeeds but poorly in integrating the tale. Though we *can* read it as an extended fiction and in part do (several articles by Arthur Voss have best shown how), most of us have little sense of any enhancement of the individual pieces; the story of the ill-considered revision for the 1848 edition, told by Mr. Howard in his stimulating biography, goes a long way toward explaining our ultimate dissatisfaction.

Yet in one or two of the parts we again find Lowell operating in the direction which marks the best. "Sunthin' in the Pastoral Line," from the second series, presents most ingratiatingly the sense of controlled improvisation. Starting out as an attack against the denationalization of nature by American poets ("Why, I'd give more for one live bobolink Than a square mile o' larks in printer's ink"), the poet describes spring in Massachusetts and then (with digressions, as that on modern education) presents a dream vision of the Pilgrim Father with his prophetic advice on the Civil War. All this coheres loosely by the demand for a realistic view of native life, whether of nature or politics, but it must be admitted that the links are weak both in appearance and in actuality. The poem does not have the sense of mastery in its form that we find in such a work as "Agassiz."

Along with all the poems of *The Biglow Papers*, "Sunthin' in the Pastoral Line" also has another quality that Lowell never thoroughly practiced in his poetry but which he did use with distinction. That is native idiom, which receives its best expression in this series. One of the finest defenses anywhere by anyone is the introduction that Lowell wrote for the second series in 1862.

> It has long seemed to me that the great vice of American writing and speaking was a studied want of simplicity, that we were in danger of coming to look on our mother-tongue as a dead language, to be sought in the grammar and dictionary rather than in

the heart, and that our only chance of escape was by seeking it at its living sources along those who were, as Scottowe says of Major-General Gibbons, "divinely illiterate." . . . No language after it has faded into *diction*, none that cannot suck up the feeding juices secreted for it in the rich mother-earth of common folk, can bring forth a sound and lusty book. True vigor and heartiness of phrase do not pass from page to page, but from man to man, where the brain is kindled and the lips suppled by downright living interest and by passion in its very throe. . . . There is death in the dictionary.

But in spite of this noble passage on the source of vigor in language, in *The Biglow Papers* Lowell used his language as rustic utterance more often to characterize Hosea than to give us a sense of "the natural stronghold of his homely dialect." In writing in the person of a provincial, Lowell acts the part of connoisseur rather than stylist. Like the French court, he is playing a game of shepherds and shepherdesses.

The distinction between Lowell's use of native language in *The Biglow Papers* and the full use he might have given to it in real poetry should not be made absolute. Henry James called these poems Lowell's "most literary production" and in so doing must have felt the force of language as one of its principal characteristics. Thackeray is said to have exclaimed, "Why a man who can delight the world with such creations as *Hosea Biglow* should insist upon writing second-rate serious verse I cannot see." In their creation of character and in their universalizing of a specific political problem, as well as in their sense of style, Lowell goes beyond the immediate into the literary. But he had the choice of writing more poetry of the school of native humor and perfecting his instrument there or of writing poems of formal literary pretension ("serious verse"). He took the latter way and most of it was second rate; yet it is probable that if he had developed the stylistic perception present in his dialect verse, his serious verse need not have been second rate at all.

When he followed a natural line of development from *The Biglow Papers* into the familiar verse essay written in colloquial style, there is no reason to disparage his accomplishment. In "The Nooning," a poem which he began in 1849 and never finished, he may have worked in this direction, though the evidence is partial and not all the completed parts of this frame-poem accord with the possibility. Yet "Fitz Adam's Story" seems central to the mature concept of "The Nooning" because after its appearance in a magazine its book publication was delayed more than twenty years with the probable hope of adding to it and rounding out the original project. If it is central, it shows what Lowell might have done in greater quantity and with more cultivation. Though one of Lowell's best, too few readers know it.

Upon completing it Lowell wrote, "It is very homely, but right from nature." The central story is about a deacon who goes to hell and tries to outsmart the devil. But this makes up only 200 of the 600 lines and reaches us through a series of obliquities. The story, though the deacon's, is told by an American expatriate, partly cynic and partly man of feeling. He had got it from an Uncle Reuben, who in turn seems to have heard it from the farmer involved in the action.

That handing on of the narrative suggests that Lowell is back in the familiar verse essay. Only now he has come into his own. We are not upset by the lack of structure as we are with *The Vision*; nor as with *A Fable* are we aware of an intention without being convinced of its realization. All 600 lines of "Fitz Adam's Story" are of New England, realized in a fashion more anticipatory of Robert Frost than even Whittier's *Snow-Bound*.

> Ah! there's a deal of sugar in the sun!
> Tap me in Indian summer, I should run
> A juice to make rock-candy of.

With its description of the expatriated narrator, his digressions on religion, authors, and scenery, his arrival at the village inn and characterization of its host and habitués, and finally with the long-delayed folktale about the deacon, the story gives a rich evocation of many lives. From the multiplicity of its materials, it achieves a center. Lowell has found the complex spirit of his province, rooted in a religion made up of stern sincerity and hard hypocrisy, realized in the variety of its growths from colonial days down to the latest pale branch—an Adam if not an Adams. "Yet still the New World spooked it in his veins, A ghost he could not lay with all his pains."

In finding this spirit and putting it into poetry, Lowell also found himself more fully than in any of his famous efforts of 1848. Lacking the breadth of these earlier poems, "Fitz Adam's Story" has greater depth; and if we could match it with a half-dozen other poems of the same kind (as Lowell probably intended we might by his plan for "The Nooning"), we could surely say that here was the poet for whom we had hoped. But we cannot. What we do find are other poems related to it in familiarity of style, and these serve to keep Lowell from complete disregard as a poet.

So far we have mostly been concerned with Lowell's failure in a great many of his poems and with his real but limited accomplishment in his two principle works, *A Fable for Critics* and *The Biglow Papers*. In our inquiry two poems have thrust themselves to the fore as superior to his failures and with advantages beyond those of the two best-known pieces. Of these, one, "Fitz Adam's Story," belongs with the familiar verse essays and the other, "Agassiz," with the odes. In these two genres I believe Lowell came closest to poetical greatness, and in our final consideration we shall turn to the work in these groups.

But first Lowell's lyrics, as a group entirely apart from these, and his miscellaneous satirical poems, as one closely related, will be worth a glance. If I find only two lyrics of Lowell worth preserving, it may seem somewhat rude to the poet. But it is better to give firm recognition to what deserves it than half-hearted assent to a number of poems that do not. What happened to a good many of Lowell's lyrics may be what Lowell recognized as occurring in "The Washers of the Shroud." "I began it as a lyric, but it *would* be too aphoristic for that, and finally flatly refused to sing at any price."

Of the two lyrics one is early and one late. The former, "To the Dandelion," shows the same breaking away from lyric intensity that Lowell remarked more fully in "The Washers." Though there may be difference of opinion at the point in which the break occurs, every reader will admit that somewhere it happens. Walter Blair writes that perhaps in the fourth stanza the imagery breaks, and others intent upon rooting out didactic heresy have found it in the sixth with the words "Thou teachest." Both views have truth. Certainly the imagery shifts in the fourth stanza; in the fifth one wonders how the poet is going to solve his further difficulties; and in the sixth one concludes that he can be credited only with a valiant try.

In the first two stanzas we have a striking series of variations around the word "gold." They come with a strong surge of language:

> Dear common flower, that grow'st beside the way,
> Fringing the dusty road with harmless gold.

The children picking them are "high-hearted buccaneers" finding an "Eldorado," and the stanzas are heavy with opulence—"wealth," "Spanish prow," "largess," "value." "Thou art my tropics and mine Italy," Lowell begins the third stanza, extending his imagery a little unsteadily but still justifiably from that of the wealth-seeking conquistadors. He is back, however, with the "golden-cuirassed bee," and now introduces new colors in "the white lily's breezy tent" and "the dark green" from which the "yellow circles burst." In the fourth and fifth stanzas Lowell sings of his own childhood, playing largely against the whiteness but with undertones of the other new color—"deep shadows on the grass" and "dark old tree." The gold is transposed into the child's spiritual recognition of nature, whether of "one white cloud" moving like a "stray lamb" or of a robin singing like an angel "with news from heaven."

But now one is watching the images pile up and wondering what the poet will do with them all. His solution is to retire into aphorism. There is some order in the retreat as again, in the sixth and final stanza, we get a backward glance at the opulence ("How like a prodigal doth nature seem") and childhood innocence ("a child's undoubting wisdom"). But the poem has lost its hold.

In "Auspex," the later poem, Lowell has kept control and working in a shorter poem with fewer images has produced his finest lyric. It is one not without pun and irony, the word "auspex" carrying the meanings of a poet and an interpreter of omens who examines both the flight of birds and the organs of an animal for his soothsaying. "Lark" and "linnet," primarily European songbirds, take us back to Lowell's early call for an American nomenclature ("square mile o' larks in printer's ink"). By means of this wit the poignancy of the loss of song and life emerges strongly.

Using a figure more violent than picturesque, that of the heart as a nest, Lowell dramatically poises his lyrics at the moment of change:

> Nest that *had* song-birds in it . . .
> Instead of lark or linnet,
> *Shall* whirl dead leaves and snow.

Briefly in the middle stanza he regrets that his poems had shown too much aspiration—"Had they been swallows only." But without carrying through the implications of this wish he breaks off in mourning the loss of any song (for "their," as I take it, may refer either to the songbirds or the swallows):

> Woe's me, I shall be lonely
> When I can feel no longer
> The impatience of their wings!

At last he recognizes that the songbirds are gone—"A moment, sweet delusion, Like birds the brown leaves hover"—and the catastrophe is at hand. With this recognition the image broadens out from that of the heart as nest to the chaotic overwhelming of author and work:

> But it will not be long
> Before their wild confusion
> Fall wavering down to cover
> The poet and his song.

Should one read the poem biographically an additional poignancy emerges when we think of Lowell's erring self-estimate and the obliteration of his work in the last half century. But in its own right the lyric furnishes all the materials for heightened feeling and dispassionate art.

In several of his satirical pieces Lowell has left work that it is pleasant, if not compulsory, to be acquainted with. In length these may go from the two-line epigram on the political boss—

> Skilled to pull wire, he baffles Nature's hope,
> Who sure intended him to stretch a rope—

to "The Unhappy Lot of Mr. Knott." The latter, an exuberantly silly story of nearly a thousand lines, has delicious sallies upon the midnineteenth-century Carpenter's Gothic and table rapping, and again makes us wish that Lowell had cultivated more fully a type in which he displays so much talent. To be sure he has left us other examples of this kind of thing—"An Oriental Apologue," "Without and Within," "Our Own," and the "Fragment of a Pindarique Ode in the manner of the late divine Mr. Abraham Cowley"—but he scarcely respected what he had done. He did not include

"Our Own" and the "Fragment" in his collected work. Of his diverting translation of the burlesque opera *Il Pesceballo,* now generally available in a collection edited by Thelma M. Smith, there was no printed recognition of his authorship until five years after his death. The well-known story of Lowell's muttering "*The Washers of the Shroud!*" and walking away when Emerson praised *The Biglow Papers* also underlies his misconception of his true literary flair.

For Lowell's real achievement, as this essay argues, was close to these satirical pieces and, in so far as those named antedate it, derived from them. We have already seen its origins in *A Fable* and *The Biglow Papers* and its full realization in "Fitz Adam's Story." *The Cathedral* also was written in this genre of the familiar verse essay, and to it we may add "An Epistle to George William Curtis, " "A Familiar Epistle to a Friend," and "Under the Willows." That two are named epistles shows the closeness of all these poems to the verse epistle. Since a substantial part of Lowell's literary accomplishment may well be, as William Smith Clark thinks, his prose letters, the closeness of the two genres further justifies the naming of the familiar verse essays as Lowell's best in poetry.

All these poems have in common a similarity of structure and language. Upon the surface they appear as awkward in their ordering as many of Lowell's poems are in essence. In language they also may first seem to be less than satisfactory, for certainly they do not cultivate the native idiom to the extent that *The Biglow Papers* do. But these later poems draw together with a final sense of wholeness, and they exhibit a learned-colloquial style, easy and efficient, that has little trace of the archaic poetical. As Barrett Wendell says, " 'Literary' you feel this man again and again; but by and by you begin to feel that, after all, this literature proceeds from an intensely human being with a peculiarly Yankee nature." Lowell admitted the colloquial when it was of good blood, and though we may think his standard of family too high, in these poems we can enjoy the liberated result.

Beginning with the 1844 volume, Ferris Greenslet has found that "whimsicality begins to sparkle through." These later poems go far beyond, in that whimsicality *is* their texture. Consciously wayward in structure and language, Lowell reveals a new kind of unity. The image of the improvising organist of *The Vision* is succeeded by another in "A Familiar Epistle":

> Not drop by drop, with watchful skill,
> Gathered in Art's deliberate still,
> But life's insensible completeness
> Got as the ripe grape gets its sweetness,
> As if it had a way to fuse
> The golden sunlight into juice.

In "An Epistle to George William Curtis," arbitrarily divided as the poem is by a gap of thirteen years in composition, the differences between the two men and the two sides of Lowell's nature are brought into a unity.

"Little I ask of Fate; will she refuse Some days of reconcilement with the Muse?" the poet asks; and by the mastery of his form gives affirmative answer. Artistic concord also emerges from "Under the Willows," in which Lowell achieves the same sense of poetic solidity. Not only in the whole but in the parts he now displays finish. Even the metaphor shows the control hitherto lacking, as the whaling image of "A Familiar Epistle" or that of the Charles River in "Under the Willows," with its sudden yet meaningful shift:

> Blue toward the west, and bluer and more blue,
> Living and lustrous as a woman's eyes
> Look once and look no more, with southward curve
> Ran crinkling sunniness, like Helen's hair
> Glimpsed in Elysium, insubstantial gold.

Of these familiar verse essays, *The Cathedral* is known best and deserves to be. Its title may be unfortunate in suggesting a kind of monumental solidity; but though naming the poem first "A Day at Chartres" and regretting he did not keep the name, Lowell was after all persuaded to make the change and probably liked having the informality held in check by the new title. Mr. Greenslet has remarked upon "a pithy and noble grandiloquence" in Lowell's style at its very best, and though in this poem Lowell's emphasis seems to have leaned toward Gothic grotesque rather than Gothic majesty, it has both elements.

More than any other poem by Lowell, whether serious or comic in intent, *The Cathedral* displays homely imagery. Partly it is of a sort which belongs to any age: "This unthrift housekeeping that will not brook A dish warmed-over at the feast of life," and "To-day's eternal truth To-morrow proved Frail as frost-landscapes on a window-pane." But more striking is Lowell's use of imagery from his own world:

> life's scenery,
> Where the same slide must double all its parts,
> Shoved in for Tarsus and hitched back for Tyre.

> That drony vacuum of compulsory prayer,
> Still pumping phrases for the Ineffable,
> Though all the valves of memory gasp and wheeze.

> Doubtless his church will be no hospital
> For superannuate forms and mumping shams,
> No parlor where men issue policies
> Of life-assurance on the Eternal Mind.

These are thrown against the traditional glory of Chartres (for admittedly Lowell "Scarce saw the minster for the thoughts it stirred") in a fine irony of effect. Yet the cathedral itself, "Imagination's very self in stone," still looms in the background as the poet tries to offer mediation between "commonplace" and "miracle."

Philosophically Lowell does not do this to the satisfaction of many of his readers, who may well find fault either with his conclusion or argument or both. But *The Cathedral* remains poetry even after its beliefs are discounted. The work has four main sections. In the first (lines 1–212), Lowell writes of his early impressions of nature, recognizing man's self-deception: "These first sweet frauds upon our consciousness That blend the sensual with its imaged world." In spite of this, the poet defends the "incomes of experience," his visit to Chartres, his dinner at a "pea-green inn," and his walk in the park. In the second part (lines 213–501) Lowell faces the cathedral and with it the problem of supernatural faith. To such faith he is partly drawn, yet at best he can propose a nostalgic religion ("seeing where God *has* been, trust in Him") or one that "Will see God rather in the strenuous doubt, Than in the creed." From this conclusion he turns (lines 502–732) to the impact of democracy on religion. Western man is sufficient in his own strength, and Lowell is attracted by "this brown-fisted rough," believing however that there will be a return to a modified tradition:

> yet he, unconscious heir
> To the influence sweet of Athens and of Rome,
> And old Judæa's gift of secret fire,
> Spite of himself shall surely learn to know
> And worship some ideal of himself,
> Some divine thing, large-hearted, brotherly,
> Not nice in trifles, a soft creditor,
> Pleased with his world, and hating only cant.

How much humorous discernment Lowell shows in this passage is hard to judge. One is reminded of a recent description in *The New Yorker* of the religion of a New York restaurant owner and his friends: "As a rule, God is referred to in the society, with an easy familiarity, as the Big Fellow Upstairs, the Big Fellow, or the Big Guy." Even Lowell's liberal Christianity and linguistics would have ill prepared him for quite this expression, and I suspect he is shocked by his own lines, for he quickly makes substitution of this concept with one of "The Cross, bold type of shame to homage turned." In different and less overt terms he comes back, contrasting the building of Chartres with building "Gothic contract-shams, because Our deacons have discovered that it pays." For a sounder religious ideal Lowell announces, "I can wait." Then in full revulsion he denounces a demagogic ideal of freedom as contrasted with one related to "private virtue strong in self-restraint." Realizing the impasse, Lowell quits the cathedral in the final part (lines 733–813): "I walked forth saddened; for all thought is sad, And leaves a bitterish savor in the brain." But looking up, he sees a sparrow-hawk. Here is an answer to the "wondrous cure-all in equality," when nature "from the premise sparrow here below" draws "sure conclusion of the hawk above,"

Pleased with the soft-billed songster, pleased no less
With the fierce beak of natures aquiline.

In an "enduring Nature, force conservative" Lowell finds a solution of the
early impressions of nature, one justified by a full view and not the deception of his earlier pantheism. Yet his evidence of God remains in his
impression and not in creed. But the experience at Chartres has warned
him that both creed and impression are delusive:

I fear not Thy withdrawal; more I fear,
Seeing, to know Thee not, hoodwinked with dreams
Of signs and wonders, while, unnoticed, Thou,
Walking Thy garden still, commun'st with men,
Missed in the commonplace of miracle.

With these lines Lowell brings his long meditation into poetic focus. The
commonplace of miracle, whether of childhood days or an adult experience
at Chartres, can still be had. Though Lowell's conclusion lacks in sharpness
or security, it has come through the materials of the poem and is more
than sentimental affirmation.

The Cathedral edges toward the outer limits of the familiar verse essay,
as we see when we compare it with the light gracefulness of "Fitz Adam's
Story." In his later odes Lowell, still close to this tradition, has definitely
stepped beyond the bounds. In a sense they represent an advance, since
they move in the direction of a deeply felt and profound poetry; and such
they might have been had Lowell not given them an increasingly severe
formality. In the order of their writing they mark a regression as each strays
farther from the center of Lowell's essential poetic accomplishment. The
"Ode Recited at the Harvard Commemoration" (1865) as most closely akin
to the familiar verse essay is best; "Agassiz" (1874) is not much inferior;
but with the "Three Memorial Poems" of 1875 and 1876 we are apt to feel
that the severity of Lowell's effort has pressed out the whimsicality of his
talent.

In speaking of the Commemoration Ode in this way, I am aware of
speaking against the influential critical voices of our day. In his *American
Renaissance* F. O. Matthiessen remarked that "a confusion between what
was really felt and the desire to move an audience vitiated Lowell's 'Commemoration Ode,' and left a stain of factitious rhetoric as unmistakable as
tobacco-juice for a token of the age's general failure to distinguish between
the nature of the two arts [rhetoric and poetry]." Possibly taken to task for
these strong terms, nine years later he repeated his judgment as sternly (if
less picturesquely) in the introduction to *The Oxford Book of American Verse.*

It is hard to argue against the charge that a poem is rhetoric rather
than poetry—or for that matter to establish it. Though commonly used as
exclusive opposites (if a poem is not poetry, it is rhetoric—or sentiment,
when we follow Yeats's threefold distinction), the terms overlap. If what
Matthiessen means is what William Van O'Connor has complained about—

that through ornamentation Lowell "expected to elevate the basically pro-saic teaching"—we have something more to work on. But even so, diffi-culties arise in discriminating between moral observation appropriate to poetry and teaching that is "basically prosaic."

In the ode Lowell deals with a subject surely proper for poetry. He mediates between absolutes and particulars; and though he uses the oc-casion of the Civil War, he consciously avoids making the poem either immediately historical or political. In the opening section he sets as the first instance of the conflict between absolutes and particulars that between song and deeds; then he moves in the next four sections to another antagonistic pairing, war and truth. But as he has made song and deed concrete with the ode itself and the lives of the Harvard soldiers, so he makes war the recent Civil War and truth the "Veritas" of Harvard's seal.

> They followed her and found her
> Where all may hope to find,
> Not in the ashes of the burnt-out mind,
> But beautiful, with danger's sweetness round her.

Only in a life embodying such truth by deed of warfare can permanence be found, and as the first example of such embodiment the poet pays tribute to Lincoln in the central (yet digressive) section of the poem. After this passage on Lincoln, that "New birth of our new soil, the first American," we turn to another pair of opposites, death and the ideal of goodness. Again in their meeting, the death for a cause, Lowell finds permanence, but not now of the individual man as Lincoln, but of American manhood. Beginning with the tenth section and extending through the twelfth and final section, we have a passage balancing the early one on Lincoln, and like it serving both as digression and climax. These deaths have redeemed the nation, producing many first Americans in Lincoln's image:

> 'T is no man we celebrate,
> By his country's victories great,
> A hero half, and half the whim of Fate,
> But the pith and marrow of a Nation
> Drawing force from all her men.

In this also is the merit of the poet, who keeps "measure with his people" by singing of their deeds and leading them in their new dedication.

This then is the subject and something of the method. Although we may smile at Lowell's optimistic hope in the aftermath of the Civil War (later on he recognized fully the evils of the period), we should not put the poem aside as rhetoric or sentiment. It is true that frequently we run into the same carelessness in imagery that we have found elsewhere in Lowell's poetry, such as in the conglomeration of sunshine, stars, clay, and fountains of lines 97–100 that Mr. O'Connor has quite rightly suspected.

But the poem is consistently oriented upon its basic images. And while we must count the blemishes, they do not obliterate the beauty that it has.

A closer glance at one of these sections may reassure us. We can properly choose the fourth, in which the sunshine, stars, clay, and fountain "image" occurs. It has three main movements, in which the hopeless flux of life and the hoped-for permanence are discriminated. In lines 66 to 74 (the first nine lines of the section), life is presented as a meaningless fluid, from the beginning in 66 ("Our slender life runs rippling by") to the ending in 73–74 ("Than such as flows and ebbs with Fortune's fickle moon?"). The second passage looks at life directly in terms of a false search for wealth (compare the earlier word "fortune"). We behave as puppets with "our little hour of strut and rave, With all our pasteboard passions and desires." Though it may be objected here that Lowell has us both as actors and bankers, even that combination might be defended, since Lowell brings the two activities together:

> But stay! no age was e'er degenerate
> Unless men held it at too cheap a rate
> For in our likeness still we shape our fate.

From lines 91 to 107 Lowell shifts to figures concerned essentially with light; as already remarked, he also slips into clay and fountains and into tears and seed as well. But in the last three lines—

> A light across the sea,
> Which haunts the soul and will not let it be,
> Still beaconing from the heights of undegenerate years—

he has brought together his two enveloping images of fluidity and light, while with the word "undegenerate" he looks back at the middle section.

Here we should take Lowell for what he is, at heart a writer of the familiar verse essay, rather than making him conform to arbitrary expectations. The section is flexible, digressive, improvised; but beneath the haphazardness is a unity that produces pleasure out of the disparateness of material. There is also further aesthetic satisfaction in the sudden exploration of the material in colloquial terms, though rather less here and in the odes generally than we have in *The Cathedral*.

These closing pages are not written with the hope of making the reader forget the enormously disheartening effect that Lowell's verses as a whole produce. What I believe is that Lowell had a real genius for a certain kind of poem. When he remained within that kind or did not depart from it widely, he wrote poetry that still serves its purpose and offers sweetness. But that poetry is so small in bulk that we are close to not having it, as he indeed was perilously close to not producing it.

As the godfather of the child whom we have come to know as the novelist Virginia Woolf, Lowell wrote some "Verses Intended to Go with a Posset Dish." They are tender, playful, and fit, even if unforeseeing how fully his goddaughter would later deserve them. But it is unfortunate that a godfather of Lowell could not have sent these verses to the poet himself to act as a charm. Filling the posset cup with wishes that the child may inherit all life's graciousness, Lowell ends:

> Thus, then, the cup is duly filled;
> Walk steady, dear, lest all be spilled.

As an artist, our poet did not walk steady; and though he did not spill all from his cup, he spilled much.

Frederick Goddard Tuckerman

Denis Donoghue

Whitman's favorite tense is the present, his favorite mood the indicative, with this qualification, that his indicatives tend to acquire the force of imperatives by pressure of tone. He is rarely content to state a fact and leave it; his "is" sounds like "ought" or "must," his facts are instruments for the transportation of value. His particular significance in American poetry is that he "made it new" by forcing issues that had never before claimed a voice. The issues wandered about the American landscape, timid and fretful, until Whitman brought them to the pitch of definition. But Whitman did not capture the entire imagination of American poetry. Even after *Leaves of Grass* it was still possible to write in one of the old ways, or even in a new way that owed nothing to Whitman's novelty. For instance, in the years immediately after *Leaves of Grass* one of the best poets in America was Frederick Tuckerman. But to read Tuckerman after Whitman is like moving into a private realm of worry and silence. The silence is heavy with questions, the only discernible movement is the movement of thought, the attendant figure is "Man Watching" rather than "Man Thinking," and the voice (when it comes) is an American voice only because it has to be. Whitman's world, more than ever in this context, is noisy, clamorous, aggressive, a world of concentration and insistence.

But at certain points the two worlds coalesce. Whitman and Tuckerman are typical American poets in assuming that for the work in hand they must rely upon their own resources. Each is, to himself, Robinson Crusoe. Tuckerman is a private man, an amateur, a scholar, astronomer, botanist, recluse; Whitman thinks of his role in much more public terms. But each poet assumes that no relevant assistance is available from other men, that

From *Connoisseurs of Chaos*. © 1964, 1984 by Denis Donoghue. Columbia University Press, 1984.

none of the work can be entrusted to others. Much of the pressure in Whitman is the force, beyond any average poetic requirement, that he must generate in the absence of relevant companions. He would praise other poets, but only on the understanding that their poetry made no essential difference to him. Bryant might be an admirable poet in his way, but his work left Whitman's still to be done in its own way. There was no question of a "common pursuit"; every job was a one-man job. Tuckerman was much less grand in his ambition—he never hoped to change the world by his sonnets. But he always assumed that value, form, and meaning were personal achievements, to be won by private resolution. Sustenance would come from those intangible powers certified by his own imagination, notably God and nature. But the relation between self, nature, and God was a closed system; no experience outside the system was relevant.

A poem by Tuckerman, therefore, tends to place an observer at a chosen point inside this "triangle," and to have him survey the scene, often a landscape, a house, a mountain, sometimes the landscape of the past, as it seems to bless or threaten him. In "Margites," for instance, the poet leans from his window in autumn and finds evidence in the landscape that his life is "well-lost," that "all things seem the same." The poet is invariably alone, and whether he finds intimations of ease or pain in the landscape, he is never tempted to blur the line of demarcation between himself and nature, the Me and the Not-Me, subject and object. A typical poem reads:

> And so the day drops by; the horizon draws
> The fading sun, and we stand struck in grief,
> Failing to find our haven of relief,—
> Wide of the way, nor sure to turn or pause,
> And weep to view how fast the splendour wanes
> And scarcely heed that yet some share remains
> Of the red after-light, some time to mark,
> Some space between the sundown and the dark.
> But not for him those golden calms succeed
> Who while the day is high and glory reigns
> Sees it go by,—as the dim pampas plain,
> Hoary with salt and gray with bitter weed,
> Sees the vault blacken, feels the dark wind strain,
> Hears the dry thunder roll, and knows no rain.

This is typical because the suffering observer is in the poem when it begins and is still there when it ends; nothing that happens in the poem releases him from the fate of merely watching and suffering. It is like *Waiting for Godot*. Tuckerman points this up by pressing down hard on the verbs in the last couplet: the one who sees the vault blacken, feels the dark wind strain, hears the dry thunder roll, and knows no rain is the one who can do nothing, take no action; he can't even move away. This is to exemplify, with a vengeance, the "point of view." Tuckerman's hero is transfixed, nailed to one spot, condemned to see, feel, hear, and—hardest of all—know.

This is why so many of Tuckerman's poems are melancholy visions—as if the Greenfield astronomer, happy enough with his telescope when it was time for stargazing, wanted in his poems the rival satisfactions of action, mobility, participation. Indeed, there are a few poems in which Tuckerman asks, literally, for something far more outgoing than his normal poetic experience. "Let me give something!" he cries at one moment, and only then do we realize how much constriction he suffered inside that triangle. The extreme point is reached when "all things seem the same," and, as Stevens says, "in such seeming all things are." If the terms of a poet's life commit him to vision and knowledge, he is well advised to still his "active" ambition and hope that the matter to be seen and known will be dense and rich enough to satisfy him. This is the only tolerable kind of silence.

Tuckerman was a recluse by choice and, for a hundred reasons, a man of vision and knowledge. We identify him with his "point of view" because this is his chief term of reference. On dog days there is for such a poet not enough to see, and one thing seems insufficiently distinct from another in the ways that count. As for taste, touch, and smell, the experience of the poems rarely comes in this fashion; he is not Keats. And as for hearing, I have said that Tuckerman's was a silent world. His "natural" mode of knowledge was by sight, vision, the interpretation of what was visibly there. This is the norm of his poems. Hence it is entirely in keeping that the great release comes, when it does at all, in sound, noise, voice. When nature "contradicts" herself and gives far more than she has promised, when she goes far beyond her contract in plenitude, the bonus comes in sound; the terrible silence is relieved and the air is full:

> For Nature daily through her grand design
> Breathes contradiction where she seems most clear:
> For I have held of her the gift to hear
> And felt, indeed, endowed of sense divine
> When I have found, by guarded insight fine,
> Cold April flowers in the green end of June,
> And thought myself possessed of Nature's ear
> When by the lonely mill-brook, unto mine,
> Seated on slab or trunk asunder sawn,
> The night-hawk blew his horn at sunny noon;
> And in the rainy midnight I have heard
> The ground-sparrow's long twitter from the pine
> And the cat-bird's silver song, the wakeful bird
> That to the lighted window sings for dawn.

This is how relief invariably comes in Tuckerman's world. When the importunities of order and chaos and knowledge are in abeyance and the poet's spirit is drenched with ease, the ease is sound. In one poem he says, "And even the present seems with voices kind / To soothe our sorrow; and the past endears. . . . " When he invokes his dead wife, as he does in several poems, he enters a world of voice, in which the questions are assuaged in answers constantly audible ("Her voice is in mine ears, her answer yet"). Indeed, when it is a case of direct response, whether the message is hard or easy, it comes as voice. The childhood memories are oral. When sorrow pours upon the poet's soul and it is too late to repair the defenses, the facts are given as sounds: the bird "seemed to cry out his warning at my ear," the night wind divides itself into two voices to express the poet's grief, and the clock that is rarely heard is heard now— "The morning bell / Into the gulfs of night dropped *one*."

But this merely emphasizes the fact that when Tuckerman stands before a world that he hopes to see and know (or that he sees and despairs of ever knowing), it is at best a world of silent, visual relations. One of his later poems begins with an invocation to the wood fern, sand grass, and pitch pine of his landscape, "and over these the incorruptible blue." Then he says:

> Here let me gently lie and softly view
> All world asperities, lightly touched and smoothed
> As by his gracious hand, the great Bestower.

It is not his finest poetic moment, but it is characteristic of Tuckerman in this respect, that he is "assuaged and soothed" when he sees evidence in landscape of the great Bestower. He was not a botanist, an astronomer, and a naturalist for nothing; these are all silent worlds. After his wife died the silence seems to have become total. In the later poetry she is a haunting absence; absent herself, she spreads absence all around. (In Tuckerman's poems one is only named to be marked absent, like the two lovely sisters, Gertrude and Gulielma: "Gertrude! with red flowerlip, and silk black hair! / Yet Gulielma was by far more fair!")

I am arguing that Tuckerman's loneliness was intensified by his commitment to the "point of view," the lexicon of vision, the interpretation of experience as silent relations, lines of influence—his position inside the triangle of self, nature, and God. We can sum up very bluntly: even if nature is, in one of Tuckerman's poems, "the old Mother," she keeps her own counsel, goes about her business without explanation or apology. And if her "invention and authority" are God's, He is not speaking. At best, God leaves silent messages, in clouds, rivers, and trees—hieroglyphs, not words, and the "scholar of one candle," to use Stevens's phrase, deciphers as best he can. This is Tuckerman's predicament in one of his greatest poems:

> But man finds means, grant him but place and room,
> To gauge the depths and views a wonder dawn,

Sees all the worlds in utmost space withdrawn
In shape and structure like a honeycomb,
Locates his sun and grasps the universe
Or to their bearings bids the orbs disperse;
Now seems to stand like that great angel girt
With moon and stars; now, sick for shelter even,
Craves but a roof to turn the thunder-rain—
Or finds his vaunted reach and wisdom vain,
Lost in the myriad meaning of a word,
Or starts at its bare import, panic-stirred:
For earth is earth or hearth or dearth or dirt,
The sky heaved over our faint heads is heaven.

The motto for this is given in the preceding poem:

Where they prefigure change, all signals must yet
Fail in the dry when they forebode the wet . . .
I know not.

The beau linguist, bent on interpreting the marks, demands that the words stay still; Tuckerman often feared that they wouldn't. T. S. Eliot in *Burnt Norton* says:

Words strain,
Crack and sometimes break, under the burden,
Under the tension, slip, slide, perish,
Decay with imprecision, will not stay in place,
Will not stay still.

Tuckerman's sonnet begins as if by quoting Marlowe it could get over the problem of deceptive signals: "But man finds means. . . . Sees all the worlds in utmost space withdrawn." Then it calls to Milton for reinforcements: "Now seems to stand like that great angel girt/With moon and stars." But the slip from "sees" to "seems" throws Tuckerman off his rhetorical guard, and almost before he knows it he is in a starker tradition, *King Lear*-land: ". . . now, sick for shelter even,/Craves but a roof to turn the thunder-rain—," and the relation between word and matter, parodied by Goneril, is known to be askew. William Empson, ephebe of ambiguity and complex words, says in "Manchouli":

I find it normal, passing these great frontiers,
That you scan the crowds in rags eagerly each side
With awe; that the nations seem real; that their ambitions
Having such achieved variety within one type, seem sane;
I find it normal;
So too to extract false comfort from that word.

But the interpreter who stands and stares at the scene, hoping to read the signs, always extracts false comfort from the words. The Fool in *Lear* says, "He's mad, that trusts in the tameness of a wolf, a horse's health, a boy's love, or a whore's oath." But if all our evidence is on earth, and if "earth is earth or hearth or dearth or dirt," what then? What then, to the visualist who must either read the signs or die? "I know not." Knowledge amounts to this: "The sky heaved over our faint heads is heaven."

Tuckerman was not always so keen. But he always knew that reading the signals is a complex affair. In several of the early poems he grieves because the "import" of natural forms is alien to him. And there is always "that dark doubt." Sometimes he tries to tease himself out of doubt by dreaming and asserting the validity of the dream, clearly to escape the despotism of the eye. Sometimes he recites a transcendentalist lesson: "If evil sneereth, yet abides the good." But he is never convincing in this note. More often when he invokes transcendentalist terms ("And ills seem but as food for spirits sage"), he goes on to say that for him they simply don't work: "But vain, oh vain, this turning for the light!" When the past drops away, the signs are few, there is not enough to read:

> As when down some broad river dropping, we
> Day after day behold the assuming shores
> Sink and grow dim, as the great water-course
> Pushes his banks apart and seeks the sea,
> Benches of pines, high shelf and balcony
> To flats of willow and low sycamores
> Subsiding, till where'er the wave we see
> Himself is his horizon utterly—
> So fades the portion of our early world.
> Still on the ambit hangs the purple air;
> Yet while we lean to read the secret there,
> The stream that by green shore-sides splashed and purled
> Expands, the mountains melt to vapours rare,
> And life alone circles out flat and bare.

To a writer like Tuckerman who is deeply committed to the reading of signals, leaning to read the secrets, it is natural to draw comfort from the imaginative or "faith-ful" techniques of interpretation, especially from the procedures exemplified by such terms as *analogy, metaphor,* and *correspondence.* If nature is a text, the words should mean and mean abundantly, else the reader is frustrated. But Tuckerman was very scrupulous on this point. He read the text, but he would not go beyond it or "amplify" it for a sounding rhetoric. Indeed, in one of his finest poems (which is also one of the best short poems in the language) he examines with great severity the entire myth of "correspondence":

> Yet wear we on, the deep light disallowed
> That lit our youth. In years no longer young

> We wander silently and brood among
> Dead graves and tease the sun-break and the cloud
> For import. Were it not better yet to fly,
> To follow those who go before the throng,
> Reasoning from stone to star, and easily
> Exampling this existence? Or shall I—
> Who yield slow reverence where I cannot see
> And gather gleams where'er by chance or choice
> My footsteps draw, though brokenly dispensed—
> Come into light at last?—or suddenly,
> Struck to the knees like Saul, one arm against
> The overbearing brightness, hear a voice?

Tuckerman walks broodingly; others "fly," relieved of his scholarly scruple. Those who go before the throng are, presumably, the popular preachers who achieve great awakenings by the suppression of evidence and common sense. But "reasoning from stone to star" seems particularly directed against Swedenborg and the Swedenborgians. In the *De Caelo* Swedenborg distinguishes things of the earth as three kinds, called kingdoms, one of which is the mineral kingdom. "The things in the mineral kingdom are correspondences in the third degree because they neither live nor grow"; that is, they are of the "lowest" degree. To reason from stone to star is therefore an extreme leap of reason in faith. When he comes to effect his translations, Swedenborg says that "Stone . . . signifies the truth of faith"; elsewhere he equates it with " the Divine Truth." But the leap is made a good deal "safer" when Swedenborg discusses the stars. "Glittering stars, which are at the same time wandering," he says, "signify what is false; but glittering and fixed stars signify what is true." Again, "Stars in the Word signify the knowledge of good and truth, consequently truths." Reasoning from stone to star is therefore an easy matter, if you start by taking the validity of correspondence for granted, on faith or trust. Emerson, now predictable, praised Swedenborg for the spirit of this trust, and drew the line only when Swedenborg insisted on translating the "things of the earth" into purely theological terms. Emerson wanted the things translated into moral terms, and was grieved by Swedenborg's theological pedantry. But Tuckerman was not impressed one way or the other; we have to give full weight to his saying that he yielded slow reverence "where I cannot see." In the second half of the sonnet the idea of finding the truth as seeing the light is linked in the two "ways" of conversion. In "The Wreck of the Deutschland" Hopkins invokes this idea, citing as its exemplars Saint Paul and Saint Augustine:

> Whether at once, as once at a crash Paul,
> Or as Austin, a lingering-out sweet skill.

Tuckerman takes the ways more slowly but just as effectively. The best he can hope for is the Augustinian way, by gathering broken lights to "come into light at last." And the tentative nature of the hope is given in the syntax, the separation of the subject from its verb by three lines and a multitude of slow footsteps. The second possibility, Saul's conversion into Paul, is given as an emblem, the victim struck by the blow of the sublime truth. And because this would be the greatest consolation of all, it is given as sound—"hear a voice." In another poem, when Tuckerman finds in heaven "no sign," "the lights are strange and bitter voices by." And in a third he says of the stars, so cozily touched by Swedenborg:

> Nor reck those lights, so distant over us,
> Sublime but helpless to the spirit's need
> As the night-stars in heaven's vault.

It is clear from the poems that Tuckerman yielded up the consolations of "correspondence" very reluctantly but with a scruple that he could not put by. Indeed, this was deeply involved in his melancholy, and it went along with a particular part of it, the feeling that he was cut off from the public analogies of his time. We don't know what he thought of Darwin and the Evolutionists, for instance, but there is a poem in which he laments that evolutionary metaphors are alien to him:

> What profits it to me, though here allowed
> Life, sunlight, leisure, if they fail to urge
> Me to due motion or myself to merge
> With the onward stream, too humble, or too proud?—
> That find myself not with the popular surge
> Washed off and on, or up to higher reefs
> Flung with the foremost when the rolling crowd
> Hoists like a wave.

And there are other poems in which he grieves that by failing these metaphors he has lost the faculty of action altogether ("No onward purpose in my life seems plain"). Even when his conscience spurs him on by telling him that "Truth is not found by feeling in the pocket, / Nor wisdom sucked from out the fingers' end!" the best he can manage for consolation is the hope that he may still make something of his sorrow. And he keeps returning to his fear:

> Where will the ladder land? Who knows?—who knows?
> He who would seize the planet zone by zone
> As on a battle-march, for use alone,
> Nor stops for visionary wants and woes
> But like the Bruce's, on, his heart he throws
> And leaves behind the dreamer and the drone?
> Great is his work indeed, his service great,
> Who seeks for Nature but to subjugate,

Break and bereave, build upward and create
And, hampering her, to carry, heave and drag
Points to results,—towns, cables, cars and ships.
Whilst I in dim green meadows lean and lag,
He counts his course in truth by vigorous steps,
By steps of stairs; but I add crag to crag.

The easy way out is to turn back to early Wordsworthian recollections of childhood and mastery:

> when glorying
> I stood a boy amid the mullein-stalks
> And dreamed myself like him the Lion-King.

Tuckerman has two or three poems in this spirit. But normally the past was no escape. For one thing, Tuckerman's sense of the past was a feeling for the human acts and sufferances that it disclosed. Looking at a house with lights and curtains and vases, he recalls that "but a lifetime back," "Here in the forest-heart, hung blackening/The wolf-bait on the bush beside the spring." And in the next poem he thinks back to "The Shay's-man, with the green branch in his hat,/Or silent sagamore, Shaug or Wassahoale." Indeed, if it is a question of reading the signals of nature, Tuckerman is much more inclined to trust his "quick savage sense," as if he were an Indian trapper, than to sentimentalize with the analogists. And knowing a hawk from a handsaw, he knows that a loss is a loss, untranslatable:

> Under the mountain, as when first I knew
> Its low black roof and chimney creeper-twined,
> The red house stands; and yet my footsteps find,
> Vague in the walks, waste balm and feverfew.
> But they are gone: no soft-eyed sisters trip
> Across the porch or lintels; where, behind,
> The mother sat,—sat knitting with pursed lip.
> The house stands vacant in its green recess,
> Absent of beauty as a broken heart.
> The wild rain enters; and the sunset wind
> Sighs in the chambers of their loveliness
> Or shakes the pane—and in the silent noons
> The glass falls from the window, part by part,
> And ringeth faintly in the grassy stones.

Tuckerman was committed, then, to the hieroglyphs of nature. There were moments in which he felt that he was dealing with a corrupt text, but generally he thought it fairly reliable, if read with a stubborn concern for scholarship. It was possible to say that nature brings a "consenting color" to "heal" a place blasted by storm, provided you saw with equal accuracy that the place was in fact blasted. You could say, "Look, where the gray is white!" provided you retained a clear distinction between the two colors. "We see what is not shown/By that which we behold"; yes, but "Nature's secrecies" are still intact. Tuckerman speaks of "the natural heart" and on one extreme occasion refers to nature as "an embracing Friend," but he is not committed to these assurances. Wordsworth speaks in the "Prospectus" of 1800 of the "great consummation" by which "the discerning intellect of Man" is "wedded to this goodly universe in love and holy passion." Tuckerman thought the universe goodly enough, but he was never tempted to spousal metaphors. At best, the relation between himself and nature was a cool affair, a matter of knowledge, signals, ciphers; there were no further intimacies. And when the situation was extreme, especially after his wife's death, there was no sign of the embracing friend:

> Each common object too—the house, the grove,
> The street, the face, the ware in the window—seems
> Alien and sad, the wreck of perished dreams;
> Painfully present, yet remote in love.
> The day goes down in rain, the winds blow wide.
> I leave the town. I climb the mountain-side,
> Striving from stumps and stones to wring relief,
> And in the senseless anger of my grief,
> I rave and weep. I roar to the unmoved skies;
> But the wild tempest carries away my cries.
> Then back I turn to hide my face in sleep,
> Again with dawn the same dull round to sweep,
> And buy and sell and prate and laugh and chide,
> As if she had not lived, or had not died.

Impersonal nature is exemplified by the sea, which comes and goes "as though the wet were dry and joy were grief." So Tuckerman is never tempted to identify himself with nature beyond the limit of discretion. Whitman's equations are Whitman's business. Tuckerman always felt that even if you went to the outer limit of nature's observances, you would still leave many of your strivings unfulfilled. Wordsworth might talk of "the individual Mind" and "the external World" as being exquisitely "fitted" to one another, but Tuckerman played this theme very softly. For one thing, he thought that man's religious motive was a separate thing, not at all to be assuaged by a "religion of Nature." This follows, of course, from his distrust of "correspondences":

> Still craves the spirit: never Nature solves
> That yearning which with her first breath began
> And in its blinder instinct still devolves
> On god or pagod, Manada or man
> Or, lower yet, brute-service, apes and wolves.
> By Borneo's surf, the bare barbarian
> Still to the sands beneath him bows to pray.

The new problem is, What happens now, when man can worship only himself?

> And what remains to me who count no odds
> Between such Lord and him I saw today,
> The farmer mounted on his market-load,
> Bundles of wool and locks of upland hay—
> The son of toil that his own works bestrode,
> And him, Ophion, earliest of the gods?

Mostly, Tuckerman implies, we "falsely claim and blindly say, / 'I am the Truth, the Life too and the way.' " But we don't take the full weight of this, and fend it off by present gratifications:

> Watching my fancy gleam, now bright, now dark,
> As snapping from the brands a single spark
> Splits in a spray of sparkles were it fall,
> And the long flurrying flame that shoots to die.

What more can one do? Tuckerman suggests that if nature's text is baffling, there is one consolation; the human mind itself has a certain stock of light. He says this in one of his most beautiful passages:

> Nay, for the mind itself a glimpse will rest
> Upon the dark; summoning from vacancy
> Dim shapes about his intellectual lamp,
> Calling these in and causing him to see;
> As the night-heron wading in the swamp
> Lights up the pools with her phosphoric breast.

However, this is not final. There are several poems in which Tuckerman speaks of God in the old way: "the round natural world" does not hold "the reconcilement," nor does "the deep mind"—only God. And God is to be sought by giving up the meretricious struggle, "leaving straining thought and stammering word":

> Across the barren azure pass to God:
> Shooting the void in silence, like a bird,—
> A bird that shuts his wings for better speed.

Often Tuckerman's answer is, Lie quietly within yourself, contain the vaunting will. It is as if, in a world of necessary silence, he were to make silence his ethic. And he did so. Just as time will bring "oblivion of annoy," so also silence will "bind the blows that words have lent." In the later poems, giving up his claims to action and the name of action, he makes "giving up" his "way," his decorum:

> And peace will come, as evening comes to him,
> No leader now of men, no longer proud
> But poor and private, watching the sun's rim,
> Contented too to fade as yonder cloud
> Dim fades and, as the sun fades, fading likewise dim.

In another poem the soul defends itself, like an embattled city, by retiring "even to her inmost keep and citadel." And in a third the soul is warned to keep within its tower, thoughtful, meditative, quiet:

> But shun the reveries of voluptuous thought,
> Day-musings, the floralia of the heart
> And vain imaginations.

This is one of the major tensions in Tuckerman: the pull between the official commitment to rest, quiet, limitation, and the unofficial, wild desire to pursue things "to the end of the line." Briefly, he wanted a wider scene, a larger circle of reference. His official commitment to thought and meditation disclosed other possibilities, and if these seemed "vain imaginations" on cool days, there were other days in which they were exciting precisely because of the wider circumference they ensured. There is a sonnet in which Tuckerman faces this:

> Nor strange it is, to us who walk in bonds
> Of flesh and time, if virtue's self awhile
> Gleam dull like sunless ice; whilst graceful guile—
> Blood-flecked like hematite or diamonds
> With a red inward spark—to reconcile
> Beauty and evil seems and corresponds
> So well with good that the mind joys to have
> Full wider jet and scope nor swings and sleeps
> Forever in one cradle wearily:
> Like those vast weeds that off d'Acunha's isle
> Wash with the surf and flap their mighty fronds
> Mournfully to the dipping of the wave,
> Yet cannot be disrupted from their deeps
> By the whole heave and settle of the sea.

It is one of Tuckerman's most daring poems. He does not deny to the human mind its mighty fronds and deeps or its implacable vote for virtue, but he confronts the possibility that meditative quiet may be nothing more than inertia, a static, graceless condition. This is the observer, in moments of greatest pressure, detaching himself from his "point of view" and making it his local object for challenge and scrutiny. If the poem is also one of Tuckerman's most "modern" pieces, it is for this reason, that it achieves immunity to irony by taking up, itself, a rival stance. Tuckerman rarely does this. He makes his commitments as each occasion offers, but he rarely hedges his bet. He votes and takes the consequence. The poorer poems are propaganda for "the deep soul that knoweth heaven and hell." To swing and sleep forever in one cradle is like lying in Abraham's bosom all the time, with this difference: that Tuckerman for once finds the experience a weary matter, hardly human at all, "like those vast weeds." What he is rejecting, if only for the time of fourteen lines, is not only his own commitment to the esthetic-ethic of "content" and limitation but the entire tradition of which Milton's Platonist scholar in the lonely tower is a central manifestation. Tuckerman is not merely giving Byronism its due, he is challenging himself by pointing beyond the sleek ensolacings in which he has often indulged himself. And if some of the blame falls upon Wordsworth, let it fall. In the "Esthétique du Mal" Stevens speaks of syllables that would form themselves, in time, "and communicate / The intelligence of his despair, express / What meditation never quite achieved." This is what Tuckerman's poem does, expressing what his official meditation fended off. Indeed, the "Esthétique" is a useful parallel text. The moon, Stevens says,

> evaded his mind.
> It was part of a supremacy always
> Above him. The moon was always free from him,
> As night was free from him.

Hence the despair. But Tuckerman's despair is his feeling that the vaunted relation between man and nature, Wordsworth's exquisite fitting of mind and world, amounts to a very inert relation. When nature, like the sea, is impersonal, aboriginal, subhuman, the mind reacts by acquiring immunity, narrowing its vision, closing itself into itself, to its own loss. The poem is therefore much closer to Coleridge's "Dejection" ode than to anything in Wordsworth; except that Coleridge blames himself for his "sullenness," while Tuckerman blames the tradition of which he is a part.

Tuckerman's masterpiece is "The Cricket." The best introduction to the poem is a sonnet in which Tuckerman meditates upon the cricket's cry and the sea break:

> Yet even mid merry boyhood's tricks and scapes,
> Early my heart a deeper lesson learnt,—
> Wandering alone by many a mile of burnt
> Black woodside, that but the snow-flake decks and drapes.
> And I have stood, beneath Canadian sky,
> In utter solitudes where the cricket's cry
> Appalls the heart and fear takes visible shapes,
> And on Long Island's void and isolate capes
> Heard the sea break like iron bars. And still
> In all I seemed to hear the same deep dirge
> Borne in the wind, the insect's tiny trill,

> And crash and jangle of the shaking surge,
> And knew not what they meant.—Prophetic woe?
> Dim bodings? Wherefore? Now, indeed, I know.

What he knows is the burden of "The Cricket," an ode in five long stanzas.

The poem begins by setting up a courtly relation between the poet and the cricket. As the bee purrs over his flower, so the poet attends the cricket, serving him with a promise of reward. In the second stanza the relation is animated by placing it in a dense setting, a collusion of the senses. What is common to the participants is the burden of their different natures. The "burdened brook" flows by, muttering and moaning; the horizon is "swooning-blue"; "Let the dead fragrance round our temples beat, / Stunning the sense to slumber"; the day "declines," and the noise of the crickets, louder still, is like the rising and falling of the sea. The third stanza is Tuckerman's greatest achievement and one of the finest passages in modern poetry. I quote it in full:

> Dear to the child who hears thy rustling voice
> Cease at his footstep, though he hears thee still,
> Cease and resume, with vibrance crisp and shrill,
> Thou sittest in the sunshine to rejoice!
> Night-lover too; bringer of all things dark,
> And rest and silence; yet thou bringest to me
> Always that burthen of the unresting sea
> The moaning cliffs, the low rocks blackly stark;
> These upland inland fields no more I view,
> But the long flat seaside beach, the wild seamew,
>   And the overturning wave!
> Thou bringest too, lost accents from the grave
> To him who walketh when the day is dim,
> Dreaming of those who dream no more of him—
> With edg'd remembrances of joy and pain:
> And heyday looks and laughter come again;
> Forms that in happy sunshine lie and leap,
> With faces where but now a gap must be
> Renunciations, and partitions deep,
> And final tears, and crowning vacancy!
> And to thy poet at the twilight's hush
> No chirping touch of lips with laugh and blush,
> But wringing arms, hearts wild with love and woe,
> Closed eyes, and kisses that would not let go.

Paraphrased, the fourth stanza reads thus: So also were you loved in ancient Greece, when the setting was different—gods, heroes, great ships; there too you brought pain as well as the skill of its expression. In the fifth stanza Tuckerman associates himself with "the Enchanter old," who sought among the poisonous plants for magical powers:

> And touched the leaf that opened both his ears
> So that articulate voices now he hears
> In cry of beast or bird or insect's hum—

This is Tuckerman's prayer: "Might I but find thy knowledge in thy song." The cricket's knowledge would be "ancient as light," aboriginal, a foreign tongue, all the more precious for that reason. I paraphrase again (because the next lines are difficult): If the poet could acquire this alien knowledge, he would dare to sing it to the human world, driving through "denser stillness" and even deeper darkness than the cricket penetrated to come here. The world might then listen. It might even applaud the poet, modestly of course; these are high matters, minority communications, and a larger applause would only prove that the truth itself, the communication, was diminished in the handling:

> For larger would be less indeed, and like
> The ceaseless simmer in the summer grass
> To him who toileth in the windy field
> Or where the sunbeams strike
> Naught in innumerable numerousness.
>   So might I much possess
>   So much must yield.

This may be otherwise put: Because there are so many sounds, we do not attend to any; because there are so many illuminations, sunbeams, we do not attend to any. The poet loses everything between the little actual and the possible. Nonetheless the cricket is still dear, even if its secrets remain alien to man:

> Then cricket, sing thy song! or answer mine!
> Thine whispers blame, but mine has naught but praises.
> It matters not.—Behold! the autumn goes,
>   The Shadow grows,
> The moments take hold of eternity;
> Even while we stop to wrangle or repine
>   Our lives are gone
>   Like thinnest mist,
> Like yon escaping color in the tree:—
> Rejoice! rejoice! whilst yet the hours exist
> Rejoice or mourn, and let the world swing on
> Unmoved by Cricket-song of thee or me.

And the poem ends. It began with a courtly relation, at one stroke meant to establish a relation between the poet and everything represented by the cricket: his antique "otherness," the primitive, prehuman element, the element that resists the sentimental harmonies imposed by man on nature.

The relation once established, Tuckerman thinks of it as the truth of things, especially the truth of pain and time and death. He must bring this truth to the world, like Shelley proposing a similar purpose to the west wind in a more hectic aspiration. But this public purpose is null, Tuckerman reflects; the same misunderstandings would persist. So he turns back. But now he identifies himself not with the human world that he proposed to inform, but with the cricket—each a fretful, noisy being, speaking to deaf ears. One can only persist, rejoicing or mourning—Tuckerman's *materia poetica*. In a poem of the same title Emily Dickinson thinks of the crickets celebrating their rituals under the grass, utterly foreign to man, "enlarging loneliness." But in this case the ritualists, like the ancient Druids, are thought to "enhance" nature. If the crickets have secret lore, antique disciplines, Emily Dickinson is content that this should be so and that the secrets remain intact, the discipline contained. If she claims such privacy for herself, why deny it to the crickets? Tuckerman, so fully committed to reading the text of nature, cannot bear the thought that there are parts of the text that are indecipherable. It is as if a scholar, studying the received texts, came upon certain fragments of a great sacred book, prophetic in tone, and gave the rest of his life to their company. The cricket's noise, like the sound of the sea, is unknowable; hence its fascination as an image of that chaos of which we must become the connoisseurs. In "A Grave" Marianne Moore says:

> Man looking into the sea,
> taking the view from those who have as much right to it as
>   you have to it yourself,
> it is human nature to stand in the middle of a thing,
> but you cannot stand in the middle of this;
> the sea has nothing to give but a well excavated grave.

And the next lines annotate the grave with footnotes on the sea's rapacious look. Then the poem ends:

> and the ocean, under the pulsation of lighthouses and noise of
>   bell-buoys,
> advances as usual, looking as if it were not that ocean in
>   which dropped things are bound to sink—
> in which if they turn and twist, it is neither with volition
>   nor consciousness.

This is our parable. Wallace Stevens's voice in "Sunday Morning" says that "we live in an old chaos of the sun." Tuckerman looks into the sea as into an old chaos of the sun, but he does not hope to take its measure, to stand in the middle of it. He is as decorous in his way as Marianne Moore in her different way. But to both poets the sea is the place where volition and consciousness die, even if bones deposited in that grave continue to twitch and roll as if they were human. The sea, as Williams said in *Paterson Five*, is not our element. American poets are brought up to know this. "The river is within us, the sea is all about us," as one of the voices says in "The Dry Salvages."

"The Cricket" is therefore an exemplary American poem and one of the greatest poems in its tradition. Tuckerman is the isolated figure caught between two worlds: behind him is the human world, deaf, obtuse, vulgar; in front and all around is a world that owes no obeisance to man. This second world is an impenetrable text, "sublime but helpless to the spirit's need"; it contains all of life that we have never known or, knowing, have forgotten. The human world has given itself over to its gross Now. So if the equities are frustrate and it comes to a choice, Tuckerman chooses to be a scholar of one candle, even if most of the text is impenetrable. And he leaves the human world "unmoved."

Henry Timrod

Roy Harvey Pearce

The people's poetry for which so many longed was a by-product of the Civil War and the conditions in American culture which preceded and followed upon it. The problem was to make that kind of poetry which would have as its end the establishing of a national identity—a community of men whose solidarity, whose mutual sense of themselves, would be sufficient to hold a nation together. To be sure, the high poetry of the period was in this broad sense a war poetry too; but its end was to transform its readers into individuals who would make the sort of community for which war would be unthinkable. Thus, for all their varying degrees of commitment to the forces of right and righteousness, as poets Emerson and Whitman would not let themselves be rushed into celebrating the group at the expense of the individual. They knew that the crisis of a house divided was first of all a crisis of man divided. When their contemporaries noted this, they were put off—put off by what they could hardly comprehend. Often, indeed, they did not note this, and . . . conceived of their betters as no different from themselves: concerned above all with the good of *res publica.*

The Civil War was crucial for the growth of southern poetry too. Yet in the South there was no tradition of Puritan individualism and grace in which to seek an authorization for working toward the renewal and transformation of man. Southern literary institutions before the war were those of the amateur and dilettante, products of the careless ease of the busy but noble lord. The great tradition in the South was that of rhetoric and public speech, the tradition of the community whose solidarity seemed (so long as an agrarian, slave-based economy would maintain it) to render meaningless questions as to the ultimate inviolability of the simple, separate

From *The Continuity of American Poetry.* © 1961 by Princeton University Press.

person. Southerners were already obsessed with their own history—
another aspect of their existence as a community—and novelists like Ken-
nedy and Simms wrote according to that obsession. The major southern
orators and historical novelists grounded their claims for southern rights
in a sense of the continuity of the community, not of the individuals who
made it up. When, during the Civil War period, an authentically southern
poetry developed, it reflected this oratorical, communal tradition and issued
immediately into a people's poetry—at worst rabble-rousing, at best
prayerful.

To be sure there were southern poets who aspired to the individualistic
lyric. But they are, as we read them now, mere epigones of the English
Romantics whom they so much admired and yet failed to understand—
mistaking Romantic insight for *frisson;* I think of Paul Hamilton Hayne, for
example. Or, in one notorious case—that of Chivers—the poet grossly
misunderstood the southern writer, Poe, whom he imitated, producing
frenetic pieces of no substantial integrity. Moreover, southern poets were
trapped by northern domination of the apparatus for publishing. One of
them, Henry Timrod, put the case thus, in his "Literature in the South"
(1859):

> [The Southerner] publishes a book. It is the settled conviction of
> the North that genius is indigenous there, and flourishes only in
> a Northern atmosphere. It is the equally firm conviction of the
> South that genius—literary genius, at least—is an exotic that will
> not flower on a Southern soil. Probably the book is published by
> a Northern house. Straightway all the newspapers of the South
> are indignant that the author did not choose a Southern printer,
> and address himself more particularly to a Southern community.
> He heeds their criticism, and of his next book,—published by a
> Southern printer—such is the secret though unacknowledged prej-
> udice against Southern authors—he finds that more than one half
> of a small edition remains upon his hands. Perhaps the book con-
> tains a correct and beautiful picture of our peculiar state of society.
> The North is inattentive or abusive, and the South unthankful,
> or, at most, indifferent. Or it may happen to be only a volume of
> noble poetry, full of those universal thoughts and feelings which
> speak, not to a particular people, but to all mankind. It is censured
> at the South as not sufficiently Southern in spirit, while at the
> North it is pronounced a very fair specimen of Southern com-
> monplace. Both North and South agree with one mind to condemn
> the author and forget his book.

Timrod himself soon learned, under the pressures of the war, that he
could do his best by directing his universal thoughts and feelings to a
southern audience. Doing so, whether he knew it or not, he wrote in the

oratorical-historical mode and so made a people's poetry, answering the wartime need to ensure the solidarity of the community.

The memorable Timrod poems are a handful of ode-like pieces. There is "Ethnogenesis," which begins:

> Hath not the morning dawned with added light?
> And shall not evening call another star
> Out of the infinite regions of the night,
> To mark this day in Heaven? At last, we are
> A nation among nations; and the world
> Shall soon behold in many a distant port
>   Another flag unfurled!

The South discovers that it is not only another community, another nation, but another race. The poet goes on to detail the glories of the southern past, so as to set them against the recent iniquities of the North, where religion itself has been corrupted by power politics. At the end he looks to the glorious future:

> The hour perchance is not yet wholly ripe
> When all shall own it, but the type
> Whereby we shall be known in every land
> Is that vast gulf which lips our Southern strand,
> And through the cold, untempered ocean pours
> Its genial streams, that far off Arctic shores
> May sometimes catch upon the softened breeze
> Strange tropic warmth and hints of summer seas.

The Gulf Stream, that is to say, figures the future role of the South—warming the North. That Timrod draws only in black and white should not discourage the industrious reader of Whittier and Lowell, for example. For Timrod, granting his convictions and his situation, must draw thus, as Whittier and Lowell must. The poet's task is not to discover but to confirm. The counterpart of Timrod's tradition of oratory is Whittier's and Lowell's of sermonizing. In a poem of this order issues are settled before they are dealt with. Since argument pro and con centers on the issues and not the way in which they are treated, the morality of the poem centers on the morality of the issue. The purpose of the poem would be utterly defeated if the poet dared in any way even to consider the possibility that—looking beyond the communal morality of the issue to the private morality of the simple, separate person—he might build greater than he knows, or seek to build differently.

In another of his "odes," "The Cotton Boll," Timrod imaged himself as lost in rapt contemplation of a haze of soft white fibers and came finally to call for a poet who would answer to the South's present needs:

Where sleeps the poet who shall fitly sing
The source wherefrom doth spring
That mighty commerce which, confined
To the mean channels of no selfish mart,
Goes out to every shore
Of this broad earth, and throngs the sea with ships
That bear no thunders; hushes hungry lips
In alien lands;
Joins with a delicate web remotest strands;
And gladdening rich and poor,
Doth gild Parisian domes,
Or feed the cottage-smoke of English homes,
And only bounds its blessings by mankind!

Timrod did not live long enough to be this poet. (He died in 1867 of tuberculosis contracted during the war.) But he put as specifically as he could his understanding of the problems that poet would have to confront: to deal somehow with the South as a special kind of civilization, agrarian, with a special mission to the world. In the South's more "natural" economy lay the source of strength for the poet who might best evoke a sense of its "nature."

Dickinson and Despair

Charles R. Anderson

Emily Dickinson was no visionary intent on escaping the prison of this flesh. What gives weight to her poems that tug to be free and soar is her solid sense of reality, not just of scene and thing but of thought and feeling. More than most of her contemporaries she knew how to discriminate between vision and fact, and was aware how small a part ecstasy makes in the sum total that comprises life. Her normal impulse is to load the scales against it, as in this early poem:

> The Heart asks Pleasure—first—
> And then—Excuse from Pain—
> And then—those little Anodynes
> That deaden suffering—.

Then permission to sleep and finally, if the "Inquisitor" wills it, "The privilege to die." With a different emphasis, reversing the compensatory doctrine of heavenly reward for a life of suffering, she says in a late letter: "To have lived is a Bliss so powerful—we must die—to adjust it."

Her effect of reality is achieved not by an accent on pleasure or pain but by her dramatic use of their interaction. As an artist she took full advantage of contrast as a mode of definition, making the pleasure-pain antithesis a running strategy in her poetry. As "Water is taught by thirst," so "Transport—by throe." Again:

> Delight—becomes pictorial—
> When viewed through Pain— . . .
> Transporting must the moment be—
> Brewed from decades of Agony!

From *Emily Dickinson's Poetry: Stairway of Surprise.* © 1960 by Charles R. Anderson. Holt, Rinehart & Winston, 1960.

And finally, from among her earliest efforts, there is a poem constructed entirely of such contrasts, in terms of intensity and duration, beginning:

> For each extatic instant
> We must an anguish pay
> In keen and quivering ratio
> To the extasy.

"Time is a pain lived piecemeal," as one critic astutely epitomizes this poem, "and the sum of the pieces equals a moment of joy." But this is just an exercise in hedonistic calculus.

There is a wide range of pain explored in her poetry. She distinguishes misery, as a hurt that can be relieved, from suffering which stresses the act of enduring. But these milder aches and griefs did not challenge her powers of analysis like the extreme forms from affliction to woe that are recurrent in her poems. She discriminates among them somewhat as her copy of Webster did. He defines "agony" as the pain so excruciating as to cause bodily contortions "similar to . . . the sufferings of our Savior in the garden of Gethsemane"; "anguish" as any keen distress of the mind "from sorrow, remorse, despair, and the kindred passions"; and "despair" itself as the extremest form of all, resulting in hopelessness, though with only subordinate theological connotations. But the purpose of her poems is something far other than the niceties of the lexicographer. She simply separates the lesser pains that will heal from the greater pains that will not and chooses the latter as her special concern, noting with precision their qualities and above all their effects.

If she had emphasized their causes, as from a loss of love or fame or religious faith, there would be more justification for biographical inquiry. Even so, her very obsession with the theme of extreme pain has made inevitable the conjecture that some experience of unusual intensity was the source of it. There is scattered evidence for this in the letters, but only one explicit statement. Written to Higginson in 1862, at the beginning of her creative flood tide, it has often been taken as explaining why she turned to poetry as a career: "I had a terror—since September—I could tell to none—and so I sing, as the Boy does by the Burying Ground—because I am afraid." It is doubtful that the nature of this "terror" will ever be clarified by further external data. But the poems of this period likewise seem to reflect an extreme emotional and psychological crisis that tempts speculation. Some fifty of them have been arranged recently by one of her biographers in an impressive display of the severity and many-sidedness of such a conjectured crisis.

A number of her poems, though not usually the best, seem to relate this extreme suffering to a loss in love. One of the quieter ones, written in 1864 on the theme of renunciation until "He" and "I" can be reunited, presumably in heaven, begins and ends with phraseology remarkably similar to her statement in the letter to Higginson just quoted: "I sing to use the Waiting . . . To Keep the Dark away." Another, ten years later, makes a memorable song out of pain as one of the pressures that wrings poetry from the heart, though declining to name the instrumentality as love:

> Not with a Club, the Heart is broken
> Nor with a Stone—
> A Whip so small you could not see it
> I've known
>
> To lash the Magic Creature
> Till it fell,
> Yet that Whip's Name
> Too noble then to tell.
>
> Magnanimous as Bird
> By Boy descried—
> Singing unto the Stone
> Of which it died—.

Singing to conquer pain is again the theme. The images are sharp—"Club," "Stone," "Whip," culminating in the evocative "Magic Creature" that makes the heart a living person. Nor is the third stanza an extraneous prose trailer, but a flash that brings the whole into focus. The boy, Eros with a slingshot, kills the bird of his desire heedless of its song. But the very real stone here links back to the invisible one at the beginning, denied into a whip, which makes the smitten heart sing too, now that the oblivious lover-killer has faded out. The suffering has been mastered and the beauty remains.

Her most anguished record of a hopeless love, "I cannot live with you," never quite rises out of pain into poetry, though some of the lines sing. For the most part it is a discursive monologue (fifty lines, her longest single effort in verse), struggling vainly to resolve an impossible dilemma. I cannot live with you or without you; I cannot die, or go to heaven, or even desire heaven without you. Yet there is no hope of reunion in Paradise either, because of some obscure flaw in their love. The reader is shaken by an eruption of emotion that is threatening from somewhere behind the poem to break out into the text, but it is never sufficiently under control to be channeled into language except to a modest degree in the final stanza:

> So We must meet apart—
> You there—I—here
> With just the Door ajar
> That Oceans are—and Prayer—
> And that White Sustenance—
> Despair—.

The prerequisite for mastery, as in all Dickinson's best poetry, was to abandon the cumulative and logical for the tight symbolic structure that was her forte. Closely connected with this was the narrowing of her concern to one emotion at a time. Two of her better poems on the pain of renunciation deal, respectively, with the acceptance of loss as an inescapable part of the human condition and with the sheer quality of the resulting agony. In both, the specific event of a love-parting is reduced to a generalized idea of deprivation. The first of these achieves conciseness of theme if not of form:

> I should have been too glad, I see—
> Too lifted—for the scant degree
> Of Life's penurious Round—
> My little Circuit would have shamed
> This new Circumference—have blamed—
> The homelier time behind.
>
> I should have been too saved—I see—
> Too rescued—Fear too dim to me
> That I could spell the Prayer
> I knew so perfect—yesterday—
> That Scalding One—Sabacthini—
> Recited fluent—here—
>
> Earth would have been too much—I see—
> And Heaven—not enough for me—
> I should have had the Joy
> Without the Fear—to justify—
> The Palm—without the Calvary—
> So Savior—Crucify—
>
> Defeat whets Victory—they say—
> The Reefs in Old Gethsemane
> Endear the Shore beyond—
> 'Tis Beggars—Banquets best define—
> 'Tis Thirsting—vitalizes Wine—
> Faith bleats to understand—.

The search for peace begins creatively with two concentric symbols, one circle for the mortal lot and one for the heavenly expansion unattainable on earth. If they had been developed to control the whole poem, their interaction might have encompassed not only the fact and the vision but the adjustment between the two, in a more satisfying fusion of theme and form. Though this advantage is not followed through, the first stanza sets up the limits of the human condition as a realized center for measuring the pressure of pain to follow. Justifying to herself why she was deprived of ecstasy, the ecstasy of heavenly love presumably, she says that it would have made her unjustly disdainful of the "penurious Round" of ordinary life. One cannot escape from the "little Circuit" of petty realities by leaping directly into a "new Circumference." Had such heavenly bliss actually been bestowed on her she would have proved inadequate to it. Being still limited by the human capacity for expansion, she would have dishonored ("shamed") the potentialities of such love and could only have "blamed" her failure on the deficient preparation of the "homelier" life she had known before. The uplifting from a "scant degree" to an exalted one is not so easily obtained. Mortal experience will never become a center from which the inner self can expand toward limitless joy. The geometry of earthly and heavenly circumference is drawn with inflexible and mutually exclusive precision.

Leaving these two encompassing images, the poem develops instead by linear argument to prove that the human way is not the easy but the hard one, the way that must go through pain to a fuller understanding of what heaven can be. Some sort of logical unity is preserved by the syntactical pattern. The conditional mood, "I should . . . ," is maintained throughout (except in the last stanza), giving the whole poem the quality of a hypothetical case history. Again, "Too rescued . . . too saved" in the second stanza echoes "Too lifted . . . too glad" in the first and is answered by "too much" in the third. Once in a letter she used the syllogistic paradox with shock effect to argue: "To be human is more than to be divine, for when Christ was divine, he was uncontented till he had been human." Similarly here: as Jesus before reaching his divine expanse had to experience mortal suffering to the point of temporary despair and utter his *Sabachthani*, so must she in order to spell out the human prayer, "My God, my God, why hast thou forsaken me." She can say it fluently now because she has been forsaken, though "Recited" gives it the air of ritualistic formula, as if she were rehearsing the words of Another to make them her own.

A more important kind of unity derives from thematic linkages. The "little Circuit—new Circumference" antithesis reappears at the beginning of the third stanza in the exalted earthly life that would blot out the heavenly. At its close the "Scalding" prayer that gives the poem its center is balanced by a daring redaction of the historic renunciation in Gethsemane ("Not my will, but thine, be done") in her startling plea: "So Savior— Crucify." The personal intensity ends with this climactic juxtaposition of opposites that began with Joy and Fear, Palm and Calvary. The last stanza seems on the surface like a mere appendix of aphorisms in further illustration of the pleasure-pain contrast. But this is the truth as "they say" it, and two submerged metaphors identify "them" as the authors of the Gospel story. "Gethsemane" recalls the night before the crucifixion, "Defeat-Victory" the agony of Golgotha that must follow the triumphal entry into Jerusalem, "Banquets" and "Wine" the spiritual feast of the Last Supper. That this was also the celebration of the Passover evokes the image of the Paschal Lamb, slain and eaten at that time, which reappears indirectly in the final line: "Faith bleats to understand." This brings to mind many biblical references to the Savior as the Good Shepherd, but also in its plaintiveness links back to the cry from the cross that forms the poem's passionate center. If glory must first be denied into despair for Christ, how much more so for mortals? Pain and loss, sharpened by a momentary vision of ecstasy, constitute the human condition she has been trying to adjust herself to throughout. For all her attempt to verbalize this, in the end she can only cry as a sheep.

The nature of despair itself, rather than the story of how she rebelled against it or finally accepted it, called out her finest talents:

> The Auctioneer of Parting
> His 'Going, going, gone'
> Shouts even from the Crucifix,
> And brings his Hammer down—
> He only sells the Wilderness,
> The prices of Despair
> Range from a single human Heart
> To Two—not any more—.

This poem comprises the most remarkable pun in nineteenth-century Anglo-American literature, reviving that clowning Elizabethan device for the purposes of serious poetry long before Joyce and Pound rediscovered its efficacy. What is being sold, what is "Going," is gone-ness itself. What is being knocked down from the cross—and the verbal play makes the horrific extension inescapable—is death, the symbolic last "Parting" of all. The wooden rap of the ordinary auctioneer's gavel makes all sales final, and this one transformed into a "Hammer," such as drove the nails into God's body, has the finality of Fate. The purchaser cannot back out, he must take possession of what he has bought.

He has bought the "Wilderness," not in the American sense of a primeval forest but as in biblical references to those waste places where life cannot be supported. Her Lexicon, differing from modern dictionaries, gives prominence to this definition, "a barren plain . . . , uncultivated and uninhabited by human beings," citing by way of example the deserts of Arabia in which the Israelites wandered for forty years. The presence of "Crucifix" in her poem makes her meaning unmistakable: a desert where the lost wander. "Wilderness" is her new designation for "that White Sustenance—Despair," the utter desolation of the human heart. That any one should buy the wilderness voluntarily may seem strange. Yet parting short of death is an act of free will, however desperate the circumstances that force the choice. The price of this "death" is a living heart, two if both make the renunciation, a single one if the other is unaware of love's commitment. (It is only in these last two lines that there is any suggestion of love-parting; otherwise the theme seems to be separation from God, made doubly poignant by its unuttered cry from the cross.) So the figure of the auction carries through to the end. The movement of the poem is unavoidably downward, dictated by the hammer's stroke. The powerful conceit reaches its climax in the second line, the devastation spends itself in the center, and the force of both is dissipated in the cool air of calculation at the end. The violent emotion comes to rest here in quiet analysis, it is true, but this is the mood that creates her best poems on the extremity of pain.

Her justification for such bold adaptations of the great Christian symbol to human agony is made explicit in another poem. "One Crucifixion is recorded—only," she says, but there are as many unrecorded ones as there are people: "Gethsemane—/Is but a Province—in the Being's Centre." The theme of her own "Calvary" in many poems is generally taken to be her suffering through the frustration of an earthly love. Yet this assumption must be balanced against references to herself as a creature "Of Heavenly Love—forgot" and the general tenor of poems like the two just discussed. Her use of "Despair" sometimes comes close to the traditional Christian definition, the last one cited in her Lexicon: "Loss of hope in the mercy of God." Such a suggested meaning in these poems is usually supported by a pervasive religious language—Sabachthani, Calvary, Crucifix. In others she uses despair simply as the extremest form of mortal suffering, "the anguish of despair" as Webster phrased the secular illustration, which is similar to but not identical with the soul's helplessness of heaven. It seems wisest to read the whole range of her poems on pain, as in the case of those on ecstasy, simply as poems, free of entanglement in autobiographical conjecture or the formalism of theology. Let the "I" be fictive, the "supposed person" who stands for Everyman, and let the pain be secular unless the evidence of the whole poem makes it otherwise.

Anguish confined entirely to this world can be devastating enough, by reason of its very intensity. It is aggravated by the realization that man can find no help for it outside himself, as he can with spiritual despair through the hope of God's grace. Contrary to many of the Romantic poets who preceded her, she found no healing balm in nature for human hurt. The absolute cleavage between man and the external world was one of her basic convictions, as previous chapters have demonstrated, and its indifference to his plight is the theme-song in many of her poems. Her best one on the theme of human suffering confronted by nature's gay parade seems on the surface to be in danger of a reverse use of the pathetic fallacy, for here the indifference is threatening at several points to break out into open hostility, but a close reading proves she has not lapsed into the error of making nature sentient. On the contrary, she has made deliberate use of emotional extravagance to create a sense of nightmare, such as might result when anguish had reduced its victim to irrational terror:

> I dreaded that first Robin, so,
> But He is mastered, now,
> I'm some accustomed to Him grown,
> He hurts a little, though—
>
> I thought if I could only live
> Till that first Shout got by—
> Not all Pianos in the Woods
> Had power to mangle me—

I dared not meet the Daffodils—
For fear their Yellow Gown
Would pierce me with a fashion
So foreign to my own—

I wished the Grass would hurry
So—when 'twas time to see—
He'd be too tall, the tallest one
Could stretch—to look at me—

I could not bear the Bees should come,
I wished they'd stay away
In those dim countries where they go,
What word had they, for me?

They're here, though; not a creature failed—
No Blossom stayed away
In gentle deference to me—
The Queen of Calvary—

Each one salutes me, as he goes,
And I, my childish Plumes,
Lift, in bereaved acknowledgement
Of their unthinking Drums—.

She feared the sounds of spring would "mangle" her, its colors "pierce" her, and so on. Nature is not only personified but on the warpath, the poet's soul so hypersensitive it can be wounded by anything, her emotions exaggerated to the point of being ludicrous. These certainly seem like the signposts of sentimentalism, and the casual reader may easily misinterpret them. Aware she was using a precarious technique, she matched her skill to the risk. The overwrought center is deftly set apart by being related in the past tense and is provided with a frame of irony by the opening and closing stanzas, which enable her and the reader to view it objectively from the calmer present. The nightmare is confined to stanzas two through five. They record not what actually happened but what she "dreaded" would happen. The past tense, and the subjunctive mood, shows that for this part of the story's enactment spring had not yet come; the section opens with the clue "I *thought* if I could only live/Till. . . ." The events that follow never existed anywhere except in her deluded imagination, but in that interior world they constituted the whole of reality and they function with terrifying precision. For an adult to hide behind grass blades for protection against the spears of attacking daffodils would indeed be insane, but that is just the point. This and the other imagined events are paranoid images skillfully objectifying the hallucinatory world of her fears.

The initial image sets the tone by evoking the exact sense of unreality desired: "Not all Pianos in the Woods/Had power to mangle me." In one sense "Pianos" is a metaphor for the treble of birds, the bass of frogs, and all the range of natural sounds in between, with their wild harmony and counterpoint. In a letter to Higginson she once said, "the noise in the Pool, at Noon—excels my Piano." In a lesser poem on the same theme she uses a similar figure, the black birds' "Banjo," accurate enough for their twanging monotone and with the added humor of an oblique reference to the Negro minstrels popular in that day. But the humor appropriate to anguish is macabre, not grotesque, and the "Pianos" here give just that touch. For in another sense they are not metaphorical but real, or rather surrealistic, like the objects in a painting by Dali. Placed in the woods instead of in the parlor, by the distortion of terror, they could become instruments of torture. Caught behind the keyboard of a gigantic piano she would be "mangled" by its hammers even as she was driven mad by the booming strings, helplessly dodging blows whose source, timing, and spacing she could not guess. This is indeed the world of nightmare, induced by dread when unbearable pain has unhinged the reason.

The framing stanzas are not for the purpose of ridiculing this terror or repudiating it as mere insanity. Their relation to the center of pain is much more intricate. The opening one is mainly in the present tense, after spring has come, but it begins with a throwback to the fear that had gripped her earlier, "I dreaded that first Robin, so." The following lines appear to modify the excess of terror by saying calmly, "He is mastered now," all the more reassuring by being couched in homely idiom ("I'm some accustomed to Him grown"). But the reader is the one who is actually reassured, knowing that the creator of the poem has mastered herself rather than the robin, though the experience lingers vividly in her memory and still "hurts a little." He is now prepared to accept as true her account in the succeeding stanzas of the dread produced by coming spring, in all the intensity of its psychic reality. As her mind reviews that past time of nightmare her language breaks into the turgid and improbable. One surrealistic scene after another flashes before her in a fantastic parade, the shouting mob of birds, daffodils, grass, and bees she "could not bear . . . should come."

The conclusion returns to the quiet mood of adjustment, in the present tense, with which the poem began: "They're here, though; not a creature failed." Arrogating to herself the title "Queen of the Calvary" might seem to indicate that some of the distorted vision still remains, but this is undercut by irony. Her imagined subjects do not obey her wish by staying away "In gentle deference" to her grief. Instead, they file past her with gay sounds and colors quite as "foreign" to her present state as she had feared in the nightmare. This, of course, is not the parade conjured up by her terrified imagination. It is the orderly procession of spring, which follows winter just as a resurrection should follow her "Calvary."

Whether she desires it or not spring brings renewal of life to nature taunting the stricken soul with its signs of health. It is only in this root sense that it "salutes" her, the assumed deference of subject to sovereign being part of the calculated mockery. She can do nothing but accept this false promise of a return to well-being. Hence her "bereaved acknowledgement" of spring's greeting by lifting her "childish Plumes." They are the insignia of her royalty and of her grief, as in the purple plumes of traditional monarchy and the black ones of the hearse and horse in the funerals of her own day. Her recognition that both are childish is the mark of a certain stage of her recovery, the awareness that at least her irrational terror is now dead. For all that she has outlived it, "mastered" it, it was none the less real while it lasted. And the new wisdom she has gained from this adjustment is perhaps even more awesome. It is apparently the conviction that her anguish was not insane but the processes of nature are, in the sense that they have no relation to her interior world. Its loud and meaningless life continues to beat on her consciousness with "unthinking Drums." Any outward demonstrations of terror and grief in the face of nature's indifference are childish, just as man's claim of sovereignty over it would be. The anguish that remains, though not named, is her sense of the suffering mind's isolation in an alien universe.

The pain that Dickinson explores in the major poems is of a sort the victim never fully recovers from. "Split Lives—never 'get well' " she commented in a letter. "It is simple, to ache in the Bone, or the Rind," according to one of her poems, "But Gimlets—among the nerve—/Mangle . . . terribler." Such pain goes to the quick. It usually involves a "death" to some part of the person's life and an awareness of change to a new dimension of being. There is nothing occult or morbid about all this. Certain basic human experiences are universally recognized as answering exactly to this description, though the resulting anguish is usually glossed by wit or otherwise played down in popular speech, probably because of its very intensity. The more obvious ones may be readily agreed upon: the struggle out of adolescence into maturity, with its loss of freedom; the breaking of the dream, whether of glory or love or joy; the benumbing discovery that the grave is not just for others, with the consequent first experience of "dying." The vocabulary of utility desperately applied to them (growing pains, disillusionment, common sense) stresses the gain in wisdom, but it cannot conceal the loss to the spirit. This kind of anguish, the distinguishing mark of the human consciousness as opposed to animal and vegetable being, is valid subject matter for the artist and she made it one of her special provinces. Though she rarely makes the experience specific, it may be indicated in a general way as that whole area of crisis, looming behind the record of the years 1859–1866, which transformed her from an obscure woman into a great poet.

Her best poetry is not concerned with the causes but with the qualities of pain, an emphasis that removes it effectively from the category of the sentimental. She even takes care to differentiate between the kind manufactured by poetasters and that which engages her attention: "Safe Despair it is that raves—/Agony is frugal." Her own approach at times seems almost clinical, but this is simply the mode she adopted to gain the proper distance between her personal emotions and her art. It separates her sharply from the subjective lyricism of an older tradition and reveals her kinship with the twentieth century. The qualities she sought to fix with greatest precision are its intensity, its duration, and the change it brings about. In several minor poems she used time as a measure of degree in defining that extremity of pain that was her real concern. To the readiest cliché of both the sentimentalist and the pragmatist, that "Time assuages," she replied, not when it is "Malady"; and in a letter: "to all except anguish, the mind soon adjusts." Extreme suffering even changes the very nature of time, she demonstrated in a pair of dialectical quatrains: "Pain—expands the Time— . . . Pain contracts—the Time." It makes clock and calendar meaningless and annihilates the very idea of eternity; the true center of pain exists in a temporal vacuum, containing its own past and future. Spatially it is equally limitless and without definable locality: it "ranges Boundlessness." Unlike contentment, which resides lawfully in a "quiet Suburb," agony cannot stay "In Acre—Or Location—/It rents Immensity." It absorbs the whole of consciousness, condensed to a measureless, momentless point.

Pain is thus a quality of being that exists outside time and space, the only two terms in which it can possibly be externalized. Her dilemma in describing this formless psychic entity was how to contrive outward symbols that would make the internal condition manifest. In solving this difficulty she borrowed from the techniques of the theatre, man's supreme contrivance for presenting illusion by making scene and action a set of appearances through which the spectator must penetrate to the reality beneath. With the aid of this device, supplemented by the rituals of formal ceremonies like trials and funerals, the effects of extreme pain are rendered by her in a series of unusually interesting poems.

In the most extraordinary of them, the abstract concept of "death" as inflicted on the consciousness by despair is projected in one of those courtroom scenes of nightmare made vivid to modern readers by Kafka. The victim is on trial for his life, though for some nameless crime, and the machinery of an inexorable justice grinds to its conclusion, without moving, in a kind of wordless horror:

> I read my sentence—steadily—
> Reviewed it with my eyes,
> To see that I made no mistake
> In its extremest clause—
> The Date, and manner, of the shame—
> And then the Pious Form
> That 'God have mercy' on the Soul
> The Jury voted Him—
> I made my soul familiar—with her extremity—

That at the last, it should not be a novel Agony—
But she, and Death, acquainted—
Meet tranquilly, as friends—
Salute, and pass, without a Hint—
And there, the Matter ends—.

The proliferation of pronouns here is not a sign of artistic confusion but a grammatical echo of the dream chaos, whose intricate meaning can be parsed readily enough if the analyst follows the mode of the subconscious drama. "I," "Him," and "She" are all aspects of the persona of the poem, as in the dream all characters are projections of the dreamer.

The poem falls into two equal parts of eight lines each, though the climactic quatrain that introduces the second is written as an extended couplet, thus giving emphasis to the previously unnamed "Agony." This twofold division corresponds roughly to the duality of body and soul. The fictive "I" stands for the whole of the mortal life that dominates the first half, as mind-heart-body react to the sentence of death. The extrapolated "she," the filmy protagonist of the second half, is the immortal part, this section being primarily concerned with the effect of the verdict on the soul. Yet both are spoken by "I," for Dickinson could not indulge in an outright *Debate between the Body and the Soul* as the medieval poet could, his belief in the absolute reality of both not being available to her. The law refuses to take any cognizance of such duality and addresses the reunited halves of the prisoner as "Him," though it does so at the very point where the jury in condemning his body to death makes use of a formula from traditional piety to recommend mercy on his soul. "Him," placed exactly at the juncture between the two halves of the poem, likewise unifies them and at the same time gives the persona wholeness of being for the duration of a single word, though even then only as the third person condemned in the nightmare, anonymous and detached from the agonized dreamer-narrator.

The legal language, concentrated in the first half, not only sets the scene but controls the meaning throughout. Brought up in a family of lawyers, she came by it naturally. But far more important than her precision in handling its terminology is the imaginative fitness with which she puts it to work. The dramatic appeal of a criminal trial comes from the contrast of the lawless emotions involved in the original actions and the ordered procedure by which the court reenacts them, with the possibility that at any moment the violently human may erupt through the formalism of its jargon. From this situational irony she creates her strategy, giving it a unique twist by having one actor, the masking "I," slip successively into all the leading roles—prisoner-in-the-dock, defense counsel, judge, jury, and courtroom spectators.

The poem opens with the flat statement that the unidentified speaker, completely subdued to the mechanism of the ritual, has read his sentence "steadily," or as her Lexicon defines it "without tottering, shaking," such as might be expected of one condemned to die. This air of professional disinterestedness holds throughout the first eight lines, as the speaker performs both judicial and counselling functions. "Reviewed it" suggests that this is a court of appeal, perhaps of last resort, reviewing the decision of a lower trial court; also that the defense, counsel and client, are going over a familiar document, not with the heart but "with my eyes," alert to any technicalities of "date," "clause," or "manner" that might serve as a basis for requesting a reversal of the opinion; finally that the condemned is even looking for an extra-legal loophole in the one human phrase that has crept into this otherwise formally pronounced judgment, but the jury's vote of "God have mercy" is just a "Pious Form" without legal consequences. All the ingenuity of the profession and the meticulous care of the accused have revealed "no mistake," however, and the sentence stands in its "extremest clause." So ends the first scene.

The same elaborate device of a dream-trial is used in another poem in the form of a simile to stand explicitly for the "death" that can come from "Agony." It crept nearer every day until the benumbed victim dropped "lost [as] from a Dream." Then, "As if your Sentence stood—pronounced," she says, and you were led from the luxurious doubts of the dungeon to the gibbet and sure death, suppose some creature should gasp "Reprieve" at the last moment, would this lessen the anguish? Only temporary relief, not pardon and remission, is possible for the pain of the human condition, she is saying, and death itself might well be preferable. But in that poem the agony, being insufficiently controlled, shatters the form with fragmentary and conflicting images. The superior mastery of the one under consideration consists in the skill by which the metaphor of the legal nightmare becomes both cover and contents, so that the thematic meaning of pain can be gradually unfolded by what the poem enacts, clarified in the last part even as it is given a new direction.

Beneath the stylized language of this drama the speaker knows he is none of these other parties, judge or jury or attorney, not even the disinterested spectator, a role reserved for the reader. He is the one condemned to death. (The exigencies of discourse require the use of the third person throughout the rest of the discussion of what happens to the "I" of the poem, but this must not be confused with her special use of "Him" in line eight.) He is also aware that the whole ritual is simply a nightmarish image of another and worse kind of death, the dying of consciousness under the pressure of despair. But he has lost his sense of identity, and this is what accounts for his apparent apathy. His detachment is such that he can read his own death sentence as if it applied to someone else. As she put it elsewhere: "A Doubt if it be Us" assists the mind, staggering under extreme anguish, until it finds a new footing.

To lose one's identity by such a living death is in a sense to be separated from one's soul, which justifies the colloquy in the second section. But the mortal part still does all the talking, "I made my soul familiar" answering in uninterrupted sequence to the opening line, "I read my sentence—steadily." The continuity of speaker binds the two parts together, and this limited point of view provides a further irony by relating an immortal sequence in mortal terms. The soul, previously introduced only in the jury's callous formula, now becomes an entity, and the theme of death-dealing pain emerges with an effect of shock from the metaphor of a legal death-sentence. The scene has now dissolved from the courtroom to some shadowy anteroom, perhaps the death-cell or even the execution chamber itself, with that inconsequent shifting so familiar in dreams. Fearing that what killed his consciousness may also kill his soul, the speaker is solicitous that "she" should be prepared for "her extremity" so that in the end "it should not be a novel Agony." "Novel" means not only unexpected, the final shock he wants to make her familiar with in advance, but also new, implying that she has gone through all his past agonies with him too.

In his ignorance of the nature of souls he apparently thinks they are subject to death as well as to suffering. So the last irony is that the "novel Agony" is reserved for him, not her. "She and Death" it turns out are old acquaintances, as symbols of mortality and immortality, but since they have no common ground save the moment of passing they simply "Salute" courteously and go their respective ways, "without a Hint" to him of what they are really like or where they have gone. His surprise discovery is that in this friendly meeting it is only he, "the Matter," which has been annihilated. His sentence has been executed not by legal but by verbal machinery. In the triple pun, "And there, the *Matter* ends," the fictive "I" experiences a new death by losing his soul as well as his identity in the depths of despair, the curtain is rung down on the bad dream along with all the legal theatricalities that bodied it forth, and the poem destroys itself in a tour de force. The reader, if any one, suffers shock.

That Dickinson could make a macabre joke out of agony will offend only those who take poetry solemnly. Perhaps it was one mode of rescue, as literal death would have been another, from a pain that was unbearable. Still another kind of escape, into a state of trance, proved most fruitful of all to the maker of poems on pain. She put it succinctly once in prose: "Anguish has but so many throes—then Unconsciousness seals it." Again, as a compact metaphor:

> There is a pain—so utter—
> It swallows substance up—
> Then covers the Abyss with Trance—
> So Memory can step
> Around—across—upon it—
> As one within a Swoon—
> Goes safely—where an open eye—
> Would drop Him—Bone by Bone.

The alternations of substance and abstraction make an intricate structure here. The inner quality of suffering "swallows up" the reality of self and world and turns them into a bottomless "Abyss," which her Lexicon illustrated by quoting the description of pre-Genesis chaos, "Darkness was upon the face of the abyss." To cover this nothingness, pain makes itself concrete in the insubstantiality of "Trance," so that consciousness can step upon it or around it and blot out the memory of it in a kind of living death. Otherwise, if the victim should materialize again, the intensity of the pain would drop him "Bone by Bone." This makes a striking definition of the mind's protection against its own suffering by falling into the blankness of "Swoon," but not a very memorable poem.

Her best poems on the extremity of pain, the kind producing a state of trance, make its quality of spiritual death concrete in terms of physical death and at the same time dramatize it in the ritual of burial. In the first of these, the levels of sinking down to unconsciousness follow step by step the ceremony so familiar in her village world:

> I felt a Funeral, in my Brain,
> And Mourners to and fro
> Kept treading—treading—till it seemed
> That Sense was breaking through—
>
> And when they all were seated,
> A Service, like a Drum—
> Kept beating—beating—till I thought
> My Mind was going numb—
>
> And then I heard them lift a Box
> And creak across my Soul
> With those same Boots of Lead, again,
> Then Space—began to toll,
>
> As all the Heavens were a Bell,
> And Being, but an Ear,
> And I, and Silence, some strange Race
> Wrecked, solitary, here—
>
> And then a Plank in Reason, broke,
> And I dropped down, and down—
> And hit a World, at every Crash,
> And Got through knowing—then—.

The stage lies within the cortex of the brain, and the drama is rendered exclusively in terms of unarticulated sounds, transformed into motions which enact the pantomime through its inexorable progress to extinction.

The subdued step of mourners in the real world became in the first stanza a heavy relentless "treading" to this tortured consciousness, until it feared that "Sense was breaking through." The twofold meanings here, of the mind giving way and of the sensations threatening to quicken again from their comfortable state of numbness, are picked up in the following stanza and the concluding one. When the funeral service began, its incessant droning made the mind at last actually begin "going numb," though with the disquieting echo of a pagan ritual in its beating "Drum." By the time the third stanza is reached, the mind is so dissociated it is now both the extinct life in the coffin and the agonized soul across which the pallbearers creak. "With those same Boots of Lead, again" implies that the experience was reenacted over and over yet simultaneously, with the lead of the coffin grotesquely transferred to the boot soles of the attendants. This same duality of consciousness continues as the procession leaves the church and the funeral knell sounds, announcing the death of the body of agony and at the same time killing the listening spirit. This sound is so cosmic only the most extravagant simile will compass it: "As all the Heavens were a Bell, / And Being, but an Ear." Such a climax has an absolute rightness about it. For the poem has consisted exclusively of a succession of images all auditory and reiterated—treading, beating, creaking. And with this final tolling, the consciousness is "Wrecked, solitary," except for the companioning "Silence," more harrowing than any sounds had been.

For the mind to apprehend beyond the pale of death, even the hallucinatory death of obliterating pain, would be to go beyond the limits of judgment. To avoid this the poem ends with the mind simply giving way, but this too in terms of the last act of burial. Just as the coffin is about to be lowered into the grave, "a Plank in Reason broke," and the persona dropped down through level after level of unconsciousness, hitting a new "World" of extinction "at every Crash." These were the last soundless sounds of agony, as the mind "got through knowing." Being has been swallowed up in trance. Perhaps the only flaw in this poem is that the metaphor of "Funeral" comes near stealing the show. The powerfully dramatized ceremony, with all its ghastly detail, tends to draw the reader's attention away from the spiritual death it was intended to illuminate. That extreme form of mortal pain she likened to "despair" did not need to be named as her theme, to be sure, but its qualities and effects should have been more vividly evoked as the final meaning of the whole sequence of images. Since this was not quite adequately done, there is some danger of the poem being misread as merely the fantasy of a morbid soul imaging its own death, which would certainly diminish its significance.

There are two kinds of death, however, not counting the death of the soul in the theological sense of "despair." One may literally die away from the world, but she never made the mistake of trying to embody her own decease in a serious poem. On the other hand, the world may die away from the perceiving consciousness under stress of pain, and the resulting death to the spirit can be experienced and rendered. Such pain overwhelmed Emily Dickinson during her last years, as death thinned the ranks of her intimate circle and all but extinguished her small world. The cumulative impact of all this brought on a nervous breakdown, which she recorded in almost clinical fashion:

> I saw a great darkness coming and knew no more until late at night. I woke to find Austin and Vinnie and a strange physician bending over me, and supposed I was dying, or had died, all was so kind and hallowed. I had fainted and lain unconscious for the first time in my life. . . . The doctor calls it "revenge of the nerves"; but who but Death wronged them?

Such actual experiences do not produce poems but collapse, as she phrased it in another letter about the same time: "Blow has followed blow, till the wondering terror of the Mind clutches what is left, helpless of an accent." Twenty years earlier she projected her imagined spiritual death from excessive pain in "I felt a Funeral, *in my Brain.*" No specific autobiographical source is needed to explain this poem, for its close similarity to the preceding and following ritual dramas make its meaning unmistakable.

In her most remarkable poem rendering the extinction of consciousness by pain in terms of a funeral, the deftness of her strategy shows just what could be done with this technique. Its three stanzas faintly shadow forth three stages of a familiar ceremony: the formal service, the tread of pallbearers, and the final lowering into a grave. But metaphor is subdued to meaning by subtle controls:

> After great pain, a formal feeling comes—
> The Nerves sit ceremonious, like Tombs—
> The stiff Heart questions was it He, that bore,
> And Yesterday, or Centuries before?
>
> The Feet, mechanical, go round—
> A wooden way
> Of Ground, or Air, or Ought—
> Regardless grown,
> A Quartz contentment, like a stone—
>
> This is the Hour of Lead—
> Remembered, if outlived,
> As Freezing persons, recollect the Snow—
> First—Chill—then Stupor—then the letting go—.

This poem has recently received the explication it deserves, matching its excellence. But its pertinence to this whole group of poems is such as to justify a brief summary of the interpretation here.

"In a literal sense," according to the critic, there is "neither persona nor ritual, and since it describes a state of mind, neither would seem to be necessary." Instead, as befits one who has lost all sense of identity, the various parts of the body are personified as autonomous entities (*the* nerves, *the* heart, *the* feet), belonging to no one and moving through the acts of a meaningless ceremony, lifeless forms enacted in a trance. As a result, attention is centered on the feeling itself and not on the pattern of figures that dramatize it. As the images of a funeral rite subside, two related ones emerge to body forth the victim who is at once a living organism and a frozen form. Both are symbols of crystallization: "Freezing" in the snow, which is neither life nor death but both simultaneously; and "A Quartz contentment, like a stone," for the paradoxical serenity that follows intense suffering. This recalls her envy of the "little Stone," happy because unconscious of the exigencies that afflict mortals, and points forward to the paradox in another poem, "Contented as despair." Such is the "formal feeling" that comes after great pain. It is, ironically, no feeling at all, only numb rigidness existing outside time and space.

In two final poems, her use of "despair" seems to be unmistakably in the direction of the Christian meaning, though her treatment of this theological term is unorthodox to say the least. From the point of view of the poet, the chief problem is that despair is amorphous and needs to be bodied forth in some palpable form, such as the ritual drama she used so successfully, in order to be fully realized. But this may tend to restrict its meaning since, from another point of view, it is a protean condition. It feels somewhat like this and somewhat like that, like none and yet like all. To give shape to this quality she used the technique of throwing up a shower of varied images, the great feat of skill requisite being to make them at once discrete and sequential, capable of coalescing into an unexpected whole.

In one attempt the power of the separate images is undeniable, though the fusion is not quite made:

> It was not Death, for I stood up,
> And all the Dead, lie down—
> It was not Night, for all the Bells
> Put out their Tongues, for Noon.
>
> It was not Frost, for on my Knees
> I felt Siroccos—crawl—
> Not Fire—for just two Marble feet
> Could keep a Chancel, cool—
>
> And yet, it tasted, like them all,
> The Figures I have seen
> Set orderly, for Burial,
> Reminded me, of mine—
>
> As if my life were shaven,
> And fitted to a frame,
> And could not breathe without a key,
> And 'twas like Midnight, some—

When everything that ticked—has stopped—
And Space stares all around—
Or Grisly frosts—first Autumn morns,
Repeal the Beating Ground—

But, most, like Chaos—Stopless—cool—
Without a Chance, or Spar—
Or even a Report of Land—
To justify—Despair.

The opening and closing words, "It was not Death" but it was "Despair," pose the problem and set up the surface dialectic. In between are a series of negations, or mere similes of possibility, each followed by an opposing statement or qualification. Occasionally they are interlocked in series by turning the affirmation of one pair into the thing denied in the next, notably in the second stanza. It becomes immediately apparent, however, that these are not statements at all but figures of speech, and the relations between them are far more poetic than their superficial resemblance to Hegelian logic indicates.

The first sequence begins with an image of the recumbent dead in contrast with her own erect figure, which rules out death as her status even while the quality of it is retained. This is picked up in the third stanza where her feeling of going through a living death recalls the figures of the dead she has seen "Set orderly, for Burial." Out of her local experience she undoubtedly knew about country funerals, where corpses were laid out in the parlor in unrelieved *rigor mortis*, but these are the dead that "lie down." This image is blended with one evoked out of her knowledge of old cathedrals, like Westminster Abbey, with their stone effigies raised up above the horizontal sarcophagi. These are the erect "Figures" of the dead whose cold semblance of life "Reminded me, of mine." This carries back to her own "Marble feet" in the preceding stanza, which are lifeless enough to "keep a Chancel cool," whether buried beneath its floor or standing in some niche nearby. The burial theme also follows over into the fourth stanza, without even a break in the syntax, "As if my life were shaven,/ And fitted to a frame." In this image of death, seemingly nearer to the rural kind she was acquainted with, the body is not being placed in a box for burial, however. It is itself being carpentered into one, "shaven and fitted," and the new "frame" into which the old one of bone and flesh is being transformed is a kind of humble wooden effigy answering to the marble ones of the great. The "key" referred to in this passage may seem somewhat out of place since corpses are sealed in coffins rather than locked. But spirits are locked in bodies, and since coffin and corpse are one here, her vital life "could not breathe without a key" to release it from the body of this despair.

Another set of relations works out from the second half of the opening stanza: "It was not Night, for all the Bells/Put out their Tongues, for Noon."

The brilliance of midday, reinforced by the clangorous sound of bells and their swinging motion, seems the very image of life in contrast to the night of death, but there are overtones of irony in all this. "Tongues," borrowed directly from the folk metaphor for bell clappers, has the inevitable connotation of wagging, and the colloquial idiom "put out" completes the suggestion of brazen mockery of her state. Bells also toll notably for death, which links this with the funeral imagery already pointed out. Though "Noon" is the height of the day's life it is also the beginning of the sun's decline. For this reason it is a recurrent image for the escape out of time in her poetry, as in the conceit of the stopped clock which went out of decimals "into degreeless Noon."

In the present poem she also uses the other end of the clock's cycle for the moment of death and, after denying that her state was one of "Night," returns twelve lines later to admit that it was "like Midnight, some." This is the hour "When everything that ticked—has stopped," with no friendly reassurance from such commonplaces as the pendulum of measured time or the visible objects of a familiar room or landscape. Instead, "Space stares all around" with the glazed eyes of death. Then the scene moves on from the midnight of black despair to the even more blank whiteness of an autumn morning when "Grisly frosts . . . Repeal the Beating Ground." The ticking life that had ceased in the silence of night is reinforced by more powerful phrasing, the pulsing life of earth abrogated by the coming death of winter. The sound effects from the verbal play of "Beating" and "Repeal" make this at last the actual funeral knell so long hinted at. There is also a final link back to the earlier "Frost" that had been denied in line 5 as the true symbol of despair.

The obscurity of this second stanza is symptomatic of the risks inherent in the technique employed for this poem. The reader is left with more to explain than to experience in the unresolved disparity of its images: "not Frost" but "Siroccos," not "Fire" but—whatever it is that is going on in the "Chancel." She seems to have felt the need to clarify, for her only suggested revisions in the manuscript come exactly at this crucial point: "on my Flesh>my Knees." . . . and "just my>just two Marble feet." One can only clutch wildly at meaning. As the poet knelt at the chancel rail, beyond which sacrament and conviction are at white heat, did she feel first cold whiteness, then a hot oppressive wind off the desert, then fire that cooled her feet to marble? The functioning of the Eucharist in relation to "Despair," if such was her intention, never quite comes through. The very obscurity of the rite hinted at in this stanza suggests that she is trying to use despair here in the traditional Christian sense, for Holy Communion is exactly what would be beyond the reach of one who had lost hope in the mercy of God, and any attempt to partake of it would be baffled and confused. This theological doctrine was almost as unavailable to her as the sacrament would be to the lost, and they find only a dim embodiment in this poem.

The spate of images flows on, however, mostly similes. It was none of these—not death or night or noon, not stone effigies or flesh turned to wood, not blank silence whether black or white—"yet, it tasted like them all." Is "tasted" a final effort to bring off the communion metaphor: the sense organs must feed on and incorporate these sensations until substance and experience are one? The next to last image for despair is most harrowing of all, its effect increased by the insistent beat of four accented syllables in succession that fall like hammer blows: "But, most, like Chaos—Stopless—cool—. . . ." By extending measurable time into eternity and familiar locale into staring space, beyond the ordered universe, this image removes the last signs by which suffering man can identify himself as human. The cumulative effect of all this overwhelms the consciousness, but the images refuse to coalesce into a whole. The poem is as chaotic as despair itself, its only form being multiform formlessness. If the harried reader may be allowed one despairing quip, he may express his fear that the method itself as here employed is "stopless." For a final anticlimactic image of shipwreck is added ("Without a . . . Spar—/Or even a Report of Land"), which fails even more to "justify," in the Miltonic sense, all this suffering.

The ultimate problem then, was not to master despair, which she presumably succeeded in doing as a woman when she took the artist's path to peace, but to manage the images evoked by her sensibility so as to transform the experience into great poetry. The same technique used in the preceding attempt was brought under perfect control in her finest poem on despair:

> There's a certain Slant of light,
> Winter Afternoons—
> That oppresses, like the Heft
> Of Cathedral Tunes—
>
> Heavenly Hurt, it gives us—
> We can find no scar,
> But internal difference,
> Where the Meanings, are—
>
> None may teach it—Any—
> 'Tis the Seal Despair—
> An imperial affliction
> Sent us of the Air—
>
> When it comes, the Landscape listens—
> Shadows—hold their breath—
> When it goes, 'tis like the Distance
> On the look of Death—

For more than half a century this poem was placed by her editors under the category of nature. But winter sunlight is simply the over-image of despair, inclosing the center of suffering that is her concern. Grammatically, the antecedent of the neutral "it" whose transformations make up the action of the poem is this "certain Slant" of light, but in figurative meaning "it" is the "Heavenly Hurt." This is a true metaphor, sensation and abstraction fused into one, separable in logic but indistinguishable and even reversible in a poetic sense. The internal experience is not talked about but is realized in a web of images that constitutes the poem's statement, beginning with one drawn from nature, or rather from the firmament above it, and returning to it in the end with a significant change of meaning.

These multiple images exemplifying the protean condition of despair are vividly discrete, but they grow out of each other and into each other with a fitness that creates the intended meaning in shock after shock of recognition. Its amorphous quality is embodied at the outset in "light," a diffused substance that can be apprehended but not grasped. Further, this is a slanting light, as uncertain of source and indirect in impact as the feeling of despair often is. Finally, it is that pale light of "Winter Afternoons," when both the day and the year seem to be going down to death, the seasonal opposite of summer which symbolized for her the fullness and joy of living. It is when he feels winter in his soul, one remembers, that Melville's Ishmael begins his exploration of the meaning of despair. Next, by the shift of simile, this desolation becomes "like the Heft/Of Cathedral Tunes." The nebulous has now been made palpable, by converting light waves into sound waves whose weight can be felt by the whole body. The strong provincialism, "Heft" (smoothed away to "Weight" by former editors), carries both the meaning of ponderousness and the great effort of heaving in order to test it, according to her Lexicon. This homely word also clashes effectively with the grand ring of "Cathedral Tunes," those produced by carillon offering the richest possibilities of meaning. Since this music "oppresses," the connotation of funereal is added to the heavy resonance of all pealing bells. And since the double meaning of "Heft" carries through, despair is likened to both the weight of these sounds on the spirit and the straining to lift the imponderable tonnage of cast bronze.

The religious note on which the prelude ends, "Cathedral Tunes," is echoed in the language of the central stanzas. In its ambiguousness "Heavenly Hurt" could refer to the pain of paradisiac ecstasy, but more immediately this seems to be an adjective of agency, from heaven, rather than an attributive one. The hurt is inflicted from above, "Sent us of the Air," like the "Slant of light" that is its antecedent. In this context that the natural image takes on a new meaning, again with the aid of her Lexicon which gives only one meaning for "slant" as a noun, "an oblique reflection or gibe." It is then a mocking light, like the heavenly hurt that comes from the sudden instinctive awareness of man's lot since the Fall, doomed to mortality and irremediable suffering. This is indeed despair, though not in the theological sense unless Redemption is denied also. As Gerard Manley

Hopkins phrases it in "Spring and Fall," for the young life there coming to a similar realization, "It is the blight man was born for."

Because of this it is beyond human correction, "None may teach it— Any." Though it penetrates it leaves "no scar," as an outward sign of healing, nor any internal wound that can be located and alleviated. What it leaves is "internal difference," the mark of all significant "Meanings." When the psyche is once stricken with the pain of such knowledge it can never be the same again. The change is final and irrevocable, sealed. The biblical sign by which God claims man for his own has been shown in the poems of heavenly bridal to be a "Seal," the ring by which the beloved is married into immortal life. But to be redeemed one must first be mortal, and be made conscious of one's mortality. The initial and overwhelming impact of this can lead to a state of hopelessness, unaware that the "Seal Despair" might be the reverse side of the seal of ecstasy. So, when first stamped on the consciousness it is an "affliction." But it is also "imperial . . . Sent us of the Air," the heavenly kingdom where God sits enthroned, and from the same source can come Redemption, though not in this poem.

By an easy transition from one insubstantial image to another, "Air" back to "a certain Slant of light," the concluding stanza returns to the surface level of the winter afternoon. As the sun drops toward the horizon just before setting, "the Landscape listens" in apprehension that the very light which makes it exist as a landscape is about to be extinguished; "Shadows," which are about to run out to infinity in length and merge with each other in breadth until all is shadow, "hold their breath." This is the effect created by the slanting light "When it comes." Of course no such things happen in nature, and it would be pathetic fallacy to pretend they did. The light does not inflict this suffering nor is the landscape the victim. Instead, these are just images of despair.

Similar figures are used in two other poems. In one the declining motion of the sun seems just a symbol of the inexorability of death:

> Presentiment—is that long Shadow—on the Lawn—
> Indicative that Suns go down—
>
> The Notice to the startled Grass
> That Darkness—is about to pass—.

But in relation to the whole body of her poetry such apprehensiveness of the coming of "Darkness," like a dreaded king whose approach has already been heralded, suggests that this "Presentiment" is one of unbearable pain. In the other poem it is so named. When lives are assailed by little anguish they merely "fret," she says, but when threatened with "Avalanches . . . they'll slant,"

> Straighten—look cautious for their Breath—
> But make no syllable—like Death—.

So with the slant of light "When it goes," as the sun finally sets and darkness covers all, " 'tis like the Distance/On the look of Death." Such is the difference between the coming of despair and the aftermath of extinction. The latter calls up an image of the staring eyes of the dead, the awful "Distance" between life and death, and, as the only relief in sight, the distance between the poet and her experience that has made this sure control of form and language possible. The final and complete desolation of the landscape is the precise equivalent of that "internal difference" which the action of the poem has brought about.

Such is the mortal view of despair, the quality and effects of which are the exclusive theme of this poem. Yet certain ambivalent phrases in it, like "Heavenly Hurt" and the great "Seal" of God (which by implication, at least, has a reverse side), seem related to the curious conjoining of ecstasy and despair that pervades much of her writing. In one poem it is explicit. The moment of ecstasy, given then withdrawn, is rendered in a series of paradoxes culminating in the lines:

> A perfect—paralyzing Bliss—
> Contented as Despair—.

This is strikingly similar to Andrew Marvell's conjunction of joy and pain in "The Definition of Love." Seeking to discriminate a love so rare that mortal hope could never reach it on "tinsel wing," he concludes:

> Magnanimous Despair alone
> Could show me so divine a thing.

Whether she was acquainted with this poem is not known but it is analogous to several of her own, in its shock imagery and the technique of juggled ambiguities more than in theme. For when she sought heavenly fulfillment for earthly denial it was directly through biblical metaphor, without the mediating convention of the cult of platonic love. Fortunately for her originality, she derives as an artist from the Calvinism of New England rather than from the tradition of metaphysical poetry.

For a final exploration of dual meaning, one may return to that ambiguous *"certain* Slant of light" which pierced her from above with "an imperial affliction." It calls to mind the "waylaying Light" that struck her once like lightning, and brought the heavenly "gleam" with which the preceding chapter on "Ecstasy" concluded. It is notable that she used exactly the same metaphor in another poem to describe a blistering pain, that came not once but continually and "burned Me—in the Night":

> It struck me—every Day—
> The Lightning was as new
> As if the Cloud that instant slit
> And let the Fire through—.

By spiritual insight she had discovered the close relation between human despair and the yearning for heavenly ecstasy, just as a kind of primitive wisdom had led her back to the juncture of love and death in the instinctual world. But these were only motions of the heart, up and down.

Always thrusting itself between was the conscious mind, that flickering identity that tries to give meaning to the bafflingly familiar pilgrimage from cradle to grave by defining, discriminating, questioning. This is what saves her from the sentimentalism that would have resulted had she adopted either extreme of ecstasy or despair as her whole view. Instead, she created her poems out of the tensions that issue from the clash of such powerful opposites. Further, she declined the gambit of an easy escape into paradox, for she never made an exact equation between love and death, ecstasy and despair. In her poetry their relations are much more complex: they form interlocking and reversible sequences. What gives this especial novelty is the direction of her emphasis, which is the opposite of that taken by her New England predecessors in the orthodox handling of these ambiguities. For example, in place of the Puritan view that earthly suffering is the ordained path to a heavenly reward of bliss, she makes the momentary glimpse of ecstasy both measure and cause of the despair that is the essence of the human condition. As she wrote in a late stanza:

> The joy that has no stem nor core,
> Nor seed that we can sow,
> Is edible to longing,
> But ablative to show.

To be human is to yearn for the heavenly ecstasy we are deprived of on earth, "ablative" being the Latin term for the case of deprivation. And so with the subtle interrelations of love and death. When her friend Higginson lost his wife she said in her letter of consolation: "Do not try to be saved—but let Redemption find you—as it certainly will—Love is its own rescue, for we—at our supremest, are but its trembling Emblems." These themes, fused from polar opposites, permeate her writings in prose and verse.

Her absolute loyalty to mind was the instrument by which she achieved this balance and maneuvered her emotions into forms. But she rarely lost sight of the fact that it was merely a technique of control, not the source of her poems. It is true that in her later years she indulged her penchant for aphorism in a number of verses that tend to run off into sheer intellectualism, even as some of her earliest efforts had been pure expressions of personal sentiment. Her best poems, however, present their themes in the full context of intellect and feeling, concerned not with exploiting either as such but with rendering the experiences that fuse them both. An eminent critic has put this succinctly: "Unlike her contemporaries, she never succumbed to her ideas, to easy solutions, to private desires . . . ; like Donne, she *perceives abstraction and thinks sensation*." And he makes this the basis for a high claim to distinction, that she was probably the only Anglo-American poet of her century who achieved a fusion of sensibility and thought, attaining "a mastery over experience by facing its utmost implications."

Inevitably, her search for meaning within the self, as well as in the nonself outside, led to a search for rediscovery of the maker of these selves. A poem written in midcareer, of small intrinsic worth, has considerable interest as a statement of her progressive concern with nature, man, and God. At first she thought that "nature" was a sufficient subject for her poetry, she says, until "Human nature" came in and absorbed the other "As Firmament a Flame"; then, when she had just begun her exploration of that, "There added the Divine." All of her major themes are listed here in order: the outer world and the inner, the other world and, by implication at least, the paradise of art as the nearest she could come to attaining the "Divine." As a schoolgirl she had explained her inability to make peace with God because "the world holds a predominant place in my affections." Her withdrawal from society after maturity merely changed the terms of her loyalty, first to external nature then to the interior world of the self. As a poet she concluded that this last was the only reality she could know. It was also, she discovered, her best instrument for perceiving the processes of time and for conceiving the stasis of eternity, so that the reader today sees the ultimate purpose of all her explorations as religious in the profoundest sense of that term. And she would have rejoiced in the confirmation of her world view by modern thinkers, as in the recent definition of religion by an eminent scientist as "a search for the relation between human desire and purpose on the one hand and cosmic change and indifference on the other."

In contrast with the orthodoxy of her own day this approach could only seem heretical, however, which explains her tendency to discountenance herself as a religious person, as in her terse self-portrait late in life, "I am but a Pagan." The letter containing this phrase encloses a poem which furnishes the title for this section and brings it to a fitting conclusion:

> Of God we ask one favor,
> That we may be forgiven—
> For what, he is presumed to know—
> The Crime, from us, is hidden—
> Immured the whole of Life
> Within a magic Prison
> We reprimand the Happiness
> That too competes with Heaven.

Her pained sense of estrangement from the religion of her fathers lingered to the end, but so did the integrity that gave her courage to go her own way, to continue her search for heaven through poetry rather than through a theology she could not accept. This debate frames her perfect image for the earthly paradise where she wrestled with her angel. The mind and heart, the consciousness, the self, the soul—whatever word one wishes—

this was the "Magic Prison" she always explored in her poetry. "Immured the whole of Life" within its walls she accepted the mortal lot as inescapable, trapped in time and wavering perpetually between doubt and belief in another life beyond. There she dedicated herself to creating the one thing of absolute value that, in her view, the human being is capable of. It goes under the rather inadequate name of religion, or art, the vision that comes with man's utmost reach towards truth and beauty. Its essence is longing, with ecstasy at one end and pain at the other, the leap of the heart and the despair of the mind.

Emily Dickinson

Margaret Homans

Dickinson thought of herself not just as a poet but as a woman poet. The first and most obvious evidence for this statement is that she searched for models among the famous women writers of her day, admiring George Eliot, the Brontës, and Elizabeth Barrett Browning in particular. This interest was more personal or biographical than it was literary, but this indicates no disparagement, since her poetry was scarcely influenced by literary men, either. In her letters she mourns the deaths of these great women as vehemently as she admires their work. She inquired insistently after the prospects for a biography of George Eliot in an exchange of letters with the Boston publisher Thomas Niles in April 1882. In March 1883 Niles sent her Mathilda Blind's *Life of George Eliot*, and in 1885 she received the first volume of Cross's *Life* from her literary correspondent Thomas Wentworth Higginson. After reading Blind's biography she commented, "A Doom of Fruit without the Bloom, like the Niger Fig," which echoes an earlier comment, made shortly after Eliot's death, indicating a range of biographical affinities between the two women:

> Now, *my* George Eliot. The gift of belief which her greatness denied her, I trust she receives in the childhood of the kingdom of heaven. As childhood is earth's confiding time, perhaps having no childhood, she lost her way to the early trust, and no later came. [*The Letters of Emily Dickinson*, ed. Thomas H. Johnson and Theodora Ward (Cambridge: The Belknap Press of Harvard University Press, 1958), III, 700. Quotations from *Letters* are cited hereafter as *L*, followed by volume and page, and by date, where appropriate. Quotations from Dickinson's poems are from *The Poems of Emily Dickinson*, ed. Thomas H. Johnson (Cambridge: The

Belknap Press of Harvard University Press, 1955), cited as P followed by the poem number assigned by Johnson.]

She possessed portraits of Mrs. Browning and was even sent a picture of her grave, testifying to her friend's knowledge of her interest. She found A. Mary F. Robinson's biography of Emily Brontë "more electric far than anything since 'Jane Eyre' " (L, III, 775). Again alluding not to Brontë's own work but to what was written about her—Charlotte Brontë's 1850 Biographical Notice—Dickinson refers to Brontë as a person more than as a writer in the following comparison with her friend Mrs. Holland: she was

> humbled with wonder at your self-forgetting, . . . Reminded again
> of gigantic Emily Brontë, of whom her Charlotte said "Full of ruth
> for others, on herself she had no mercy."
>
> (L, III, 721)

In these comments she extends her sympathies to these women as suffering human beings, not as women, but she also considers them as women, and is aware of special difficulties that were perhaps similar to hers.

> That Mrs. Browning fainted, we need not read *Aurora Leigh* to
> know, when she lived with her English aunt; and George Sand
> "must make no noise in her grandmother's bedroom." Poor children! Women, now, queens, now!
>
> (L, II, 376)

She also uses womanhood specifically as a literary classification. In 1871 she wrote to Higginson, "Mrs Hunt's Poems are stronger than any written by Women since Mrs—Browning, with the exception of Mrs Lewes" (L, II, 491). She must be making a special point in referring to George Eliot as Mrs. Lewes and in using a dash to emphasize Elizabeth Barrett's marriage, but it is unclear whether this is a private reference to her metaphor of wife and bride for poetic power, or whether she is thinking of the difference marriage might make to a woman writer. In 1870 she held a curious exchange with Higginson about another married woman poet.

> You told me of Mrs Lowell's Poems.
>   Would you tell me where I could find them or are they not for
> sight?
>
> (L, II, 480)

Maria White Lowell's poems were published in 1855, but Higginson had apparently been referring to her poems in a metaphoric sense, because in her next letter Dickinson says

> You told me Mrs Lowell was Mr Lowell's "inspiration" What is
> inspiration?
>
> (L, II, 481)

Dickinson is incensed that, when she has a chance to read a woman's poetry, or, just as good, to learn of another woman poet as private as herself, Higginson, a self-proclaimed champion of women's rights, asks her to consider the poetess in her more acceptably feminine role as her husband's muse.

That Dickinson can compare reading Emily Brontë's life with reading *Jane Eyre* indicates that she groups real and fictive biographies under the category of exemplary lives. When she turns from the lives to the works of these women writers, it is usually without reference to gender. Her comments on Eliot and Emily Brontë suggest affinities between their work and aspects of her own work that seem to have nothing to do with femininity. She characterizes Eliot as "she who Experienced Eternity in Time" (*L,* III, 689).

> "What do I think of *Middlemarch?*" What do I think of glory-except that in a few instances this "mortal has already put on immortality."
>
> George Eliot is one. The mysteries of human nature surpass the "mysteries of redemption," for the infinite we only suppose, while we see the finite.
>
> > (*L,* II, 506)

Dickinson is perhaps expressing her surprise and delight that a novel can do what she expects of poetry; in any case it is Eliot's encompassing mind that she is considering, and not "Mrs Lewes." Several very late letters quote one "marvelous" stanza from Brontë's "No coward soul is mine," each time subsuming it to the expression of her own sentiment (*L,* III, 802-3, 844, 848). One of these quotations includes an illuminating misinterpretation. Writing in 1883 of the "sorrow of so many years" brought by the deaths of so many beloved friends and relatives, she says "As Emily Bronte to her Maker, I write to my Lost 'Every Existence would exist in thee—' " (*L,* III, 802–3). Dickinson must have known that Brontë was referring not to "her Maker" but to a more personally defined deity, a conception much closer to Dickinson's own than Dickinson seems willing to acknowledge. She treats Brontë the poet as a rival and distances her, while at the same moment welcoming an affinity on the personal level.

Just as Dickinson compartmentalized her own interest in women writers, studies of her have tended to consider her femininity at the level of biography and to leave her femininity out of critical readings of her poems. Even though she seems to have been more openly conscious than Dorothy Wordsworth or Emily Brontë about the difficulties of being a woman and a poet, any treatment of her specifically as a woman poet runs the risk of being either confining or tangential, because she has too large and brilliant a body of poetry to be adequately interpreted from any single perspective. However, this chapter will argue that Dickinson derives her unique power from her particular way of understanding her femininity, and that her work is as complex and profuse as it is, at least in part, because she is able to put behind her problems of identity that make Dorothy and Brontë linger over the same themes and issues in poem after poem. For example, in the letter discussed above in which she quotes from Brontë, she telescopes Brontë's long and arduous struggle to center an external poetic power within herself, and although this telescoping may be unfair, it suggests what Dickinson views as a crucial difference between Brontë's concept of language and her own: for Brontë linguistic power is a single entity, which may or may not be possessed, but Dickinson goes on in the rest of the letter to sketch obliquely her concept of language's doubleness. The most recent and stunning of those deaths, that of her eight-year-old nephew Gilbert, has broken language into its components. Naming is difficult and self-conscious:

> Sweet Sister.
> Was that what I used to call you?
>
> . . . .
>
> The Physician says I have "Nervous prostration."
> Possibly I have—I do not know the Names of Sickness.

Her disease is unnameable because it is a disease of referents lost through the recent deaths. Gilbert's last words—" 'Open the Door, open the Door, they are waiting for me' "—have set her thinking about what is for her an ultimately missing referent, where just previously she has supplied one for Brontë. "*Who* were waiting for him, all we possess we would give to know. . . . All this and more, though *is* there more? More than Love and Death? Then tell me it's name!" She splits language to find genuine mysteries, and she finds in language's doubleness, paradoxically, a way around the hierarchizing dualism that impedes Dorothy Wordsworth and Brontë.

In a letter to her friend Abiah Root written when she was nineteen, Dickinson tells an extravagant and amusing story about a cold, and then, in a gesture that distinguishes artist from anecdotist, she exposes her fictive strategy:

> Now my dear friend, let me tell you that these last thoughts are fictions—vain imaginations to lead astray foolish young women. They are flowers of speech, they both *make*, and *tell* deliberate falsehoods, avoid them as the snake, and turn aside as from the *Bottle* snake, and I dont *think* you will be harmed.
>
> (*L*, I, 88; 29 Jan. 1850)

Although this letter dates from well before Dickinson's first serious poetry, such self-consciousness establishes this and related passages as the proper place to begin an investigation of her sense of identity as a writer and as a woman. The writer here is logically, though never overtly, associated with the snake, since she is the inventor of the "vain imaginations," and in a postscript she refers to her story about the cold as "mistakes" and "sin." Her interlocutor, so innocent that she must be told that the story is a fiction, plays Eve to Dickinson's Satan. At the end of the passage the writer renounces her guise as a fiction-maker and turns abruptly to what she announces to be her sincerer feelings. Searching for a better topic she says, "Oh dear I dont know *what* it is! Love for the absent dont *sound* like it, but try it, and see how it goes." She signs the letter "Your very sincere, and *wicked* friend," as if to demarcate, retrospectively, two separable styles of address and of self.

These are sins in jest, of course, but the reader is provoked to take this language seriously because of the context in which it occurs. In a letter to her friend and former teacher Jane Humphrey, written only six days earlier, she uses the same language to describe her own life as genuinely wicked. Charitable works would provide an opportunity "for turning my back to this very sinful, and wicked world. Somehow or other I incline to other things—and Satan covers them up with flowers, and I reach out to pick them" (*L*, I, 82; 23 Jan. 1850). The letter to Abiah simply transfers the metaphor of flowers and falsehood to a less serious tenor. The origin of this fatal view of herself is her failure to become converted to the evangelical Christianity that most of her friends were then embracing. She herself views it as a failure: in the sad discussions of religion of this period and earlier she never expresses a doubt that Christianity has a patent on goodness and that in not accepting Christ it is she who is in the wrong. In 1846 she had, from her report, experienced a temporary conversion, and in describing its aftermath she uses the unequivocal language of true and false: "I had rambled too far to return & ever since my heart has been growing harder & more distant from the truth" (*L*, I, 31; 28 March 1846). If truth is a place, then her dislocation from it repeats the Fall:

> I think of the perfect happiness I experienced while I felt I was an heir of heaven as of a delightful dream, out of which the Evil one bid me wake & again return to the world & its pleasures. Would that I had not listened to his winning words! . . . I determined to devote my whole life to [God's] service & desired that all might taste of the stream of living water from which I cooled my thirst. But the world allured me & in an unguarded moment I listened to her syren voice.
>
> (*L*, I, 30)

Her transfer of religious metaphor to fiction-making later on is not fortuitous. Religious and literary concerns converge at the idea of truth. In the passage above, both orthodoxy and her fall are portrayed as fictive: one was a delightful dream, the other the product of winning words and a siren voice. Her insistence in these religious passages that there is such a thing as the truth may be a defense against her growing knowledge that there is no absolute truth or literal meaning. The Bible is said to be a true text, yet her own experience shows her how easily figurative language can deceive, and the Bible is figurative. That the satanic storyteller in the letter about the cold is a guise does not necessarily make the contrasting sincerity genuine. If she can speak in one invented style, all forms of address may be fictive. When she writes to her more religious friends, her apparently genuine self-depreciation may be as fictive as the most extravagant of her announced fantasies. She is writing to please her readers, and she may also be convinced of her own sincerity, writing to please herself as well. But she depicts such a worldy sinner and such a radical fall that it is hard to believe that she did not see, or even intend, the melodrama. The modern reader prefers to think that she saw the religious fervour of her day as a delusion, and in retrospect it is easy to doubt that she would ever have considered entrusting her mental faculties to the keeping of her saviour. But a parodic element is coextensive with whatever sincere religious sorrow she expresses; and to mean two opposing things at the same time would very likely debase the writer's faith in the possibility of a literal truth, whether secular or Christian.

A few months prior to the letter in which she invokes the language of the Fall, she jokingly identifies herself with Eve on the grounds that there is no account of her death in the Bible, and the Bible must be taken at its word. "I have lately come to the conclusion that I am Eve, alias Mrs. Adam. You know there is no account of her death in the Bible, and why am I not Eve?" (*L*, I, 24; 12 Jan. 1846). This is the kind of remark that is entirely parodic and entirely serious at once. If the Bible is the source of the truth, then she is indeed Eve, because she has picked Satan's flowers and fallen from an Eden of perfect belief. In the letter about the cold she transforms herself from tempted into tempter. There, Abiah is an innocent Eve, and Dickinson as the writer of fictions is implicitly identified as the tempter. In the letter to Jane Humphrey of the same week, excerpted above, in which the writer pictures herself as led astray by Satan, she also identifies herself as the tempter: "you are out of the way of temptation—and out of the way of the tempter—I did'nt mean to make you wicked—but I was—and am—and shall be—and I was with you so much that I could'nt help contaminate" (*L*, I, 83). Again there is a note of parody, even though the tone of the whole letter is sincerely pained: "I was—and am—and shall be" makes her wickedness as immutable as God's divinity. It disturbs her to find that the fictions she delights in are indistinguishable from the words of the "Evil one," in that she is the speaker of both, and they are equidistant from the truth. Implicitly her own fanciful words led her astray: she is self-tempted. The difference between Eve and Satan is enormous, but that she moves between the two as metaphors for herself reminds the reader that Eve became Satan's accomplice and is a tempter herself—both tempted and temptor.

Later in the same letter she speaks of her angry impatience to see Jane and again condemns herself. "Is it wicked to talk so Jane—what *can* I say that isn't? Out of a wicked heart cometh wicked words." Though hating the intervening time may be reprehensible, her friendship, the source of that animosity, is not. The wickedness may refer instead to the vivid metaphor with which she describes her impatience, just previously: "Eight weeks with their bony fingers still poking me away—how I *hate* them—and would love to do them harm! Is it wicked to talk so" (*L*, I, 83). The danger of fictions, here or in the story about the cold, is that they tempt her to say things that she does not literally mean, but which will be read literally by others. Such talk is "wicked" only if those vividly personified weeks are really animate, but a vocabulary of hate leaves corrupting traces in the minds of writer and reader. Furthermore, the use of metaphor may itself be wicked, since orthodoxy might call fiction a falsehood.

It must have made a considerable difference to one's sense of self to have been a girl instead of a boy growing up in a context in which biblical history was the dominant metaphorical framework in which human activity was viewed. Even if Dickinson's Puritan heritage did not plentifully reinforce the cultural prejudice that, if we are all sinners, women are a little more sinful than men, to read Genesis (and Milton) and see oneself in Eve rather than in Adam would lead to an entirely different sense of self in relation to language. Emerson's attack on orthodoxy, if that might have furnished the young Dickinson with support for her own independent views, only strengthens the identification of poetic language with a masculine tradition. By insisting on the proximity between poetic speech and the divine Word in "The Poet," Emerson makes poetry as masculine a province as does Coleridge with his inheritance of the "infinite I AM, despite other differences in their theories of poetry. Emerson invokes the tradition that Adam was the first and best speaker when he says that the poet is "the Namer or Language-maker," who gives to every thing "its own name and not another's. . . . The poets made all the words." Dorothy Wordsworth may have been discouraged from writing poetry in part by the appropriation of poetic language by those who can consider themselves the inheritors of a masculine divinity. However unlike the God of orthodoxy Emerson's powers of divinity may be, he retains the masculinity of the verbal tradition. Eve's words are secondary and stray from the truth. Because she learns Adam's language rather than inventing it with him (Adam having named the living creatures before Eve's creation), she can learn another as well, and she learns Satan's. Satan teaches her to doubt the literal truth of the language that God and Adam share, and to interpret and demystify God's prohibition about the tree of the knowledge of good and evil. Wrong though she is to take the fruit, she proves God's words to be not literally true, because it is not, in fact, the case that "in the day that thou eatest thereof thou shalt surely die." Satan's words are no less accurate than God's: her eyes are opened, as he promises, and she learns good and evil. It is Eve's discovery that both God and Satan are fictive speakers, and that no discourse is literally true. Adam becomes the traditional symbol for literal language in which words are synonymous with meaning, but Eve is the first to question that synonymity, the first critic, the mother of irony. It is in this sense that she is similar to Satan, and in making tempter and tempted synonymous Dickinson is recognizing this aspect of her inheritance from Eve. When she talks about wickedness, then, in the context of fiction or of religion, what she fears is not the conventional notion of sin, but rather the figurativeness of language that allows even the most sincere speech to be a fiction among other fictions.

When male Romantic writers identify themselves with Satan it is in order to annex the energy of his revolt against a bland orthodoxy. In *Paradise Lost*, by the time Satan is instructing Eve in the ways of deceptive speech nothing admirable remains, but it is this aspect of Satan's history that Dickinson invokes, an entirely different paradigm from that provided by his earlier career.

An enormous change takes place in Dickinson's tone concerning tempters between the two letters of January 1850 and a letter of April of the same year. Writing again to Jane Humphrey, she extols, as she has before, the "marvellous change" that belief brings to those around her. But when she turns to her own doings, she suggests for the first time that she may be as justified as the orthodox believers. "I have dared to do strange things—bold things, and have asked no advice from any—I have heeded beautiful tempters, yet do not think I am wrong" (*L*, I, 95; 3 Apr. 1850). Whatever her belief is, she views it as a center of truth rather than as a deviation. Or rather she uses the metaphor of religious belief without any worry that she is infecting orthodoxy by pairing it with "tempters." "I hope belief is not wicked, and assurance, and perfect trust— . . . I hope human nature has truth in it—Oh I pray it may not deceive—confide—cherish, have a great faith in."

Between January and April, Dickinson wrote her first (extant) poem— a valentine addressed to a friend, dated March 4—and a prose valentine published in the Amherst College paper, *The Indicator*, in February. The prose valentine's exuberant effect comes from its deliberate word consciousness. It revels in language, using many words where one would suffice, as if the lethal fictiveness of language had become a matter of delight. "Sir, I desire an interview. . . . And not to *see* merely, but a chat, sir, or a tete-a-tete, a confab, a mingling of opposite minds is what I propose to have" (*L*, I, 92). Those "beautiful tempters" might be words themselves, like Whitman's "dumb, beautiful ministers," so that her use of the word "tempter" might itself be the first evidence of her own "marvellous change:" one word with two happily opposite meanings. The extensiveness of her language, which both multiplies language and elevates the speaker into "Judith the heroine of the Apocrypha, and you the orator of Ephesus," is figurative speech.

> That's what they call a metaphor in our country. Don't be afraid
> of it, sir, it won't bite. If it was my *Carlo* now! The Dog is the

noblest work of Art, sir. I may safely say the noblest—his mistress's rights he doth defend—although it bring him to his end—although to death it doth him send!

This kind of fanciful language is exactly that which she told Abiah jokingly to "avoid . . . as the snake;" the directive not to fear its bite might be better directed at herself than at the "sir." The passage in effect frees her, by parodying it, from the connection she had created between falsehood in language and real "wickedness." The vehicle of this parody is the contrast between harmless language and the bite of a real dog, but the last sentence in the passage renders the dog fictive, too. Because the dog dissolves into a nursery rhyme, there is no difference, at the level of the letter, between a metaphoric bite and a "real" one. This glimpse of the nonreferentiality of language has a momentary liberating effect, regardless of whether or not she would subscribe to the theories of deconstructive criticism. The biblical names she adopts remind the reader that her identification with Eve, earlier, both in play and in earnest, depended on a literal reading of the Bible. If orthodoxy depends on literal reading, then this is a declaration of freedom from orthodoxy, and from her notion that she must define herself as an exile from orthodoxy, either as the fallen Eve, as Satan, or as both.

The virtue of this provisional freedom from referentiality is that it enables her to use metaphoric language without anxiety. In the letter about the cold, fictions were dangerous only figuratively. Fictions, momentarily personified, tell falsehoods but are not synonymous with them, and she advises Abiah to avoid fictions "as the snake." In the April letter she uses metaphoric language to describe her special "truth," that belief that has resulted from heeding "beautiful tempters," showing how far she has advanced from her belief that metaphor and truth were incompatible:

> What do you weave from all these threads, for I know you hav'nt been idle the while I've been speaking to you, bring it nearer the window, and I will see, it's all wrong unless it has one gold thread in it, a long, big shining fibre which hides the others—and which will fade away into Heaven while you hold it, and from there come back to me.

(L, I, 95)

Never before has she found an explicit metaphor to be adequate for the expression of heartfelt concerns. She emphasizes its status as metaphor by privileging the signifier, asking her reader to believe that the golden fibre is a tangible and visible object as well as a verbal figure. At the same time, the image she chooses is a neat transformation of her earlier metaphor for metaphor. The "long, big shing fibre" must be art's redeemed version of the snake, serpentine but crafted and beautiful, issuing from and returning to the artist rather than invading her integrity.

The snakes in the letter about the cold belong to a sequence of images of the Fall, and take their significance from this association with wickedness and with questioning literal truth. An equally traditional interpretation would be to read them as phallic images, related to but distinct from satanic imagery. As a personal expression, the passage may or may not be about sexual fears, but what is important is that the text engages the idea of masculinity as a literary term. That Dickinson combines these two sets of significations is already an interpretive gesture. For wickedness and temptation to be characterized as masculine presents an alternative to or defense against the identification of Eve with Satan that also lurks in the passage. Instead of reading her own words as vain falsehoods, as when she says, "Out of a wicked heart cometh wicked words," identifying falsehood with masculinity would allow her to see it as alien and therefore not a reflection on herself. Her flights of fancy would be proper extravagances: moments when she borrows a language not her own. (This would hardly be a helpful paradigm for her poetic vocation, and is not long retained.)

At the same time that she identifies lies as masculine, she also sees religious orthodoxy as masculine. In the early letters about religion she limits herself to a choice between her saviour and "the world," but each alternative is equally alien to her own identity, if she characterizes them both as masculine. For the girls in her adolescent circle, "loving Christ" clearly had romantic overtones. Religion was the one permissible romance, and provided a sanctioned outlet for feelings otherwise suppressed. She loses female friends to Christ as she later loses them to husbands. Wishing she could console Jane Humphrey for the loss of her father she says, "She has the 'Great Spirit' tho', and perhaps, she does'nt need me" (*L*, I, 100). A long passage about marriage in a letter to Sue Gilbert, the future wife of Dickinson's brother Austin, begins by using marriage as a metaphor for religion and turns imperceptibly to its major subject by transforming the vehicle into a new tenor. Walking with Sue's sister Mattie, we "wished for you, and Heaven. You did not come, Darling, but a bit of Heaven did, or so it *seemed* to us, as we walked side by side and wondered if that great blessedness which may be our's sometime, is granted now, to some" (*L*, I, 209; early June 1852). This blessedness, so far, seems to refer to a religious state of grace, but the passage continues, without a break:

> Those unions, my dear Susie, by which two lives are one, this sweet and strange adoption wherein we can but look, and are not yet admitted, how it can fill the heart, and make it gang wildly beating, how it will take *us* one day, and make us all it's own, and we shall not run away from it, but lie still and be happy!

By the end of the sentence it is clear that the subject is marriage, but it is impossible to say where the transition occurs. "It" renders all mysteries equivalent. The next paragraph is explicitly about marriage, but it uses language drawn from orthodoxy. The terms of secular romance and marriage include a sacrifice of autonomy, as does, by analogy, "loving Christ:"

I was almost inclined to yeild to the claims of He who is greater than I. . . . I hope the golden opportunity is not far hence when my heart will willingly yield itself to Christ, . . .

I know that I ought now to give myself away to God & spend the springtime of life in his service.

(*L*, I, 28, 31)

This sacrifice of autonomy goes far to explain Dickinson's resistance both to marriage and to orthodox religion.

Dickinson's way of characterizing many external things as masculine—truth and falsehood, the world and its renunciation—illustrates a mind defining its own interior operations as feminine. It is also typical of a rhetorical pattern, prevalent throughout her work and not just at this early period, of rendering equivalencies from polarities. Her freedom from literal meaning originates in her sense of femininity, from her identification with Eve, and it permits her a special use of irony to draw disparate meanings from a single term. This pattern is not the same as a satanic equivalency of good and evil, even though Eve and the Tempter are closely related. If it verges on the satanic, it is only because Dickinson pursues language's own logic to that point. It is a question more of tonal than of moral values, and the manipulation of tone readily permits such divergent readings. One case in point is the way in which an apparently transparent poem invites two mutually exclusive readings. Published anonymously in 1878, Dickinson's "Success is counted sweetest" (P 67) was taken to be the work of Emerson. Slipped in to the volume of poetry Emerson published in 1876, or read in the context of the later essays, it might well be taken as a straightforward account of a pessimistic view of the doctrine of compensation. Read as early Dickinson, the poem is surely a bitter parody both of orthodox thinking and of the principle of compensation that the Emersonian reading would endorse.

> Not one of all the purple Host
> Who took the Flag today
> Can tell the definition
> So clear of Victory
>
> As he defeated—dying—
> On whose forbidden ear
> The distant strains of triumph
> Burst agonized and clear!

By compensation Emerson means a tendency in nature for all oppositions to balance out: losses are compensated for here on earth, not in heaven. In this context, the soldier is compensated for his dying by a gain in understanding. But Dickinson may be undermining the poem's ostensible moral as she utters it: "forbidden ear" suggests not just that the soldier is dying as he hears the "distant strains of triumph" but rather that he cannot hear them at all and that with his death he has purchased nothing whatsoever. The poem suggests that where Emerson would find a balance of price and purchase, Dickinson finds an equivalence of valuelessness. That the attribution of this poem could even today be mistaken is a measure of one of the challenges of reading Dickinson: it is often very difficult to know when she is being ironic and when we are to take her at her word, and often she seems to have contrived this difficulty. To speak of opposing readings of the same poem is in itself risky with Dickinson, because the poems seldom permit such comforting distinctions. But the difference between these two readings is characteristic of Dickinson's way of treating oppositeness. The poem makes its critique of an idea about oppositions, compensation, by entertaining two irreconcilable readings. It is also characteristic of a major disagreement between Dickinson and Emerson: Emerson begins with polarities and works toward reconciling them, but Dickinson works toward undermining the whole concept of oppositeness.

The language Dickinson uses to describe her idea of heaven is often the same as the language she uses to satirize the heaven of orthodoxy, so that there is only a difference of tone between heaven and one version of hell.

> "Heaven"—is what I cannot reach!
> The Apple on the Tree—
> Provided it do hopeless—hang—
> That—"Heaven" is—to Me!
>
> (P 239)

However, "the unknown is the largest need of the intellect." The vanishing and the elusive are genuine objects of faith and desire, as in "A Light exists in Spring" (P 812). This rare light "passes and we stay,"

> A quality of loss
> Affecting our Content
> As Trade had suddenly encroached
> Upon a Sacrament.

If we suddenly recall that communion is only a transaction, belief vanishes; the vanishing light is an image of faith. But the same light is found in the nasty orthodoxy of the last stanza of poem 239: "Her teazing Purples—Afternoons—/The credulous—decoy—." The second stanza includes "The interdicted Land—" among examples of teasing heavens. This is one of several references to Jehovah's cruelty in letting Moses see but not enter Canaan. It is not Canaan itself as an image of desirability that she satirizes, but God's method of consecration, inflating the value of Canaan for others by depriving Moses, making unattainability a pure and empty status symbol.

"Success is counted sweetest" is one of many poems, early and late, that take up the theme of the relativity of knowledge, of emotion, or of achievement. These poems have largely been taken as straightforward statements of her belief, as is also true of a similar group of poems by Brontë. Joy is apparently unknown without the experience of pain, and only what is inaccessible is attractive.

> Water, is taught by thirst.
> Land—by the Oceans passed.
> Transport—by throe—
> Peace by it's battles told—
> Love, by Memorial Mold—
> Birds, by the Snow.
>
> (P 135)

She rarely punctuates with periods, and her use of them here is the first signal of irony, as their authority and finality suggest dogmatism. The problem in the poem is that the innocent speaker seems not to know the qualitative differences among the six pairs. The first and last refer to simple and remediable absences: thirst teaches the value of water, winter teaches us to miss the birds. But to group with these innocuous forms of relativism "Transport—by throe—"is overtly bitter. Though the speaker seems to miss its power, the bland context makes the line stand out for the reader: it is not just different, but nonsensical, too.

Our appreciation of the bitterness of the line depends on our seeing its contrast to the other lines' variations on the same structure. The speaker who believes in the instructional value of relativity can do so only through deafness to the poem's tonal contrast, but we can criticize the poem's ethic of relativity only by relying on such a principle in reading the poem's language.

Two poems overtly consider the idea of oppositeness by name. "The Zeroes—taught us—Phosphorus" is, like poem 135, organized on an instructional principle, but the instruction is faulty. Not only are mild and bitter mixed indiscriminately, as if for camouflage, but some of the pairs of oppositions are simply not opposite. The speaker's critical faculties may be oppressed by orthodoxy.

> The Zeroes—taught us—Phosphorus—
> We learned to like the fire
> By playing Glaciers—when a Boy—
> And Tinder—guessed—by power
> Of Opposite—to Balance Odd—
> If White—a Red—must be!
> Paralysis—our Primer—dumb—
> Unto Vitality!
>
> (P 689)

The exclamation marks raise a facade of false assertiveness, in the manner of the periods in poem 135. "When a Boy" denotes a time prior to cultural or linguistic differentiation, just as, in a different context ("A narrow Fellow in the Grass," P 986), the same expression denotes innocence of sexual difference. Zeroes and phosphorus, like red and white, are as opposite to him as are glacier and fire. We learn that there is no innate sense of relativity, because it must be acquired, and it can be acquired faultily. Because the poem mixes faulty and true oppositions, the final one, for which the others are a preparation, is undecidable. We may learn to value vitality by experiencing paralysis, but as in "Success is counted sweetest" that is a final frustration, not an educatuion, and it invites an ironic reading. Or if paralysis refers to the constrictions of life on earth and vitality to a freer life after death, the logic is that of an oppressive orthodoxy that endorses suffering by reversing the meanings of life and death. Either way, the poem invites both ironic and nonironic readings, and having established that the simple reversal of meaning is central to orthodox rhetoric, the poet allows orthodoxy's own principles to undermine themselves.

"'Tis Opposites—entice" considers the satanic deception, corollary to this orthodox belief in deferred rewards, that whatever the believer lacks must be the good. Opposites may entice but it is because they are constructed to do so; the valuation conferred by lack is a distortion.

> 'Tis Opposites—entice—
> Deformed Men—ponder Grace—
> Bright fires—the Blanketless—
> The Lost—Day's face—
>
> The Blind—esteem it be
> Enough Estate—to see—
> The Captive—strangles new—
> For deeming—Beggars—play—
> (P 355)

The final form of these overvaluations is projection:

> To lack—enamor Thee—
> Tho' the Divinity—
> Be only
> Me—

Assuming that "Thee" has all that "Me" lacks is not far from saying that what this divine interlocutor has is what the self has too but cannot recognize. Divinity is only as powerful as the mind of its imaginer.

Most of the poems that consider the idea of opposites or of relativity admit of ironic readings, but Dickinson's use of irony is itself involved in what she criticizes. Saying one thing in order to mean its opposite is the rhetorical analogue of what she criticizes. Her ironies are so fine that it is quite hard to say if she is in earnest or ironic, and several poems do in fact celebrate what she elsewhere mocks, or, like poem 355, combine sincerity with irony. She mocks the very structure of language by writing ironically about irony. Read without irony, these poems would celebrate antithesis as the fundamental of knowledge or desire, as when transport is known by pain. Taken ironically they decry that definition of knowledge. But to take them ironically the reader must use a principle of antithesis; to decry antithesis the reader must concede antithesis. Or, in the first case, to read these as celebrations of antithesis requires that the reader become—or be, innocently—deaf to antithesis.

Poem 1036 is one of many poems about deferment whose ostensible theme is that unattainability confers value, and proximity or achievement is disappointing.

> Satisfaction—is the Agent
> Of Satiety—
> Want—a quiet Comissary
> For Infinity.

This stanza plays on the idea that one polarity demands or requires the other, not on the instructional model of poems 67, 135, and 689, but in terms of an economy of feeling. Satisfaction and satiety, used here as opposites, come from the same root, *satis* or enough. That an affective opposition ought to be or once was an identity is a self-critique of the cultural shaping of language, and threatens the poem with collapse by undermining the validity of its apparently valorized oppositions, such as want and infinity. Presenting want and infinity as a pair of opposites renders infinity a plenitude, but etymologically infinity is as negative a concept as want. The second verse complements the thought of the first by apparently opposing possession and joy:

> To possess, is past the instant
> We achieve the Joy—

All the oppositions in this poem are slightly askew. The achievement of joy may precede possession, but nothing except traditional expectation precludes joy from continuing into possession. Achieve and possess are close enough to reproximate "possess" and "the instant we achieve the Joy."

> Immortality contented
> Were Anomaly.

"Immortality contented" is presented as if it ought to be an oxymoron, since it parallels the pairing of want and infinity in the first verse, as if immortality were a process of constant desire. Anomaly usually implies deviance, more than simply difference, with negative connotations that enforce the inappropriateness of "immortality contented," but since it derives from "without law" it may have positive value here as well. To be without or outside the law, if it is the law of orthodoxy, would be freedom. The poem has used a commercial or legal metaphor throughout, in "Agent," "Comissary," and possibly "possess." If that is the kind of law that "Immortality contented" violates, then it is to the discredit of those already dubious transactions, not of the immortality. The poem would then double back and mean that satisfaction is not the agent of satiety, or that the two terms are simply returned to their original identity, cancelling the poem.

In order to show that "Immortality contented" is not an oxymoron or a self-opposition, it was necessary to show that anomaly is, in that it suggests two opposing sets of meanings. On one level the poem states that satisfaction and satiety are opposites, affectively, at the same time reminding us that they are the same, by reminding us of their common root. But these readings make sense only when opposed to first or nonironic readings: they deny an impossibility rather than making a positive statement. Like her self-contradictory use of irony described above, this poem opposes opposition only by way of a rhetorical strategy based on oppositions.

Despite the transparency between self and world that Emerson prophecies, and the infinitude of his individual man, his philosophic universe depends on dualism as much as any in tradition. Though he parodies the orthodox preacher of deferred rewards in "Compensation," the dualism that that essay extols includes a dichotomy between matter and spirit among others, and from Dickinson's point of view there cannot have been much difference between parodier and parodied. The essay *Nature* is dualistic throughout. His account of the origin of language assumes a basic dualism: "Every word which is used to express a moral or intellectual fact, if traced to its root, is found to be borrowed from some material appearance." The purpose of his essay is to prove the congruence of spirit and nature, but manifestly there would have been no need for such a proof if the reverse were the accepted case, and his proof of the transparency between natural facts and spiritual facts begins with their separation.

> All the facts in natural history taken by themselves, have no value,
> but are barren like a single sex. But marry it to human history,
> and it is full of life.

His manner of arguing demands that he postulate an original division. His first example of the uses of nature is the orthodox analogy between the germination of seeds and the rising of the spirit after the body's death. This analogy and that between the seasons and the sequence of human life, which Emerson lists next, figure largely in Dickinson's poems but their validity is constantly questioned. Her reason for using them is probably not that Emerson does, but for the same reason: they are clichés, the most accessible examples of orthodox metaphor. She does not take that "marriage" to be inevitable, perhaps because Emerson assumes subservience on the part of the bride. Oppositions in orthodoxy are kept apart by deprivation. Blake's chimney sweeper in the *Songs of Experience* tells of "God &

his Priest & King / Who make up a heaven of our misery." Figurative language depends on, or brings about, the absence of the tenor.

The account of the origin of language presented by Freud in "The Antithetical Meaning of Primal Words" is very different from Emerson's in *Nature* but also centers on a dualism, that of relativity. Freud's account sounds very much like the relativity that Dickinson parodies as orthodox. I cite Freud here, even though Dickinson could not have known the work, because it helps demonstrate that certain assumptions are held in common by a wide range of phallogocentric philosophies. Freud's essay is a review of a work by the philologist Karl Abel (1884) and the theory of language is not so much Freud's own as his interpretation of Abel's interpolation of the philosopher Bain. Because of "the essential relativity of all knowledge" language ought theoretically to have originated (according to Bain), and did originate, according to Abel's discoveries about the ancient Egyptian language, in antithesis. No concept is imaginable without being measured against its opposite: we know darkness only because we know light; we understand far only in comparison with near. In this primitive language, the word for far and the word for near are conjoined, and take one of the other of the two meanings according to the speaker's gesture. But although conjoined, the word must already be read or heard as two, because it is a compound. As in *Nature*, which assumes the existence of division in order to insist on its closure, the speakers of this primitive language must have recognized difference at the same time that they denied it (or they were emerging from not recognizing to recognition). Although *Nature*'s dualism is different, Emerson's "Compensation" matches Abel's theory in designating those qualitative oppositions as a primal dualism.

> Polarity, or action and reaction, we meet in every part of nature; in darkness and light; in heat and cold; in the ebb and flow of waters; in male and female; . . . An inevitable dualism bisects nature, so that each thing is a half, and suggests another thing to make it whole.

This passage sweeps the dualism of spirit and matter of *Nature* into an encompassing, universal structural principle.

Freud's interest in Abel's work stems from his perception that it supports one aspect of his theory of dreams. In *The Interpretation of Dreams* he notes that reversals occur frequently in representations in dreams because something can be said in reverse that would be censored in its proper shape. The idea of the antithetical meanings of primal words provides a paradigm and possibly a source for the reversals formulated by dreams, by showing how close in the primitive levels of the brain oppositions lie. The analogy in Dickinson's rhetoric is to the moments when she brings back together words that have come to have opposite meanings, as when satiety and satisfaction are made compatible through the irony of poem 1036. But what about the complementary case in Dickinson, when one word is taken apart and shown to have two opposing meanings? There is a corresponding phenomenon in Freud's essay, which he does not explain, although he implies, by offering no other account, that Bain's theory of the relativity of all knowledge explains both the compound words mentioned above and this other sort. In addition to compounds that rely on relativity for meaning, there are in the same language unitary words that have two opposing meanings simultaneously. For these, a different sort of conceptualization seems necessary. Rather than containing two opposing meanings, they are prior to differentiation into opposites. We must translate Latin *altus* by deep *and* high, but the Romans must have known the word as a unitary concept. It is a strain on the imagination to conceive of a language that differentiates only between ranges of qualities, for example between the spectrum of color and the range of temperature, but this is what Abel tells us was the habit of the primitive mind. This is a language (or a part of a language) without value judgments, which already appear in the compounds analyzed later in the essay. Relativity simply does not account for this phenomenon. There is a slight but crucial difference between saying that a primitive language system entertains mutually exclusive oppositions (in the same word) and saying that it does not know that they are opposite, or what opposition means.

None of this enters into Freud's considerations; rather, he considers that there is conceptually no difference between the two phenomena, except to say that the compound words are "a further stage in this unintelligible behaviour of the Egyptian language." This conflation is surprising in the light of Freud's own views. His essay opens with a reference to the problematic discovery that dreams often represent two opposites as one thing. Anna Freud offers this unity of opposites as one of the defining characteristics of the id:

> In the id the so-called "primary process" prevails; there is no synthesis of ideas, affects are liable to displacement, opposites are not mutually exclusive and may even coincide and condensation occurs as a matter of course.

It is the ego that makes value judgments. Anna Freud notes that children are able to counteract experienced pain by means of fantasy without asking that the fantasy be experientially true. Prior to the development of a powerful ego, the young child is capable of feeling two contradictory states of mind to be equally valid, and two reports about experience that adults perceive as opposite to be equally true, without experiencing a sense of conflict or contradiction. In "The Zeroes—taught us—Phosphorus—" the boy must acquire his knowledge of contradiction. It is the synthesizing ego, by all accounts, that objects to contradictions. Because of the hierarchical nature of relations between id and ego, and because they develop sequentially, Anna Freud suggests that the id is prior to differentiation, unfallen rather than simply resistant to progress. The id, if it spoke, might invent a unitary term that meant both of two opposites, unperceived as opposites;

the ego would be the one to insist that this is not one term but a composite, and would separate it into two. Abel's unintended implication that there was once a time when the mind did not discriminate between what we perceive as opposites may not be verifiable, but his suggestion makes a suitable myth of the id; and his account of the compound words sounds like an account of the ego.

Dreams do not exclude the use of consciousness's language, and they may function in ways analogous to the functioning of language, but they originate in the unconscious, which for Anna Freud is synonymous with the id. It is therefore curious that Freud blurs the distinction between the two ways of experiencing opposites which offers so excellent an analogy for his own structures. The reversals that occur in dreams are closest to the idea of the unitary word that contains two meanings, but the explanation he favors is the one that accounts only for the compound words. This lapse on his part is consistent with the pervasive dualism of his thinking, but it also shows how difficult it is to escape dualism. Dickinson's language is a departure from dualistic thinking, and from the phallogocentrism in which it originates, but it is difficult to comprehend the extent and value of this departure, so firmly are her readers' imaginations shaped by dualism.

The price often paid for this departure is loss of communicability, as she indicates in a poem that enacts the departure as a journey.

> I saw no Way—The Heavens were stitched—
> I felt the Columns close—
> The Earth reversed her Hemispheres—
> I touched the Universe—
>
> And back it slid—and I alone—
> A Speck upon a Ball—
> Went out upon Circumference—
> Beyond the Dip of Bell—
>
> (P 378)

The hemispheres here are the concentric spheres of the earth and the heavens, and they are halves in the sense that neither is complete without the other, but by calling them hemispheres the poet limits them to the oppositeness of east and west or north and south. Then by referring to them as "it" she puts oppositeness behind her. This departure from a dualistic universe takes her "Beyond the Dip of Bell," or beyond signification, especially beyond a system of signs with ties to conventional religion, if the bell here is a church bell. The poet knows that by forgoing the tradition of language that relies on oppositions or relativity for meaning, as she often does, she may forgo the possibility of communicating what she discovers. To the extent that her poems are readable, she is still relying on the conventions of unreversed hemispheres.

Hierarchy or relativity in language is fundamentally the same as pro-priation in language, because both fulfill the need for the center to posit an eccentricity, or for the primary to posit a secondary. Emerson's definition of language balances human spirit against nature's matter, in a neat sym-metry of relativity. This use of nature as the ground for human meaning is also propriative, in the manner of Derrida's account of the operation of language, because it subjects nature to human usage and denies its separate identity. Dickinson's objections to hierarchy in language extend, as might be expected, to language's appropriation of nature, and to overthrow this subjection of nature she makes use of strategies similar to those that she employs in her disruption of language's hierarchical structure. Dickinson's sense of the foreignness of nature is commonly recognized, but nature's distance is due as much to her sense of the fictiveness of language as to qualities inherent in nature. Nature's defiance of human comprehension should not be credited entirely to nature's power, or to Dickinson's sup-posed timidity; nature is "graspless" at least in part because of a conscious and voluntary resistance to possessiveness on Dickinson's part. Nature's resistance to human language could be a model for Dickinson's own project to overthrow ordinary terminology, yet to call it a model of any kind is to violate the first principle of that nonappropriative project.

"What mystery pervades a well!" is often cited as the extreme case of Dickinson's wariness about human efforts to possess nature. The poem's rhetorical mode is paradox, which stretches the oxymoronic style of poems like "Success is counted sweetest" to a limit where it approaches mean-inglessness. Whether or not the contradiction is resolvable, paradox artic-ulates the possibility of pure contradiction, which also typifies relations between the human and nature. The water in the well is "A neighbor from another world," the first of a series of paradoxical epithets about the mis-taken belief that nature participates in the human community of under-standing. Here are the final stanzas:

> But nature is a stranger yet;
> The ones that cite her most
> Have never passed her haunted house,
> Not simplified her ghost.
>
> To pity those that know her not
> Is helped by the regret
> That those who know her, know her less
> The nearer her they get.
>
> (P 1400)

Those who know her know that she is inaccessible to language, so that even to make such a statement is to make nonsense of terms like knowledge. Her apparent presence seems to invite knowledge but her absence makes knowledge impossible; furthermore, presence and absence are imposed terms. The terms "her ghost" and "her haunted house" demonstrate the difficulty that even the sardonic speaker has in writing any account of nature. They implicate her in the same error made by "The ones that cite her most," because to separate matter from spirit is to impose on her an artificial system. The ones who cite her most are the more at fault, however, because they have reduced nature to her matter component.

"The ones that cite her most" perform an act of naming that implies appropriation of the named. Citing is naming with the specially active sense of bringing forward for purposes of argument, so that what is cited is made secondary to the argument. The ones who cite her most believe that they can use her as, for example, a metaphor for human activity. But nature escapes and leaves language a husk. Those citers, if they can be cited, must be Emerson and the Transcendentalists. Insisting that nature and spirit are indissolubly linked, their rhetoric depends on a separation. Emerson cites nature in *Nature* as the matter that human history elevates when the two are wed. He also cites nature according to the whim of his argument. At the outset he distinguishes between two uses of nature, nature as the "NOT ME" and the nature of "the river, the leaf." As his argument continues, nature becomes the reverenced repository of spirit, or the barren matter which the mind must enliven. "Nature is thoroughly mediate. It is made to serve." Dickinson is warning against such an appropriative project because it risks an ignorance of fatality. Those who get near to nature know her less by comprehending her resistance to our inquiries, but they also know her less because to get near to nature is to die, and to know everything less.

"What mystery pervades a well!" is often grouped with other poems apparently concerned with nature's inaccessibility, particularly to the poet's art, in order to arrive at a general statement about Dickinson's distance from nature. " 'Nature' is what we see—" exposes the futility of efforts to master nature by finding linguistic equivalencies for it:

> "Nature" is what we see—
> The Hill—the Afternoon—
> Squirrel—Eclipse—the Bumble bee—
> Nay—Nature is Heaven—
> Nature is what we hear—
> The Bobolink—the Sea—
> Thunder—the Cricket—
> Nay—Nature is Harmony—
>
> (P 668)

The listing of natural elements is insufficient and provokes a "Nay" each time, but the abstract terms that seem intended to correct that insufficiency—"Nature is Heaven," "Nature is Harmony"—not only remain distant from nature but they also produce a stuttering effect that threatens to bring the poem to a halt. Putting "Nature" in quotation marks in the first line is Dickinson's way of separating herself from the poem's definitions of nature, and it may also be a specific reference to the essay *Nature*. The poem's rapid shifting from one definition of nature to the next suggests that Dickinson is again mocking Emerson's belief that nature "is made to serve" the ends of whatever argument he happens to be pursuing. If the poem is in this way a response to the essay *Nature*, the poet is suggesting that Emerson's appropriative definitions are damaging not so much to nature (that was Dorothy Wordsworth's fear) as to Emerson himself: he is wasting his efforts. The poem's conclusion cautions the reader against trying to "say" nature:

> Nature is what we know—
> Yet have no art to say—
> So impotent Our Wisdom is
> To her Simplicity

Even "her Simplicity" is an imposed and abstract term, even though what it stands for is nature's resistance to human language.

Dickinson elaborates elsewhere on the way that nature surpasses human language:

> The Veins of other Flowers
> The Scarlet Flowers are
> Till Nature leisure has for Terms
> As "Branch," and "Jugular."
>
> We pass, and she abides.
> We conjugate Her Skill
> While She creates and federates
> Without a syllable.
>
> (P 811)

A conjugation is an uncreative exercise in repetition that is set against nature's highly efficient substitute for language, the soundless federation of the scarlet flowers with the apparently bloodless ones. Typical of Dickinson's rhetorical mobility, a poem from the same packet precisely reverses this poem's metaphor for nature's separateness. Where poem 811 has "We pass, and she abides," poem 812, referring to the fleeting "Light" that "exists in Spring," says, "It passes and we stay—." This juxtaposition, of opposite expressions that have the same import for human relations to nature, expresses nature's inaccessibility as effectively as could any single expression. It seems to make no difference what language is used, because, although the two lines would seem to cover all possibilities, they play against each other rather than touching nature.

As Charles Anderson points out, language relates happily to nature only where it forgoes the effort to imitate nature literally. It is worth considering here that Dickinson welcomes a limitation in language that Dorothy

Wordsworth also celebrates, but for very different purposes. Dorothy's wish not to try to appropriate nature by means of language contributes to her resistance to poetic identity, because to her that is the characteristic operation of poetic language. Dickinson's art is not impeded in any way by her recognition that nature is not to be possessed, because she understands and makes use of a general dislocation between words and their referents that includes, but is not limited to, language's relation to nature. Because she knows that all language is figurative, she feels no special distress at the discovery that actual nature is not the same as the words used to name it. Emerson, even though he shares some of Dickinson's knowledge of the vertiginous freedom of language, is disconcerted by nature's elusiveness, because his views of language include its powerful propriation of nature.

The test of Dickinson's equanimity about language's supposed failure to possess nature is that for every poem about nature's evasion of language there is a poem in which poetry matches or surpasses nature, or in which such comparative terms may be discarded in favor of an indication of pure difference. Something small (a poem) can be larger than something big (the summer, a sunset), when the terms of relativity are abandoned. "When I count at all—," the poets merely head a numbered list of priorities, but "looking back," reversing the order of the counting, poets "Comprehend the Whole" (P 569). In a mock competition with the day the poet makes two sunsets "and several Stars—/While He—was making One—." The day's was "ampler," but "Mine—is the more convenient/To Carry in the Hand—" (P 308). In a similar stalemate, poem 811 appears to value nature's visual language over human language, but to conjugate is to conjoin as well as to repeat, and in fact it is only through the poem's juxtaposition that the scarlet flowers have any relation to the others. Nature's language is at once superior to and dependent on a human viewpoint. The first two verses of "The Brain—is wider than the Sky—," in which the brain contains the sky and absorbs the sea, demonstrate that scale is irrelevant to power, by lifting the small over the large (P 632). But the poem presses past this point. The third stanza violates the expectation raised by the first two, of a pattern of such displacements, by abandoning the language of scale altogether, even as a metaphor. Competition for status as the largest in the first two stanzas gives way to a recognition of difference that is neither spatial nor temporal. The brain and God differ here "As syllable from Sound—." They may be coextensive, or even occupy the same place. Syllable is articulate and sound is unintelligible, but articulation may equally be a diminishing of pure and primal sound. It is impossible to find here an order of valuation, and the poem teaches us not to wish to impose one.

Both Dorothy Wordsworth and Emily Brontë have difficulty writing about nature because they inherit a tradition in whch nature is Mother Nature, and, in the mythic family dynamic, the mother is the object of their jealousy rather than of their devotion. Dickinson's sense of the fictiveness of language finally frees her from this problematic tradition. But at the same time that she is learning to become a daughter of Eve, she is also a daughter of Mother Nature, and it is evidence of the tenacity of this tradition that Dickinson's liberation from it is a process that extends past the time of her understanding of the powers of irony. Mother Nature holds her to the terms of literal competition or identification. Dickinson is, however, helped in this regard by the fact that her American predecessors are not so prolifically enamored of nature as are their British counterparts. Nature is not so unavoidable a subject of verse for an American poet.

Dickinson very early becomes involved in a minor competition with maternal nature when the love of a beloved male figure is in question, though it is a competition that stirs her to write, not to stop writing. The second poem in the Harvard edition, actually the prose conclusion to a letter written to her brother Austin in 1851, is read by some critics as a veiled sexual invitation, and certainly it is a love poem with a female speaker. Out of context, as verse, the alternative nature that the speaker offers is a metaphor for her love, in the tradition of the Song of Solomon, where the woman is a garden:

> There is another sky,
> Ever serene and fair,
>
> . . . .
> Here is a brighter garden,
> Where not a frost has been;
> In its unfading flowers
> I hear the bright bee hum;
> Prithee, my brother,
> Into *my* garden come!
>
> (P 2)

While the "another sky" and "brighter garden" retain their status as metaphors when restored to their context in the letter, that they follow a passage about actual nature puts them in a slightly different light:

> The earth looks like some poor old lady who by dint of pains has bloomed e'en till *now,* yet in a forgetful moment a few silver hairs from out her cap come stealing, and she tucks them back so hastily and thinks nobody *sees.* . . . Dont think that the sky will frown so the day when you come home! She will smile and look happy, and be full of sunshine *then*—and even *should* she frown upon her child returning, there is *another* sky ever serene and fair.
>
> (L, 1, 149)

The "brighter garden" is called into being in response to an inadequacy in real nature, so that as well as functioning as a metaphor for the writer's love, those lovely images compete with real nature on the literal level. That nature is characterized as a woman in this passage emphasizes the femininity of the speaker, making the sequence a competition between two women for the love of the man.

Because the rhyming lines seem to grow spontaneously out of prose, they appear (whether or not Dickinson contrived the effect) to represent the untutored origins of poetry, as if poetry originated in imitation of nature. This moment of origination stands at the beginning of a project for poetry quite different from that which her objections to hierarchical language produce. Many of the poems from her first year of writing seriously (1858, seven years later) enact this implicit competition with nature by assuming nature's voice. Domesticating small natural objects by personifying them, she then joins them as if to test the hypothesis that poetry might substitute for nature. Other poems were sent with flowers as greetings, making an equation between flowers and speech and between nature and the speaker.

> She slept beneath a tree—
> Remembered but by me.
> I touched her Cradle mute—
> She recognized the foot—
> Put on her carmine suit
>   And see!
>
> (P 25)

If nature wakes the tulips with a touch and without voice ("I touched her Cradle mute—"), then she is hardly a model for the aspiring poet, but the poet here seems to desire nothing further than simple presence ("And see!"), deferring to nature. Elsewhere the poet constructs a rose out of language, but her speaker's purpose, as before, is only to approximate nature's activity, and no more:

> A sepal, petal, and a thorn
> Upon a common summer's morn—
> A flask of Dew—A Bee or two—
> A Breeze—a caper in the trees—
> And I'm a Rose!
>
> (P 19)

The impulse to compete with or correct nature seems to have disappeared in favor of an apprenticeship in innocence.

This apprenticeship is essentially stultifying, and Dickinson knows it. Another letter from the 1851 correspondence with Austin anticipates and characterizes the feminine voice of the 1858 poems so accurately that she cannot have been unaware of their trite effect. Austin has apparently admonished her for a grandiose style in previous letters and has recommended a simpler one. Her letters at this time are full of the flights of borrowed fancy that she identifies as masculine. Perhaps he objected to her satiric tone in her letter of June 15, or her hyperbole of June 22, the two letters just previous to this response. In either case, his admonition causes her to be defensive about pirating an alien style.

> I feel quite like retiring, in presence of one so grand, and casting my small lot among small birds, and fishes—you say you dont comprehend me, you want a simpler style. *Gratitude* indeed for all my fine philosophy! I strove to be exalted thinking I might reach *you* and while I pant and struggle and climb the nearest cloud, you walk out very leisurely in your slippers from Empyrean, and without the *slightest* notice request me to get down! As *simple* as you please, the *simplest* sort of simple—I'll be a little ninny—a little pussy catty, a little Red Riding Hood, I'll wear a Bee in my bonnet, and a Rose bud in my hair, and what remains to do you shall be told hereafter.
>
> (L, I, 117; 29 June 1851)

The humor here almost makes us forget that this letter represents the usual relations between men and women. The godlike admonisher and the little ninny are all too recognizable, and Dickinson portrays them repeatedly in the letters and poems about Master and the daisy, satirized there as they are here. She outwits her critic but she also sketches what will become, strangely, a serious program of poetry writing. The nature poems of 1858 may represent an effort to show that wearing a rosebud does not necessarily make the wearer a little ninny, but benighted as her attempt may have been, it is necessary to put into context her lack of success. Identifying the empyrean style as alien, she chose to begin writing by first investigating the possibilities of a style that was definably feminine and ought to have felt native.

Fortunately, among these early poems are some that perform the salutary task of proving to their writer the impossibility of an innocent or entirely natural speaker. She deduces figuration out of the context of her loyalty to this natural style, and so makes the use of figuration more genuinely her own.

> The morns are meeker than they were—
> The nuts are getting brown—
> The berry's cheek is plumper—
> The Rose is out of town.
>
> The Maple wears a gayer scarf—
> The field a scarlet gown—
> Lest I sh'd be old fashioned
> I'll put a trinket on.
>
> (P 12)

The innocent "I" thinks that she is deficient in ornament relative to nature, but the poem shows us that her deficiency is in her critical faculties, in that she misinterprets the meaning of nature's bright coloring. Like Blake's *Songs of Innocence*, this poem is ironic without having an ironic speaker. Reading nature with the assumption that it participates in the community of human meaning, the speaker takes brilliant color to signify decoration, not death. This misreading may be innocent, but it is dangerous. Rather than humanizing nature, the speaker risks her life in naturalizing herself: for her to put on a trinket is, in the context of nature's language of gayer scarf and scarlet gown, to prepare for death. The speaker requires the concept of metaphor in order not to make this error, even though metaphor would confirm the separation between nature and a no longer innocent speaker.

This natural speaker finds that there is no equivalent for nature's voice, and that nature cannot be spoken of without the defense of figuration. Mother Nature disappears as a major subject after these very early poems, and when she does appear it is her silence and her defiance of poetic language that are emphasized. As for Dorothy, nature's real power is no help to those among her daughters who aspire to be poets, because it is a power against articulation. "Nature—the Gentlest Mother is" is a counterpart to Dorothy's "Irregular Verses" ("To Julia Marshall—A Fragment") in presenting a maternal figure who conceals oppression beneath kindness:

> Her Admonition mild—
>
> In Forest—and the Hill—
> By Traveller—be heard—
> Restraining Rampant Squirrel—
> Or too impetuous Bird—
>
> (P 790)

In what way can a bird be "too impetuous"? What is the need for these restraints? Nature inspires worship, a traditional notion, but the description of her worshipers emphasizes their inferiority. Her voice

> Incite the timid prayer
> Of the minutest Cricket—
> The most unworthy Flower—

Granted that crickets are small, it makes no sense to say that a flower is unworthy. Earlier in the poem, Mother Nature is called gentle because she is "Impatient of no Child—/The feeblest—or the waywardest." The poem makes Nature superior to and separate from natural objects, an odd notion that reappears in another poem naming nature as mother:

> If Nature smiles—the Mother must
> I'm sure, at many a whim
> Of Her eccentric Family—
> Is She so much to blame?
>
> (P 1085)

Where nature is Mother Nature she is outside nature, making herself implicitly the center from which nature (with a small n) is eccentric.

In "Nature—the Gentlest Mother is," Mother Nature is primarily represented as a voice, speaking "Her Admonition mild" and vocally inciting prayer; a day's beauty is "How fair Her Conversation—/A Summer Afternoon—." Though this voice is metaphoric, it is perhaps a sign that the poet's own voice has been preempted. The last two stanzas are about the silence Mother Nature condescends to confer on nature:

> When all the Children sleep—
> She turns as long away
> As will suffice to light Her lamps—
> Then bending from the Sky—
>
> With infinite Affection—
> And infiniter Care—
> Her Golden finger on Her lip—
> Wills Silence—Everywhere—

This might have been a charming allegory of the coming of night, except that Mother Nature "Wills Silence" only after her children are asleep. This silence must be more than sleep, then. "Infiniter Care" is also overabundant. "Infiniter" makes no sense in natural terms and, like "Silence—Everywhere—," goes beyond the harmonious imagery of night and sleep that Nature is promulgating. "Infiniter" is also parodic, undermining the hypnotic effect of "Her Golden finger on Her lip—." The "Silence—Everywhere—" must be death masquerading, as in the Lucy situation, as an entirely harmonious part of natural process.

In these two poems (P 790 and P 1085) Mother Nature is separate from nature. This separation is in distinct contrast to Mother Nature in both the Wordsworths and in Brontë, where she is by definition a presence immanent in nature. Knowing that nature is not to be possessed by means of any human construct, Dickinson is not taking Mother Nature to be a personification of nature, but a figure imported from tradition and extrinsic to nature. To Dorothy and to Brontë, Mother Nature appears to be part of nature's reality, because they do not separate literary tradition from actuality. Dickinson, with her greater sense of the potential detachment of words from their referents, is able to see with greater clarity the difference between Mother Nature and actual, unnameable nature. The concept of Mother Nature is only a fiction among other fictions. This is the most effective answer to the women poets' struggles with that maternal figure. Dickinson abandons the struggle after her earliest attempts at verse, and simply removes the grounds for the struggle altogether. Nature, "graspless," is alien, but its foreignness ceases to pose a threat to the existence of poethood. With nature no longer maternal, the woman poet need not feel a daughter's conflicting wishes to subdue and at the same time to identify.

This recognition of the fictionality of nature's traditional sexual identification is part of Dickinson's larger discovery about language's fictiveness.
Her resistance to appropriating nature is one model for improving the status
of the woman writer in relation to the tradition; another lies in her challenge
to the assumption that opposition is necessary for language to have meaning. Her undoing of rhetorical dualism becomes a model for a revised
pattern of relations between the sexes in her recognition that the opposition
of the sexes is as figurative as any other kind of opposition, not a literal
necessity. The traditional determinisms that have maintained this opposition need no longer operate, just as the tradition of Mother Nature, once
it is recognized as a tradition and therefore figurative, not actual, ceases to
be confining. A tradition of masculine dominance may be at the root of
dualistic language, and her feminine identity, particularly her sense of
inheritance from Eve, may be the origin of her readiness to object to that
structure of language. She disrupts traditional relations between the sexes
by means of the kind of undoing of hierarchical language that she employs
in poems about the idea of opposition itself. Dickinson brings to those
poems in which the poet's identity is explicitly feminine her knowledge
that her best power lies in the manipulation of language to reverse its
ordinary meanings. She uses that linguistic power first to reverse the ordinary direction of power between a feminine self and a masculine other,
and then, as in the poems where she undoes antithetical language, uses it
to discard the idea of dominance altogether.

There is a group of poems in which she pictures herself as a tiny being,
typically a daisy and typically in relation to some figure of masculine power.
As in the many poems in which she criticizes dualism or polarity, she
entertains, in order to challenge it, the convention that women remain
childlike or regress in romantic relations. In all these poems the positions
are reversed by a slight disjunction. In the manner of the poems that mock
human competition with nature, the daisy may be tiny, but she is also
larger than Master. If the poet's purpose were simply to prove her power,
she would hardly portray herself as a daisy in the first place. Her point is
that power is not relative, and cannot be described in the terms of relativity.

> In lands I never saw—they say
> Immortal Alps look down—
>
> (P 124)

"They say" always signals the false authority of convention, which she
defies. In this case the "they say" refers to both expressions, preceding
and following. She doubts "their" view that she never saw these lands;
but she also reports that they say that immortal Alps look down. In the
world of "they say," hierarchies of up and down obtain, but she has never
seen such a place, which is to say that she never herself entertains such
hierarchical thoughts. The ambiguous positioning of "they say" makes
equally plausible two readings that contradict each other, in that she insists

both that she might have seen and that she has not, and this confusion is paradigmatic of the procedure of the poem. An apparent opposition is resolved by lifting the convention; the poet can see perfectly clearly if her vision is not occluded by "them".

The power of these condescending Alps is next reduced by the contrivance of a figure that miniaturizes them:

> Whose Bonnets touch the firmament—
> Whose Sandals touch the town—
>
> Meek at whose everlasting feet
> A Myriad Daisy play—

"Daisy" was printed as "daisies" in the 1891 edition of Dickinson's poems, accurately destroying the very precise effect of these lines. A myriad daisy turns multiplicity into a fantastic unity. Where bonnets and sandals rationalize Alps, by rendering their size accessible, the myriad exalts the daisy, because "Myriad Daisy defies not only sense but logic and reason too.

> Which, Sir, are you and which am I
> Upon an August day?

These lines have been cited as an example of the poet's confusion, intentional or not, about sex roles. But if she were genuinely confused, she would hardly make so bald a statement. Instead, she voices the form of such a confusion in order to show its inapplicability: by now the reader ought to see that the question is not a question. Most sirs would still opt for the Alps, but the choice has been minimized; there is no longer a clear opposition of high and low. The poem is about the invidiousness of ascribing conventional characteristics to the sexes.

This poem offers an interpretive key to related poems. Poem 106 presents the daisy again at someone's feet, shy here instead of meek, using the sun's grandeur to enlarge her own.

> The Daisy follows soft the Sun—
> And when his golden walk is done—
> Sits shily at his feet—
> He—waking—finds the flower there—
> Wherefore—Marauder—art thou here?
> Because, Sir, love is sweet!
>
> We are the flower—Thou the Sun!
> Forgive us, if as days decline—
> We nearer steal to Thee!

The daisy is better at most things than is the admired sun. She knows him, but he is ignorant of her. Her gentility is superior to his, as is her command of articulation. When, surprised, he calls her "Marauder," she not only has a loving answer, but also manages to transform his rudeness into the language of her own adoration: "We nearer steal to Thee!" As in poem 124, the daisy multiplies her size and number till she becomes an omnipresent "we" who attends the sun's every motion, east and west. Her name means "day's eye," making her etymologically a mock sun. Having equalized their powers, the poet now renders the daisy and the sun even more similar by giving them the same view of each other. Her apparent reliance on his power parodies the dependence of the weak on the strong, because it is his absence that she desires, not his presence.

> Enamored of the parting West—
> The peace—the flight—the Amethyst—
> Night's possibility!

The daisy is in the end no less self-centered than the sun, who resented her presence at the opening, because "We nearer steal to Thee" in order to look beyond. Self-representation makes the other disappear, and the daisy has the last word in the poem because she has made the sun vanish. The poem parodies the faulty relations between the sexes that obtain when the conventional attributes are assigned, such as the equation of weakness with femininity and of power with masculinity. This exclusiveness isolates the sexes. The daisy can acquire power in this system only by mocking the sun, thereby depriving him of some of his power.

The daisy does not just desire the sun's absence, however. The last three lines (quoted above) project a kind of presence as well as absence: amethyst as well as parting, flight, and peace. "Night's possibility" suggests transcendence, a third term outside the narrow competition between the daisy and the sun, but, like the moment of leaving the dualistic universe defined by hemispheres and going "out upon Circumference—/Beyond the Dip of Bell—"(P 378), if it represents a possibility beyond the isolation of sexual characteristics, it is also beyond communicable terminology. Incommunicability is the risk of any strategy that denies or surpasses oppositions, whether rhetorical or thematic, where conventional terminology depends on relativity.

Many of the Daisy poems simply enact reversals of size and power as related to gender. Poem 85 elevates the daisy to Christlike status. Jesus' brave statement is

> "They have not chosen me," he said,
> "But I have chosen them!"

The daisy's response is that although Jesus hasn't chosen her, she has chosen him, so that she is the inheritor of his position:

> Sovreign! Know a Daisy
> Thy dishonor shared!

In the Master letters the writer uses Daisy as a proper name for herself. The first of these letters, from about the same period as the Daisy poems, opens with a reversal similar to that of the poems: "I am ill, but grieving more that you are ill, I make my stronger hand work long eno' to tell you"(*L*,II, 333; about 1858). Competition is not far from the surface of this apparently self-abasing text. She slights his faulty powers of understanding: "You ask me what my flowers said—then they were disobedient—I gave them messages." Stooping to explain, she says that her message was no less than apocalyptic, and should not have been difficult to read. "They said what the lips in the West, say, when the sun goes down, and so says the Dawn." Though she defends the possibility of intelligibility, the role reversal here does not simply cause unintelligibility, it is founded on it.

The daisy that addresses the sun as sir and the humble voice that speaks to her Master have, among other sources, a literary source in the manipulation of power in the relationship between Jane Eyre and Mr. Rochester in Charlotte Brontë's novel, which Dickinson greatly admired. Jane refers to Rochester as her master, at first in the literal sense that he is her employer and later generically, as her private deity. She always addresses him as sir, as a form of deference behind which she conceals her growing sense of equality with him. It permits her to exercise what powers she chooses without ever deserving a reproach, from herself or from the critical world, for forwardness or immodesty. He is her superior in every way— as her employer, in age and experience, and by virtue of being a man—so that her language is initially unremarkable. At the end of the novel when Jane, now independent both financially and morally, returns to find Rochester blind and helpless, the balance of power has become reversed. She torments him briefly with jealousy, ritually, in order to cancel the symmetrical power he once held over her. She profits from his crippling: "I love you better now, when I can really be useful to you, than I did in your state of proud independence, when you disdained every part but that of the giver and protector." But the special quality of his dependence is that she retains the form of the usual relation of power. Walking, she leads him by letting him place his arm around her shoulders, as if it were he who protected her: "being so much lower of stature than he, I served both for his prop and guide." She retains the same form of address throughout, though in these last pages her "sir" becomes almost a parody of servility:

> "Am I hideous, Jane?"
> "Very, sir: you always were, you know."

The daisy's mock humility is similar in tone to Jane's. It is not disrespectful, but at the same time that it pretends to a continuity of relationship it measures the change in it, and it emblemized the way in which power is augmented by disarming the governed. Jane Eyre's "sir" permits both of them to be powerful, as does the daisy's. When, in poem 124, she asks "Which, Sir, are you and which am I/Upon an August day?" she is not confused about sex roles but rather she is demonstrating their dispensability.

This alteration of ordinary relations between male and female figures may extend beyond the patently fictive voice of the daisy to a relationship that involves the poet's identity as a poet. Like Emily Brontë, Dickinson invokes an array of masculine figures of power in reference to the poetic process. Brontë's visitants—her dream, her God of Visions, her Wanderer, and others—invite comparison with a similar group in Dickinson. Many of Dickinson's poems on poetry are also about, or enact, relationships between the speaker and a range of powerful masculine figures. The speaker's attitude shifts, from poem to poem, between love, anguish, desire, fear, and humility, and the figure addressed may be God, an apparently human lover, death, awe, Master, or some other being or abstraction, but they are all masculine and they are all addressed as other, while the speaker characterizes herself as queen or wife or some other female figure. These poems sometimes follow the Daisy poems' pattern of inverting our expectations about gender roles, but sometimes they do not. For both poets these masculine figures function as something like a muse. Both poets both love and fear these figures, and both indicate a sense of alienation from their poetic powers, though Dickinson far less than Brontë.

Two critics have directly and extensively considered the gender or genders of Dickinson's mind, and though their arguments differ greatly, both find those figures to be a masculine component of Dickinson's mind. Albert J. Gelpi, addressing the issue of Dickinson's femininity along Jungian lines in *The Tenth Muse*, describes the masculine figures listed above as versions of the animus and discusses the poems in terms of their negotiations between feminine self and a masculine part of the self that is nonetheless other. He is clearly right in associating these figures and in emphasizing their status as figures rather than as actual persons (every reader of Dickinson should be grateful for his putting to rest the search for the biographical identity of Master). But the Jungian system leads Gelpi to a reductive formula—feminine self plus masculine mind equals complete poet—and to a static critical program of demonstrating Dickinson's ceaseless effort to "adapt the masculine characteristics of mind and will to the achievement of an integral identity as a woman." Dickinson assimilates those internalized figures to varying degrees, but by identifying intellect, will, and imagination as perpetually masculine, Gelpi (with Jung) insures that these powers must be uneasily appropriated and are never inherent. As with Emerson's marriage of natural history to human history, the objection to this sytem, both for Dickinson's criticism and for human experience, is that while proposing to restore humanity to its primordial integrity, it only further divides and creates hierarchies.

Joanne Feit Diehl (in the works already cited) identifies an analogous range of masculine figures as the poet's internalization of her poetic precursors, arguing persuasively from Freudian and Bloomian theory for a structure of mind that is similar to, though more complex than, the one Gelpi describes with reference to Jung. Because these masculine figures double as precursor and as muse, the poet's antithetical struggle to defend herself against her precursors, which she shares with male poets, causes her at the same time to defend against the beloved sources of her own inspiration, which for male poets are feminine and therefore distinguishable from the paternal precursors. This identification of precursor and muse accounts for Dickinson's ambivalence about the poetic art that she experiences as a dangerous, destructive power. Although Joanne Feit Diehl does not discuss Brontë, there is a remarkable similarity between this reading of Dickinson and Brontë's identification of the sources of poetry both with masculine figures of power and with death. This similarity could make one of the strongest cases for the existence of a common and recurrent experience of feminine poethood. However, while this alienation is Brontë's major experience of poetry, for Dickinson it is only one aspect, perhaps a stage, of her endeavor to establish her own poetic voice outside the tradition of masculine discourse. Brontë is genuinely "stalled" by the danger and power of the masculine figures she invokes, but to say this about Dickinson is to overrate the importance of the masculine in a poetics that endeavors to liberate itself from restrictive terms like those of gender.

Both of these ways of reading are persuasive, but both privilege poems that delineate internal struggles between masculine and feminine in such a way as to retain the hierarchical terms of self and other or subject and object. It may be that Dickinson's greatest originality is in her breaking out of the terms of gender altogether, in other poems in which the mind appears to be divided into identical halves and in which identical terms replace the expected terms of opposition or complementarity. Gelpi cites in support of his argument about Dickinson's difficulties in controlling her masculine mind several poems, including the following one, that sketch a balance, or sometimes a stalemate, between parts of the mind that are explicitly unlabelled, and that are, in fact, not separable parts at all.

> Me from Myself—to banish—
> Had I Art—
>
> . . . . .
>
> And since We're mutual Monarch
> How this be
> Except by Abdication—
> Me—of Me?
>
> (P 642)

Written out of her recognition that to use gender terms is unavoidably to use the hierarchical terms of self and other, these termless poems indicate Dickinson's objections to the conventional language of sexual opposition (as exemplified in Brontë's poetry) and her effort to do without it.

This balance within the mind is not a confrontation between qualitatively different parts of the mind, nor a mirroring of one part by another, but a balance of two parts that are neither different nor the same. This self-doubling is a form of irony carried from rhetoric to the level of poetic identity. Just as a word may be asked to bear antithetical meanings, thereby denying the reader's expectation of a stable or consistent reading, the self may split into antithetical parts; but this irony of the self is even less easily read than the rhetorical ironies of other poems. Rhetoric demonstrates the self's divisions by a doubling in language, as in "Abdication—/Me—of Me?" or in lines like "Ourself behind ourself" or "Itself—it's Sovreign—of itself." These repetitions seem to reach the limit of meaning, because meaning depends on difference. As in the poems in which the poet exploits the antithetical meanings of words, that she avoids labeling her various powers of mind, either sexually or hierarchically, creates a risk of obscurity. These parts of the self may be provisionally labeled with gender or other terms, but that these terms are variable suggests that these characterizations are not proper differences:

> The Soul unto itself
> Is an imperial friend—
> Or the most agonizing Spy—
> An Enemy—could send—
> (P 683)

The terms "friend" and "Spy" represent the poet's efforts to render comprehensible this division between the soul and itself. The poet falls back on the oppositional structure of language, as a self-defense, even though she has elsewhere proved to herself that that structure is obsolete. The language of hierarchy is used in these poems only in order to be undone. The poem closes,

> Itself—it's Sovreign—of itself
> The Soul should stand in Awe—

The soul should stand in awe, but it cannot. Could the soul transform its self-duplicated friend or enemy into sovereign or into monarch, the doubling would cease to be so problematic. Hierarchy would restore a temporary and inauthentic calm. (It is instructive to compare this structureless structure to the hierarchy that preserves Whitman's divisions of the self from becoming a splintering.)

Most of these poems intensify the concept of rhetorical opposition through a metaphor of combat or defense within the self. The poem that begins "Me from Myself—to banish—" represents a fortress within the self that cannot resist when "Myself—assault Me—;" and in the poem "One need not be a Chamber—to be Haunted—"(P 670), "Ourself behind ourself" is "a superior spectre" whose dangerousness exceeds that of "External Ghost" or "Assassin." This violence is due not to the problem of masculine power, because these poems use no terms of gender, but to the sense of risk implicit in the act of self-division. Language's capacity for splitting into antithetical or free meanings is a powerful weapon when turned against itself and against sexual hierarchy, and when applied to identity it is equally dangerous. Eve's discovery of irony is liberating, but it is, after all, fatal. Yet at the same time that the poet is demonstrating this strategy's dangers she is using it to enlarge language's possibilities. Her repititions cause difference to emerge from sameness: when she says "Itself—it's Sovreign— of itself," the two words are distinct without being separately characterized. She makes us understand how richly duplicitous any word can be.

Dickinson's sense of herself as two selves, rather than as a unitary self in relation to others or as the other in relation to a self perceived elsewhere, is probably the most radical and conceptually challenging answer possible to the dualism of self and other that empowers the masculine tradition and that troubles its female inheritors. The same structural principle pervades and underlies the poetic strategies sketched in this chapter: it makes her ironies undecidable, it stalemates potential power struggles as they arise, and it splits words into etymological and connotative meanings while re- fusing to hierarchize them. Brontë's efforts to master her master never quite succeed because of her assumption that there is a unitary power of speech and that it can reside ony in one place. The external and powerful keepers of language make imaginative experience either unavailable or fearful as death. Because Dickinson places linguistic power in the context of her understanding of the fictiveness of language, she denies the singleness of that control, democratizing the structure of poetry. At the same time she revises for positive use what was a major difficulty for Dorothy Words- worth. Dorothy allows her lack of a central sense of self to arrest her writing poetry, because her inherited definition of poetry necessitates a central speaking self. Dickinson's self-division allows her to avoid direct compe- tition with the masculine unitary self, while at the same time also allowing her a power of her own. Dickinson's self-division approaches a stoppage like Dorothy's, but she uses it to press more meaning out of a word, and in the end to extend language rather than to collapse it.

It must not be forgotten that Dickinson's recognition of language's fictiveness, which has the effects charted above, came originally from her sense of femininity and of its place within the tradition that she then un- does. Once she has used her femininity as a force for disruption, she liberates herself from that too, because sexual determinism of any kind must be antithetical to her concerns.

The proof of her freedom is that where she sees an image of power she is free to consider adopting it as her own, late in her life, even though it represents the masculine tradition from which she was originally alien- ated. "A Word made Flesh is seldom" aligns the poet's linguistic powers with the incarnation of the Word that represents a masculine God's spe- cifically masculine powers of creation. The poem has been cited for its resemblance to other poems about the power and efficacy of language, but this way of reading, though it describes the religious content of the poem, does not indicate its significance in relation to her sense of identity. Dickinson is not simply making use of a clever metaphor for language's power; she is entertaining a long tradition of the inheritance of divine language by human language. Conflating the sequential transformation of word into flesh and of flesh into bread and wine, incarnation and Eucharist, the poet claims a protestant privilege of individual communion:

> A Word made Flesh is seldom
> And tremblingly partook
> Nor then perhaps reported
> But have I not mistook
> Each one of us has tasted
> With ecstasies of stealth
> The very food debated
> To our specific strength—
>
> (P 1651)

As the poem continues, the poet's operations are revealed as being like these manifestations of the Word. The Spirit dwells in the poet's words as much as in the divine Word: "Made Flesh and dwelt among us" is "Like this consent of Language/This loved Philology."

Neither the poem nor a prose fragment that it resembles (*L*, III, 912) can be securely dated, but the poem is likely to have been written late in the poet's life because of its similarity to a passage from a late letter.

> All grows strangely emphatic, and I think if I should see you again,
> I sh'd begin every sentence with "I say unto you—" The Bible
> dealt with the Centre, not with Circumference—
>
> (*L*, III, 849–50; late autumn, 1884)

The "Word made Flesh" of the undated poem is the speaker of "I say unto you." The Bible makes pronouncements and requires that its language be taken as the literal truth. The incarnation is the type of literal language, and that is what is meant by language as a center, as opposed to Dickinson's usual rhetorical indirection, which she often identifies as "circumference." To model her poetry after God's or Christ's speech would be to change to an entirely new paradigm, and to concede her fictive gains.

But have I not mistook? This alternate source of power would not be incorporated into poetic identity without qualification. "A Word that breathes distinctly"

> may expire if He—
> "Made Flesh and dwelt among us
> Could condescension be
> Like this consent of Language
> This loved Philology

A living word in a poem may lose its inspiriting power if the incarnation, as a provisional model for poetry, is a condescension. Consent is an agreement among equals, and that is how Dickinson's language normally operates. The phrase "This loved Philology" enacts that "consent of Language" by pairing two etymologically equivalent words. The difference between consent and condescension is small in sound and appearance, but the poet splits a sound to find a vast difference in meaning: where consent implies equality, condescension is a reversion to hierarchical ways. That love of the Logos is loved only as long as it is a consent. It would be too easy for the rhetoric of the center of "I say unto you—" to become a hierarchy of condescension. She would adopt a masculine prototype for the self's power, but only if it could be free from determinism. Rather than a revision of her own model for poetry, she proposes a revision in the entire structure of patriarchal religion, to the effect that the incarnation might become more like her poetry, instead of poetry aspiring to resemble the incarnation.

Emerson, Dickinson,
and the Abyss

Joanne Feit Diehl

> *He who fights with monsters should be careful lest he thereby become a monster. And if thou gaze long into an abyss, the abyss will also gaze into thee.*
>
> —FRIEDRICH NIETZSCHE

Arachne, maiden of legendary audacity, claimed she could weave more splendidly than the goddess Minerva herself; the challenge ended in self-inflicted death and metamorphosis into a spider—the cunning revenge of the divine weaver. Dickinson betrays a similar boldness, placing her poems against the most powerful voices for her generation—the poets of Romanticism. Like the Romantics, she writes quest poems, for they seek to complete the voyage, to prove the strength of the imagination against the stubbornness of life, the repression of an antithetical nature, and that "hidden mystery," the final territory of death. The form of the poems reflects their subject. She writes poems of "radical inquiry," riddles that tease the intelligence or alternatively achieve startling definitions which testify to the authority of her own consciousness. Such authority depends on power, and it is power that lies at the center of Dickinson's relation to Emerson. It is from Emerson that she learns the terms of the struggle and what she needs to conquer—to write poems that win from nature the triumph of freedom for the imagination.

Each of us holds a particular, if hidden, resentment towards the voice that first liberates us. How strong the antagonistic joy for Dickinson to read, almost in "credo" form, a validation of her initial aims in Emerson's essay, "The Poet"! The controlling image of poet as reader of the universe leads to his observing minute particulars, studying his relation to the text, his subject-symbol, finding what will suffice as an adequate symbol for the self. The poet must be more than a scrupulous reader, for "there is no fact in nature which does not carry the whole sense of nature," and even he is part of the process itself: "We are symbols and inhabit symbols." To

From *Dickinson and the Romantic Imagination.* © 1981 by Princeton University Press.

carry the creative emphasis further, the "poet is the Namer or Language-maker." In conclusion, all is in nature, and the force of the poet's imagination determines his success in hearing and reading the natural world. Emerson had yet to learn, in 1842, what he knew later—that such certain knowledge, a complete ability to read a text, was beyond any human poet. In "Experience," Emerson was to envision both life and the man living it as the result of illusions. The individual is limited to creating the illusion determined by his own qualities; we are left with the power to live within our self-created deceptions: "Dream delivers us to dream, and there is no end to illusions. . . . We animate what we can, and we see only what we animate. Nature and books belong to the eyes that see them." And, a little later in the essay, Emerson emphasizes the negative aspects of this personal dream: "Temperament also enters fully into the system of illusions and shuts us in a prison of glass which we cannot see."

In response to the Emerson of "The Poet," Dickinson works out her own solution as she asserts that nature is not the sacred text, ready to reveal all if we read it right. She contends not only that we can never attain to full knowledge of nature, that our view is dominated by our eye; she extends the negative cast of Emerson's opening pages of "Illusions": "There is illusion that shall deceive even the elect. There is illusion that shall deceive even the performer of the miracle. Though he make his body, he denies it." For her, nature becomes an antagonist, a deeply equivocal mystery, certainly exquisite at times, but with an exotic power that withholds its secrets as it dazzles. No matter how well one reads or imagines, nature as text withdraws and guards its final lesson; morality departs from the natural world to depend solely upon the individual. Consequently, the self perceives nature as an adversary and seeks to go beyond it into an anti- or postnaturalistic environment, pursuing questions in a self-dominated sphere that rejects the province of a communal, natural life. Finally, nature becomes not a sacred ground but a place that fails to protect, from which she must withdraw to ask other kinds of questions. Dickinson cannot accept the uneasy position Emerson maintains at the close of "Illusions": "If life seem a succession of dreams, yet poetic justice is done in dreams also." Nor can she subscribe to the conclusion to "Experience": a reiteration of justice and the rather belated assurance that "the true romance which the world exists to realize will be the transformation of genius into practical power." Abandonment of the problem fails to satisfy; nor is she temperamentally able to achieve the solace Emerson rises to attain: "For we transcend the circumstances continually and taste the real quality of existence. . . . We see God face to face every hour, and know the savor of Nature." Such compromises appear evasions to Dickinson, and she turns from them to seek her own accommodation to the dilemma Emerson described in his "Ode to Beauty":

> I dare not die
> In Being's deeps past ear and eye;

> Lest there I find the same deceiver
> And be the sport of Fate forever.
> Dread Power, but dear! if God thou be,
> Unmake me quite, or give thyself to me!

If nature is no longer at the center and cannot hold the answers she seeks, what of vision, the significance of sight? What becomes of the crucial Emersonian "eye" if the "text" cannot be read anyway? Although vision remains a major concern, she antithetically praises what she cannot see, either because the moment is past, distant, or denied. She defines through negation the positive values Emerson had praised in "Nature," "Circles," and "The Poet." She cannot believe that "a flash of his eye burns up the veil"; and the pattern of this failure, its procedures and disappointments, assumes priority for her imagination.

> Sweet Skepticism of the Heart—
> That knows—and does not know—
> And Tosses like a Fleet of Balm—
> Affronted by the snow—
> Invites and then retards the Truth
> Lest Certainty be sere
> Compared with the delicious throe
> Of transport thrilled with Fear—
>
> (P 1413)

Internal qualities developed in response to an impenetrable natural world determine her strength and inform her character; she chooses to fly "with Pinions of Disdain."

If Dickinson turns from the nature espoused by the early Emerson, denying its moral imperative, she also simultaneously relinquishes his doctrines of compensation and correspondence. No justice can be expected, no resemblance between self and the landscape maintained, once morality disappears from the universe of things. Emerson, at the age of twenty and writing for himself, stated most strongly what was to be an essential element for his own philosophical position: his ability to rise above circumstance into moments of ecstatic fulfillment. "Rend away the darkness," he writes, "and restore to man the knowledge of this principle [a moral universe], and you have lit the sun over the world and solved the riddle of life." Dickinson abjures this possibility, for when she surveys the landscape for evidence of the moral imperative she finds it lacking. Instead, Dickinson learns that nature is often capricious, disinterested, or cruel. By rejecting a moral nature, she cuts herself off from the comforts of a compensatory philosophy and a benevolent view of life which allows Emerson the privilege, when he can reach it, of escaping the ground of discouraging circumstance.

Dickinson, however, does seek correspondence between herself and nature, but her own consciousness must dictate the relationship; the landscape becomes an allegorical projection of her internal drama as her poems present a spectrum of reaction to the amorality of nature—from hope and exultation to despair. If nature cannot be relied upon as a way to approach the spiritual world and lead us from Secondary to Primary Causes, she must go by another route, approach immortality not through nature but in a direct confrontation with death. The poems' most ambitious attempt is, therefore, to provide us, the living, with the experience of hearing a voice speaking from the dead. They anticipate, observe, and follow the movements of the dying. This concentration on final moments is Dickinson's protest against the inviolate silence of death. What she wants, what "is best," the poems tell us, lies beyond her power, in realms of impossibility. It is past life that Dickinson wishes to draw her circle. If consciousness bestows power, she must carry her awareness beyond the grave, invading the forbidden territory with her voice. Emerson had asserted the potency of the energizing spirit to break through all boundaries, to rise above circumstance. Dickinson, with a daring literalism, attempts to face her central antagonist directly, to draw a circle around the fact of death. Emerson preaches the strength of the individual: "But if the soul is quick and strong it bursts over that boundary on all sides and expands another orbit on the great deep, which also runs up into a high wave, with attempt again to stop and to bind. But the heart refuses to be imprisoned; in its first and narrowest pulses it already tends outward with a vast force and to immense and innumerable expansions."

Dickinson's poems face the barrier of mortality and confront Emerson's challenge: "There is no outside, no inclosing wall, no circumference to us. . . . His only redress is forthwith to draw a circle outside of his antagonist." He perceives this power during isolated moments; the freedom of that moment from the past determines its potential for imaginative transformation: "In nature every moment is new; the past is always swallowed and forgotten; the coming only is sacred. Nothing is secure but life, transition, the energizing spirit." Her poems strive not for the moment in nature that is new but a space beyond it which provides a retrospective vision on life—the freedom of evaluation after the event. During life, however, there are moments which potentially speak of the mysteries to be disclosed in death, and it is the poet's task to witness these occasions and discover their meaning:

> The Moments of Dominion
> That happen on the Soul
> And leave it with a Discontent
> Too exqisite—to tell—
>
> (P 627)

The secret of the landscape will reveal itself only after life departs, when the taunts of an unknowable nature cease. Until then, "The Pleading of the Summer—" and "That other Prank—of Snow—" will not disclose their secret:

> Their Graspless manners—mock us—
> Until the Cheated Eye
> Shuts arrogantly—in the Grave—
> Another way—to see—
>
> (P 627)

Only the thinnest of veils, life, prevents her from winning this necessary vision. Another poem, in the same packet, and most probably written in the same year, 1862, asserts Dickinson's frustration in divine, mercantile terms which combine the bitterness of defeat with an attack on the doctrine of compensation itself:

> I asked no other thing—
> No other—was denied—
> I offered Being—for it—
> The Mighty Merchant sneered—
>
> Brazil? He twirled a Button—
> Without a glance my way—
> 'But—Madam—is there nothing else—
> That We can show—Today?'
>
> (P 621)

She finds other subjects, but Brazil—the ultimate exotic—remains an adequate symbol for the unifying quest of her poems. The challenge she faces is the inability to speak clearly from the other side of the grave. Deploring the inevitable silence, Dickinson will write poems that go so far as to deny death's inevitability and hover on the threshold between life and death. Prolepsis becomes a crucial strategy because it allows her to supersede the strictures of life. Moreover, passion extends to others' final moments as well; for, it is through death that the mutual condition of solipsism is simultaneously consolidated and dissolved.

Loss of belief, of a Christian or even an Emersonian faith, points toward the origins of her grim obsession:

> Those—dying then,
> Knew where they went—
> They went to God's Right Hand—
> That Hand is amputated now
> And God cannot be found—
>
> The abdication of Belief
> Makes the Behavior small—
> Better an ignis fatuus
> Than no illume at all—
>
> (P 1551)

Nullifying the integrity of the flame as the poem names it denies the possibility of belief. Always haunted by the forbidden, Dickinson merges memories of childhood lures, the "Flower Hesperian," with the promise of the dead. A worksheet draft written late in the poet's life specifies this preeminent concern with the moment of another's death:

> Still own thee—still thou art
> What surgeons call alive—
> Though slipping—slipping I perceive
> To thy reportless Grave—
>
> Which question shall I clutch—
> What answer wrest from thee
> Before thou dost exude away
> In the recallless sea?
>
> (P 1633)

The poem wants answers and is willing to clutch the question, to wrestle with the dying, for response. No other thing is denied, and the intensity of inquiry stems not from a life of despair but from an increasingly complete hegemony of consciousness that is deprived only of what it most craves to make it complete. Such extremity accounts, in large measure, for the polarities of the poems—the radically fluctuating moods that confront us as we read.

No forward or backward can be measured when the goal remains inviolate. Acknowledging that "no man saw awe," Dickinson asserts that we cannot come back bearing the vision, for "returning is a different route, The spirit could not show." Dickinson describes this geography of impossibility, a terrain one needs to cross before the journey begins: "Three Rivers and a Hill to cross/One Desert and a Sea." At the moment of completion, the fulfillment of her quest, mortality intercedes. With customary boldness, she names Death itself as the agent of usurpation; he walks off with the prize rightfully her own. In the face of this defeat, Dickinson places her poems, literally experiments that presume against the possible. She writes, "Experiment escorts us last—" and beneath "escorts" she places, then crosses out, "accosts." The polarity of feeling, the inner dialectic of what her "experiments" mean to her, cannot be more adequately conveyed than by these two words and their "correction."

Emerson challenges Dickinson to explore her power, but what saves him fails her needs. His darkest voice forms the background against which she composes poems. The opening to "Circles," an essay that deeply affected Dickinson, states the potency of expansion for the eye.

> The eye is the first circle; the horizon which it forms is the second; and throughout nature this primary figure is repeated without end. It is the highest emblem in the cipher of the world. St. Augustine described the nature of God as a circle whose centre was every-

where and its circumference nowhere. We are all our lifetime reading the copious sense of this first of forms. One moral we have
already deduced in considering the circular or compensatory character of every human action. Another analogy we shall now trace,
that every action admits of being outdone. Our life is an apprenticeship to the truth that around every circle another can be drawn;
that there is no end in nature, but every end is a beginning; There
is always another dawn risen on mid-noon, and under every deep
a lower deep opens.

The possibility of a "lower deep," a more potent mystery to conquer,
becomes, for Dickinson, the abyss; expansion opens into emptiness. She
cannot abide the thought of fathomless depths, for they offer not opportunity but the terror of imminent destruction, an utter dissolution of the
self. Emerson's faith in our capacity to expand into such depths depends
upon his effect as a teacher—his ability to awaken us from our lapse, our
temporary degeneracy. Only in such a state of slipping degradation are we
estranged from nature and God. "As we degenerate, the contrast between
us and our house is more evident. We are as much strangers in nature as
we are aliens from God." He heralds the need for a liberating poet to restore
us to an adequate awareness of our own possibilities. Through a series of
comparisons between this sublime potential and our current condition,
Emerson asserts the illimitable power lurking within: "Once man was all;
now he is an appendage, a nuisance." The fault can be remedied, if only
we heed his call. And throughout all the later, more sober, modulations
of his thought, the belief that "intellect annuls Fate. So far as a man thinks,
he is free," remains firm. In his early proclamation "Nature," Emerson
states this essential center to his future meditations: "The ruin or the blank
that we see when we look at nature, is in our own eye." The material world
remains subordinate to the power of the single mind, and, though he may
sink into a temporary despair, or realize the necessity of accepting some
principle of Fate, Emerson retains his belief in the power of the imagination
to rise above despondency and conquer the conditions of life.

But there are moments in Emerson when despair takes over, and it is
during these that he sounds most like Dickinson. In a journal entry marked
"Skepticism," Emerson states, "There are many skepticisms. The universe
is like an infinite series of planes, each of which is a false bottom, and
when we think our feet are planted now at last on the adamant, the slide
is drawn out from under us." Over twenty years later, he expresses the
relation of the Me and the Not-Me when the false bottom slips: "There
may be two or three or four steps, according to the genius of each, but for
every seeing soul there are two absorbing facts,—*I and the Abyss*." This
comes closest to Dickinson's vision of the problem she confronts. Here is
a struggle to know, to dive into the abyss and extract from it the knowledge
she cannot win from nature or any other mediate experience. She agrees

with Emerson when he remarks: "I am very content with knowing, if only I could know. That is an august entertainment, and would suffice me a great while." But the salves Emerson applies to heal the wound between "I and the Abyss" remain temperamentally unavailable to Dickinson. She cannot rely on a central self, a single, inner core. When she turns to it, she finds a consciousness that hides when she approaches, an inner adversary as threatening as any she faces from outside. And so experience becomes for her, literally, a "going through peril" a walk along broken planks over the abyss of annihilation; a vertiginous threshold which offers only the terror of defeat. Though the pit remains a threat to Emerson, he marshals against it the promise of the "over-seer," one who rises above, who stands erect, and climbs "the stairway of surprise" to freedom. If "the world is nothing, the man is all," he will take advantage of his sovereignty. "Let me ascend above my fate and work down upon my world." The stance of the beholder yields him the safety he requires. To stand above and aside allows him the leisure to recollect experience. And in this act he imitates the Spirit beyond—"For it is only the finite that has wrought and suffered; the infinite lies stretched in smiling repose." The eye of the observer is the gift of the poet and offers him imaginative freedom from the circumstances of life, the pain of existence. Such a perspective serves the world, for without man it would remain only "a remoter and inferior incarnation of God, a projection of God in the unconscious." The human mind provides the consciousness that lends meaning to an otherwise un-self-conscious, hence powerless nature. Man is the vital, necessary force that unites God to his works. Moreover, if one goes deep enough into the self, he discovers this truth is applicable to all men: the Other for Emerson is the Self, whereas for Dickinson the self can and most often does become the demonic Other.

The fluid conception of Self with its boundless potency allows Emerson to push past the border of confining limitations. In "Spiritual Laws," Emerson describes his concept of a self that asserts the requisite flexibility to enact his challenge: "A man is a method, a progressive arrangement; a selecting principle, gathering his like to him wherever he goes. He takes only his own out of the multiplicity that sweeps and circles round him. He is like one of those booms which are set out from the shore on rivers to catch driftwood, or like the loadstone amongst splinters of steel." The self has a pattern, a set of tendencies, which attracts only complimentary forms to it. This fluid self becomes in Emerson's own career an evolving identity that alters its strategies but returns to address itself to fundamental questions. Dickinson's transformation of this fluid self is among her more devastating achievements: from many selves, she names two, the self and the other. This "other" is consciousness, that awful internal stranger that she must repeatedly confront. Dickinson further polarizes the internal structure, for that other self is sexualized. He embodies the masculine, prepotent force that must be at once wooed and denied.

This choosing up sides and severely narrowing options determines the intensity of Dickinson's strongest poems. Lovers and friends feed the identities of self and other, but crucial action occurs within the single, split consciousness. Such internal duality serves as a structure that governs her poems, demanding the exchange of worlds and encouraging an essentially dramatic form. This primal split in the self finds corollaries, most notably in an intense psychomachia—the struggle between the body and the soul. Self-division hardens into a basic austerity when the Emersonian multiplicity reduces to two. This process of consolidation, a toughening of position, points toward the central split between the poets themselves.

In his confrontation with Necessity, Emerson adopts specific strategies for survival. By summoning his ability to distance at least a part of the self, he is able to embrace an acquiescence that accepts the fact of a finally unknowable nature and an unalterable Fate. Saadi, the Emersonian fictive poet, maintains his cheerful equanimity because of his absence from immediate involvement; he sits a little to one side and concentrates on writing poems. The development of such an independent poet-figure is itself a part of Emerson's creation of the Observer within the self. As R. A. Yoder writes:

> The personality of the poet was a matter of long and serious concern which Emerson tried to resolve in poems, essays, and even in bits of fiction scattered through the journals. Much of the character of the emerging poet-figure is clearly autobiographical and an attempt to state his own concept of the poet's role. But gradually Emerson loosened the identification between himself and the character he created, so that in his later essays, as Whicher pointed out, there are a number of dramatic characters or alter egos who speak for different, often opposite, sets of ideas.

By contrast, although Dickinson states that the "I" of her poems is not herself but a "supposed person," this separation exists outside the province of the text; it occurs before the formation of the "I" that speaks to us so directly from the heart of her poems.

Emerson, however, rather than force solutions to what he perceives as a deepened division between the Me and Not-Me, exploits this detachment which performs so incalculable a service: "What was food for remorse and regret on the plane of action, on the plane of intellection was matter for wonder. Even in his time of greatest enthusiasm some part of him had stood disengaged and aloof, and answered all interrogations, 'I, oh, I am only here to see.' " Although in times of disillusion, the privilege of spectatorship assumes a more ominous cast and threatens numbness; the relief, stasis, and aesthetic distance offered by this power earn it a permanent role within the flux of Emersonian identity.

Alternative vision—the observing eye—becomes literalized and expanded in Whitman's version of the self that stands apart and above. But in Dickinson's poems the self assumes neither an Emersonian nor a Whitmanian form. Her observer is potentially a spy, for his sight is directed not toward nature, the Not-Me, but focuses inward, on the self from which he grew. He most often takes the shape of an adversary, another consciousness that inhabits her mind and whose struggle Dickinson converts to poems. This other self may be best friend or deadly enemy—a love-hate relationship that assumes priority over any external commitment.

> The Soul unto itself
> Is an imperial friend—
> Or the most agonizing Spy—
> An Enemy—could send—
>
> Secure against it's own—
> No treason it can fear—
> Itself—it's Sovreign—of itself
> The Soul should stand in Awe—
> (P 683)

Despite this fundamental difference in their concepts of the Self, Emerson and Dickinson both find the origin of power within the individual. They assume a vocabulary normally ascribed to external, natural phenomena, and apply it to the inner life. Instances of this process of internalization recur throughout Emerson, and one does not have to look far to find him celebrating his own use of such language. Of man he declares: "But the lightning which explodes and fashions planets, maker of planets and suns, is in him." And, in what was to become a favorite trope for Dickinson, Emerson elaborates further upon the power that resides within:

> The human mind cannot be enshrined in a person who shall set a barrier on any one side to this unbounded, unboundable empire. It is one central fire, which, flaming now out of the lips of Etna, lightens the capes of Sicily, and now out of the throat of Vesuvius, illuminates the towers and vineyards of Naples. It is one light which beams out of a thousand stars. It is one soul which animates all men.

The lips of Etna and throat of Vesuvius, the oral and the volcanic, anticipate Dickinson's coupling of voice and flame. Threat of eruption, for both poets, emanates from the mouth:

> When Etna basks and purrs
> Naples is more afraid
> Than when she shows her Garnet Tooth—
> Security is loud—
> (P 1146)

Whereas Emerson and Dickinson are both drawn to the vision of an imminent power that smoulders undetected, Dickinson "personalizes" this vision. Volcanic force is no longer associated with universal man as in "The

American Scholar," but, instead, with the single life. Power does not run through all of us, as Emerson maintains; furthermore, it cannot be apprehended by anyone who observes the seemingly quiet, single self. The one soul which animates all men now stands isolated and alone.

> A still—Volcano—Life—
> That flickered in the night—
> When it was dark enough to do
> Without erasing sight—
>
> A quiet—Earthquake Style—
> Too subtle to suspect
> By natures this side Naples—
> The North cannot detect
>
> The Solemn—Torrid—Symbol—
> The lips that never lie—
> Whose hissing Corals part—and shut—
> And Cities—ooze away—
>
> (P 601)

This single life erupts irrevocably. Hidden, mysterious, still, the power floods mechanically; corals "part and shut"—destroying cities. What distinguishes this from Emerson's volcano is Dickinson's insistence on secrecy, on individuality, and on destruction. The poems will go further to identify this oral potency with both poetry and the self.

Moreover, Dickinson's practice of defining her self against Emerson's while drawing upon his language recurs in varying forms. Although she may alter the thrust of an Emersonian image or impose her own priorities on his diction, the new poem lies hidden in its parent text. Characteristically, a Dickinson poem takes an example that Emerson introduces into an essay and invests it with the strength of a subversive, anti-Emersonian vision. For instance, in his essay "Fate," Emerson develops a series of paragraphs that open with a general, declarative sentence followed by specific occasions which enumerate the forms his generalizations assume. One paragraph in this series supplants the "listing" of examples with an encapsulated narrative:

> The force with which we resist these torrents of tendency looks so ridiculously inadequate that it amounts to little more than a criticism or protest made by a minority of one, under compulsion of millions. I seemed in the height of a tempest to see men overboard struggling in the waves, and driven about here and there. They glanced intelligentlly at each other, but 'twas little they could do for one another; 'twas much if each could keep afloat alone. Well, they had a right to their eye-beams, and all the rest was Fate.

Emerson's example comes at the close of a series that climaxes in his assertion of our utter helplessness against the facts of nature, the fatality of our gestures against the end: "We cannot trifle with this reality, this cropping-out in our planted gardens of the core of the world. No picture of life can have any veracity that does not admit the odious facts. A man's power is hooped in by a necessity which, by many experiments, he touches on every side until he learns its arc." Emerson uses the drowning swimmers to enlist our sympathy while driving home the truth of the reality that affects us all. Dickinson's description of a related drowning is instructive.

> Two swimmers wrestled on the spar—
> Until the morning sun—
> When One—turned smiling to the land—
> Oh God! the Other One!
>
> The stray ships—passing—
> Spied a face—
> Upon the waters borne—
> With eyes in death—still begging raised—
> And hands—beseeching—thrown!
>
> (P 201)

One swimmer appears to *cause* the other's drowning, or, at least, offers him no help. He is clearly victorious, and at dawn returns triumphant toward shore. Dickinson shifts our attention to the "Other One," who is spied but ignored by the ships that pass as he sinks, still pleading, toward death. Emerson left his swimmers to Fate, choosing to emphasize that the glances exchanged by the drowning men could not save them, that indeed men are helpless to save even themselves in the presence of such a force; but Dickinson stresses the accountability of one swimmer for the other's death, as well as the prolonged moment of helplessness of the drowned. Ships that pass do not even attempt to help; they are "stray," random, without purpose, yet they do not pause; without so much as the excuse of destination, they abandon the pleading man to his death. The poem explodes the event, opening it to its own narrative emphases—wrestling, human responsibility, the concentration on the eyes in death. Paradoxically, this sharpening of focus magnifies the moment by an act of compression. Blame is localized; the point of view partial. With these shifts in emphasis, Dickinson renders impossible Emerson's acceptance of an impersonal, impenetrable Fate; agencies of solution—the power of the self, its relation to the Over-Soul, a capacity to grow erect—fail Dickinson. Her self is split, and nature remains a mystery immune to the power of even so masterful an intellect as her own. The mediating experience of nature deceives more than it satisfies. She defines existence as a series of descents in the abyss:

Emerging from an Abyss and entering it again—that is Life, is it not?

Dickinson's poems announce how it is to live on the edge of such danger. Fear of falling assumes precedence over the possibility of flight.

> A Pit—but Heaven over it—
> And Heaven beside, and Heaven abroad;
> And yet a Pit—
> With Heaven over it.
>
> To stir would be to slip—
> To look would be to drop—
> To dream—to sap the Prop
> That holds my chances up.
> Ah! Pit! With Heaven over it!
>
> The depth is all my thought—
> I dare not ask my feet—
> 'Twould start us where we sit
> So straight you'd scarce suspect
> It was a Pit—with fathoms under it
> Its Circuit just the same
> Seed—summer—tomb—
> Whose Doom to whom
>
> (P 1712)

The circuit of the pit (the path around it) is marked by the stages of life: the seed = birth, summer = maturity, and the tomb of death. The cycle of life itself walks on the edge, with no possibility of escape except a heaven that remains tantalizingly beside, abroad, and above it. The "I" is left with awe and the abyss, extremes that cause her to guard each step she takes as she rounds the circle.

> I stepped from Plank to Plank
> A slow and cautious way
> The Stars about my Head I felt
> About my Feet the Sea.
>
> I knew not but the next
> Would be my final inch—
> This gave me that precarious Gait
> Some call Experience.
>
> (P 875)

As the danger of her position increases, as her world is reduced to heaven and the abyss, to the stars and the sea, her own figure enlarges to fill the gap. Self assumes the gigantic proportions of one who touches the extremities of the universe. The radical severity of her world demands a self that will fill "the Term between." This giantism corresponds to the aims of the expanded self that desires to measure the abyss. Thus, her poems speak with the power of an enclosed solipsism, the voice of compression. By single moments alone can Dickinson chart her course into the heart of the abyss and map her way out of it. She warns both herself and us that "slipping—is Crashe's law"; the next moment may signal another descent.

What both Emerson and Dickinson call the abyss finds at least one of its origins in Jonathan Edwards' blazing pit of Hell. The terror his description instilled in the hearts of the congregation echoes in his wayward disciples: "Unconverted men walk over the pit of hell on a rotten covering, and there are innumerable places in this covering so weak that they will not bear their weight, and these places are not seen." The void of the unknown, the mystery of the abyss, has replaced the certainty of the flames of Hell, but the central image of our own thoughtless instability as we walk on rotten planks remains. By placing the supreme power within the individual, Emerson removed much of the fear of the emptiness beneath us, but Dickinson restores to the pit its rightful terror, not by an orthodox vision of Divine retribution, but with her own forbidding gift. She would have been moved by Edwards' vision of "the dreadful pit of the glowing flames of the wrath of God," substituting only her doubt for his certainty. Identical, however, is her tenuous position, the precariousness of the self: "You hang by a slender thread, with the flames of divine wrath flashing about it." She recognizes this condition, except in her abyss the flames are self-generated, created by the power of her own imagination. Furthermore, hers is an abyss that she tells us she can enter, and so it must be an internal, deeper part of the mind to which she descends and from which she emerges through the act of writing poems.

The fact that Dickinson's abyss lies within, that it resides in her psyche, grows from Emerson's assertion that the mind contains limitless possibilities. Ironically, what Dickinson acheives by fusing the threat of the Edwardsean pit with the Emersonian faith in the self is a devastating subversion of Emersonian power. She couples the mind's power with the terrors of hell to create, in an act of daring perversion, an unfathomable creature of her own mind—a pit she must enter for her salvation but a pit that holds within it the capacity to destroy the creative self.

Dickinson, in this radical act, recalls the specter of Arachne, who claims her superiority, usurping the sovereignty of others to weave a taut web above a pit of her own making. If the points of Dickinson's web touch the bottom of the pit, they also stretch to the heaven above it. The poems alone prove the wisdom of her demonic maneuver, a power won through the subversive risk of Arachnean form.

The Blind Poet: Sidney Lanier

Robert Penn Warren

More than half a century has elapsed since the death of Sidney Clopton Lanier, a period sufficient for the ordinary sifting of literary reputation. His body was interred in the Greenwood Cemetery of Baltimore in September 1881; his fame has been entrusted to the usual repositories. He has had his biography, his official edition of prose and verse, his courteous commentary in the textbooks, and even a circle of pious enthusiasts. It is doubtful if his new biography [*Sidney Lanier, A Biography and Critical Study*] will augment his fame.

It is doubtful, in the first place, because the biographer, Aubrey Harrison Starke, has nothing important to add to the body of common discussion. Certainly he has assembled a mass of material more formidable than has been previously accessible, but this material is, generally, of only corroborative value. It alters in neither outline nor meaning the more expert presentation made by Edwin Mims in his biography of Lanier, on which, as a matter of fact, the present writer seems sometimes to lean too heavily: Lanier's character remains unchanged for our contemplation.

In the second place, Mr. Starke entices with no novelty or acuteness of interpretation. "Professor Mim's biography makes beautifully clear the relation of Lanier to the South," Mr. Starke remarks, "but the time has come, I feel, for us to see Lanier first of all as a Southerner who grew beyond all sectional limitation." Again, Lanier's identification with the "New South," on which Professor Mims bestows emphasis, was nothing more nor less than identification with the national (*i.e.*, northern) ideal and programme. But on this issue Professor Mims is crystal clear:

From *The American Review* 2, no. 1 (November 1933). © 1934 by the Bookman Publishing Company, Inc.

He was national rather than provincial, open-minded not preju-
diced, modern and not mediaeval. His characteristics . . . are all
in direct contrast with those of the conservative Southerner. . . .
He therefore makes his appeal to every man who is today working
for the betterment of industrial, educational, and literary conditions in the South. . . . He was a pioneer worker in building up
what he liked to speak of as the New South:

> The South whose gaze is cast
> No more upon the past,
> But whose bright eyes the skies of promise sweep,
> Whose feet in paths of progress swiftly leap;
> And whose fresh thoughts, like cheerful rivers run
> Through odorous ways to meet the morning sun!

To this interpretation, it may be said, Professor Mims has given adequate
documentation.

On the critical side Mr. Starke's performance seems at best superficial;
that is, he rarely attempts analysis and, when he does, concentrates on
some detail which is almost irrelevant. In reference to the "Song of the
Chattahoochee," he says: "Any child can hear in it the music of the water,
but the child who has heard this too often, may fail later to note the varied
metre of the poem, the use of short vowels, liquid consonants, alliteration,
internal rhyme, and skilful repetition by means of which the music is recorded. Nor does early familiarity with the poem make for intelligent appreciation of its central idea, the river's swift answer to the call of duty."
Or again about another poem: "There the inclusion of an extra syllable,
e'en, in the fifth line of the second stanza spoils the metre." Elsewhere
grandiose analogy is Mr. Starke's most congenial method: "The *Symphony*
possesses a music more varied and more beautiful than that of *Corn*, and
a richness of imagery that comes from a close observation unsurpassed by
that of Marlowe or Shakespeare or Keats for accuracy." The Archbishop of
Canterbury might be added to the list.

But Mr. Starke has defined his own impulse as evangelical rather than
critical.

> Because he was and is one of us, a living figure of our own world,
> we need to know him, and so long as he becomes known to us
> for what he was, so long as he becomes known not merely to some
> but to all who love and cherish the American spirit and our great
> men, it matters little whether we find him in his poetry or in his
> letters, or in the tradition that lingers, or in the beautiful face of
> Keyser's bronze bust. It is only essential that we come to know
> him: until we have, discussion of his final rank as a poet is some-
> what futile, and after we have, it appears unnecessary.

To quarrel with this would be churlish.

But, specifically, what does a more profane curiosity discover in the Lanier who was born in Macon, Georgia, on February 3, 1842, and died of consumption at Lynn, in the mountains of North Carolina, on September 7, 1881? As a boy he drilled a company of archers and read Scott, Bulwer, and the *Arabian Nights;* later he attended Oglethorpe College, served creditably the Confederate cause as a mounted scout, and read Shelley, Coleridge, Keats, Wordsworth, Chatterton, Carlyle, Tennyson, Ruskin, Elizabeth Browning, and the German Romantic writers—Richter, Novalis, Heine, Schiller, Lessing, Schelling, Tieck, and Goethe, whose territory "was ever afterwards Lanier's spiritual home." In 1865 he was released from Point Lookout Prison, where his flute had comforted a fellow sufferer, Father Tabb, and returned to Macon with a few poor poems, a poorer novel, a determination to be an artist, either musical or literary, and a ruined constitution.

In this period, of which he could say "pretty much the whole of life has been merely not dying," Lanier had married. The rest of his short life was a twofold struggle, a heroic struggle against disease and a struggle, sometimes a trifle less than heroic, to gratify his literary ambition. By Lanier's own account Stedman once had to advise him in a friendly way, "not to be asking poets to dinner lest I might be thought to be pushing my way." And again, when the *Nation* rather soundly criticized the lack of clarity in his Centennial Ode for the Philadelphia celebration of 1876 as evidence "not so much of want of practice in composition as of discipline of thought," Lanier wrote: "it has naturally caused me to make a merciless arraignment and trial of my artistic purposes; and an unspeakable content arises out of the revelation that they come from an ordeal confirmed in innocence and clearly defined in their relation to all things. I do not hate people who have so cruelly maltreated me; they knew not what they did; and my life will be of some avail if it shall teach even one of them a consideration that may bloom in tenderer treatment of any future young artist." Such was

> The artist's pain—to walk his blood-stained ways,
> A special soul yet judged as general—
> The endless grief of art, the sneer that slays,
> The war, the wound, the grave, the funeral pall.

In fact, although Lanier demanded of the South a stern and nonsectional literary criticism, he himself adopted in the face of critics an attitude either querulous or Christ-like; on the whole, he seemed to find the latter more satisfying.

The German Romantics, we are told, and the English Romantics with their Victorian brethren for that matter, defined the demesne that was always to remain Lanier's "spiritual home." But there was some commerce between the spiritual home and the perfectly substantial, though disordered, home Lanier occupied in the South of Reconstruction. From the spiritual abode he brought a message which, according to Mr. Starke, is "particularly worth listening to in the present period of economic and social unrest." The message appears in varying forms, in the poems and in the several volumes of collected prose. It is a message sometimes contradictory or vague, as a communication from the realm of spirits is apt to sound in perverse mundane ears. Coleridge said that his early reading gave him a mind "habituated to the vast"; Lanier's early reading gave him a mind habituated not to the vast but to the confused, to the blurred. Or possibly it was not the fault of the reading.

"For as time flows on," Lanier wrote in "Retrospects and Prospects," an early essay, but one which differs from later work only in the greater naïveté of detail and example, "For as time flows on, man and nature steadily etherealize. As time flows on, the sense-kingdom continually decreases, and the soul-kingdom continually increases, *and this not by the destruction of sense's subjects, but by a system of promotions in which sensuous things, constantly etherealizing, constantly acquire the dignity of spiritual things, and so diminish their own number and increase the other.*" This sentiment is a sort of text for Lanier's work, equally for his applause of science and his applause of small diversified farms, for the "Psalm of the West" and the *English Novel*, for "The Marshes of Glynn" and his nationalism, for his admiration of Beethoven and his admiration of big business.

Nature, he said, etherealizes. "In Greek times Nature rose halfway to the dignity of man, with her oreads and nymphs and fauns; in our times she has risen all the way." This new relation, this etherealization, is expressed in the "nature-metaphor," which is a union "of human nature with physical nature," the embodiment of man's broadened love of the universe, and in the advances of the studies in physical science.

For man this etherealization seems to correspond to the development of "personality," which since the Renaissance has assumed three characteristic new relations. Lanier's little chart in the *English Novel* sums up the whole matter. And all of these new relations, which find their characteristic expressions in Music, the Novel, and Science, respectively, are rooted in Love.

The Unknown (Music)

Personality ⟶ *Fellowman (The Novel)*

Nature (Physical Science)

The little chart, in itself, may be irrelevant. The important thing is this: where did it guide Lanier? In literature it led him to prefer Tennyson to Milton, because Tennyson is "more spiritual" and has purged himself of Milton's "purely physical accessories." He preferred George Eliot to Fielding, that "muck of the classics," and, incidentally, to Shakespeare, presumably because she "shows man what he may be, in terms of what he is." In architecture it led him to regard the rapidity and lightness of commercial construction as an indication of "the veritable etherealizing change which it has undergone." It led him to applaud photography as an "etherealized" painting, an art which now "has risen and floated away free as air and sunshine into all homes and all wastes, simply by having lightened itself of the purely material load of colour."

Few people, however, have taken Lanier seriously as a critic; but many people have taken him seriously as a prophet, as a man with a message. The element of this message which, in the not-so-distant past, received most approbation was his nationalism, that doctrine transcending merely sectional concern or prejudice. This nationalism represented, I surmise, an "etherealization." Actually, it can be cast in terms of his formula: "The soul kingdom increases . . . by a system of promotions in which sensuous things [*i.e.*, the States, the individual localities with conflicting traditions and interests], constantly etherealizing, constantly acquire the dignity of spiritual things [*i.e.*, the Nation]." The basis of such new etherealized relations, it is worthy of recollection, is Love—that "key to Lanier's philosophy." The Civil War, recently concluded, had been the great single step toward the achievement of the new nationalism. The Civil War, we may infer, was, if not itself an act of love, a step toward a loving synthesis. As a matter of fact, in the "Psalm of the West," that favourite document for Lanier's nationalism, the fratricidal and sanguine years of 1861–65 are represented allegorically as a joust between two knights, *Heart* (the South) and *Brain* (the North):

> They charged, they struck; both fell, both bled;
> Brain rose again, ungloved;
> Heart fainting smiled, and softly said,
> *My love to my beloved.*
>
> Heart and Brain! no more be twain;
> Throb and think, one flesh again!
> Lo! they weep, they turn, they run;
> Lo! they kiss: Love, thou art one!

In the year 1876 this must have struck some as slightly unrealistic.

Lanier was not realistic. He wrote as a poet of the new nationalism, and at the same time he protested (although he once found it in his heart to approve big corporations because they were "needed") against the domination of Trade, by which he meant, apparently, commerce and industry. "The worker must pass to his work in the terrible town," he complained. Or he surveyed the "hell-coloured smoke of the factories." Specifically, as in the "Symphony," his objection is that Trade dries up the springs of Love, that its ethics are those of war, that it does not permit the labourer to recline "where Art and Nature sing and smile." Mr. Starke submits that the "Symphony" "presents an intelligible program for social amelioration." This program is Love, and the instrument of its execution is music: "Love

God utterly, and thy neighbour as thyself—so I think the time will come when music rightly developed to its now-little-foreseen grandeur, will be found to be a revelation of all gospels in one." But what Mr. Starke fails to see, as Lanier failed, is that the nationalism mystically embodied in the "Psalm of the West" was a nationalism of Trade. *Amor vincit omnia*—even the contradiction.

Lanier's evangelical concern with science meant a similar contradiction, or rather a two-edged one, as related to art and to society. Science, along with the nature-metaphor, he regarded as an indication of the Love of Nature . . . the new *rapport* between Man and Nature. "We found," he said to his audience in Baltimore, "that science and poetry had been developing alongside each other ever since early in the seventeenth century; inquiring into the general effect of this long contact, we could only find that it was to make our general poetry greatly richer in substance and finer in form." It is, probably, a defect of taste to prefer "darling Tennyson" to Milton; it is a defect of another order to confound science with art, the abstract with the concrete, the practical with the contemplative.

> And Science be known as the sense making love to the All,
> And Art be known as the soul making love to the All,
> And Love be known as the marriage of man with the All—
> Till Science to knowing the Highest shall lovingly turn,
> Till Art to loving the Highest shall consciously burn,
> Till Science to Art as a man to a woman shall yearn.

It is no wonder that Lanier likewise failed to perceive that the science he adored was the handmaid of the industrial system he detested. But in enthusiasm for his American myth he sometimes even forgot that science was a Venus and made her into a sort of amazon with brand and buckler.

> Yea, where the taunting fall and grind
> Of Nature's Ill doth send
>
> Such mortal challenge of a clown
> Rude thrust upon the soul,
> That men but smile where mountains frown
> Or scowling waters roll,
> And Nature's front of battle down
> Do hurl from pole to pole.

In such moments he did achieve realism.

Now all of Lanier's judgements on the arts, as judgements, are devoid of interest except such interest as is felt in eccentricity. His social judgements in themselves are interesting only insofar as they illustrate the peculiar and sometimes irresponsible confusion into which the southern liberal lapsed. The artistic judgements, to put it bluntly, simply mean that Lanier, despite his professions of extreme sensitivity, was really lacking in capacity for aesthetic perception. He did not *see* anything. He was a doctrinaire; that is, he appreciated a work of art to the degree in which it supported his especial theory of progress. But that very theory of progress, and his particular social applications of it, means that he did not think except in obvious and incomplete analogy. These various judgements are worthy of discussion at all only because they may clarify, to some extent, the properties of his poetry.

Lanier's fame depends on his poetry. If he had not written the poems, he would now be a scarcely remembered flute-player with liberal views and a handsome head. His personality, Mr. Starke to the contrary, would not command us.

Lanier's conception of himself, of the poet's role, was a paradoxical one, but one characteristic of the century in which he lived. The poet was a "special soul yet judged as general," a sufferer who indulged the "endless grief of art." There is an element of self-dramatization in much of his poetry, for instance, in "Sunrise," in "The Marshes of Glynn," and in "Clover"; the poet, withdrawn from the humming haunts of men, is presented in the throes of an experience. But in his letters this characteristic is most obvious: the critics "knew not what they did." He was "a pard-like spirit, beautiful and swift," but unlike Shelley, he was never unsure as to whether it was the mark of Cain or Christ he bore on the brow. Paradoxically, the poet is not only a special soul set apart, but a social prophet. That is, the business of the poet is twofold: he must "express" his own etherealizing personality and must reform the personalities of other people. Or perhaps it was not as paradoxical as it seems; the egotist imposes himelf.

The difficulty, for Lanier, was insoluble. No poem of his represents a single vision, for the fatal self-consciousness intervenes. The obvious criticism is that he is didactic. But, more fundamentally, the trouble was that he never understood the function of idea in art. He regularly performed an arbitrary disjunction, both in creation and in criticism, between the idea and the form in which it might be embodied. Painting etherealizes by freeing itself of the "purely material load of colour." "The Princess" is superior to *Paradise Lost.* Or religion etherealizes by losing its "material props," by which, I suppose, he meant dogma, ritual, and, finally, the Church itself. Lanier's poetry, by consequence, was intellectual in a bad sense—in the sense that Browning or Tennyson, or better, Elizabeth Browning, all better poets, were frequently intellectual. The idea is never realized; it remains abstract; it does not achieve the status of experience.

Lanier's imagery, in this respect, is instructive. Early in his poetical career he wrote to his father: "I have frequently noticed in myself a tendency to a diffuse style; a disposition to push my metaphors too far, employing a multitude of words to heighten the patness of the image and so making of it a *conceit.*" This self-criticism has been almost consistently echoed by writers on Lanier, such as Professor Howard Mumford Jones, with the assumption that the conceit is necessarily bad. Lanier occasionally did employ images that might be termed conceits, but they were bad conceits, "yoked by violence." For instance, in an early poem revised in 1879:

> A star that had remarked her pain
> Shone straightway down that leafy lane,
> And wrought his image, mirror-plain,
> Within a tear that on her lash hung gleaming.
> "Thus Time," I cried, "is but a tear
> Someone hath wept 'twixt hope and fear,
> Yet in his little lucent sphere
> Our star of stars, Eternity, is beaming."

Compare this with Donne's more famous tear:

> On a round ball
> A workman that hath copies by, can lay
> An Europe, Afrique, and an Asia,
> And quickly make that, which was nothing, *All*,
>   So doth each teare
>   Which thee doth weare,
> A globe, yea world by that impression grow,
> Till thy teares mixt with mine doe overflow
> This world, by waters sent from thee, my heaven dissolved
>   so.

Lanier's so-called conceit is bold and vague; Donne's is bold, but precise on each term of comparison. Lanier's is, by reason of its vagueness, artificial; Donne's is artificial only in the sense that all imagery is artificial, that is, from the scientific view.

But more generally, in the attempt to communicate a poetic idea, Lanier resorted to something that is more like a fragmentary allegory than like the conceit. The conceit, I believe, differs structurally from the images commonly called metaphor or simile only in that it affords more than one point of contact between the two elements involved in the image, more than one term of comparison. The extension of contact invites a prolonged contemplation; by calling attention to the purely logical form of the comparison it provokes a scientific criticism of that comparison which is really pseudo-scientific. The resolution of what might, for lack of a better term, be called the *internal strain* of the conceit gives that special effect associated with metaphysical poetry. But the resolution, the success of the conceit, depends on precisely the same factors as those involved in the other types of imagery. Now an allegory seems to be a system of assigned equivalents. Such a system is comprised by the Ox representing the "Course-of-Things" and the heads of clover representing the poets in "Corn"; or by the "young Adam of the West" representing America in "Psalm of the West." Cases of incidental allegory are numerous, as in the much admired "Stirrup-Cup," the first division of "Sunrise," the next to the last stanza of "Corn," "Song of the Future," or "Marsh Song." The last is interesting because it presents in protracted form a mannerism which often occurs in Lanier's work, the use of literary allusion with allegorical implication. I shall only quote the first stanza:

> Over the monstrous shambling sea,
>   Over the Caliban sea,
> Bright Ariel-cloud, thou lingerest:
> Oh wait, oh wait, in the warm red West,—
>   Thy Prospero I'll be.

Except for the first line this stanza conveys no perception, and even the literal, the intellectual, meaning is dependent on a knowledge of *The Tempest* for comprehensibility. The allegory, even, is second-hand. This is perfectly arbitrary, arbitrary in the same way that the assignment to various instruments of different attitudes in regard to Trade is arbitrary in the "Symphony." It is but another example of Lanier's failure to realize an idea poetically.

Lanier was right, however, when he commented on his tendency to diffuseness, a fault which arose from vagueness of perception. In Andrew Marvell's "Bermudas" occur the lines:

> He hangs in shades the orange bright
> Like golden lamps in a green night.

By insistence (again something related to his allegorical bias) Lanier debases a similar image in "Tampa Robins":

> Burn, golden globes in leafy sky,
> My orange-planets: crimson I
> Will shine and shoot among the spheres
> (Blithe meteor that no mortal fears)
>   And thrid the heavenly orange-tree
>   With orbits bright of minstrelsy.

Lanier confuses the visual image, orange-planets, with "orbits bright of minstrelsy," which is no image at all. But a better instance appears in "Clover":

> Now the little winds, as bees,
> Bowing the blooms come wandering where I lie
> Mixt soul and body with the clover-tufts,
> Light on my spirit, give from wing and thigh
> Rich pollens and divine sweet irritants
> To every nerve, and freshly make report
> Of inmost Nature's secret autumn thought
> Unto some soul of sense within my frame
> That owns each cognizance of the outlying five
> And sees, hears, tastes, smells, touches, all in one.

Aside from a vile and pedestrian versification, the chief fault of this passage is vagueness which results in diffuseness. Compare with this the precison, the poised hypnotic quality, of Marvell's couplet from "Thoughts in a Garden," of which it is reminiscent:

> Annihilating all that's made
> To a green thought in a green shade.

If Lanier read Marvell, he read him without understanding.

Much of Lanier's imagery, much that has been excessively admired, reduces to nothing more than verbalism.

> Tolerant plains, that suffer the sea and the rains and the
>   sun
> Ye spread and span like the catholic man who hath mightily
>   won
> God out of knowledge and good out of infinite pain
> And sight out of blindness and purity out of a stain.

To me this conveys nothing. But again:

> Far down the wood, a one-desiring dove
> Times me the beating of the heart of love

And this

> To bend of beauty the bow, or hold of silence the string.

Or this

> The beech dreams balm, as a dreamer hums a song

These lines, as far as I can make out, exemplify the "nature-metaphor," that "union of human nature with physical nature." Abstractness is the quality most apparent; the reader neither sees the *plains*, nor understands the *tolerence*.

With this usually goes another variety of abstractness, a variety expressed in Lanier's fondness for adjectives like *dear, sweet, adorable*, and *thrilling*, and for lines like

> Of the dim sweet woods, of the dear dark woods.

This abstractness, it seems, derives from Lanier's sentimentality, a property quite as common and offensive in his prose as in his verse. ("That adorable sonnet," "our adorable John Keats.") That is, Lanier insists on an emotional attitude for which he can provide no stimulus; the reader is asked to accept the poet's experience on trust, the one thing a reader declines to do, unless he, like the poet, is a sentimentalist.

This sentimentality is not confined to detail, but appears, naturally enough, at the very root of Lanier's inspiration. It is a result of his basic bewilderment. The general theme of all his poetry, the critics say, is Love, which apparently was the name he bestowed on any emotional disturbance. I have shown, I hope, that when he tried to define his attitudes in presumably sober prose, he merely resolved a confusion or contradiction by appeal to that term. In poetry his theme is most commonly manifested in what has been called his "nature-worship." (It is well to remember that Lanier, in his fairly acute criticism of Whitman in the *English Novel*, said realistically enough: "Nature is the tyrant of tyrants.") Despite the fact that he has been frequently praised as an observer of Nature, most recently by Mr. Starke and Mr. Ludwig Lewisohn, he exhibited a remarkably feeble capacity for seeing anything; his use of imagery makes that clear. He referred to Nature as a vague embodiment of his private agitations, his desire for marriage with the All.

> I am fain to face
> The vast sweet visage of space.

'Tis here by the marsh, he said

> 'Tis here, 'tis here thou canst unhand thy heart
> And breathe it free, and breathe it free.

As with all sentimentalists, Lanier's emotionalism was a species of self-indulgence, which probably accounts for the fact that he was able to communicate nothing. It was a species of self-indulgence both sensual and effeminate, as his relaxed rhythmic effects often imply. But rhythm is not the only evidence. The glades in the marshes are

> Cells for the passionate pleasure of prayer to the soul
>   that grieves.

And he could commit himself to these lines:

> Tell me, sweet burly-barked, man-bodied Tree
> That mine arms in the dark are embracing, dost know
> From what fount are these tears at thy feet which flow?

The most charitable pronouncement on this, as on much of Lanier's poetry, is that it is absurd.

Lanier has only a doubtful importance for us. What he had to say has been said by better men in a better way: Wordsworth, Coleridge, Tennyson, Shelley, Emerson, Carlyle, Browning, Longfellow, Ruskin, Swinburne. Lanier merely recapitulated in a vulgar and naïve version what today may appear as their fallacies and confusions, the unsatisfying quality of their work. He was the final product of all that was dangerous in Romanticism: his theory of personality, his delusion of prophecy, his aesthetic premise, his uninformed admiration of science, his nationalism, his passion for synthesis, his theory of progress. What was valuable in his century passed him by. He was admired because, as Tennyson to England, he spoke to America, and tardily to the South, in the accent of its dearest anticipations:

> Now the glittering Western land
> Twins the day-lit Eastern Strand;
> Now white Freedom's sea-bird wing
> Roams the Sea of Everything;
> Now the freemen to and fro
> Bind the tyrant sand and snow,
> Snatching Death's hot bolt ere hurled,
> Flash new life around the world,
> Sun the secrets of the hills,
> Shame the gods' slow-grinding mills,
> Prison Yesterday in Print,
> Read To-morrow's weather-hint,
> Haste before the halting Time,
> Try new virtue and new crime,
> Mould new faiths, devise new creeds,
> Run each road that frontward leads,
> Driven by an Onward-ache,
> Scorning souls that circles make.

After all, Mr. Starke may be right. Perhaps we should know Lanier. He may help us to assess our heritage.

Sidney Lanier and "Musicality"

John Hollander

A poet who is also a skilled professional musician would appear to have all sorts of advantages. Not only would he or she reunite the sundered halves of the power of control over melody and text which the Greeks called *mousiké*, thus reconstructing as well the type of Orpheus *in propria persona*. Having intimate knowledge of literal musical structure—its schemata of repetition, variation, and the modulation of relationships; its metaphors of gesture, event, and emotion—might seem to give one added insights into the so-called music of poetic language. Instances are of course rare: in the Renaissance, there is the case of Thomas Campion (yet even he was not a "professional" in the modern sense), and we are told of Herbert and Milton and their knowledge and love of music, their being able to play the lute, and so forth (but this is rather like being able to play the piano today: it doesn't make one a musician). Of nineteenth-century English poets, only Leigh Hunt and Robert Browning display much technical musical knowledge at all; in America, Whitman's exuberant love of opera is somewhat exceptional, and in general the English language has not tended to produce, in its writers of genius, the relations between literary and musical skills that we find in a Rousseau, an E. T. A. Hoffman, or a Nietzsche.

Sidney Lanier was extremely conscious of a dual heritage: a literal musical ancestry (Nicholas Lanier composed music for some of Ben Jonson's masques) and the figurative, but sometimes even more powerfully significant, literary paternity which is so fascinating in its manifest and latent variations. A professional orchestral flute-player of presumably great skill, Lanier was devoted to music and that devotion generally overflowed into

---

his concern to sanctify poetry itself. But there is a danger for poetry always lurking in the literal, and this danger looms large in the literal conflation of poetry and music—save for that continuingly remarkable and tentative series of brief assignations which the long-since divorced couple, text and music, contrive for themselves from time to time in art-song. It can manifest itself in the proto-symbolist attempt to dissolve signification in what is thought to be "pure" sound, as in Poe: this is in itself a weakly literal misreading of the notion that Walter Pater would eventually put in canonical form as "All art constantly aspires toward the condition of music." Fortunately for Lanier's best poems, they are able to escape the reductive literalism that affected his prosodic and rhythmic theorizing and, as we shall see, the tropes of music in his poetry have much more to do with those of the major romantic tradition than with their author's own musicianship.

But even to consider the theory for a moment is instructive. Lanier's *The Science of English Verse,* finished in the penultimate year of the poet's life, when the final stages of tuberculosis were yet insufficiently debilitating to daunt his prodigious energies, is a touching monument to the mistake that organized linguistic sound patterns can be analyzed with the methods developed over centuries to notate musical tones. "Music is *not* a species of Language. Language is a species of music," Lanier insisted (appendix 7 in the Centennial Edition volume containing *The Science of English Verse*). In this he seemed unaware that some German romantic theorists before him, and much of the serious treatment of meaning and representation in music today, would either want to put it exactly the opposite way or argue that the very terms of the formulation are misleading. Lanier's concept of musicality in poetry, while it takes on an almost religious significance for him in itself, is derived from the sophisticated practical knowledge of a working musician; nevertheless, it is that very technical power which seems to turn the gentlest of spirits into an unwitting intellectual Procrustes.

Lanier's equivocal musical notations of prosodic entities—transcribing lines and passages of English accentual-syllabic verse in regularly barred rhythmic notation—dictated a reading of the text rather than describing the activity of rhythmic linguistic events occurring in a metrical frame. He seemed unaware—as most nineteenth-century musicians were—of unbarred medieval and Renaissance notation, or of the utility of ad hoc rebarrings as in later music. The notational possibilities open to him were thus rather narrow in the first place, causing him to interpret in triple or quadruple musical meters what are in fact subtle variations of what is only metaphorically speaking "length" or "duration" in accentual-syllabic verse. In essence, Lanier's musical notations were unpitched musical settings of the text, declamatory and inexpressive, seemingly responsible only to regularities of poetic accent better rendered by the standard notation of stressed and unstressed syllables in any case. None of his paradigms could be right or wrong, save for doing unreasonable violence to English word accent.

Thus, for example, he notates the Old English "Wanderer," beginning "Oft him anhaga are gebideth," in musical 3/8 time; yet doing so in 2/4 would preserve similarly the downbeats on the primary stresses (*"oft," "an," "ar-,"* and *"bid-"*), and even allow the secondary stress on the fourth syllable of the line a more viable rhythmic treatment than a triple rhythm does (unless Lanier were to have specified something like a muzurka rhythm for his second measure). But the point is ultimately that equal timing of syllables is in the case of English an irrelevant imposition of a declamatory chant upon the far more subtle, variable, and dynamic rhythms of the spoken language, and, even more important, that with a stressed language like English, the interplay of syntax and rhythm, the subtle dispositions of metrically stressed syllables to differentiate meanings (rather than, as Lanier felt, to set up an authenticating undersong of transcendence) is the heart of the rhythmic matter.

In such questions as that of rhyme too, odd, vague analogies between vowel sound, musical timbre, and visual "color," curiosities of some late eighteenth-century aesthetic theories, again come up in despite of deeper questions of signification. Lanier is concerned with feeling and not with meaning, both in music and in poetic language. His remarks on Beethoven's Seventh Symphony in one of his essays concern not the structure of the work but a program of emotionally mimetic moments and devices which he reads into it. In short, his technical writing on the music of verse generally expands upon a typical late-romantic trope, and as such might be considered part of his poetry.

His own verse on formal musical subjects reflects not so much his musical ability per se as it does his rather broadly held association of music with the divine. The poems to Beethoven and Wagner praise the composers as myth-makers and heroes of the imagination, and a sonnet to a Baltimore pianist both in German and in English invokes the conceptual hyperbole that, in her, Beethoven "lives again." Robert Browning, an amateur musician but a very hard-thinking one, might have been far more specific, as well as far more conditional, in a case like this, making very specific emblems and conceits out of sudden modulations, the architectonic character of certain kinds of musical structure (Beethoven's in particular, although for Lanier it is just that quality which ceases to exist in his sweeping but undifferentiated praise). It is indeed rare to find such precise musical imagery in Lanier's poems, as in the Browningesque moment from the fine, late "Sunrise" when a line of almost pure Whitman is followed with a varied repetition: "So, with your question embroid'ring the dark of the question of man,—/So, with your silences purfling this silence of man." Here, "purfling," used so as to seem simply synonymous with "embroid'ring," is actually operating in its musical application—the purfling of black around the borders of violins, violas, and cellos—to reinforce the relation of "dark" to "silence." Similarly, the moment in "The Symphony" when "A velvet flute-note fell down pleasantly/Upon the bosom of that harmony," a precisely observed effect of orchestration, of flute against thick string-writing, is being remembered. The interplay of flute and violin, frequent in this and other poems, reverses a very traditional sort of emblematic distinction (between the rational string and the emotive wind), neoclassical in origin and ubiquitous since the Renaissance, in another, far more personal musical iconography. The violin of passion, whose sounds are produced by active bowing, is opposed frequently in his images to the more controlled and rational flute. Again, from "Sunrise":

> Oh, what if a sound should be made!
> Oh, what if a bound should be laid
> To this bow-and-string tension of beauty and silence
>   a-spring,—
> To the bend of beauty the bow, or the hold of silence the
>   string!
> I fear me.

Aside from the remarkable complexity of the image of bow and string and the sense of their dialectic, these lines suggest some of what G. M. Hopkins was writing at the same time, but which would remain unpublished for so long.

Indeed, many of Lanier's remarkable lines have a power that seems to be sapped by the overall structure of the poems that contain them—and this is particularly true of the chant-like Hymns. Three lines near the opening of "Sunrise" need only to be deprived of the rhyme at the end of the middle one to gain a Whitmanian strength:

> The little green leaves would not let me alone in my sleep;
> Up-breathed from the marshes, a message of range and of
>   sweep,
> Interwoven with waftures of wild sea-liberties, drifting.

Or the opening line of "The Marshes of Glynn," when separated from the weaker, rhyming second one: "Glooms of the live-oaks, beautiful-braided and woven"; here again we feel that the music of Lanier's verse lies closer to the ebb and flow of Whitman's than to the brilliant contraptions of Swinburne's. These are both poets whose mighty conceptions of art, self, and sexuality could not but cause Lanier some concern, given his milder-natured belief in music as "Love in search of a word."

His most ambitious poems are the long, ode-like chants: "The Symphony," "Sunrise," "The Marshes of Glynn," "The Psalm of the West," the earlier "Corn." It is primarily moments in these that are most profoundly successful (with the exception, probably, of "Sunrise" and "The Marshes of Glynn," which are two of his finest poems). When he writes in a smaller compass, as in the very fine "A Ballad of Trees and the Master" or in "The Song of the Chattahoochee," he avoids the impulse to call attention to the expansive repetitions and modulating line-lengths of the

more self-proclaimedly "musical" form, and this tends sometimes to undercut—as we have seen from a few examples—the particular rhetorical
power of particular lines. It is instructive to compare the last-mentioned
lyric, the voice of the poet-river dutifully shunning distractions of folly or
dalliance (despite its "lover's pain to attain the plain," the Georgia river
must shun the patently erotic "lures with the lights of streaming stone / In
the clefts of the hills of Habersham, In the beds of the valleys of Hall"),
with a later poet's revision of it. Hart Crane's "Repose of Rivers" recasts
Lanier's stream as strongly as the earlier poet had recast Tennyson (both
in "The Brook" and in other lyrics); "The pond I entered once and quickly
fled—/I remember now its singing willow rim," is part of a meditative lyric,
brooding over a refigured journey whose distractions and byways are as
much its matter as is its mere termination.

This poem, along with the wonderful sonnet "To the Mockingbird,"
"Clover," and the longer poems mentioned earlier, comprise the canon of
Lanier's poetry, and are of a stature far above that of his occasional verses,
or of his best-forgotten verses in dialect. In them, he continually invokes
literal and figurative music as a trope for universal expressiveness. What
is so interesting about this is how often he employs or develops a figure
from the history of English poetry after Milton, such as the adaptation of
the Aeolian harp image into a natural instrument, in "The Psalm of the
West":

> And the sun stretched beams to the worlds as the shining
>   strings
> Of the large hid harp that sounds when an all-lover sings.

Again, a few lines later in the same poem, the raising of Pandemonium in
book 2 of *Paradise Lost* is echoed in the musico-poetic artist's creation:

> And the spirals of music e'er higher and higher he wound
> Till the luminous cinctures of melody up from the ground
> Arose as the shaft of a tapering tower of sound.

It is more important for Lanier as a poet that this represents the discerning
ear of the reader of texts rather than that of the performing reader of scores;
Lanier's music is here drawn from the repository of romantic musical mythology rather than actual concert-hall practice, and it allows the verse in
which it is framed to become truly poetry rather than versified essay or
journalism.

It is by the very virtue of the way in which Lanier's work in verse and
prose embraces two modes of considering music, then, that he holds such
interest for readers interested in the relation of the two arts. If his prosodic
theories do not hold up, largely because of the weakness of their theoretical
grasp of linguistic structure, they certainly support in another, figurative
way the larger thematic image, the realm of the Sublime, that music becomes in his best poems. Lanier's life as a practical musician could double

with his vocation as a poet, and allowed him to sanctify artistic work—as against a rather simplistic vision of trade and industry—in more than one way. One cannot tell whether, had he lived beyond the age of thirty-nine, this vision might have acquired more complexity, or its expression more tension. But that the poems of 1880 (the year before his death) show him beginning to hit a remarkable stride, there can never be any doubt.

The Poetry of Stephen Crane: War in Heaven

Daniel G. Hoffman

What fame Stephen Crane has as a poet largely rests upon half a dozen anthology pieces, and most of these present him in iconoclastic defiance of a wrathful Jehovah. "God fashioned the ship of the world carefully," begins one well-known poem (*The Black Riders* no. 6), "Then—at fateful time—a wrong called," and God, distracted, allowed the hull to slip away "slyly, / Making cunning noiseless travel down the ways." Thus the world is doomed from its creation: "forever rudderless, it went upon the seas / Going ridiculous voyages." The final couplet places this cosmic irony in its proper relation to the Universal Plan:

> And there were many in heaven
> Who laughed at this thing.

This view could hardly win accolades from a large public in 1895, although a similar mood of ironic despair was being expressed—or soon would be—in the writings of many other authors of the decade. Mark Twain was rapidly moving toward the nihilism of *The Mysterious Stranger* (begun in 1898) and *What Is Man?* (1904); five years after *The Black Riders* Dreiser was to complete, and Doubleday to suppress, *Sister Carrie*, which dramatized the irrelevance of faith in such a cosmos as Crane envisaged. Interpreting history and the times against a more complex background and with a more disciplined intelligence than any of theirs, Henry Adams too was approaching the "mechanistic catastrophism" which would characterize his autobiography, first issued in 1907. When Crane's poems appeared, a columnist in the *Bookman* (probably H. T. Peck) suggested that one of them "might serve some purpose if pinned to the title page of *Jude the Obscure*,"

From *The Poetry of Stephen Crane*. © 1956 by Columbia University Press. Columbia University Press, 1957.

since Crane epitomizes the "bitterness of Mr. Hardy's pessimism, his keen remorseless sense of the ironies of life, the passionate insurgence of his heart against Nature's injustice, and the revolt of his soul against this mad, sad world." The poem concerned a man who ate his own heart and liked it, because it was bitter. We shall return to this mordant fable a little later.

To most readers of *The Black Riders* it seemed that when the heedless God who set the world adrift did turn His attention to mankind, the result is "the cruel injustice of omnipotence torturing weakness." One poem, for instance, carries as its epigraph this passage from Exod. 20:5: "And the sins of the fathers shall be visited upon the heads of the children, even unto the third and fourth generation of them that hate me."

> Well, then, I hate Thee, unrighteous picture;
> Wicked image, I hate Thee;
> So, strike with Thy vengeance
> The heads of those little men
> Who come blindly.
> It will be a brave thing.
>
> (*BR* 12)

The theme seems obsessive. Crane states it again:

> If there is a witness to my little life,
> To my tiny throes and struggles,
> He sees a fool;
> And it is not fine for gods to menace fools.
>
> (*BR* 13)

And he returns to it again and again (in *BR* 19, 25; *War Is Kind* 10; and, as will be seen, in many other poems by implication).

In view of these uncompromising, gnomic statements, it is not surprising that some critics should see no other theme in Crane's verse than the smashing of idols. Harriet Monroe, for one, dismissed his work on these grounds. "*The Black Riders* is full of the wisdom of yesteryear. . . . as old-fashioned as Bob Ingersoll's fiery denunciations. Crane's startling utterances . . . somehow cease to startle after twenty years." Amy Lowell, more perceptive, finds Crane haunted by his religious background. "He disbelieved it and he hated it, but he could not free himself from it. . . . Crane's soul was heaped with bitterness and this bitterness he flung back at the theory of life which had betrayed him." And Miss Lowell wisely proposed the Bible as a source for the form of his poems. "Its cadences, its images, its parable structure" must have been "ground into his consciousness." It was of course beyond the scope of her introduction to trace in detail the influence she here suggests.

Since there is general agreement that Crane was in revolt against his religious background, it would seem logical to investigate the exact climate of belief and opinion against which he was rebelling. Most recently, Marcus

Cunliffe had this to say (in another connection) of Crane and the religion of his immediate family:

> he is anti-clerical though belonging to a clerical heritage. In his early work, I do not think he knows where he stands—whether it is religion or religiosity he disapproves of, whether he is adapting or burlesqueing. He reacts against the familiar elements of his world where these seem to him hypocritical, but they shape his thought.

Quoting the character of Crane's father given by the *Dictionary of American Biography*, Cunliffe adds that his "one serious fault seems to have been his monumental innocence," and mentions that Crane's mother, too, came from "a clerical family."

> What Crane was reacting against, therefore, was nothing very rigid or terrible; hence, his adolescent reversal of what he had been taught consisted in condemning *false* religion; in showing that there was "greater viciousness" than Jonathan Townley Crane ever suspected, in smoking and drinking; and in not only reading "trashy novels" but actually writing some.
>
> In fact, Stephen Crane strives to be free not of merely a family but a national atmosphere. Its restrictions are irksome, just because they are on the whole, kindly.

Mr. Cunliffe's view is at variance with the suggestions given in John Berryman's biography of Crane. Berryman remarks that Crane's mother held religious views "evidently much narrower and more insistent than her husband's." The biographer presents his estimate of the Reverend Dr. Crane based upon Stephen's reminiscence, the *DAB*, and the father's book on *Popular Amusements*, a gently earnest warning against sinful pleasures known only vicariously to the author. Berryman concludes that Crane's father led "a saintlike life." Of his mother Mr. Berryman has little to say biographically, although she looms as a stern and forceful figure in the fantasies which, according to the psychoanalytic interpretation this critic proposes, lie at the source of Crane's creativity. With respect to the poetry, Berryman makes this valuable suggestion:

> God is the brutal villain of *The Black Riders*, and some pieces that set this Old Testament swaggerer against an interior pitying God (xxix, li, liii) went unnoticed. His mother's had been warring with his father's God in Crane's thought. Neither won; both perhaps disappeared and were replaced by a notion we shall come to— already now when the little book appeared, some of it had ceased to represent his thought, transformed in the Southwest.

Berryman recognizes that Crane's anticlerical verse is not all of a piece, that his treatment of religious themes is marked by a tension between Divine

Justice and Divine Mercy, and suggests that his parents had different conceptions of God. But the cryptic unclarity of the last sentence is less than helpful, and the assertion that "Neither won" seems to me unsubstantiated by the verse itself.

In the following pages I shall try to show that such poems as attack the brutal God represent only the first phase of Crane's war in heaven. It would indeed be surprising were this all there was: as though a youth growing up with a crowd of distinguished clergymen in his own family could defy God a dozen times in verse and be done with the theme. In fact there is in Crane's treatment of God and of religion a progress from the utter denial of "Well, then, I hate Thee" to an affirmation of faith in the "interior pitying God." Crane goes even beyond proposing an alternative deity: in his best and most neglected poem there is an apocalyptic vision of the triumph of this God of love. But between the denial and "When a people reach the top of a hill" (*WK* 27) there are many poems and several stages. As we trace them we shall have to look further into the doctrines and dogmas of both sides of Crane's clerical family.

II

"In doctrine . . . a strict Methodist of the old stamp, filled with the sense of God's redeeming love. . . . In controversy he was gentlemanly, in his judgments charitable. . . . He leaves the impression of an unusually noble mind straightened by dogma and a narrow education." So is Jonathan Townley Crane characterized in the *Dictionary of American Biography*; to his youngest son he was "so simple and good that I often think he didn't know much of anything about humanity." Yet Stephen Crane owed much to the loving, unworldly soul of his father, who may not have known much of human iniquity but felt passionately what he did know of the merciful nature of his God. His biographer in the *DAB*, like the critics and biographers of his son, seems to have depended chiefly upon his books *Popular Amusements* (1869) and *Arts of Intoxication* (1870) for this description, which Berryman uses and Cunliffe quotes: "deeply concerned about such sins as dancing, breaking the sabbath, reading trashy novels, playing cards, billiards, and chess, and enjoying tobacco and wine, and too innocent of the world to do more than suspect the existence of greater viciousness."

But a more useful guide to the influence of Jonathan Crane's thought upon his son's is a theological tract published when Stephen was three years old. We can reasonably assume that the religious sensibility exhibited in *Holiness the Birthright of All God's Children* (1874) represents the man young Stephen knew as his father. Nor is it unlikely that the Reverend Dr. Crane drew upon the ethical attitudes, the researches, and the occasional exempla in this book for his sermons and family devotions in the six years of life that remained to him. In it he undertakes to refute Wesley himself on the doctrine that innate depravity remains in the soul of the regenerate believer.

This view the Reverend Crane denies with a fine sense of historical relativity, showing that Wesley held different positions on the question over a period of years, each being the reply or defense of the founder of Methodism against specific arguments of critics and dissidents who threatened his early religious societies by proclaiming their own complete perfection after conversion. The historical arguments need not concern us here, but we should note the view of human nature Crane's father propounds in the course of refuting the "residue theory." Interpreting a passage in Wesley's *Sermon on Sin in Believers*, Dr. Crane remarks, "By the term 'sin' . . . he cannot mean that there is guilt in a believer, nor any state of mind or heart which involves condemnation. Consequently, instead of sin, properly so-called, he means simply temptation." And "All trial life implies temptation." But is not temptation itself sinful? Consider the first temptation and the first sin:

> Eve was pure in her whole being; with no defect, no taint of depravity of any kind. By the craft of her adversary she was drawn into discourse. . . . Her eyes and her thoughts were kept upon the tree until she *saw that it was good for food, and that it was pleasant to the eyes, and a tree to be desired to make one wise.* Here were three enticements, each of which appealed to an element of perfect human nature, and tended to create a desire which in itself was wholly innocent. . . . The elements of her nature to which appeal was made were holy.

Sin did not begin until "at last she began to weigh the question of obedience or disobedience. . . . to ponder that question is to begin to yield."

This analysis may not be as wise in the psychology of human frailty as Milton's, but what is noteworthy is its recognition of the holiness of natural impulses; among these is the "inner taste, which delights in beautiful forms and colors." Such convictions Stephen Crane was to share. His father continues:

> To be human is to be endowed with appetites and passions, innocent in themselves, but unreasoning, required to be guided by the intellect and the conscience, and controlled by the will. These appetites and passions may ally themselves to thought, but in themselves are void of thought, and know only to press onward. Man's duty and safety demands that they be subjugated, taught to obey. . . . There are affections, also, in themselves not only innocent, but essential to a perfect humanity, which at times impel in the direction of sin.

Jonathan Crane, returning in bitter weather from an errand of charity, took sick and died when Stephen was only ten. In the next few years the boy was exposed to another variety of Methodist profession, less tolerant of "affections . . . essential to a perfect humanity, which . . . impel in the direction of sin."

Crane's mother had been before her marriage Mary Helen Peck, daughter of the Reverend George Peck, D.D., a prominent Methodist clergyman. She was a forceful woman who did not fear to risk censure by "taking care of a girl who had an accidental baby. . . . Mother was always more of a Christian than a Methodist," Stephen Crane recalled. In the same reminiscence, transcribed by a young admirer—a circumstance to be remembered in evaluating these remarks—Crane said,

> My mother was a very religious woman but I don't think she was as narrow as most of her friends or her family. . . . After my father died, mother lived in and for religion. We had very little money. Mother wrote articles for the Methodist papers and reported for the [New York] *Tribune* and the [Philadelphia] *Press*. Every August she went down to Ocean Grove and reported proceedings at the Methodist holy show there. . . . My brother Will used to try to argue with her on religious subjects such as hell but he always gave it up. Don't understand that mother was bitter or mean but it hurt her that any of us should be slipping from Grace and giving up eternal damnation or salvation or those things. You could as well argue with a wave.

There are several things to remark in this passage. First, that his mother's family and friends seemed narrower in religion than she herself— evidently Crane felt he had to defend her against the reputation of these associates to his young admirer. We may add to this a passage from a letter of Crane's about her family: "In those old times the family did its duty. Upon my mother's side everybody as soon as he could walk became a Methodist clergyman—of the old ambling-nag, saddlebag, exhorting kind." Indeed they did: her father and his four brothers, one of whom, Jesse Truesdell Peck, rose to the eminence of Bishop of Syracuse. Partly because of the weight such an office would have in a family so ecclesiastical, and partly too because Stephen was sent to Syracuse University, which his great-uncle Jesse had helped to found, the views of Bishop Peck will merit further consideration.

A second point is the obvious one that Mrs. Crane supported herself by religious journalism. This, as well as the plethora of preachers in the family circle, suggests that the sermon and evangelical tract, as well as the Bible, may have been influential upon Crane's poetry. Third, when he says it hurt his mother that any of the children should be backsliding, is it not curious that he mentions her concern with their defection from "eternal damnation" before her hope that they be saved? They should not give up damnation! This is most suggestive of the nature of her belief, of the language of her persuasions. And finally, her persuasions: "You could as well argue with a wave."

Yet, says Mr. Berryman, "His father's had been warring with his mother's God in Crane's thought." It is time to look at this war. We may well begin with a poem which seems to have nothing to do with God. Its subject, in fact, is not immediately apparent. One critic takes it to be "the positive, ethical side" of Crane's verse, as contrasted to the negativism of the "unrighteous picture"; in this poem "he celebrates integrity."

III

> In the desert
> I saw a creature, naked, bestial,
> Who, squatting upon the ground,
> Held his heart in his hands,
> And ate of it.
> I said, "Is it good, friend?"
> "It is bitter—bitter," he answered;
> "But I like it
> Because it is bitter,
> And because it is my heart."
>
> (*BR* 3)

"It is not clear that these [lines] were verse," Berryman remarks after quoting them; Stallman examines the structure of this poem and finds it to be syllogistic. But what does the poem mean?

If, as Gillis suggests, the poem celebrates integrity, why are we "in the desert"? And what are we to make of its *persona,* more a brute than a human being, "a creature, naked, bestial, . . . squatting"? Despite the brutishness of the heart-eater and the bitterness of his feast, the lines somehow lend his stubborn gesture a kind of dignity. Such intransigence suggests that not to eat his own heart might be a still more bitter experience than his present unsavory feast.

By a chain of lucky coincidences we can find the passage which may reveal the elusive significance of this parable of Crane's. Among the fifty-five books from Crane's library (exclusive of his own writings) preserved by Cora Crane there is a much-battered pocket edition of a little manual, its green binding waterstained and gnawed at the edges. This work is "intended to lead the unconverted to a grave consideration of the wrong of sin, and the duty of immediate efforts to secure forgiveness." In the course of analyzing the sinner's present condition the book presents this passage, in a chapter called "The Depraved Heart":

> To understand in how deep a sense you are lost, you must know your own heart; but "the heart is deceitful above all things, and desperately wicked, who can know it?" "From within, out of the heart of men, proceed evil thoughts, adulteries, fornications, murders, thefts, covetousness, wickedness, deceit, lasciviousness, an

evil eye, blasphemy, pride, foolishness; all these evil things come from within and defile the man." And *you* are the sinner thus depraved. It is *your* "heart" that is thus "deceitful above all things, and desperately wicked." . . . No healthy human figure can illustrate this fallen moral state. A mass of loathsome corruption alone can show how vile is the depravity of man.

It would be rash to assume that just because a book is found among an author's effects that he must have read and been influenced by it—especially when, like Crane, he scarcely annotated a line in any of his volumes. Yet one can make a strong case for the probability that Crane had not only read this book, but for a time had been practically reared on it, steeped in it, and that much of his mother's family's Methodism and her own can be represented by the grim unrelenting didacticism of *What Must I Do to Be Saved?* The copy in the Columbia University collection is inscribed on the flyleaf, "Rev. Dr. Crane/With the respects of/the author"; below this is written, in Stephen's clear hand, his autograph and the year 1881. The author who gave this book to Crane's father was Jesse T. Peck, D.D., who by 1881 had been a bishop for nine years. The Reverend Dr. Crane had died the year before. We can reconstruct the scene with fair confidence: "Mother lived in and for religion. . . . it hurt her that any of us should be slipping from Grace and giving up eternal damnation or salvation or those things." We can imagine with what hopes and admonishments Mrs. Crane gave her favorite youngest son this volume, inscribed from her most eminently religious uncle to her lately deceased husband. It made interesting reading for a boy of ten.

Did he read it? At that time, he would have been of a mind to. "I used to like church and prayer meetings when I was a kid," he wrote in the year of his death, "and when I was thirteen or about that, my brother Will told me not to believe in Hell after my uncle had been boring me about the lake of fire and the rest of the sideshows." This was another uncle—they were all clergymen. From them, from his mother, from Great-uncle Jesse's salvation tract, Stephen had by the age of thirteen learned all about "the sideshows."

This work by Crane's great-uncle is not produced in order categorically to state that it is the single source of Crane's poems on religious themes. There are, it is true, several instances—"In the desert" is among them—where parallels in idea and even in statement are close enough to make fair an assumption of direct indebtedness. But rather than insist upon immediate influence it seems more valuable to use Bishop Peck's book to indicate the climate of religious opinion in which Crane grew up, particularly in the years after his father's death. It is most valuable—perhaps more so than the Bible itself—as an index to the attitudes toward God, man, and the universe of Methodists "of the old ambling-nag, saddle-bag, exhorting kind," as Crane described them. And although Great-uncle Jesse was a bishop and founded a university, and Grandfather George Peck "through half a century of the Church's history . . . had an important part in shaping its legislation," Crane's evocation of a backwoods revivalist does them no injustice.

For George Peck had been born in a log cabin in the wilds of Otsego County, New York, in 1797—only six years after the death of Wesley. From *The Life and Times of Rev. George Peck, D.D., Written by Himeslf* (1874), we get a vivid picture of the emotional frenzy of frontier Methodism and the arduous dangers the circuit-riding preachers faced from forest, beast, and hostile settlers. The fortnightly arrival of the exhorter was the one ray of human fellowship in the isolated cabins along his route. Camp meetings, held on grounds hewn out of virgin forests, were occasions of great communal feeling. Singing mighty hymns together, hearing out the long oratory from the pulpit, kneeling in common prayer—these eagerly shared experiences made the most welcome contrast to the weeks and months of bleakly lonely frontier life. The climax of the camp meeting was the conversion of sinners. Just after George Peck had been licensed to preach, in 1816, he attended such a meeting at which "Father" Timothy Dewey "preached a terrific sermon on the words, 'Prepare to meet thy God' ":

> Father Dewey . . . stood before the crowd like a giant among pigmies, and his voice was clear as a trumpet, and terrible as thunder. He came down upon the wicked in such sort that hundreds . . . listened with amazement and terror. . . . There was an unbroken roar of fervent supplication all over the ground, while the awful voice of the preacher resounded above the tempest of prayer, and every word was heard as distinctly as if in the silence of midnight. "O sinner, sinner," thundered the preacher, "are you determined to take hell by storm? Can you dwell with devouring fire? Can you stand eternal burnings? Are your bones iron, and your flesh brass, that you plunge headlong into the lake of fire?"

The effect of such preaching under such conditions was often "the curious experience which has been termed religious ecstasy":

> Perhaps while engaged in fervent prayer or joyous song a man would fall prostrate, his eyes fixed, his whole form rigid, and remain thus sometimes for several hours. . . . Unconverted persons, deeply convinced of sin, not infrequently "fell," as the current phrase expressed it, "under the power of God.". . . often while the lips were silent, and the powers of voluntary motion were suspended, the soul passed through a great moral crisis, surrendered to the Divine rule, trusted in Christ; and when the physical effects of the intense mental conflict began to subside, the first words uttered were exultant praise and thanksgiving.

However we may reason or doubt in regard to these phenomena, one thing is certain, they occurred in connection with genuine religious emotions, and a truly Divine work.

George Peck, seeing such conversions at the camp-meetings, "leaped to the conclusion that they were indicative of a great grace" and "earnestly desired to share the joy and the benefit." Great was his disappointment that his own conversion at fifteen was unaccompanied by this frenzy.

George and his youngest brother Jesse were the sons of a Half-Covenant Congregationalist who, soon after his removal to the frontier from Connecticut, was converted to Methodism by a terrifying dream. Two dead friends summoned him "to the eternal world. . . . He expected at once to be ushered into the presence of a God whose repeated warnings he had disregarded. . . . The most intense horror seized his soul. He had no hope of mercy." Awaking in terror, "He expected to die before morning, and saw nothing before him but 'the blackness of darkness forever.' " But Luther Peck survived the dawn, joined the Methodist Society, and "his house became the home of preachers, and a true house of God." When the service was held at a neighbor's, the Peck family attended; one sermon, on "the end of the world," delivered "in a voice of thunder," haunted George Peck's imagination "for years."

Such was the apocalyptic religion of the early nineteenth-century frontier to which Stephen Crane's great-grandfather, grandfather, and great-uncle were converted in their adolescence. Moderate as their Methodism seemed to their contemporaries, in theology, forensics, and tractarian fervor they preserved to the end of the century the essential features of frontier evangelism. Crane's mother, reared in such a family, carried on its tradition in her own household in turn. Thus in the 1880s Stephen Crane was brought up on a tract written in 1858 by a forebear whose great religious experience—his own conversion—had occurred under circumstances like those Crane's grandfather describes, in a frontier clearing in 1827. Jesse Peck's book, *What Must I Do to Be Saved?* is, like the above-quoted sermons of half a century earlier, redolent with the fumes of sulphur. The effort is to frighten the sinner out of hell on earth, not to win him by love to heaven. Throughout the seventy-four-page admonition to sinners (later sections, less germane to our inquiry, give counsel to penitents and converts), there is continual emphasis upon the temerity of the sinful individual, the terrifying jeopardy in which his unrepentant rebellion against God prolongs his soul. The section preceding "The Depraved Heart" is called "The Sinful Life": "God has spoken to you in the language of paternal kindness and authority, but how criminally you have shut your ears to his voice. . . . you have rebelled against the only perfect government in the universe." This is the actual theme of Stephen Crane's poem in which a creature in the desert gnaws his own heart.

He squats in the desert, the Waste Land traditional in Christian literature as the home of those lacking in Grace. "O the bitter wrong of sin!" writes Bishop Peck, "it sears, as a burning fire, the land once lovely with blooming virtue." The creature—he is unworthy to be called a man—is naked, bestial, a brute, as we have seen. "I said, 'Is it good, friend?' " I, the poet, call this vile and wretched thing my friend: I recognize in his posture and lineaments that which is akin to my own. "It is bitter—bitter. . . . But I like it/Because it is bitter,/And because it is my heart." Loathsome, filled with corruption, the source of all sin and evil, his heart is still good to him, because it is his. That is his condition, his humanity. And he would rather taste it, though to do so is to consume himself, than renounce his humanity for those transcendent goods which require that more-than-human renunciation. So to will is to defy God's will. But in both his bestiality and his intransigent self-assertion the "creature" appears to the poet as a "friend," a kindred spirit.

Crane's poem may thus be read as a denial of the Peck family's relentless insistence upon natural depravity. From his father he may have taken not only the ethical view, as he interpreted it to himself, but also a hint as to the narrative element. In *Holiness the Birthright of All God's Children*, Jonathan Crane recounts his personal acquaintance with "a man who, when convinced of his sin and danger, prayed for a new heart, found pardon and peace." But, as Dr. Crane afterward learned, "when he prayed for a new heart he thought, in his simplicity," that the heart in his breast "had been so long the home of Satan that it must be taken out of his body and a new one substituted." The good Dr. Crane tells this to illustrate that "God's answer was wiser than the prayer"; it is the kind of exemplum, based on personal experience, he would surely have often used in his sermons, and the tale is so odd that young Stephen could hardly have forgotten it. A sinner removes his own heart: this may have been the notion that originally stirred Crane's imagination.

This poem gathers into itself several of Crane's most important themes: rebellion against the wicked God, the kinship of fallen man in his sin, and the insistence upon a human fate—though it be damnation—rather than the transcendent beatitudes that follow superhuman renunciation. These themes account for almost half of the poems in *The Black Riders*. But before we go on to them we must first complete our scrutiny of Crane's poems on the rebellion of man against the vengeful Jehovah—and his final reconciliation with a more merciful God. It is well at this point to reconstruct the moral universe of the young Stephen Crane, as it was probably given him by motherly and avuncular precept and in the pages of *What Must I Do to Be Saved?*

IV

Since Jesse Peck's tract is, half a century later, a scarce book, an extended quotation may prove useful not only for its content but as an example also of the Bishop's hortatory style. The following passage, from a chapter on "The Creature and the Creator," is one of several perorations in the book. Here Peck reiterates in a rhetorical tide his arguments against rebellion, his presentiments of the joys of submitting to the Divine Will:

> Whence came your powers of life and motion, of thought and reason, of feeling and will. No finite agency could produce them. Is it right that these noble powers should be turned against the very God who made them? that he should be attacked and insulted by the very organs of speech he has formed to utter his praise? that he should be treated with scorn or neglect by the thinking, feeling, determining mind he has made? that these deathless powers should instigate revolt in the empire of their Creator, bring desolation into his fair heritage, and stir up the world to treason against the only faultless government in the universe? O the bitter wrong of sin! What tears and groans of anguish it has wrung from the crushed heart of humanity! What untold misery it has inflicted upon the conscious soul! The blight of death is in it. It turns the very pleasures of life into gall. It sears, as a burning fire, the land once lovely with blooming virtue. It tears down and tramples in the dust the rights of conscience, the rights of God, the hopes of mortals. Its track may be traced in the blood of the slain, in the fainting, writhing, agonizing throng it leaves to curse, and wail, and die beyond the reach of mercy. But you know not even yet of its horrors. You must open the pit of woe, where wrath has come upon souls whose immortality is turned into a fearful curse by this deadly evil. You must hear the language of despair as it comes up from the place where there is "weeping, and wailing, and gnashing of teeth." Nay, you must need feel through every power of your deathless being the undying worm and the burnings of unquenchable fire, to have a just idea of the infinite wrong of sin. But even here you have felt the sentence of death in yourself, because you are a sinner, and you mourn over it as your most humiliating and crushing calamity, that you are a rebel against the Lord of hosts.
>
> On the other hand, how fair and lovely is everything that is still in harmony with the plans of the Creator.

By this time one's ears are so split by the wailing, the gnashing, "the language of despair," that the harmony of the spheres can scarcely be heard above the tumult. Filled though it is with pulpit clichés, the Bishop's description of hell on earth is vivid, sensory in conception, tactile, and terrifying. It is also twice as long as the ensuing description of the joys to be gained only by renouncing the claims of this world:

> How sweet are the charms of what yet remains of his earthly paradise! What gladness and delight run through the animal

natures that move in harmony with the Creator's plans! What beauty and glory sparkle in the heavens above! What holy rapture glows in the bosoms of those who are saved from the power of sin! What beatific visions rise before the eyes of faith! What thrills of holy joy, what shouts of triumph gladden the world of light, where angels and the ransomed from among men ascribe "glory, honor, and power, and might, and dominion to Him that sitteth upon the throne, and to the Lamb forever!" O, this is right. This shows the just relation of the creature to the Creator. Here is the play of created powers in the sphere of their original glory. This is the glad acclaim in which you long to join.

Perhaps. This vision of joy is abstract, bodiless, qualified, unconvincing; it requires the abnegation of the senses and of the self—for what? For a clergyman's expostulation, "O, this is right."

> Supposing that I should have the courage
> To let a red sword of virtue
> Plunge into my heart,
> Letting to the weeds of the ground
> My sinful blood,
> What can you offer me?
> A gardened castle?
> A flowery kingdom?
>
> What? A hope?
> Then hence with your red sword of virtue.
>
> (*BR* 30)

Not only is the reward illusory, but the Creator of the latter part of Bishop Peck's sermon is no less fierce than the terrible God of the first. Yet, the book insists, the chief end of man is to make himself worthy, by denying his own nature, of the approbation of this tyrannical ruler. To rebel is to fling oneself forever into the burning wilderness.

Crane's poems may well derive their strangely abstract characters from this work, for in the course of repudiating the Bishop's brimstone theology his young nephew adopted some of the unbodied personages from his manual. Chapter headings tell us who they are: in addition to "The Creature and the Creator," we find "The Sinner and the Redeemer," ". . . an Enemy," "The Good and the Wicked," "Sinful Men and Demons," "Good Men and Angels," "The Omniscient God." There are but few parables among the Bishop's exhortations, and in these too the characters are faceless and nameless. Were the Bible the only source of Crane's own parables, would he not have inclined to follow the examples there of delineating individuals as well as types? Crane seems to have combined the structure of the biblical parable with the disembodied allegorical figure from pulpit oratory and the evangelical tract. The sinners, demons, angels, and wrath-

ful gods of the verse—not one of whom is named or given any indi-
vidualizing features—are creatures from Bishop Peck's own sermon. It is
almost as though Crane had taken *What Must I Do to Be Saved?* as his text,
and proceeded to write commentaries on what seemed to him the mon-
strousness and inhumanity of the creed of his mother's family. " 'The wrath
of God abideth on you.' Condemned already, already lost!" roars Great-
uncle Jesse; Stephen replies,

> A god in wrath
> Was beating a man:
> He cuffed him loudly
> With thunderous blows
> That rang and rolled over the earth.
> All people came running.
> The man screamed and struggled,
> And bit madly at the feet of the god.
> The people cried,
> "Ah, what a wicked man!"
> And—
> "Ah, what a redoubtable god!"
> (BR 19)

We may imagine which people Crane has in mind: his mother's people. In
another poem their God threatens the rebellious mortal again:

> Blustering God,
> Stamping across the sky
> With loud swagger,
> I fear You not.
> No, though from Your highest heaven
> You plunge Your spear at my heart,
> I fear You not.
> No, not if the blow
> Is as the lightning blasting a tree.
> I fear You not, puffing braggart.

Crane does not deny that this God exists, nor that he is powerful; there is
such a God, active in malice, and yet the poet defies Him.

> Withal, there is One whom I fear;
> I fear to see grief upon that face.
>
> . . . .
> Ah, sooner would I die
> Than see tears in those eyes of my soul.
> (BR 53)

Crane opposes the "Blustering God" not, like Ingersoll, with the void of
agnosticism, but with another One—whom he fears, not to be injured by,

but to injure. This gentle personal God is vulnerable only to some unstated possible injury He may receive from the man who believes in Him. What would bring "tears in those eyes"? The eyes, we note, are not glaring down from the brows of heaven; they are "of my soul"—in transcendental fashion Crane merges the divine in himself with the Divinity. Those eyes would weep were he to violate the compassionate nature of the divinity within him.

It is important to remark that much as Crane opposes the damnatory Methodism of his mother's family, he nowhere denies that man is a fallen sinner. But this fact, accepted from the background against which he rebels, has quite a different significance to Crane's inner God of mercy from what it meant to Bishop Peck. We scarcely need the Bishop to tell us what the "Blustering God" makes of man in his depravity; yet the following pasage is useful, since another poem of Crane's is a counterstatement to these admonitory words:

> And your sins are remembered. The omniscient God knows every one of them, and will hold you to a stern responsibility. . . . You cannot endure to meet the least of these in the presence of the Judge; but what will you do when in countless numbers they throng your memory, when every one charges upon your soul its infinite wrong, and demands the wrath of your offended Sovereign without mixture of mercy forever. . . . "Depart from me, ye cursed, into everlasting fire."
>
> The Savior himself has condescended to inform you of the fearful doom which awaits you. You shrink from it with indescribable terror.

The relation of Crane's poem to this passage is made clear by a manuscript in the Columbia collection in which the pronouns "one" in the first line and "he" in the last are capitalized; the published text, from another manuscript, suppresses these indications of the Deity and leaves the significance of the poem ambiguous:

> There was one I met upon the road
> Who looked at me with kind eyes.
> He said, "Show me of your wares."
> And this I did,
> Holding one forth.
> He said, "It is a sin."
> Then held I forth another;
> He said, "It is a sin."
> Then held I forth another;
> He said, "It is a sin."
> And so to the end;
> Always, he said, "It is a sin."

> And finally, I cried out,
> "But I have none other."
> Then did he look at me
> With kinder eyes.
> "Poor soul!" he said.
>
> (*BR* 33)

The theme of compassion for humility appears again in poem 17, where the one who could not remember having done any good deeds is deemed by God "O best little blade of grass." In still another poem, "The God of his inner thoughts," as opposed to "The God of many men," regards him "With soft eyes / Lit with infinite comprehension," and calls him "My poor child!" (*BR* 51).

"The God of many men" had a voice that "thundered loudly, / Fat with rage, and puffing."

> The livid lightnings flashed in the clouds;
> The leaden thunders crashed.
> A worshipper raised his arm.
> "Hearken! hearken! The voice of God!"
>
> "Not so," said a man.
> "The voice of God whispers in the heart
> So softly
> That the soul pauses,
> Making no noise,
> And strives for these melodies,
> Distant, sighing, like faintest breath,
> And all the being is still to hear."
>
> (*BR* 39)

This inner voice of mercy, of direct reverberation, with the Love that is God, takes the man who hears it out of the fellowship of Christians assembled in their churches. There, ministers and bishops echo the threats of the other God, menacing in thunder. Bishop Peck, wise in the snares of Satan, had warned Stephen against that alluring voice which softly subverts the Divine Order and the Church by promising forgiveness for human frailty. One chapter of *What Must I Do to Be Saved?* is called "The Whisperings of an Enemy":

> There has been another voice within you, a rebel voice, whispering treason against the Lord of lords and King of kings; a voice which has dared to oppose the communication of Divine wisdom, saying: "There is no great harm in this carnal indulgence; there is no immediate danger in a life of pleasure; God is merciful, he will punish you according to your sins, he will still follow you with offers of pardon.

But Stephen Crane knew very well where he had first heard the voice of mercy that whispers "so softly" that "All the being is still to hear." He had heard it from his father. He knew that his father was "simple and good." And he knew what to make of a creed that heaped such malign threats upon his own. Crane's own creed was that of "a radical, un-churched, defaithed, Christian gentleman," as the editors of his most re-vealingly personal letters describe him. "Trained to believe in the great tradition of the Christian gentleman as it had been Americanized in the generations of Jefferson and Emerson and Robert E. Lee, Crane made the tempermentally natural gesture of taking it seriously . . . he was moved in the name of the ideal to revolt desperately against the smothering conven-tionalities of moralism and respectability by which the world evaded the ideal." As Crane put it himself, "The final wall of the wise man's thought . . . is Human Kindness of course. . . . Therefore do I strive to be as kind and as just as may be to those about me and in my meagre success at it, I find the solitary pleasure of life."

Opposed though the Christian ethics of Jonathan Crane were, in Ste-phen's mind, to the iron rule of Jesse Peck, it is well to emphasize that if his "mother's had been warring with his father's God in Crane's thought," it was a war which neither parent nor maternal grandfather nor great-uncle recognized or fought themselves. There is no indication whatever that the Reverend Dr. Crane's mildness was regarded as heretical by his wife's family or by any authority of the Methodist Church; indeed, his father-in-law gave Dr. Crane's books the encouragement of four pages of advertising among the flyleaves of his autobiography. Probably Dr. Crane used George Peck's publisher at the latter's behest. And Jesse Peck, as we have noted, was considered "not bigoted" as regards doctrinal differences. Although two such intrepid logicians as the brothers Peck would certainly have rec-ognized their differences with Jonathan Crane, relations between them seem not to have been strained. Nor is there evidence that Dr. Crane and his wife had any serious fallings-out on theological grounds—or on any other. The conflict became a conflict only in the mind of their son.

The psychological burden of his inner battle may be reckoned from two poems in *The Black Riders*, the longest and the last. In "I stood musing in a black world" (no. 49), not knowing where to go, he hears a thousand voices call "Look! look! There!" A radiance flickers "in the far Sky"—and disappears; "I hesitated." But the torrent of voices calls again, and he leaps "unhesitant":

> The hard hills tore my flesh;
> The ways bit my feet.
> At last I looked again.
> No radiance in the far sky,
> Ineffable, divine;
> No vision painted upon a pall;
> And always my eyes ached for the light.

But the torrent again cries "Look! look! There!"—

> And at the blindness of my spirit
> They screamed
> "Fool! fool! fool!"

This theme of faith desperately sought and not found is paralleled in poem 68, significantly placed as the final "lines" in the book:

> A spirit sped
> Through spaces of the night;
> And as he sped, he called,
> "God! God!"

Seeking "into the plains of space," his calls are mocked by echoes;

> Eventually then, he screamed,
> Mad in denial,
> "Ah, there is no God!"
> A swift hand,
> A sword from the sky
> Smote him,
> And he was dead.

We remember the spear of the "Blustering God" was "as the lightning blasting a tree": the terrible God of wrath is ever-present, most known when most denied. This is the burden of guilt Crane must bear for his temerity. "You must go alone to the bar of God," warned Jesse Peck. "You must answer for your own life of guilt, and you yourself must, if finally impenitent, obey the terrific words, 'Depart, ye cursed, into everlasting fire.' You alone must suffer for your obstinate rebellion."

But Stephen Crane is not in quite the same case as the God-denying spirit of this last poem. Unlike him, Crane, as we have seen, does not at the end of his quest scream "Mad in denial, / 'Ah, there is no God!' " What Crane denies is the God he fears, while he acclaims and seeks the Spirit of Love. Behind the denial we may trace again the ethical vision of his father. In this poem, the controlling image and the unstated logic derive from *Holiness the Birthright*, or from Jonathan Crane's oral repetition of this theme:

> God could, if he deemed it best, so reveal himself that unbelief would be impossible. He might write his laws upon the azure skies. . . . He could smite every sinner at the very moment of his transgression with so stern and visible a hand that obedience would have little moral value. . . . That moral liberty may not be destroyed, God withdrew himself from human vision. . . . And because He is not seen, the fool hath said in his heart, *There is no God*.

The spirit in the last poem, then, was a fool. (The speaker in "I stood musing" is called a fool by the faithful, but for his blindness, not his unbelief.) But those whose God is lightning in a swift hand are not so wise. "Not to thrust one's hand into a blazing furnace is not proof of uncommon sagacity. . . . For children to obey when the father stands holding the rod over them, is no proof that they posssess the spirit of true obedience." It is from such knowledge that Crane took courage in his own rebellion and in his quest.

V

The death of the faithless spirit concludes *The Black Riders*, but it does not bring to an end Stephen Crane's preoccupation with God in his poems. Two or three poems from that book remain to be mentioned, in which are prefigured themes he takes up again in *War Is Kind* or in verse hitherto unpublished. Significantly, there is nothing in his later book as nihilistic as "God fashioned the ship of the world carefully," as embittered as "Well, then, I hate Thee, unrighteous picture." The remaining themes, to state them in rough generalizations, are these: (1) there is one code appropriate for gods and angels, but men live by another; (2) the Church is a fallible institution, not the Body of God; (3) men are brothers in sin; and (4) God is inscrutable.

When Copeland and Day, publishers of *The Black Riders*, conveyed to Crane their reservations about bringing out his manuscript, his reply was typically candid and uncompromising: "It seems to me that you cut all the ethical sense out of the book. All the anarchy, perhaps. It is the anarchy which I particularly insist upon. . . . The ones which refer to God, I believe you condemn altogether. I am obliged to have them in when my book is printed." Although Crane did offer to withdraw "some which I believe unworthy of print," he may have had to drop others in whose worth he believed, for two of the seven omissions he later included in *War Is Kind* (3 and 16); but these were not about God. Two which are about God have turned up in the Columbia collection; the other three are still untraced.

Two codes. In what way did Crane see anarchy as essential to "the ethical sense" of his verse? If by anarchy he meant self-determination in defiance of institutions, the connection is plain. It was Crane's fate to find his paternal heritage of integrity, kindness, humanism, and love irreconcilable with the attitudes and institutions his mother's tutelage put before him as the Christian tradition to which he ought to belong. Jonathan Crane, in his gentleness, had yet made peace with the same church over which the Pecks presided; indeed, he had been converted to it at eighteen from his Presbyterian backgound. But for Stephen the way was harder, perhaps because, as we have seen, the Peck variety of Methodism was by his boyhood anachronistic in a long-settled urban society. The social forces which had made it attractive were no longer operative.

So it is that when Stephen Crane envisaged the Fall, he agreed with his father that the "elements of [human] nature to which appeal was made were holy. . . . There are affections, also, in themselves not only innocent but essential to a perfect humanity, which may at times impel in the direction of sin." But Stephen cannot go on to believe that "Man's duty and safety demand that [his appetites and passions] be subjugated," even as his father believed, for here the gentle voice of paternal reasonableness is drowned out by the thunderer. In the following poem, not before available, Crane, like his father, interprets Genesis. But where the father had absolved Eve of guilt in being tempted, his son interpolates a human reply to the commandment to abstain from the fruit (Gen. 2:16-17). Stephen implies a question that would never have occurred to Jonathan crane: How can God be good if he demands the impossible of man? For his father, "To ponder that question [of obedience] is to begin to yield."

> A god came to a man
> And said to him thus,
> "I have a glorious apple
> "It is a glorious apple
> "Aye, I swear by my ancestor
> Of the eternities before this eternity
> "It is an apple that is from
> The inner thoughts of heaven's greatest.
> And this will I hang here
> And then I will adjust thee here
> Thus—you may reach it.
> And you must stifle your nostrils
> And control your hands
> And your eyes
> And sit for sixty years
> But,—leave be the apple.
>
> The man answered in this wise:
> "Oh, most interesting God
> What folly is this?
> Behold, thou hast moulded my desires
> Even as thou hast moulded the apple.
>
> How then?
> Can I conquer my life
> Which is thou?
> My desires?
> Look you, foolish god
> If I thrust behind me
> Sixty white years
> I am a greater god than god
> And then, complacent splendor,

Thou wilt see that the golden angels
That sing pink hymns
Around thy throne-top
Will be lower than my feet.

(Columbia MS)

In another poem the argument is condensed and the presentation, while still allegorical, is made lyrical by a functional refrain:

"It was wrong to do this," said the angel.
"You should live like a flower,
Holding malice like a puppy,
Waging war like a lambkin."

"Not so," quoth the man
Who had no fear of spirits;
"It is only wrong for angels
Who can live like the flowers,
Holding malice like the puppies,
Waging war like the lambkins."

(*BR* 54)

Those are ambiguous puppies and lambkins. Even in heaven these gentle beasts own something of the malice and aggressiveness of animal nature.

Irrelevance of the church. After his father's death Stephen Crane probably never again attended a church in which the voice of his inner God was heard. In *The Black Riders*, poem 32, we see the irrelevance of the conventional church to the worship of the true God:

Two or three angels
Came near to the earth.
They saw a fat church.
Little black streams of people
Came and went in continually.
And the angels were puzzled
To know why the people went thus,
And why they stayed so long.

In this new poem, probably written after his trip to Mexico in the summer of 1895, Crane uses a ruined Indian temple to symbolize the transience of human creeds:

A row of thick pillars
Consciously bracing for the weight
Of a vanished roof
The bronze light of sunset strikes through them,
And over a floor made for slow rites.

There is no sound of singing
But, aloft, a great and terrible bird
Is watching a cur, beaten and cut,
That crawls to the cool shadows of the pillars
To die.

(Columbia MS)

Here, as in "It was wrong to do this," he concludes with animal images. The "great and terrible bird" is the condor, a huge and disgusting vulture which prefers carrion to live prey. Waiting for the "beaten and cut" dog to die in the treacherously inviting shadows, the bird is the only occupant of a Heaven as vacant as the deserted temple.

Two poems in *War Is Kind* carry further the "anarchy" of Crane's assault on institutionalized religion:

Even the sky and the opulent sea,
The plains and the hills, aloof,
Hear the uproar of all these books.
But it is only a little ink more or less.

This refers to the voluminous clerical writings of Crane's family. The aloofness of nature from man's aspirations we are to meet again. The poem continues:

What?
You define me God with these trinkets?
Can my misery meal on an ordered walking
Of surpliced numskulls?
And a fanfare of lights?
Or even upon the measured pulpitings
Of the familiar false and true?
Is this God?
Where, then, is hell?
Show me some bastard mushroom
Sprung from a pollution of blood,
It is better.

Where is God?

(*WK* 4)

This poem is a curious jumble of Crane's verse at its best and worst. From the third through the seventh lines above there is a fusion of language, rhythm, and concept. But this requires a psychological distance from the subject; in the rest of the quotation this distance is lost, and with it the verbal control. The result is jejune invective, too self-conscious of its own iconoclasm. The extent of such lapses is shown in Crane's note to Elbert Hubbard, to whom he had submitted this poem: "Oh, Hubbard, mark this well. Mark it well! If it is overbalancing your discretion, inform me." Hubbard must have marked it well indeed, for he never printed the poem. But in April, 1898, the back-wrapper of his *Philistine* carried this terse declaration:

> You tell me this is God?
> I tell you this is a printed list,
> A burning candle, and an ass.
> (WK 10)

Here again Crane has condensed a long poem into a short one. Although "a printed list" may be as good a phrase as "a little ink" (neither is remarkable), surely "a burning candle" lacks the suggestiveness of "a fanfare of lights," while "an ass" is flat and puerile compared to "an ordered walking / Of surpliced numskulls." One danger of Crane's poetic practice— the result of his condensation and directness—is a tendency toward flat statement instead of evocative indirection.

Brothers in sin. A dozen poems in *The Black Riders* elaborate one of the implications we have found in the fable of the heart-eater: the kinship of fallen man in his sin. Most of the poems of which this is the theme are short and unambiguous:

> I stood upon a high place,
> And saw, below, many devils
> Running, leaping,
> And carousing in sin.
> One looked up, grinning,
> And said, "Comrade! Brother!"
> (BR 9)

This poem, as Mr. Stallman remarks, "epitomizes Hawthorne's story *Young Goodman Brown.*" But if these lines look backward to Hawthorne's theme and his use of allegory, "Comrade! Brother!" reminds us also of Baudelaire's "Hypocrite lecteur—mon semblable—mon frère." Crane does not yet resemble Baudelaire in poetic strategy; that will come later, as he develops his own means to express attitudes and states of feeling far more complex than the theme of these early poems. Although one-sixth of his first book is given to categorical fables like the foregoing, not a single poem in *War Is Kind* treats this theme directly. There is however one manuscript poem—"The patent of a lord"—that does so, in a way more ambiguous than those in *The Black Riders.*

The world appears in this group of poems as "a reptile-swarming place" (BR 29), or "a desert" of sand, heat, and vacant horizon, despite God's voice assuring him "It is no desert" (42). The evil truth of the human heart is envisaged in no. 44:

I was in the darkness;
I could not see my words
Nor the wishes of my heart.
Then suddenly there was a great light—

"Let me into the darkness again."

Earlier, the poet had summoned a "Mystic shadow" to "tell me—is it fair
/ Or is the truth bitter as eaten fire? . . . / Fear not that I should quaver. /
For I dare—I dare" (*BR* 7). Now he knows the bitterness of truth: "There
was a man who lived a life of fire . . . / Yet when he was dead, / He saw
that he had not lived" (62). And again, more personally,

Many red devils ran from my heart
And out upon the page.
They were so tiny
The pen could mash them.
And many struggled in the ink.
It was strange
To write in this red muck
Of things from my heart.

(*BR* 46)

This confession may explain an unnoticed significance to the title poem of
The Black Riders. Since this is the only poem in the book in which the action
involved horses, why, one wonders, did Crane head the book with it and
give the whole collection its name? Crane is so deliberate about such matters
as his titles that it must be this: in a metaphorical sense, *all* the poems are
like the black riders that come from the sea (conventionally a symbol of
the unconscious), and in them, as in his imagined warriors, there is

clang and clang of spear and shield
And clash and clash of hoof and heel.
Wild shouts and the wave of hair
In the rush upon the wind:
Thus the ride of Sin.

In succeeding chapters [elsewhere] we will trace in Crane's verse the themes
of sensual life ("the wave of hair") and of war. As in the poems discussed
in the present chapter, these too are concerned primarily—obsessively—
with Sin.

Knowledge and admission of one's own sinful nature has the immediate effect of isolating one from human kinship, sympathy, and love.
Crane's verse shows three directions in which the isolated individual may
try to reestablish the love and kinship lost with his innocence. He may
recognize that all men are as sinful as he; he may seek to share the sinful
love of a fallen woman; and, in two poems only, he presages a triumph of
regenerate believers over the agony of mortal life. This vision, in "The Blue

Battalions," we will reach at the end of the fifth chapter; his love poems are the subject of the next. But now we have four poems attacking the hypocrisy of pious gestures hiding a heart of shame, for the isolation that follows sin cannot be denied.

In two of these poems (*BR* 50 and 57) the same line, "You say you are holy," is repeated; in these and in a third (63) the "you" is obviously a clergyman; in the fourth (58) he is a "sage." Mr. Berryman interprets the image this way: "in poems the father-image (sage or seer) is generally on a high place and hypocrisy is the usual charge, suggesting that the original incredulous revulsion on learning that the parent who preaches on Sunday 'does it too' is still governing the poet's fantasies." It may well be that such poems as the following represent masked rivalry against the father:

> There was a great cathedral.
> To solemn songs,
> A white procession
> Moved toward the alter.
> The chief man there
> Was erect, and bore himself proudly.
> Yet some could see him cringe,
> As in a place of danger,
> Throwing frightened glances into the air,
> A-start at threatening faces of the past.
>
> (*BR* 63)

Berryman might, in fact, have used this poem to strengthen his case, for *songs* and *chief man* connect with analogous images in Crane's story "The King's Favor"; there the biographer finds them symbolic disguises of self and father-image. Freudian considerations enlighten achievements artistically more interesting in the love poetry. Here, however, there is another possible source for—or at last contributory to—Crane's animus against religious hypocrites in high places.

From one periodic sentence three pages long in Great-uncle Jesse Peck's tract, I select six clauses on the incapacities of ministers to win mercy for unrepentant sinners:

> Christian ministers can present to you the gracious message from the lips of Jehovah; . . . they can uncover a life which you would fain conceal from the world, from angels, and from God; . . . they can lead you to Sinai trembling to its base under the frown of a revealing Jehovah . . . they can uncover the pit of endless woe, where wicked men and devils walk, and curse, and writhe forevermore; . . . they can range the world of love and wrath for motives to sway your purpose and bring you to the foot of the cross; they can do all this, but they cannot yield, or repent, or believe for you.

Now the effect of this passage is to glorify Christian ministers, not to insist upon the need of repentence. I do not doubt that Berryman is at least partly right: the "you" of these poems is Crane's father. But "you" is also, partly, the whole tribe of preaching Pecks. Phrases in this passage collate neatly with these poems, which, turned against the ministers, "uncover a life which you would fain conceal from the world." Where Crane "stood upon a high place," Bishop Peck leads him to Sinai. As for the rest, the Bishop with resplendent redundance restates all the reasons Stephen Crane had to hate his doctrines and to turn them against the sinners who believed in his damnation but assumed their own perfection in rhetoric as arrogant as this.

One further poem, a manuscript at Columbia, completes this group, implying rather than proclaiming the familial ties of sin:

> If you would seek a friend among men
> Remember: they are crying their wares.
> If you would ask of heaven of men
> Remember: they are crying their wares.
> If you seek the welfare of men
> Remember: they are crying their wares
> If you would bestow a curse upon men
> Remember: they are crying their wares
>   Crying their wares
>   Crying their wares
> If you seek the intention of men
> Remember:
> Help them or hinder them
>   As they cry their wares.

(Columbia MS)

This relates of course to *The Black Riders* 33, in which "One I met upon the road" asked, "Show me of your wares" and all the traveler's wares proved to be sins. There God regarded him "with kinder eyes"; here that compassion is invoked as a code of human conduct. Technically the repetitions are too insistent and monotonous; Crane will later achieve a tense equilibrium between the harshness of his "tongue of wood" and the lyricism of balanced structure, incremental repetition, and refrain.

The Lord is unknowable. The theme in Crane's verse which I represent by this statement is expressed in a group of interesting poems which differ surprisingly in technique and in content. It is stated outright in *The Black Riders* 59: "Walking the sky, / A man in strange black garb / Encountered a radiant form," but when he bowed to do it reverence, "the Spirit knew him not." More complex is "In the night", first published in the *Chap-book* for March, 1896. Like many of the poems in *War Is Kind*, this one differs from most of those in *The Black Riders* in its stanzaic organization and the use of a refrain. The poem is cyclical, these opening lines being repeated at the end:

> In the night
> Grey heavy clouds muffled the valleys
> And the peaks looked toward God alone.

The thrice-stated refrain consists of their prayers which, with incremental repetition, beg "that we may run swiftly across the world / To huddle in worship at Thy feet"; implore "Give voice to us, we pray, O Lord, / That we may sing Thy goodness to the sun"; and affirm "We bow to Thy wisdom, O Lord— / Humble, idle, futile peaks." The central stanza contrasts to the imperturbable humility of the peaks the daylit bustle of humanity:

> In the morning
> A noise of men at work came the clear blue miles
> And the little black cities were apparent.

But at the end it is night again and "Grey heavy clouds muffle the valleys." Man is enshrouded in darkness, and the mountains, with the wisdom of humble resignation, "looked toward God alone." We are not told that they see Him.

The contrast between the humble serenity of the natural world and the egotistic striving of man for knowledge and personal salvation is made again in two other poems from *War Is Kind*. Amy Lowell cited these, apparently on technical grounds, as "Crane's high-water mark in poetry." With respect to the first (*WK* 14) she noted "the vigorous handling of colour in the first two lines" and "the noise and tremor whirling into one stupendous shout." "He had got beyond the stage of mere expression to where he can . . . make a thing of beauty." The "thing of beauty" is in this case a Whitman-like iteration of the purposelessness, the futile noises, of human striving.

> A slant of sun on dull brown walls,
> A forgotten sky of bashful blue.
>
> Toward God a mighty hymn,
> A song of collisions and cries,
> Rumbling wheels, hoof-beats, bells,
> Welcomes, farewells, love-calls, final moans,
> Voices of joy, idiocy, warning, despair,
> The unknown appeals of brutes,
> The chanting of flowers,
> The screams of cut trees,
> The senseless babble of hens and wise men—
> A cluttered incoherency that says at the stars:
> "O God, save us!"
>
> (*WK* 14)

As first published in the *Philistine* for December, 1895, the last line read "O, God save us!" In any case the plea is directed not, as the wise men think, "Toward God," but "at the stars." These, fixed in their orbits, regard the "cluttered incoherency" without concern. Part of the "senseless babble" is man's own din, of which this later three-line bit, not included in *Collected Poems*, is reminiscent:

> Rumbling, buzzing, turning, whirling Wheels,
> Dizzy Wheels!
> Wheels!

But the rest of the babble is the cries of brutes and flowers. "The screams of cut trees": Nature crying against man's abuse.

In poem 25 of *War Is Kind* there is a synesthetic evocation of natural beauty, regarded as praise of God and proof of His existence. The technique resembles the impressionism and colorfulness of "A slant of sun."

> Each small gleam was a voice,
> A lantern voice—
> In little songs of carmine, violet, green, gold.
> A chorus of colours came over the water;
>
>   .   .   .   .
>
> Small glowing pebbles
> Thrown on the dark plane of evening
> Sing good ballads of God
> And eternity, with soul's rest.
> Little priests, little holy fathers,
> None can doubt the truth of your hymning,
> When the marvellous chorus comes over the water,
> Songs of carmine, violet, green, gold.

The point of course is that even this "marvellous chorus" fails to appease man's doubt. In contrast to this sacramentalizing of Nature, Crane elsewhere regards it as a force which "at fateful time" reveals "grim hatred" for man, as we shall see.

Crane's most successful poem on the inscrutability of God is only five lines long, a hitherto unpublished poetic cryptogram on the problem of evil. Nowhere in his published verse did Crane achieve such evocative compression:

> The patent of a lord
> And the bangle of a bandit
> Make argument
> Which God solves
> Only after lighting more candles.
>   (Columbia MS)

The slightness of dimension is deceptive, as an attempt at paraphrase makes clear. The first three lines are plain enough; the reality of privilege and plunder raises the question of evil, for how can such things be if God is good? But what is meant by the answer implied to the argument "Which God solves / Only after lighting more candles"? We must first note that the argument is solved by God, not man; but what signify the candles He lights? In one sense they signify both light and enlightenment: God makes light and is the source of our knowledge. Mere candles then are an ironic comment on how little light omniscient God, creator of suns and stars, has thus far given us. But God Himself may be baffled for want of light. On the other hand, candles are lit for the souls of the dead; that is to say, God will solve the argument for us only after death, when He will enlighten our immortal souls on such points of Divine Truth as lie beyond human sight. The candles then indicate that more faith than we have now is needed to "solve" the problem. But with more faith the problem is not really solved, it simply ceases to exist. The "argument" begins when man has the temerity to question the Divine Will as it appears in the world about him. This, to paraphrase Crane's father on the Fall, is where sin begins. In this poem Crane has come a long way from his blatant rebuttals in *The Black Riders* to Great-uncle Jesse's damnation tract. A more absolute economy of diction, based on an aesthetic of poetry as the spoken language rather than the sung, would be perhaps impossible to imagine.

VI

Crane's personal Redeemer is, as we have seen, a private deity; his own sanctification of an ideal compassion, an ideal love, which he found embodied in neither the world of natural forces man inhabits nor in the world of social forces man creates. As I have intimated throughout this chapter, Crane did, in one important poem, eventually achieve a resolution of the almost unbearable tensions which give his best poems and stories their validity and power. Since that resolution involves not only the war between his mother's and his father's gods, but all of his major themes, I must postpone analysis of "The Blue Battalions" until these other contributory matters have been explored.

There remains to be examined here a group of poems in which the Blustering God wears as his mask the visible forms of Nature. His wrath and rod are our hostile environment; part of our weakness is our illusion that Nature, because occasionally beautiful, has any care for us in the vistas we admire:

> To the maiden
> The sea was a blue meadow,
> Alive with little froth-people
> Singing.
>
> To the sailor, wrecked,
> The sea was dead grey walls

> Superlative in vacancy,
> Upon which nevertheless at fateful time
> Was written
> The grim hatred of nature.
>
> (WK 3)

Thus, a year and a half before he watched the snarling waves from an open boat. That experience did not alter his convictions about man's relation to nature; it simply confirmed them. After that ride in the open boat, though, he was to dramatize the hatred of nature in another poem far more subtle and profound than this one, a poem on the coldness of God. The poem quoted above is titled "The Sea—Point of View" in a holograph list of magazine acceptances of his verse. The first point of view, that Nature is beautiful and, implicitly, benificent, Crane attributes to a sensibility not only feminine but virginal; to one inexperience in what, as the next chapter will show us, was for him the exquisite sin and supreme source of terror in life. Only those innocent of the mysterious terror of sin can be so innocent as not to know the terror of being abhorred by the elements in which we live.

Once, in *The Black Riders*, Crane himself had been almost as innocent as that about his favorite emblem of Nature, the sea:

> The ocean said to me once,
> "Look!
> Yonder on the shore
> Is a woman, weeping. . . .
> Go you and tell her this—
> Her lover I have laid
> In cool green hall.
> There is wealth of golden sand
> And pillars, coral-red:
> Two white fish stand guard at his bier.
>
> . . . .
> . . . the king of the seas
> Weeps too, old, helpless man.
> The bustling fates
> Heap his hands with corpses
> Until he stands like a child
> With surplus of toys."
>
> (BR 38)

Copyright to the volume in which these sentiments appeared was applied for on January 14, 1895. Six weeks later, the author was in Eddyville, Dawson County, Nebraska—far from the ocean, yet learning something of Nature that would never again let him pity the sea as an unwilling slave of the fates, nor let him think that Nature might pity him. Crane describes the oncome of disaster in "Nebraska's Bitter Fight for Life," one of the best of his uncollected sketches:

> Then from the southern horizon came the scream of a wind hot as an oven's fury. Its valor was great in the presence of the sun. . . . From day to day, it raged like a pestilence. The leaves of the corn and of the trees turned yellow and sapless like leather. For a time they stood the blasts in the agony of a futile resistance. The farmers, helpless, with no weapon against the terrible and inscrutable wrath of nature, were spectators at the strangling of their hopes, their ambitions, all that they could look to from their labor. It was as if upon the massive altar of the earth, their homes and their families were being offered in sacrifice to the wrath of some blind and pitiless deity.

This is a face of Nature unknown to Emerson, undescribed in Bishop Peck's encomia of the bounteous blessings with which God has furnished the habitations of mankind. We realize with a start that this sketch is date-lined February 22: Crane has witnessed not this withering heat but the blizzards of half a year later. His imagination has endowed other persons' descriptions of the summer's blight with these forceful metaphors of futile suffering and ritual sacrifice.

Nature's malignity and omnipotence are accentuated in Crane's work by the gnatlike stature of man. The world has no need for man, and can readily dispense with his strivings:

> A man said to the universe:
> "Sir, I exist!"
> "However," replied the universe,
> "The fact has not created in me
> A sense of obligation."
>
> (WK 21)

The individual's disproportionate sense of his own magnitude is a constant source of Crane's irony. Thus, in *George's Mother* (written in 1893-94), when the hero perceived "that the earth was not grateful to him for his presence upon it," he relished "the delicious revenge of a partial self-destruction. The universe would regret its position when it saw him drunk." In "The Open Boat" we find the same irony as in the last poem, but the dialogue device is reversed. Now Nature does not acknowledge the tiny man's existence with so much as a reply:

> When it occurs to a man that nature does not regard him as important, and that she feels she would not maim the universe by disposing of him, he at first wishes to throw bricks at the temple, and he hates deeply the fact that there are no bricks and no temples. Any visible expression of nature would be pelleted with his jeers.

Then if there be no tangible thing to hoot, he feels, perhaps, the desire to confront a personification and indulge in pleas, bowed to one knee, and with hands supplicant, saying, "Yes, but I love myself."

A high cold star on a winter's night is the word he feels that she says to him. Thereafter he knows the pathos of his situation.

Crane has reversed the usual techniques of prose and verse, using personification and dialogue in his poem and elaborating a cluster of symbols in the story. Philosophically the selections are identical, and the implications of such a world-view is the terrible aloneness with which Crane's puny protagonists must face their fates.

VII

Where in "The Open Boat" the unconcern of the high cold star revealed the pathos of man's situation, in the last poem we are to read on this theme the destiny of man making his little struggles against the hostility of the universe is heightened instead to tragedy. This poem, "A man adrift on a slim spar," was written before *War Is Kind* appeared, yet Crane never published it; first printed posthumously in the *Bookman* (1929), it was appended to the 1930 edition of *Collected Poems*.

"A man adrift" resembles in theme the bitter poems with which this chapter began. But unlike those "Godless" poems, and unlike the poems immediately preceding in which the ocean or the universe reveals its grim hatred in abstract terms, this one reflects Crane's mature experience rather than exclusively his early religious training. Yet personal as is the experience, the poem itself is impersonal, objective, and detached in a way impossible to the younger Crane of *The Black Riders*. Writing of *The Red Badge of Courage*, a work artistically more mature than most of the contemporaneous poems in *The Black Riders*, Crane observed, "Preaching is fatal to art in literature. I try to give readers a slice out of life, and if there is any moral or lesson in it, I do not try to point it out, I let the reader find it for himself. . . . As Emerson said, "There should be a long logic beneath the story, but it should be kept carefully out of sight.' " The earlier poems allow some justice to Harriet Monroe's complaint that Crane was "tempted to orate, to become cosmic and important, to utter large truths in chanting tones." But "A man adrift" follows the precepts just stated, and they bring Crane to a remarkable success of indirection. In this poem Crane does not need to raise his voice, for "the incessant raise and swing of the sea" is terrifying.

Each poem thus far examined has told a story. In this one there is a narrative implied—implied because nothing of the tale is actually stated. Instead we have a succession of images, most of them visual, of how the drowning man sees his own situation:

> A man adrift on a slim spar
> A horizon smaller than the rim of a bottle
> Tented waves rearing dark lashy points
> The near whine of froth in circles.
> > God is cold.

This creation of a point of view identical to that of the suffering character parallels the achievement of "The Open Boat." After another stanza of like impressions, in which "growl after growl of crest" suggests the malign animism of the sea, there is a shift from the eyes of the victim to those of an objective observer. His nine-line interpolation remarks some implications of the scene:

> The seas are in the hollow of The Hand;
> Oceans may be turned to a spray
> Raining down through the stars
> Because of a gesture of pity toward a babe.
> Oceans may become grey ashes,
> Die with a long moan and a roar
> Amid the tumult of the fishes
> And the cries of the ships
> Because The Hand beckons the mice.

Without interruption the point of view shifts again to the man on the spar; we see his dying moment through his eyes:

> A horizon smaller than a doomed assassin's cap,
> Inky, surging tumults
> A reeling, drunken sky and no sky
> A pale hand sliding from a polished spar.
> > God is cold.

The final stanza returns to the observer, who like the survivors in "The Open Boat," can be an "interpreter":

> The puff of a coat imprisoning air;
> A face kissing the water-death
> A weary slow sway of a lost hand
> And the sea, the moving sea, the sea.
> > God is cold.

This poem is Crane's most complete denial of God—not only of the God of vengeance, but, worse, of the God of mercy. What the observer interprets is a truth of terrible simplicity; Nature endures—the triple iteration of that last line *makes* it endure—and the God who, Christian doctrine assures us, is concerned with every sparrow's fall, takes not the slightest heed of "A face kissing the water-death," not even to judge his soul. The man is drowned; the sea goes on forever. The refrain had been until now the despairing lament of the dying man betrayed by his God; but the final "God is cold" is a judgment made by another who survives to interpret his death to the living.

But the poem demands closer attention. For all its grim bravura and the memorableness of such lines as "A horizon smaller than a doomed assassin's cap," is it really a coherent whole? What difficulties the poem presents may be dispelled by an explicatory paraphrase.

The observer interpolates two statements, parallel in structure, conditional in mood, on the possibilities of merciful action open to God if He would but follow them. God holds all creation in His hand; He has the power to transform "Inky, surging tumults" of this menacing ocean into the gentleness of spring rain, were he pitiful. (This accurate allusion to the water cycle is one of the few images Crane derived from science.) God in his omnipotence could blast the sea to ashes, bringing consternation to the fishes and the ships (how they come alive in that line!), if He should care to save even the mice aboard them.

But, to the man adrift on the slim spar, the horizon is "smaller than a doomed assassin's cap," doomed because he is being executed through God's nonintervention just as surely as though he were a murderer, condemned, unworthy of mercy. The irony of the epithet "assassin" is turned against God too, for He in effect murders the man by refusing to save him, by considering him less worthy of sustenance than the mice. This term "assassin," which Crane, like Emily Dickinson, was curiously given to using in nonpolitical contexts, combines in portmanteau fashion the word *sin* with the signification of murder or killing. So the drowning man may be an assassin after all, since natural depravity, as first inherited by Cain and by him passed on, led to the murder of a brother. "Assassin" further suggests the desperation of the victim (the term derives from *hashish*, smoked in the Orient by hired murderers to induce frenzy); and the cap of a doomed assassin is a powerful image of what the drowning man sees as the waves close over his head. In the first stanza the waves were "tented," which ironically suggests both land and sleep. Now the tent has shrunk to a fez or stocking cap, contracting the round horizon to the funneled darkness of a diminishing sky no larger, at its widest diameter, than his own headband.

The "lashy dark points" come together above him and break as he surfaces into "A reeling drunken sky," then sinks: "and no sky." He loses his hold on the spar, and nothing remains but the sea. "A weary slow sway of a lost hand" is the drifting of both the hand that has lost its grip and of the man himself—sailors are "hands"—whose soul is lost. The "slim spar" that fails him is the debris of the wreck from which he has been cast adrift: the "ship of the world" which God had abandoned in *The Black Riders* (6). The slim spar also evokes the correlated images in "The Open Boat," the "thin little oar" of Billy Higgins, the oiler who dies, which "seemed ready to snap"; and "The breaking of a pencil's point" which expresses the correspondent's unconcern with the deaths of others before his initiation into the fellowship of those who do not know the color of the sky.

"There is no probation beyond the cold river." Perhaps Stephen Crane remembered this sentence from the tract that thundered over his boyhood. The coldness of the waters has become the coldness of God, and all that can matter to man is the integrity with which he meets the perils in life and the death from which an uncaring Deity will not save him.

A Matter of Autumn: Trumbull Stickney and "Mnemosyne"

John Hollander

Trumbull Stickney, who died at 30 in 1904, left behind him a largely ignored book of verse and some remarkable poems in manuscript. These, with additional material, were brought out posthumously in 1905 by his friends George Cabot Lodge and William Vaughn Moody. F. O. Matthiessen included some of these in his *Oxford Book of American Verse,* and Conrad Aiken included some in his wonderful Modern Library anthology of twentieth-century American poetry, from which my whole generation learned so much. Edmund Wilson wrote a short but intense essay on Stickney in 1940, and there was an unpublished Princeton dissertation on him in 1947. But it was only in England, and in 1968, that there appeared a good collection of his poems, both published and from manuscript, with a bibliography and critical introduction by James Reeves and Sean Haldane.

In an attempt to remedy this and at the urging of Edmund Wilson a complete collection of Stickney's verse has been published in a series that started out recently with the overrated Yale poet H. Phelps Putnam (whose "Hasbrouck and the Rose," a great undergraduate favorite in my time, has withered) and which promises Edith Wharton's poems in a future volume. The Stickney text has been edited and introduced by Amberys R. Whittle (who neglects in his bibliography to mention Sean Haldane's *The Fright of Time,* published in 1970, the only book-length study of the poet); the volume includes Wilson's essay, Stickney's early lyrics and fragments of verse drama (such as one on Julian the Apostate, who so fascinated Swinburne, Pater, Ibsen, and Gore Vidal) and the remarkable group of poems that give Stickney, along with John Brooks Wheelwright of a later generation, such urgent priorities for revival.

From *The New York Times Book Review* (July 16, 1972), © 1972 by the New York Times Company; and from *Lyric Poetry: Beyond New Criticism* edited by Chaviva Hosek and Patricia Parker, © 1985 by Cornell University Press.

Joseph Trumbull Stickney came from an expatriate New England family. Born in Geneva, he grew up, like someone in a Henry James story, in London, Italy, and Switzerland. He studied classics (and perhaps became romantically involved with an older woman) at Harvard (graduating six years before Wallace Stevens) and returned to France to study at the Sorbonne, where in 1903 he took the first D. es L. degree, in Greek, ever awarded an American. The final year of his life was spent teaching Greek at Harvard and in suffering the physical pain of a brain tumor, from which he died the following spring. His Harvard was that of Santayana; his émigré Europe that of his friends Henry Adams and Bernard Berenson. His poems, all sonnets and strophic lyrics full of a romantic Hellenism and a formal sense sometimes stronger than their rhetoric, needed half-apologizing-for under the strictures of modernism. With the current rediscovery of American romantic-verse tradition, his work appears more central than ever.

Stickney was a romantic in the major American tradition: dying young, his imaginative life never edged onto the dry summer dust of those that "burn to the socket," in Wordsworth's phrase. And yet his vision was always an autumnal one:

> Men live who say there's gain in loss!
> And yet Desire
> Revives like ferns on a November fire,

he calls out in a cycle of love poems called *Eride*. His most successful prospects are like those of American romantic landscape painting of the midcentury, framed with a touch of ironic distancing.

Stickney's vision was transformed by the actual landscape of Greece, which he visited, for the only time, in the final summer of his life. The Arcadian mountain scenery, read through Wordsworthian filters, becomes for him a vision that cries out for mediation, in an ironically anti-Wordsworthian turn; thus, from "Mount Lykaion":

> Below within the chaos last and least
> A river like a curl of light is seen.
> Beyond the river lies the even sea,
> Beyond the sea another ghost of sky,—
> O God, support the sickness of my eye
> Lest the far space and long antiquity
> Suck out my heart.

But that "sickness," that clouding of the eyeball's transparency, brings an imaginative health in poems like "Near Helikon"; or the sonnet on Sunion, with its major reworking of the romantic aeolian harp theme in which the temple's columns themselves become "the strings of the Aegean lyre"; the poem to Mount Ida, where "as adoring I look after thee,/My eyes see white."

Even in earlier sonnets, as Edmund Wilson indicates, the demands of closure could tighten up the language at the end of the poem to a pitch that modernism could acknowledge. Thus, the image of Delos breaking out in "Thou are divine, thou livest—as of old/Apollo springing naked to the light,/And all his island shivered into flowers," or, again, at the end of "Tho' Inland Far with Mountains Prisoned Round" (full of other Wordsworthian echoes as well), "the mellow evening falls;/Alone upon the shore in the wet light/I stand, and hear the infinite sea that calls." But here, as elsewhere, the interest is not in style, but in the grasp of the visionary moment.

The longer lyrics, like "In Ampezzo" (which Aiken reprinted) and "Lakeward" (which he did not), and part of the over-ambitious *Liederkreis*, "Eride" (from Eridanus, the river Po, although the muse may have been a Jewish girl the poet knew in Paris), like "Now in the Palace Gardens Warm with Age," are all suffused, like most imaginative vision, with the light of other poetry. Just as "the far space *and long antiquity*" (my emphasis), the dimension of myth, rather than merely historical time, combined with the visual to overpower the poet's sight on Mount Lykaion, so the wind blowing past Hölderlin, past Leopardi and Ugo Foscolo can be heard on nearby hills in these later lyrics. And, writing in 1898, near the Tyrol and far from Miltonic Tuscan ground, Stickney begins "In Ampezzo" with a delicate recollection of the "Yet once more . . ." that opens Milton's *Lycidas*:

> Only once more and not again—the larches
> Shake to the wind their echo, "Not again,"—
> We see, below the sky that over-arches
> Heavy and blue, the plain

Stickney, an excellent Greek scholar, may be specifically hearing the New Testament Greek behind Milton's English "yet once more"—*eti hapax*, ("once and for all"). He is certainly attentive to the fallen leaves passage in *Paradise Lost* ("Where th' Etrurian shades/High overarch't imbow'r"). This is a late, sad shaking and echoing, and a late revision both of a visionary moment and a poetic mode of self-conscious recapitulation. The echo scheme, allusively echoing an earlier allusive echo scheme: both of these generated originally by a biblical "yet once more" and its repetition in the canonical mode of the interpreter.

Ultimately, Stickney's major poem remains the unique and perfect "Mnemosyne," written fairly close to 1900. It represents one of the most beautiful uses of refrain in modern literature. Its epigraph might have been from one of his own sonnets ("The melancholy year is dead with rain") where his own diction speaks of itself: "So in the last autumn of a day/Summer and summer's memory returns./So in a mountain desolation burns / Some rich related flower." His major summoning up of what he elsewhere calls "memory's autumnal paradise" is the poem originally called (on the manuscript) "Song," but then retitled:

It's autumn in the country I remember

How warm a wind blew here about the ways!
And shadows on the hillside lay to slumber
During the long sun-sweetened summer-days.

It's cold abroad the country I remember.

The swallows veering skimmed the golden grain
At midday with a wing aslant and limber;
And yellow catttle browsed upon the plain.

It's empty down the country I remember.

I had a sister lovely in my sight:
Her hair was dark, her eyes were very sombre;
We sang together in the woods at night.

It's lonely in the country I remember.

The babble of our children fills my ears,
And on our hearth I stare the perished ember
To flames that show all starry thro' my tears.

It's dark about the country I remember.

There are the mountains where I lived. The path
Is slushed with cattle-tracks and fallen timber,
The stumps are twisted by the tempests' wrath.

But that I know these places are my own,
I'd ask how came such wretchedness to cumber
The earth, and I to people it alone.

It rains across the country I remember.

Structurally, the refrain here is complicated by the ambiguity of its role; starting out the poem, it seems more like a thematic, expository opening, immediately qualified (a) by the white space separating it from the tercet which it should else have joined to make a regular quatrain, and (b) by the implied opening-up of the syntax. In the exposition of autumn as the condition of remembering summer, the full stop is almost put back two words, and "I remember" enjambed to the tercet. With one's realization, at the first repetition, that a varying refrain has indeed been thereby instituted, comes the further problem of the Janus-like line in its very liminal placement. We have to ask whether the *rentrement* introduces or concludes, whether the line in its paradigmatic recurrence is epistrophic to its proceeding tercet, or anaphoric to its following one. The meticulously shaded echoic quality of the half-rhymes with the middle lines of the tercets, not to speak of the deep, inner resonance of the white space surrounding the refrain lines, underscores their liminal role. In their very placement, they control the mode of crossing from one chamber of remembrance, from one topos, to another. The white spaces are full of ellipsis: *But* (after the first tercet) "It's cold" or *"But now* it's empty" or *Yet now* it's lonely." And yet the last two returns are not governed by those *and yets*—"You see, it's dark . . ." then leads to the vision of a ruined landscape in the next tercet, and the ellipsis of the refrain itself before the final one. The poem has a bipartite structure, controlled by the pattern of variation of the refrain line. Not only do we have the sequential narrative which leads us through the five successive predicates *autumn, cold, empty, lonely, dark,* but in addition, there is the mode of attributing the adjectives, which we come to hear as a superimposed sequence of varied predication: *it's . . . in, it's . . . abroad, it's . . . down. It's . . . in* returns to open the second sequence (followed by *it's dark about*) which concludes with the ellipsis of the last intermediate refrain, and its displacement to the end of the poem, where it forms a kind of sonnet-sestet of the last two tercets, replacing the predicatory sequence of adjectives in the previous ones with a verb. And so much is going on in those tercets: the introjection of the landscape cumbered by what has come to pass; the realization that "the ruin, or blank," as Emerson calls it, is in his own eye, which causes the speaker to reject the rhetorical posture of a Noah; and the rain of the *rentrement* which follows (I shall refrain from calling it, in the manner of my colleague Geoffrey Hartman, a ref-rain, despite its saturated allusiveness, of which more later) portends no new deluge. (For the "wretchedness" came to "cumber" the earth in an array of that word's senses: *overwhelm, destroy, trouble, fill or block up, benumb with cold.*)

The second section of the poem is also distinguished by the only full rhyme in the sequence. The "lonely in . . . remember" and the "dark about . . . remember" lines embrace the remarkable trope of "staring the perished ember/To flames," which itself revivifies the latent allusion to Shakespeare's "glowing of such fire/That on the ashes of his youth doth lie," a precursor text of belated, autumnal, not-yet-totally posterotic mediation. The "ember" morpheme is elicited by punning analysis, from "remember." The emphasis of that analysis in the one perfect rhyme underscores an etymological trope of Mnemosyne's scene as one of flame reduced to its hotter spores, rather than one of recollection or regathering. The poem organizes its own derivately autumnal quality (the late September of Stickney's almost Parnassian romanticism) in specific relation to Shakespeare and Keats (its swallows as yet ungathered, but like swift Camillas that "skim" the plain); to its scene of present hearth and wasted outdoors; to its autumnal time-scale, in which recent summer seems so very bygone (one of the effects of the biblical diction evoking the "sister lovely in my sight"); and, of course, to its own schematic form of threshold refrain, of the chant of the word "remember" itself.

The interwoven narratives of tercet and repetend here are also effective in allegorizing the poem's structure. The movement from summer's re-membered "here" to autumn's present "there"; the extended meditative and moralizing moment of the last two tercets and the way in which the interposition of the refrain between them would seem a transgression of some more than structural line; the final avowal of the mythological nature of "these places"—they are the speaker's "own," fully possessed, fully, in Wallace Steven's sense, "abstract"—this movement is played out against the refrain sequence noted before, which could be said to name autumn and then unpack some of its store of predicates. *Autumn in . . . cold abroad . . . empty down . . .* (where the preposition is troped with such plangency), then the repeated preposition starting out the second part, in *lonely in . . . dark about* (with its echoes of "empty down"); then the displacement, and, at the end (one wants to say, "in the end," for this is what it all *comes down to*), "It rains across the country I remember." The rain is out of sequence in that it is not one of the attributes of the scene, and the refrain is framing a very different kind of statement from the others. Whether projecting (again, echoically and thereby belatedly) an original introjection of Verlaine (as if to say: "Il pleut sur le pays/Comme il pleure dans ma memoire"); or momentarily realizing again the visionary geography of the now rainy coun-try, Baudelaire's "pays pluvieux," the falling rain now plunging the whole poem in *"l'eau* verte du Lethé"; or indubitably evoking the refrain of rain raining every day in Feste's song in *Twelfth Night,* the final return is most complex. Apparently turning from emotional moralizing to the plenitude of plain statement, it cannot help but be over-determined, both by virtue of, and in demarcation of, its terminal position. It is no longer liminal, save that on the other side of its threshold is the endless Lethean flood.

This remarkable poem by a rather young man fictionalizes his very youth as latecoming and therefore, figuratively, old enough to look—we cannot say, "back at," but rather "across"—such a long landscape. "Mem-ory," said Swift, "is an old man's observation"; here, imagination is a young man's memory. And yet Walter Savage Landor's octogenarian observes, in a great poem called "Memory," that the names of his dearest surviving friends get lost to him. Specifically, they cumber like blocked river water the threshold between storage and retrieval: "To these, when I have written and besought/Remembrance of me, the word *Dear* alone/Hangs on the upper verge, and waits in vain." And then Landor concludes: "A blessing wert thou, O oblivion,/If thy stream carried only weeds away/But vernal and autumnal flowers alike/It hurries down to wither on the strand." (If not, as for Spenser, "Flowers + flow-ers, things that move in water," then at least the flow of what has been remembered into re-membered in the retrieval and articulation of it is seen as a flood that staves off the transverse flow of Lethe.) But for the young poet, there is no terror of a damming-up of the flow of eloquence. He is in sure control of the returning sequence of half-rhymes and its own structural narrative (*slumber—limber—sombre—ember—timber—cumber*): framed by the *slumber* that comes to *cumber,* bracketed within that by the *limber* now felled to *timber*, mediated by the Janus faces of "remember."

Stickney's poem clearly tropes its scheme of refrain as a fable of memory, but less obviously, it makes refrain a matter of autumn, and a figure for his entire, lovely, fragile but inescapable body of poetry.

Biographical Notes

Anne Bradstreet (ca. 1612–72), daughter of Thomas Dudley, a governor of the Massachusetts Bay Colony, was born in England and married at sixteen to Simon Bradstreet, also a governor of the Colony. In 1630 the family sailed on the *Arbella* to Massachusetts, where Bradstreet assumed the heavy household duties typical in Puritan life. A volume of her poems, entitled *The Tenth Muse Lately Sprung Up in America*, was published in 1650 in England, having been sent off by an enthusiastic brother-in-law without Bradstreet's knowledge. The first American edition was published post-humously in 1678 in Boston. While acknowledging Du Bartas and Sir Philip Sidney as her influences, Bradstreet is responsible for an original oeuvre in a New England Puritan, feminine voice.

Edward Taylor (ca. 1644–1729) emigrated in 1668 from his native England to Boston, where he graduated from Harvard in 1671. He then served as a Puritan preacher in Westfield, Massachusetts, where he spent the rest of his life. His sacred verse and all his poetical works remained unpublished until 1939, when the volume *Poetical Works* including *Preparatory Meditations in Verse* was finally printed. Sermons delivered by Taylor between 1701 and 1703 were published in 1962 as *Christographia*. Modern readers typically compare his work to that of such English metaphysical poets as Herbert and Crashaw.

Philip Freneau (1752–1832) was born in New York of Huguenot ancestry and attended Princeton. After serving as a private secretary to a plantation owner in the West Indies, Freneau traveled on the seas, having various misadventures. His term of imprisonment on a British prison ship is described in *The British Prison Ship* (1781). Between 1784 and 1790 he returned to sea, journeying in the Atlantic and Caribbean. His first collection, *Poems*, appeared in 1786, followed by *Miscellaneous Works* in 1788. He began to publish *The National Gazette* in 1791 and was appointed by Jefferson to a clerkship in the State Department. After retiring to New Jersey he published a series of essays, *Letters on Various Interesting and Important Subjects* (1799). Freneau's early historical and satirical verse won him the title "poet of the American Revolution"; his later work includes occasional verse and poems on democracy and romantic themes.

Phillis Wheatley (ca. 1753–84) was brought from Africa to America in 1761 as a seven- or eight-year-old slave. She was purchased by the Wheatleys of Boston at whose home she spent her childhood. She was tutored in English, Latin, and the Bible and began to publish poems in local periodicals as a young woman. She was sent in 1773 to London, where her volume *Poems on Various Subjects, Religious and Moral* was printed after her return to Boston, at which time she was manumitted. Her poem to George Washington was published in 1776. Wheatley's work was widely read by contemporary intellectuals, including Jefferson who publicly disparaged it. Married to a free man, she died in Boston.

William Cullen Bryant (1794–1878) was born in Cummington, Massachusetts, and attended Williams College. He left his most famous early poems, "Thanatopsis" and "To a Waterfowl," unpublished while pursuing what was to be a short-lived legal career. "Thanatopsis" was published in 1817, establishing his reputation as a poet. A leading Democratic editor and journalist of his day, Bryant's opposition to slavery eventually brought him into the Republican party. He became coeditor of *The New York Review and Atheneum Magazine* and the *New York Evening Post*, positions he maintained for nearly a half-century. In his poetic concern for themes of nature, Bryant was aligned with his friends of the Hudson River School of painting, such as Thomas Cole. Bryant's first collection, *Poems*, appeared in 1821. Other publications include: *Poems* (1832); *The Fountain* (1842); *The White-Footed Deer* (1844); prose discourses on other writers, *Letters of a Traveller* (1850); *Hymns* (1869); translations of the *Iliad* (1870) and *Odyssey* (1871–72); *Orations and Addresses* (1873); and *The Flood of Years* (1878).

Ralph Waldo Emerson (1803–82) was born in Boston, graduated from Harvard in 1821, and ordained as a Unitarian minister in 1826. He gave up his ministry for a literary career, and in 1835 settled in Concord where he became the central figure of the Transcendentalist movement. His friends and colleagues included Thoreau, Bronson Alcott, Jones Very, Margaret Fuller, and Nathaniel Hawthorne. Emerson's first book, *Nature*, appeared in 1836, followed by his oration *The American Scholar* (1837); *The Divinity School Address* (1838); and *Essays* (1841). His first volume of *Poems* was published in 1847. His later important works include *Representative Men* (1850); *English Traits* (1856); *The Conduct of Life* (1860); and *May-Day and Other Pieces*

(1867). Emerson, leader of the American Renaissance and a major influence on the subsequent history of American letters, died in Concord at the age of 79.

Henry Wadsworth Longfellow (1807–82) was born in Portland, Maine, and attended Bowdoin College. After studying and traveling in Europe and a brief period teaching at Bowdoin, he began an eighteen-year professorship at Harvard in 1836. In Cambridge, Longfellow became a prominent literary figure, heralding an American romantic movement and popularizing American folk themes at home and abroad. His prose romance, *Hyperion*, was published in 1839, followed in the same year by his first book of poems, *Voices of the Night*. Other publications include *Ballads and Other Poems* (1841); *Poems on Slavery* (1842); a poetic drama, *The Spanish Student* (1843); *Evangeline* (1847); *The Seaside and the Fireside* (1849); *The Song of Hiawatha* (1855); *The Courtship of Miles Standish* (1858); and what he considered his magnum opus, *Christus: A Mystery* (1872). Longfellow's translation of Dante's *Divine Comedy* appeared in three volumes from 1867 to 1870.

John Greenleaf Whittier (1807–90) was born on a farm near Haverhill, Massachusetts, and began his career by publishing in country journals. His early romantic period is represented by his first collection, *Legends of New England in Prose and Verse* (1831). In 1835 Whittier was elected to the Massachusetts legislature and commenced an ardent abolitionist phase. His antislavery verse of this era is collected in *Voices of Freedom* (1846). A long work of fiction, *Leaves from Margaret Smith's Journal in the Province of Massachusetts Bay, 1678–79* (1849), addressed the Salem witchcraft trials. Whittier also founded the Liberty party, edited the *National Era*, and contributed regularly to other periodicals. Returning to sentimental and natural themes, his later work includes *The Chapel of the Hermits* (1853); *The Panorama* (1856); and *Home Ballads, Poems, and Lyrics* (1860). Regarded as his finest poetic work, *Snow-Bound* appeared in 1866, followed by *The Tent on the Beach* (1867); *Among the Hills* (1869); and, in the year he died, *At Sundown* (1890).

Edgar Allan Poe (1809–49) was born to traveling actors in Boston. After his father's death in 1810, his mother wandered with him and his brother and sister until her death in Richmond a year later. Poe was then taken into the home of a merchant, John Allan, with whom he was never to achieve a happy relationship. After traveling in England with the Allans, Poe attended the University of Virginia. Using a false name and age, he entered the U.S. army in 1827; three years later he was admitted to, and expelled from, West Point. Poe's bizarre personal life included a marriage in 1836 to his thirteen-year old cousin, Virginia Clemm, who died of tuberculosis a decade later. During the period of his marriage, Poe worked as an editor for the *Southern Literary Messenger*, *Graham's Magazine*, and *The Broadway Journal*, which he also owned. His prolific literary career began with early publications of *Ligeia* (1837); *Pym* (1838); *Tales of the Grotesque and Arabesque* (1839); and various stories. His popularity grew with further publications, including the prize-winning "The Gold-Bug" (1845); *Tales* (1845); *The Raven and Other Poems* (1845); and *Eureka* (1848). In 1849, after a year of rapid decline marked by heavy drinking and paranoid delusions, Poe was discovered delirious outside a polling booth in Baltimore, suggesting the subsequent legend that he had been dragged from poll to poll as an alcoholic "repeater." He died four days later on October 7.

Jones Very (1813–80) was born in Salem, Massachusetts, and graduated from Harvard in 1836. While attending Harvard Divinity School and studying classics, he had radical spiritual visions which he claimed communicated to him his religious sonnets. In 1838 he was committed to an insane asylum where he continued his writing. His admirer Emerson called Very "profoundly sane" and in 1839 helped edit Very's *Essays and Poems*, the only book Very published during his lifetime. Very's mystic theology set him apart from his Transcendentalist friends. After he was discharged from the mental institution, he delivered ad hoc sermons in Maine and Massachusetts, then retired to his sister's home where he lived the rest of his life as a recluse. *Poems* (1883) and *Poems and Essays* (1886) appeared posthumously.

Henry David Thoreau (1817–62) was born in Concord, Massachusetts, and went to school at a local preparatory facility in the woods of Concord and at Harvard College. After graduating from Harvard in 1837, he taught school with his brother John, following the method of Bronson Alcott. A trip with his brother in 1839 became the subject of *A Week on the Concord and Merrimack Rivers* (1849). Shortly thereafter, he closed his school to live with his friend Emerson as a disciple and handyman. Later Thoreau began contributing to *The Dial* and affiliating with other Transcendentalists. Between July 4, 1845, and September 6, 1847, Thoreau lived in a hut at Walden Pond. His book *Walden* (1854) refers to that period, which included his one-day imprisonment for refusing to pay a tax, in political protest—the record of this action being his "Civil Disobedience" essay of 1849. Thoreau's later essays and lectures include "Life without Principle" (1863); "Slavery in Massachusetts" (1854); and three lectures on John Brown. His various travels provided material for posthumously published books: *Excursions* (1863); *The Maine Woods* (1864); *Cape Cod* (1865); and *A Yankee in Canada* (1866). Selections from his journals appeared posthumously in *Early Spring in Massachusetts* (1881); *Summer* (1884); *Winter* (1888); and *Autumn* (1892). Thoreau's significant body of poetic work was collected in *Poems of Nature* (1895); a modern edition of the *Complete Poems* appeared in 1943.

Herman Melville (1819–91) was born in New York City to an English and Dutch colonial family. After his father's bankruptcy and early death, Melville ended schooling at age 15. After being a teacher, clerk, and farmer, Melville began his career at sea as a cabin boy on a merchant ship to Liverpool. In 1841 he set sail on a whaler for the South Seas, but he jumped ship in 1842 at the Marquesas, where he lived among the natives for a month. Further adventures took him to Tahiti and Hawaii. In 1843, Melville traveled home on the frigate *United States*, where he then joined literary society in Boston and New York and achieved immense popularity with his novels *Typee* (1846); *Omoo* (1847); *Mardi* (1849); *Redburn* (1849); and *White-Jacket* (1850). After moving to Massachusetts with his wife and the first of four children, he began his long friendship with Hawthorne. Though he wrote what is now acknowledged as his most successful fiction during the post-1850 period, none of it was well received at the time. Melville's masterpiece *Moby-Dick* (1851) was followed by *Pierre* (1852); various stories and sketches between 1853 and 1856; *Israel Potter* (1855); *The Piazza Tales* (1856); *The Confidence Man* (1857); and *Billy Budd*, written just before his death. His travels and tour of the Holy Land in 1857 provided inspiration for *Clarel*, the long poem of 1876. Melville's other poetry includes *Battle-Pieces and Aspects of the War* (1866); *John Marr and Other Sailors* (1888); and *Timoleon* (1891). Many uncollected shorter poems were first published in the 1924 collected edition of his works.

Walt Whitman (1819–92), America's most legendary poet, was born on Long Island to a Quaker family with a carpenter father. After attending public school in Brooklyn and working as a printer and schoolteacher, he campaigned for Martin Van Buren in 1840 and 1841. From that time he lived in New York City, where he was a newspaperman and active member of the Democratic party. In 1842 he began to publish stories as well as the "temperance novel," *Franklin Evans*. The crucial years of return to his family from 1849 to 1854 produced the notebooks which were the embryo of *Leaves of Grass*. In 1855 he published *Leaves of Grass*, including what would later be titled "Song of Myself" and "The Sleepers." In 1856 the second edition appeared with Emerson's laudatory letter, Whitman's reply, and new poems including what he later called "Crossing Brooklyn Ferry." The third edition of 1860 included the "Calamus" poems and what later would be titled "Out of the Cradle Endlessly Rocking" and "As I Ebb'd with the Ocean of Life." Whitman returned to journalism in 1861 and 1862. During these "Wound-Dresser" years, Whitman visited soldiers at New York Hospital and sought his wounded brother George at the Virginia battlefront in December 1862. In Washington, D.C., he visited regularly in military hospitals. He was dismissed from a clerkship with the Indian Bureau of the Department of the Interior on a scandal related to the purported immorality of *Leaves of Grass*. In 1865 he met the young Peter Doyle, the object of a long and troubled love. Whitman's later publications include further editions of *Leaves of Grass* (1867 and 1871); a prose text, *Democratic Vistas* (1871); *Passage to India* (1871); and *Goodbye, My Fancy* (1891). In his later years he traveled, but suffered a severe paralytic stroke in 1888. He died in quiet retirement in Camden.

James Russell Lowell (1819–91) was born in Cambridge, Massachusetts, to a colonial family and graduated from Harvard as class poet in 1838. In 1841 he received a Harvard degree in law. Under the influence of his liberal wife, Maria White Lowell, he worked as an abolitionist journalist until her death in 1853. After his initial two books of verse, *A Year's Life* (1841) and *Poems* (1844), his crucial work of 1848 included *Poems . . . Second Series; A Fable for Critics; The Biglow Papers;* and *The Vision of Sir Launfal.* Lowell taught at Harvard from 1855 to 1886 and continued to write mostly criticism, collected as *Among My Books* (1870 and 1876) and *The Old English Dramatists* (1892). Lowell served as the first editor of the *Atlantic Monthly* from 1857 to 1861 and worked with Charles Eliot Norton as editor of *The North American Review* in 1864. Lowell's *Political Essays* (1888) and addresses such as *On Democracy* (1884) represent his later involvement in Republican politics. He served as Hayes's minister to Spain from 1877 to 1880 and as Garfield's minister to England from 1880 to 1885. He died in Cambridge.

Frederick Goddard Tuckerman (1821–73) was born to a distinguished Boston family and attended Harvard. He practiced law for several years, but after marrying Hannah Jones in 1847 moved to Greenfield, Massachusetts, where he lived reclusively. During his second trip to Europe in 1854 he began a long friendship with Tennyson. Tuckerman published only one book, *Poems,* privately printed in 1860, followed by a British edition in 1863 and an American edition in 1864. A modern edition of the *Complete Poems* was issued in 1965, and three previously unpublished sonnet sequences with some additional poems appeared as *Sonnets* in 1931.

Henry Timrod (1828–67) was born in Charleston, South Carolina, and educated at Franklin College (the present University of Georgia). Trained in the classics and concerned with nature, Timrod was known for only one volume, *Poems* (1860), but still was recognized as "the laureate of the Confederacy." He was a member along with Paul Hamilton Hayne and William Gilmore Simms of Russell's Bookstore Group in Charleston. Because he was tubercular, Timrod was declared unfit to serve in the war and led a brief, unhappy life. After his death, his friend Hayne collected his work in *Poems* (1873) with an insightful and sympathetic introduction. Timrod's other posthumous publications include a long lyric to his wife, *Katie* (1884), and the *Complete Poems* (1899).

Emily Dickinson (1830–86) was born in Amherst, Massachusetts, where she lived her entire life in her family home. The second of three children, she attended Mount Holyoke Female Seminary. A few intellectual companions, notably the Reverend Charles Wadsworth (reputedly a prototype for her figurative lover), fostered her poetic and spiritual development. She also maintained a long correspondence with Thomas Wentworth Higgins. Dickinson's intense, lonely, and isolated life produced over 1,000 short lyrics marked by a concern with the dichotomy between the material and spiritual worlds. Only six of her poems were published, in newspapers, during her lifetime. From a mass of papers found after her death, *Poems* was compiled in 1890, followed by *Poems: Second Series* in 1891.

Sidney Lanier (1842–81) was born in Macon, Georgia, and attended Ogelthorpe University, where he received early training as a musician. His service in the Civil War, four months in prison, a serious illness, and financial troubles left him discouraged and despairing. But after his novel *Tiger-Lilies* was published successfully in 1867 he decided on a dedicated artistic career. He traveled throughout the South in 1875 to produce the "guide-book" narrative *Florida* (1875), and his collection of *Poems* appeared in 1877. He also became a flutist with a Baltimore orchestra. Various lectures (published posthumously as *Shakspere and His Forerunners* [1902]) brought him a teaching position at Johns Hopkins in 1879. His classes there resulted in *The Science of English Verse* (1880) and *The English Novel* (1883). Lanier's book on prosody is distinguished for asserting that metrical theories can be applied similarly in music and verse, an understanding which he realizes in his own lyrics.

Stephen Crane (1871–1900) was born in New Jersey and grew up in upstate New York. He attended Lafayette College and Syracuse University before moving to New York City to work as a reporter and to write fiction. *Maggie: A Girl of the Streets* was published privately in 1893. In the same year, Crane wrote his masterpiece of war, *The Red Badge of Courage*, without personal experience of war. In 1896 he was sent as a war correspondent to Cuba. He was shipwrecked off the coast of Florida in 1897 and based his best-known story, "The Open Boat," upon the incident. In 1898 *The Open Boat and Other Tales of Adventure* was published and Crane became a correspondent in the Spanish-American War. His two books of poetry include *The Black Riders* (1895) and *War Is Kind* (1899). His poetry is thought to be a prototypical "free" verse. Escaping a reputation of alcoholism and drug addiction in New York, Crane went to England in 1899 and died soon after of tuberculosis in Bandweiler, Germany.

Trumbull Stickney (1874–1904) was born and raised in New England. He attended Harvard College, where he began a friendship with Henry Adams. He was known as a distinguished classical scholar excelling at Greek, and published only one book during his lifetime, *Dramatic Verses* (1902). After his death, William Vaughn Moody published the *Poems* (1905).

Contributors

Harold Bloom, Sterling Professor of the Humanities at Yale University, is the author of *The Anxiety of Influence, Poetry and Repression*, and many other volumes of literary criticism. His forthcoming study, *Freud: Transference and Authority*, attempts a full-scale reading of all of Freud's major writings. A MacArthur Prize Fellow, he is general editor of five series of literary criticism published by Chelsea House.

Robert Daly is Professor of English at the State University of New York at Buffalo. He is the author of *God's Altar: The World and the Flesh in Puritan Poetry*.

Louis L. Martz, Sterling Professor of English Emeritus at Yale University, is the author of *The Poetry of Meditation* (1954), *The Paradise Within* (1964), *The Poem of the Mind* (1966), *The Wit of Love* (1969), and *Poet of Exile* (1980).

Annette Kolodny is Professor of Literature at Rensselaer Polytechnical Institute. She is the author of *The Lay of the Land: Metaphor as Experience in American Life and Letters*.

Terrence Collins is Associate Professor of English in the General College at the University of Minnesota.

Donald Davie is a distinguished poet and critic. His books include *Purity of Diction in English Verse* and *Articulate Energy: An Inquiry into the Syntax of English Poetry*, as well as several volumes of verse.

Rebecca Rio-Jelliffe teaches in the English Department at the University of Redlands.

David Porter is Professor of English at the University of Massachusetts, Amherst. His books include *The Art of Emily Dickinson's Early Poetry* and *Emerson and Literary Change*.

533

Howard Nemerov, a distinguished poet, is Edward Mallinckrodt Professor of English at Washington University. His books include *Sentences, Inside the Onion*, and *New and Selected Essays*.

Robert Penn Warren, our Poet Laureate, is also famous as novelist, critic, and social historian. His central books include *All The King's Men* and the five versions of his *Selected Poems*.

Richard Wilbur is one of the principal lyric poets of his generation and the most accomplished translator of Molière into English.

Lawrence Buell, Professor of English at Oberlin College, is the author of *Literary Transcendentalism: Style and Vision in the American Renaissance*.

Henry W. Wells is the author of many studies in western and oriental literature, including *The Ameican Way of Poetry*.

Roy Harvey Pearce is Professor of English at the University of California at San Diego. His books include *The Continuity of American Poetry*, probably the best general study of its subject.

R. W. B. Lewis is Neil Gray Professor of Rhetoric at Yale University. His books include studies of Hart Crane and Edith Wharton, and the celebrated study of nineteenth-century American literature, *The American Adam*.

Bryan C. Short is Chairman of the English Department of North Arizona University at Flagstaff. He is at work on a study of Melville's sources.

George Arms, Professor of English Emeritus at the University of New Mexico, Albuquerque, is the author of *The Fields Were Green*, a classic study of the "fireside" poets.

Denis Donoghue is Henry James Professor of English and American Literature at New York University. His books include *The Third Voice, The Sovereign Ghost, Connoisseurs of Chaos*, and *Ferocious Alphabets*.

Charles R. Anderson retired in 1969 as Caroline Donovan Professor of English at Johns Hopkins University. Besides his work on Dickinson, he is known for his writings on Melville, Thoreau, and Henry James.

Margaret Homans is Associate Professor of English at Yale University. She is the author of *Women Writers and Poetic Identity* and *Bearing the Word*, a book on women writers in the Victorian period.

Joanne Feit Diehl teaches English and American Literature at the University of California at Davis, and is the author of *Dickinson and the Romantic Imagination*.

John Hollander, A. Bartlett Giamatti Professor of English at Yale University, is widely known both as poet and as critic. His most recent books are *Powers of Thirteen*, a long poem, and *The Figure of Echo*, a critical study of allusion in poetry.

Daniel G. Hoffman is Professor of English at the University of Pennsylvania. His recent critical works include *Barbarous Knowledge: Myth in the Poetry of Yeats, Graves, and Muir* and *"Moonlight Dries No Mittens": Carl Sandburg Reconsidered.* He is also the author of several volumes of verse including *Able Was I Ere I Saw Elba,* and *Brotherly Love.*

Bibliography

GENERAL

Allen, Gay Wilson. *American Prosody*. New York: American Book Co., 1935.

Anderson, Quentin. *The Imperial Self: An Essay in American Literary and Cultural History*. New York: Knopf, 1971.

Arms, George. *The Fields Were Green*. Palo Alto: Stanford University Press, 1953.

Bloom, Harold. *Figures of Capable Imagination*. New York: Seabury, 1976.

——. *The Ringers in the Tower*. Chicago: University of Chicago Press, 1971.

Brooks, Van Wyck. *New England: Indian Summer, 1865–1915*. New York: Dutton, 1940.

Buell, Lawrence. *Literary Transcendentalism: Style and Vision in the American Renaissance*. Ithaca, N.Y.: Cornell University Press, 1973.

Duffey, Bernard. *Poetry in America: Expression and Its Values in the Times of Bryant, Whitman, and Pound*. Durham, N.C.: Duke University Press, 1978.

Fussel, Edwin. *Lucifer in Harness: American Meter, Metaphor, and Diction*. Princeton: Princeton University Press, 1973.

Gelpi, Albert. *The Tenth Muse: The Psyche of the American Poet*. Cambridge: Harvard University Press, 1975.

Harbert, Earl N., and Robert A. Rees, eds. *Fifteen American Authors before 1900: Revised Edition*. Madison: University of Wisconsin Press, 1984.

Irwin, John T. *American Hieroglyphics*. New Haven: Yale University Press, 1980.

Kazin, Alfred. *An American Procession*. New York: Knopf, 1984.

Kolodny, Annette. *The Lay of the Land: Metaphor as Experience and History in American Life and Letters*. Chapel Hill: University of North Carolina Press, 1975.

537

Kreymborg, Alfred. *Our Singing Strength*. New York: Coward-McCann, 1929.

Lewis, R. W. B. *Trials of the Word*. New Haven: Yale University Press, 1965.

Marx, Leo. *The Machine in the Garden, and the Pastoral Ideal in America*. New York: Oxford University Press, 1964.

Matthieson, F. O. *American Renaissance*. New York: Oxford University Press, 1941.

Miller, Perry. *The Raven and the Whale*. New York: Harcourt Brace, 1956.

Morrison, Claudia C. *Freud and the Critic*. Chapel Hill: University of North Carolina Press, 1968.

Pearce, Roy Harvey. *The Continuity of American Poetry*. Princeton: Princeton University Press, 1961.

———. *Historicism Once More*. Princeton: Princeton University Press, 1969.

Poirier, Richard. *A World Elsewhere: The Place of Style in American Literature*. New York: Oxford University Press, 1966.

Spiller, Robert E. *The Oblique Light*. New York: Macmillan, 1948.

Stauffer, Donald B. *A Short History of American Poetry*. New York: Dutton, 1974.

Waggoner, Hyatt. *American Poets from the Puritans to the Present*. Boston: Houghton Mifflin, 1968.

Williams, Kenny J. *They Also Spoke: An Essay on Negro Literature in America, 1787–1930*. Nashville: Townsend, 1970.

Wilson, Edmund. *Patriotic Gore*. New York: Oxford University Press, 1962.

Ziff, Larzer. *Literary Democracy*. New York: Viking, 1981.

ANNE BRADSTREET

Arner, Robert D. "The Structure of Anne Bradstreet's Tenth Muse." In *Discoveries and Considerations: Essays on Early American Literature and Aesthetics Presented to Harold Jantz*, edited by Calvin Israel, 46–66. Albany: State University of New York Press, 1976.

Berryman, John. *Homage to Mistress Bradstreet*. New York: Farrar, Straus & Giroux, 1956.

Cowell, Pattie, and Ann Stanford, eds. *Critical Essays on Anne Bradstreet*. Boston: G. K. Hall, 1983.

Hildebrand, Anne. "Anne Bradstreet's Quaternions and 'Contemplations.'" *Early American Literature* 8 (1973): 118.

Hutchinson, Robert. "Introduction." In *Poems of Anne Bradstreet*, 1–33. New York: Dover, 1969.

McElrath, Joseph G., Jr., and Allan P. Robb, eds. *The Complete Works of Anne Bradstreet*. Boston: Twayne, 1981.

Margerum, Eileen. "Anne Bradstreet's Public Poetry and the Tradition of Humility." *Early American Literature* 17 (Fall 1982): 152–60.

Martin, Wendy. *An American Triptych: Anne Bradstreet, Emily Dickinson, Adrienne Rich*. Chapel Hill: University of North Carolina Press, 1984.

Piercy, Josephine K. *Anne Bradstreet*. New York: Twayne, 1965.

Rich, Adrienne. "Anne Bradstreet and Her Poetry." In *The Works of Anne Bradstreet*, edited by Jeannine Hensley. Cambridge: Harvard University Press, 1967.

Rosenmeier, Rosamund. "Divine Translation: A Contribution to the Study of Anne Bradstreet's Method in the Marriage Poems." *Early American Literature* 12 (1977): 121–35.

Stanford, Ann. *Anne Bradstreet: The Worldly Puritan*. New York: Burt Franklin, 1974.

White, Elizabeth Wade. *Anne Bradstreet: The Tenth Muse*. New York: Oxford University Press, 1971.

EDWARD TAYLOR

Ball, Kenneth R. "Rhetoric in Edward Taylor's Preparatory Meditations." *Early American Literature* 4 (1969–70): 79–88.

Benton, Robert M. "Edward Taylor's Use of His Text." *American Literature* 39 (1967): 31–41.

Bercovitch, Sacvan, ed. *Typology and Early American Literature*. Amherst: University of Massachusetts Press, 1972.

Blake, Kathleen. "Edward Taylor's Protestant Poetic: Nontransubstantiating Metaphor." *American Literature* 43 (1971–72): 1–24.

Brumm, Ursula. "Edward Taylor's Meditations on the Lord's Supper." In *American Thought and Religious Typology*, translated by John Hoaglund, 56–85. New Brunswick, N. J.: Rutgers University Press, 1970.

Bush, Sargent, Jr. "Paradox, Puritanism and Edward Taylor's God's Determinations." *Early American Literature* 4 (1969–70): 48–66.

Carlisle, E. F. "The Puritan Structure of Edward Taylor's Poetry." *American Quarterly* 20 (1968): 147–63.

Curtis, Jared R. "Edward Taylor and Emily Dickinson: Voices and Visions." *Susquehana University Studies* 7 (1964): 159–67.

Davis, Thomas M. Edward Taylor's 'Valedictory' Poems." *Early American Literature* 7 (1972–73): 38–63.

———. "Edward Taylor and the Traditions of Puritan Typology." *Early American Literature* 4 (1969–70): 27–47.

Gefvert, Constance J. *Edward Taylor: An Annotated Bibliography, 1668–1970*. Kent, Ohio: Kent State University Press, 1971.

Grabo, Norman S. *Edward Taylor*. New Haven, Conn.: College and University Press, 1961.

———. "Edward Taylor on the Lord's Supper." *Boston Public Library Quarterly* 12 (1960): 22–36.

———. "Edward Taylor's Spiritual Huswifery." *PMLA* 79 (1964): 554–60.

——. "God's Determinations: Touching Taylor's Critics." *Seventeenth-Century News* 28 (1970): 22–24.

Griffith, Clark. "Edward Taylor and the Momentum of Metaphor." *ELH* 33 (1966): 448–60.

Howard, Alan B. "The Word as Emblem: Language and Vision in the Poetry of Edward Taylor." *American Literature* 44 (1972–73): 359–84.

Junkins, Donald. "Edward Taylor's Creative Process." *Early American Literature* 4 (1969–70): 67–78.

——. "Edward Taylor's Revisions." *American Literature* 37 (1965): 135–52.

——. "Should Stars Wooe Lobster Claws?: A Study of Edward Taylor's Poetic Practice and Theory." *Early American Literature* 3 (1968): 88–117.

Keller, Karl. *The Example of Edward Taylor.* Amherst: University of Massachusetts Press, 1975.

——. " 'The World Slickt Up in Types': Edward Taylor as a Version of Emerson." *Early American Literature* 5 (1970): 124–40.

Lynen, John. "Literary Form and the Design of Puritan Experience." In *The Design of the Present: Essays on Time and Form in American Literature*, 49–73. New Haven: Yale University Press, 1969.

Mignon, Charles W. "Edward Taylor's Preparatory Meditations: A Decorum of Imperfection." *PMLA* 83 (1968): 1423–28.

Pearce, Roy Harvey. "Edward Taylor: The Poet and Puritan." *New England Quarterly* 23 (1950): 31–46.

Prosser, Evan. "Edward Taylor's Poetry." *New England Quarterly* 40 (1967): 375–98.

Reed, Michael D. "Edward Taylor's Poetry: Puritan Structure and Form." *American Literature* 46 (1974–75): 304–12.

Russell, Gene. *A Concordance to the Poems of Edward Taylor.* Washington, D.C.: Microcard Editions, 1973.

Scheick, William J. " 'The Inward Tacles and the Outward Traces': Edward Taylor's Elusive Transitions." *Early American Literature* 12 (1977–78): 163–76.

——. "A Viper's Nest, The Featherbed of Faith: Edward Taylor on the Will." *Early American Literature* 5 (1970): 45–56.

——. *The Will and the Word: The Poetry of Edward Taylor.* Athens: University of Georgia Press, 1974.

Stanford, Donald E. *Edward Taylor.* Minneapolis: University of Minnesota Press, 1965.

——. "Edward Taylor and the Lord's Supper." *American Literature* 27 (1955): 172–78.

——. "The Puritan Poet as Preacher: An Edward Taylor Sermon." In *Studies in American Literature*, edited by Waldo McNeir and Leo Levy, 1–10. Baton Rouge: Louisiana State University Press, 1960.

Warren, Austin. "Edward Taylor." In *Rage for Order*, 1–18. Ann Arbor: University of Michigan Press, 1948.

———. "Edward Taylor's Poetry: Colonial Baroque." *The Kenyon Review* 3 (1941): 355–71.

PHILIP FRENEAU

Adkins, Nelson F. *Philip Freneau and the Cosmic Enigma*. New York: New York University Press, 1949.

Andrews, William L. "Goldsmith and Freneau in 'The American Village.' " *Early American Literature* 5 (1970): 14–23.

Arner, Robert D. "Neoclassicism and Romanticism: A Reading of Freneau's 'The Wild Honey Suckle.' " *Early American Literature* 9 (1974): 53–61.

Axelrad, Jacob. *Philip Freneau: Champion of Democracy*. Austin: University of Texas Press, 1967.

Bowden, Mary Weatherspoon. *Philip Freneau*. Boston: G. K. Hall, 1976.

Brown, Ruth W. "Classical Echoes in the Poetry of Philip Freneau." *The Classical Journal* 45 (1949–50): 29–34.

Clark, Harry Hayden. "The Literary Influences of Philip Freneau." *Studies in Philology* 22 (1925): 1–33.

Fender, Stephen. "Philip Freneau and Joel Barlow." In *American Literature in Context, I: 1620–1830*, 143–61. London: Methuen, 1983.

Gibbens, V. E. "A Note on Three Lyrics of Philip Freneau, and Their Similarity to Collins's Poems." *Modern Language Notes* 59 (1944): 313–15.

Haviland, Thomas P. "A Measure of the Early Freneau's Debt to Milton." *PMLA* 55 (1940): 1033–40.

Hedges, William L. "The Myth of the Republic and the Theory of American Literature." *Prospects* 4 (1979): 101–20.

Itzkowitz, Martin E. "Freneau's 'Indian Burying Ground' and Keats's 'Grecian Urn.' " *Early American Literature* 6 (1971): 258–62.

Kyle, Carol A. "That Poet Freneau: A Study of the Imagistic Success of the Pictures of Columbus." *Early American Literature* 9 (1974): 62–70.

Leary, Lewis. *That Rascal Freneau: A Study in Literary Failure*. New Brunswick, N.J.: Rutgers University Press, 1941.

Marsh, Philip M. *Philip Freneau: Poet and Journalist*. Minneapolis: Dillon, 1967.

———. *The Works of Philip Freneau: A Critical Study*. Metuchen, N.J.: Scarecrow Press, 1968.

Vitzhum, Richard C. *Land and Sea: The Lyric Poetry of Philip Freneau*. Minneapolis: University of Minnesota Press, 1978.

PHILLIS WHEATLEY

Richmond, Merle A. *Bid the Vassal Soar: Interpretive Essays on the Life and Poetry of Phillis Wheatley and George Moses Horton*. Washington, D.C.: Howard University Press, 1974.

Robinson, William, H., ed. *Critical Essays on Phillis Wheatley*. Boston: G. K. Hall, 1982.

———. *Phillis Wheatley in the Black American Beginnings*. Detroit: Broadside Press, 1975.

Scheick, William J. "Phillis Wheatley and Oliver Goldsmith: A Fugitive Satire." *Early American Literature* 19 (Spring 1984): 82–84.

Wheatley, Phillis. *The Poems of Phillis Wheatley*, edited by Julian Mason, Jr. Chapel Hill: University of North Carolina Press, 1966.

WILLIAM CULLEN BRYANT

Arms, George. "William Cullen Bryant: A Respectable Station on Parnassus." *The University of Kansas City Review* 15 (1949): 215–23.

Brodwin, Stanley, and Michael D'Innocenzo, eds. *William Cullen Bryant and His America: Centennial Conference Proceedings, 1878–1978*. New York: AMS Press, 1983.

Brown, Charles Henry. *William Cullen Bryant*. New York: Scribner's, 1971.

Budick, Miller E. " 'Visible' Images and the 'Still Voice': Transcendental Vision in Bryant's 'Thanatopsis.' " *Emerson Society Quarterly* 22 (1976): 71–77.

Donovan, Alan B. "William Cullen Bryant, Father of American Song." *New England Quarterly* 41 (December 1968): 505–20.

Free, William J. "William Cullen Bryant on Nationalism, Imitation, and Originality in Poetry." *Studies in Philology* 66 (July 1969): 672–87.

Harrington, Evans. "Sensuousness in the Poetry of William Cullen Bryant." *University of Mississippi Studies in English* 7 (1966): 25–42.

Hollander, John. "Introduction." In *William Cullen Bryant*, by John Bigelow. New York: Chelsea House, 1980.

Jones, Howard Mumford. "Landscape as Religion—Irving, Cooper, Bryant." In *Belief and Disbelief in American Literature*, 24–47. Chicago: University of Chicago Press, 1967.

McLean, Albert F. "Bryant's 'Thanatopsis': A Sermon in Stone." *American Literature* 31 (1960): 474–79.

———. *William Cullen Bryant*. New York: Twayne, 1964.

Phair, Judith Turner. *A Bibliography of William Cullen Bryant and His Critics: 1808–1972*. Troy, N.Y.: Whitson, 1975.

Poger, Sidney. "William Cullen Bryant, Emblem Poet." *Emerson Society Quarterly* 43 (1966): 103–6.

Ringe, Donald A. "Bryant and Whitman: A Study in Artistic Affinities." *Boston University Studies in English* 2 (Summer 1956): 85–94.

———. "Painting as Poem in the Hudson River Aesthetic." *American Quarterly* 12 (Spring 1960): 71–83.

———. *The Pictorial Mode: Space and Time in the Art of Bryant, Irving, and Cooper*. Lexington: University Press of Kentucky, 1971.

Sanford, Charles L. "The Concept of the Sublime in the Works of Thomas Cole and William Cullen Bryant." *American Literature* 37 (1957): 434–48.

Sillen, Samuel, ed. *William Cullen Bryant, Selections from His Poetry and Prose.* New York: International Publishers, 1945.

Spiller, Robert E. "The Men of Letters: Irving, Bryant, Cooper." In *The Cycle of American Literature, an Essay in Historical Criticism*, 24–46. New York: Macmillan, 1956.

Untermeyer, Louis, ed. *The Poems of William Cullen Bryant.* New York: The Heritage Press, 1947.

RALPH WALDO EMERSON

Allen, Gay Wilson. *Waldo Emerson: A Biography.* New York: Viking, 1981.

Baker, Carlos. "Emerson and Jones Very." *New England Quarterly* 7 (1934): 90–99.

Bishop, Jonathan. *Emerson on the Soul.* Cambridge: Harvard University Press, 1964.

Bloom, Harold, ed. *Ralph Waldo Emerson: Poetry and Later Writings.* New York: The Library of America, 1987.

Bode, Carl, ed. *Ralph Waldo Emerson: A Profile.* New York: Hill & Wang, 1969.

Brittin, Norman A. "Emerson and the Metaphysical Poets." *American Literature* 8 (1936): 1–21.

Burke, Kenneth. "I, Eye, Ay—Emerson's Early Essay 'Nature': Thoughts on the Machinery of Transcendence." In *Transcendentalism and Its Legacy*, edited by Myron Simon and Thornton H. Parsons, 3–24. Ann Arbor: The University of Michigan Press, 1966.

Cavell, Stanley. "An Emerson Mood" and "Thinking of Emerson." In *The Senses of "Walden": An Expanded Edition.* San Francisco: North Point, 1981.

Chapman, John Jay. "Emerson." In *The Selected Writings of John Jay Chapman*, edited by Jacques Barzun. New York: Farrar, Straus & Cudahy, 1957.

Cheyfitz, Eric. *The Trans-Parent: Sexual Politics in the Language of Emerson.* Baltimore: Johns Hopkins University Press, 1981.

Cowan, Michael. *City of the West: Emerson, America, and Urban Metaphor.* New Haven: Yale University Press, 1967.

Ellison, Julie. *Emerson's Romantic Style.* Princeton: Princeton University Press, 1984.

Emerson, Edward Waldo, ed. *The Complete Works of Ralph Waldo Emerson.* 12 vols., Centenary Edition. Boston and New York: Houghton Mifflin, 1903–4.

Emerson, Edward Waldo, and Forbes Waldo Emerson, eds. *The Journals of Ralph Waldo Emerson.* 10 vols., Centenary Edition. Boston and New York: Houghton Mifflin, 1910–14.

Emerson Society Quarterly, 1955–.

Firkins, O. W. *Ralph Waldo Emerson*. Boston and New York: Houghton Mifflin, 1915.

Gillman, William, et al., eds. *The Journals and Miscellaneous Notebooks of Ralph Waldo Emerson*. Cambridge: Belknap, 1960.

Hopkins, Vivian. *Spires of Form: A Study of Emerson's Aesthetic Theory*. Cambridge: Harvard University Press, 1951.

Hughes, Gertrude. *Emerson's Demanding Optimism*. Baton Rouge: Louisiana State University Press, 1984.

Konvitz, Milton R., ed. *The Recognition of Ralph Waldo Emerson: Selected Criticism since 1837*. Ann Arbor: University of Michigan Press, 1972.

Konvitz, Milton R., and Stephen E. Whicher, eds. *Emerson: A Collection of Critical Essays*. Englewood Cliffs, N.J.: Prentice-Hall, 1962.

Levin, David, ed. *Emerson: Prophecy, Metamorphosis, and Influence: Selected Papers from the English Institute*. New York: Columbia University Press, 1975.

Loving, Jerome. *Emerson, Whitman, and the American Muse*. Chapel Hill: University of North Carolina Press, 1982.

Lowell, James Russell. "Emerson the Lecturer." In *The Literary Criticism of James Russell Lowell*, edited by Herbert F. Smith. Lincoln: University of Nebraska Press, 1969.

McAleer, John. *Ralph Waldo Emerson: Days of Encounter*. Boston: Little, Brown, 1984.

Miller, Perry. "From Edwards to Emerson." In *Errand into the Wilderness*. New York: Harper, 1964.

Packer, Barbara L. *Emerson's Fall*. New York: Continuum, 1982.

Paul, Sherman. *Emerson's Angle of Vision*. Cambridge: Harvard University Press, 1952.

Porte, Joel. *Representative Man: Emerson in His Time*. New York: Oxford University Press, 1979.

————, ed. *Emerson in His Journals*. Cambridge: Belknap, 1982.

————, ed. *Ralph Waldo Emerson: Essays and Lectures*. New York: The Library of America, 1983.

Porter, David. *Emerson and Literary Change*. Cambridge: Harvard University Press, 1978.

Reaver, J. Russell. "Mythology in Emerson's Poems." *Emerson Society Quarterly* 39 (1965): 56–63.

Richardson, Robert D., Jr. *Myth and Literature in the American Renaissance*. Bloomington: Indiana University Press, 1978.

Rusk, Ralph L., ed. *The Letters of Ralph Waldo Emerson*. 6 vols. New York: Columbia University Press, 1964.

————, ed. *The Life of Ralph Waldo Emerson*. New York: Columbia University Press, 1949.

Slater, Joseph, ed. *The Correspondence of Emerson and Carlyle*. New York: Columbia University Press, 1964.

Spiller, Robert, Alfred Fergusen, et al., eds. *The Collected Works of Ralph Waldo Emerson*. Cambridge: Belknap, 1971–.

Waggoner, Hyatt H. *Emerson as Poet*. Princeton: Princeton University Press, 1974.

Wellek, René. "Emerson and German Philosophy." *New England Quarterly* 16 (1943): 41–62.

Whicher, Stephen E. *Freedom and Fate: An Inner Life of Ralph Waldo Emerson*. Philadelphia: University of Pennsylvania Press, 1953.

———, ed. *Selections from Ralph Waldo Emerson: An Organic Anthology*. Boston: Houghton Mifflin, 1957.

Whicher, Stephen E., Robert Spiller, et al., eds. *The Early Lectures of Ralph Waldo Emerson*. 3 vols. Cambridge: Belknap, 1960–72.

Wilson, Edmund, ed. "Emerson and Whitman: Documents on Their Relations (1855–58)." In *The Shock of Recognition*. New York: Doubleday, Doran, 1943.

Woodbury, Charles J. *Talks with Ralph Waldo Emerson*. New York: Baker & Baker, 1890.

Yoder, R. A. *Emerson and the Orphic Poet in America*. Berkeley and Los Angeles: University of California Press, 1978.

HENRY WADSWORTH LONGFELLOW

Arvin, Newton. *Longfellow: His Life and Work*. Boston: Little, Brown, 1962.

Cameron, Kenneth Walter, ed. *Longfellow among His Contemporaries*. Hartford: Transcendental, 1978.

———. *Longfellow's Reading in Libraries: The Changing Records of a Learned Poet Interpreted*. Hartford: Transcendental, 1973.

Franklin, Phyllis. "The Importance of Time in Longfellow's Works." *Emerson Society Quarterly* 58 (1970) 14–22.

Hammer, Carl, Jr. *Longfellow's "Golden Legend" and Goethe's "Faust."* Baton Rouge: Louisiana State University Press, 1952.

Hirsch, Edward L. *Henry Wadsworth Longfellow*. Minneapolis: University of Minnesota Press, 1964.

Longfellow, Henry Wadsworth. *The Complete Poetical Works of Longfellow*. Boston: Houghton Mifflin, 1893.

———. *The Works of Henry Wadsworth Longfellow*. New York: Davos, 1909.

Matthews, J. Chesley. *Henry W. Longfellow Reconsidered: A Symposium*. Hartford: Transcendental, 1970.

Millward, Celia, and Cecilia Tichi. "Whatever Happened to Hiawatha?" *Genre* 6 (September 1973): 313–32.

Nemerov, Howard, ed. *Longfellow*. Laurel Poetry Series. New York: Dell, 1959.

Nyland, Waino. "*Kalevala* as a Reputed Source for Longfellow's *Song of Hiawatha*." *American Literature* 22 (March 1950): 1–20.

Rodale, J. I., ed. *The Continental Tales of Longfellow*. New York: Barnes, 1960.

Schramm, Wilbur L. "Hiawatha and Its Predecessors." *Philological Quarterly* 11 (October 1932): 321–43.

Tichi, Cecilia. "Longfellow's Motives for the Structure of Hiawatha." *American Literature* 42 (January 1971): 548–53.

Wagenknecht, Edward C. *Henry Wadsworth Longfellow: Portrait of an American Humanist.* New York: Oxford University Press, 1966.

———. *Longfellow: A Full-Length Portrait.* New York: Longmans, Green, 1955.

Williams, Cecil Brown. *Henry Wadsworth Longfellow.* New York: Twayne, 1964.

Zimmerman, Michael. "War and Peace: Longfellow's 'The Occultation of Orion.' " *American Literature* 39 (January 1967): 540–47.

JOHN GREENLEAF WHITTIER

Bennett, Whitman. *Whittier: Bard of Freedom.* Chapel Hill: University of North Carolina Press, 1941.

Cady, Edwin Harrison, and Harry Hayden Clark. *Whittier on Writers and Writing: The Uncollected Critical Writings of John Greenleaf Whittier.* Syracuse: Syracuse University Press, 1950.

Currier, Thomas Franklin. *A Bibliography of John Greenleaf Whittier.* Cambridge: Harvard University Press, 1937.

Foerster, Norman. *Nature in American Literature.* New York: Macmillan, 1923.

Hall, Donald. "Whittier." *Texas Quarterly* 3 (Autumn 1960): 165–74.

Jones, Howard Mumford. "Whittier Reconsidered." *Essex Institute Historical Collections* 93 (1957): 231–46.

Leary, Lewis. *John Greenleaf Whittier.* New York: Twayne, 1961.

Miller, Perry. "John Greenleaf Whittier: The Conscience in Poetry." *Harvard Review* 2 (1964): 8–24.

Mordell, Albert. *Quaker Militant: John Greenleaf Whittier.* Boston: Houghton Mifflin, 1933.

Pickard, John B. *The Basis of Whittier's Critical Creed: The Beauty of the Commonplace and the Truth of Style. Rice Institute Pamphlet* 47 (October 1960): 34–50.

———. "Imagistic and Structural Unity in Snow-Bound." *College English* 21 (1960): 338–42.

———. *John Greenleaf Whittier: An Introduction and Interpretation.* New York: Barnes & Noble, 1961.

Pickard, Samuel. *Life and Letters of John Greenleaf Whittier.* 2 vols. Boston: Houghton Mifflin, 1894.

Pollard, John A. *John Greenleaf Whittier: Friend of Man.* Boston: Houghton Mifflin, 1949.

Scott, Winfred Townley. "Poetry in America: A New Consideration of Whittier's Verse." *New England Quarterly* 7 (1934): 258–75.

Wagenknecht, Edward. *John Greenleaf Whittier: A Portrait in Paradox.* New York: Oxford University Press, 1967.

Waggoner, Hyatt. "What I Had I Gave: Another Look at Whittier." *Essex Institute Historical Collections* 95 (1959): 32–40.

Whittier, John Greenleaf. *The Complete Poetical Works of John Greenleaf Whittier*. Boston: Houghton Mifflin, 1894.

—————. *Legends of New England*. Gainesville, Fla.: Scholars' Facsimiles & Reprints, 1965.

EDGAR ALLAN POE

Auden, W. H., ed. "Introduction." In *Selected Prose and Poetry*. New York: Rinehart, 1950.

Bonaparte, Marie. *The Life and Works of Edgar Allan Poe*. Translated by John Rodker. London: Imago, 1949.

Carlson, Eric W., ed. *The Recognition of Edgar Allan Poe*. Ann Arbor: University of Michigan Press, 1966.

Davidson, Edward Hutchins. *Poe: A Critical Study*. Cambridge: Belknap, 1957.

Eliot, Thomas Stearns. *From Poe to Valéry*. New York: Harcourt-Brace, 1948.

Hoffman, Daniel. *Poe Poe Poe Poe Poe Poe Poe*. Garden City, N.Y.: Doubleday, 1972.

Howarth, William, ed. *Twentieth Century Intepretations of Poe's Tales*. Englewood Cliffs, N.J.: Prentice-Hall, 1971.

Huxley, Aldous. *Music at Night and Other Essays*. London: Fountain Press, 1931.

Ketterer, David. *The Rationale of Deception in Poe*. Baton Rouge: Louisiana State University Press, 1979.

Lacan, Jacques. "The Seminar on 'The Purloined Letter.' " Translated by J. Mehlman. *Yale French Studies* 48 (1972): 38–72.

Levin, Harry. *The Power of Blackness: Hawthorne, Poe, Melville*. New York: Knopf, 1958.

Mabbot, Thomas Ollive, ed. *Collected Works of Edgar Allan Poe*. Cambridge: Belknap, 1969–78.

Mankowitz, Wolf. *The Extraordinary Mr. Poe*. New York: Summit Books, 1978.

Ostrom, John, ed. *The Letters of Edgar Allan Poe*. Cambridge: Harvard University Press, 1948.

Pollin, Burton R., ed. *The Imaginary Voyages: In the Collected Works of Edgar Allan Poe*. Boston: G. K. Hall, 1981.

Quinn, Arthur Hobson. *Edgar Allan Poe: A Critical Biography*. New York: Appleton-Century-Crofts, 1963.

Quinn, Patrick Francis. *The French Face of Edgar Poe*. Carbondale: Southern Illinois University Press, 1957.

Regan, Robert, ed. *Poe: A Collection of Critical Essays*. Englewood Cliffs, N.J.: Prentice-Hall, 1967.

Stovall, Floyd, ed. *The Poems of Edgar Allan Poe*. Charlottesville: University Press of Virginia, 1965.

Tate, Allen. *The Forlorn Demon*. Chicago: Ayer, 1953.

Wagenknecht, Edward Charles. *Edgar Allan Poe: The Man behind the Legend*. New York: Oxford University Press, 1963.

Whitman, Sarah Helen Power. *Poe's Helen Remembers*. Edited by John Carl Miller. Charlottesville: University Press of Virginia, 1979.

Wilson, Edmund. *The Shores of Light*. New York: Farrar, Straus & Giroux, 1952.

Woodberry, George Edward. *Edgar Allan Poe*. Boston and New York: Houghton Mifflin, 1885.

Woodson, Thomas, ed. *Twentieth Century Interpretations of* The Fall of the House of Usher. Englewood Cliffs, N.J.: Prentice-Hall, 1969.

JONES VERY

Baker, Carlos. "Emerson and Jones Very." *New England Quarterly* 7 (1934): 90–99.

Bartlet, William I. *Jones Very: Emerson's "Brave Saint."* Durham, N.C.: Duke University Press, 1942.

Gittleman, Edward. *Jones Very: The Effective Years 1833–1840*. New York: Columbia University Press, 1967.

Herbold, Anthony. "Nature as Concept and Technique in the Poetry of Jones Very." *New England Quarterly* 40 (1967): 244–59.

Levernier, James A. "Calvinism and Transcendentalism in the Poetry of Jones Very." *Emerson Society Quarterly* 24 (1978): 30–41.

Reese, Helen R. "Unpublished and Uncollected Poems of Jones Very." *Emerson Society Quarterly* 30 (1984): 154–62.

Robinson, David. "The Exemplary Self and the Transcendent Self in the Poetry of Jones Very." *Emerson Society Quarterly* 24 (1978): 206–14.

———. "Four Early Poems of Jones Very." *Harvard Library Bulletin* 28 (1980): 146–51.

———. "Jones Very, the Transcendentalist, and the Unitarian Tradition." *Harvard Theological Review* 68 (1975): 103–24.

Winters, Yvor. "Jones Very and R. W. Emerson: Aspects of New England Mysticism." In *Maule's Curse*, 125–46. Norfolk, Conn.: New Directions, 1938.

HENRY DAVID THOREAU

Beston, Henry. *Henry David Thoreau*. New York: Rinehart, 1951.

Bode, Carl J., ed. *Collected Poems of Henry Thoreau*. Baltimore: Johns Hopkins University Press, 1964.

Bridgman, Richard. *Dark Thoreau*. Lincoln: University of Nebraska Press, 1982.

Cavell, Stanley. *The Senses of Walden*. New York: Viking, 1972.

Colquitt, Betsy F. "Thoreau's Poetics." *The American Transcendental Quarterly* 11 (1971): 74–81.

Dennis, Carl Edward. "Correspondence in Thoreau's Nature Poetry." *Emerson Society Quarterly* 58 (1970): 101–9.

Ford, Arthur Lewis, Jr. *A Critical Study of the Poetry of Henry Thoreau.* Ann Arbor: University of Michigan Microfilms, 1972.

————. "The Poetry of Henry David Thoreau." *Emerson Society Quarterly* 61 (1970): 1–26.

Garber, Frederick. *Thoreau's Redemptive Imagination.* New York: New York University Press, 1977.

Glick, Wendell. *The Recognition of Henry David Thoreau.* Ann Arbor: University of Michigan Press, 1969.

Harding, Walter. *Thoreau: A Century of Criticism.* Dallas: Southern Methodist University Press, 1972.

Harding, Walter, and Michael Meyer, eds. *The New Thoreau Handbook.* New York: New York University Press, 1980.

Lane, Laurist, Jr. "Finding a Voice: Thoreau's Pentameters." *Emerson Society Quarterly* 60 (1970): 67–72.

McIntosh, James. *Thoreau as Romantic Naturalist.* Ithaca, N.Y.: Cornell University Press, 1974.

Monteiro, George. "Redemption through Nature: A Recurring Theme in Thoreau, Frost, and Richard Wilbur." *American Quarterly* 20 (1968): 795–809.

Paul, Sherman, ed. *Thoreau: A Collection of Critical Essays.* Englewood Cliffs, N.J.: Prentice-Hall, 1962.

Rukeyser, Muriel. "Thoreau and Poetry." In *Henry David Thoreau: Studies and Commentaries,* edited by Walter Harding, et al. Rutherford, N.J.: Fairleigh Dickinson University Press, 1972.

Sampson, H. Grant. "Structure in the Poetry of Thoreau." *Costerus* 6 (1972): 137–54.

Thoreau Journal Quarterly, 1969–.

Tuerk, Richard Carl. "The One World of Thoreau's Verse." *Thoreau Journal Quarterly* 6 (1974): 3–14.

Wagenknecht, Edward. *Henry David Thoreau.* Amherst: University of Massachusetts Press, 1981.

Williams, Paul Osborne. "The Concept of Inspiration in Thoreau's Poetry." *PMLA* 79 (1964): 466–72.

————. "Thoreau's Growth as a Transcendental Poet." *Emerson Society Quarterly* 19 (1973): 189–98.

HERMAN MELVILLE

Arvin, Newton. *Herman Melville.* New York: Sloane, 1950.

Barrett, Lawrence. "The Differences in Melville's Poetry." *PMLA* 70 (1955).

Beaver, Harold. "Melville and Modernism." *Dutch Quarterly Review of Anglo-American Letters* 13 (1983): 1–15.

Bowen, Merlin. *The Long Encounter.* Chicago: University of Chicago Press, 1963.

Brodhead, Richard H. *Hawthorne, Melville and the Novel.* Chicago: University of Chicago Press, 1976.

Dryden, Edgar A. *Melville's Thematics of Form.* Baltimore: Johns Hopkins University Press, 1968.

Fischer, Marvin. *Going Under.* Baton Rouge: Louisiana State University Press, 1977.

Fogle, Richard Harter. "The Themes of Melville's Later Poetry." *Tulane Studies in English* 11 (1961): 65–86.

Kemper, Steven. "*Omoo*: Germinal Melville." *Studies in the Novel* 10 (1978): 420–30.

Lewis, James W. "The Logic of Broken Promises: Religion and Sex in Melville's Shorter Fiction." *North Dakota Quarterly Review* 47 (1979): 19–33.

Mason, Ronald. *The Spirit above the Dust.* Mamaroneck, N.Y.: Appel, 1972.

Melville, Herman. *Clarel.* Edited by Walter Bezanson. New York: Hendricks, 1960.

———. *Selected Poems of Herman Melville.* Edited and with an introduction by Robert Penn Warren. New York: Random House, 1969.

———. *Poems of Herman Melville.* Edited by Douglas Robillard. New Haven, Conn.: College and University Press, 1976.

Mumford, Lewis. *Herman Melville.* New York: Harcourt Brace, 1929.

Murray, Henry A. "In Nomine Diaboli." *New England Quarterly* 23 (1951): 435–52.

Pullin, Faith, ed. *New Perspectives on Melville.* Kent, Ohio: Kent State University Press, 1978.

Rosenberry, Edward H. *Melville.* Boston: Routledge & Kegan Paul, 1979.

Sewall, Richard B. *The Vision of Tragedy.* New Haven: Yale University Press, 1959.

Sherrill, Rowland A. *The Prophetic Melville: Experience, Transcendence and Tragedy.* Athens: University of Georgia Press, 1979.

Short, Bryan. " 'The Redness of the Rose': The Mardi Poems and Melville's Artistic Compromise." *Essays in Arts and Sciences* 5 (1976): 100–112.

Stein, William Bysshe. *The Poetry of Melville's Late Years.* Albany: State University of New York Press, 1970.

———. "Melville's Poetry: Two Rising Notes." *Emerson Society Quarterly* 27 (1962): 10–13.

Stern, Milton R. *The Fine Hammered Steel of Herman Melville.* Urbana: University of Illinois Press, 1968.

WALT WHITMAN

Allen, Gay Wilson. *The Solitary Singer.* New York: New York University Press, 1967.

———. *The New Walt Whitman Handbook.* New York: New York University Press, 1975.

Allen, Gay Wilson, and S. Bradley, eds. *The Collected Writings of Walt Whitman*. New York: New York University Press, 1963–.

Arvin, Newton. *Whitman*. New York: Macmillan, 1938.

Asselineau, Roger. *The Evolution of Walt Whitman*. 2 vols. Cambridge: Belknap, 1960 and 1962.

Black, Stephen. *Whitman's Journey into Chaos*. Princeton: Princeton University Press, 1975.

Blodgett, H. W., ed. *Walt Whitman: An 1855–56 Notebook toward the Second Edition of Leaves of Grass*. Carbondale: Southern Illinois University Press, 1959.

Blodgett, H. W., and S. Bradley, eds. *Leaves of Grass: Comprehensive Reader's Edition*. New York: Norton, 1968.

Bloom, Harold. *A Map of Misreading*. New York: Oxford University Press, 1975.

———. *Poetry and Repression*. New Haven: Yale University Press, 1976.

Borges, Jorge Luis. "The Achievements of Walt Whitman." *Texas Quarterly* 5 (1962): 43–48.

Bowers, F., ed. *Whitman's Manuscripts: Leaves of Grass (1860): A Parallel Text*. Chicago: University of Chicago Press, 1955.

Bradley, S., A. Blodgett, A. Golden, and W. White, eds. *Leaves of Grass: A Textual Variorum of the Printed Poems*. New York: New York University Press, 1980.

Bucke, R. M., ed. *Notes and Fragments*. London, Canada: Talbot, 1899.

Bucke, R. M., T. H. Harned, and H. L. Traubel, eds. *The Complete Writings*. New York and London: Putnam's, 1902.

Burke, Kenneth. *Attitudes toward History*. 2d ed., rev. Los Altos, Calif.: Hermes, 1959.

Carlisle, E. G. *The Uncertain Self: Whitman's Drama of Identity*. East Lansing: Michigan State University Press, 1973.

Chase, Richard. *Walt Whitman Reconsidered*. New York: Sloane, 1955.

Coffman, Stanley. " 'Crossing Brooklyn Ferry': A Note on the Catalog Technique in Whitman's Poetry." *Modern Philology* 2 (1954): 225–32.

———. "Form and Meaning in Whitman's 'Passage to India.' " *PMLA* 70 (1955): 337–49.

Crawley, Thomas. *The Structure of* Leaves of Grass. Austin: University of Texas Press, 1970.

Furness, C., ed. *Walt Whitman's Workshop*. New York: Russell & Russell, 1964.

Golden, A., ed. *Walt Whitman's Blue Book*. New York: New York Public Library, 1968.

Griffith, Clark. "Sex and Death: The Significance of Whitman's 'Calamus' Themes." *Philological Quarterly* 39 (1960): 18–38.

Hindus, Milton, ed. *Walt Whitman: The Critical Heritage*. New York: Barnes & Noble, 1971.

———. Leaves of Grass: *One Hundred Years After*. Palo Alto, Calif.: Stanford University Press, 1955.

Kaplan, Justin. *Walt Whitman: A Life.* New York: Simon & Schuster, 1980.

Lewis, R. W. B., ed. *The Presence of Walt Whitman.* New York: Columbia University Press, 1962.

Loving, Jerome. *Emerson, Whitman and the American Muse.* Chapel Hill: University of North Carolina Press, 1982.

Miller, Edwin Haviland. *Walt Whitman's Poetry: A Psychological Journey.* New York: New York University Press, 1969.

———, ed. *A Century of Whitman Criticism.* Bloomington: Indiana University Press, 1969.

Miller, James E., Jr. *The American Quest for a Supreme Fiction: Whitman's Legacy in the Personal Epic.* Chicago: University of Chicago Press, 1979.

———. *A Critical Guide to "Leaves of Grass."* Chicago: University of Chicago Press, 1957.

———. *Walt Whitman.* New York: Twayne, 1962.

———. *Whitman's "Song of Myself": Origin, Growth, Meaning.* New York: Dodd, Mead, 1964.

Murphy, Francis, ed. *Walt Whitman.* Harmondsworth, England: Penguin, 1969.

Musgrave, S. *T. S. Eliot and Walt Whitman.* Wellington: New Zealand University Press, 1952.

Pearce, Roy Harvey, ed. *Whitman.* Englewood Cliffs, N.J.: Prentice-Hall, 1962.

———, ed. *Leaves of Grass (Facsimile Edition of the 1860 Text).* Ithaca, N.Y.: Great Seal Books, 1961.

Rubin, Joseph Jay. *The Historic Whitman.* University Park: Pennsylvania State University Press, 1973.

Stovall, Floyd. *The Foreground of* Leaves of Grass. Charlottesville: University Press of Virginia, 1974.

Strom, Susan. " 'Face to Face': Whitman's Biblical References in 'Crossing Brooklyn Ferry.' " *Walt Whitman Review* 24 (1978): 7–16.

Symonds, John Addington. *Walt Whitman: A Study.* New York: AMS Press, 1968.

Trilling, Lionel. "Sermon on a Text from Whitman." *The Nation* 160 (1945): 215–20.

Waskow, Howard. *Whitman: Explorations in Form.* Chicago: University of Chicago Press, 1966.

White, William, ed. *Daybooks and Notebooks.* 3 vols. New York: New York University Press, 1978.

Zweig, Paul. *Walt Whitman: The Making of the Poet.* New York: Basic Books, 1984.

JAMES RUSSELL LOWELL

Anderson, John Q. "Lowell's 'The Washers of the Shroud' and the Celtic Legend of the Washer of the Ford." *American Literature* 35 (1963–64): 361–63.

Bandy, W. T. "James Russell Lowell, Sainte-Beuve, and *The Atlantic Monthly*." *Comparative Literature* 11 (1959): 229–32.

Beatty, Richmond Croom. *James Russell Lowell*. Nashville: University of Tennessee Press, 1942.

Clark, Harry Hayden. "Lowell—Humanitarian Nationalist, or Humanist?" *Studies in Philology* 27 (1930): 415–41.

———. "Lowell's Criticism of Romantic Literature." *PMLA* 41 (1926): 209–28.

Duberman, Martin. *James Russell Lowell*. Boston: Houghton Mifflin, 1966.

Griffin, Max L. "Lowell and the South." *Tulane Studies in English* 2 (1950): 75–102.

Harder, Jayne Crane. "James Russell Lowell: Linguistic Patriot." *American Speech* 29 (1954): 181–86.

Howard, Leon. *A Victorian Knight Errant: A Study of the Early Career of James Russell Lowell*. Berkeley: University of California Press, 1952.

Lombard, C. M. "Lowell and French Romanticism." *Revue de Littérature Comparée* 38 (1968): 582–88.

McGlinchee, Claire. *James Russell Lowell*. New York: Twayne, 1967.

Nye, Russell B. "Lowell and American Speech." *Philological Quarterly* 18 (1939) 249–56.

Oggel, L. Terry. "Lowell's Humor and His Other Review of Thoreau." *The American Transcendental Quarterly* 41 (1979): 45–60.

Pritchard, John P. *Return to the Fountains*. Durham, N.C.: Duke University Press, 1942.

———. "A Glance at Lowell's Classical Reading." *American Literature* 21 (1949–50): 442–55.

Simpson, Lewis P. "Introduction." In *James Russell Lowell and His Friends* by Edward Everett Hale. New York: Chelsea House, 1980.

Voss, Arthur W. M. "James Russell Lowell." *The University of Kansas City Review* 15 (1948): 224–53.

———. "Backgrounds of Lowell's Satire in *The Biglow Papers*." *New England Quarterly* 23 (1950): 47–64.

Wagenknecht, Edward. *James Russell Lowell: Portrait of a Many-Sided Man*. New York: Oxford University Press, 1971.

Warren, Austin. "Lowell on Thoreau." *Studies in Philology* 27 (1930): 442–61.

FREDERICK GODDARD TUCKERMAN

Eberhart, Richard. "A Quiet Tone from a Rich Interior." *New York Times Book Review* (June 20, 1965): 5.

England, Eugene. "Tuckerman's Sonnet I:10: The First Post-Symbolist Poem." *The Southern Review* 12: 323–47.

Golden, Samuel A. *Frederick Goddard Tuckerman*. New York: Twayne, 1966.

———. *Frederick Goddard Tuckerman: An American Sonneteer*. Orono.: University of Maine Press, 1952.

————. "Frederick Goddard Tuckerman: A Neglected Poet." *New England Quarterly* 29 (1956): 381–93.

Howe, Irving. "An American Poet." *The New York Review of Books* (March 25, 1965): 17–19.

Lynch, T. Patrick. "Still Needed: A Tuckerman Text." *Papers of the Bibliographical Society of America* 69: 255–65.

Marcus, Mordecai. "Frederick Goddard Tuckerman's 'The Cricket': An Introductory Note." *The Massachusetts Review* 2 (Autumn 1960): 33–38.

————. "The Poetry of Frederick Goddard Tuckerman: A Reconsideration." *Discourse* (Concordia College, Moorhead, Minn.) 5 (Winter 1961–62): 69–82.

Tuckerman, Frederick Goddard. *The Complete Poems of Frederick Goddard Tuckerman.* Edited and with an introduction by N. Scott Momaday. New York: Oxford University Press, 1965.

————. *The Sonnets of Frederick Goddard Tuckerman.* Edited and with an introduction by Witter Bynner. New York: Knopf, 1931.

Wilson, Edmund. *Patriotic Gore,* 489–97. New York: Oxford University Press, 1962.

Winters, Yvor. "A Discovery." *The Hudson Review* 3 (Autumn 1950): 453–58.

HENRY TIMROD

Green, Claude B. "Henry Timrod and the South." *The South Carolina Review* 2 (May 1969): 27–33.

Hubbell, Jay B., Jr. "Henry Timrod." In *The South in American Literature, 1607–1900,* 466–74. Durham, N.C.: Duke University Press, 1954.

————. "Literary Nationalism in the Old South." In *American Studies in Honor of William Kenneth Boyd,* 175–220. Durham, N.C.: Duke University Press, 1940.

McMichael, James. "Review of *The Collected Poems of Henry Timrod: A Variorum Edition.*" *The Southern Review* 3 (Spring 1967): 434–35.

Parks, Edd Winfield. *Henry Timrod.* New York: Twayne, 1964.

————. "Henry Timrod, Traditionalist." In *Ante-Bellum Southern Critics.* Athens: University of Georgia Press, 1958.

————. "Timrod's Concept of Dreams." *The South Atlantic Quarterly* 48 (October 1949): 584–88.

Rubin, Louis D., Jr. "Henry Timrod and the Dying of the Light." *Mississippi Quarterly: The Journal of Southern Culture* 11 (Summer 1958): 101–11.

Timrod, Henry. *The Uncollected Poems of Henry Timrod.* Edited and with an introduction by Guy A. Cardwell, Jr. Athens: University of Georgia Press, 1965.

Young, Thomas D. "Review of *The Collected Poems of Henry Timrod: A Variorum Edition.*" *Mississippi Quarterly: The Journal of Southern Culture* 19 (Spring 1966): 92–99.

EMILY DICKINSON

Anderson, Charles R. *Emily Dickinson's Poetry: Stairway of Surprise*. New York: Holt, Rinehart & Winston, 1960.

Blake, Caesar R., and Carlton F. Wells, eds. *The Recognition of Emily Dickinson*. Ann Arbor: University of Michigan Press, 1964.

Cambon, Glavco. "Emily Dickinson's Circumference." *The Sewanee Review* 84 (1976): 342–50.

Cameron, Sharon. *Lyric Time: Dickinson and the Limits of Genre*. Baltimore: Johns Hopkins University Press, 1979.

Capps, Jack L. *Emily Dickinson's Reading: 1836–1886*. Cambridge: Harvard University Press, 1966.

Chase, Richard. *Emily Dickinson*. New York: Sloane, 1951.

Cody, John. *After Great Pain: The Inner Life of Emily Dickinson*. Cambridge: Harvard University Press, 1971.

Cunningham, J. V. "Sorting Out: The Case of Dickinson." *The Southern Review* 5 (1969): 436–56.

D'Avanzo, Mario. "Dickinson's 'The Reticent Volcano' and Emerson." *The American Transcendental Quarterly* 14 (1972): 11–13.

Davis, Thomas M., ed. *Fourteen by Emily Dickinson*. Glenview, Ill.: Scott, Foresman, 1964.

Diehl, Joanne Feit. *Dickinson and the Romantic Imagination*. Princeton: Princeton University Press, 1981.

Donoghue, Denis. *Emily Dickinson*. Minneapolis: University of Minnesota Press, 1966.

Eitner, Walter H. "Emily Dickinson's Awareness of Whitman: A Reappraisal." *Walt Whitman Review* 22 (1976): 111–15.

Ford, Thomas W. *Heaven Beguiles the Tired: Death in the Poetry of Emily Dickinson*. University: University of Alabama Press, 1966.

Franklin, R. W., ed. *The Manuscript Books of Emily Dickinson*. 2 vols. Cambridge: Belknap, 1981.

Frye, Northrop. *Fables of Identity: Studies in Poetic Mythology*. New York: Harcourt, Brace & World, 1963.

Gelpi, Albert J. *Emily Dickinson: The Mind of the Poet*. Cambridge: Harvard University Press, 1966.

Gilbert, Sandra M., and Susan Gubar. *The Madwoman in the Attic: The Woman Writer and the Nineteenth-Century Literary Imagination*. New Haven: Yale University Press, 1979.

Griffith, Clark. *The Long Shadow: Emily Dickinson's Tragic Poetry*. Princeton: Princeton University Press, 1964.

Hagenbüchle, Roland. "Precision and Indeterminacy in the Poetry of Emily Dickinson." *Emerson Society Quarterly*: 74 (1974): 33–56.

Homans, Margaret. *Women Writers and Poetic Identity*. Princeton: Princeton University Press, 1980.

Johnson, Thomas H. *Emily Dickinson: An Interpretive Biography.* Cambridge: Harvard University Press, 1964.

————, ed. *Selected Letters.* Cambridge: Belknap, 1971.

————, ed. *The Complete Poems of Emily Dickinson.* Boston: Little, Brown, 1960.

————, ed. *The Poems of Emily Dickinson.* 3 vols. Cambridge: Belknap, 1958.

Johnson, Thomas H., and Theodora Ward, eds. *The Letters of Emily Dickinson.* 3 vols. Cambride: Belknap, 1958.

Keller, Karl. *The Only Kangaroo among the Beauty: Emily Dickinson and America.* Baltimore: Johns Hopkins University Press, 1979.

Kher, Inder Nath. *The Landscape of Absence: Emily Dickinson's Poetry.* New Haven: Yale University Press, 1974.

Laverty, Carroll. "Structural Patterns in Emily Dickinson's Poetry." *Emerson Society Quarterly* 44 (1966): 12–17.

Leyda, Jay. *The Years and Hours of Emily Dickinson.* New Haven: Yale University Press, 1960.

Lindberg-Seyersted, Brita. *The Voice of the Poet: Aspects of Style in the Poetry of Emily Dickinson.* Cambridge: Harvard University Press, 1968.

Lubbers, Klaus. *Emily Dickinson: The Critical Revolution.* Ann Arbor: University of Michigan Press, 1968.

Lucas, Dolores Dyer. *Emily Dickinson and Riddle.* DeKalb: Northern Illinois University Press, 1969.

MacLeish, Archibald, Louise Bogan, and Richard Wilbur. *Emily Dickinson: Three Views.* Amherst, Mass.: Amherst College Press, 1960.

Miller, Ruth. *The Poetry of Emily Dickinson.* Middletown, Conn.: Wesleyan University Press, 1968.

Porter, David. *The Art of Emily Dickinson's Early Poetry.* Cambridge: Harvard University Press, 1966.

Rosenbaum, S. P. *A Concordance to the Poems of Emily Dickinson.* Ithaca, N.Y.: Cornell University Press, 1966.

Sewall, Richard. *The Life of Emily Dickinson.* 2 vols. New York: Farrar, Straus & Giroux, 1974.

————, ed. *Emily Dickinson.* Englewood Cliffs, N.J.: Prentice-Hall, 1963.

Sherrer, Grace B. "A Study of Unusual Verb Constructions in the Poems of Emily Dickinson." *American Literature* 7 (1935): 37–46.

Sherwood, William. *Circumference and Circumstance: Stages in the Mind and Art of Emily Dickinson.* New York: Columbia University Press, 1968.

Ward, Theodora. *The Capsule of the Mind: Chapters in the Mind of Emily Dickinson.* Cambridge: Belknap, 1961.

Weisbuch, Robert. *Emily Dickinson's Poetry.* Chicago: University of Chicago Press, 1975.

Whicher, George. *This Was a Poet.* New York: Scribner's, 1938.

Wolff, Cynthia Griffin. *Emily Dickinson.* New York: Knopf, 1986.

Wolosky, Shira. *Emily Dickinson: A Voice at War.* New Haven: Yale University Press, 1984.

Yetman, Michael. "Emily Dickinson and the English Tradition." *Texas Studies in Literature and Language* 15 (1973): 129–47.

SIDNEY LANIER

Abel, Darrell. "Sidney Lanier." In *American Literature.* Vol. 2, 498–517. Woodbury, N.Y.: Barrons, 1963.

Coulson, Edwin R., and Richard Webb. *Sidney Lanier: Poet and Prosodist.* Athens: University of Georgia Press, 1941.

De Bellis, Jack. *Sidney Lanier.* New York: Twayne, 1972.

Fleissner, Robert F. "Frost and Lanier: An Immediate Literary Source of 'Once by the Pacific.' " *Papers on Language and Literature* 16: 320–25.

Fletcher, John Gould. "Sidney Lanier." *The University of Kansas City Review* 16 (Winter 1949): 97–102.

Graham, Philip. "A Note on Lanier's Music." *University of Texas Studies in English* 17 (1937): 107–11.

———. "Sidney Lanier and the Pattern of Contrast." *American Quarterly* 11 (Winter 1956): 54–56.

Hendren, Joseph W. *Time and Stress in English Verse, with Special Reference to Lanier's Theory of Rhythm. Rice Institute Pamphlet* 46 (July 1959): 1–72.

Lanier, Sidney. *The Centennial Edition of the Works of Sidney Lanier.* Edited and with an introduction by Charles R. Anderson. Baltimore: Johns Hopkins University Press, 1945.

Leary, Lewis. "The Forlorn Hope of Sidney Lanier." In *Southern Excursions: Essays on Mark Twain and Others.* Baton Rouge: Louisiana State University Press, 1971.

Martin, Jay. "Sidney Lanier: The Real and the Ideal." In *Harvests of Change: American Literature 1865–1914,* 92–96. Englewood Cliffs, N.J.: Prentice-Hall, 1967.

Parks, Edd Winfield. *Sidney Lanier: The Man, the Poet, the Critic.* Athens: University of Georgia Press, 1968.

Petry, Alice Hall. "Death as Etherealization in the Poetry of Sidney Lanier." *South Dakota Review* 17, no. 1 (Spring 1979): 46–55.

Ransom, John Crowe. "Hearts and Heads." *American Review* 2 (1934): 554–71.

Reamer, Owen J. "Lanier's 'Marshes of Glynn' Revisited." *Mississippi Quarterly: The Journal of Southern Culture* 23 (May 1969): 57–63.

Ross, Robert. "The Marshes of Glynn: Studies in Symbolic Obscurity." *American Literature* 32 (1961): 403–16.

Rubin, Louis D., Jr. "The Passion of Sidney Lanier." In *William Elliott Shoots a Bear: Essays on the Southern Literary Imagination.* Baton Rouge: Louisiana State University Press, 1976.

Starke, Aubrey. *Sidney Lanier.* Chapel Hill: University of North Carolina Press, 1933.

Tate, Allen. "A Southern Romantic." *The New Republic* 76 (August 30, 1933): 67–70.

Warfel, Harry R. "Mystic Vision in 'The Marshes of Glynn.' " *Mississippi Quarterly: The Journal of Southern Culture* 19 (Winter 1965): 39–40.

Williams, William Carlos. "The Present Relationship of Prose to Verse." *Seven Arts* 1 (1953): 140–49.

STEPHEN CRANE

Bassan, Maurice, ed. *Stephen Crane: A Collection of Critical Essays*. Englewood Cliffs, N.J.: Prentice-Hall, 1967.

Beer, Thomas. *Stephen Crane: A Study in American Letters*. New York: Knopf, 1923.

Bergon, Frank. *Stephen Crane's Artistry*. New York: Columbia University Press, 1975.

Berryman, John. *Stephen Crane*. New York: Sloane, 1950.

———. "Stephen Crane." In *The Freedom of the Poet*, 168–84. New York: Farrar, Straus & Giroux, 1976.

Cady, Edwin H. *Stephen Crane*. New York: Twayne, 1962.

———. "Stephen Crane and the Strenuous Life." *ELH* 28 (1961): 376–82.

Colvert, James. "The Origins of Stephen Crane's Literary Creed." *University of Texas Studies in English* 34 (1955): 179–88.

———. *Stephen Crane*. San Diego: Harcourt Brace Jovanovich, 1984.

Franchere, Ruth. *Stephen Crane*. New York: Cromwell, 1961.

Gross, Theodore L., and Stanley Wertheim. *Hawthorne, Melville, Stephen Crane: A Critical Bibliography*. New York: Free Press, 1971.

Gullason, Thomas A., ed. *Stephen Crane's Career: Perspectives and Evaluations*. New York: New York University Press, 1972.

Hoffman, Daniel G. *The Poetry of Stephen Crane*. New York: Columbia University Press, 1957.

Katz, Joseph. *The Merrill Checklist of Stephen Crane*. Columbus, Ohio: Merrill, 1969.

———, ed. *Stephen Crane in Transition: Centenary Essays*. DeKalb: Northern Illinois University Press, 1972.

Kazin, Alfred. "American Fin de Siècle." In *On Native Grounds*. New York: Reynal & Hitchcock, 1942.

LaFrance, Marston. *A Reading of Stephen Crane*. Oxford: Clarendon, 1971.

Miller, Ruth. "Regions of Snow: The Poetic Style of Stephen Crane." *Bulletin of the New York Public Library* 72 (1968): 328–49.

Nelson, Harlan D. "Stephen Crane's Achievement as a Poet." *Texas Studies in Literature and Language* 4 (1963): 564–82.

Stallman, R. W. *Stephen Crane*. New York: Braziller, 1968.

———. *Stephen Crane: A Critical Bibliography*. Ames: Iowa State University Press, 1972.

Weatherford, Richard M., ed. *Stephen Crane: The Critical Heritage.* London: Routledge & Kegan Paul, 1973.

Westbrook, Max. "Stephen Crane's Poetry: Perspective and Arrogance." *Bucknell Review* 11 (1963): 24–34.

TRUMBULL STICKNEY

Dickey, James. *Exchanges . . . Being in the Form of a Dialogue with Joseph Trumbull Stickney.* Bloomfield Hills, Mich.: Adagio Press, 1971.

Haldane, Seán. *The Fright of Time: Joseph Trumbull Stickney, 1874–1904.* Ladysmith, Quebec: Ladysmith Press, 19780.

Meyers, J. William. "A Complete Stickney Bibliography." *Twentieth Century Literature* 9 (January 1964): 209–12.

Reeves, James, and Seán Haldane, eds. *Homage to Trumbull Stickney: Poems.* London: Heinemann, 1968.

Stickney, Trumbull, *Dramatic Verses by Trumbull Stickney.* Boston: C. E. Goodspeed, 1902.

———. *The Poems of Trumbull Stickney.* Boston: Houghton Mifflin, 1905.

———. *The Poems of Trumbull Stickney.* Edited by Amberys R. Whittle. New York: Farrar, Straus & Giroux, 1972.

Whittle, Amberys R. "The Dust of Seasons: Time in the Poetry of Trumbull Stickney." *The Sewanee Review* 74 (Autumn 1966): 899–914.

Wilson, Edmund. "Foreword." In *The Poems of Trumbull Stickney*, edited by Amberys R. Whittle. New York: Farrar, Straus & Giroux, 1972.

Acknowledgments

"Introduction" (originally entitled "Bacchus and Merlin: The Dialectic of Romantic Poetry in America") by Harold Bloom from *The Ringers in the Tower* by Harold Bloom, © 1971 by the University of Chicago. Reprinted by permission of the University of Chicago Press.

"Anne Bradstreet and the Practice of Weaned Affections" by Robert Daly from *God's Altar: The World and the Flesh in Puritan Poetry* by Robert Daly, © 1978 by The Regents of the University of California. Reprinted by permission of the University of California Press. The notes have been omitted.

"Edward Taylor: *Preparatory Meditations*" by Louis L. Martz from *The Poem of the Mind* by Louis L. Martz, © 1966 by Louis L. Martz. Reprinted by permission of the author and Oxford University Press. This essay originally appeared as the foreword to *The Poems of Edward Taylor*, edited by Donald Stanford, Yale University Press, 1960.

"The Visionary Line: The Poetry of Philip Freneau" (originally entitled "Laying Waste Her Fields of Plenty: The Eighteenth Century: The Visionary Line: The Poetry of Philip Freneau") by Annette Kolodny from *The Lay of the Land: Metaphor as Experience and History in American Life and Letters* by Annette Kolodny, © 1975 by the University of North Carolina Press. Reprinted by permission of the publisher.

"Phillis Wheatley: The Dark Side of the Poetry" by Terrence Collins from *Phylon: The Atlanta University Review of Race and Culture* 36, no. 1 (March 1975), © 1975 by Atlanta University. Reprinted by permission.

"William Cullen Bryant: 'To a Waterfowl' " (originally entitled "William Cullen Bryant: To a Waterfowl") by Donald Davie from *Interpretations: Essays on Twelve English Poems*, edited by John Wain, © 1955 by Routledge & Kegan Paul Ltd. Reprinted by permission.

"Bryant's 'Thanatopsis' and the Development of American Literature" (originally entitled " 'Thanatopsis' and the Development of American Literature") by Rebecca Rio-Jelliffe from *William Cullen Bryant and His America: Centennial Conference Proceedings 1878–1978*, edited by Stanley Brodwin and Michael D'Innocenzo, © 1983 by AMS Press, Inc. Reprinted by permission.

"The Muse Has a Deeper Secret: Emerson's Poetry" (originally entitled "The Muse Has a Deeper Secret") by David Porter from *Emerson and Literary Change* by David Porter, © 1978 by the President and Fellows of Harvard College. Reprinted by permission of Harvard University Press.

"On Longfellow" by Howard Nemerov from *Poetry and Fiction: Essays* by Howard Nemerov, © 1963 by Rutgers, The State University. Reprinted by permission of Rutgers University Press. This essay originally appeared in the *Laurel Poetry Series* published by Dell Publishing Company.

"John Greenleaf Whittier" (originally entitled "Whittier") by Robert Penn Warren from *The Sewanee Review* 79 (January–March 1971), © 1971 by Robert Penn Warren. Reprinted by permission of the William Morris Agency.

"The House of Poe" by Richard Wilbur from *Anniversary Lectures 1959*, © 1966 by Richard Wilbur. Reprinted by permission of the author. This essay was originally presented as a lecture at the Library of Congress.

"Transcendental Egoism in Very and Whitman" by Lawrence Buell from *Literary Transcendentalism* by Lawrence Buell, © 1973 by Cornell University. Reprinted by permission of Cornell University Press.

"An Evaluation of Thoreau's Poetry" by Henry W. Wells from *American Literature* 16, no. 2 (May 1944), © 1944, renewed 1971 by Duke University Press. Reprinted by permission.

"Whitman: The Poet in 1860" (originally entitled "Introduction") by Roy Harvey Pearce from *Leaves of Grass, by Walt Whitman: Facsimile Edition of the 1860 Text* by Roy Harvey Pearce, © 1961 by Cornell University. Reprinted by permission of Cornell University Press.

"Walt Whitman: Always Going Out and Coming In" by R. W. B. Lewis from *Trials of the Word* by R. W. B. Lewis, © 1965 by R. W. B. Lewis. Reprinted by permission of Yale University Press.

"Whitman's Image of Voice: To the Tally of My Soul" by Harold Bloom from *Agon* by Harold Bloom, © 1982 by Oxford University Press. Reprinted by permission.

"Melville the Poet" by Robert Penn Warren from *Selected Essays* by Robert Penn Warren, © 1966 by Vintage Books. Reprinted by permission of Random House, Inc. and the William Morris Agency.

"Form as Vision in Herman Melville's *Clarel*" by Bryan C. Short from *American Literature* 50, no. 4 (January 1979), © 1979 by Duke University Press. Reprinted by permission.

"James Russell Lowell" (originally entitled "Lowell") by George Arms from *The Fields Were Green: A New View of Bryant, Whittier, Holmes, Lowell, and Longfellow, with a Selection of Their Poems* by George Arms, © 1953 by the Board of Trustees of the Leland Stanford Junior University. Reprinted by permission of Stanford University Press.

"Frederick Goddard Tuckerman" by Denis Donoghue from *Connoisseurs of Chaos* by Denis Donoghue, © 1964, 1984 by Denis Donoghue. Reprinted by permission of the author and Columbia University Press.

"Henry Timrod" (originally entitled "Timrod and Lanier") by Roy Harvey Pearce from *The Continuity of American Poetry* by Roy Harvey Pearce, © 1961 by Princeton University Press. Reprinted by permission of Princeton University Press.

"Dickinson and Despair" (originally entitled "Despair") by Charles R. Anderson from *Emily Dickinson's Poetry: Stairway of Surprise* by Charles R. Anderson, © 1960 by Charles R. Anderson. Reprinted by permission of the author and Holt, Rinehart & Winston. The notes have been omitted.

"Emily Dickinson" by Margaret Homans from *Women Writers and Poetic Identity* by Margaret Homans, © 1980 by Princeton University Press. Reprinted by permission of Princeton University Press.

"Emerson, Dickinson, and the Abyss" by Joanne Feit Diehl from *Dickinson and the Romantic Imagination* by Joanne Feit Diehl, © 1981 by Princeton University Press. Reprinted by permission of Princeton University Press.

"The Blind Poet: Sidney Lanier" by Robert Penn Warren from *The American Review* 2, no. 1 (November 1933), © 1934 by the Bookman Publishing Company, Inc. Reprinted by permission.

"Sidney Lanier and 'Musicality' " by John Hollander reprinted from *Poems of Sidney Lanier*, edited by Mary Day Lanier, published by Charles Scribner's Sons, New York, 1884, 1916; Reprinted 1981 by the University of Georgia Press, with Afterword by John Hollander, © 1981 by the University of Georgia Press. Reprinted by permission.

"The Poetry of Stephen Crane: War in Heaven" (originally entitled "War in Heaven") by Daniel G. Hoffman from *The Poetry of Stephen Crane* by

Daniel G. Hoffman, © 1956 by Columbia University Press. Reprinted by permission.

"A Matter of Autumn: Trumbull Stickney and 'Mnemosyne' " (originally entitled "The Poems of Trumbull Stickney" and "Breaking into Song: Some Notes of Refrain") by John Hollander from *The New York Times Book Review* (July 16, 1972), © 1972 by the New York Times Company, and from *Lyric Poetry: Beyond New Criticism*, edited by Chaviva Hosek and Patricia Parker, © 1985 by Cornell University Press. Reprinted by permission.

Index

ADG 3635

9/4/96

PS
305
A54
1987